CEDU쎄듀는 A **C**omprehensive **E**nglish e**DU**cation(**종합적 영어교육**)**의 약자입니다.**

펴낸이 김기훈 I 김진희
펴낸곳 (주)쎄듀 I 서울특별시 강남구 논현로 305 (역삼동)
발행일 2020년 10월 12일 1쇄
내용문의 www.cedubook.com
구입문의 콘텐츠 마케팅 사업본부
Tel. 02-6241-2007
Fax. 02-2058-0209
등록번호 제 22-2472호
ISBN 978-89-6806-207-0

파워업

독해실전편

모의고사 15회

POWER Up

저자

김기훈

現 ㈜쎄듀 대표이사
現 메가스터디 영어영역 대표강사
前 서울특별시 교육청 외국어 교육정책자문위원회 위원

저서 천일문 / 천일문 Training Book / 천일문 GRAMMAR
첫단추 BASIC / 쎄듀 본영어 / 어휘끝 / 어법끝 / 문법의 골든룰 101
절대평가 PLAN A / 리딩 플랫폼 / ALL씀 서술형
Reading Relay / The 리딩플레이어 / 빈칸백서 / 오답백서
첫단추 / 파워업 / 수능영어 절대유형 / 수능실감 등

쎄듀 영어교육연구센터

쎄듀 영어교육센터는 영어 콘텐츠에 대한 전문지식과 경험을 바탕으로
최고의 교육 콘텐츠를 만들고자 최선의 노력을 다하는 전문가 집단입니다.

장정문 선임연구원

Project Managing | **박순정**
개발에 도움을 주신 분 | **조원웅** 선생님(클라비스 학원) · **최대호** 선생님(전북과학고)

마케팅 콘텐츠 마케팅 사업본부
제작 정승호
영업 문병구
인디자인 편집 한서기획
디자인 윤혜영
영문교열 Adam Miller · Janna Christie

Preface

본 교재는 2014년 발간된 <Power Up! 쎄듀 독해 모의고사>를 토대로 한 것으로, 실전 모의고사 12회와 고난도 모의고사 3회로 구성된 <파워업 독해유형편>의 후속 교재이다. 고2~고3 학력평가 수준의 난이도이므로 반드시 <파워업 독해유형편>이 아니더라도 유형별 전략을 익혔다면 실전에서 적용해볼 수 있는 데 최적의 교재가 되리라 생각한다. 유형별로 어떤 포인트를 잡아 어떤 부분에 주목하고 어떻게 풀이를 해야 하는지를 빠짐없이 신속하게 적용할 수 있도록 하자.

이와 함께 실전 모의고사 교재는 본인의 예상되는 현재 등급을 알려주고 실력을 한층 업그레이드 할 수 있는 좋은 학습서의 기능도 겸한다. 수능을 바로 코앞에 두지 않은 이상, 아래와 같은 실질적인 학력 증진을 함께 도모하기에 좋다. 좀 더 자세하게는 How to Use This Book(p.6)을 참고하기 바란다.

1 버려야 할 습관은 찾아내 버리고 **익혀야 할 좋은 습관을 체화**한다.
특히, 실수는 습관이 되기 쉬우므로 똑같은 실수를 반복하지 않도록 해야 한다.

2 본인의 **강약점을 파악하여 약점을 해결**한다.
유독 자주 틀리는 유형이 있다면 유형별 해결전략을 다시 점검해 보도록 한다. 만약 어휘에서 자주 막힌다면 어휘 복습에 중점을 두고 본인의 전반적인 어휘 학습을 좀 더 강화해서 이를 보강할 수 있을 것이다.

3 풀이 속도를 향상시켜 **제한 시간을 넘기지 않도록** 한다.
풀이 속도는 전반적인 실력 향상과 함께 자연히 해결될 수도 있지만 제한 시간을 습관적으로 넘긴다면 이를 해결하기 위해 시간을 효율적으로 사용할 수 있는 전략을 강구해서 차츰차츰 풀이 시간을 줄여나가도록 해야 한다.

우리 모두의 바람은 목표 등급에 도달하고 이를 잘 유지하여 수능에서도 이루는 것이다. 학년이 올라갈수록 난이도는 예상을 뛰어넘게 높아지므로 목표 등급 달성이나 점수 유지는 절대로 녹록지 않다. 독해 실력의 기본이 되어주는 어휘, 구문의 학습도 중요하고 실전에서의 능력을 확인하면서 적용 능력을 기르는 것도 중요하다. 항상 목표 등급을 마음에 새기면서 품질 좋은 실전 모의고사로 꾸준히 그리고 전략적으로 학습하라. 모든 독자 여러분의 선전과 건승을 진심으로 기원한다.

저자

이 책의 구성과 특징

Before & After Testing

시험 전후로 학습을 계획하고 복습하는 데
도움을 주는 가이드를 제공합니다.

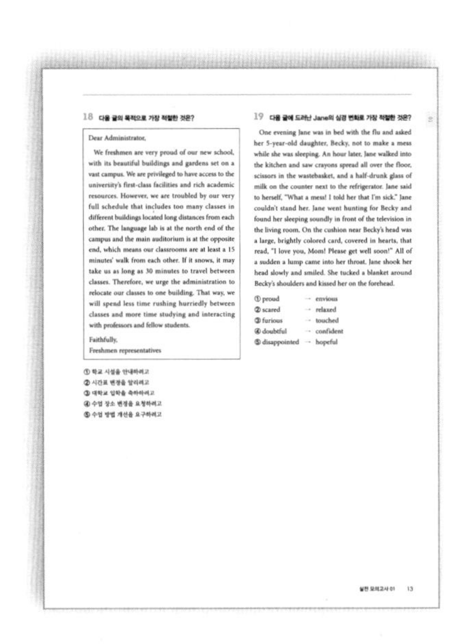

독해 모의고사

최신 수능 출제 경향을 100% 반영한
고품질 모의고사 15회분으로
수능시험에 완벽하게 대비합니다.

정답 및 해설

혼자서 학습하는 데에도 어려움이 없도록
글의 소재와 주제문, 친절한 해설과 구문풀이,
어휘를 수록하였습니다.

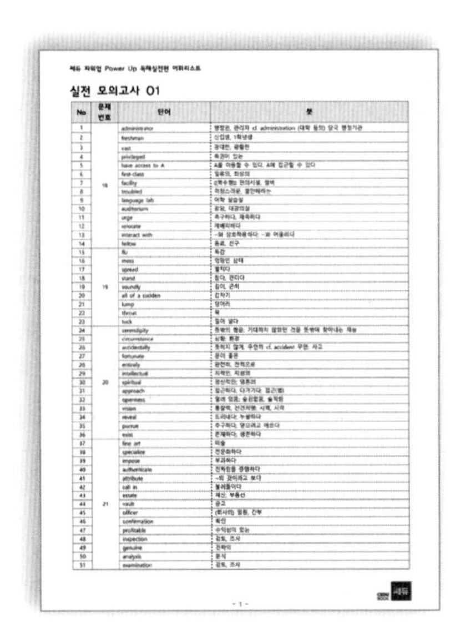

어휘리스트·어휘테스트·어휘출제프로그램

교재에 나온 중요 어휘를 모두 정리한 어휘리스트로
단어를 암기하고, 어휘테스트로 확인해보세요.
(무료 다운로드 www.cedubook.com)

Contents

How to Use This Book

1 Before Testing

1 제한 시간을 답안지 OMR 마킹시간을 포함하여 45분으로 설정한다.
만약 문제를 다 풀고 채점 및 해설 확인 시간이 충분치 못하거나 버겁게 느껴진다면 문제를 14문제씩 절반으로 나눠서 학습할 것을 권한다.

2 어휘는 예습하지 않고 문맥을 통해 최대한 추론한 뒤에 나중에 해설지로 확인하는 것이 좋다. 그러나 어휘 때문에 막히는 경우가 너무나 많아서 유형별 전략 적용 훈련을 제대로 할 수 없다면, 예습을 하고 문제 풀이를 할 것을 권한다.

2 During Testing

1 문제를 풀며 실전과 동일하게 OMR 답안지(p. 223)에 정답을 마킹한다.

2 제한 시간 내에 문제를 다 풀었더라도 애매한 문제를 다시 검토하는 등 주어진 시간을 모두 활용하도록 한다. 제한 시간을 넘어가면 총 몇 문제를 못 풀었는지 체크하고, 추가시간이 얼마나 필요했는지를 기록하여 초과한 시간은 문제 풀이에 적응하면서 차차 줄여나가도록 한다. 시간이 모자라더라도 대충 풀지 말고 추가시간을 들여서라도 반드시 문제를 다 풀어야 한다.

3 정답의 근거라고 생각되는 부분에 표시하여 해설지의 정오답 해설과 맞춰본다. 정답을 맞혔다고 해도 간혹 본인이 생각하는 정답의 근거와 해설지의 정답 근거가 틀릴 경우가 있으므로 이를 확인하고 수정하는 과정이 필요하다.

4 모르거나 헷갈리는 문제의 번호에 따로 표시를 해두어 추후에 해설지를 참고할 수 있도록 한다. 정답을 맞혔더라도 실력 향상을 위해 꼭 필요하다.

5 이해가 잘 안 되는 어휘나 문장(선택지 포함)에 표시하여 해설지를 참고할 수 있도록 한다.

<예시>

→ 자신 없는 문제에 ✓표시

34 다음 빈칸에 들어갈 말로 가장 적절한 것을 고르시오. [모의]

Interestingly, in nature, ______________________. The distinction between predator and prey offers a clarifying example of this. The key feature that distinguishes predator species from prey species isn't the presence of claws or any other feature related to biological weaponry. The key feature is *the position of their eyes*. Predators evolved with eyes facing forward — ⟨which allows for binocular vision that offers accurate depth perception when pursuing prey⟩. Prey, on the other hand, often have eyes facing outward, maximizing peripheral vision, which allows the hunted to detect danger that may be approaching from any angle. Consistent with our place at the top of the food chain, humans have eyes that face forward. We have the ability to gauge depth and pursue our goals, but we can also miss important action on our periphery.

→ 정답 근거에 밑줄

→ 잘 모르는 부분에 < > 표시

→ 정답 근거에 밑줄

*depth perception: 거리 감각 **periphery: 주변

✓① the more powerful species have a narrower field of vision
② eyes facing outward are linked with the success of hunting
③ humans' eyes facing forward enable them to detect danger
④ eyesight is closely related to the extinction of weak species
⑤ animals use their eyesight to identify members of their species

위와 같이 본인이 표시한 모든 부분은 바로 본인의 약점을 고스란히 알려주는 바로미터가 된다. 이를 잘 활용할 줄 알아야 실질적인 학습 능력의 향상을 꾀할 수 있으므로 일일이 표시하는 이 과정이 다소 번거롭더라도 반드시 실천하기를 권한다.

3 After Testing

1 채점을 진행하여 등급을 확인한 후, 어떤 유형의 문제를 틀렸는지 살펴보고 전략 적용에 문제가 있다면 유형별 전략을 복습하고 다른 어려움이 있다면 해설지를 통해 해결한다.

2 틀린 문제들만을 확인하고 학습을 마칠 것이 아니라 전체 문제에서 정확히 알지 못하는 모든 부분에 대한 학습을 가능한 세세하게 진행할 것을 권한다. 시험을 보면서 표시한 정답 근거나 잘 모르는 부분을 해설지에서 참고하여 암기할 것은 암기하고 다음 회차 문제를 풀 때 유념할 것을 확실히 알아둔다.

3 점수에 일희일비하지 않는다. 모의고사 결과를 지금까지 해온 학습에 대한 피드백이라 생각하고 부족한 점을 보완할 기회로 삼도록 한다.

Reading & Vocabulary

1 모든 단어를 알아야 한다고 생각하지 마라.

알다시피 수능 독해는 한 문장 한 문장을 빠짐없이 정확한 번역을 해야 하는 시험이 아니라 주어진 문제에 답하는 형태이다. 즉, 지문 내의 모든 단어를 알아야만 정답을 낼 수 있는 것이 아니다. 정답의 근거는 보통 주제문과 주요 세부사항에 있기 때문에 그 이외의 사소한 정보는 무시해도 대개는 정답 도출에 지장을 받지 않는다.

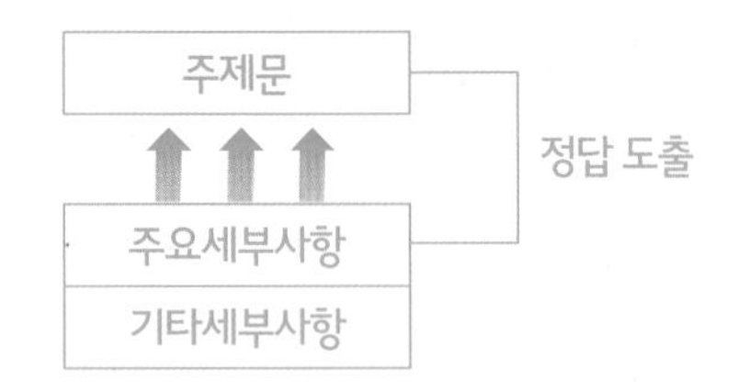

물론 한 지문의 사소한 정보에 해당하는 단어가 다른 지문의 주제문에 포함될 수도 있기 때문에 학습을 할 때는 출제 예상 단어를 가급적 많이 암기해야 하지만, 독해문제를 풀 때는 몰라도 지장이 없는 단어가 있다는 것을 명심하고 과감히 무시할 수 있는 용기를 가져라.

2 독해 지문을 어휘 암기용으로 적극 활용하라.

대개 전문 어휘서로 학습할 때는 단어와 한두 가지 뜻에만 집중하는 경제적인 학습을 하게 된다. 그러나 독해에서는 그 단어의 중요한 제2, 3의 뜻이 사용되는 경우가 적지 않다. 알고 있는 단어인데 문맥상 잘 들어맞지 않는 경우 대부분 제2, 3의 뜻으로 사용된 것이다. 어휘서에서 그냥 넘어갔던 중요한 뜻을 독해를 통해 접하게 되면 암기 효과가 크다. 분명 외웠는데 잘 생각이 안 나는 단어들, 어렴풋하게 알고 있던 단어들도 독해로 접하면 마찬가지로 학습효과가 배가된다.

3 문맥을 이용하는 어휘 의미 추론의 범위를 넓혀라.

문제 해결의 관건이 되는 어휘의 의미를 모를 때 문맥의 도움을 받아 최대한 의미를 추론하게 되는데, 사실 그 어휘의 아주 정확한 의미를 추론하는 데 충분한 문맥이 제공되는 경우는 많지 않다. 우리가 어렸을 때 했던 스무고개를 예로 들어보자. 정답이 되는 단어를 맞추기까지 몇 단계의 과정을 거치게 되는데, 그러한 과정들이 모두 문맥으로 주어지는 독해지문은 거의 없다.

Quiz I am not alive, but I grow.
I don't have lungs, but I need air.
I don't have a mouth, but water kills me.
What am I?

Answer Fire

그러므로 문맥으로 완벽하게 해결할 수 있다는 기대보다는 그 어휘의 대강의 의미 파악에 목표를 두는 것이 현실적이다. 예를 들어 성격을 말하는 것, 직업을 말하는 것, 질병을 말하는 것 등이나 긍정적인 것인지 부정적인 것인지에 대해서만이라도 감을 잡을 수 있으면 충분하다.

When I tried to pay in pounds sterling, the clerk explained that the store accepted only American dollars.

· pounds sterling의 뜻은?
· American dollars는 허용된다는 문맥을 통해, pounds sterling은 화폐 종류일 것으로 추론 가능
· 실제로 pounds sterling은 '영국의 파운드화'를 의미한다.

How to Tackle Unfamiliar Vocabulary: Using Context Clues (출처: 어휘끝 수능 p. 24)

1 유사 의미 표현을 활용하라.

단서 어구 as / also / like / likewise / similar to / the same as 등
'signal words'가 명시적으로 드러나지 않는 경우도 있으나, 이때도 문맥과 약간의 논리력을 발휘하여 판단이 가능할 수 있다.

> The number of people who need medical help for breathing problems like asthma tends to increase during very windy weather.
> (breathing problems ≒ asthma)

· asthma의 뜻은?
· breathing problem(호흡 장애) 증상을 보이는 어떤 질병의 이름일 것으로 추론 가능
· asthma → 천식

2 상반되는 의미의 표현을 활용하라.

단서 어구 but / whereas / however / although / on the contrary / by contrast / in contrast to / on the other hand 등

> I tried reading his notes but I found them illegible. However, yours were easy to read.
> (illegible ↔ easy to read)

· illegible의 뜻은?
· illegible ↔ easy to read(읽기 쉬운)
· illegible → 읽기 어려운

> The economy faltered badly last year but has now started to improve.
> (faltered ↔ improve)

· falter의 뜻은?
· 경기가 나아지는 것과 상반되는 개념으로 추론 가능
· falter → 불안정해지다, 흔들리다

3 정의하거나 부연 설명을 해주는 표현을 찾아라.

단서 어구 be동사 / 대시(—) / 콜론(:) / 세미콜론(;) / 동격을 나타내는 콤마(,)나 of / that is / refer to / mean 등
'A=B'라고 직접적으로 정의되거나 뒤에 부연 설명이 이어진다.

> Temporocentrism is the belief that your times are the best of all possible times. All other times are thus inferior. [수능]
> (Temporocentrism = the belief that your times are the best of all possible times)

· temporocentrism의 뜻은?
· temporocentrism → 자기 시대 중심주의

4 이어지는 예시나 설명을 활용하라.

단서 어구 such as / for example / for instance / including 등

Recently, sales of major home appliances such as refrigerators and ranges have risen. [수능]

· home appliance의 뜻은?

· home appliance = refrigerator, range와 같은 것 → 가전제품

5 원인과 결과 구조를 활용하라.

단서 어구 because / since / therefore / consequently / as a result / when 등

Sunny became incensed when I refused to give her my biology notes, and she hasn't spoken to me since.

· incensed의 뜻은?

· 내가 Sunny에게 생물학 노트를 보여주지 않자, 그녀가 incensed되었고 그 이후로 내게 말을 하지 않았으므로 Sunny가 화가 났다는 의미일 것으로 추론 가능

· incensed → 몹시 화난

POWER UP!

실전 모의고사

01

: BEFORE TESTING

시작 시 분

학습 목표

1 **제한시간** (OMR 마킹시간 포함) ☐ 40분 ☐ 45분
2 **어휘예습** ☐ 해당 없음 ☐ 완료
3 **문제풀이순서** ☐ 순서대로 ☐ 2점 → 3점 ☐ 기타
4 **기타 목표**

Check Point

1 **정답 근거** *e.g.* 밑줄 긋기
2 **잘 모르는 부분** *e.g.* 〈 〉 또는 ? 표시
3 **자신 없는 문제** *e.g.* 문제 번호에 ✓표시

18 다음 글의 목적으로 가장 적절한 것은?

Dear Administrator,

We freshmen are very proud of our new school, with its beautiful buildings and gardens set on a vast campus. We are privileged to have access to the university's first-class facilities and rich academic resources. However, we are troubled by our very full schedule that includes too many classes in different buildings located long distances from each other. The language lab is at the north end of the campus and the main auditorium is at the opposite end, which means our classrooms are at least a 15 minutes' walk from each other. If it snows, it may take us as long as 30 minutes to travel between classes. Therefore, we urge the administration to relocate our classes to one building. That way, we will spend less time rushing hurriedly between classes and more time studying and interacting with professors and fellow students.

Faithfully,
Freshmen representatives

① 학교 시설을 안내하려고
② 시간표 변경을 알리려고
③ 대학교 입학을 축하하려고
④ 수업 장소 변경을 요청하려고
⑤ 수업 방법 개선을 요구하려고

19 다음 글에 드러난 Jane의 심경 변화로 가장 적절한 것은?

One evening Jane was in bed with the flu and asked her 5-year-old daughter, Becky, not to make a mess while she was sleeping. An hour later, Jane walked into the kitchen and saw crayons spread all over the floor, scissors in the wastebasket, and a half-drunk glass of milk on the counter next to the refrigerator. Jane said to herself, "What a mess! I told her that I'm sick." Jane couldn't stand her. Jane went hunting for Becky and found her sleeping soundly in front of the television in the living room. On the cushion near Becky's head was a large, brightly colored card, covered in hearts, that read, "I love you, Mom! Please get well soon!" All of a sudden a lump came into her throat. Jane shook her head slowly and smiled. She tucked a blanket around Becky's shoulders and kissed her on the forehead.

① proud → envious
② scared → relaxed
③ furious → touched
④ doubtful → confident
⑤ disappointed → hopeful

20 다음 글에서 필자가 주장하는 바로 가장 적절한 것은?

The word "serendipity" describes the wonderful circumstance of accidentally discovering something fortunate, usually while one is looking for something else entirely. Many of the greatest scientific discoveries in history have resulted from serendipity, simply because it happens most often to those who are adventurers and searchers. Whether our adventures are physical, intellectual, or spiritual, if we approach all that we do with an attitude of openness, our true vision is more likely to be revealed to us. On the other hand, if we close our minds, we'll probably miss the one great thing that is worth more or is better than what we were looking for. Even if the thing you are pursuing does not yet exist, you must not quit too soon, for a happy accident may be waiting just for you.

① 다양한 경험을 통해 통찰력을 키워야 한다.
② 끊임없이 노력하면 위대한 과학적 발견을 할 수 있다.
③ 현재 자신이 가지고 있는 것에 감사할 줄 알아야 한다.
④ 행운보다는 노력의 대가를 더 가치 있게 생각해야 한다.
⑤ 열린 마음으로 새로운 것에 대한 도전을 계속해야 한다.

21 밑줄 친 You don't have to put them back in the vault가 다음 글에서 의미하는 바로 가장 적절한 것은?

As fine-art dealers, my partner Sidney and I do many appraisals. Appraising fine art is a highly specialized art. One of the most challenging tasks imposed upon the fine art appraiser is that of authenticating the artist to whom the art may have been attributed. Some time ago, Sidney was called in by a bank to study some paintings that were part of a large estate. He examined the works of art by famous artists as they were taken one by one from the vault, while the bank officer waited expectantly for confirmation of their value and to discuss the most profitable method of sale. "Well," the bank officer asked after the inspection, "what should I do?" "I'll tell you what you don't have to do," Sidney replied. "You don't have to put them back in the vault."

*appraisal: 감정, 평가

① The paintings have been sold.
② The paintings were found to be not genuine.
③ The paintings need more analysis and examination.
④ The paintings should be kept somewhere besides the vault.
⑤ The paintings are in poor condition and need to be restored.

22 다음 글의 요지로 가장 적절한 것은?

The media constantly report the results of opinion polls, and many people pay attention. They are impressed because the polls have an air of scientific authority, and the results are reported with what seems like super precision. Also, people tend to believe that the newspaper or radio or TV station or whatever is unbiased, authoritative, and intelligent. However, we all need to learn to be more critical. Understand that, because of their nature, polls can be unreliable. When you read the results of a poll, ask "What if the poll questions were written in such a way that the respondents were fooled into giving certain answers?" and "What if the sample of people polled is not a fair representation of the general population?" and "What if the author of the poll and the media reporting the results have a private aim?" The answers should help you see opinion polls in a very different light.

① 객관적이고 정확한 여론조사는 쉽지 않다.
② 여론조사 결과의 신뢰성이 점차 낮아지고 있다.
③ 여론조사 결과를 맹신하는 것은 위험할 수 있다.
④ 여론조사 결과는 전체의 의견을 대변하지 못한다.
⑤ 현상을 비판적으로 바라보는 태도가 공정한 사회를 만든다.

23 다음 글의 주제로 가장 적절한 것은?

Strange as it may sound, arms of a snow crystal that are quite separate can send signals to each other. Snow crystals have distinctive sets of vibrations. The vibrations are formed by atoms that move in time with other atoms located at matching positions in other parts of the crystal. When atoms are moving in a formation, a change in one part may spread evenly to other parts of the formation, just as a soldier who alters his pace in a marching group usually sets off a steady change of pace throughout the entire group. Thus, the arms of a developing snow crystal may not touch each other, but still they are affected by each other's changes. As in a mirror, changes in one arm are likely to occur in the other and that's why all the structures of snow crystals are symmetrical.

① diversity of snow crystal shapes
② conditions that make snow crystals
③ factors that affect the types of snow crystals
④ reasons the arms of a snow crystal are the same
⑤ lessons that people can learn from snow crystals

24 다음 글의 제목으로 가장 적절한 것은?

Perception refers to the meaning we assign to information when it is received by our senses. Our eyes may work like cameras, but what we see (or perceive) is affected by the information contained in our brains. For example, look at the following: I3. If you were asked what *number* this is, you would probably say "13." Yet if you were asked to name the *letter*, you might answer "B." There is only one figure, but your perception changes based on what you are asked and your existing knowledge of numbers and letters. To a young child with no stored information of either numbers or letters, these would be meaningless marks on paper. The assignment of meaning to incoming stimuli, therefore, depends on prior knowledge and on what we expect to see. In a sense, the brain is always checking new information against what has previously been encountered.

① The Role of Senses in Perception
② Factors Influencing Our Perception
③ Commonly Misunderstood Symbols
④ How Your Brain Can Trick Your Senses
⑤ Why We Assign Meaning to Information

25 다음 도표의 내용과 일치하지 않는 것은?

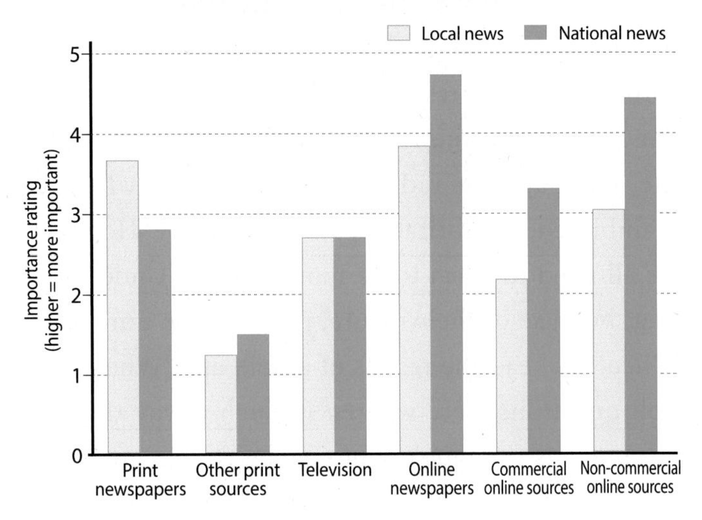

The chart above shows how our readers rated the importance of six different sources of local and national news. ① Among the six, only two sources of local news were considered less important than television. ② Perhaps unsurprisingly, the category "other print sources," which might include magazines and newsletters, was rated the least important source of all news. ③ The only news source considered more important for local news than for national news was print newspapers. ④ Readers preferred online newspapers to print newspapers as a source of national news. ⑤ It is also interesting to note that non-commercial online sources were rated the most important source of national news.

26 John Nash에 관한 다음 글의 내용과 일치하지 않는 것은?

John Nash, a genius American mathematician, was diagnosed with paranoid schizophrenia when he was 28 and spent the next 30 years in and out of mental hospitals. In 1970, however, he stopped taking antipsychotic medication, and gradually began to recover. He was awarded the 1994 Memorial Nobel Prize in Economic Sciences in recognition of the work he did in game theory as a graduate student at Princeton. He had theorized that an individual's success in a game depends on the choices of the other players. In Princeton legend, Nash was "The Phantom of Fine Hall," a ghost-like figure who would scribble equations on blackboards in the middle of the night in Fine Hall, the center of mathematics at Princeton. Nash was the subject of the Oscar-winning Hollywood movie *A Beautiful Mind*.

*paranoid schizophrenia: 편집증적 조현병

① 미국의 천재 수학자로, 30년간 조현병을 앓았다.
② 약물 치료를 중단한 후 병이 더욱 악화되었다.
③ 대학원 시절에 발표한 이론으로 노벨상을 받았다.
④ 한밤중에 대학 강당 칠판에 수학 방정식을 갈겨쓰곤 했다.
⑤ 그의 이야기는 영화로 제작되어 오스카상을 수상했다.

27 Graduation Ceremony에 관한 다음 안내문의 내용과 일치하지 않는 것은?

PATTISON COLLEGE
Graduation Ceremony

Date: Friday, September 18, 2020
Time: 2:00 p.m. to 3:30 p.m. (Students should arrive between 12:30 – 1:00 p.m. to receive gown & ceremony instructions)
Place: Pattison Auditorium
Guests: Up to 4 guests per graduate (Additional guests will be seated in a separate location.)

Please let us know if you will attend
and the number of guests.
We will also need your height
for your graduation gown.

ALL GRADUATES – RSVP by calling 604-580-1770 or emailing admin@pattison.com. Complimentary childcare will be available for children ages 3-11. Please contact Mahsa at 604-580-2772 or msa@pattison.com for more details.

① 졸업식은 1시간 30분 동안 진행된다.
② 학생들은 늦어도 오후 1시까지는 도착해야 한다.
③ 초대 손님은 졸업생 1명당 4명을 초과할 수 없다.
④ 본인의 참석 여부와 초대 손님의 수를 회신해야 한다.
⑤ 3세부터 11세까지의 아이들을 돌보는 시설이 운영된다.

28 Earth Day Recycling Event에 관한 다음 안내문의 내용과 일치하는 것은?

Earth Day Recycling Event!

Open to All Blain County Residents

If you're interested in helping your family gain a better understanding of recycling and waste reduction, come to the Earth Day Recycling Event at the DHS ReStore. We will be collecting a variety of used goods for reuse and recycling as well as offering educational workshops.

Date and Time: Saturday, April 22, from 11 a.m. to 4 p.m.

Location: 430 N. Front Ave., Sturgeon Bay

What to Bring

- books and DVDs
- glasses and sunglasses
- electronics (no cell phones, please)
- lightly worn clothing and shoes

* Free entry does not include lunch. Burgers will be available for $3 and hot dogs for $2.

Please visit us online for more information about what to recycle: blaincountyhabitat.org.

① Blain County 주민 중 성인을 대상으로 한다.
② 프로그램으로 교육 워크숍이 있다.
③ 토요일 오후에 다섯 시간 동안 진행된다.
④ 핸드폰을 포함한 전자기기를 가져갈 수 있다.
⑤ 입장료는 무료이며, 점심식사도 무료로 제공된다.

29 다음 글의 밑줄 친 부분 중, 어법상 틀린 것은? [3점]

Why is it legal to drive while eating or drinking ① but not while talking on a cell phone? It is not convincing enough to argue that cell phone use is more ② distracting than those activities. When all other attempts to explain the reason for a law ③ fails, a good strategy is to ask how it might change the income of those affected by it. If legislators banned the consumption of coffee and soda and hamburgers while driving, sales at fast food restaurants ④ would decline suddenly. But by allowing headsets as an exception to the ban on cell phone use while driving, legislators do not run that risk. Moreover, mobile phone companies stand to earn ⑤ even higher profits through the sale of additional headsets.

30 다음 글의 밑줄 친 부분 중, 문맥상 낱말의 쓰임이 적절하지 않은 것은? [3점]

A way to more effective handling of written information is to quickly ① scan the whole of it before you actually read it. When you read the newspaper, read the headline of a story first, and you will get the ② detailed idea of what it concerns. Then, when you read the story, you look for more information to explain it further. The material isn't ③ unfamiliar to you if you are working from a base of information and adding to it. Actually, you wouldn't pick up a magazine from a newsstand and buy it without ④ previewing its contents. When doing this, you look over the whole magazine and get an idea of what it is about and what it contains before spending your money on it. In this way, you ensure a more ⑤ sensible purchase and use of your money.

[31~34] 다음 빈칸에 들어갈 말로 가장 적절한 것을 고르시오.

31 Jumbo jets have enabled Korean computer consultants to fly to Silicon Valley as if popping next door, and Singaporean entrepreneurs now reach Seattle in a day. The borders of the world's greatest ocean have been joined as never before. But what about the people on the islands that the jumbos fly over five miles above? Has the mighty jumbo brought them greater communion with those whose shores are washed by the same water? It hasn't, of course. Air travel may have enabled travelers to buzz across the ocean, but the concurrent decline in ocean travel has only increased the ______________ of many island communities. Pitcairn, like many other Pacific islands, has never felt so far from its neighbors. [3점]

*concurrent: 동시(발생)의

① identity ② strength
③ isolation ④ unity
⑤ competition

32 As children, the most common problem-solving strategy we employed was likely ______________. For instance, let's say the problem a child faces is how to retrieve a toy his mother has put up on a shelf. The child may try to stretch his arms to reach the toy. That doesn't work. Next, he tries to climb up on the shelf to reach the toy. He falls; that doesn't work. When he can't get it on his own, he asks his mother for the toy. She says no; that doesn't work. Still undeterred, the child cries a bit for the toy. The mother ignores the cries; that doesn't work. Finally, he throws a full-blown tantrum, complete with screams, kicks, and tears. Exasperated, the mother gives the child the toy to appease him. Bingo—the tantrum worked.

① trial and error
② copy and imitation
③ reasoning and analysis
④ reward and punishment
⑤ association and visualization

33 The experience of live performance is ______________. As an example, let's look at a live theater performance and the three main parties involved: the playwright or director, the actors, and the audience. The playwright means the play to express certain ideas, and this meaning is affected by both the actors' performances and audience responses. Actors add layers of meaning to the playwright's words with the personal experiences they bring to their roles, and their performances are affected in turn by audience reactions. Audiences respond to the playwright's ideas not only through the actors but also through the physical experience of being in the theater. During any performance, something amazing happens: each party experiences the action not only from that party's perspective but also from the perspective of two others. [3점]

① often challenging for certain audiences
② a wild gathering of the most creative people
③ a mutual experience for the parties involved
④ like an amazing party that everyone will remember
⑤ something whose meaning is best interpreted individually

34 Aggression, an act of hostility by one person toward another, is something that is seen everywhere. In fact, it's one of the defining characteristics we have in common with other species within the animal kingdom. While the cause of aggression in animals is mainly about scarce food resources and land territory, human beings usually show aggressive behavior ______________________. Think of a little brother and his teenage sister, who are constantly arguing with each other because the younger sibling won't leave the teenage sibling alone, bothering her with questions about this or that and constantly looking over her shoulder. Or recall a situation where an acquaintance came too close to you during a conversation, in which you felt your comfort zone had been violated so you had to take a few steps back or you might have pushed the person away from you. [3점]

① when reacting to being treated badly
② to other people who are smaller and weaker
③ in regard to violations of their personal space
④ when necessary to protect their family and property
⑤ toward strangers, or newcomers in their community

35 다음 글에서 전체 흐름과 관계 없는 문장은?

Each autumn, when daylight hours become fewer and temperatures fall, animals take action against the coming cold. Many species travel thousands of kilometers to spend the winter in warmer southern lands or oceans. ① Earthworms, which cannot survive in freezing temperatures, start on a vertical migration from soil at the surface of the earth to soil deeper underground. ② Having no eyes, earthworms respond to changes in light through their skin, which is so sensitive that chemicals can easily kill them. ③ Meters below the surface of the earth, the temperature remains comfortable for earthworms. ④ Using little barbs that stick out of their bodies to grasp the earth, they dig deep down to an area where the soil will not freeze. ⑤ When they reach the safe area, they curl up into a ball and spend the entire winter inactive and warm.

*barb: (동식물에 난) 수염 모양의 것

[36~37] 주어진 글 다음에 이어질 글의 순서로 가장 적절한 것을 고르시오.

36

> Intelligent drivers understand that traffic lights are a fact of life, and that they will encounter roughly equal numbers of red and green lights over time. They don't take it personally if a light ahead turns red; they simply stop and put up with the short interruption to their trip.

(A) So they drive stupidly, speeding through yellow lights and blocking intersections so that other vehicles and pedestrians cannot pass. Or even worse, they cause a collision.

(B) These drivers should change their perception and see a red traffic light as a welcome sight. If they saw red lights as a signal to relax for a moment, driving would be a more pleasant experience, and the roads would be safer for everyone.

(C) Other drivers, however, have a decidedly unhealthy attitude; they see red lights as enemies that have to be beaten and getting stopped by one as a sign of weakness.

① (A) — (C) — (B)
② (B) — (A) — (C)
③ (B) — (C) — (A)
④ (C) — (A) — (B)
⑤ (C) — (B) — (A)

37

Bank runs or bank panics have occurred multiple times throughout American history. Because banks operate with far less than 100% required reserves, it is possible that if enough customers demand their account balances on a single day, the bank will not be able to meet the demand.

(A) However, if the speculation or rumors are pervasive, then banks may become unwilling to lend to each other. When this happens, it sparks even more speculation, and can create a run on the entire financial system.

(B) Once the line starts forming at the bank's door, other customers will notice and the rumor will spread. Banks can avert a run if they are able to borrow from other banks and provide their customers' balances.

(C) Many bank panics have been caused because of rumor or speculation about a bank's financial health. If enough people believe the rumor, they will logically want to withdraw their funds and move them to another financial institution or stuff them under the mattress. [3점]

① (A) — (C) — (B)　② (B) — (A) — (C)
③ (B) — (C) — (A)　④ (C) — (A) — (B)
⑤ (C) — (B) — (A)

[38~39] 글의 흐름으로 보아, 주어진 문장이 들어가기에 가장 적절한 곳을 고르시오.

38

The night owls, however, ate and slept inconsistently each day and, as a result, suffered "mini jet lag" symptoms.

When it comes to health, early birds have the advantage over night owls. (①) A study has found that early risers tend to be consistent in their habits, and that this regularity leads to better health. (②) The study noted that the early birds were more likely to eat, exercise, and sleep at about the same time each day. (③) It also noted that their regular routines promoted better sleep. (④) Having better sleep meant they had more energy during the day. (⑤) They were advised to fix their irregular routines by going to bed 15 minutes earlier each night until they reached an 11 p.m. bedtime, not exercising or eating before sleep, and avoiding sleeping in on weekends.

39

> This attribute of the tourism industry presents a significant challenge to tourism suppliers who must figure out how to advertise their products to potential customers.

Before making a purchase, it is always wise to compare products. Consumers can see, touch, and maybe smell or taste a product before deciding to buy it. (①) On the other hand, services are difficult to compare because consumers cannot inspect them first before purchase. (②) For example, the tourism industry — hotels, souvenir shops, and tourist attractions — is composed mostly of services. (③) Those products whose attributes can be determined only after purchase are called experience goods. (④) In buying experience goods, consumers must often rely on the reputation of the seller, a professional advisor, the experience of friends and relatives, and their own past experiences in making a purchase decision. (⑤) In sum, tourism is largely an information business prior to and through the actual sale of services.

40 다음 글의 내용을 한 문장으로 요약하고자 한다. 빈칸 (A), (B)에 들어갈 말로 가장 적절한 것은?

> Pablo Britiol, a psychology professor at the Autonomous University of Madrid, performed a study about the relationship between the body and the mind. He assigned their subjects to either sit up straight and push out their chests or sit slouched forward with their faces looking at their knees. As they held these poses for a few minutes, they were asked to describe themselves with either three positive traits or three negative traits that would be likely to either help or hurt them in their future professional lives. Not only did those in the upright position find it easier to think positive, empowering thoughts about themselves, they also believed more strongly in the traits they listed. The slouchers, on the other hand, weren't convinced of their positive or negative traits; they struggled even to know who they were.

> According to the experiment above, the way subjects ___(A)___ themselves was influenced by their ___(B)___ when they described their traits.

	(A)		(B)
①	rated	……	mentality
②	rated	……	posture
③	introduced	……	environment
④	treated	……	mentality
⑤	treated	……	posture

[41~42] 다음 글을 읽고, 물음에 답하시오.

The blame instinct is the instinct to find a clear, simple reason for why something bad has happened. It seems that it comes very naturally for us to decide that when things go wrong, it must be because of some bad individual with bad intentions. We like to believe that things happen because someone wanted them to, that individuals have power and agency; otherwise, the world feels unpredictable, confusing, and frightening. The blame instinct makes us (a) exaggerate the importance of individuals or of particular groups. This instinct to find a (b) guilty party hinders our ability to develop a true, fact-based understanding of the world. It (c) blocks our learning because once we have decided who to punch in the face, we stop looking for explanations elsewhere. For example, blaming an airplane crash on a sleepy pilot will not help to stop future crashes. To do that, we must ask: Why was he sleepy? How can we regulate sleepy pilots in the future? If we stop thinking when we find the sleepy pilot, we make no progress. To understand most of the world's significant problems we have to look to the (d) individual. The same instinct is triggered when things go well. When something goes well, we are very quick to give the credit to an individual or a simple cause, when again it is usually more complicated. If you really want to change the world, you have to understand it. (e) Following your blame instinct isn't going to help.

41 **윗글의 제목으로 가장 적절한 것은?**

① Blame Instinct: A Double-Edged Sword
② How Can We Control the Blame Instinct?
③ Stop the Blame Game in Your Relationship
④ Why We Should Coordinate Different Views
⑤ Blame Instinct Undermines the Problem-solving Ability

42 **밑줄 친 (a)~(e) 중에서 문맥상 낱말의 쓰임이 적절하지 않은 것은?** [3점]

① (a) ② (b) ③ (c) ④ (d) ⑤ (e)

[43~45] 다음 글을 읽고, 물음에 답하시오.

(A)

Nicole and Joe, my mother and father, first met in New York. Nicole was sitting alone in a cafe reading Charles Dickens' *Great Expectations*. The cafe was full, so Joe asked if he could share her table. They were instantly attracted to one another, and talked for hours. When she had to leave, Nicole wrote her phone number in the book and gave it to Joe.

(B)

She took a new copy of *Great Expectations* with her. After a long day of sightseeing, she found a table in a cafe, opened her book to the first page, and started thinking once again about the man she had met in New York. She was interrupted by (a) a young man carrying a tray of dishes and asking in French if she would share her table. She nodded and returned to her reading. Then, she heard his voice. It said, "I should never have lost that book." Looking up again, she saw Joe, smiling back at her.

(C)

Joe had forgotten to ask for my mother's last name. The phone number in the book was his only link to her. The call Nicole longed for never came from (b) the young man she met in New York. Joe kept returning to the cafe, but (c) he never found Nicole. Three summers later, my mother went to England to take a literature course. During a three-day break in her studies, she flew to Paris to spend 72 hours sightseeing.

(D)

After she left, Joe couldn't stop thinking about her. The next day, after a sleepless night, (d) my father went to visit his parents in Brooklyn, and brought the book to read on the subway. He was tired, so he slipped the book into the pocket of his coat, laid it on the seat next to (e) him, and closed his eyes. When my father opened his eyes, he had already passed Brooklyn, and his coat was gone. Someone had stolen it, and with it, the book. My mother's telephone number was lost.

43 주어진 글 (A)에 이어질 내용을 순서에 맞게 배열한 것으로 가장 적절한 것은?

① (B) — (D) — (C)
② (C) — (B) — (D)
③ (C) — (D) — (B)
④ (D) — (B) — (C)
⑤ (D) — (C) — (B)

44 밑줄 친 (a)~(e) 중에서 가리키는 대상이 나머지 넷과 다른 것은?

① (a) ② (b) ③ (c) ④ (d) ⑤ (e)

45 윗글에 관한 내용으로 적절하지 않은 것은?

① Nicole과 Joe는 뉴욕에서 처음 만났다.
② Joe는 *Great Expectations*라는 책을 선물 받았다.
③ Nicole은 파리의 한 카페에서 Joe를 생각했다.
④ Nicole은 학업을 위해 파리에 머물러 있었다.
⑤ Joe는 지하철에서 코트와 책을 도난당했다.

: AFTER TESTING

종료 시 분
소요시간 분

학습 마무리

1 채점하기 | 정답 및 해설 p.2
주의 틀린 문제를 다시 풀 수 있도록 정답을 본문에 표기하지 마세요.
2 등급 확인
3 틀린 유형 확인 후 전략 적용 복습 및 해설지 확인

How to Review

1 틀린 문제와 ✓ 표시한 문제는 다시 풀고 해설 확인하기
2 내가 표시한 정답 근거가 해설과 일치하는지 확인하기
3 잘 모르는 부분으로 표시한 내용은 해설을 통해 완전히 이해하기
4 어휘 외우기 (어휘 목록 다운로드 www.cedubook.com)
5 다음 회에 개선할 점 정리하기 (시간 엄수, 취약 유형 보완 등)

POWER UP!

실전 모의고사

02

: BEFORE TESTING

시작 시 분

학습 목표

1 **제한시간** (OMR 마킹시간 포함) ☐ 40분 ☐ 45분
2 **어휘예습** ☐ 해당 없음 ☐ 완료
3 **문제풀이순서** ☐ 순서대로 ☐ 2점 → 3점 ☐ 기타
4 **기타 목표**

Check Point

1 **정답 근거** e.g. 밑줄 긋기
2 **잘 모르는 부분** e.g. 〈 〉 또는 ? 표시
3 **자신 없는 문제** e.g. 문제 번호에 ✓표시

18 다음 글의 목적으로 가장 적절한 것은?

Dear Ms. Ellen,

We're so pleased that you came to our daughter's wedding and enjoyed yourself so much. Victoria and our new son-in-law will soon return from their honeymoon, but their wedding album has not yet been prepared. The reason for this is that the official photographs were useless. Most were out of focus, others were poorly composed, and in several photographs the image was covered by the photographer's finger! Thus, we have informed him that he will not be paid. We noticed that you had a camera at the wedding. I would be most grateful if you could email me any pictures you have so that we can assemble a wedding album of photographs taken by guests. I look forward to hearing from you soon.

Best regards,
Janet Miller

① 결혼식에 참석해준 것에 대해 감사하려고
② 결혼식 앨범을 보내주지 못한 것을 사과하려고
③ 결혼식 때 사진 촬영을 해줄 수 있는지 문의하려고
④ 가지고 있는 결혼식 사진을 보내달라고 부탁하려고
⑤ 결혼식 사진을 형편없이 찍은 것에 대해 항의하려고

19 다음 글에 드러난 Keenan의 심경 변화로 가장 적절한 것은?

Two weeks before John Assaraf's son Keenan started kindergarten, John took Keenan up to the kindergarten building and looked through the window with him. Keenan showed no emotion and said nothing. He just played with a toy he had brought. John told his son all kinds of stories about kindergarten and what a great time it was going to be for Keenan. But his son didn't listen. Worried but not knowing what to do, John decided not to mention kindergarten again. Surprisingly, when the first day of school arrived, Keenan had completely changed. As John and he walked up the steps together to enter the building, John could hardly keep him from running in ahead of him. It was a brand-new experience, but Keenan was completely prepared. His face brightened up as though he were floating on air. John realized that Keenan just had needed some more time to be ready.

① bored → disappointed
② delighted → frightened
③ nervous → ashamed
④ horrified → proud
⑤ indifferent → excited

20 다음 글에서 필자가 주장하는 바로 가장 적절한 것은?

Plants, like animals, are subject to many diseases. It has been estimated that 30,000 different diseases attack our plants. Forty diseases are known to attack corn, for example, and about as many attack wheat. Since people all over the world depend on these crops for food, the results of unchecked plant diseases could be disastrous. If just one of the major crops were attacked and destroyed by disease, the resulting famines could kill millions of people. Presently, common diseases that lead to infections in major crops cannot be completely eliminated, and the plants cannot be completely physically isolated from the diseases. Therefore, many plant scientists are working on genetic modifications to help the plants develop built-in immunity. In order to maintain a sufficient food supply for the world's population, it is necessary for those involved in plant growth and management to find ways to combat plant diseases.

① 곡물에만 의존하는 식량 정책을 개선해야 한다.
② 식물 질병의 피해를 해결할 방안을 강구해야 한다.
③ 세계 식량 부족 문제에 대한 경각심을 가져야 한다.
④ 식물 질병의 확산을 막기 위해 검역을 강화해야 한다.
⑤ 유전자 변형이 생태계에 미치는 영향을 연구해야 한다.

21 밑줄 친 you never did—he quit가 다음 글에서 의미하는 바로 가장 적절한 것은?

What is the difference between those who throw in the towel on their dreams and those who struggle to maintain their dreams? It's getting back up and taking just one more small step forward. I once heard a great story of a high school basketball coach who was attempting to get his players to persevere through a difficult season. After several long and unsuccessful games, he stood before his team and said, "Did Michael Jordan ever quit?" The team responded with a "No!" He yelled, "What about the Wright brothers? Did they give up?" "No!" the team responded. "Did Walt Disney ever quit?" Again, the team yelled "No!" "Did Elmer McAllister ever quit?" There was a long silence. Finally one player was bold enough to ask, "Who's Elmer McAllister? We've never heard of him." The coach snapped back, "Of course, you never did—he quit."

① Anyone can become famous if they try harder.
② Everybody has a talent and a duty to improve it.
③ The future belongs to those who prepare for it today.
④ There is nobody who gave up and then became great.
⑤ Being famous requires natural ability and constant effort.

22 다음 글의 요지로 가장 적절한 것은?

If there is a lesson for us in the history of discovery, it is that the huge growth in our knowledge of and reverence for science may trick us into thinking we are less ignorant than we really are. We like to think that discoveries give final answers, but what we usually get instead are more questions. Every great discovery discloses unimagined realms of ignorance. It is clear that the great obstacle to progress is not ignorance but the illusion of certainty. Discoverers have always been the ones to say that we do not know as much as we think we do. The courage to believe that we don't know something is the first stage in discovery. This was (and is) the courageousness of such giants as Charles Darwin, Albert Einstein, and Stephen Hawking.

① 무지를 인정하는 데에는 용기가 필요하다.
② 사회 발전에 가장 큰 장애는 지식의 단절이다.
③ 지식과 겸손을 겸비한 과학자가 더 존경받는다.
④ 역사상 새로운 발견은 무지를 깨닫는 데서 비롯되었다.
⑤ 인간의 무지는 새로운 발견을 통해 점점 줄어들고 있다.

23 다음 글의 주제로 가장 적절한 것은?

A decisive moment occurred in the nineteenth century when those in advertising and journalism discovered that if they framed their stories and appeals with fear, they could capture our attention. It is an emotion we find difficult to resist or control, and so they continually shifted our focus to new possible sources of anxiety. They took advantage of the latest health scare, the new crime wave, a social faux pas we might be committing, and endless dangers in the environment of which we were not aware. With the increasing sophistication of the media and the overpowering quality of the imagery, they have been able to give us the feeling that we are fragile creatures in an environment full of danger — even though we live in a world infinitely safer and more predictable than anything our ancestors knew. With their help, our anxieties have only multiplied.

*faux pas: 무례, 실례

① ways to cope with unrealistic fears and anxiety
② past and current strategies used in advertisement
③ roles of the media in protecting consumers' rights
④ intensified anxiety in modern times due to the media
⑤ aspects of the media's manipulation of public opinion

24 다음 글의 제목으로 가장 적절한 것은?

Suppose you are one of a large group of participants in a study and for your time, you are given either a coffee mug or a nice pen. The two gifts are of similar value and randomly distributed. You and your fellow participants are then offered the chance to trade. Considering the random distribution, you would assume that about half the people would be happy to swap. But in fact there are very few trades. This phenomenon is called the *endowment effect*. Once something is given to you, it's yours. Even after a couple of minutes, giving it up will entail a loss. And because losses are worse than gains are good, the mug or pen with which you have been "endowed" is worth more to you than it is to a potential trading partner. And "losing" (giving up) the pen will hurt worse than "gaining" (trading for) the mug will give pleasure. Thus, you refuse the trade.

① Ownership Affects Our Valuation
② Gains Are More Powerful Than Losses
③ Pros and Cons of Trading Restrictions
④ Rational Choice in an Uncertain World
⑤ Get What You Deserve, Not What You Desire

25 다음 도표의 내용과 일치하지 않는 것은?

Proportion Exceeding Government Guidelines of Weekly Alcohol Consumption

(government guidelines: 21 units for men, 14 units for women)

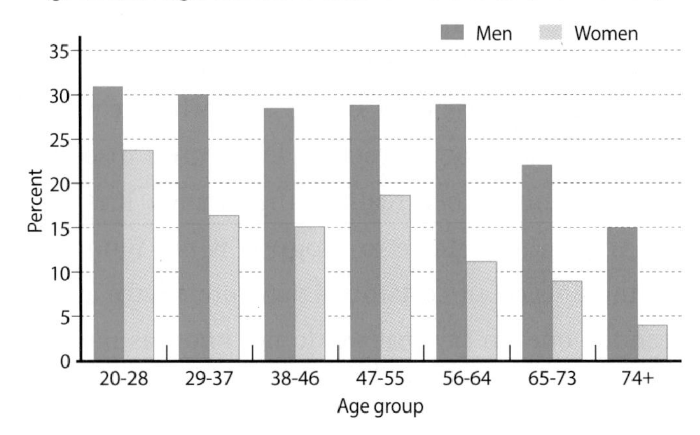

This graph shows the average weekly drinking habits of men and women by age group. A unit of alcohol is equivalent to a 250 ml glass of beer or a 125 ml glass of wine. ① Men drink more alcohol than women in all age groups, and the gap is the largest in the 56-64 age group. ② Among men, the proportion exceeding 21 units per week is fairly uniform, at around 30%, up to the 56-64 age group. ③ In older age groups of men, the proportion decreases to 22% of those aged 65-73, and 15% of those aged 74 and over. ④ Among women, it's the most senior age group that has the highest percentage of drinkers exceeding the government's 14 recommended units per week. ⑤ Those aged 47-55 are the second most excessive female drinkers, followed by women in the 29-37 year-old-age group.

26 Somerset Maugham에 관한 다음 글의 내용과 일치하지 않는 것은?

Somerset Maugham's masterpiece is generally agreed to be *Of Human Bondage*, a semi-autobiographical novel whose main character is Philip Carey, an orphan like Maugham, who was raised by his uncle. Philip has a clubfoot of which he is painfully self-conscious and embarrassed, echoing Maugham's own struggles with a speech disability. His other successful novels are also based on characters from real life, including the painter Paul Gauguin whose life is fictionalized in *The Moon and Sixpence*. Maugham's last major novel, *The Razor's Edge*, was a new departure for him in many ways. While much of the novel takes place in Europe, its main character is an American World War I soldier who travels to India seeking enlightenment. The story's theme of war weariness touched many readers.

*clubfoot: 만곡족(굽은 발)

① 자신을 닮은 소설 주인공을 만들어냈다.
② 신체적인 장애를 갖고 있었다.
③ 실존 인물의 삶을 소설화했다.
④ 미국 군인이 인도를 여행하는 소설을 썼다.
⑤ *The Razor's Edge*에서 전쟁의 피폐함을 다뤘다.

27 공연에 대한 다음 안내문의 내용과 일치하지 않는 것은?

Venue Announcement

Our staged production of Schubert's Goethe-Lieder will be hosted by the Austrian Cultural Forum at the Embassy of Austria on Friday, May 20, at 8 p.m. We are looking forward to collaborating with the embassy in creating this unusual production!

About the Production:

Two singers and a pianist will perform the Lieder in the original German in the embassy's atrium. Selections from the Lieder will be woven into a 90-minute dramatic narrative that explores the resonances of Schubert's art songs in our contemporary world.

General Admission: $25

Students/Seniors (65+): $20

About the Cultural Forum:

The Cultural Forum aims to present innovative, contemporary artistic and scientific achievements across a wide range of disciplines and to act as a forum for discussion and lectures on relevant issues in culture and politics.

*lieder: 가곡 **resonance: (소리의) 울림

① 공연은 5월 20일 밤 8시에 시작한다.
② 성악가 두 명과 피아니스트 한 명이 공연한다.
③ 공연은 90분 동안 진행된다.
④ 학생과 65세 이상은 입장료가 할인된다.
⑤ 문화 포럼은 예술 분야에 한정된 문제를 다룬다.

28 Scholarship Program에 관한 다음 안내문의 내용과 일치하는 것은?

Scholarship Program

The following is the scholarship program offered for undergraduate applicants. Students may apply for the program before or during the admission application period.

Eligibility

International applicants who wish to apply for 4-year undergraduate programs at ANU.

* *Those who wish to study in the programs that are longer than 4 years — such as medicine, veterinary medicine, pharmacy, and architecture — cannot apply for this scholarship.*

Number of Recipients

Approximately 20-40 every year

Subsidies

- Full tuition fee: tuition exemption for 8 semesters
- Airfare: one economy round-trip ticket
- Korean language training fee: one year

  * *Korean language training is mandatory.*

Application Period

July 1, 2021–August 20, 2021

Contact: ANU staff in charge: 82-2-820-6000, anuadmit@anu.ac.kr

① 입학 신청 기간 이후부터 신청을 받는다.
② 4년 이상 과정을 공부하는 국제 학생이 대상이다.
③ 매년 약 20~40명이 장학금을 받는다.
④ 8학기 동안 수업료의 일부가 면제된다.
⑤ 한국어 교육은 선택적으로 들을 수 있다.

29 다음 글의 밑줄 친 부분 중, 어법상 틀린 것은? [3점]

It was a day when, upon opening my eyes at dawn, I had no desire to do anything but ① get some rest. It was my third day in Melbourne, Australia. The day's schedule — a trip to the Dandenong Ranges National Park — didn't hold much appeal at ② that early hour. Interestingly enough, however, it was the time I spent in the Dandenong Ranges ③ that was still hovering in my memory on the day I flew back home. The Dandenong Ranges are densely forested hills ④ located to the east of Melbourne, where sky-high eucalyptus trees create a majestic atmosphere. The area is also home to Puffing Billy, a century-old steam locomotive ⑤ whom engineers, with long white beards, transport tourists from all over the world.

30 다음 글의 밑줄 친 부분 중, 문맥상 낱말의 쓰임이 적절하지 않은 것은? [3점]

For a researcher, variability is typically a ① curse. It can mean a difference between a publishable study and one that goes straight to the file cabinet. Essentially, researchers test their hypothesis by seeing whether it can improve conditions enough so that they notice a difference ② beyond that which occurs by chance or "natural" variability. If I tested a drug to make people taller and everyone who got the drug got taller, and no one got taller who didn't get the drug, it would not be difficult to see the effectiveness of the treatment. Rarely, however, are things so straightforward. The more variety there is in the conditions of the experiment, the ③ harder it is to see if the drug is effective. If some people in both groups grew but the drug group got a little taller on average, the effect of the drug is ④ unquestionable. The drug may or may not have resulted in a statistically significant difference. If not, the paper is not published and the drug will not be ⑤ easy to promote.

[31~34] 다음 빈칸에 들어갈 말로 가장 적절한 것을 고르시오.

31 There are people who cannot form lasting friendships. Who are they? Those who cannot be a good friend. It is probably not their lack of understanding nor lack of good nature that is at fault; neither is it their lack of entertaining or useful qualities. On the contrary, they may have many attractive aspects, but they will almost certainly have one weakness that spoils all these good characteristics. That is, they care nothing about you and are not affected at all by what you think of them. They show no joy at your approach, and when you leave them, it is with a feeling that they can get along just as well without you. This is not sullenness nor absent-mindedness. They are just ____________ to others and concentrate solely on their own thoughts.

① indifferent
② arrogant
③ impolite
④ irresponsible
⑤ cruel

32 In the 20th century, architects in major cities in Europe designed structures in a way that reduced noise and yet made living as comfortable as possible. They used techniques such as making walls hollow and filling this wall space with materials that absorb noise. Thick carpets and heavy curtains were used to cover floors and windows. Air conditioners and fireplaces were designed to filter air through soundproofing materials. However, after much time and effort had been spent in making buildings less noisy, it was discovered that people also reacted negatively to ________________. Now, architects are designing structures that reduce undesirable noise but retain the kind of noise that people seem to need.

① poor designs
② extreme noise
③ low-quality materials
④ a lack of sound
⑤ excessive furnishings

33 A to-do list, a tool to help us plan and prepare our day, can be made with an appointment calendar, a schedule planner, or a host of electronic devices. Even though we are thorough when making these 'to-do' lists, inevitably something else, which cannot be pushed to the side, comes up and at the end of the day we're left with an unfinished 'to-do' list, which becomes a source of great tension and unhappiness. It's time to rethink how we plan our days so that we ________________________________. The key is not to say, "I have to deal with this important task today," but rather to say, "I need to find a good day for this important task." This will mean that what we do is actually up to us and we're not emotionally committed to actually finishing something that will just never get finished. [3점]

① have more free time to do our household chores
② choose the right form of tool to make our list with
③ make time planning a real tool that is under our control
④ are able to control our emotions whenever it's necessary
⑤ have completely finished our 'to-do' list at the end of the day

34 While electrical energy is an exceptionally clean and convenient form of energy for a wide array of uses, it is ______________________________. Generating stations have to be built and operated, and high-voltage transmission lines constructed, all of which consume a substantial amount of energy. The earliest generating stations lost all but 4 percent of what they produced, and this rose to about 13 percent in the mid-1920s, and then to about 25 percent by the 1950s. However, since then there has been almost no further improvement. This means that although a third of the world's energy is used to produce electricity, at least two-thirds of it is wasted in generation and transmission. Furthermore, since it is exceedingly difficult to store, electricity is generally produced on demand. When demand does not meet predictions, the result is a blackout which can affect thousands of people and cost millions of dollars. [3점]

① an outdated method of transmitting power
② a highly inefficient way of powering our world
③ the leading cause of today's world energy crisis
④ a misapplication of the law of supply and demand
⑤ the perfect example of an unpredictable commodity

35 **다음 글에서 전체 흐름과 관계 없는 문장은?**

In Australia, failure to vote is punishable by fines or even by imprisonment. Some of us think this is an abusive exercise of power, while many others insist that our government consider adopting the same system to secure greater democratic involvement of the population. ① Currently, our democracy is deeply endangered through a lack of participation in elections. ② If local elections are held simultaneously with national elections, generally a higher voter turnout is achieved. ③ Low participation rates mean our politicians are not representative of the population as a whole. ④ Since the poor and disadvantaged are far less likely to vote than any other socio-economic group, they can safely be ignored by mainstream politicians. ⑤ Liberal democracy relies upon a balance of rights, and thus the resolution of such a democratic crisis may in a small way restrict some personal liberties, but it is in the interests of society as a whole.

[36~37] 주어진 글 다음에 이어질 글의 순서로 가장 적절한 것을 고르시오.

36

A paradigm is a set of beliefs, assumptions, and values. It's your way of judging reality or seeing things, rather like wearing glasses.

(A) Then I got new glasses and was astonished at how wonderfully clear and detailed everything now looked. That's often the way it is. Until we fix our incorrect paradigms, we don't know how much we're missing.

(B) Then, you will probably behave in ways that are stupid. What you should do is change your prescription! I thought my eyesight was great until I had it tested and was shocked to discover that it was actually quite bad.

(C) If you have faulty paradigms regarding yourself or the world in general, it's like wearing the wrong prescription glasses, because what you see is what you get. For example, let's say that according to your paradigm, you see yourself as stupid.

① (A) — (C) — (B)
② (B) — (A) — (C)
③ (B) — (C) — (A)
④ (C) — (A) — (B)
⑤ (C) — (B) — (A)

37

How did astronomy start? Imagine being a cave person, laboring away with hunter-gathering tasks day after day and then hiding in your rocky home after dark so the creatures of the night don't eat you and your family. If you do venture out at night, it's for short trips not far from the cave.

(A) You hardly know what to make of all this. Everything you see is beyond your reach, but you've noticed over the years you've been watching them that the lights in the sky follow the same paths year after year.

(B) Perhaps you decide to make a record of what you see — in a painting on the wall of a cave, or on an animal hide. That way you can teach others about it and add that knowledge to the information you and your clan need to survive.

(C) So one night after the bright thing in the sky has gone down below the horizon, you're just about to head back to the cave when you happen to look up and really notice the night sky in all its glory. Little bright points of light twinkle at you.

① (A) — (C) — (B)
② (B) — (A) — (C)
③ (B) — (C) — (A)
④ (C) — (A) — (B)
⑤ (C) — (B) — (A)

[38~39] 글의 흐름으로 보아, 주어진 문장이 들어가기에 가장 적절한 곳을 고르시오.

38

However, contrary to popular belief, pirates did not routinely compel large numbers of prisoners to join them.

During the classical period of piracy, sailors from captured ships sometimes voluntarily joined pirate crews. (①) If the pirates needed extra hands, the volunteers might be accepted and allowed to sign the Articles of Agreement, or the Pirate's Code. (②) In cases where the pirates were in great need of men, they might force unwilling sailors into piracy. (③) Carpenters, navigators, and other men with valuable skills were especially likely to be forced to join a pirate crew. (④) This is because adding too many new crew members would overburden the pirates' existing supplies and decrease the value of each man's share of plunder. (⑤) Therefore, even willing men might be turned away when not needed.

*plunder: 약탈품

39

Therefore, a respondent may not feel that consumer researchers are asking merely about a simple preference.

People may misrepresent themselves to interviewers when questioned about their opinions or surveyed about the products they prefer. (①) Because of this potential source of distortion, some consumer psychologists believe that it is not productive to ask persons directly for their opinions or preferences. (②) They claim that the direct question being asked may differ from what the respondents actually heard. (③) For example, by asking what brand of beverage a person prefers, we are, essentially, asking what kind of person he or she is. (④) Rather, he or she hears the question asking: "Do you drink the cheap stuff or the expensive, high-status brand?" (⑤) Critics of the survey method argue that we cannot uncover true human motivations and feelings through direct questions that allow the respondents to distort their feelings. [3점]

40 다음 글의 내용을 한 문장으로 요약하고자 한다. 빈칸 (A), (B)에 들어갈 말로 가장 적절한 것은? [3점]

Some of the most convincing neuroscience data for the benefits of getting just scared enough comes from studies of squirrel monkeys. When they were but 17 weeks old, monkeys were taken from their cozy cage once a week, for 10 weeks. They were put in another cage for an hour with adult monkeys they did not know — terrifying for squirrel monkey youngsters. Later, when they had just been weaned, the same monkeys were placed with their mothers in a strange cage. Those monkeys who had earlier been exposed to the stressful cages were able to meet the challenge of their new circumstances and proved far braver and more curious than others their age who had never left their mothers' side. The regular visits to a scary place acted as a vaccination against stress. Neuroscientists conclude that if humans as well as monkeys are exposed to stress they learn to handle, this mastery becomes imprinted in their neural circuitry, acting as a vaccination against stress.

*wean: (아기의) 젖을 떼다

↓

Studies suggest that if people are ____(A)____ exposed to stress they can handle, they will become more ____(B)____ when facing stress later.

(A)		(B)
① repeatedly	……	reluctant
② repeatedly	……	adaptable
③ accidentally	……	resistant
④ accidentally	……	adjustable
⑤ regularly	……	vulnerable

[41~42] 다음 글을 읽고, 물음에 답하시오.

"Prospect theory" explains why we don't act when we should. The theory says that when people are shown a high number of choices (or "prospects"), they are less likely to be able to decide quickly than when they have very few options. Also, when the options are very attractive, the decision becomes harder to make. Further, the longer it takes them to make a decision, the less likely it is that they will stop hesitating. Essentially, they become paralyzed by too much freedom of choice. Clearly, having ________________ is not always preferable.

One study asked people to complete a questionnaire in return for a reward; some were told they had five days to submit the completed questionnaire, others were told 21 days, and a third group had no deadline. Results: 66 percent of those with the five-day deadline returned their questionnaires, 40 percent of those with the 21-day deadline returned theirs, and only 25 percent with no time limit returned theirs. People with decision paralysis are advised by psychologists to remember that not doing something is itself a decision — and the worst decision you can make. Instead, just do something!

41 윗글의 제목으로 가장 적절한 것은?

① Your Single Greatest Choice
② How to Make a Quick Decision
③ Doing Nothing Is the Best Decision
④ Your Decisions Will Make Your Life Better
⑤ Prospect Theory: Ideas about Decision-making

42 윗글의 빈칸에 들어갈 말로 가장 적절한 것은? [3점]

① financial rewards
② a deadline for projects
③ a wider range of options
④ too much freedom in life
⑤ a time limit for decisions

[43~45] 다음 글을 읽고, 물음에 답하시오.

(A)

In his book *The Wings of Joy*, Sri Chinmoy tells an interesting story of perseverance and self-discipline. Once there was a young Indian boy named Bopdeb who was the worst possible student. Eventually, his teacher gave up and threw him out of school. His father said he didn't want (a) <u>him</u> around anymore. So, feeling miserable, Bopdeb left his home and went to the park in his village.

(B)

A few days later, he started reading his old Sanskrit grammar books again. He had been terrible in Sanskrit, but now he was able to remember what he read. He asked his father to look for a 'less harsh' tutor, and the tutor taught him to write Sanskrit step by step. Each step brought him closer to achieving (b) <u>his</u> objective and, in the process, he accomplished other goals — gaining confidence and self-esteem — as well. With the help of his tutor, he went on to become the greatest Sanskrit scholar in India.

(C)

Frustrated and confused, Bopdeb sat under a tree and said to himself, "I am useless." Day after day, Bopdeb sat under that tree beside a large pond in the village. From there, (c) <u>he</u> watched a young man carrying empty pitchers to the pond and filling them. Bopdeb observed that the man would fill the pitchers, place them on the stone steps, and then go and bathe in the pond. After getting refreshed, (d) <u>he</u> returned home with his pitchers of water.

(D)

One day, when no one was there, Bopdeb noticed that the part of the step on which the young man placed his pitchers was no longer flat like the rest. (e) <u>He</u> said to himself, "Because the man placed his pitchers here repeatedly, the stone has worn down. If even a stone can wear down, then what is wrong with my brain?" From this experience, Bopdeb came to understand patience and perseverance.

43 주어진 글 (A)에 이어질 내용을 순서에 맞게 배열한 것으로 가장 적절한 것은?

① (B) — (D) — (C)　② (C) — (B) — (D)
③ (C) — (D) — (B)　④ (D) — (B) — (C)
⑤ (D) — (C) — (B)

44 밑줄 친 (a)~(e) 중에서 가리키는 대상이 나머지 넷과 <u>다른</u> 것은?

① (a)　② (b)　③ (c)　④ (d)　⑤ (e)

45 윗글의 Bopdeb에 관한 내용으로 적절하지 <u>않은</u> 것은?

① 성적이 나빠 퇴학당했고 아버지도 그를 외면했다.
② 가정교사와 공부하면서 자신감을 갖게 되었다.
③ 인도에서 가장 위대한 산스크리트어 학자가 되었다.
④ 연못 근처에 갔다가 한 청년과 대화를 나누었다.
⑤ 마모된 돌계단을 보고 깨달음을 얻었다.

: AFTER TESTING

종료	시 분
소요시간	분

학습 마무리

1 채점하기 | 정답 및 해설 p.10
주의 틀린 문제를 다시 풀 수 있도록 정답을 본문에 표기하지 마세요.
2 등급 확인
3 틀린 유형 확인 후 전략 적용 복습 및 해설지 확인

How to Review

1 틀린 문제와 ✓ 표시한 문제는 다시 풀고 해설 확인하기
2 내가 표시한 정답 근거가 해설과 일치하는지 확인하기
3 잘 모르는 부분으로 표시한 내용은 해설을 통해 완전히 이해하기
4 어휘 외우기 (어휘 목록 다운로드 www.cedubook.com)
5 다음 회에 개선할 점 정리하기 (시간 엄수, 취약 유형 보완 등)

POWER UP!

실전 모의고사

03

: BEFORE TESTING

시작 시 분

학습 목표

1 **제한시간** (OMR 마킹시간 포함) ☐ 40분 ☐ 45분
2 **어휘예습** ☐ 해당 없음 ☐ 완료
3 **문제풀이순서** ☐ 순서대로 ☐ 2점 → 3점 ☐ 기타
4 **기타 목표**

Check Point

1 **정답 근거** *e.g.* 밑줄 긋기
2 **잘 모르는 부분** *e.g.* 〈 〉 또는 ? 표시
3 **자신 없는 문제** *e.g.* 문제 번호에 ✓표시

18 다음 글을 쓴 목적으로 가장 적절한 것은?

Dear Customer,

Thank you for your online purchase of goods from Office Wares. We are confident you will be satisfied with our high-quality merchandise. Please inspect the contents of this delivery carefully to ensure all your goods have arrived in undamaged condition. In the event that you are not totally satisfied with your purchase for any reason, you can return it to us within 30 days for a full refund, no questions asked. Just repack it in the same box in which it was delivered to you, and stick the enclosed return shipping label on the outside of the box. Return shipping fees will be paid by the customer. If you wish to return a product more than 30 days after the purchase date, please call the customer service office at 800-232-1002, and a purchase order representative will assist you.

Thank you.

① 제품 반송 날짜를 확인하려고
② 환불 절차에 대해 안내하려고
③ 구매 고객에게 감사를 전하려고
④ 고객의 주문 내역을 확인하려고
⑤ 온라인 판매 제품을 광고하려고

19 다음 글에 드러난 'I'의 심경 변화로 가장 적절한 것은?

The network news images of the storm's damage troubled me: catastrophic flooding, crowds desperately seeking shelter. It was just days after Hurricane Katrina tore through the Gulf Coast, and I hadn't heard from my great-aunt Iva and great-uncle Bob, who lived in River Ridge, a New Orleans suburb. I searched the Internet. Then I saw a link for a real estate office. They'll know the area, I thought. I clicked on the page. Their number was listed. I dialed it. Finally, a man picked up. "I hope you can help me," I started. "How bad is it in River Ridge?" "Minor flooding and some downed trees," the man answered. "Oh, good," I said. "Are you looking for someone?" the man asked curiously. "My great-aunt and uncle," I said. "I don't suppose you know anything about the condition of Rural Street?" "I sure do," he said. "I live there." Two hours later Aunt Iva called. "The man down the street said you were looking for us." She and Uncle Bob were fine; their house suffered only minor damage.

① worried → relieved
② excited → disappointed
③ curious → bored
④ ashamed → proud
⑤ comfortable → frightened

20 다음 글에서 필자가 주장하는 바로 가장 적절한 것은?

Millions of us enjoy competitive events of every kind without ever leaving the comfort of our sofas. What's the attraction? For me, the fun comes from cheering on my team and cursing at the opposition. But some people actually watch a game without rooting for anyone. They won't risk being on the losing side. They sit in their grey-colored neutral zone, never tasting the joy that comes from picking a winner. Don't be like them. Pick a side to pull for. Cheer and boo. Laugh and sigh. Enjoy not only the color and action but also the intense fight. Sure, your team might lose. But then again, they might win. Either way your experience as a spectator will have been rich and alive, not pale and passive and poor.

① 성숙한 운동 경기 관람 태도를 가져야 한다.
② 경기의 승패보다 최선을 다하는 것이 중요하다.
③ 운동 경기는 직접 경기장에 가서 관람해야 한다.
④ 한쪽 팀을 응원하는 능동적인 관중이 되어야 한다.
⑤ 운동 경기를 내기의 수단으로 사용하지 말아야 한다.

21 밑줄 친 the Swiss cheese method가 다음 글에서 의미하는 바로 가장 적절한 것은?

When a task seems difficult, unpleasant or overwhelming, you are likely to put it off. The more we put tasks off, the more difficult they become to start. If you are suffering from the presence of an overwhelming task, try <u>the Swiss cheese method</u>. As soon as you receive a big assignment, set aside just 10 or 15 minutes a day for one week to work on it. By the end of the first week, you'll have spent at least an hour on the task, and you may have found that it's not quite as bad as you may have thought. By spending only a few minutes each day, you are accomplishing a small and therefore less intimidating task. Once you are involved and maybe even interested in the task, you may be motivated to spend more time on it.

① breaking big projects into smaller sections
② taking regular breaks while working
③ establishing priorities for each task
④ making a detailed plan in advance
⑤ avoiding distractions at work

22 다음 글의 요지로 가장 적절한 것은?

I have yet to meet a perfectionist who is also filled with inner peace. That's because the need for perfection and the ability to be contented are in conflict with each other. Whether the imperfections are yours or those you perceive in another person, the very act of focusing on them pulls you away from the possibility of being kind and contented. Constantly fixing things has nothing to do with being a better person but much to do with being overly attached to and focused on negatives. If you have this problem, then what you need to do is to start catching yourself in the act of insisting that a thing should be other than it is. Then immediately replace your insistent thoughts with this one: "Life is OK the way it is, right now." As you learn to let more things just be as they are, you'll discover more perfection in life itself.

① 외면의 완벽함보다 내면의 안정이 더 중요하다.
② 다른 사람의 결점을 비판하는 것을 자제해야 한다.
③ 시작한 일은 끝낼 때까지 완벽을 기할 필요가 있다.
④ 완벽을 버리고 있는 그대로를 인정하면 평안을 찾을 수 있다.
⑤ 모든 일에 온 힘을 기울이기보다는 선택과 집중을 하는 것이 낫다.

23 다음 글의 주제로 가장 적절한 것은?

The more women go out to work, it has been said, the lower the birthrate will be. The idea is that it's so much more difficult for parents to raise children when both parents work full-time. Yet, in some countries, the facts suggest otherwise. Countries with high female labor participation rates, such as Sweden, tend to have higher fertility rates than Italy and Japan, where fewer women work. Indeed, the decline in fertility has been greatest in countries where female employment is low. It seems that if female labor participation is supported by the right policies, it need not reduce fertility. In general, countries in which more women have stayed at home offer less support for working mothers, which causes lower birth rates. In countries where women and men participate fairly equally in the workforce and childcare services are affordable and widely available, birthrates do not tend to be lower than average.

① national approaches to childcare services
② advantages of countries with higher birthrates
③ reason why fewer women choose to be mothers
④ changing perspectives regarding working mothers
⑤ misconception about working women and lower birthrates

24 다음 글의 제목으로 가장 적절한 것은?

A group of researchers reported an experiment in which students were asked: "How happy are you with your life in general?" and "How many dates did you have last month?" For the average person, there is some connection, but not a strong one, between the answers to these questions. After all, dating is only one part of a complete life. And when students in the experiment were asked these questions in this order, the correlation between the answers to these questions was not statistically different from 0, but the correlation rose to 0.66 when the order was reversed with another sample of students. The dating question evidently caused that aspect of life to become relevant and its importance to be exaggerated when the respondents encountered the more general question about their happiness. Similar effects were observed when attention was first called to respondents' marriage or health.

① Factors Affecting Our Satisfaction in Life
② Moments of Joy: Appreciating the Little Things
③ The Influence of Order on Responses to Questions
④ The Correlation Between Dating and Quality of Life
⑤ Good Questions: The Key to a Successful Experiment

25 다음 도표의 내용과 일치하지 않는 것은?

The American Food Budget

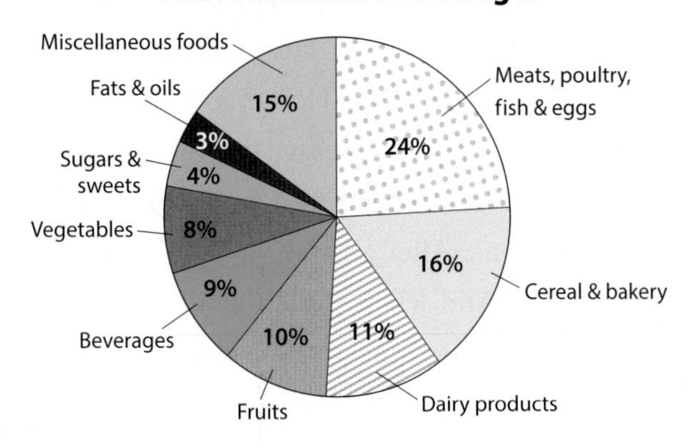

This pie chart shows American spending on food for the home. ① Overall, the three categories of miscellaneous foods; cereal & bakery; and meats, poultry, fish & eggs constitute more than half of the total expenditure. ② Americans spend almost the same percentage of their food budget on vegetables as they do on beverages. ③ The total amount spent on sugars & sweets plus vegetables is less than that spent on dairy products. ④ Dairy products comprise just over one-tenth of expenditure on food, while fruits and vegetables combined account for under 20 percent. ⑤ The smallest categories are fats & oils, and sugars & sweets, both of which fall under 5 percent of household food budgets.

26 Cuscuta pentagona에 관한 다음 글의 내용과 일치하지 않는 것은?

Cuscuta pentagona is not your typical plant. It's a tall and thin orange vine that can grow up to a meter high, produces tiny white flowers of five petals, and is found all over North America. What's unique about Cuscuta is that it has no leaves and it isn't green because it lacks chlorophyll, the pigment that absorbs solar energy, which allows plants to turn light into sugars and oxygen through photosynthesis. Cuscuta obviously cannot perform photosynthesis, as most plants do, so it doesn't make its own food from light. With all of this in mind, it would seem that Cuscuta would starve, but instead it thrives. Cuscuta survives in another way: it gets its food from its neighbors. It is a parasitic plant. In order to live, Cuscuta attaches itself to a host plant and sucks out the nutrients provided by it. Unsurprisingly, Cuscuta is an agricultural nuisance and is even classified as a "harmful weed" by the U.S. Department of Agriculture.

*chlorophyll: 엽록소 **photosynthesis: 광합성

① 하얀색 꽃이 피는 덩굴 식물이다.
② 북아메리카 전역에 걸쳐 서식한다.
③ 잎 이외의 기관에서 광합성을 한다.
④ 다른 식물로부터 양분을 얻는다.
⑤ 농사에 해로운 잡초로 분류된다.

27 학교 방문 발레 공연에 관한 다음 안내문의 내용과 일치하지 않는 것은?

A Unique Experience Where Professional Dancers Visit Your School

Each year, the professional dancers of Richmond Ballet present lecture demonstrations in elementary schools. These demonstrations feature a theme based on classic ballet stories. The theme for this season is Cinderella, and the full-length story ballet will be performed in February 2021 at the Carpenter Theatre.

Performance
A 45-minute performance will be presented by five dancers of the professional company. It consists of several dance pieces, dialogue relating to the theme, and a student interaction/participation section.

Q&A Session
Following the performance, the dancers will answer students' questions in a Q&A session.

For more information, please call Tanya Dolphin, education coordinator, at (802) 310-0900 or send an e-mail to tdolphin@richmondb.com.

① 초등학교에 가서 하는 연례 시범공연이다.
② 올해의 공연 테마는 Cinderella이다.
③ 다섯 명의 전문 무용수들이 45분간 공연한다.
④ 학생들이 공연에 직접 참여하지는 않는다.
⑤ 공연 후에 무용수와 학생 간의 질의응답 시간이 있다.

28 Cranberry Harvest Day에 관한 다음 안내문의 내용과 일치하는 것은?

Cranberry Harvest Day

Held annually on the first Saturday of October, the event is sponsored by the Cranberry Discovery Center (CDC) and the Warrens Area Business Association.

We'll have several pairs of hip boots available so you can walk out into a pool of floating cranberries.

Free tours of the marsh will be offered from 10 a.m. to 11 a.m. After touring the marsh, the CDC will offer free cranberry wine tasting and gourmet cranberry food sampling.

Date: October 3, 2020
Venue: Cranberry Discovery Center
Phone: 608-300-2800
Address: 202 Main Street, Warrens, WI

About CDC:
A nonprofit center dedicated to educating the public about the state's cranberry growing heritage

*marsh: 습지

① 매년 10월 마지막 토요일에 열린다.
② 체험 행사를 위해 장화를 가져가야 한다.
③ 습지 투어는 오전에 유료로 진행된다.
④ 크랜베리 와인과 음식을 저렴한 가격으로 맛볼 수 있다.
⑤ CDC는 크랜베리 재배 전통을 교육하는 비영리기관이다.

29 다음 글의 밑줄 친 부분 중, 어법상 틀린 것은? [3점]

The feathers of birds serve a variety of functions in the day-to-day lives of birds, and feathers on different parts of the body have evolved for a range of purposes. Those that cover the majority of the body ① provide necessary insulation from the cold and, to varying amounts, waterproofing, too. And, of course, there are the feathers on the wing that enable flight in all ② its forms to take place. From the birdwatcher's point of view, feathers are there to be admired but, when ③ interpreting correctly, they can also provide a wealth of information about the bird in question. For example, the sex of a bird can often ④ be told at a glance. In addition, its age and ⑤ whether it has breeding or non-breeding feathers can also be discerned in many cases. Such details are interesting in their own right, but more fundamentally they offer clues to birdwatchers with regards to identification.

*breeding feathers: 번식깃(번식기에 평상시와 달라지는 조류의 깃)

30 (A), (B), (C)의 각 네모 안에서 문맥에 맞는 낱말로 가장 적절한 것은? [3점]

The invention of air conditioning had a radical impact on the southern manner of living. Perhaps most notably, and especially visually, it altered southern architecture. Prior to this invention, southerners constructed homes with covered verandas, but with the increasing use of air conditioning in the domestic context, verandas became increasingly (A) [scarce / abundant]. Second, air conditioning decreased casual opportunities for social interaction. Once it arrived on the scene, people tended to remain inside their houses, thus becoming more (B) [withdrawn / outgoing] from their communities. Third, it virtually revolutionized summertime leisure activities. Before air conditioning, people gathered at beaches and pools and avoided hot, (C) [confined / wide-open] spaces. However, with the arrival of air conditioning, people were at liberty to attend concerts, films, and plays without the concern of stifling heat.

	(A)		(B)		(C)
①	scarce	……	withdrawn	……	confined
②	scarce	……	withdrawn	……	wide-open
③	scarce	……	outgoing	……	confined
④	abundant	……	outgoing	……	wide-open
⑤	abundant	……	withdrawn	……	confined

[31~34] 다음 빈칸에 들어갈 말로 가장 적절한 것을 고르시오.

31 Most people are more or less ticklish, especially in tender areas such as the armpits, the belly, and the soles of the feet. A few different theories seek to explain why being tickled makes some people laugh. Some scientists say that it has something to do with ________________. We laugh when we are tickled, but it's not because we find it funny. Laughter that happens during tickling is caused by anxiety. We panic a little because it feels threatening when the tender parts of our body are attacked. The threatening feeling arises from the element of surprise, and of not knowing where you might be tickled next. Therefore, the more anxious you normally are, the more ticklish you tend to be. This is why you react that way when someone tickles you. [3점]

① culture
② heredity
③ satisfaction
④ self-defense
⑤ health and fitness

32 Dreams expand the world. That is why James Allen suggested that "dreamers are the saviors of the world." If we are to promote the freedom to dream, we need, first and foremost, a creative environment. But what if the place where you work or study has an environment hostile to creativity, and you possess little ability to change it? Your best option is to ________________________________. Creativity is contagious. Have you ever noticed what happens during a good brainstorming session? One person throws out an idea, which is used as a springboard to discover another idea by another person, who finds that someone else has taken his idea in yet another, even better direction. It's a fact that you begin to think like the people you spend a lot of time with, so if you want to dream, you ought to spend your time with other dreamers who bring ideas to whole new levels.

① interact with other creative people
② remember what you dreamed about
③ look at things from a new perspective
④ change your job to a more creative one
⑤ try to think creatively every moment of the day

33 If you spent hours learning a musical instrument as a child only to lose interest when you reached your teens, ____, according to a leading scientist. Learning to play an instrument has major advantages for a child's growing brain and should be a stable part of school education, says neuroscientist Professor Nina Kraus, who points out that there is strong evidence to show that music lessons help children improve their language skills. Prof. Kraus conducted research which demonstrated that playing a musical instrument significantly improves not only the sensitivity of a normal child's brain to speech sounds but also that of children with developmental problems such as dyslexia and autism. [3점]

*dyslexia: 난독증 **autism: 자폐증

① the left side of your brain will have developed
② your family has wasted a lot of money in vain
③ it may not have been a complete waste of your time
④ it may have hindered the development of your language skills
⑤ it may have been because you became interested in other subjects

34 With long-distance travel becoming ever faster and easier, people and cargo are traveling a greater number of intercontinental miles every year. But on those trips to new lands, they are often accompanied by tiny, unwanted passengers: insects. Hidden in baggage and cargo containers, these bugs can cause a lot of trouble if they escape and multiply. Consider, for example, the Asian longhorned beetle. The larvae of this pest tunnel through trees, killing them. The beetles, brought to America from China in crates, pallets, and other wooden packing materials used to protect cargo, have been detected in warehouses nationwide. Currently, there is ______________________________, so New York City and Chicago had to cut down more than 5,500 trees in an effort to stop the insect spreading to other areas. [3점]

*Asian longhorned beetle: (곤충) 유리알락하늘소

① a great diversity of insects in American forests
② not enough old wood or roots for insects to eat
③ no known chemical or biological defense against them
④ a growing sense of guilt over the destruction of species
⑤ a demand for the least toxic methods for protecting crops

35 다음 글에서 전체 흐름과 관계 없는 문장은?

Market research is too often focused on the average user. We, as business people, tend to rely on this paradigm in order to simplify matters, but it means that we lose the essence of what is relevant for each consumer. ① On too many occasions, products are designed with a user type in mind which is believed to represent the whole of a chosen segment. ② It is easy to miss the key point: each individual consumer wants a satisfying experience while consuming a product or service. ③ Studies on the average consumer help firms and organizations improve their marketing strategies. ④ Pause for a moment and consider whether your company fully satisfies its consumers, regardless of their build, age, intellectual abilities, visual abilities, religious beliefs, type of family, gender, and so on. ⑤ If it does not, your company has fewer consumers than it could have.

[36~37] 주어진 글 다음에 이어질 글의 순서로 가장 적절한 것을 고르시오.

36

Attention is a necessary prerequisite for conscious perception. In fact, you may not perceive something that is right before you unless you are paying attention to it.

(A) For example, imagine you are sitting in a library reading a book and someone shouts, "Is that a fire?" Even though you are paying attention to the book, you still perceive the shout.

(B) Indeed, if there were absolutely no processing of stimuli in the background, it would be necessary to periodically make a conscious decision to scan your surroundings to see if anything important was happening: Let's see, is anyone shouting "fire"?

(C) But there must be more to the explanation than just that. What if you're focused completely on one stimulus, and another stimulus in the environment requires your attention? [3점]

*prerequisite: 전제 조건

① (A) — (C) — (B)
② (B) — (A) — (C)
③ (B) — (C) — (A)
④ (C) — (A) — (B)
⑤ (C) — (B) — (A)

37

> Some people think that the "democratization of knowledge" made possible by the Internet means that we no longer need to rely on experts and can request directly to the collective intelligence of amateurs.

(A) This is not to criticize Wikipedia, but to point out that there is no escape from requesting to experts. The broad spectrum of topics covered by Wikipedia is in many ways to be welcomed, and it is sometimes a good place to begin your research. It is, however, a bad place to end it.

(B) As evidence for this, they point to the online encyclopedia Wikipedia — which is written largely by amateurs. Its science articles, in particular, are said to be remarkably accurate.

(C) However, it is important to note that Wikipedia is not in the business of content creation, but of summarizing content that has been created elsewhere — usually by experts. Moreover, the much-vaunted accuracy of its articles can itself only be judged by experts.

*democratization: 민주화 **vaunted: 칭찬받는

① (A) — (C) — (B)
② (B) — (A) — (C)
③ (B) — (C) — (A)
④ (C) — (A) — (B)
⑤ (C) — (B) — (A)

[38~39] 글의 흐름으로 보아, 주어진 문장이 들어가기에 가장 적절한 곳을 고르시오.

38

> However, there has been no real change in the number of sunspots in the last 20 years, but Earth's temperature has continued to rise.

Sunspots have been observed on the Sun and their numbers recorded since 1610. (①) The recordings, taken over the past few hundred years, show that the number of sunspots has steadily increased. (②) This trend accelerated in the 20th century, coinciding with the period when Earth started to warm noticeably. (③) It seems to suggest that changing solar activity is somehow causing Earth's warming. (④) We may attribute this to the greenhouse effect caused by farming and human burning of fossil fuels. (⑤) This latest analysis shows that the Sun has had a considerable indirect influence on Earth's climate in the past, and that human activity is magnifying the Sun's latest attempt to warm the planet.

39

This signals to the other person that you need to talk, but you're finding it a bit difficult to start the discussion.

When you need to have a discussion with someone about a sensitive matter, your fears about approaching the person are invariably worse than the discussion itself. (①) You probably find yourself postponing bringing up the tough subject, telling yourself that you're waiting for the "perfect opportunity." (②) But in real life, the right time rarely comes along, so you have to make the conversation happen regardless. (③) In these circumstances, it's best to start with an indirect approach, such as a text message asking for time to chat about something "delicate." (④) Once you've sent your text, you'll find the conversation has been put in motion already, with the recipient preparing to talk with you. (⑤) Sure, you may still feel anxious before you actually sit down together, but that's okay; you've initiated the conversation you needed to have.

40 다음 글의 내용을 한 문장으로 요약하고자 한다. 빈칸 (A), (B)에 들어갈 말로 가장 적절한 것은?

Repeated exposure makes us respond positively to strangers who just happen to look familiar to us. The mere fact that a person looks like our uncle Harry, our old friend Mary, or the cashier at our neighborhood grocery store is enough to make him or her seem familiar and thus less threatening. This occurs even when we are not consciously aware that we were exposed to a particular face. In a study that demonstrated this, subjects were asked to talk about some neutral topic with two people who were confederates of the experimenter. Before the conversation, a photograph of one of the confederates was flashed on a screen so quickly that the subjects were unaware of it. Despite their lack of awareness of this subliminal exposure, the subjects still responded more favorably toward the familiar person than they did toward the person whose photograph was not flashed.

*confederate: 공모자, 일당 **subliminal: 부지불식간에 영향을 미치는

↓

Whether aware of it or not, we are inclined to respond ____(A)____ to a person whose face is not ____(B)____ to us.

	(A)		(B)
①	positively	……	exposed
②	agreeably	……	strange
③	promptly	……	known
④	strongly	……	familiar
⑤	negatively	……	attractive

[41~42] 다음 글을 읽고, 물음에 답하시오.

For any nation, the recruiting of students from overseas evokes mixed feelings. There are two myths about the influx of international students. One is the brain-drain myth, according to which the countries of origin are being (a) <u>robbed</u> of talent. Take the case of the large numbers of graduate students recruited from India over the past three or so decades — mostly in science and engineering. The dire warnings about a brain drain have proved (b) <u>false</u>. The students have formed a bridge between India and the U.S. that is providing the two countries with new economic opportunities along with a stable political relationship. The global matching of talent with opportunity is not (c) <u>limited</u> to science and engineering. The great American conservatories of music are filled with students of Japanese, Chinese, and Korean descent, as are the stages of our concert halls.

A second myth about the movement of students across borders is that the host country bears a net cost. If we again take the example of American universities recruiting Indian graduate students in science and engineering, the truth is that the host nation is getting a (d) <u>return</u> on this investment. American graduate programs in science and engineering have long relied on the graduating classes of the Indian Institute of Technology in order to meet the U.S. economy's demand for scientists and engineers. Knowledge knows no national borders, and learning shouldn't either. Institutions of higher learning are taking the lead in reaching across nations to prepare global citizens and leaders for a world in which cultures are more (e) <u>individualized</u> than ever before.

*influx: 밀어닥침 **brain-drain: 두뇌 유출의
***conservatory: 음악 학교

41 윗글의 제목으로 가장 적절한 것은?

① We Must Dispel the Myths of Higher Education
② How Does Globalization Affect Higher Education?
③ Higher Education Globalization: Myths and Realities
④ Negative Effects of the Globalization of Higher Education
⑤ Globalization of Education and Cross-border Student Mobility

42 밑줄 친 (a)~(e) 중에서 문맥상 낱말의 쓰임이 적절하지 <u>않은</u> 것은? [3점]

① (a) ② (b) ③ (c) ④ (d) ⑤ (e)

[43~45] 다음 글을 읽고, 물음에 답하시오.

(A)

George Hull, a farmer, had an unusual idea to make money — by having a huge human figure made from stone and advertising it as the body of a giant, petrified by centuries in the grave. (a) He bought a five-ton block of stone and hired a sculptor to carve a statue.

*petrify: 석화(石化)하다

(B)

Amid the growing suspicions, an expert examined it and declared it to be of very recent origin. Finally, (b) he was forced to admit that his giant was a fake. Despite the truth coming out, people still flocked to see the giant. It changed owners several times over the years, and was eventually bought by the Cooperstown Farmers' Museum, New York, where it remains on display today.

(C)

It took three months of hard work for (c) him to finish the statue. And George gave it a final touch by pouring a chemical over it to make its exterior look like old, petrified skin. Then the giant was put in a wooden crate and carried to a farm in Cardiff, New York. There, the giant was buried next to a barn, where it remained for a year. Then, he hired workers to dig a well by the barn, and they made the "discovery" that (d) he had planned for a long time.

(D)

Two days after the giant was uncovered, (e) he began charging tourists 50 cents each to see it. Between 300 and 500 visitors came daily, and more than 2,000 on weekends. Soon after, he sold the giant for $5,000. Its new owners moved the giant to Syracuse, New York, and put it on display, but suspicions about its origin had already started to grow.

43 주어진 글 (A)에 이어질 내용을 순서에 맞게 배열한 것으로 가장 적절한 것은?

① (B) — (C) — (D)　② (C) — (B) — (D)
③ (C) — (D) — (B)　④ (D) — (B) — (C)
⑤ (D) — (C) — (B)

44 밑줄 친 (a)~(e) 중에서 가리키는 대상이 나머지 넷과 다른 것은?

① (a)　② (b)　③ (c)　④ (d)　⑤ (e)

45 윗글에 관한 내용으로 적절하지 않은 것은?

① 거인 석상이 가짜임이 밝혀졌다.
② 거인 석상은 현재 박물관에 전시되어 있다.
③ 거인 석상은 우물을 파다가 우연히 발견되었다.
④ 농부는 관광객들에게 석상 관람료를 받았다.
⑤ 농부는 거인 석상을 다른 사람에게 팔았다.

: AFTER TESTING

종료 시 분
소요시간 분

학습 마무리

1 채점하기 | 정답 및 해설 p.18
주의 틀린 문제를 다시 풀 수 있도록 정답을 본문에 표기하지 마세요.
2 등급 확인
3 틀린 유형 확인 후 전략 적용 복습 및 해설지 확인

How to Review

1 틀린 문제와 ✓ 표시한 문제는 다시 풀고 해설 확인하기
2 내가 표시한 정답 근거가 해설과 일치하는지 확인하기
3 잘 모르는 부분으로 표시한 내용은 해설을 통해 완전히 이해하기
4 어휘 외우기 (어휘 목록 다운로드 www.cedubook.com)
5 다음 회에 개선할 점 정리하기 (시간 엄수, 취약 유형 보완 등)

POWER UP!

실전 모의고사 04

: BEFORE TESTING

시작 시 분

학습 목표

1 **제한시간** (OMR 마킹시간 포함) ☐ 40분 ☐ 45분
2 **어휘예습** ☐ 해당 없음 ☐ 완료
3 **문제풀이순서** ☐ 순서대로 ☐ 2점 → 3점 ☐ 기타
4 **기타 목표**

Check Point

1 **정답 근거** *e.g.* 밑줄 긋기
2 **잘 모르는 부분** *e.g.* 〈 〉 또는 ? 표시
3 **자신 없는 문제** *e.g.* 문제 번호에 ✓표시

18 다음 글의 목적으로 가장 적절한 것은?

Dear Ms. Hayes,

Thank you for offering me the position. The interview process was incredibly challenging, and I am very proud to be your first choice. I also appreciate your having given me time to consider the offer and your frank discussion of the details. As you may recall, I stated that I was exploring several other employment opportunities. This week the Ministry of Environment made an offer that provides the ideal match for my goals at this stage of my career. After careful consideration, I have decided to accept the offer. I want to thank you sincerely for your confidence in me; meeting you and learning about the innovative community programs being implemented by the school this year was most enjoyable. I wish you and your staff all the very best.

Respectfully,
Lindsay Jones

① 취업 제의를 수락하려고
② 다른 일자리를 구했음을 알리려고
③ 일자리에 맞는 취업자를 주선하려고
④ 면접 기회를 준 것에 대해 감사하려고
⑤ 직원 채용 방식에 대한 아이디어를 주려고

19 다음 글에 드러난 Kevin의 심경 변화로 가장 적절한 것은?

At last, Kevin was set to deliver a talk on financial products to a group of clients. The weekend before the talk, he practiced his speech over and over again. He walked into the seminar room with pride because he had rehearsed his speech several times. Kevin knew his lines without fault. He got up in front of the audience and started speaking with a smile. He even got a laugh from the audience as he made a joke. Then... he forgot his lines. He didn't know what he was going to say next. He started breaking out in beads of sweat. They rolled down his forehead and pretty soon, it was like Niagara Falls. He felt as if he had gone into *America's Got Talent* without any prior rehearsal. He wished that he could disappear at the moment.

① hopeful → worried
② furious → satisfied
③ anxious → relieved
④ ashamed → pleased
⑤ confident → embarrassed

20 다음 글에서 필자가 주장하는 바로 가장 적절한 것은?

Because we are wired for interdependence, we need help from others to do our best. Within the theory of self-directed learning is the discovery that "you need others to identify your ideal self or find your real self, to discover your strengths and gaps, to develop an agenda for the future, and to experiment and practice." Everyone needs the support of trustworthy friends and colleagues to help them stay true to their goals. Make sure you establish at least a few relationships with people who will tell you the truth about yourself, even when you might not want to hear it. Find trusted people who know your values and goals and will let you know when you are not living up to them. When you are attempting to change your behavior, let them know what changes you are trying to make and ask them to tell you if they see you hesitate.

① 도움을 받기보다 베풀어주는 사람이 되어라.
② 스스로 해결할 수 있는 일을 남에게 미루지 마라.
③ 진실한 조언을 해줄 수 있는 사람들을 주변에 두어라.
④ 다른 사람의 기대에 부응하려고 지나치게 노력하지 마라
⑤ 남의 단점을 비판하기보다는 장점을 찾아 칭찬해 주어라.

21 밑줄 친 there is no one size fits all이 다음 글에서 의미하는 바로 가장 적절한 것은?

When it comes to the human mind, there is no one size fits all. I've seen Deepak Chopra, the author of more than eighty books, work on a book surrounded by the noise and bustle of a train station, and on an airplane. Physicist Richard Feynman liked to get ideas while sipping 7Up in a noisy, crowded bar in Pasadena. On the other hand, Jim Davis, the creator of the *Garfield* comic strip, told me that he had to isolate himself in a hotel room for four days in order to have the uninterrupted peace of mind he needed to create that concept. Jonathan Franzen, a novelist and essayist, works alone in an office at the University of California, Santa Cruz, often under a spell so fragile that it is broken by the fragrance of an Indian professor down the hall heating curry in a microwave. I myself cannot do imaginative work if I feel there is a fixed time at which I must quit.

① writers make an effort to find ways that boost their creativity
② the personality trait of high sensitivity makes a writer more creative
③ there are some relationships between creativity and time management
④ the best place to write has much to do with a writer's daily biological cycle
⑤ the optimal environment for creative activities varies from person to person

22 다음 글의 요지로 가장 적절한 것은?

Organic foods are produced without conventional pesticides, hormones, or artificial chemicals; are free from contamination by industrial waste; and are promoted as being vital for a sustainable planet and better for our health. However, another school of thought challenges the idea that all organic food is always good. According to this school of thought, we have to count "food miles," defined as the distance food travels from the field to the grocery store, when we calculate the benefits of buying organic. The more food miles any product has, the greater damage it does to the environment. When you choose an organic apple that has traveled great distances by truck and airplane instead of a locally grown conventional apple, you personally encourage excessive and unnecessary pollution, fossil fuel consumption, and carbon emissions.

① 유기농 식품이 일반 식품보다 더 안전하다.
② 유기농 음식은 건강에 큰 도움이 되지 않는다.
③ 유기농 식품과 일반 식품은 영양소 차이가 없다.
④ 유기농 식품이 환경에 나쁜 영향을 미칠 수 있다.
⑤ 유기농 식품의 재배는 지역 경제를 활성화시킨다.

23 다음 글의 주제로 가장 적절한 것은?

Groups of ants can be just as irrational as stampeding soccer fans. Panicking ants, like panicking people, follow the herd, even when the herd makes stupid decisions. A stampede can be fatal, especially in enclosed areas like sports stadiums, dance clubs, and department stores. When there is a fire or other cause of panic, people frequently—and illogically—try to escape through just one door, jamming it up, while leaving other exits free. People who are panicked forget about reasonable strategies and just follow the crowd, behaving rather like ants. In a University of Havana study, researchers trapped ants in a circular chamber and then opened two identical exit doors. Calm ants used both doors equally. But ants panicked by insect repellent jammed one exit while ignoring the other.

*stampede: 우르르 몰려가다; 우르르 몰려감

① ways to avoid stampede behaviors
② tendency of people to panic in crowds
③ problems caused by irrational soccer fans
④ stupid behavior shared by people and ants
⑤ reactions of different ant groups when panicked

24 다음 글의 제목으로 가장 적절한 것은?

The majority of shoppers respond very strongly to the prospect of a sale. As shoppers learn more about the markdown strategies of retailers, however, they come to expect larger and larger discounts. Where 10 or 20 percent off might have given shoppers a thrill before, today they want 50 or even 60 percent off. Retailers must explore other ways to stimulate the shopper beyond the simplistic 50 percent off sales approach. Inevitably, retailers and manufacturers pay the price for an overstocked selling floor and extreme discounts. They need to make use of other emotional drivers, and there are many, besides just offering a sale, that stimulate shoppers and get them in the mood to spend money.

① Bargain Sales, the Last Resort of Retailers
② Are Price Cuts the Best Marketing Strategy?
③ How Can We Evoke Curiosity in Customers?
④ How to Build a Customer Interaction System
⑤ Understanding the Markdown Strategy of Retailers

25 다음 도표의 내용과 일치하지 않는 것은?

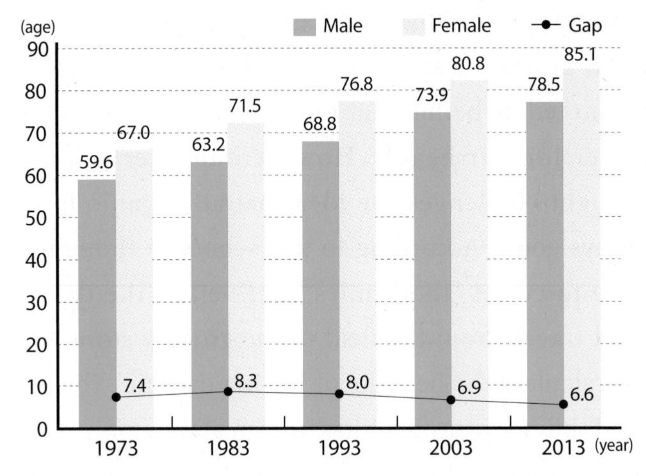

This chart shows the life expectancies of Korean men and women in 1973, 1983, 1993, 2003, and 2013. The chart clearly indicates that the life expectancy of both Korean men and women increased steadily and dramatically over the period. ① As for Korean men, life expectancy increased by 18.9 years over the 40-year period. ② At the same time, Korean women gained 18.1 years in life expectancy. ③ It's interesting to note that the expected life span of Korean women has been more than 80 years since 2003. ④ Meanwhile, the gap between male and female life expectancies averaged around six to eight years. ⑤ However, the gap between male and female life expectancies has been steadily increasing since 1983, when it reached 8.3 years.

26 Norman Myers에 관한 다음 글의 내용과 일치하지 않는 것은?

Born on August 24, 1934, Norman Myers is a British environmentalist specializing in the study of biodiversity. Myers now lives in Headington, Oxford, England. He has been an advisor to organizations including the United Nations, the World Bank, and numerous scientific academies around the world. In the 1970s, his work focused mainly on the loss of tropical forests. In the following decade, he began to focus on the environmental damage caused by raising cattle. His book *Ultimate Security: The Environmental Basis of Political Stability* has had a major influence on local and international politics. In 1991, he was awarded the Blue Planet Prize, and he was elected as a Foreign Associate of the U.S. National Academy of Sciences in 1994. In 2007, he was named *Time* magazine's "Hero of the Environment" for his work discovering regions with very high numbers of different species.

*biodiversity: (균형 잡힌 환경을 위한) 생물의 다양성

① 생물의 다양성을 연구하는 환경운동가이다.
② UN 등 세계 여러 기관에서 고문을 맡아왔다.
③ 목축으로 인한 환경 훼손에 주목했다.
④ 그의 저서는 국내외 정치에 큰 영향을 미쳤다.
⑤ 극소수의 생물 종이 사는 지역을 발견했다.

27 Akron Marathon에 관한 다음 안내문의 내용과 일치하지 않는 것은?

Akron Marathon
9.25.2021

The Akron Marathon is known for its great giveaways, and this year's official race jacket given to all full marathoners (those participating in the full 26.2 mile race) is no exception! Sponsored by K Sports, this lightweight track jacket has a $65 value and will be your go-to jacket for those cool morning runs.

Event Details
- Start Time: 7 a.m.
- Cut-off Time: 1 p.m. (The course will close on a continuous pace of 13 minutes, 44 seconds per mile.)
- Minimum Age: 16 years of age on race day

Package Pick-up
Runners must pick up their race package at the Expo on Friday, September 24, 2021 between 11 a.m. and 9 p.m. This is the only place to get your race number, jacket and goodie bag. There will be no pick-up the day of the race.

① 풀코스 참가자에게 행사 공식 재킷이 제공된다.
② K Sports에서 65달러 상당의 상품을 후원받는다.
③ 여섯 시간 동안 열리는 마라톤 대회이다.
④ 참가자는 16세 이상이어야 한다.
⑤ 마라톤용품은 개최 당일에 지급받을 수 있다.

28 Seattle International Film Festival에 관한 다음 안내문의 내용과 일치하는 것은?

SIFF 2021 Call for Entries

Seattle International Film Festival is seeking full-length movies, documentaries, short films, and animated movies for its 47th annual festival. SIFF is one of the largest and most highly attended film festivals in the United States. What is more, it has an audience of over 150,000 annually.

This year, SIFF is proud to offer $8,000 in cash prizes in the following categories:

- $2,500 New Directors Competition
- $2,500 Documentary Competition
- $1,000 Short Film: Live Action
- $1,000 Short Film: Animation
- $1,000 Short Film: Documentary

These international awards are given for excellence in filmmaking, form, and content.

Submission Deadlines

Regular submission deadline: November 4, 2020
Final submission deadline: January 3, 2021
EXTENSION – Online (only) submission deadline: February 3, 2021

① 출품작 모집에 애니메이션은 포함되지 않는다.
② 매년 열리는 미국 최대 규모의 국제 영화제이다.
③ 영화제의 누적 관객 수가 15만 명에 이른다.
④ 단편 영화에는 총 1,000달러의 상금이 책정되어 있다.
⑤ 온라인 출품을 제외한 최종 마감일은 2월 3일이다.

29 다음 글의 밑줄 친 부분 중, 어법상 틀린 것은? [3점]

All writing is personal, more or less. Even a shopping list tells us quite a bit about the person who wrote it. It seems Napoleon was well aware of this fact, given that he demanded to see a sample of an officer's writing before promoting the officer to one of ① the highest ranks. Explanation, argument, description, and narration all gradually but surely show us ② who the writer is. Equally revealing ③ are the writer's choice of topic, the depth of knowledge displayed, and the skill with which the material is shaped. If all this is true, then you may well ask why any particular piece of writing ④ should be labeled "personal." The answer is that the personal element is always present in essays but ⑤ varying widely in its prominence.

30 다음 글의 밑줄 친 부분 중, 문맥상 낱말의 쓰임이 적절하지 않은 것은? [3점]

Emotions play a critical function: they provide ① fuel for action. While they can sweep over us, leading us into temptation, they can also compel us to take appropriate action, giving us courage and resolve. No one demonstrated this ② latter process of transformation better than Mahatma Gandhi, who, without a single weapon, succeeded in putting an end to the centuries-long colonial domination of India by the British Empire. He explained his secret as follows: "I had learned through bitter experience the one supreme lesson to ③ conserve my anger. And as heat is transmitted into energy, even so our anger controlled can be transformed into a power which can move the world." As Gandhi suggested, refrain from ④ impulsive reaction, which is only a reckless waste of your precious energy. Finally, at the right moment, purposively ⑤ conceal your emotional energy as resolve.

[31~34] 다음 빈칸에 들어갈 말로 가장 적절한 것을 고르시오.

31 Researchers of motor vehicle accidents have spent a great deal of time investigating the average driver's reaction time, visual acuity, and ability to estimate speed and distance, in the hope of better understanding and explaining the causes of accidents. However, dangerous driving may have more to do with the opportunities that a car provides for ______________. The thing is, when some people — young men in particular — get behind the wheel, they use the power of their car to show the rest of the world how fast, clever, strong, or angry they are. They see their vehicle as an extension of their own body or personality, which means trouble if they are feeling reckless.

① status
② convenience
③ pleasure
④ competition
⑤ self-expression

32 A certain amount of bureaucracy, accountability and organization is vital for the world we live in. The benefits of bureaucracy do not need urging. Yet the hidden costs are very considerable. A harmful effect of over-active bureaucracies is that they ______________. In almost all organizations, the higher the pay and the higher the status, the less practical work and the more administration. A head teacher who was perhaps an excellent communicator does not teach any more. An excellent surgeon ends up doing paperwork as head of a hospital. A brilliant academic is finally the administrative head of a university. None of them any longer do the thing they most enjoy or are good at. They spend their time as fundraisers, personnel officers, and chairs of committees. It is a widespread tendency: if you can do anything really well, stop doing it and become an administrator. [3점]

① divert talent
② waste budgets
③ justify injustices
④ provoke corruption
⑤ reinforce inequalities

33 Modern English is the dominant international language in diplomacy, communications, aviation, radio, business, science, tourism, and entertainment and is spoken by as many as 1.8 billion people around the world. So, it takes quite an effort of the imagination to understand ______________________________. Just four centuries ago, for example, when William Shakespeare was writing and producing plays, the language was almost completely confined to England and southern Scotland and virtually unknown to everyone else in the world. It had not yet even penetrated far into neighboring Ireland or Wales. Back then, the total number of people who could have been expected to understand the language of a Shakespeare play was, at most, around five million. [3점]

① that it hasn't always been like this
② that this is not good news for Scotland
③ that Shakespeare is responsible for its success
④ how Old English changed into Modern English
⑤ why other European languages aren't as widespread

34 I sometimes try to explain to people who don't use a computer how a computer could make their job easier. Often enough, their attitude is a perfect expression of the words "Thanks, but no thanks." Why do some people resist learning something that could make their job better or easier? In most cases, the reason is fear. People who don't know much about technology may worry that computers will replace them, or that a computer will make them look incompetent. That's why it's a good idea to see teaching as like asking someone to go on a trip. Just as nobody would accept an invitation to go to a place that they've heard is dangerous or unpleasant, people are reluctant to learn things that they think will make them worse off. When you try to teach anyone something new, you have to make it clear from the start that ______________________________. [3점]

① every job will be changed by computers
② enjoyable trips can give our lives energy
③ you promise to make his or her job easier
④ the destination is a place we'd all like to go to
⑤ change is an obligation in the information age

35 다음 글에서 전체 흐름과 관계 없는 문장은?

In an argument, the ability to see the situation as the other side sees it, as difficult as it may be, is one of the most important skills you can possess. ① It is not enough to know that the other person sees something differently. ② If you want to influence people, you also need to feel real empathy for their point of view and the emotional force with which they believe in it. ③ It will not do to study them like bugs under a microscope; you need to know what it feels like to be that bug. ④ To accomplish this, you must be prepared to withhold your judgement for a while as you try to understand their views. ⑤ An argument is not won by the person with the loudest voice; it is won by the person with the most compelling arguments.

[36~37] 주어진 글 다음에 이어질 글의 순서로 가장 적절한 것을 고르시오.

36

> Space and time are interesting things. They can both be affected by matter — particularly large amounts of matter that have strong gravitational influences.

(A) The eclipse blocked sunlight, allowing observers to see stars they normally wouldn't see, and they succeeded in measuring a tiny shift in light due to gravitational lensing.

(B) This is the basis for the work that Albert Einstein did, spurred on by a solar eclipse that occurred in 1919. He predicted that light rays from distant stars would be bent as they passed by the Sun due to the Sun's gravitational influence.

(C) This observation led Einstein to publish work describing how the mass of an object curves local space-time, thus forcing light rays to bend ever so slightly. The 1919 eclipse produced the first experimental confirmation of gravitational lensing. [3점]

① (A) — (C) — (B)
② (B) — (A) — (C)
③ (B) — (C) — (A)
④ (C) — (A) — (B)
⑤ (C) — (B) — (A)

37

> There are a couple of ways of interpreting a situation in which someone is isolated socially. On one hand, it's healthy for people to seek to be by themselves from time to time.

(A) For example, a homebound elderly man whose daughter visits every day may still feel isolated and depressed. A satisfying social life is determined by the quality and shared sense of give-and-take, not by the number and frequency of one's social interactions.

(B) That's why the isolated person's perception of the situation is key in understanding social isolation. Simply counting the number and frequency of someone's social interactions is not enough to decide whether he or she is okay.

(C) On the other hand, it becomes a real problem when people feel trapped, unhappy, and distressed because of their lack of social and emotional interactions. Isolation by choice is pleasant solitude; without choice, it is depressing loneliness.

① (A) — (C) — (B)　② (B) — (A) — (C)
③ (B) — (C) — (A)　④ (C) — (A) — (B)
⑤ (C) — (B) — (A)

[38~39] 글의 흐름으로 보아, 주어진 문장이 들어가기에 가장 적절한 곳을 고르시오.

38

> Unfortunately, the hybrid potato's sticky hairs also trap and kill beneficial insects.

The nutritious and tasty potato is an important food crop, feeding millions around the world. (①) But potatoes are vulnerable to insect pests that can destroy entire crops. (②) Therefore, plant researchers have developed a new potato species with unique sticky hairs that can trap and kill insects. (③) This sticky hair potato is a cross between the common potato and a wild Bolivian variety. (④) It has been shown to lower populations of common insect pests by 40 to 60 percent, including the Colorado potato beetle, one of the most destructive potato pests. (⑤) The plant researchers are working on this problem now by trying to reduce the density of the sticky hairs.

39

CEOs should then meet with this cabinet periodically to see how its perspective on key strategic issues differs from what they are hearing from the members of the senior management team.

Young people often have a keen early understanding of important societal trends. (①) They tend to have great familiarity with the latest ideas and products in fields such as technology, fashion, healthy living, and the environment. (②) For that reason, Gary Hamel argues that CEOs should go out of their way to stay connected with the youngest and brightest in their organization. (③) He recommends that CEOs form a "shadow cabinet" of highly capable employees in their twenties and thirties. (④) Hamel believes that interacting with young people will help CEOs see opportunities and threats that senior leaders may not perceive. (⑤) Moreover, Hamel recognizes that the perspectives of these young people are often filtered out if left to the normal machinations of the organizational hierarchy.

*shadow cabinet: (야당이 집권을 예상하고 만든) 예비 내각
**machination: 교묘한 술책

40 다음 글의 내용을 한 문장으로 요약하고자 한다. 빈칸 (A), (B)에 들어갈 말로 가장 적절한 것은?

Do you know a girl's secret to selling cookies? She asks her neighbors if they can donate a bicycle to Africa. If the neighbors turn her down, she then asks if they can help children in Africa by purchasing a box of cookies for $5. Then the neighbors are happy to make up for not donating a bike. This technique was what psychologist Robert Cialdini discovered in an experiment. Cialdini had his assistants disguise themselves as volunteer workers. They were instructed to approach college students and ask them if they were willing to volunteer two hours per week, for at least two years. When this request was rejected, as expected, it was followed up with a more reasonable request, which was to lead a group of juvenile delinquents on a two-hour trip to the zoo. Nearly 85% of their requests were accepted.

*juvenile delinquent: 비행 청소년

↓

The ____(A)____ of the initial larger request ____(B)____ compliance with the secondary smaller request.

	(A)		(B)
①	target	⋯⋯	increases
②	target	⋯⋯	decreases
③	refusal	⋯⋯	increases
④	refusal	⋯⋯	decreases
⑤	hesitance	⋯⋯	blocks

[41~42] 다음 글을 읽고, 물음에 답하시오.

Fatigue does not necessarily occur at fixed points. To a large extent, mental and physical exhaustion may be determined by unquestioned expectations. Psychologist Anita Karsten studied situations that at first feel good, but with (a) repetition become neutral or uncomfortable. She put subjects in "(b) semi-free situations" in which they were given tasks to do but were instructed that they could stop working whenever they were tired. They were told to do the work as long as they enjoyed it. Tasks were of two types: continuous activities such as drawing or writing, and tasks that come to a quick end but are repeated, such as reading a short poem again and again. For each type of task, the subjects worked until they grew weary.

The investigator then changed the context. For instance, after the subjects had drawn until exhausted, the investigator asked them to turn the page over and re-draw the last picture they had drawn, to show the experimenter how fast they could draw it. The "totally exhausted" subjects had no difficulty repeating the drawing in the new context. Another subject was given the task of writing ababab... until he had had enough. He went on until he was mentally and physically (c) exhausted. His hand felt numb, as though it couldn't move to make even one more mark. At that moment the investigator asked him to sign his name and address for a different purpose. The context created by the new request seemed to act as a new (d) stimulus to him. He did so quite easily. Similarly, other subjects, who read short poems repeatedly, did the same thing. When Karsten had subjects read poems aloud, after a while they became hoarse. When they complained to her how they hated the task, however, the hoarseness (e) appeared.

41 윗글의 제목으로 가장 적절한 것은?

① Does Boredom Cause Fatigue?
② How to Refresh Your Brain Immediately
③ Mental Exhaustion: Causes and Treatment
④ Change of Context Brings Renewed Energy
⑤ Fatigue: A Symptom of Psychological Disorders

42 밑줄 친 (a)~(e) 중에서 문맥상 낱말의 쓰임이 적절하지 않은 것은? [3점]

① (a) ② (b) ③ (c) ④ (d) ⑤ (e)

[43~45] 다음 글을 읽고, 물음에 답하시오.

(A)

In the tenth grade Kevin joined his high school music club, and he played first trumpet there. He worked hard rehearsing for their May Festival performance with the members of the music club and has presented many ideas for the club. Kevin became popular among the members, and ran for president of the club last year. He had tied with Dave Hamilton on the first round of voting but lost in the final voting. This year Kevin was again hoping to be elected president of the music club.

(B)

The secretary was giving out voting papers. Kevin bit on his pencil nervously. "I could print my name," he thought. "No one would know I voted for myself." Kevin almost voted for himself, but his conscience stopped (a) <u>him</u>. "If I don't respect the club traditions," he said to himself, "I really don't deserve to be president." So (b) <u>he</u> wrote Bill Cummings on the voting paper and passed it in.

(C)

The secretary collected the voting papers and silently counted them. Then he handed the voting papers and the total to Dave Hamilton, the retiring president. (c) <u>He</u> smiled and then spoke: "This is quite remarkable. All members but one have voted for Kevin Moore, our next club president. Congratulations, Kevin." Kevin smiled happily. (d) <u>He</u> was glad he had listened to his conscience.

(D)

Now it was time for another election. His friends said he would win the election this year, but Kevin didn't know. He couldn't forget tying with Dave and then losing last year. If only (e) <u>he</u> had voted for himself then! Of course, the club tradition was for each candidate to vote for an opponent. But with so many members voting, who would know? After all, the voting was secret.

43 주어진 글 (A)에 이어질 내용을 순서에 맞게 배열한 것으로 가장 적절한 것은?

① (B) — (D) — (C)
② (C) — (B) — (D)
③ (C) — (D) — (B)
④ (D) — (B) — (C)
⑤ (D) — (C) — (B)

44 밑줄 친 (a)~(e) 중에서 가리키는 대상이 나머지 넷과 <u>다른</u> 것은?

① (a) ② (b) ③ (c) ④ (d) ⑤ (e)

45 윗글의 Kevin에 관한 내용으로 적절하지 <u>않은</u> 것은?

① 음악 동아리에서 트럼펫을 연주했다.
② 동아리 회장으로 선출되기를 원했다.
③ 투표용지에 자신의 이름을 쓰지 않았다.
④ 전임 회장에게서 당선 축하를 받았다.
⑤ 선거 전에 이미 승리를 확신하고 있었다.

: AFTER TESTING

종료 시 분
소요시간 분

학습 마무리

1 채점하기 | 정답 및 해설 p.26
주의 틀린 문제를 다시 풀 수 있도록 정답을 본문에 표기하지 마세요.
2 등급 확인
3 틀린 유형 확인 후 전략 적용 복습 및 해설지 확인

How to Review

1 틀린 문제와 ✓ 표시한 문제는 다시 풀고 해설 확인하기
2 내가 표시한 정답 근거가 해설과 일치하는지 확인하기
3 잘 모르는 부분으로 표시한 내용은 해설을 통해 완전히 이해하기
4 어휘 외우기 (어휘 목록 다운로드 www.cedubook.com)
5 다음 회에 개선할 점 정리하기 (시간 엄수, 취약 유형 보완 등)

POWER UP!

실전 모의고사

05

: BEFORE TESTING

시작 시 분

학습 목표

1 **제한시간** (OMR 마킹시간 포함) ☐ 40분 ☐ 45분
2 **어휘예습** ☐ 해당 없음 ☐ 완료
3 **문제풀이순서** ☐ 순서대로 ☐ 2점 → 3점 ☐ 기타
4 **기타 목표**

Check Point

1 **정답 근거** e.g. 밑줄 긋기
2 **잘 모르는 부분** e.g. 〈 〉 또는 ? 표시
3 **자신 없는 문제** e.g. 문제 번호에 ✓표시

18 다음 글의 목적으로 가장 적절한 것은?

Dear Brianna,

It was great reading your last email. I especially enjoyed the pictures of your family at the beach. It looked like an amazing time, and it reminded me of just how long it's been since our two families got together. In the interest of correcting that, I'd like to suggest a trip to the National Baseball Hall of Fame. Brad's been talking about it non-stop, and the kids are very excited too. They have overnight packages for children ages 7-12 that let families sleep among the artifacts of past players, as well as hands-on activities for the kids. I know there are a few baseball fans in your family too, so it seems like a great opportunity for us to do something enjoyable together. Let me know soon if you are interested, as there are discounts for early registration.

Your friend, Sarah

① 동반 가족 여행을 제안하려고
② 지난 휴가 경험을 공유하려고
③ 명예의 전당 행사를 알려주려고
④ 가족 여행에 동참하지 못한 것을 사과하려고
⑤ 여행 패키지에 대한 추가 정보를 요청하려고

19 다음 글에 드러난 'I'의 심경 변화로 가장 적절한 것은?

On my way to the market, I saw the same homeless woman I'd seen dozens of times before. She was looking at me in that odd way she always did, so I started to speed up. It always seemed like she wanted something from me. Then she started walking toward me. My mind started racing. She wouldn't attack me, would she? When she got close enough, she said, "I'm sorry, honey, I didn't mean to upset you." Then she pulled out an old photograph of a woman who looked like me. She explained, "That's my sister, Claire. She died ten years ago. You look just like her. I miss her so much." My heart sank as I realized I'd been thinking such horrible things about a person in pain. Even at home, I couldn't forget the sad look in her eyes.

① upset → excited
② scared → guilty
③ happy → horrified
④ calm → surprised
⑤ anxious → relieved

20 다음 글에서 필자가 주장하는 바로 가장 적절한 것은?

No one will fit in perfectly in every situation. Personality traits that are merits in one circumstance may be considered shortcomings in another circumstance, and vice versa. Those who are admired for their deliberate and careful handling of things in one workplace, for example, may find themselves criticized as boring and unadventurous in another workplace. Or a friend who is considered too aggressive in many ordinary situations may be a hero in an emergency. Everyone has both their strong points and weak points, and these are not absolutes; instead, they are relative to situations. So it is important to see the other side of everyone's drawbacks and assets. Those who are always digging out and focusing on the weak points of others are likely to have few friends or admirers.

① 사람들의 다양한 특성을 존중해주어야 한다.
② 잘못을 겸허히 시인할 줄 아는 용기가 필요하다.
③ 사람을 단정 짓지 말고 그 이면을 보도록 해야 한다.
④ 상대방의 잘못된 행동을 통해서 자신을 반성해야 한다.
⑤ 모든 일을 완벽하게 해야 한다는 강박관념을 버려야 한다.

21 다음 글의 요지로 가장 적절한 것은?

Before making any significant purchase, take advantage of those websites that allow consumers to post personal reviews of products for sale. These days, more and more people are posting reviews of anything and everything — from pizzas to luxurious cars. Because the reviews are independent, they reflect a wide range of opinion, whether favorable or unfavorable. It's easy to find places on the Internet where you can get an idea of the general opinion about a particular company or product. These consumer forums can actually have a powerful effect on a product or company's reputation and sales. Companies now understand what it really means to say that the customer is always right. They try to make better products and offer better service in order to reduce the possibility of online complaints.

① 온라인 상품평은 편향된 정보를 제공한다.
② 인터넷 쇼핑의 발달로 상품 구매가 편해졌다.
③ 개인정보 유출 등 온라인 거래의 폐해가 늘고 있다.
④ 온라인상의 상품평이 소비자의 권리를 증대시키고 있다.
⑤ 기업들이 상품평을 주요 판매 촉진 수단으로 이용하고 있다.

22 다음 글의 주제로 가장 적절한 것은?

Attached to the large intestine like a little worm, the appendix seems to have no effect on digestion. In fact, for many years, scientists couldn't say what the appendix was built for. But Dr. Parker and his team at Duke University claim that the appendix is a "safe house" for important beneficial bacteria that produce films to protect our organs. According to him, the human appendix acts as a back-up storage area for good bacteria. The shape of the appendix is perfectly suited as a safe place for bacteria. Thus, in the event of a bacteria-killing sickness, which causes severe pain in the intestine, a great concentration of the bacteria shelters in the appendix and later refills the intestine. "Where this kind of disease is common," Dr. Parker says, "without the appendix to contain safe bacteria, you have less of a survival advantage."

*appendix: 맹장

① various roles of bacteria in the appendix
② new discovery revealed about the appendix
③ accurate shape and location of the appendix
④ proper and adverse functions of the appendix
⑤ controversy about the function of the appendix

23 다음 글의 제목으로 가장 적절한 것은?

No one I know has yet found a way to live in the future. Maybe someday we'll invent inexpensive time machines that allow us to vacation a hundred years into the future. Right now, if we want to live in 'tomorrow'—that place which is just a little better than today—the best we can do is live in the most forward-looking city on Earth. In a city there are increased choices and possibilities. Every day, a million people move from the countryside into cities, a journey that is less a trip in space than in time. These migrants are really moving decades of years forward, relocating from old villages into 21st-century sprawling urban areas. The ills of the slums are highly visible but don't stop the arrivals. They keep coming—as we all do—for the greater number of freedoms and options, which they never had before. This is why we live where and the way we do—to have more choices.

① How We Will Live in the Future
② Time Travel: A New Perspective
③ Every Day We Live Is the Future
④ Cities Are Where the Future Happens
⑤ Population, Urbanization, and Quality of Life

24 다음 도표의 내용과 일치하지 않는 것은?

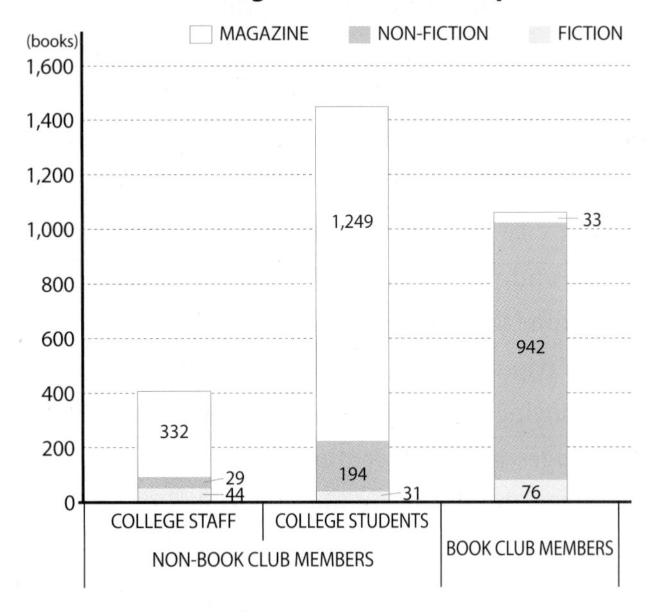

This chart shows the kinds of items bought by different groups of customers in a college bookstore in one month. According to the graph, each group has a distinctively different preference. ① Book club members and non-book club members bought roughly equal numbers of fiction books. ② However, sales of non-fiction books differed significantly according to customer group. ③ Book club members purchased the most non-fiction books, and college students bought the fewest. ④ Among the three categories of items purchased, magazines were the biggest sellers, and most were bought by college students. ⑤ Overall, the biggest buyers were college students, who were followed secondly by book club members, and then by college staff.

25 *Dia de Muertos*에 관한 다음 글의 내용과 일치하지 않는 것은?

Mexico's *Dia de Muertos* ("Day of the Dead") is one of the country's most important festivals. It's a time when families celebrate their memories of deceased loved ones, who return to earth as spirits to see their families again. Those who died as children visit on the first day, the spirits of adults on the second. To welcome them, families clear spaces in their homes and prepare flowers, candles, sweets, photographs, dishes of the deceased's favorite foods, and so on. Some families even set out towels and soap so that a spirit visitor can wash before eating. It's also a time when Mexicans visit family graves to clean and decorate them, often remaining at the grave throughout the night. Daytime brings uproarious street parties with music, dancing, and parades of people dressed as ghosts, devils, and other death-themed characters.

① 죽은 이들의 영혼을 맞이하는 축제일이다.
② 첫째 날은 어린아이의 영혼을 위한 날이다.
③ 죽은 이들을 위해 목욕용품을 준비하기도 한다.
④ 묘지에 찾아가 밤을 새우는 사람들이 있다.
⑤ 죽은 이들이 입었던 옷을 입고 거리를 행진한다.

26 *Cooking Country* 잡지에 관한 다음 안내문의 내용과 일치하지 않는 것은?

Cooking Country
Claim Your Free Trial Issue!

Try our FREE TRIAL issue of *Cooking Country*. If you like it, you will pay just $19 for one full year (six issues, including the FREE TRIAL issue), saving 45% off the newsstand price of $35.

In Every Issue

- **Guaranteed Simple Recipes:** Prepare easy weeknight meals
- **Lost Recipes:** Find recipes you thought were gone forever, which have been made easier for the modern cook
- **Regional Favorites:** Get Introduced to little-known local specialities from across the country
- **Objective Equipment Reviews and Ratings:** Find information about which brands and models to buy — and which to avoid

Please click here and enter your full name & address along with your subscription information.

① 무료 증정본 잡지를 받아 볼 수 있다.
② 1년 구독 시 가판대 가격보다 16달러가 절약된다.
③ 사라진 요리법을 되살리는 코너가 있다.
④ 전국 각지의 이름난 요리의 요리법을 소개한다.
⑤ 요리 기구에 대한 평가를 싣는다.

27 Sunburn Treatment에 관한 다음 안내문의 내용과 일치하는 것은?

Sunburn Treatment

1. Rehydrate

- Replace body fluids with water, juice, or sports drinks.

2. Treat Symptoms

- Apply aloe or over-the-counter moisturizing lotion to skin as directed.
- To soothe and cool skin, bathe in lukewarm water or apply cool compresses to the area.

Call a health care provider if:

- The burn has blisters or the skin is numb or appears white, which are symptoms of more serious sunburn.
- The sunburned person is a child under one year old.

Call 911 if the person:

- Does not seem to be responding to treatment appropriately.
- Has a seizure, visual changes, or any other neurological symptoms.

*blister: 물집

① 체내 수분을 보충하되, 주스는 좋지 않다.
② 환부에는 아무것도 바르면 안 된다.
③ 피부의 열을 식히기 위해 찬물로 씻어야 한다.
④ 피부가 하얗게 되면 회복되고 있는 것이다.
⑤ 치료 반응이 보이지 않으면 911에 전화한다.

28 (A), (B), (C)의 각 네모 안에서 어법에 맞는 표현으로 가장 적절한 것은? [3점]

Pansori is a Korean folk tradition of musical storytelling, sometimes (A) [referred / is referred] to as "Korean opera," that first emerged around the middle of the Joseon dynasty (1392-1910). Performances feature a solo vocalist and a solo drummer who share the stage to tell epic narrative tales. The identities of pansori's original creators and the exact year of its emergence are unknown; (B) [it / they] began as an oral tradition that was adopted by professional entertainers. These people were looked down on by the Joseon gentry, (C) [what / which] may explain why pansori long remained the preserve of peasants. Audiences for pansori expanded with the growing interest shown in the art form by the gentry of late Joseon, and in 2003, UNESCO officially recognized pansori as an outstanding example of the world's intangible cultural heritage.

*gentry: (조선시대) 양반, 상류 계층

	(A)		(B)		(C)
①	referred	……	it	……	what
②	referred	……	it	……	which
③	referred	……	they	……	what
④	is referred	……	it	……	which
⑤	is referred	……	they	……	what

29 다음 글의 밑줄 친 부분 중, 문맥상 낱말의 쓰임이 적절하지 <u>않은</u> 것은?

The meanings of talk and silence ① <u>vary</u> among cultures. I once made a presentation in Bangkok to local staff. I was sure it was going to be a success, but for some reason it was not. The staff stared at me ② <u>blankly</u> and just smiled. Nobody asked any questions. I had expected my presentation to start a lively discussion; instead there was an ③ <u>uncomfortable</u> silence. After getting to know Thai ways better, I realized that the staff thought I had talked too much. In my own culture, we express meaning mainly through words. We speak a great deal to express what we feel and think, and silence makes us ④ <u>nervous</u>. In some other cultures, people understand a lot of what is happening from the context, and usually feel a lot of words are ⑤ <u>necessary</u>. People communicate in an unspoken way.

30 밑줄 친 <u>It[it]</u>이 가리키는 대상이 나머지 넷과 <u>다른</u> 것은?

The fear of public speaking is sometimes called "stage fright." ① <u>It</u> is believed to be the single most common phobia — affecting as much as 75% of the population. ② <u>It</u> is even said to be ranked higher than the fear of death. The famous American comedian Jerry Seinfeld joked about ③ <u>it</u>, saying "The average person at a funeral would rather be in the coffin than doing the eulogy." However, many careers require some ability in public speaking, such as making presentations to clients or colleagues. The ability to do public speaking is sometimes considered one of the most valuable skills that an individual can possess. Most great speakers possess a natural ability for ④ <u>it</u>, but this does not mean they don't also suffer from stage fright, and the difference between a great public speaker and a poor one is knowing how to control ⑤ <u>it</u> when it happens.

*eulogy: (고인에 대한) 추도문

[31~34] 다음 빈칸에 들어갈 말로 가장 적절한 것을 고르시오.

31 Education researchers at the University of Sussex have found major ________________ in the British Prime Minister's education policy, which aims to have ability groupings as the norm in key subjects. Two new independent studies have shown that organizing schoolchildren into sets is unfair, and not an accurate means of assessing ability. Research by Jo Boaler, a professor of Education at Sussex, revealed that children in mixed ability mathematics classes outperformed those grouped by ability. The other new study by Sussex researchers has revealed that children are being assigned to a group according to their social background, with middle-class pupils more likely to be placed in higher-ability sets, irrespective of their prior scholastic achievements.

① benefits ② flaws
③ insights ④ changes
⑤ surprises

32 In the mid-1970s, two social psychologists asked students at a large university to spend five minutes completing a brief test designed to measure the complexity of their thoughts. The students had to unscramble a series of anagrams, but there was no way they could finish the entire series within the allotted five-minute period. The researcher told the students that a bell would ring after five minutes, and they shouldn't continue working past the bell, since that would be cheating. Some of the students completed the test across from a large mirror, whereas others couldn't see themselves while they worked on the anagrams. Meanwhile, the experimenter looked through one-way glass and counted how many of the students continued to work past the five-minute bell. The results were astonishing: only 7 percent of the students who saw themselves in the mirror cheated, whereas a massive 71 percent cheated when they weren't forced to look at themselves as they decided whether to behave honestly. When people consider behaving badly, their mirror images ________________________. [3점]

*anagram: 철자 순서를 바꾼 어구

① are mutually reversed
② tend to create conflicts
③ distort them in every way
④ reflect a different persona
⑤ become moral police officers

33 People seek to be anonymous for all kinds of reasons. Some of these reasons are lawful, as when people vote in elections. Other reasons are illegal and immoral, as when criminals use false names to commit crimes and avoid capture. Another kind of anonymity isn't created by an individual's choices but by ________________________. This especially happens with quotations. Many quotations have no known authors, so are signed "Anonymous." Each of these quotations must have started out as an original with a single author, but over the decades or even centuries, the author's name may have been misspelled, omitted, changed, and then finally lost altogether. Or the quotation itself may have been slightly modified in modern times by different people who couldn't claim to "own" the original words or idea, and in this way the quotation came to be authored by "Anonymous." [3점]

① pretending not to hear and see
② copying an original work for sale
③ a modern modification in current times
④ the efforts of a concerned citizens' group
⑤ a gradual eroding of ownership information

34 Popular people are the trendsetters of society, especially when it comes to the outbreak of diseases. During the H1N1 pandemic, researchers tracked and compared the spread of the disease in a random sample of students and a group of more socially dominant students at one university. While both groups ended up coming down with the flu in similar numbers, the more "popular" group of students got sick about two weeks ahead of their less socially-connected peers, and this fact makes them a potentially useful gauge of when and to what extent a future flu outbreak might occur. Because individuals who are more connected within their social network come into contact with individuals in that network more frequently, the logic goes that these social butterflies are also more likely to ______________________. [3점]

*H1N1: 신종 인플루엔자

① find it difficult to isolate themselves from others
② be exhausted due to their wide ranges of activities
③ recover more quickly from any contagious disease
④ get everything they want even under bad conditions
⑤ be the first to catch a communicable bug going around

35 **다음 글에서 전체 흐름과 관계 없는 문장은?**

Our environment affects every aspect of life on Earth — including the air we breathe, the water we drink, and the food we eat. ① While you might think environmental protection would top all other priorities, the reality is that conservation efforts are often made secondary to other pressures like economic development. ② For example, a government or company might decide that building up industry is more important than maintaining air and water quality or protecting other natural resources. ③ Some companies are trying to construct "green buildings" designed to reduce the overall impact on the natural environment. ④ Generally speaking, people are not educated about the impact their actions can have on the planet, and many of those who are aware of problems simply avoid changing their behavior. ⑤ When it comes to protecting the environment, the challenge isn't that some people are against conservation but that they are unwilling or unable to make more Earth-friendly choices.

[36~37] 주어진 글 다음에 이어질 글의 순서로 가장 적절한 것을 고르시오.

36

When trying to influence opinion and persuade listeners or readers to agree with a certain way of thinking, people often use words that are carefully selected for their ability to stir up emotions instead of logic.

(A) This is called using loaded language. For example, a liberal journalist might write about government spending on "the military" where a conservative would use the expression "national defense" instead.

(B) However, if she were anti-abortion, she would call those who share her views "pro-life," for the same reason. Thus, recognizing loaded language reveals important clues about the user's points of views.

(C) Similarly, if a writer favors abortion, she will call those who share her views "pro-choice," since the expression has strong positive connotations, and the people such expressions are associated with will be seen in a positive light.

① (A) — (C) — (B) ② (B) — (A) — (C)
③ (B) — (C) — (A) ④ (C) — (A) — (B)
⑤ (C) — (B) — (A)

37

As hunter-gatherer societies grew and eventually exhausted their natural food supplies, some survived by becoming sedentary farmers. With the advent of farming came a need for an organized system of planting, harvesting, and storing crops.

(A) The advantage of this type of system is the ability for decision-makers to produce rapid changes in their society. For example, Soviet dictator Josef Stalin's five-year plans quickly transformed the Soviet Union from a peasant-based agricultural society into one of the world's industrial superpowers.

(B) This required a greater amount of structure than what existed in a traditional economy. In order to ensure the survival of the society, decisions had to be made about what crops to grow and how much of the harvest to store.

(C) Over time, decision-making became centralized, and the command economic system developed. One leader or a group of powerful individuals makes the key economic decisions for the entire society.

*sedentary: 한 곳에 머물러 사는

① (A) — (C) — (B) ② (B) — (A) — (C)
③ (B) — (C) — (A) ④ (C) — (A) — (B)
⑤ (C) — (B) — (A)

[38~39] 글의 흐름으로 보아, 주어진 문장이 들어가기에 가장 적절한 곳을 고르시오.

38

> We may think those steps are a more polite approach, but they are not effective.

When we really want something from someone, many of us take predictable steps, each one making us more upset than the last. (①) We may start by waiting, not saying anything. (②) Next, we may talk "around" the need we have, but never directly mention it. (③) Later, we may start asking in an irritated manner, or even making angry demands. (④) We should focus on solving the problem we have, rather than on our desire to seem polite. (⑤) When we are focused on finding solutions, it's clear that a simple request is the most productive approach to take, whereas a winding path of steps is not.

39

> With the Sun at its highest point, and the days at their longest, common sense would tell you that June should be the hottest month of the year.

Why is the longest day of the year not also the hottest? Thermal inertia — the tendency of temperatures to remain the same — keeps the land and water from getting instantly hot. (①) On June 21, known as the summer solstice, the Sun's rays beat directly down on the Northern Hemisphere. (②) Because Earth is tilted at 23.5 degrees, the Sun shines straight above 23.5 degrees latitude, an imaginary line around Earth called the Tropic of Cancer. (③) If you stand on this line on the first day of summer, the Sun will be directly overhead, seemingly paused for a moment before beginning to sink lower in the sky each day. (④) But due to an effect, the ocean and landmasses take time to heat up. (⑤) As a result, the hottest weather usually arrives about six weeks after the summer solstice. [3점]

*summer solstice: 하지(夏至) **Tropic of Cancer: 북회귀선

40 다음 글의 내용을 한 문장으로 요약하고자 한다. 빈칸 (A), (B)에 들어갈 말로 가장 적절한 것은? [3점]

> Most of us are taught to pay attention to what is said — verbal language. Words do provide us with some information, but the meanings are derived from so many other sources. Take a simple phrase like, "I'll give you a lesson." If a counselor tells his client in a polite voice, "I'll give you a lesson," the counselor could imply that he could help him by sharing his personal experiences. However, if a sergeant says the same thing to a private with firmness in his voice, he would imply that the private would get some sort of punishment for his wrongdoing. When a guest comments to a host with the emphasis in his voice, "It's a bit chilly in here," the host understands that this is not simply an observation but really a request to have the window closed.
>
> *sergeant 병장 **private 이등병

> The meaning of a message is influenced by the ____(A)____ accompanying the message and the ____(B)____ that a speaker uses.

	(A)		(B)
①	culture	······	tone
②	culture	······	gesture
③	emotion	······	accent
④	context	······	tone
⑤	context	······	gesture

[41~42] 다음 글을 읽고, 물음에 답하시오.

Test anxiety is one of the most common problems students experience. The brainpower necessary to successfully complete the test can be hijacked by worrying. Sian Beilock, a professor of psychology at the University of Chicago, and her colleagues studied students who seemed to choke under pressure and didn't perform as well as expected in stress-filled situations. They asked a group of 20 college students to solve a series of math problems, telling them that the highest scorers on the test would be rewarded with money. To really pile on the pressure, students were also told they would be videotaped during the exam and both their professors and peers would be watching.

One group of students was instructed to sit quietly for 10 minutes before the test; the rest spent the time writing down their thoughts and feelings about the upcoming exam. Those who put pen to paper outperformed the others, enjoying a 5 percent boost on their test scores. "Writing down these negative thoughts gives you a chance to see them on paper and rethink your negativity. Then those thoughts are less likely to enter your head during the test and distract you," says Sian Beilock. "It's almost as if you've ______________ your mind. Now you have the cognitive power to perform at your best." Beilock repeated similar tests with more than 50 ninth-graders taking a final exam in biology. Students who wrote down their worries before the final earned a B+ on the exam, while students who wrote about something else earned a B−.

41 윗글의 제목으로 가장 적절한 것은?

① What Are the Secrets of the Brain?
② Students Speak Out About Test Anxiety
③ Writing About Emotions Beats Test Anxiety
④ Test Anxiety: A Major Educational Problem
⑤ The Negative Effects of Being Watched During a Test

42 윗글의 빈칸에 들어갈 말로 가장 적절한 것은? [3점]

① ignored
② emptied
③ disturbed
④ explored
⑤ intensified

[43~45] 다음 글을 읽고, 물음에 답하시오.

(A)

In the late 1990s, a family arrived at the public elementary school where I taught deaf students. They planned to enroll their deaf daughter as a first grader. They were upset because their child's kindergarten teacher warned them not to have high hopes for her academically. Based upon assessment results, (a) she painted a gloomy picture for their little girl's future. Standing behind them was their daughter, Katherine.

(B)

From that point forward she had a new appreciation for writing. (b) She is a young woman now and has developed into an excellent writer, public speaker, and student leader. She enrolled at the University of Northern Colorado intent on becoming a teacher. Katherine stays in touch and I especially treasure (c) her e-mails with term papers attached. This young lady is armed with a very powerful pen!

(C)

The entire time her parents were there she didn't make a sound or use sign language. After a few weeks with Katherine, I discovered she was a very bright, very strong-willed child. Although I did manage to engage (d) her in various learning activities, writing was a constant struggle. Every time the pencils came out, she would shut down and refuse to participate.

(D)

One day Katherine got off her bus and stood in front of the school crying loudly. The staff members, who didn't know sign language, brought (e) her a pen and notepad. Katherine wrote: "PAC BAK." Immediately the office staff realized she left her backpack on the bus. They summoned the bus back to school and Katherine was reunited with her backpack. That day Katherine finally saw the power of the pen.

43 주어진 글 (A)에 이어질 내용을 순서에 맞게 배열한 것으로 가장 적절한 것은?

① (B) — (D) — (C)
② (C) — (B) — (D)
③ (C) — (D) — (B)
④ (D) — (B) — (C)
⑤ (D) — (C) — (B)

44 밑줄 친 (a)~(e) 중에서 가리키는 대상이 나머지 넷과 다른 것은?

① (a) ② (b) ③ (c) ④ (d) ⑤ (e)

45 윗글의 Katherine에 관한 내용으로 적절하지 않은 것은?

① 학업 전망이 밝지 않다는 평가를 받은 적이 있다.
② 선생님이 되겠다고 결심하고 대학에 입학했다.
③ 필자와 더 이상 연락하고 지내지 않는다.
④ 다양한 학습 활동에 참여해도 글쓰기는 거부했다.
⑤ 사람들의 도움으로 잃어버린 가방을 되찾았다.

: AFTER TESTING

🕒 종료 시 분

⌛ 소요시간 분

학습 마무리

1 채점하기 | 정답 및 해설 p.34

(주의) 틀린 문제를 다시 풀 수 있도록 정답을 본문에 표기하지 마세요.

2 등급 확인

3 틀린 유형 확인 후 전략 적용 복습 및 해설지 확인

How to Review

1 틀린 문제와 ✓ 표시한 문제는 다시 풀고 해설 확인하기

2 내가 표시한 정답 근거가 해설과 일치하는지 확인하기

3 잘 모르는 부분으로 표시한 내용은 해설을 통해 완전히 이해하기

4 어휘 외우기 (어휘 목록 다운로드 www.cedubook.com)

5 다음 회에 개선할 점 정리하기 (시간 엄수, 취약 유형 보완 등)

POWER UP!

실전 모의고사

06

: BEFORE TESTING

시작 시 분

학습 목표

1 **제한시간** (OMR 마킹시간 포함) ☐ 40분 ☐ 45분
2 **어휘예습** ☐ 해당 없음 ☐ 완료
3 **문제풀이순서** ☐ 순서대로 ☐ 2점 → 3점 ☐ 기타
4 **기타 목표**

Check Point

1 **정답 근거** e.g. 밑줄 긋기
2 **잘 모르는 부분** e.g. 〈 〉 또는 ? 표시
3 **자신 없는 문제** e.g. 문제 번호에 ✓표시

18 다음 글을 쓴 목적으로 가장 적절한 것은?

To Whom It May Concern,

I recently participated in one of the tennis programs offered by the Orange County Fitness Club. It was advertised as a 4-week lesson for students of all ages taught by a certified pro. Now, as a long-time tennis enthusiast who has competed at the amateur level, I might not be the typical student. Still, I am nowhere near the professional level and certainly have much to learn from a pro. So, I was beyond disappointed when my $60 entry fee got me nothing more than basic advice on how to hold a racket. It was a complete waste of time and money. If any advanced students ask for my opinion on this program in the future, I'll simply offer to teach them myself.

Sincerely,
David Blain

① 테니스 강습비의 환불을 요구하려고
② 경험 많은 테니스 강사 소개를 부탁하려고
③ 학생 대상 무료 테니스 강습을 제안하려고
④ 추후에 있을 테니스 강습 일정을 문의하려고
⑤ 테니스 강습을 제대로 받지 못한 것을 항의하려고

19 다음 글에 드러난 'I'의 심경 변화로 가장 적절한 것은?

My brother Ethan and I were once out in the Gallatin Mountains of southern Montana for hunting elk. At night, we camped in our favorite free spot out in the national forest. It was a quiet and peaceful night for the two of us. I felt refreshed from the hustle and bustle of city life. The next morning, when we started hunting, it began to snow heavily. Within a very short time it became apparent that snow conditions were extremely perilous — snow layers around my brother and me collapsed with that scary whumping sound. Ethan looked at me with a concerned look on his face. I tried to force a smile but wasn't very successful. I didn't know what to do. To make matters worse, the wind was so strong that I couldn't stand upright and walk in a normal fashion.

① pleased → lonely
② calm → annoyed
③ ashamed → envious
④ comforted → worried
⑤ hopeful → disappointed

20 다음 글에서 필자가 주장하는 바로 가장 적절한 것은?

Well-meaning parents rush to book their infants and toddlers into swimming classes because they worry about the safety of their children. Over the years, I have witnessed many children completely out of control at swimming lessons—toddlers of two or three sobbing, screaming and clinging to their parents because they are terrified of even one toe touching the water. Other toddlers are glued to their parents and won't put their heads under, or are afraid to let go of the side of the pool. When parents ask me what they should do, I tell them to forget lessons for a while—forcing their toddlers will only make them more anxious about water. "Give her a splash in the bath or fill a big plastic bucket with water and lots of toys. Or just go to the pool as a family. Make water fun, not a chore. Then maybe try again in twelve months." It's not the end of the world if your child doesn't learn to swim until primary school or even later.

① 수영장에 어린이를 위한 안전시설을 확충하라.
② 어린 자녀에게 수영 강습을 억지로 시키지 마라.
③ 초등학교에 수영 강습 프로그램 도입을 의무화하라.
④ 자녀의 안전을 위해 반드시 수영 강습을 시켜주어라.
⑤ 어린이 수영 강습 프로그램에서 경쟁적 요소를 배제하라.

21 밑줄 친 an unforgettable lesson이 다음 글에서 의미하는 바로 가장 적절한 것은?

My thirty years of work with the Pirahã of the Amazon rainforest has taught me a great deal. I once thought it might be fun to teach the Pirahã about Western games, so I organized a field day, with a foot race, a sack race, and a tug-of-war, among other things. In the foot race, one fellow got out in front of everyone else. He then stopped and waited for the others to catch up so they could cross the finish line together. The idea of winning was not only novel but unappealing. We cross the line together or I don't cross it. The same went for the sack race. The tug-of-war was a joke—just guys keeping the slack out of the rope and talking. They loved it all, laughing and talking all day long and telling me what a good time they had. They taught me an unforgettable lesson. That's not a bad lesson—that's a fine lesson.

*Pirahã: 피라항(브라질 아마존강 유역에 사는 부족)

① Sometimes you have to lose, just to win again.
② You can have a great time and have everyone win.
③ The outcome of the game is unpredictable and changeable.
④ Some of your greatest pains become your greatest strengths.
⑤ The primary purpose of games is not to teach but to entertain.

22 다음 글의 요지로 가장 적절한 것은?

For thousands of years, farmers have improved their crops by crossbreeding plants that have good traits. They take pollen from one plant and add it to the flowers of another plant to produce a plant with the traits they want. But crossbreeding is slow and unreliable. Now, there are amazing shortcuts. Scientists can take a gene from one living thing and put it directly into another plant. That way, changes can be made more precisely in a much shorter time period. This new technique can create crops that are pest-proof, disease-resistant, and more nutritious. For example, a rice plant has been modified so it gets an extra boost of vitamin A from a daffodil gene. The plant was made for those who don't get enough vitamin A in their diet.

*crossbreed: 이종 교배하다 **daffodil: 나팔수선화

① 이종 교배의 단점을 유전자 조작으로 극복할 수 있다.
② 유전자 조작의 안전성은 과학적으로 검증되지 않았다.
③ 유전자 조작 식품의 규제를 위한 법적 조치가 필요하다.
④ 이종 교배를 통해 농촌 지역의 수익을 증가시킬 수 있다.
⑤ 유전공학을 농업에 적용하기 위해서는 신뢰도를 높여야 한다.

23 다음 글의 주제로 가장 적절한 것은?

Depending on the field or industry, 25 to 40 percent of workers are temporarily hired workers, part-timers, or contract workers, and employment in these nontraditional roles is growing while full-time employment is shrinking. Clearly, the smart job seeker today should look for a variety of paid work and not just an old-fashioned full-time job. However, the full-time job is still held as the ideal, and so many job seekers do not make use of this more flexible strategy. Many refuse to accept the legitimacy of any option outside of the traditional career model. But these narrow-minded people will have to compete for a declining supply of "conventional" permanent positions. They should instead see that to make a good living today, one must be flexible and pursue work in any of its many forms.

① ways to get hired at popular companies
② necessity of changing our perception of jobs
③ reasons for pursuing traditional full-time jobs
④ strategies for getting the most desired positions
⑤ deepening social problems due to the lack of jobs

24 다음 글의 제목으로 가장 적절한 것은?

We used to think that with age there was a progressive deterioration in brain cell structure and function. But that widespread assumption has been proved wrong. New nerve cells have been found to be generated in the brains of old animals, and we're learning more and more how this amazing property of the aged brain can be manipulated. Low levels of regular exercise, for instance, have been found to significantly generate new nerve cells in the hippocampus, a brain structure that deals with memory. Moreover, a recent study showed that certain nerve cells in the eyes of old people are capable of growing new processes. We will be able to regenerate parts of the brain that have worn out or been damaged in the course of a lifetime, providing renewed capabilities to those who are currently considered old folks.

*hippocampus: (뇌의) 해마

① Myths and Facts about Anti-ageing
② Your Nerve Cells Decide How Well You'll Age
③ Why Your Cognitive Functions Decline with Age
④ New Brain Cells Are Made Throughout Your Life
⑤ Think of Ageing as a Positive Growth Experience

25 다음 도표의 내용과 일치하지 않는 것은?

Energy Demand and Availability in Victoria

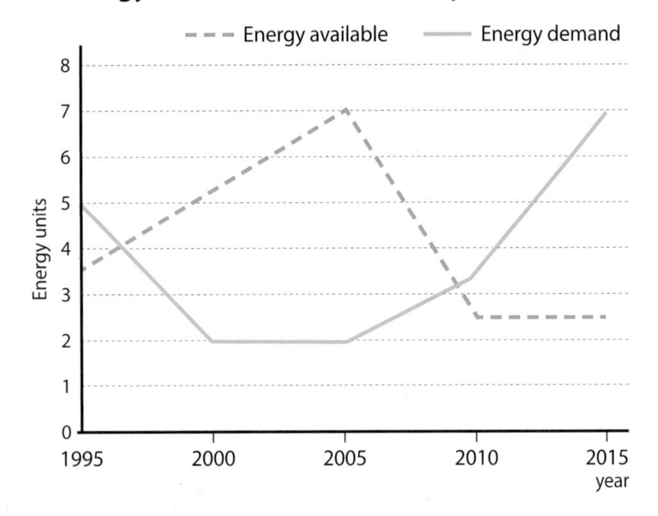

This chart shows the relationship between demand for energy and the energy available from fossil fuels in Victoria from 1995 to 2015. One energy unit represents 100 billion megajoules. ① The demand for energy dropped steadily between 1995 and 2000 from 5 units of energy to approximately 2 units. ② For the next five years, demand remained constant, and then from 2005 onwards, it climbed steeply, reaching 7 units by the year 2015. ③ In contrast, the amount of energy available from fossil fuels increased steadily from about 3.5 units in 1995 until it reached a peak of 7 in 2005. ④ From its peak it declined sharply until it finally leveled out at around 2.5 units from 2010 onwards. ⑤ As for the gap between energy demand and availability, it was the biggest in 2015, reaching 4.5 units.

*megajoule: 메가줄(에너지의 단위; 100만 줄)

26 James McNeill Whistler에 관한 다음 글의 내용과 일치하지 않는 것은?

James McNeill Whistler was a U.S.-born British painter who was highly influential in the late 19th century. He was born on July 11, 1834, in Lowell, Massachusetts. He was educated in St. Petersburg, Russia, then attended the United States Military Academy at West Point. Establishing himself as a painter in Paris and London, Whistler developed his distinctive style, utilizing soft colors and simple forms. His masterpiece is largely credited as *Whistler's Mother* (*Arrangement in Grey and Black No. 1*). Now held in Paris, it is one of the few American paintings that is widely known outside the United States, often being referred to as a Victorian *Mona Lisa*. Whistler would go on to found an art school in 1898, but it was forced to close soon after when Whistler became sick. He died in London in 1903. His work later provided the inspiration for Oscar Wilde's novel *The Picture of Dorian Gray* (1890).

① 미국 태생의 영국인 화가이다.
② 파리와 런던에서 화가로 자리 잡았다.
③ 그의 작품 *Whistler's Mother*는 현재 파리에 있다.
④ 미술 학교를 설립했지만 곧 문을 닫았다.
⑤ 소설 *The Picture of Dorian Gray*에서 영감을 받았다.

27 Student Summer Program에 관한 다음 안내문의 내용과 일치하지 않는 것은?

Student Summer Program

The Student Summer Program gives high school students the unique opportunity to volunteer at the National Aquarium and spend a summer sharing the aquarium's mission and magic.

Requirements

Applicants:
- have successfully completed ninth grade and at least one high school biology course
- are environmentally aware
- are interested in marine biology
- enjoy smiling and talking to people

Benefits

As a guide in the galleries, you will enjoy:
- a realistic look at marine biology as a career
- an opportunity to fulfill your school's community service requirements
- staff discounts and privileges
- the possibility of a part-time paid position

How to Apply

Please send the completed application form to recruit@nationalaquarium.org.

① 국립 수족관에서 자원봉사하는 프로그램이다.
② 9학년을 마친 사람만 지원할 수 있다.
③ 지원자는 해양 생물학에 흥미가 있어야 한다.
④ 학교에서 지역 봉사활동으로 인정해준다.
⑤ 추후 정규직 입사 기회가 주어질 수 있다.

28 The Bedford Bridge Park에 관한 다음 안내문의 내용과 일치하는 것은?

The Bedford Bridge Park

Buy Tickets Online

Purchase your tickets online for the Bedford Bridge Park and bypass the ticket lineup!

Bedford Residents: Please bring your photo identification along with your ticket to get a complimentary annual pass!

Terms and Conditions:

1. Tickets are non-refundable. No exceptions.
2. Tickets are valid for one year from the date of purchase and can be used on any day.

* Rates and conditions are subject to change. For ticket delivery problems, please email help@bedfordpark.au.

① 입장권은 온라인으로만 구매할 수 있다.
② Bedford 주민은 신분증이 있으면 무료입장할 수 있다.
③ 환불 불가가 원칙이지만 몇 가지 예외 규정이 있다.
④ 입장권은 미리 지정한 날짜에만 사용 가능하다.
⑤ 입장권 가격과 약관은 변동될 수 있다.

29 다음 글의 밑줄 친 부분 중, 어법상 틀린 것은? [3점]

A study of 7,400 civil service workers in London yielded some ① surprising statistics. Workers who felt they had little control over their work had a 50 percent higher risk of developing symptoms of heart disease than ② those with more job flexibility. In other words, feeling little control over the demands and pressures of the work we have to do ③ hold as great a risk of heart disease as risk factors like hypertension. That is why, of all the relationships we have at work, the one with our boss or superior has the greatest impact on our physical health. When volunteers at a British cold research unit ④ were exposed to a cold virus and followed for five days to see who would get sick, it turned out that those caught up in social tensions were the most susceptible. One tough day at the office was not a problem. However, ⑤ having persistent trouble with a boss was stressful enough to lower immune system strength.

30 (A), (B), (C)의 각 네모 안에서 문맥에 맞는 낱말로 가장 적절한 것은? [3점]

The famous mountaineer Edmund Hillary possessed a strange mix of extreme confidence and genuine modesty. With a(n) (A) [aggressive / passive] manner, he once said he was drawn to conquer Mt. Everest by the idea of smashing his rivals into the ground. Yet, after reaching the top, one of the greatest conquests of all time, he devoted much of his life to the poor Nepalese Sherpas who had so often helped him. Raising funds through his Himalayan Trust, Hillary helped (B) [remove / install] water pipes and built thirty schools, two hospitals, twelve medical clinics, several bridges, and more. The amount of work he (C) [undertook / avoided] could have kept 10 men busy, but Hillary never slowed down. In 1996, at the age of 87, he said, "I would like to see myself not going to Nepal quite so often. But at the moment, the responsibility is there. It has to be done."

	(A)		(B)		(C)
①	aggressive	……	remove	……	undertook
②	aggressive	……	install	……	avoided
③	aggressive	……	install	……	undertook
④	passive	……	remove	……	undertook
⑤	passive	……	install	……	avoided

[31~34] 다음 빈칸에 들어갈 말로 가장 적절한 것을 고르시오.

31 Eye contact seems to be particularly important in white Anglo-Saxon cultures. It is part of traditional British culture, for example, that others should be kept at a distance, and that contact with another person's body should be avoided in all but the most intimate situations. Because of this social convention of dealing with others at a distance, the English and other white Anglo-Saxon cultures rely very much on their eyes for personal communication. In many other cultures, however, people come closer together, and intimate physical interaction in social situations is as __________ as eye contact is in England. In Mediterranean cultures, for example, both the touch and the smell of others are expected while interacting. [3점]

① exciting
② routine
③ cold
④ intense
⑤ impolite

32 According to a survey conducted annually over a period of 17 years, and which gathered responses from more than 188,000 students, today's college freshmen are ______________________________ than at any other time in the 17 years of the poll. Given that the economy is in such bad shape today, it's hardly surprising that the stated major objective of most students was "to make as much money as possible." Fewer students than ever indicated that it was important for them to develop a meaningful philosophy of life. It follows then that the most popular course these days is not literature or history but accounting. Interest in teaching and social service fields is at an all-time low while, also unsurprisingly, enrollment in business courses, engineering, and computer science is way up.

① more stingy and less wasteful
② more impartial and less biased
③ more instinctive and less rational
④ more introverted and less ambitious
⑤ more materialistic and less impractical

33 Several years ago gas prices suddenly began to climb. As a result, there was considerable political pressure to alleviate the squeeze placed on the pocketbooks of many Americans. Instead of driving less, many wanted to continue their lifestyle of driving a vehicle without having to pay higher prices. So, here is what happened. As gas prices increased, demand for alternative fuels increased. This increase in demand for alternative fuels was popular among corn growers who had a product called ethanol. In order to provide ethanol at a lower cost, corn growers lobbied Congress for greater subsidies. This resulted in more land being placed into corn production at the expense of other crops, namely wheat. As wheat supplies decreased and wheat prices rose, the price of the substitute crop, rice, also rose because there was now more demand for rice. This led to the price of rice increasing to the point where people in South and Southeast Asia were unable to afford their basic staple. Starvation quickly followed. People overlooked the fact that ______________________________. [3점]

*subsidy: 보조금

① sellers can control prices
② markets talk to each other
③ starvation occurs unexpectedly
④ businesses are motivated by profits
⑤ labor mobility creates supply shocks

34 Common sense suggests that the best way to get somebody to improve himself is to give him positive feedback and praise about the things he does well before pointing out mistakes in a constructive, rather than critical, way. Many parents, however, tend to forcefully rebuke their children for their weaknesses, while at the same time purposely underrating the significance of their achievements. One common reason for this is that often parents are eager to ensure their children don't grow up to have too good an opinion of themselves, becoming what is commonly known as "big-headed." Many parents fear that their children may become conceited or complacent. They are keen for their children to outdo the neighbors' kids but ______________________________. [3점]

① don't want them to become arrogant and boastful
② want them to be popular and sociable at the same time
③ believe that they are already sufficiently active at school
④ want them to explore and discover the world themselves
⑤ don't teach them the traditions and values of their culture

35 **다음 글에서 전체 흐름과 관계 없는 문장은?**

Our society is rapidly becoming cashless as more and more people are using bank cards and credit cards to pay for goods. ① People can get a free loan for up to a month because they do not have to pay for the goods until the credit card bill comes in a month later. ② This allows people to earn interest on the savings in the bank that have technically already been spent. ③ When people use their credit card for nonessential items, they usually lose track of how much they spend. ④ Also, if a person loses his or her card or it is stolen, he or she can contact the bank and have the card canceled so the finder or thief cannot use the card. ⑤ Credit cards can be an advantage to consumers as they are inherently useful in the respect that they offer both financial and security benefits.

[36~37] 주어진 글 다음에 이어질 글의 순서로 가장 적절한 것을 고르시오.

36

"Purple snowflake" is a metaphor for standing out in a crowd. In business, it's more important than ever that people notice you, your products, or the services you offer.

(A) To get this attention when nearly everything is equal among you and your competitors, you need to do something unique. When I want a busy magazine editor to open an invitation from me, for example, I use the finest stationery, my very best pen, and elegant handwriting.

(B) Obviously, not every purple snowflake is going to get you the attention you want. But instead of giving up, see if you can create another purple snowflake. As the old saying goes, "If at first you don't succeed, try, try again."

(C) Of course, there are cheaper and less time-consuming ways to do it. But a magazine editor is far less likely to open an ordinary business envelope than a lovely handwritten one, which in this case is my purple snowflake!

*stationery: 편지지

① (A) — (C) — (B)
② (B) — (A) — (C)
③ (B) — (C) — (A)
④ (C) — (A) — (B)
⑤ (C) — (B) — (A)

37

> How many times have you set a goal only to realize later that you've lost all your energy for it and have to give it up?

(A) After adding up your potential losses, calculate the benefits that the prize will bring, and decide whether the benefits outweigh the losses. If they don't, then don't make the commitment. Counting the costs and benefits always adds a healthy dose of realism when you're considering setting a goal.

(B) Before you set it as your goal, figure out how much you will have to pay. For instance, you may have to spend many hours writing essays and practicing speeches, which means you won't have as much time to hang out with friends, play on the computer, or watch TV.

(C) It's a very common experience, because many people don't pause to weigh up sacrifices they'll have to make to achieve their goals. Let's say that your school awards an annual English prize.

① (A) — (C) — (B)　　② (B) — (A) — (C)
③ (B) — (C) — (A)　　④ (C) — (A) — (B)
⑤ (C) — (B) — (A)

[38~39] 글의 흐름으로 보아, 주어진 문장이 들어가기에 가장 적절한 곳을 고르시오.

38

> The interesting thing is that although the upsurge in obesity has a number of causes, genetics doesn't appear to be among them.

A recent study found that the rate of obesity is increasing in every American state, regardless of gender, age, race, or educational level. (①) In 1991, only four states had obesity rates of 15 percent or higher; today at least 37 states do. (②) The makeup and structure of American genes has not changed in the past few decades. (③) What has changed is the nation's diet and way of life: when people eat more and do less, they get fat. (④) In America, people drive everywhere rather than walk; they even drive to places within easy walking distance. (⑤) When this addiction to the car is combined with a daily diet that is exceptionally high in fat and calories, widespread obesity is sure to occur.

39

> However, it could be argued that our ability to manipulate things is just as unique, and that the hand with its flexible thumb is as good a symbol of human intelligence as the head with its large brain.

When we discuss knowledge, we often focus on theoretical "knowledge of the head" and overlook practical "knowledge of the hand." (①) Indeed, there seems to be something of a prejudice against the latter. (②) For example, the abstract knowledge of the scientist is generally held in higher esteem than the practical knowledge of the car mechanic or the craftsman. (③) This prejudice may derive from the widespread assumption that our capacity for reason is what distinguishes us from the rest of the animal kingdom. (④) There is a sense in which practical knowledge is prior to, and more fundamental than, abstract knowledge. (⑤) After all, we need basic skills, such as the ability to speak and manipulate objects, before we can acquire any kind of knowledge. [3점]

40 다음 글의 내용을 한 문장으로 요약하고자 한다. 빈칸 (A), (B)에 들어갈 말로 가장 적절한 것은?

> Do you have a good sense of what those around you are thinking and feeling, even when they're reluctant to open up? If not, you can improve this valuable ability by spending quality time with some imaginary friends. Jessica Black and Jennifer Barnes conducted a study. It featured 100 college students who were randomly assigned to watch an extended excerpt from either an award-winning television drama (*Mad Men* or *The West Wing*) or a documentary (*How the Universe Works* or *Shark Week: Jaws Strikes Back*). Participants were then shown 36 images of sets of eyes and asked which of the four words best described the person in the photograph: jealous, panicked, arrogant, or hateful. Not surprisingly, the researchers found women were better than men at choosing the correct emotion. But for both genders, those who watched one of the dramas scored higher on average than those who saw a documentary.
>
> *feature: (특별히) 포함하다 **excerpt: 발췌, 인용

↓

> Watching high-quality ____(A)____ programs such as television dramas can increase our ability to ____(B)____ other people's feelings.

	(A)		(B)
①	fictional	……	read
②	fictional	……	control
③	entertaining	……	internalize
④	entertaining	……	control
⑤	instructive	……	read

[41~42] 다음 글을 읽고, 물음에 답하시오.

For years, social psychologists have written about the differences between the perspective of an actor and that of an observer. For instance, we are likely to blame (a) circumstances for our own negative behavior: "The subway always makes me late." If the very same behavior is engaged in by someone else, however, we tend to blame that individual: "He is chronically behind schedule."

Once we become mindfully aware of views other than our own, we start to realize that there are as many different views as there are different observers. Such awareness is potentially (b) liberating. For instance, imagine that someone has just told you that you are rude. You thought you were being frank. If there is only one perspective, you can't both be right. But with an awareness of many perspectives, you could accept that you are both right. If we cling to our own point of view, we may be blind to our impact on others; if we are too vulnerable to other people's definitions of our behavior, we may feel (c) undermined, for observers are generally less favorable to us than we are to ourselves.

As we said, there are potentially as many (d) interpretations as there are observers. Every idea, person, or object is potentially simultaneously many things depending on the perspective from which it is viewed. A cow is steak to a rancher, a sacred object to a Hindu, and a collection of genes and proteins to a molecular biologist. Being mindful does not mean that we can plan certain defined ways of interacting with others that will produce certain outcomes; rather, it means that we remain aware that the various possible perspectives will never be (e) cultivated. We can see this on a grand scale or in the most ordinary circumstances.

41 윗글의 제목으로 가장 적절한 것은?

① Expand Perspectives to Be Happy
② Be Open to Different Points of View
③ Perspective Shifts Make a Difference
④ Change Your Perspective, Change Your Life
⑤ How to See Things from Different Perspectives

42 밑줄 친 (a)~(e) 중에서 문맥상 낱말의 쓰임이 적절하지 않은 것은? [3점]

① (a) ② (b) ③ (c) ④ (d) ⑤ (e)

[43~45] 다음 글을 읽고, 물음에 답하시오.

(A)

Two angels in disguise asked a wealthy family if they could stay the night. The angels were treated with contempt by the family, and were refused a bed. Instead, (a) <u>they</u> were shown to the cold, dark basement.

(B)

"The night we stayed in the mansion's basement, I inspected that hole in the wall and found piles of gold. Since the owners were so mean to us, I sealed the hole so the gold could never be found. Then, last night, the angel of death came for the farmer's wife as we slept in her bed. I made the angel take the farmer's cow instead. Things may not always be what they seem."

(C)

The next morning the companions found (b) <u>them</u> weeping. Their prized cow, the only thing of value they had ever owned, was dead. The younger angel lost his temper. "How could you let this happen? The rich people treated us badly but you helped them!" he accused the older angel. "Then, these poor people were willing to share everything with (c) <u>us</u>, but you let their cow die!" "Things may not always be what they seem," the older angel replied.

(D)

As the younger angel tried to sleep on the cold, hard floor, the older angel set to repairing a hole in the wall. This puzzled the younger angel, but the other said, "Things may not always be what they seem." The next night (d) <u>the pair</u> went to the home of a very poor farmer and his wife. They shared all their food with the angels, then gave them their own bed so that (e) <u>they</u> would feel comfortable and welcome.

43 주어진 글 (A)에 이어질 내용을 순서에 맞게 배열한 것으로 가장 적절한 것은?

① (B) — (C) — (D)　② (C) — (B) — (D)
③ (C) — (D) — (B)　④ (D) — (B) — (C)
⑤ (D) — (C) — (B)

44 밑줄 친 (a)~(e) 중에서 가리키는 대상이 나머지 넷과 <u>다른</u> 것은?

① (a)　② (b)　③ (c)　④ (d)　⑤ (e)

45 윗글에 관한 내용으로 적절하지 <u>않은</u> 것은?

① 천사들은 부잣집 지하실에서 하룻밤을 묵었다.
② 부잣집 지하실 벽 속에 금 무더기가 있었다.
③ 천사는 가난한 농부와 소의 목숨을 맞바꿨다.
④ 천사가 부잣집 지하실의 벽을 수리해 주었다.
⑤ 가난한 농부는 천사들에게 침실을 내주었다.

: AFTER TESTING

⏱ 종료	시	분
⌛ 소요시간		분

학습 마무리

1 채점하기 | 정답 및 해설 p.42
주의 틀린 문제를 다시 풀 수 있도록 정답을 본문에 표기하지 마세요.
2 등급 확인
3 틀린 유형 확인 후 전략 적용 복습 및 해설지 확인

1 틀린 문제와 ✓ 표시한 문제는 다시 풀고 해설 확인하기
2 내가 표시한 정답 근거가 해설과 일치하는지 확인하기
3 잘 모르는 부분으로 표시한 내용은 해설을 통해 완전히 이해하기
4 어휘 외우기 (어휘 목록 다운로드 www.cedubook.com)
5 다음 회에 개선할 점 정리하기 (시간 엄수, 취약 유형 보완 등)

POWER UP!

실전 모의고사 07

: BEFORE TESTING

시작 시 분

학습 목표

1 **제한시간** (OMR 마킹시간 포함) ☐ 40분 ☐ 45분
2 **어휘예습** ☐ 해당 없음 ☐ 완료
3 **문제풀이순서** ☐ 순서대로 ☐ 2점 → 3점 ☐ 기타
4 **기타 목표**

Check Point

1 **정답 근거** *e.g.* 밑줄 긋기
2 **잘 모르는 부분** *e.g.* 〈 〉 또는 ? 표시
3 **자신 없는 문제** *e.g.* 문제 번호에 ✓표시

18 다음 글의 목적으로 가장 적절한 것은?

Dear Mr. Palmer,

I was present at the Music Educators' Conference where your school's orchestra performed. When I heard that you have 360 students out of a total enrollment of 500 actively participating in your instrumental music program, I was very impressed. As I'm sure you know, that number is quite remarkable. Do you have any advice for new music teachers trying to increase the number of student musicians in their schools? If you don't have the time to answer this e-mail, perhaps you could indicate a time and date when I could call you. I'd appreciate any tips you might have.

Sincerely,
Olivia Wright

① 학교 대항 합주대회 참가를 요청하려고
② 음악 교사 연수 프로그램 참가를 독려하려고
③ 효과적인 악기 연주 교육 방법을 소개하려고
④ 학교 관현악단에서 사용할 악기 기증을 부탁하려고
⑤ 학생 연주자 수를 늘리는 방법에 대한 조언을 구하려고

19 다음 글의 상황에 나타난 분위기로 가장 적절한 것은?

The noisy alarm clock buzzed and buzzed. I reached a hand out from under the warm covers, switched off the buzzer, and snuggled back down. Outside the window was a cold, wet, grey day—just the right kind for lazing about in bed and dozing. Almost every Monday morning for the past forty-four years, I had leapt out of bed and busied myself getting ready for work. Not today. I listened for noises in the house but then remembered that my wife plays golf early every Monday morning. Lazily I stretched, yawned, and thought about breakfast. Coffee would be nice. I swung my legs slowly out of bed, put on my slippers, and reached for my bathrobe. Today was the beginning of my retirement.

① busy and noisy
② lively and festive
③ boring and gloomy
④ relaxed and leisurely
⑤ urgent and frightening

20 **다음 글에서 필자가 주장하는 바로 가장 적절한 것은?**

It seems that punctuation, diction, and grammar are of little importance to many people these days. At supermarket express checkout aisles, for example, the signs always say "12 items or less," when "12 items or fewer" is correct. Indifference and a general decline in education standards have made Standard English go downhill. Some people are terribly bothered by this. They believe everybody should respect Standard English as much as they do, and are very angry whenever they see English abused. Sadly, these people are setting themselves up for a lifetime of stress. They should just accept the fact that standards have declined. Poor English is everywhere — in menus, street signs, ads, newspapers, and even academic papers. Don't let yourself be obsessed with it or upset by it.

① 정확한 문법을 사용하도록 노력하라.
② 폭넓은 어휘력의 중요성을 이해하라.
③ 자신의 영어 실력 때문에 좌절하지 마라.
④ 언제나 올바른 문법만을 기대하지는 마라.
⑤ 실생활에서 사용되는 언어 표현을 익혀라.

21 **다음 글의 요지로 가장 적절한 것은?**

Listen to football announcers during a game, and you'll hear them talking about risks, especially those associated with trying to score — like throwing the ball too far or going for a big play. But they never talk about the risk of *not trying* risky things. In the attempt to avoid a loss or a setback in play, teams can be so conservative that they will lose anyway because they didn't take the risks needed. The same applies to your career. It's easy to see risks associated with aiming high, such as when you go for a challenging new job. But if you don't take the risk, you won't get anywhere. Failing to take risks is the biggest risk of all — that's the way to lose all your opportunities for success.

① 원하는 것이 커지면 그만큼 책임감도 커진다.
② 큰 위험을 감수할수록 큰 이익을 얻을 수 있다.
③ 계획은 세우는 것보다 실천하는 것이 중요하다.
④ 실패에 대한 걱정이 많을수록 실패할 확률이 높다.
⑤ 실패가 두려워 어떤 시도도 하지 않는 것이 가장 위험하다.

22 **다음 글의 주제로 가장 적절한 것은?**

Many events, facts, observations, and changes can be mathematically correlated with others, but such correlations do not prove any cause-effect relationship, whatsoever. Just to "prove" this fallacy, try on this silly correlation: Carbon dioxide levels have increased in the air above every nation on earth over the last 100 years. Similarly, the number of reported crimes committed has increased in the world over the last 100 years. Therefore, one concludes that there is a causative relationship between carbon dioxide in the air and the number of crimes committed. Of course, that is pure nonsense. But politicians, media reporters, and the public at large all fall for that kind of reasoning. Then, "solutions" to problems that are thought to be understood are generated, and they often require raising taxes and borrowing money from future generations. In the end, time and money have been lost, but no problem has been solved.

① effects of air pollution on crime rates
② danger of following the majority's opinion
③ necessity of finding causes for phenomena
④ cause-and-effect analysis as a problem-solving tool
⑤ misconceptions about mathematically correlated events

23 다음 글의 제목으로 가장 적절한 것은?

It may be unpleasant to smell someone else's sweat, but here's a fun fact. Researchers at Utrecht University in the Netherlands knew from previous studies that negative emotions could be transferred by scent via "chemosignals," so they wanted to know if the opposite emotion could be conveyed, too. They gathered 12 men and showed them movies that either generated fear or happiness in them, along with a control group that was shown neutral scenes. The researchers collected sweat samples from each man by placing pads under their arms. All of the sweat samples were then presented to 36 female participants to smell while their facial expressions were recorded. The researchers were able to conclude the women smiled more when they smelled the sweat of the happy men than when they smelled the sweat of those who watched a neutral clip.

*chemosignal: 화학 신호
**clip: (영화) 클립(필름 중 일부만 따로 떼어서 보여주는 부분)

① Happiness May Be Contagious via Smell
② When the Sense of Smell Meets Emotion
③ Do Scents Affect People's Work Performance?
④ The Secret of People Who Always Smell Good
⑤ Scenes That Can Positively Transform Your Mood

24 다음 도표의 내용과 일치하지 않는 것은?

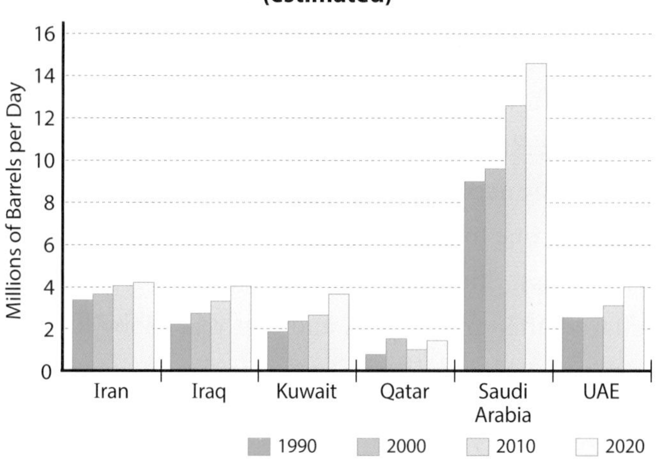

This graph, which compares estimates of the oil production capacity of six Middle Eastern countries, has several notable points. ① The most significant is that oil production was estimated to increase year by year in all countries. ② Both Kuwait and Iraq were expected roughly to double their output between 1990 and 2020. ③ After remaining steady at 2.5 million barrels per day from 1990 to 2000, the UAE's output was expected to approach 4.0 million in 2020. ④ Saudi Arabia's 1990 output was estimated to exceed that of Iran, Iraq and Kuwait combined. ⑤ The graph also predicts that Saudi Arabia would maintain and strengthen its position as the leader in production capacity, with 14.5 million barrels per day expected in 2020.

25 Susan Butcher에 관한 다음 글의 내용과 일치하지 않는 것은?

Pursuing her love of animals and the wilderness, Susan Butcher moved to Alaska when she was 20 and began training to compete in the Iditarod Trail Sled Dog Race. Incredibly tough, the Iditarod tests the endurance of mushers and their dogs over the course of one to two weeks and 1,100 miles of Alaskan wilderness. She was forced to pull out of the 1985 Iditarod after an accident, and that year Libby Riddles survived a blizzard to become the first woman ever to win the race. Later that same year, Susan married fellow dog racer David Monson, and the pair went on to compete successfully in almost every major sled dog race in the world. Susan won the Iditarod in 1986, '87, '88, and '90. The reason she missed the race of '89 was only because she was pregnant with her first daughter.

*musher: (개썰매를 이용한) 크로스컨트리 경주 참가자

① 20세 때 알래스카에서 훈련을 시작했다.
② 1985년 눈보라를 이겨내고 경주에서 우승했다.
③ 개썰매 동료 선수와 결혼해서 함께 경주에 참가했다.
④ 결혼 이후 참가한 경주에서 4회 우승했다.
⑤ 아이를 임신했을 때 경주에 참가하지 않았다.

26 학생회 선거 운동 규칙에 관한 다음 안내문의 내용과 일치하지 않는 것은?

Rules for Campaigning ☑

1. Students can only campaign using posters. All posters must be approved by Mr. Little.
2. Students can have a total of eight campaign posters.
   a. One on the student's locker
   b. Seven in general spaces (cafeteria and hallways)
3. Posters must be positive and cannot mention other candidates.
4. Students cannot hand anything out (candy, prizes, cards, etc.).
5. Students running for office will need to prepare a speech.
   a. Speeches will be recorded before school on Wednesday, October 9.
   b. Speeches will need to be at least one minute long but not longer than three minutes.
6. Parents are not permitted to participate in any part of the campaigning.

① 포스터는 총 여덟 장을 게시할 수 있다.
② 포스터에 다른 후보를 언급하면 안 된다.
③ 후보자 연설은 수요일 방과 후에 녹화한다.
④ 후보자 연설은 1~3분 동안 이루어져야 한다.
⑤ 선거 운동에 학부모가 관여해서는 안 된다.

27 Holiday party에 관한 다음 안내문의 내용과 일치하는 것은?

HOLIDAY PARTY

You are invited to the annual Franklin Alumni & Faculty Celebration

December 29, 6 p.m. to 10 p.m.
at Chiba at 8312 Oak Street

Come celebrate our finest past & present faculty while talking with fellow alumni! Enjoy traditional holiday fare as well as Chiba's cuisine, specialty cocktails, and live jazz music by *The Courtyard Kings*.

Alumni

There is no admission fee for Alumni Association members, and members can each bring one guest. Pay your annual membership fees at the door or online at fafa.org. All members receive one complimentary Franklin-inspired specialty cocktail, "The Big Ben," created especially for us by Chiba.

Donations: Suggested donations are $30, but don't let that stop you from attending. Donations, at any level, are welcome and appreciated.

We hope to see you at this special opportunity!

① 파티는 12월 29일에 6시간 동안 열린다.
② 파티에 참석하는 교수들은 모두 현직 교수들이다.
③ 동창회 회원에게만 입장료가 무료이다.
④ 동창회비는 온라인과 현장 납부 모두 가능하다.
⑤ 기부금은 최소 30달러부터 자율적으로 낼 수 있다.

28 다음 글의 밑줄 친 부분 중, 어법상 틀린 것은?

We humans, ① compared to other land mammals, are the best distance runners in the animal kingdom. Our upright posture and ability to shed heat are ② what allow people to run more than 20 miles during a race. Our superior cooling system makes it ③ easily for us to run long distances on hot days. We also have a superior breathing system, which enables us to change speeds without losing efficiency. And our diet allows us to store energy longer than most other animals ④ do. Very few other animals can run long distances, especially at the speeds that top human athletes perform. All this adds up to one simple fact: we were born to run, especially to run ⑤ such long distances.

29 다음 글의 밑줄 친 부분 중, 문맥상 낱말의 쓰임이 적절하지 않은 것은? [3점]

Don't expect too much from your future trip to space. You might be disappointed to find lots of trash ① floating around you instead of beautiful stars. More than 5,000 satellites have been launched into space since 1957, and all that activity has led to large amounts of space trash. Space trash, also called space debris, is any man-made object, such as a satellite or anything that assisted a satellite in any stage of its ② productive life, that is now no longer serving a useful purpose. Understanding its seriousness, the United Nations is working on guidelines to ③ limit the creation of debris. In addition, a space shuttle has been picking up ④ functioning spacecraft orbiting the Earth for many years. Without continuous efforts like this, space will turn into a big ⑤ dumping place.

30 밑줄 친 them[they]이 가리키는 대상이 나머지 넷과 다른 것은?

In France, from time to time, efforts have been made to "purify" its national language, and some nationalist language authorities have led ① them. They have attempted to expel foreign words from the vocabulary and to replace ② them with "pure French" words that have become neglected and in some cases even forgotten. Some language theorists are even of the view that when a native word of the same meaning exists, no word of foreign origin should be used. However, any effort to make rules to ban the use of ③ them in French would be doomed to failure. Foreign words that have long been in common use in French are just as much part of the language as if ④ they had been invented by Voltaire, a prominent French writer and philosopher. There is no sound reason for which ⑤ they should be considered inferior or abandoned.

[31~34] 다음 빈칸에 들어갈 말로 가장 적절한 것을 고르시오.

31 Spontaneous expressions of pride appear to be ________________. Tracy and David Matsumoto analyzed photos of athletes from more than thirty countries taken after they won or lost judo matches in the 2004 Olympics and Paralympics. 15 athletes from all over the world tended to show the same behaviors after winning (smiling, head tilted back, arms raised in a V, chest out) and losing (shoulders slumped, chin down, and chest narrowed). This was true even in competitors from collectivistic cultures, where pride is less appreciated — even discouraged, in some cases. But perhaps the strongest evidence of the innateness of these expressions is the fact that even athletes who were born blind — athletes who had never seen another person express pride or power or victory — did the same thing with their bodies when they won.

① functional　② predictive
③ contagious　④ universal
⑤ unreadable

32 Your nature is designed to ________________. In other words, you're designed rather like an elevator, ready for your buttons to be pushed. An elevator has special circuitry, called a switch, which closes to "remember" which button was pushed and how to respond to it. Some human genes act as switches, too. They respond to, or "remember," certain experiences by closing a circuit and activating a complex, one-way process of development, after which there is no option of going back to your previous state. That's one reason genetically identical twins aren't exactly the same. One twin may have an experience which triggers a genetic switch to permanently close. If the other twin does not have the same experience, the switch remains open. In the same manner, two elevators may have an identical design (nature), but are sent to different floors because different buttons were pressed (nurture). [3점]

① tolerate many ups and downs
② be both patient and impulsive
③ produce hormones to forget something bad
④ respond at the genetic level to your experiences
⑤ be open to some experiences and closed to others

33 Ecological disaster has been unfolding in the icy waters off Alaska. Since the 1970s, populations of seals, sea lions, and sea otters have plummeted. Some scientists have blamed changes in ocean currents, while others have pointed their finger at human overfishing of the marine mammals' food supplies. But a recently published paper has attributed the devastation to ____________________. In the aftermath of World War II, commercial whaling expanded rapidly, and the great whales of the North Pacific Ocean were almost entirely wiped out. This removed a major source of food for killer whales, who then began to fish down the food web, beginning with harbor seals (populations collapsed in the early '70s), then moving on to fur seals, then sea lions, and finally, sea otters (today), collapsing these populations one after another. [3점]

*plummet: 급격히 줄다 **killer whale: 범고래

① an ecological domino effect
② an international armed conflict
③ ignorance about ocean currents
④ a natural predator of killer whales
⑤ the hunting of small marine mammals

34 Mistakes can play a critical role in personal and professional development. If the error was a result of a poor decision, explain to your boss and other interested parties how you will avoid making the same or a similar misstep in the future, but remember that you have to act quickly before people make judgments about your competence or expertise. By demonstrating that you've changed as a result of your mistake, you can reassure your superiors or peers that you can be trusted with equally important tasks or decisions in the future. Perhaps your boss or co-workers will make you pay a price for making the mistake, such as a higher workload or less responsibility, but whatever the consequences you need to show that you get it. This is far easier in a learning-focused culture than in a performance-focused culture, in which mistakes are often judged more harshly. But regardless of the office environment, you need to figure out how you can ____________________. [3점]

① adapt yourself to a different company's culture
② accept the mistake you made and boldly admit it
③ stop yourself from making the same mistake again
④ avoid situations in which you might make a mistake
⑤ translate the mistake from a drawback into an asset

35 다음 글에서 전체 흐름과 관계 없는 문장은?

It's a fact of human behavior that some people lie in interviews or aren't perfectly truthful in their answers on questionnaires. Psychologists call this "dissimulation" and say it comes in two distinct varieties. ① The first is called impression management, which is all about presenting yourself in a positive light by "forgetting" certain facts or telling little lies about yourself. ② The second is called self-deception, which is believing something about yourself that isn't true; for instance, that you're fashionable even though everyone who knows how you dress can tell you are not. ③ Researchers have found that the more well-dressed you are, the more likely strangers are to give you money if you ask them for it. ④ Self-deception can also be based on negative false ideas, as when a girl believes she is ugly when she obviously is not. ⑤ In any case, self-deceptive thinking is harmful, but it can be reduced or even cured with professional help.

*dissimulation: (감정의) 위장

[36~37] 주어진 글 다음에 이어질 글의 순서로 가장 적절한 것을 고르시오.

36

Imagine you're building a chair. The first thing you will check on your "rough draft" is whether it performs the essential functions of a chair. Even the most artistic chair has to have a seat and some legs.

(A) Next, you will test whether the chair is solidly put together. There's no point in having a chic new chair if it falls over the first time someone sits on it.

(B) If you concentrate on minor grammatical points and on trying to impress the reader with your vocabulary, but you fail to notice weak connections between sentences and paragraphs, your readers may misunderstand your point. Keep the bigger picture in mind.

(C) Each part should be strong, and the joints must be stable. This also holds true for your writing. You need to have a solid basic structure, with strong connections.

① (A) — (C) — (B)
② (B) — (A) — (C)
③ (B) — (C) — (A)
④ (C) — (A) — (B)
⑤ (C) — (B) — (A)

37

In my job as a psychiatrist, I see many people who are "stuck" in their lives and unfulfilled. In most cases, it's not because of a lack of money or opportunity, neither is it because of incompetence or a lack of intelligence.

(A) My job is to show them how their beliefs about themselves are keeping them trapped and to help them open their minds and try new things.

(B) Instead, it's because they don't want to do anything new, go anywhere different, or change themselves in the slightest way. Over and over again they say, "I've always done things that way" or "That's just the type of person I am," as if their thoughts were carved in stone, or as if they had no choice in the matter.

(C) Progress is when they make tiny changes and get excited about the new doors that open for them. Then, it isn't long before they really start moving again and truly enjoying the ride. [3점]

① (A) — (C) — (B)
② (B) — (A) — (C)
③ (B) — (C) — (A)
④ (C) — (A) — (B)
⑤ (C) — (B) — (A)

[38~39] 글의 흐름으로 보아, 주어진 문장이 들어가기에 가장 적절한 곳을 고르시오.

38

And instructions may also be given by a police officer, either routinely at busy intersections or as temporary road traffic control around construction zones and accidents.

Rules of the road are the general practices and procedures that must be followed by all road users, including motorists, cyclists, and pedestrians. (①) They govern interactions with other vehicles and pedestrians. (②) Driving safely is usually easy if a driver can adapt to both the written and unwritten rules of the road. (③) As a general rule, all drivers are expected not to hit other vehicles, pedestrians, or anything near the road. (④) In addition to the general rules that always apply, there are traffic signals including traffic lights. (⑤) These rules should be distinguished from the mechanical procedures required to operate one's vehicle.

39

> But many musicians act like it's the end of the world if they don't get a contract the night they meet a potential team member.

I am often shocked at how fast musicians think business relationships develop. In all my years of working with musicians, I've rarely seen an A&R person or manager come out on the first day they see a musician and say they want to sign them. (①) Despite what you may have seen in the movies, this isn't how it usually goes. (②) There is no contract waiting to be signed inside a briefcase. (③) They don't understand that this is the beginning of a relationship. (④) Just as someone isn't a fan after they hear your song one time, it also takes time to develop and explore a working relationship with potential team members. (⑤) Slowly showing someone how enjoyable it would be to work together is the way to build a team ... not asking for a contract on day one.

*A&R: (음반 회사의) 신인 발굴 팀

40 다음 글의 내용을 한 문장으로 요약하고자 한다. 빈칸 (A), (B)에 들어갈 말로 가장 적절한 것은? [3점]

> In 1966, social psychologist Elliot Aronson conducted an experiment about likability in individuals. In the experiment, a panel of 48 students from the University of Minnesota listened to tape recordings of contestants (in reality just one actor) trying out for a College Quiz Bowl team. In one of the tapes, the contestant accidentally spilled a cup of coffee on himself, and in the other he didn't. The panel of students perceived this individual as more likeable when he spilled the cup of coffee on himself than when he didn't. However, this truth only held when the students perceived the contestant as highly capable. In this instance, the contestant had answered 92 percent of difficult quiz questions correctly. Yet in tapes showcasing an "average" contestant, who answered only 30 percent of quiz questions correctly, spilling coffee made that contestant appear less likeable to the panel.

↓

> According to the study above, the subjects liked a contestant better when he showed human ____(A)____, on the premise that he was highly ____(B)____.

	(A)		(B)
①	weakness	……	popular
②	emotion	……	popular
③	interaction	……	attractive
④	weakness	……	competent
⑤	emotion	……	competent

[41~42] 다음 글을 읽고, 물음에 답하시오.

In developing countries, as opposed to developed countries, a large proportion of the population is engaged in farming activities. The conventional agricultural practices in developed countries are designed to minimize a scarce resource: labor. This is achieved by using pesticides, chemical fertilizers, and heavy machinery where manual labor would be used in developing countries. When these kinds of farming systems are moved from wealthy to poor countries, the results can be ________________. For example, developing countries often have limited space available for cultivation, and the soil in many countries is not very fertile to begin with. When cultivation techniques further degrade the soil, it becomes less useful for cultivation. Farmers notice this loss of production and move to a different spot, leaving the nutrient-poor soil to turn into wasteland. In some cases fertilizer is overused, causing soil degradation. The excess fertilizer can contaminate groundwater, as does pesticide residue.

A lack of education and regulation means that pesticides are sometimes overused in developing countries. Poor irrigation practices are also indicative of a lack of research and education. It is becoming increasingly evident that conventional agriculture is not a long-term option in developed or developing countries. While developed countries are beginning to make policy decisions which recognize the importance of environmentally-friendly agriculture, many developing nations are not afforded this luxury. Whether environmentally-friendly agricultural processes are an achievable proposition in developing countries is the subject of much current research.

41 윗글의 제목으로 가장 적절한 것은?

① The History of Farming Practices
② Agriculture: The Promise of a Better Life
③ The Opposition to Eco-friendly Agriculture
④ How Poor Policy Is Ruining Agricultural Labor
⑤ Issues of Modern Agriculture in Developing Countries

42 윗글의 빈칸에 들어갈 말로 가장 적절한 것은? [3점]

① sustainable
② fruitful
③ overlooked
④ devastating
⑤ economical

[43~45] 다음 글을 읽고, 물음에 답하시오.

(A)

On the eve of my wedding day, one worry troubled me. Steve and I came from different backgrounds — I was a city girl from Scottsdale, Arizona. He was born in Oklahoma and grew up in Kansas. His dad was a minister, (a) mine was a trucker — but the boy who bothered me in freshman biology class at college quickly won my heart. He proposed senior year, and we decided to marry at the college church two days after graduation. My parents and Steve's would drive in to celebrate. Living so far from one another, our parents had never met. And my parents weren't that outgoing. Would they get along?

(B)

Later, I told Mom how amazed I was by Dad and Steve's dad's meeting all those years before. "There's more," Mom said. "Your dad met a lot of people on his routes, but I definitely remember (b) him talking about that couple. He was so impressed by them. He thought it was funny our kids were about the same age.... And he told me one more thing." "What was that?" I asked. "He said he'd be proud if one of our kids married into a family like theirs."

(C)

At the rehearsal dinner, I saw Steve's parents looking curiously at my dad. "Don't worry, Lana, they just think (c) he looks familiar," Steve said. I hoped that was a good thing. The ceremony and reception went beautifully, and afterward we headed to Steve's parents' house for a family dinner. I was anxious to get there. "I'm sure our parents are getting on fine without us," Steve told me. (d) He tried to put me at ease, but the butterflies in my stomach wouldn't stop.

(D)

When we finally pulled up, I was relieved to see our dads happily walking together in the yard. "We figured out how we know each other," Steve's dad said. Twenty years ago Dad was driving long-distance when a snowstorm forced him to detour through Oklahoma. "It was Sunday morning, so I pulled my truck over and stopped at a church for services," Dad said. "Afterward, the minister and his wife invited (e) me home for a meal." "That was us!" Steve's dad said.

43 주어진 글 (A)에 이어질 내용을 순서에 맞게 배열한 것으로 가장 적절한 것은?

① (B) — (D) — (C)
② (C) — (B) — (D)
③ (C) — (D) — (B)
④ (D) — (B) — (C)
⑤ (D) — (C) — (B)

44 밑줄 친 (a)~(e) 중에서 가리키는 대상이 나머지 넷과 다른 것은?

① (a) ② (b) ③ (c) ④ (d) ⑤ (e)

45 윗글에 관한 내용으로 적절하지 않은 것은?

① 필자와 Steve는 서로 다른 환경에서 자랐다.
② 필자와 Steve는 대학 졸업 후 결혼하기로 했다.
③ 필자의 아버지는 목사 부부의 친절에 감동했다.
④ Steve는 불안해하는 필자를 안심시키려고 애썼다.
⑤ 필자의 부모님과 Steve의 부모님은 넷이 함께 만난 적이 있었다.

: AFTER TESTING

종료 시 분

소요시간 분

학습 마무리

1 채점하기 | 정답 및 해설 p.50
 주의 틀린 문제를 다시 풀 수 있도록 정답을 본문에 표기하지 마세요.
2 등급 확인
3 틀린 유형 확인 후 전략 적용 복습 및 해설지 확인

How to Review

1 틀린 문제와 ✓ 표시한 문제는 다시 풀고 해설 확인하기
2 내가 표시한 정답 근거가 해설과 일치하는지 확인하기
3 잘 모르는 부분으로 표시한 내용은 해설을 통해 완전히 이해하기
4 어휘 외우기 (어휘 목록 다운로드 www.cedubook.com)
5 다음 회에 개선할 점 정리하기 (시간 엄수, 취약 유형 보완 등)

POWER UP!

실전 모의고사 08

: BEFORE TESTING

시작 시 분

1 **제한시간** (OMR 마킹시간 포함) ☐ 40분 ☐ 45분
2 **어휘예습** ☐ 해당 없음 ☐ 완료
3 **문제풀이순서** ☐ 순서대로 ☐ 2점 → 3점 ☐ 기타 ....
4 **기타 목표** ....

Check Point

1 **정답 근거** *e.g.* 밑줄 긋기
2 **잘 모르는 부분** *e.g.* 〈 〉 또는 ? 표시
3 **자신 없는 문제** *e.g.* 문제 번호에 ✓표시

18 다음 글의 목적으로 가장 적절한 것은?

Dear Mr. Richardson,

I was delighted to have the opportunity to meet you in person during your visit to our college for the second Presidential Public Leadership Program. As chair of the Committee for the Restoration of Roosevelt House, I wish to express our great pleasure at the success of the program and the recognition it has brought to Hunters and the Campaign, another organization involved in the restoration of Roosevelt House. The program was an experience, I am sure, that the students will reflect upon as they make their career and life choices. On behalf of all of the staff and students of our college, I want to express to you our tremendous appreciation.

Regards,
Billy Wright

① 대학의 재정 지원을 요청하려고
② Roosevelt의 업적을 설명하려고
③ Roosevelt 추모 단체를 소개하려고
④ 리더십 프로그램의 성공에 대해 감사하려고
⑤ Roosevelt 생가 복원 프로그램을 홍보하려고

19 다음 글에 드러난 Chad의 심경 변화로 가장 적절한 것은?

Chad sat on the edge of his bed lazily bouncing a ball off his bedroom wall. His dream of going to college to play football was no longer a possibility. Doctors had told him he wouldn't be able to play again for at least six months. He sighed and looked out the window at unending gray skies. "Why me?" he thought, as his father walked into his room. Chad's father had always seemed indifferent to him, so he didn't expect what happened next. His father sat down beside him, put his arm around him, and told him about the end of his own sports career many years before. This was a side of his father he'd never seen before, and he felt a warmth inside him from being trusted with this story. If his own father suffered through a similar situation and became the strong man he knew today, perhaps Chad would be okay, too.

① relaxed → confused
② depressed → romantic
③ anxious → excited
④ amused → sorrowful
⑤ gloomy → comforted

20 다음 글에서 필자가 주장하는 바로 가장 적절한 것은?

Many people are uncomfortable asking others not to do something, so when something upsets them, they let anger build up inside of them. Then, if they do speak, they sound unnecessarily angry and often direct their anger at the wrong person. It is much better to speak your feelings clearly and calmly right away, and to the right person. For example, if you are a non-smoker and someone near you lights a cigarette, ask them politely not to smoke near you. Don't sit there suffering and getting angry, and don't go complaining to a friend about how much you hate smokers. The smoker may have been completely unaware of your discomfort. Don't let other people's ignorance and inconsiderateness cause you to suffer, and don't complain to people who can't fix the problem.

① 상대방에게 배려를 강요하지 말아야 한다.
② 분노의 감정은 시간을 두고 다스려야 한다.
③ 다른 사람에게 불쾌감을 주는 행동을 삼가야 한다.
④ 불편한 감정을 억누르지 말고 즉시 표현해야 한다.
⑤ 감정을 효과적으로 표현하는 데는 훈련이 필요하다.

21 밑줄 친 one hard and fast rule이 다음 글에서 의미하는 바로 가장 적절한 것은?

Once upon a time, there was a teacher who declared that she would only read a paper for as long as it held her interest. As soon as a report became dull, she would stop reading and grade only the part she had read. If that meant reading only the first half, or the first quarter of the paper, then it was just too bad for the student. She used to say, "Attention spans are short! Nobody watches boring TV shows or listens to boring music. They'll change to something interesting. Nobody reads boring writing! If you don't hook your reader with your first few sentences, they are gone!" This teacher's students avoided a boring topic and didn't write in an old-fashioned style with a slow-moving plot. They became good writers. The reason is obvious. They were able to learn <u>one hard and fast rule</u> from their teacher.

① Keep practicing if you want to get better at writing.
② Maintain your readers' attention from the start to the end.
③ Say what you are going to say in a clear and concise way.
④ Find someone who will give honest feedback on your writing.
⑤ Believe that if you write it, your reader will read it with interest.

22 다음 글의 요지로 가장 적절한 것은?

When the boat overturns a mile out to sea, optimism about one's ability to swim to shore is deadly. When deciding whether to invade a foreign country, optimism about receiving a warm welcome can result in a catastrophe that changes the whole course of history for the worse. The tendency to view optimism as superior to pessimism is a deep-rooted illusion. Optimism is useful in favorable situations, but pessimism is useful in dangerous situations. For the fortunate, life now is vastly safer and more secure than it once was, so pessimism is less necessary. But unintended consequences of blocking pessimism are likely. The world will be better in many ways and worse in others that are hard to predict. Thus, pessimism is not a problem, but a useful emotional state.

① 낙관주의는 역경을 견디는 동기를 부여한다.
② 어려운 상황에서는 비관주의가 더 유용하다.
③ 낙관주의는 성공 가능성을 과대평가하기 쉽다.
④ 현실성 없는 비관주의는 문제 해결을 어렵게 한다.
⑤ 낙관주의와 비관주의의 균형이 역사를 발전시킨다.

23 다음 글의 주제로 가장 적절한 것은?

Although certain types of events (such as the loss of a loved one) are probably viewed as stressful in virtually all human societies, cultures vary greatly in the predominant forms of stress their people experience. Obviously, the challenges of daily living encountered in modern, western cities like Montreal or Philadelphia are quite different from the day-to-day difficulties experienced in indigenous societies in Africa or South America. Indeed, culture sets the context in which people experience and appraise stress. In some cases, a specific cultural group may be exposed to pervasive stress that is unique to that group. For example, the ethnic cleansing of Albanians in Kosovo in 1999 and the devastating and widespread destruction from the tsunami in Indonesia and regions of Southeast Asia in 2004 were extraordinary forms of stress distinctive to these societies.

*indigenous: 토착의

① influences of culture on sources of stress
② unrealistic desires for a stress-free society
③ universal characteristics of stressful events
④ solutions to the stress specific to each society
⑤ stress responses irrespective of the cultural context

24 다음 글의 제목으로 가장 적절한 것은?

According to some scientists, humans can thank their primate ancestors, at least in part, for the existence of war. During earlier stages of human evolution, aggressive behavior may have improved the odds of survival and become encoded in the genes of an increasing number of individuals. Ethologists and sociobiologists believe that aggressive tendencies may have been transmitted genetically from one generation to the next. One of the most famous advocates of this view is the ethologist Konrad Lorenz. Like other ethologists, Lorenz has directed his research toward the behavior of animals other than humans. From this work he has concluded that aggression is an instinct in humans, as it is in lower animals. Lorenz links aggression with territoriality. Just as animals defend their nests, burrows, and ranges, humans fight wars to defend their nations. It follows from this theory that because war stems from a natural urge, it is likely inevitable.

*ethologist: 생태학자

① Is War in Our Genes?
② The Golden Age of Peace
③ Imagine a World Without War
④ Transformations of Aggression
⑤ Coping with Aggressive Behavior

25 다음 도표의 내용과 일치하지 않는 것은?

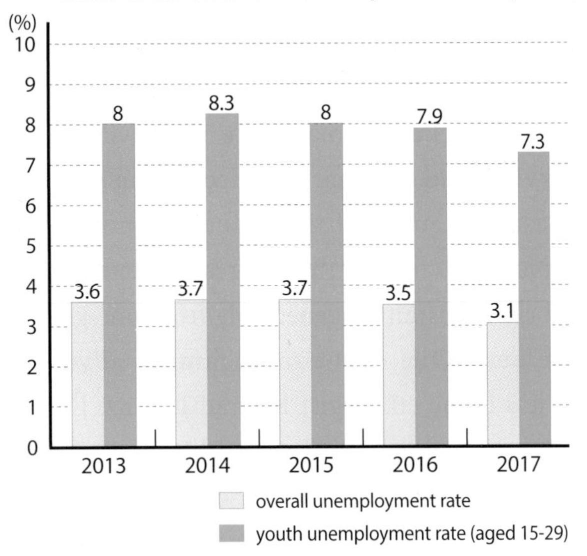

The above chart compares the overall unemployment rates with the unemployment rates for workers aged 15-29 over a five-year period. For the entire period, youth unemployment rates were much higher than overall unemployment rates. ① The overall unemployment rates ranged from 3.1% to 3.7%, while the youth unemployment rates ranged from 7.3% to 8.3%. ② The overall unemployment rate reached a record high in 2014 and 2015 and dropped to 3.1% in 2017. ③ Meanwhile, the youth unemployment rate hit a record high in 2014 before dropping to its lowest point in 2017. ④ While there was no change in the overall unemployment rate between 2014 and 2015, the youth unemployment rate dropped by 0.3%p. ⑤ Also, the gap between the two unemployment rates was greatest in 2017, and smallest in 2014.

26 James Hubert Blake에 관한 다음 글의 내용과 일치하지 않는 것은?

James Hubert Blake was born in Baltimore in 1883 to ex-slaves, their eighth child and the only one who survived infancy. When Blake began music lessons at age five, his deeply religious mother insisted he would never play "ungodly music," but he ignored her rule the minute he discovered ragtime. At age 15, without his mother's knowledge, he began playing the piano for money. It was known that he first composed the melody to his famous "Charleston Rag" when he was just 12, but didn't put it down on paper for another 16 years. At 32, he met the singer Noble Sissle and together, they wrote "It's All Your Fault." When Sophie Tucker, a famous singer and comedian, incorporated the song into her show, Blake and Sissle were instantly transformed into major songwriters.

*ragtime: 래그타임(빠른 박자의 재즈 음악)

① 노예였던 부모 사이에서 여덟째로 태어났다.
② 어머니의 원칙을 깨고 대중 음악가가 되었다.
③ 15세 때 피아노를 연주하여 돈을 벌었다.
④ 처음 작곡한 곡을 16년 후에야 악보에 옮겼다.
⑤ Sophie Tucker와 함께 부른 노래로 유명해졌다.

27 Adams Farm에 관한 다음 안내문의 내용과 일치하지 <u>않는</u> 것은?

Adams Farm

Dear Parents,

We are excited that your child will be visiting our farm for a field trip very soon! Adams Farm is a 40 acre agri-entertainment farm.

We want to invite you to join your child on the field trip if your schedule allows. The field trip will begin at 10:00 and end at approximately 1:15. Admission is $6 per person. Please come into The Adams Market upon arrival to pay your admission and receive your required wristband.

Helpful Info:
Please make sure that everyone dresses for the weather as all activities are outdoors. Don't forget to bring your camera!
Coupon: Bring this letter into The Adams Market and receive 25% off one item.

WE HOPE TO SEE YOU
DOWN ON THE FARM!

① 체험학습은 약 3시간 15분간 진행된다.
② 입장료는 1인당 6달러이다.
③ 입장료를 내면 손목 밴드를 받는다.
④ 모든 활동은 야외에서 이뤄진다.
⑤ 이 안내문을 가져가면 입장료를 할인받는다.

28 Fresh Fountain Pump에 관한 다음 안내문의 내용과 일치하는 것은?

Fresh Fountain Pump

Like people, pets require water for good health. The Fresh Fountain Pump responds to your pet's need for a continuous supply of fresh and clean drinking water.

CAUTION:
THIS IS A PET DRINKING FOUNTAIN PUMP.

- Do not use the pump in swimming pools or other situations where people are immersed.
- This pump is suitable for use in water temperatures up to 35°C.
- Do not use this pump with inflammable liquids.
- Do not install or store the appliance where it will be exposed to temperatures below freezing. Shelter the pump from direct sunlight.
- Do not allow the pump to run dry. The pump must be immersed in water completely.

① 반려동물용 수영장에 물을 공급하는 기구이다.
② 사람들이 이용하는 수영장에도 사용할 수 있다.
③ 35도 수온에서는 사용하기 적절하지 않다.
④ 영하의 온도와 직사광선에 노출되지 않게 해야 한다.
⑤ 펌프를 물에 반 정도 담가 사용하는 것이 좋다.

29 다음 글의 밑줄 친 부분 중, 어법상 틀린 것은? [3점]

The experiment I conducted in graduate school explored the problem of the single perspective. It was a pilot study to examine the effectiveness of different requests for help. A fellow investigator stood on a busy sidewalk and told people ① passing by that she had sprained her knee and needed help. If someone stopped, she asked him or her ② to get an ACE bandage from the nearby drugstore. I stood inside the store and listened while the helpful person gave the request to the pharmacist, who had agreed earlier to say that he was out of ACE bandages. After ③ telling this, not one subject, out of the twenty-five we studied, thought to ask if the pharmacist could recommend something else. People left the drugstore and returned empty-handed to the "victim" and told her the news. We speculated that ④ had she asked for less specific help, she might have received it. But, acting on the single thought ⑤ that a sprained knee needs an ACE bandage, no one tried to find other kinds of help.

30 다음 글의 밑줄 친 부분 중, 문맥상 낱말의 쓰임이 적절하지 않은 것은? [3점]

Human cognition depends on change and movement in order to ① function. Evolution has built us this way. Try staring at a blank wall for several seconds without blinking, and you will find the image eventually bleaching until you can see nothing. The eye's visual workings respond to movement and change. So, too, do the other parts of our cognitive systems. Feed them the same inputs successively and they ② cease to produce very much worth having as output. Like the shark in water, we need to keep moving or, cognitively, we die. Science, too, represents the greatest advertisement for our ③ restless natures. For as soon as a theory becomes the established orthodoxy, creative minds begin to explore the possibility that we must begin from completely different starting assumptions and seek ④ novel interpretations of the data. Without this constant movement to ⑤ encourage acceptance and stasis, we would not have the advances or excitements that fundamental science can provide.

*orthodoxy: 통설, 정설

[31~34] 다음 빈칸에 들어갈 말로 가장 적절한 것을 고르시오.

31 One way the media reinforces the justifications for eating meat is through ____________. How often have you seen media exposés on the violent treatment of farm animals and the corrupt practices of the slaughter industry? Compare this with the amount of coverage afforded to fluctuating gas prices or Hollywood fashion blunders. Most of us are more outraged over having to pay five cents more for a gallon of gas than over the fact that billions of animals, millions of humans, and the entire ecosystem are systematically exploited by an industry that profits from such unjustified violence. And most of us know more about what the stars wore to the Oscars than we do about the animals we eat. The ten billion animals that are killed every year for meat and the destructive consequences of contemporary animal agricultural practices remain conspicuously absent from public discourse. [3점]

*exposé: 폭로(기사)

① simplification
② omission
③ overemphasis
④ transparency
⑤ generalization

32 When the average person tells a lie, he or she becomes emotionally aroused and begins to fidget. However, we fidget not only when we are telling a lie, but also when we are feeling uncomfortable. Fidgeting, however, will make an observer sense that something isn't right or that you are lying about something. Consider the televised presidential debate between Richard Milhous Nixon and John Fitzgerald Kennedy, broadcast on September 25, 1960. Political experts speculate that Nixon's nervous movements, which included mopping his brow on camera, lost him the election. When what you are saying really counts and you want people to believe that you are reliable and trustworthy, try to ______________________. [3점]

① detect the listener's mood
② reveal your true emotions
③ avoid unnecessary movements
④ talk about the things you know well
⑤ make eye contact with your audience

33 The themes of nightmares ________________.
In the few studies that have been done across different cultures, the most common scenario involves the dreamer being pursued, attacked or facing imminent death. Other different scenarios may involve the thought of being in a shameful situation — being paralyzed during a school presentation or even being naked in public — or finding oneself not in the right place — being late for an important meeting or an exam. While the storylines show immense similarities across cultures, the people that appear in our nightmares are nevertheless as varied as we are. Police officers, schoolteachers, friends, family members, and unknown scary and faceless authority figures can pop in and out of our communities, neighborhoods, and houses. But in the end, while a nightmare's characters, settings, and plot twists can vary infinitely, people all over the world seem to possess the same unconscious metaphors for fear, shame, loss, mortality, and so on. [3점]

① seem to be surprisingly universal
② deal with very scary subject matter
③ show how powerful people scare us
④ explain each person's specific needs
⑤ present both great simplicity and complexity

34 In the future chatty people ________________
________________. Scientists from Korea have turned the main ingredient of calamine lotion into a tiny material that converts sound waves into electricity. The researchers explained that just as speakers transform electric signals into sound, the opposite process — turning sound into a source of electrical power — is possible. The research could lead to the manufacturing of small sound panels. After they collect energy from a phone call, these panels could be used to charge any electrical device, including the cell phone the person had been talking on. Not only could this technology be used to invent a self-charging cell phone, but it could also provide a boost of energy to the nation's electrical grid through the placement of large sound-collecting and energy-generating panels on the nation's busiest and noisiest roads. [3점]

*calamine lotion: 칼라민 로션 (피부 질환 치료제)

① will care much more about energy conservation
② could be the world's next renewable energy source
③ will be the biggest users of electricity in the country
④ could aid researchers in developing communication technologies
⑤ will want to have the most recently released electronic devices

35 다음 글에서 전체 흐름과 관계 없는 문장은?

Facebook has added a new security feature to increase levels of privacy and security on the website for its millions of users worldwide. ① The change came after mass complaints and negative public opinion about the lack of privacy protection on the world's biggest social networking site. ② With the addition of this new feature, users now have the option of security that's of a similar level to that of online banking websites. ③ Furthermore, online banking is an easy and safe way to manage your money and provides fast and easy access to all your accounts. ④ Using this feature, a user can make their account accessible only through specific computers and mobile phones they've personally authorized. ⑤ If access is attempted through an unauthorized device, the user is notified by e-mail or SMS and can block the attempt before it has a chance to succeed.

[36~37] 주어진 글 다음에 이어질 글의 순서로 가장 적절한 것을 고르시오.

36

A vibrant and active musical culture enriches life, making it more exciting, interesting, and meaningful for everyone around. Beauty is in the ear, and not just the eye, of the beholder, and enjoying a song or a piece of instrumental music depends to a certain extent on the listener's personal taste and social background.

(A) By opening up their ears and mind's eye to the "other," people can more happily engage and interact with new and different cultures.

(B) To an average Westerner, for instance, the traditional music of East Asia would probably sound mysterious and may even be uncomfortably difficult to listen to, because its mode of expression is so unfamiliar.

(C) However, people who can set aside their preconceptions about musical conventions and make an effort to understand the context of the unfamiliar music will find it more accessible and enjoyable.

① (A) — (C) — (B)　② (B) — (A) — (C)
③ (B) — (C) — (A)　④ (C) — (A) — (B)
⑤ (C) — (B) — (A)

37

> If you darken your kitchen, place a small amount of salt or soda on the end of a screwdriver or piece of tin, and hold the salt or soda in a gas flame, what will happen?

(A) If you passed the light from this flame through a prism, you would find that this light has only one color from the spectrum—a narrow region in the yellow part of the spectrum and nothing else. Any chemical that contains sodium will give off light of this same color.

(B) Even the tiniest speck of salt will cause a colorless, almost invisible flame to take on a strong yellow glow. The yellow color is due to the vapor of the chemical element sodium, which is one of the components of common salt.

(C) In the same way, a little cream of tartar or saltpeter introduced into a gas flame gives the flame a peculiar lilac color. To sum up, the flame appears in a different color depending upon the chemical additives. If you know which chemicals result in what colors, you'll be able to make fire burn in different colors whenever you want.

*tartar: 주석 **saltpeter: 초석

① (A) — (C) — (B)
② (B) — (A) — (C)
③ (B) — (C) — (A)
④ (C) — (A) — (B)
⑤ (C) — (B) — (A)

[38~39] 글의 흐름으로 보아, 주어진 문장이 들어가기에 가장 적절한 곳을 고르시오.

38

> To ensure that every research project has this protection, investigators must submit their proposed studies for formal review by a local panel of experts and community representatives prior to any data collection.

Choosing a good research design requires more than just selecting a particular method. (①) Researchers must determine whether the methods they plan on using are ethical. (②) That is, when designing a research study, investigators must do so in a way that does not violate the rights of people who participate. (③) Only with the approval of this panel can scientists begin their study. (④) If the review panel doesn't approve of some aspects of the proposed study, the researcher must revise those aspects and present them again for the panel's approval. (⑤) Likewise, each time a component of a study is altered, the review panel must be informed and give its approval.

39

Then he glanced back at the tube and, apparently, at this moment the insight came to him.

There are some reported examples of insight learning in apes. Lethmate Gebrauch describes the following sequence, suggesting insight in a young orangutan. The orangutan was given a long rod which could be inserted into a transparent plastic tube to reach a sweet and push it out. (①) The orangutan knew what the sweet was, but he did not know how to use the rod as a tool to obtain it. (②) He bit the tube and tried unsuccessfully to insert the tool. (③) He then moved away and sat down, apparently in frustration as he began to perform stereotyped repetitive behaviors with the tool. (④) He got up, walked over to the tube carrying the rod, inserted it into the tube and obtained the sweet. (⑤) Although he was, of course, rewarded by eating the sweet, this was only at the end of the sequence, and the problem appeared to be solved in a flash of insight.

40 다음 글의 내용을 한 문장으로 요약하고자 한다. 빈칸 (A), (B)에 들어갈 말로 가장 적절한 것은? [3점]

In one experiment, subjects were asked to read a short account of a series of interactions between two people. In these accounts, one person asked another person for a favor, such as a ride to work. In half the accounts, the recipient of the favor subsequently provided the same benefit to the other person (e.g., if they were given a ride to work, they offered the other person a ride to work), and in half the accounts the recipient of the favor subsequently provided a different kind of benefit to the other person (e.g., if they were given a ride to work, they offered to buy the other lunch). Subjects were asked to evaluate the quality of the friendship between the two individuals after they read these accounts. Subjects reported that individuals who exchanged the same benefits were less close than individuals who exchanged benefits of different types. Asked why they made these assessments, subjects said that they interpreted the exchange of the same benefits as a form of repayment, something that they evidently did not associate with close friendship.

↓

In the situation of giving and receiving benefits, the perceived ____(A)____ was greater when the benefits were ____(B)____.

	(A)		(B)
①	availability	......	tangible
②	availability	......	unrelated
③	closeness	......	dissimilar
④	closeness	......	substantial
⑤	impact	......	immediate

[41~42] 다음 글을 읽고, 물음에 답하시오.

We are subjected to never-ending cascades of negative news from across the world: wars, famines, natural disasters, diseases, mass layoffs, acts of terror. Stories about gradual improvements (a) rarely make the front page even when they occur on a dramatic scale and impact millions of people. And thanks to increasing press freedom and improving technology, we hear more, about more disasters, than ever before. This improved reporting is itself a sign of human progress, but it creates the impression of the exact opposite. At the same time, activists and lobbyists skillfully manage to make every dip in a trend appear to be the end of the world, even if the general trend is clearly improving, (b) scaring us with alarmist exaggerations. For example, in the United States, the violent-crime rate has been on a (c) growing trend since 1990. Just under 14.5 million crimes were reported in 1990. By 2016 that figure was well under 9.5 million. Each time something horrific or shocking happened, which was pretty much every year, a crisis was reported. The majority of people, the vast majority of the time, believe that violent crime is getting worse. The doom-laden feeling that this creates in us is then intensified by our (d) inability to remember the past. But the news agenda actually misses the key point. Things are getting better. We fail to remember that, one year ago, or ten years ago, or 50 years ago, there was a much larger number of terrible events. This illusion of (e) deterioration creates great stress for some people and makes other people lose hope. For no good reason.

*cascade: (한꺼번에 많이) 쏟아지는 것

41 윗글의 제목으로 가장 적절한 것은?

① Journalism Ethics and Standards
② How Freedom of the Press Works
③ Big Technology Curbs Misinformation
④ The Unending Stream of Bad News Is Itself Flawed
⑤ Selective Reporting: Telling and Detecting Actual Lies

42 밑줄 친 (a)~(e) 중에서 문맥상 낱말의 쓰임이 적절하지 않은 것은?

① (a) ② (b) ③ (c) ④ (d) ⑤ (e)

[43~45] 다음 글을 읽고, 물음에 답하시오.

(A)

Long ago in Egypt there lived a famous wise man named Zunnun. One day, a young man came to his house and said, "Teacher, I do not understand why you dress so simply and humbly. Isn't it better to dress in the finest clothes you can afford?"

(B)

The young man went quickly to the market. (a) He offered the ring to the textile merchants, vegetable sellers, butchers, and fish traders. Nobody was willing to pay a piece of gold. So, (b) he returned to Zunnun and reported "Teacher, nobody would offer more than one piece of silver." Zunnun smiled and said, "Now, go to the gold trader's shop at the end of the street and show the ring to the owner. Don't give your price, just ask how much he will pay you for the ring."

(C)

The young man found the shop to which (c) he was told to go. When he returned, he said, "Teacher, the gold trader offered me one thousand pieces of gold for your ring! (d) He valued it two thousand times higher than what the other traders did!" Zunnun smiled again and spoke softly, "That was the answer to your question, my friend. Do not be swift to decide value by appearance. The traders in the market did that and saw brass, but the gold trader looked closer and saw diamonds and gold."

(D)

Zunnun simply smiled at (e) him, took a ring from his finger, and said "I will answer your question, but first you must take this ring to the market and sell it for one piece of gold." Taking the dull ring from the wise man's hand, the young man thought to himself, "One piece of gold? It's impossible to sell this worthless ring for that much! But I want to know the answer to my question, so I will try."

43 주어진 글 (A)에 이어질 내용을 순서에 맞게 배열한 것으로 가장 적절한 것은?

① (B) — (D) — (C)
② (C) — (B) — (D)
③ (C) — (D) — (B)
④ (D) — (B) — (C)
⑤ (D) — (C) — (B)

44 밑줄 친 (a)~(e) 중에서 가리키는 대상이 나머지 넷과 다른 것은?

① (a) ② (b) ③ (c) ④ (d) ⑤ (e)

45 윗글에 관한 내용으로 적절하지 않은 것은?

① 현자(賢者)는 허름한 옷을 입고 있었다.
② 젊은이는 시장 상인에게 금 한 덩이에 반지를 팔았다.
③ 금을 파는 상인은 반지 값으로 금 천 덩이를 제안했다.
④ 반지는 금과 다이아몬드로 만들어진 것이었다.
⑤ 젊은이는 반지가 금 한 덩이의 가치가 없다고 생각했다.

: AFTER TESTING

⏱ 종료 시 분
⌛ 소요시간 분

학습 마무리

1 채점하기 | 정답 및 해설 p.58
(주의) 틀린 문제를 다시 풀 수 있도록 정답을 본문에 표기하지 마세요.
2 등급 확인
3 틀린 유형 확인 후 전략 적용 복습 및 해설지 확인

How to Review

1 틀린 문제와 ✓ 표시한 문제는 다시 풀고 해설 확인하기
2 내가 표시한 정답 근거가 해설과 일치하는지 확인하기
3 잘 모르는 부분으로 표시한 내용은 해설을 통해 완전히 이해하기
4 어휘 외우기 (어휘 목록 다운로드 www.cedubook.com)
5 다음 회에 개선할 점 정리하기 (시간 엄수, 취약 유형 보완 등)

POWER UP!

실전 모의고사

09

: BEFORE TESTING

시작 시 분

학습 목표

1 **제한시간** (OMR 마킹시간 포함) ☐ 40분 ☐ 45분
2 **어휘예습** ☐ 해당 없음 ☐ 완료
3 **문제풀이순서** ☐ 순서대로 ☐ 2점 → 3점 ☐ 기타
4 **기타 목표**

Check Point

1 **정답 근거** *e.g.* 밑줄 긋기
2 **잘 모르는 부분** *e.g.* 〈 〉 또는 ? 표시
3 **자신 없는 문제** *e.g.* 문제 번호에 ✓표시

18 다음 글의 목적으로 가장 적절한 것은?

Dear Readers,

It's that time of year again when the Crestford High School Drama Department puts on its final play of the school year. Past performances have highlighted the talent of our beloved drama instructor, David Banff, as well as that of our finest drama students. This year's performance of *The Wizard of Oz* is no exception, managing to capture the spirit of the original with a few exciting changes. I have nothing but great things to say about this play, and I wholeheartedly recommend it to anyone who loves the theater. Also, as this year marks the retirement of Mr. Banff, it's your final opportunity to see his work in action. Ticket prices may seem a bit high, at least without the student discount, but the profits all go toward supporting the drama department — a worthy cause, in my opinion. See you at the theater!

Maria Vasquez, Contributor

① 연극 공연 목록을 공지하려고
② 학교 연극 공연 관람을 권하려고
③ 연극 입장권 가격에 대해 비판하려고
④ 연극부 지원 모금 참여를 독려하려고
⑤ 연극 강사의 은퇴 축하 행사에 초대하려고

19 다음 글에 드러난 'she'의 심경 변화로 가장 적절한 것은?

She was beginning to get very tired of sitting by her sister on the bank, and of having nothing to do. Once or twice she had peeped into the book her sister was reading, but it had no pictures or conversations in it. "What is the use of a book without pictures or conversations?" Suddenly a white rabbit with pink eyes ran close by her. There was nothing so very remarkable in that. But when the rabbit actually took a watch out of its waistcoat-pocket, and looked at it, and then hurried on, she started to her feet, for it flashed across her mind that she had never before seen a rabbit with either a waistcoat-pocket or a watch to take out of it. So she ran across the field after it.

① sad → pleased
② sympathetic → terrified
③ lonely → jealous
④ annoyed → embarrassed
⑤ bored → curious

20 다음 글에서 필자가 주장하는 바로 가장 적절한 것은?

I was intrigued by a sports writer's interview with Bill Russell a number of years ago. Bill Russell is one of the greatest players in the history of the National Basketball Association, a man who helped bring multiple championships to the Boston Celtics. In this interview, the sports reporter asked the Hall of Famer if he ever got nervous before a game. Russell said, "Before every game, I vomit." That's high anxiety. How did Bill Russell overcome his anxiety? He started the game. Once the game started, the anxiety was gone. Action was the key. This strategy will also work for us. Sometimes the only way to overcome anxiety is to get busy doing something. At that point, one of two things will happen. If the anxiety had no basis in fact, it will dissolve in the flurry of activity. If the cause for the anxiety was legitimate, we still get some relief because we are at least doing something about it.

① 불안을 극복하기 위해 목표 행동을 실천하라.
② 불안이 일어날 때 객관적으로 문제를 바라보라.
③ 목표 기대치를 낮추고 행동하여 불안에서 벗어나라.
④ 불안 해소를 위해 최상의 결과를 마음속에 그리면서 행동하라.
⑤ 불안을 상황에 대처하기 위한 자연스러운 감정으로 받아들여라.

21 밑줄 친 the futility of papering over the persistent cracks가 다음 글에서 의미하는 바로 가장 적절한 것은?

The most strengths-focused culture is the United States, with 41 percent of the population saying that knowing their strengths will help them improve the most. The least strengths-focused cultures are Japan and China. Only 24 percent believe that the key to success lies in their strengths. However, despite the range, this general conclusion holds true: The majority of the world's population doesn't think that the secret to improvement lies in a deep understanding of their strengths. Interestingly, in every culture the group least fixated on their weaknesses was the oldest group, those fifty-five years old and above. A little older, a little wiser, this group has probably acquired a measure of self-acceptance. They have realized the futility of papering over the persistent cracks.

① they don't have to try to correct their weaknesses
② they need to keep trying to overcome their weaknesses
③ they should focus on their own strengths and maximize them
④ they have the opportunity to vary approaches to achievement
⑤ they have to set realistic expectations during challenging times

22 다음 글의 요지로 가장 적절한 것은?

Your consumption habits connect you directly to a great many people's lives. Have you ever heard of the terms "fair trade" and "ethical consumption"? Do you ever consider where your coffee came from? Most of the world's coffee is produced by multinational corporations who can keep their prices down by paying low wages to farm workers. To compete with the corporations, traditional farmers are forced to sell their produce at unfair prices, and thus they become trapped in poverty. But coffee labeled "fair trade" is produced by farmers who have been paid fair prices. Buying and drinking fair trade coffee is just one example of ethical consumption. It gives money to a wider range of people who deserve it. Now, before buying a product, read the label and see if you are making an ethical purchase.

① 빈곤 퇴치와 경제 발전은 밀접한 관계가 있다.
② 계획적인 쇼핑 습관이 충동구매를 줄일 수 있다.
③ 지나친 가격 경쟁은 공정 거래를 저해할 수 있다.
④ 활발한 구매 활동은 침체된 경제에 활력소가 된다.
⑤ 윤리적 소비가 부의 재분배를 이루는 데 기여할 수 있다.

23 다음 글의 주제로 가장 적절한 것은?

If a child is given half an hour to clean their room, the parent is obligated to check thirty minutes later. If the job is not done and the parent orders the child to return and finish the job, what does that teach the child about the meaning of a deadline (or the meaning of thirty minutes, for that matter)? The child soon realizes that there was no real deadline, no ultimatum. Ordering a child to "Get back in there and do it!" after the deadline has expired fails to teach a child about time management. It teaches the child there are further opportunities to practice arguing. Nobody needs that kind of practice. Too many second chances teach kids they can disobey, fail inspection, irritate people, and do tasks when *they* feel like doing them, and still reap the benefits.

*ultimatum: 최후통첩

① methods of motivating kids to do their chores
② importance of enforcing deadlines with children
③ consequences of rewarding a child's bad behavior
④ benefits of teaching time management skills to children
⑤ common misunderstandings between children and parents

24 다음 글의 제목으로 가장 적절한 것은?

Our faces reveal our strongest feelings — turning scarlet with rage, red with embarrassment. Now, Caltech neurobiologist Mark Changizi claims that our ability to see colors may have evolved to better interpret these emotional signals. He also claims that the trait could explain why we became "the naked ape." Changizi found that barefaced and bare-bottomed primates (a group that includes baboons, gorillas, and humans) have vision that's highly sensitive to increased redness in the skin, whereas completely fur-covered primates do not. This visual sensitivity increases the ability to read the moods of friend and foe, a highly advantageous social skill, but is useless if skin is totally covered in fur. Thus, we may have lost our hairy covering over the ages because less hair makes the body more useful at signaling emotions.

*baboon: 개코원숭이

① How to Read the Moods of Primates
② How Humankind Came to Lose Its Fur
③ Benefits of Sophisticated Human Vision
④ How Human Vision Differs from Monkeys'
⑤ How Humans and Other Primates Evolved

25 다음 도표의 내용과 일치하지 않는 것은?

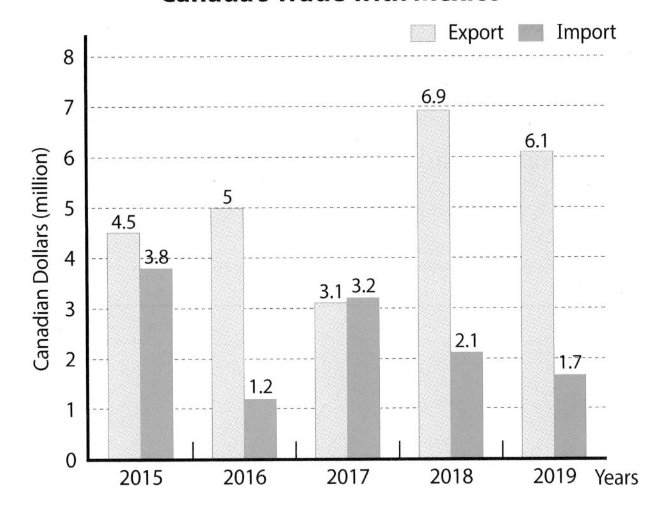

This chart shows the value, in millions of Canadian dollars, of annual trade between Canada and Mexico over a five-year period from 2015 to 2019. ① Within the five years, 2018 was the biggest for exports to Mexico, setting a record 6.9 million Canadian dollars. ② In 2017, the volume of imports slightly outdid that of exports. ③ After that, Canada's total imports decreased year by year. ④ The value of imports was far less than that of exports in 2019, but four years prior, the gap between exports and imports was only about 0.7 million Canadian dollars. ⑤ Compared to the beginning of the five-year period, Canada's exports in 2019 had increased in value by more than two million Canadian dollars.

26 Dragon's blood에 관한 다음 글의 내용과 일치하지 않는 것은?

"Dragon's blood" is a natural sap that has been in use for centuries by the native tribes of South America. The sap comes from Croton lechleri, an Amazon rainforest tree that locals named *Sangre de Drago* ("Dragon's blood" in Spanish) because when the tree is cut or injured it produces sap and looks as if it is bleeding. Dragon's blood is applied externally to skin problems such as bug bites and stings, cuts, burns, rashes, and so on. The sap is used as a kind of liquid bandage, rubbed directly on the affected area several times daily and allowed to dry. It creates a layer that seals affected areas to protect against infections, reduce bleeding and pain, and speed up the healing process. Special alkali chemicals contained in the sap are thought to be the source of its healing powers.

*sap: 수액(樹液), (식물의) 액즙

① 남아메리카 원주민들이 오랫동안 사용해왔다.
② *Sangre de Drago*라는 스페인어에서 이름이 유래되었다.
③ 수액을 섭취하면 피부 질환 치료에 도움이 된다.
④ 출혈과 통증을 줄여주는 효과가 있다.
⑤ 수액 속에 알칼리 성분이 포함되어 있다.

27 Food Poisoning Treatment에 관한 다음 안내문의 내용과 일치하지 않는 것은?

Food Poisoning Treatment

1. Control Nausea and Vomiting

- Avoid solid foods until vomiting ends. Then eat light, bland foods, such as crackers, bananas, rice, or bread.
- Sipping soda may help prevent vomiting.
- Don't eat fried, greasy, spicy, or sweet foods.
- Don't take anti-nausea or anti-diarrhea medication without asking your doctor. They may make some kinds of diarrhea worse.

2. When to See a Doctor

Go to see a doctor immediately for diarrhea:

- that lasts more than 3 days
- that happens after you eat seafood or mushrooms
- with signs of severe dehydration

① 구토가 있을 때는 단단한 음식을 피해야 한다.
② 탄산수가 구토를 막는 데 도움이 될 수 있다.
③ 구토를 멈추는 약은 의사의 처방에 따라 복용해야 한다.
④ 해산물이나 버섯을 먹은 후 설사를 하면 즉시 병원에 가야 한다.
⑤ 심한 탈수 증세가 3일 이상 지속되면 병원에 가야 한다.

28 제습기 보상 판매 행사에 관한 다음 안내문의 내용과 일치하는 것은?

Trade-in Event

When: June 20–22 (Friday–Sunday)
Where: All Brant Power store locations across Ontario
How: Bring in your old, inefficient dehumidifier and exchange it for a $50 coupon towards the purchase of a replacement ENERGY STAR qualified dehumidifier.

Not only is this your chance to save $50 towards the purchase of a new energy-efficient appliance, but with the trade-in event, you can also enjoy additional ongoing savings of up to $60 per year in electricity costs when you replace your old unit with an ENERGY STAR qualified one.

Requirements:
Old dehumidifiers must be 10 years of age or older and in working condition. Your old appliances will be discarded responsibly.

① 온타리오 주 일부 상점에서 진행하는 행사이다.
② 제습기를 구매하면 50달러 상품권을 준다.
③ 새 제습기로 바꾸면 전기료를 절약할 수 있다.
④ 고장 난 제습기도 쿠폰으로 교환할 수 있다.
⑤ 보상 판매한 낡은 제습기는 수리 후 재활용된다.

29 다음 글의 밑줄 친 부분 중, 어법상 틀린 것은? [3점]

Centuries ago when explorers traveled through new frontiers, they didn't have trails to follow or maps to tell them ① what was on the other side of each mountain. Instead, they had to create their own trail and draw their own maps. Similarly, as you explore new mental frontiers, you must blaze your own trail without any step-by-step instructions or rules to follow. After all, you're going ② where perhaps no one has ever been, so how can anyone supply you with instructions to get there? But geographic explorers learned useful strategies they could use ③ that helped them explore. They climbed high mountains to see the surrounding terrain, and they let the flow of water, in the form of rivers, ④ indicating routes that didn't involve unnecessary climbing. Analogously, there are strategies you can draw upon ⑤ to guide you through the creative problem solving process.

*blaze: 개척하다 **terrain: 지형, 지역

30 (A), (B), (C)의 각 네모 안에서 문맥에 맞는 낱말로 가장 적절한 것은?

When it comes to eating and drinking and savoring all the flavors we can possibly taste, our noses are even more important than the taste buds on our tongues. If we didn't have the aroma receptors that are (A) [situated / obtained] at the back of our nasal cavities, we probably wouldn't be able to tell the difference between kimchi and apples. The human sense of smell is much more (B) [sensitive / sensible] than that of taste and can identify thousands of different scents. From the moment we are born, everything that we smell is (C) [recorded / erased] in our brains along with the feelings and other sensations that accompany those smelling experiences. This data is important for our survival and even shapes our moods and our memories.

*nasal cavity: 비강(鼻腔, 콧구멍에서 목젖 윗부분에 이르는 코 안의 빈 곳)

	(A)		(B)		(C)
①	situated	……	sensitive	……	recorded
②	situated	……	sensible	……	recorded
③	situated	……	sensitive	……	erased
④	obtained	……	sensible	……	erased
⑤	obtained	……	sensitive	……	recorded

[31~34] 다음 빈칸에 들어갈 말로 가장 적절한 것을 고르시오.

31 David Lykken and Auke Tellegen examined reported levels of happiness in 1,300 sets of identical and fraternal twins. Identical twins reported similar levels of happiness, while fraternal twins exhibited greater variation in their reported sense of well-being. These results were found not only in families of twins raised together but in twins reared apart. They concluded that nearly half of happiness can be accounted for by ____________ factors. The other half is determined by life's everyday ups and downs. In other words, everyone is born with a certain "set point" for happiness in the same way that your household thermostat is set to maintain a certain temperature in your home. Tragedies and pleasures might affect your level of happiness. But eventually you will return to your set point, just as the temperature of your home will return to your thermostat's set point after you have let in cold air by opening a door or window. [3점]

① cultural
② temporal
③ genetic
④ accidental
⑤ geographical

32 Let's imagine what a visitor from some distant planet would think of human history. Let us look down on the museum of human history from afar. The visitor would almost certainly conclude that humans are ____________________. They are obviously just animals, yet they seem to think that they are special. They think of themselves as immortal, yet they die. They think of themselves as lords of creation, yet they are a prey to very many other species. They have excellent minds, but this just leads them into folly and unreason. Humans are cooperative creatures, yet they are also intensely selfish. They can create great art, but leave the world an ugly mess. They advocate tolerance and understanding, yet they torture each other for their beliefs. The distant observer might well be confused. [3점]

① a mysterious cycle
② a sum of sufferings
③ a bundle of fallacies
④ an embodied paradox
⑤ all composites of history

33 Older adults often have trouble understanding what someone is saying when surrounded by background noise, such as at a restaurant or party, so many people think the ears of senior citizens deteriorate with age, but according to a research study, ______________________________. Using magnetic resonance imaging (MRI), the researchers performed brain scans on 36 older and younger adults as they tested their ability to identify certain words, some of which had been filtered to make them difficult to understand. They found that, in general, older adults were significantly worse at identifying words than younger adults in challenging listening conditions. The findings could help us better understand presbycusis, a type of hearing loss brought on by aging that also involves the brain's inability to process what the ears hear. [3점]

① their ears may not be the only problem
② their ears only have trouble with certain sounds
③ young people's ears can naturally deteriorate, too
④ there are many ways to treat this type of hearing loss
⑤ the level of the background noise is the main problem

34 You're at a convention where everyone is asking "Where are you from?" When you reply, "Oh, I'm from Muscatine, Iowa" or anywhere else they haven't heard of, what can you expect except a blank stare? Even if you're a cosmopolitan and urbane big city dweller from Miami or Los Angeles, you'll receive a panicked look from all but someone from your hometown. Others will be rapidly racking their brains thinking "What do I say next?" When I tell people I'm from New York City, what are they expected to say? ________________, "Where are you from?" It's a matter of conversational politeness to give the asker some fuel for his tank so that he, so obviously a hungry communicator, can keep the conversation going by commenting about or replying to something you have said or asked. All it takes is an extra sentence or two about your city that your conversational partner can comment on. [3점]

① Be a better communicator by never asking
② Do not answer impolitely when you are asked
③ Learn how to make proper small talk such as asking
④ Take a guess about someone's hometown before asking
⑤ Never give just a one-sentence response to the question

35 **다음 글에서 전체 흐름과 관계 없는 문장은?**

Traveling medicine shows were a regular feature of entertainment in 19th-century America. The shows' comedy and musical routines provided a welcome diversion from workers' daily lives. ① Once a crowd had assembled, a distinguished-looking gentleman, who always claimed to be "Doctor" somebody, began a performance aimed at selling his cure-alls. ② Even though the sideshow doctors made outrageously exaggerated claims for their products, business was usually good. ③ Modern advertising was born during this period as medicine companies printed newsletters with humorous quotations mixed with plenty of advertising. ④ Today, these shows are things of the past, but medical fraud and trickery are not. ⑤ Like their 19th-century counterparts, modern crooks disguise themselves as health professionals and sell their "miracle" healing products by taking advantage of common fears of pain, aging, and death.

*sideshow: (중요한 것 전에 하는) 맛보기 공연, 볼거리 **crook: 사기꾼

[36~37] 주어진 글 다음에 이어질 글의 순서로 가장 적절한 것을 고르시오.

36

Appetite is instinctive in humans. So is motivation for achievement. We don't have to make an effort to create them; they exist already. Because we are born with appetite and motivation and because they are instinctive, they predate our knowledge of their existence.

(A) In the same way, we can dull or sharpen our motivation to succeed. If you constantly worry and wait for an easy life, you will reduce your motivation for success.

(B) But that doesn't mean we cannot control them. We already know how to regulate appetite: we can drink lots of water to reduce an appetite before a meal or eat a handful of salty crisps to increase it.

(C) If, on the other hand, you fill your time with activities that you care about and that make you feel stimulated, your motivation will grow. Cultivate your motivation towards your goals, and your growing motivation will make the pursuit of success easier.

① (A) — (C) — (B)
② (B) — (A) — (C)
③ (B) — (C) — (A)
④ (C) — (A) — (B)
⑤ (C) — (B) — (A)

37

When the printed word dominated the media, the definition of literacy was simply the ability to read and write, or the ability to use language to understand and communicate ideas in a society. But emerging technologies have changed what it means to be literate.

(A) Today, literacy is more than just being able to read and write. It is having the skills to use and produce information in various media. The digital age is transforming the quantity, range and speed of information we need to understand.

(B) Those who don't have these skills will be left behind. To be literate today, people must be able to decode, understand, and create information through, and with, all forms of media, including print and non-print.

(C) And most people today get most of their information from television, the Internet, and other technologies; therefore, it is necessary to have these media skills.

① (A) — (C) — (B)
② (B) — (A) — (C)
③ (B) — (C) — (A)
④ (C) — (A) — (B)
⑤ (C) — (B) — (A)

[38~39] 글의 흐름으로 보아, 주어진 문장이 들어가기에 가장 적절한 곳을 고르시오.

38

One explanation is that a drought might have forced them to move to a different area, but this couldn't have been the only reason.

The Anasazi were sophisticated people who established a flourishing culture in the Mesa Verde area about 1,500 years ago. (①) But in the late 1200s, the Anasazi suddenly left their homes and mysteriously moved away, taking only what they could carry on their backs. (②) The Anasazi must have had a good reason to leave the area, but no one really understands why they left. (③) There have been many theories. (④) They may also have lost a battle with a neighboring tribe, or there could have been an outbreak of a terrible disease. (⑤) Most likely, it was a combination of factors that caused the Anasazi to leave the elaborate stone cities that they built in the canyon walls.

39

However, if it becomes necessary to make such a reversal, it is advisable that the coach explain to his athletes why the switch is occurring.

Flip-flops occur, for example, when a coach makes a transition from one activity to a second activity and then switches back to the first activity, as though he has changed his mind. (①) For example, a gymnastics coach tells his players that Tuesday will be beam and bar day, but when his athletes arrive on Tuesday prepared to practice beam and bar, he tells them they will be working on floor and vault. (②) Then, midway through practice he instructs them to go to beam and bar. (③) The transition not only ruins the flow of practice activity but also conveys to the athletes that the coach is unsure of what to do. (④) It is important to avoid flip-flops. (⑤) For example, the gymnastics coach might gather his athletes for a brief meeting and say, "I know I told you yesterday that we would be practicing beam and bar today, but we won't be able to use the spring floor tomorrow, so we are going to work on our floor routines today."

*flip-flop: (태도 등의) 돌변 **vault: (체조) 도마

40 다음 글의 내용을 한 문장으로 요약하고자 한다. 빈칸 (A), (B)에 들어갈 말로 가장 적절한 것은? [3점]

In one experiment, which was designed to test experience and judgmental accuracy, Erik Dane asked people to look at ten designer handbags and judge whether they were real or fake. Half the participants had only five seconds to guess, which forced them to rely on their instincts. The other half had thirty seconds, which allowed them to inspect and analyze the features. Dane's team also measured their handbag experience—some had a lot, owning more than three handbags made by Coach or Louis Vuitton, whereas others had never touched a designer bag. Experienced handbag owners were 22 percent more accurate when they had just five seconds than when they had thirty seconds. For those who didn't know anything about handbags, however, their automatic verdict wasn't going to help them. They needed to take a step back and assess the handbags.

↓

In domains where we have a lot of experience, ____(A)____ can beat analysis; in unfamiliar ones, ____(B)____ judgments can only be made with a careful examination.

	(A)		(B)
①	intuition	……	flexible
②	intuition	……	sound
③	action	……	hasty
④	confidence	……	accurate
⑤	confidence	……	arbitrary

[41~42] 다음 글을 읽고, 물음에 답하시오.

We simply love flowers — perceiving them to be beautiful — which makes them beloved. According to Jack Goody, however, an English anthropologist who has studied the role of flowers in most of the world's cultures — East and West, past and present — the love of flowers is almost, but not quite, (a) universal. The "not quite" refers to Africa, where flowers play almost no part in religious observance or everyday social ritual. Africans seldom grow domesticated flowers, and flower imagery seldom shows up in African art or religion. Goody offers two possible explanations for the (b) absence of a culture of flowers in Africa. One explanation is that people can't afford to pay attention to flowers until they have enough to eat; a well-developed culture of flowers is a (c) luxury that most of Africa historically has not been able to support. The other explanation is the ecology of Africa. Relatively few of the world's domesticated flowers have come from Africa, and the range of flower species on the continent is nowhere near as (d) restricted as it is in, say, Asia or even North America. However, one question remains on all our minds: Could it mean that the beauty of flowers is in the eye of the beholder? If so, why did so many different peoples invent the idea in so many different times and places? As Goody points out, Africans quickly adopted a culture of flowers wherever others introduced it. Maybe the love of flowers is a predilection all people (e) share, but it's one that cannot itself flower until conditions are ripe — until there are lots of flowers around and enough leisure to stop and smell them.

*predilection: 애호, 편애

41 윗글의 제목으로 가장 적절한 것은?

① Why Do Humans Love Flowers?
② How Is Flower Diversity Produced?
③ Is the Preference for Flowers Universal?
④ The Diversity and Universality of Taste in Beauties
⑤ The Symbolic Meaning of Flowers in World Culture

42 밑줄 친 (a)~(e) 중에서 문맥상 낱말의 쓰임이 적절하지 않은 것은? [3점]

① (a) ② (b) ③ (c) ④ (d) ⑤ (e)

[43~45] 다음 글을 읽고, 물음에 답하시오.

(A)

I have two daughters. When the older girl entered adolescence, my wife and I experienced the usual parent-versus-adolescent struggles for control. Often, the battles with our daughter were about buying clothes. Our daughter was style-conscious and had expensive taste, and her ideas about what (a) she "needed" differed from ours.

(B)

This wasn't so easy for the younger one. Each shopping trip was accompanied by distress about whether purchasing this or that item was really the best thing to do. Would she regret a purchase two months later, when the fashions had changed? This was too much for the younger sister. Giving (b) her all this freedom was not doing her a genuine favor. Her "clothing liberation" gave her much worry and little joy.

(C)

Then we had an idea. We negotiated a clothing allowance with our daughter, allocating funds for a number of reasonably priced items. We gave her a lump sum, and (c) she could then decide how to spend it. It worked like a charm. Arguments about clothing stopped, and we could spend the rest of our daughter's adolescence fighting with (d) her about more important things.

*lump sum: 총액, 일시불

(D)

My wife and I were so pleased with our success that we decided to do the same with our younger daughter. However, the two girls are very different. The older one is a satisfier, while the younger one is a maximizer—at least with regard to clothing. What this meant was that the older one took her clothing allowance, bought things (e) she liked, and never worried about alternatives that she was passing up.

43 주어진 글 (A)에 이어질 내용을 순서에 맞게 배열한 것으로 가장 적절한 것은?

① (B) — (D) — (C)
② (C) — (B) — (D)
③ (C) — (D) — (B)
④ (D) — (B) — (C)
⑤ (D) — (C) — (B)

44 밑줄 친 (a)~(e) 중에서 가리키는 대상이 나머지 넷과 다른 것은?

① (a) ② (b) ③ (c) ④ (d) ⑤ (e)

45 윗글에 관한 내용으로 적절하지 않은 것은?

① 필자 부부는 사춘기에 들어선 큰딸과 통제권을 두고 다퉜다.
② 큰딸은 패션 유행에 민감하고 취향이 고급스러웠다.
③ 작은딸은 옷을 쇼핑할 때 쉽게 결정하지 못했다.
④ 필자 부부는 큰딸에게 용돈을 어디에 사용할지 정해주었다.
⑤ 큰딸과 작은딸은 옷을 쇼핑하는 성향이 전혀 달랐다.

: AFTER TESTING

종료 시 분
소요시간 분

학습 마무리

1 채점하기 | 정답 및 해설 p.66
주의 틀린 문제를 다시 풀 수 있도록 정답을 본문에 표기하지 마세요.
2 등급 확인
3 틀린 유형 확인 후 전략 적용 복습 및 해설지 확인

How to Review

1 틀린 문제와 ✓ 표시한 문제는 다시 풀고 해설 확인하기
2 내가 표시한 정답 근거가 해설과 일치하는지 확인하기
3 잘 모르는 부분으로 표시한 내용은 해설을 통해 완전히 이해하기
4 어휘 외우기 (어휘 목록 다운로드 www.cedubook.com)
5 다음 회에 개선할 점 정리하기 (시간 엄수, 취약 유형 보완 등)

실전 모의고사 10

: BEFORE TESTING

시작 시 분

학습 목표

1 **제한시간** (OMR 마킹시간 포함) ☐ 40분 ☐ 45분
2 **어휘예습** ☐ 해당 없음 ☐ 완료
3 **문제풀이순서** ☐ 순서대로 ☐ 2점 → 3점 ☐ 기타
4 **기타 목표**

Check Point

1 **정답 근거** e.g. 밑줄 긋기
2 **잘 모르는 부분** e.g. 〈 〉 또는 ? 표시
3 **자신 없는 문제** e.g. 문제 번호에 √표시

18 다음 글을 쓴 목적으로 가장 적절한 것은?

Dear Valued Customer,

Thank you for your order. This note is to confirm your payment and inform you of delivery arrangements. We take the utmost care to deliver your merchandise in perfect condition. Therefore, should the packaging show signs of impact or leakage, we suggest you refuse to accept the delivery. On receiving the delivery, please open the package and check the merchandise before signing the receipt form. If this is not possible, you are invited to indicate your concerns about the state of the merchandise on the form. Our company is responsible for all transport risks and will refund your payment as long as the package is returned to us with an explanatory letter of complaint.
Thank you.

Customer Service Department

① 주문이 발송되었음을 알리려고
② 주문한 물품 내역을 확인하려고
③ 배송 오류 건에 대해 해명하려고
④ 인터넷 주문 혜택에 관해 홍보하려고
⑤ 물품 수령 시 주의사항을 안내하려고

19 다음 글에 드러난 Sarah의 심경 변화로 가장 적절한 것은?

Sarah had been working in the tech department of a trading company for several years and was used to her colleagues asking her computer questions. She always did her best to be helpful and she even enjoyed the interruptions. She felt herself flattered to hear so many nice compliments from them. Then Kelly joined her department. Sarah enjoyed Kelly's company and thought she was a good addition to their office staff. Before long, Sarah noticed people started flocking to Kelly with their computer questions. At first, Sarah was relieved to be rid of the interruptions. But then it hit her. No one needed her anymore. Sarah felt she was just another office staff. Many thoughts raced through her head. "Why is she suddenly the expert? She is just a newcomer. I can answer their questions better! It's not fair that Kelly gets more attention than I do."

① proud → jealous
② anxious → grateful
③ indifferent → pleased
④ delighted → ashamed
⑤ anticipating → disappointed

20 다음 글에서 필자가 주장하는 바로 가장 적절한 것은?

A famous band recently announced that fans can pay whatever they want to download the band's latest album. Other artists have already followed their lead, which has prompted some observers to claim that it's the dawn of a new business model for the music industry. This may be fine for well-established bands, as they have millions of fans who might be willing to pay. However, everyone else is finding it harder and harder to get listeners to pay for music. The only sure way for artists to make money is through live performance. We need to make every effort to re-energize the live music scene and make it a part of daily culture. One way to enhance awareness is by increasing the number and quality of venues and festivals where we can go and see artists play.

① 음원 판매 수익의 분배 구조를 개선해야 한다.
② 라이브 공연 문화를 활성화하여 음악 시장을 넓혀야 한다.
③ 무명 음악인들은 라이브 공연을 통해 인지도를 높여야 한다.
④ 음반 산업의 활성화를 위해 불법 다운로드를 근절해야 한다.
⑤ 다수의 음악인들이 수익을 낼 수 있는 음원 시장을 구축해야 한다.

21 다음 글의 요지로 가장 적절한 것은?

Poetry is the art of words in their entirety: meaning and sound. Patterns of syllables coming at regular intervals define the shape and the rhythm of a poem, but it is sound that is the key factor for developing musicality in a poem. In fact, even when it is composed of free verses, poetry is music made of words: unusual combinations bring out the melodic aspect of language. The subtle art of weaving relations between meaning and sound is the essence of the poetic craft. So, it's nearly impossible to translate a poem into languages other than the original. If it is true that often the sense is preserved, sound and original rhythm are irretrievably lost. To fully grasp the rhythmic and musical aspect of the poem, the verses should be enjoyed in the original language, out loud, without translation.

① 시를 번역할 때는 원어의 의미와 정서를 반영해야 한다.
② 시를 다른 나라의 언어로 번역하는 것은 거의 불가능하다.
③ 시는 시인의 주관적인 감정의 표현이므로 번역하기 어렵다.
④ 시의 음악적 요소를 살리는 것이 시 번역에서 가장 중요하다.
⑤ 시를 여러 언어로 번역하여 많은 사람들이 감상할 수 있게 해야 한다.

22 다음 글의 주제로 가장 적절한 것은?

One characteristic of genius is the capacity for great intensity, which is often expressed in a cyclic fashion. That is, the personality of the genius sometimes seems to incorporate polar extremes: When inspired, he may work 20 hours a day to realize a solution while it's still fresh in his mind; these periods of intense activity tend to be scattered with intervals of apparent stasis that are actually times of fermentation, which is a necessary part of the creative process. Geniuses understand the need to make space for ideas to crystallize, for creativity occurs under appropriate inner, not outer, circumstances. The stage is often set by complete distraction — we all know stories of people who have gotten the answers to complex problems while sitting in traffic on the freeway.

*stasis: 정체, 정지

① benefit of consistent focus on creative ideas
② effect of environment on a person's ingenuity
③ ways geniuses manage to display their creativity
④ importance of structured rest periods for geniuses
⑤ best methods for geniuses to increase concentration

23 다음 글의 제목으로 가장 적절한 것은? [3점]

Early Islamic architects and artists strove to create a grand physical backdrop to provide material support and evidence for the claims of their religion. Claiming God to be the source of all understanding, Islam particularly emphasized mathematical laws as divine qualities. Elegant and complicated geometries were thought to imply the infinite wisdom of God, so Muslim artisans covered the walls of mosques and houses with repeating sequences of these patterns. This ornamentation, so pleasingly intricate on a rug or glass, produces an almost hallucinatory experience when it completely covers the interior of a hall. Eyes accustomed to looking at nothing but the dull and practical objects of daily life could, inside such a hall, imagine a world with absolutely no associations with the everyday. Such delicate yet extraordinarily complex decoration seemed like the product of a mind without earthly limitations, of a higher being uncorrupted by human failings, and therefore of a God worth surrendering to completely.

*hallucinatory: 환각의

① The Earthly and the Heavenly in Islamic Art
② Psychological Effects of Mosque Architecture
③ Divinity: A Driver of Design in Early Islamic Art
④ Pure Mathematics and Geometry in Islamic History
⑤ Delicate Ornamentation in Domestic Islamic Design

24 다음 도표의 내용과 일치하지 않는 것은?

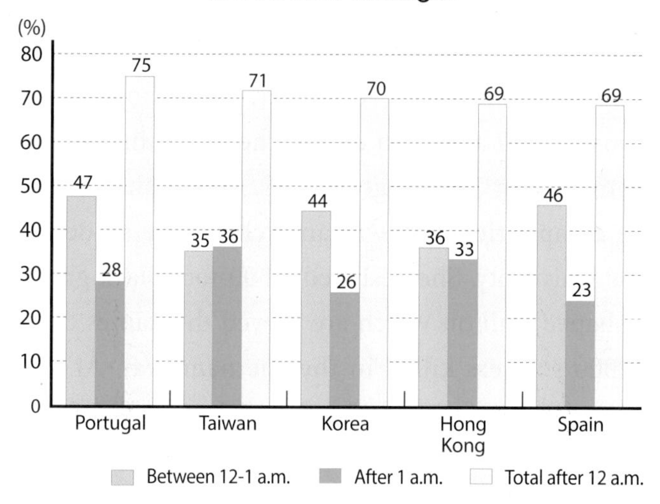

This chart shows the top five nations in terms of their numbers of people who usually go to bed late at night. ① Portugal had the highest percentage of people who go to bed between 12 a.m. and 1 a.m., followed closely by Spain and then Korea. ② There was quite a difference, of 8%p, between Korea and the next country in the 12-1 a.m. bedtime category, Hong Kong. ③ As for people who go to bed after 1 a.m., Hong Kong had the highest percentage and Taiwan had the second highest. ④ Overall, 75% of Portuguese reported having a post-midnight bedtime, followed by the Taiwanese and the Koreans. ⑤ The difference between the country with the largest number of people with a 12-1 a.m. bedtime and the country with the smallest number was 12%p, while the difference in the after-midnight category was only 6%p.

25 Maya Ying Lin에 관한 다음 글의 내용과 일치하지 <u>않는</u> 것은?

Who would dream of winning a national architectural competition at the age of twenty-one? In 1980, Maya Ying Lin, a Chinese American, was chosen from among 1,400 artists to design the Vietnam Veterans Memorial in Washington, D.C. When she entered the competition, she was an architecture student at Yale University. She designed a 500-foot black granite V-shaped wall on which are carved the names of the 58,000 soldiers killed in the Vietnam War. At first, some people attacked the design because it was so different from traditional memorials. However, the astonishingly simple yet powerful monument soon became one of the most beloved attractions. As a result, Maya Lin has become a respected architect, chosen to design many other important memorials.

① 베트남 참전용사 기념비 공모전에서 당선되었다.
② 공모전 참가 당시 건축학과 대학생이었다.
③ 기념비에 전사한 병사들의 이름을 새겼다.
④ 기념비의 독창성을 인정받는 데 오랜 시간이 걸렸다.
⑤ 많은 주요 기념비의 설계를 의뢰받았다.

26 Harvest Box에 관한 다음 안내문의 내용과 일치하지 <u>않는</u> 것은?

Harvest Box

Fresh Farmers' Goods

It's like having a farmers' market located right outside your classroom. Harvest Box is a program for students who want to purchase high-quality produce at affordable price while supporting local farms.

Options

- Value Box: costs $8.50 for 12 pounds of seasonal fruits and vegetables
- Local Box: costs $16.50 for 25 pounds of seasonal fruits and vegetables

The Harvest Box is available two times in both September and October, then once per month for the remainder of the school year. It is first come, first served, with a limited number of boxes, so get your order in early.

For a listing of all purchase and pick-up dates, check our Events Calendar posted around campus.

① 학생들을 위한 농산물 판매 행사이다.
② Value Box의 무게는 12파운드이다.
③ Local Box는 Value Box보다 8달러 더 비싸다.
④ 9월과 10월에만 한정적으로 판매된다.
⑤ 주문한 선착순으로 판매가 이루어진다.

27 **The HBS Flea Market에 관한 다음 안내문의 내용과 일치하는 것은?**

The HBS Flea Market

The HBS Flea Market is open year round (rain or shine) on the third Saturday of the month from 6:00 a.m. to 2:00 p.m. Sellers must be out of the parking lot by 3:00 p.m. or additional fees will be charged to them.

Time

Gate Opens: 6:00 a.m. (the main gate)
Gate Closes: 3:00 p.m. (all gates)

Price

- two stalls side by side cost $15.00
- three stalls in a row cost $25.00

Notification

Stalls are available on a first-come-first-serve basis and cannot be reserved. If your stall size exceeds the size for which you paid, you will be charged an additional $15.00. For more information, please contact us at (400) 620-3400.

① 우천 시에는 열리지 않는다.
② 오후 2시부터 주차장 요금이 부과된다.
③ 판매대를 세 개 사용하면 총 75달러가 든다.
④ 판매대 사용은 선착순이며 예약은 받지 않는다.
⑤ 규정된 판매대를 사용하지 않으면 15달러가 부과된다.

28 **(A), (B), (C)의 각 네모 안에서 어법에 맞는 표현으로 가장 적절한 것은?** [3점]

In the USA, "Fordism" is an economic theory which considers that widespread prosperity and high profits for corporations can be achieved through high wages that enable workers (A) [purchasing / to purchase] the products of their labor, such as automobiles. Fordism was coined around 1910, as a result of Henry Ford's successes in the automobile industry. Ford pioneered the development of mass production methods, (B) [introducing / introduced] the assembly line by 1913. He sold 10 million relatively inexpensive Model T automobiles and made a vast fortune while his employees became the highest paid factory workers in the world. From a wider perspective, Fordism was part of the Efficiency Movement, which characterized the American Progressive Era. When the Great Depression began, U.S. policy was to keep wages high in the hope (C) [what / that] Fordism would reverse the downturn.

	(A)		(B)		(C)
①	purchasing	……	introducing	……	what
②	purchasing	……	introduced	……	that
③	to purchase	……	introducing	……	that
④	to purchase	……	introducing	……	what
⑤	to purchase	……	introduced	……	that

29 다음 글의 밑줄 친 부분 중, 문맥상 낱말의 쓰임이 적절하지 않은 것은? [3점]

The great psychological ① paradox concerning money is that if you give money to people in need, you feel rich even if you have to watch your spending habits. A subsequent contradiction occurs because the very act of giving away money can lead to a ② reduction in spending and, hence, the saving of money. This is because your unconscious mind will push you to exercise financial ③ freedom after making a donation. On the other hand, some people think they would feel richer if they didn't donate anything at all and just spent a lot on themselves: elegant clothes, grand vacations. Even though the unconscious mind gives them a hard time for such ④ egotism, they cannot change their ways and sooner or later there is a disaster relating to their income that is coming in. They lose their wealth in ⑤ reckless financial choices.

30 밑줄 친 부분이 가리키는 대상이 나머지 넷과 다른 것은?

In 1822, an English bookseller and freethinker named Richard Carlile designed a vending machine ① he hoped would provide protection from censors and the police. At the time, Carlile and a handful of other booksellers and publishers were struggling to establish freedom for the English press. Carlile and some of his employees had been jailed for selling items such as Thomas Paine's *The Age of Reason*. To prevent any more such arrests, ② he decided to sell books by machine, believing that by doing so the bookseller could not be legally identified. Describing ③ his device, Carlile wrote: "In the shop is a dial on which is written every publication for sale. The purchaser enters and turns the hand of the dial to the publication he wants, when, on depositing the price, the publication drops down before ④ him." However, the court still held him responsible and convicted one of ⑤ his employees of selling offensive literature through the device.

[31~34] 다음 빈칸에 들어갈 말로 가장 적절한 것을 고르시오.

31 In a well-known study, it was found that the actions kids could perform at five months predicted not only their IQ at four and ten years of age but their academic achievement at age fourteen. These actions included "tummy time," when infants could lift their head and shoulders for several seconds at a time; when they could sit by themselves; and how often they attempted to reach out and grab objects. The researchers were able to show that the link from action to thought was explained not by the parents' intelligence or education level but by the infants' physical capabilities. When kids can sit up by themselves, their hands are free to reach out and grab objects, which allows them to learn things about the world that they wouldn't otherwise. Infants learned that their actions could change their environment, which helped shape their understanding of others' actions and intentions. In short, action and intelligence are ____________.

① inherited
② unpredictable
③ inseparable
④ developmental
⑤ unrelated

32 Researchers from Scotland's University of St. Andrews have discovered that when chimpanzees are being threatened or attacked, they __________ to get help from other chimps who are higher in rank. It was already understood that chimpanzees produce high-pitched and prolonged screams when they are being subjected to severe aggression, such as a beating. But what the study found was that the primates magnify their cries when there is a higher-ranking chimp or human in the area who could challenge the aggressor. Dr. Katie Slocombe, leader of the study, said, "The screams are normal when no higher-status animals are around, but when there are, the chimpanzee being attacked makes it sound far worse than the attack actually is."

① pretend to be badly injured
② fight far more aggressively
③ remain as quiet as possible
④ transmit scream-like signals
⑤ exaggerate their signs of fear

33 If somebody asked you, "Do things exist?" you might say something like, "What do you mean? Of course things exist! Look around you: real physical tangible things are everywhere, all existing independently of you and me!" But what if the question were "What allows any single thing — a chair or any other object — to exist?" One way to find the answer is to imagine a specific thing — say, a book — expanding and expanding until there is nothing in the universe except the book. What would happen to it? It would disappear because there would be nothing in the universe that was not the book. This is a very basic concept about reality: In order for any single thing to exist, __________. [3점]

① that exact thing must not exist
② there must also be other things
③ we should give it a proper name
④ it should have distinctive features
⑤ it must be independent of other things

10

34 Daylight saving time around the world has long been promoted as a way to save energy. Whether it does is still a matter of debate, but it does seem clear from studies that a one-hour time adjustment __________. It seems that when the clock is moved forward or back one hour, the body's internal clock — its circadian rhythm, which uses daylight to stay in tune with its environment — does not adjust. In a study of 55,000 people, for example, scientists found that on days off from work, subjects tended to sleep on standard time, not daylight time: their waking hour followed the seasonal progression of dawn. In other studies, scientists found that in spring, people's peak activity levels were more in tune with their body clock than with the actual clock. Studies suggest that this disconnect between body time and clock time can result in restlessness, sleep disruption, and shorter sleep duration. [3점]

*circadian rhythm: (생물) 24시간 주기 리듬

① can have unintended health consequences
② involves resetting our internal body clocks
③ is obviously a healthier way to start our day
④ has a beneficial effect on people with sleep disorders
⑤ can more easily be made in the spring than in the summer

35 다음 글에서 전체 흐름과 관계 없는 문장은?

If a frog is dropped into hot water, it will react very quickly to the sudden change of heat and jump out, unharmed. But if it is put into cold water, which is then warmed up very slowly, it will stay there until it boils to death. ① It's useful to bear the frog in mind when considering problems. ② Many of the most challenging and important problems in our own lives sneak up on us gradually. ③ Before we even recognize that they are there, we are deeply immersed in them. ④ A lack of motivation or patience is an especially difficult problem to deal with because it limits your ability to solve other problems as well. ⑤ Being aware of problems is essential to finding solutions to them, and dealing with small problems as they arise is better than ignoring them until they build up into problems too big to fix.

[36~37] 주어진 글 다음에 이어질 글의 순서로 가장 적절한 것을 고르시오.

36

A study of three decades of the phenomenon of "brain drain" and its relationship to Korean scientists and engineers (KSEs) who earned a PhD in the US shows economic factors were central to these professionals' decisions to return or stay.

(A) It emphasizes loyalty and duty to one's country and was found to be key to KSEs' decisions to opt for employment at home rather than in the US. Clearly, a cultural analysis is necessary for understanding the brain drain phenomenon in Korea.

(B) In the brain drain phenomenon, intellectual capital flows towards the country offering the highest salaries. However, the study found that when economic differences between the alternatives narrowed, other factors became more important in KSEs' decisions.

(C) In particular, the study suggests that Confucian values were a major influence. Confucianism is the ancient system of thought that underpins Korean society. [3점]

① (A) — (C) — (B)
② (B) — (A) — (C)
③ (B) — (C) — (A)
④ (C) — (A) — (B)
⑤ (C) — (B) — (A)

37

In a study, researchers interviewed residents of the state of Victoria over many years to see how life events and personality affected people's happiness. They wanted to know the extent to which a person's personality versus the things that happened to them affected well-being and happiness.

(A) Lucky people were lucky again and again. Likewise, people with lots of bad experiences, like relationship breakups and job losses, seemed to encounter one bad thing after another. The researchers' assumption that personality and life events would have separate influences on happiness was wrong.

(B) Instead, personality itself had the strongest influence on what happened to people. The optimists had more positive experiences, while the pessimists had more negative experiences.

(C) Personality might account for, say, 40 percent of happiness, whereas life events might account for 60 percent. Alternatively, perhaps personality would turn out to be more important. As the study progressed, it became clear that the same kind of things kept happening to the same people over and over again.

① (A) — (C) — (B)　　② (B) — (A) — (C)
③ (B) — (C) — (A)　　④ (C) — (A) — (B)
⑤ (C) — (B) — (A)

[38~39] 글의 흐름으로 보아, 주어진 문장이 들어가기에 가장 적절한 곳을 고르시오.

38

Soon enough, though, many more unskilled workers began to arrive from China.

Not including Native Americans, who probably arrived around 12,000 years ago from Siberia, the first large-scale immigration of Asians into the US was in the mid-19th century. (①) This was the time of the California gold rush, and many Chinese were lured by the dream of the "gold mountain." (②) The earliest immigrants were mainly wealthy, skilled Chinese—those who could afford the passage by ship. (③) These later arrivals, unlike the earlier settlers, willingly accepted long hours of difficult, dirty, and dangerous work in return for very little pay. (④) Because they were considered "cheap labor," these hardworking Chinese were resented by many Americans. (⑤) They felt that the new immigrants were taking jobs and wealth that rightfully belonged to themselves.

39

> In contrast, students in the productive failure group were given complex problems and then worked in groups with fellow classmates to attempt the problems.

Recent research suggests that introducing difficulties and errors can be very effective in the classroom. In a study by educationalists Kapur and Bielaczyc, for example, students were assigned to either a "productive failure" group or a "direct instruction" group. (①) Students in the direct instruction group completed typical lessons on complex math problems. (②) Their teacher helped them successfully solve problems along the way. (③) The problems were very difficult, and the productive failure group was unable to solve them. (④) During the final lesson, the teacher helped the productive failure group analyze its failed attempts and provided correct methods. (⑤) On a final test, the productive failure group scored more than the direct instruction group on both complex problems as well as more straightforward problems.

40 다음 글의 내용을 한 문장으로 요약하고자 한다. 빈칸 (A), (B)에 들어갈 말로 가장 적절한 것은? [3점]

> Man was formerly thought to be a reasoning animal. It was supposed that before forming an opinion or deciding on a course of conduct he weighed at least some of the reasons for and against the matter, and performed a more or less simple process of reasoning. But modern research has showed this belief is not true. Most of our opinions and actions are rather like shots in the dark. In fact, some authorities declare that an act of pure reasoning is very rare in the average mind. Momentous decisions are made, far-reaching actions are determined upon, primarily by the force of suggestion. Notice that word "primarily," for simple thought, and even mature reasoning, often concludes with a guess, and the thinker absurdly supposes that his conclusion is from first to last based on solid deduction.

↓

> It has been a generally accepted idea that humans are ____(A)____ decision makers, but in reality, ____(B)____ plays a more important role in such matters.

(A)		(B)
① rational	……	emotion
② rational	……	assumption
③ reasonable	……	flexibility
④ reasonable	……	convention
⑤ integrated	……	insight

[41~42] 다음 글을 읽고, 물음에 답하시오.

Students usually go to university to obtain a degree in physics, economics or history. But in Britain, it's now possible to get a university degree in less traditional subjects, including equestrian studies or aromatherapy. These degrees are known informally as "Mickey Mouse" degrees. Taken from the name of the cartoon character, anything termed "Mickey Mouse" is considered amateurish. But are these degrees, often offered at newly created universities, really inferior to conventional degrees from established universities?

People in favor of these degrees say that society benefits from having a large number of university graduates in any field because studying promotes a love of learning and respect for education. They also claim that these new courses require serious study. For example, surfing studies include meteorology, biology and business. In addition to the social benefits, there are also ___________ ones. More university students means more money for universities to improve facilities, and to expand research. Moreover, specific training can be attractive to many employers. However, some people claim that training in fields like baking technology should be acquired both on the job and at technical schools; universities exist to further knowledge rather than to help people find jobs. They say that politicians want to increase the number of university graduates, and opening these "Mickey Mouse" courses achieves this without maintaining high educational standards. They also argue that if these degrees were abolished, more scholarship money would be available to those studying "real" university subjects.

*equestrian: 승마의 **aromatherapy: 방향(芳香) 요법

41 윗글의 제목으로 가장 적절한 것은?

① Mickey Mouse Degrees: Facts and Myths
② How and Where to Get a Mickey Mouse Degree
③ Why Are Mickey Mouse Degrees Considered Inferior?
④ Is Finding a Job the Purpose of Studying at a University?
⑤ Mickey Mouse Degrees: A Helpful Innovation or a Bad Idea?

42 윗글의 빈칸에 들어갈 말로 가장 적절한 것은?

① psychological
② financial
③ cultural
④ academic
⑤ theoretical

[43~45] 다음 글을 읽고, 물음에 답하시오.

(A)

Jessica was working as a reporter for a newspaper. One winter, Jessica was in an airport, snowbound and reading the magazines in the bookshop. She intended to buy one eventually, but she was reading a magazine she did not intend to buy. It was a fluff magazine. She said to herself, "Just as calories you eat standing up don't count, fluff that you read but don't buy doesn't count, either."

*fluff: 시시한 일[것], 질 낮은 오락물

(B)

The woman behind the counter was giving Jessica a big "Are you going to buy that?" stare. Jessica hid behind a rack of books. When (a) she finished the article, she put the fluff magazine down and selected the magazine she intended to buy. As (b) she was waiting in line, Jessica noticed that the clerk never smiled at the customers and ignored the polite conversation. She seemed to be bored with her job.

(C)

After a slight delay, she smiled and said, "Yeah, they wanted a boy." Jessica said, "Mine too. I learned how to fish by the time I was six." She asked if (c) she was named after her dad. Jessica said no, but she wasn't disappointed. She matched Jessica's story. "I learned how to build things. My dad was a carpenter. I can saw, measure, and pound nails." Jessica and Eddie were both smiling then. They traded stories and it made them both feel better.

(D)

At last when it was (d) her turn, Jessica was met by a very grumpy face. The clerk had long blond hair and wore cat-eye glasses. While the clerk was packaging the book, Jessica said, "I really wish I had your blond hair." The clerk looked up, half-startled, her face beaming with a smile. "Well, it isn't as good as it used to be," (e) she said modestly. Then Jessica caught sight of her name tag, "Eddie Jo." Jessica asked with smile, "Were you named after your daddy?"

43 주어진 글 (A)에 이어질 내용을 순서에 맞게 배열한 것으로 가장 적절한 것은?

① (B) — (D) — (C)　② (C) — (B) — (D)
③ (C) — (D) — (B)　④ (D) — (B) — (C)
⑤ (D) — (C) — (B)

44 밑줄 친 (a)~(e) 중에서 가리키는 대상이 나머지 넷과 다른 것은?

① (a)　② (b)　③ (c)　④ (d)　⑤ (e)

45 윗글에 관한 내용으로 적절하지 않은 것은?

① Jessica는 공항 서점에서 사지도 않을 잡지를 읽었다.
② Jessica는 손님에게 불친절한 서점 직원을 보았다.
③ 서점 직원은 아버지에게서 낚시를 배웠다고 말했다.
④ 서점 직원은 자신의 아버지에 관해 이야기했다.
⑤ 서점 직원은 자신의 머리색에 대한 찬사를 듣고 기뻐했다.

: AFTER TESTING

종료 시 분
소요시간 분

학습 마무리

1 채점하기 | 정답 및 해설 p.74
주의 틀린 문제를 다시 풀 수 있도록 정답을 본문에 표기하지 마세요.
2 등급 확인
3 틀린 유형 확인 후 전략 적용 복습 및 해설지 확인

How to Review

1 틀린 문제와 ✓ 표시한 문제는 다시 풀고 해설 확인하기
2 내가 표시한 정답 근거가 해설과 일치하는지 확인하기
3 잘 모르는 부분으로 표시한 내용은 해설을 통해 완전히 이해하기
4 어휘 외우기 (어휘 목록 다운로드 www.cedubook.com)
5 다음 회에 개선할 점 정리하기 (시간 엄수, 취약 유형 보완 등)

POWER UP!

실전 모의고사 11

: BEFORE TESTING

시작 시 분

학습 목표

1 제한시간 (OMR 마킹시간 포함) ☐ 40분 ☐ 45분
2 어휘예습 ☐ 해당 없음 ☐ 완료
3 문제풀이순서 ☐ 순서대로 ☐ 2점 → 3점 ☐ 기타
4 기타 목표

Check Point

1 정답 근거 e.g. 밑줄 긋기
2 잘 모르는 부분 e.g. 〈 〉 또는 ? 표시
3 자신 없는 문제 e.g. 문제 번호에 ✓표시

18 다음 글을 쓴 목적으로 가장 적절한 것은?

Dear Lincolnshire Residents:

Our city's road workers ensure our streets are kept clean and safe. But help is also needed from property owners who can blow, shovel, or plow snow onto their properties from the street. We also ask property owners to bear in mind City Ordinance 7-1, which prohibits residents from moving snow from their properties onto the street. Snow deposited on the roads quickly compacts into mounds of ice, which cannot easily be detected by our snowplow drivers. If a truck's plow strikes ice, the plow can be ripped off the truck, and the truck can be sent spinning out of control. Compacted ice is equally hazardous for everyone using the roads, so please give us a hand by keeping your street clear.

Sincerely,
Jim Mckay
General Manager of Management Department

*ordinance: (지방 자치체의) 조례, 규정

① 제설 차량 운행 계획을 알리려고
② 새로운 교통법규 조항을 공지하려고
③ 폭설로 인한 도심 혼잡을 경고하려고
④ 눈길에서의 운전 속도 감속을 요청하려고
⑤ 눈을 차로 쪽으로 치우지 말 것을 당부하려고

19 다음 글에 드러난 Matt의 심경 변화로 가장 적절한 것은?

The boys decided to visit the beaver dam again. Matt was walking behind Attean, when Attean suddenly halted. Matt could see nothing unusual, and he had opened his mouth to speak, when Attean silenced him with a quick raise of his hand. Then he heard a sound in the underbrush ahead. It was unlike that of a snake or a trapped animal. This was a stirring of something moving slowly and heavily. He could feel the hair on his arms stand up. He stood beside Attean, his own muscles tight, scarcely breathing. A low bush bent sideways. Through the leaves a brown head thrust itself. Bigger than that of a dog, and covered in thick fur. It was a small bear cub. Matt could see the little eyes peering at them curiously, the brown nose wrinkling at the strange smell of human boy. The little animal looked so comical that Matt almost laughed out loud.

① worried → irritated
② relieved → nervous
③ envious → delighted
④ frightened → relaxed
⑤ anticipating → disappointed

20 다음 글에서 필자가 주장하는 바로 가장 적절한 것은?

Democracy is part of a package which ensures that individuals can pursue their economic goals in safety and indeed are encouraged to do so. So it tends to generate economic and hence military success. Yet it is clear that democracy does not automatically generate economic growth. It is possible to point to periods in the history of democratic societies, including the recession in the United States in the 1930s, where there has been economic decline. Secondly, there are forms of autocracy, as in China today with its amazing economic growth, which are temporarily more successful than most democracies. There are one-party, bureaucratic states such as Singapore or, some would argue, Japan, which have had extraordinary growth without democracy in the normal sense of the word. So democracy is neither a guarantee of growth nor is it the only path.

① 정치적 안정과 경제 성장은 서로 양립할 수 없다.
② 경제 성장을 위해 민주주의가 필수적인 것은 아니다.
③ 독재 체제가 경제 성장의 측면에서는 가장 효율적이다.
④ 민주주의의 경제적 자유가 때로는 위기를 불러올 수 있다.
⑤ 민주주의 체제의 단점을 보완한 경제 정책 수립이 필요하다.

21 밑줄 친 None of us is us가 다음 글에서 의미하는 바로 가장 적절한 것은?

A recent article in the *New York Times* by Barry Meier discussed the problems of setting guidelines for treating different patients suffering from the same disease. Creating one set of guidelines for diabetes, for example, might save money, but some people will suffer serious health consequences from a treatment that helps others. This problem will not go away by shifting the guidelines, or requiring more rigorous research as some argue. No matter how accurate the research is that the guidelines are based on, some people will suffer. There are hidden decisions in medical research — dosage, times administered, subject population, context, definition of disease severity and so on — for which a slight change in any one of these could change the results of the study. Research only yields probabilities, not absolute facts. Given that the data are only normative — what may be true for most people under the same circumstances — surely for some people it will prove to be untrue. None of us is us.

① We have to eliminate negative health mindsets.
② Guidelines for a disease don't work for everyone.
③ The guidelines used to assess our health are temporary.
④ We need to adopt new guidelines for dealing with health.
⑤ Patients need faster access to useful medical innovations.

22 다음 글의 요지로 가장 적절한 것은?

In houses and apartments alike, we start with a box and fit everything into it; a box within a box. Consider how that applies to the outside, too: the street you live on, the neighborhood, train tracks, and so on. Imagine how liberating it would feel to eliminate the sharp edges and make everything more seamless. The next time you're on a plane, look out the window at that grid and consider whether it is truly the ideal way for us to live. What if every line could be a curve? Why make an intersection when it can be seamless? Corners are a point of friction, a place where dust collects. Now consider the interior of a plane, with its angleless cabin. Think about the comforting cocoon-like feeling it evokes. The absence of corners and right angles makes for a more casual space. There are no right angles in nature. We know we find comfort in bean bags and womb-like spaces. Why fight it?

*bean bag: 빈 백(주머니에 폴리스티렌 구슬을 넣어 만든 의자)

① 생활공간이 자연친화적일수록 건강에 좋다.
② 모서리 없는 공간이 더 편안함을 느끼게 한다.
③ 집을 꾸밀 때는 큰 물건부터 배치하는 것이 좋다.
④ 공간 활용도가 높을수록 생활 만족도가 증가한다.
⑤ 직선과 곡선이 조화를 이룬 환경이 창의력을 높인다.

23 다음 글의 주제로 가장 적절한 것은?

In a sense, emotional display is like theater. We all have a backstage, the hidden zone where we feel our emotions, and a stage front, the social arena where we present the emotions we choose to reveal. This split between our public and private emotional lives is similar to how employees in a store change their behavior for customers. Emotional displays are more often carefully managed when interacting with customers and less well managed backstage, and this difference can be unfortunate. The director of a large Sunday school complained to me about her minister whose sermons were inspiring and thought-provoking, "He's completely unexpressive and so hard to understand; I don't know how to take much of what he says to me — it's very difficult to work with him." Being poor at appropriately expressing emotions can be a major handicap.

① various ways of controlling emotions on stage
② reasons why we feel it is hard to display emotions
③ necessity of concealing private emotions in public
④ health benefits of expressing emotions appropriately
⑤ difference between public and private emotional lives

24 다음 글의 제목으로 가장 적절한 것은?

Experiments sometimes produce results that have occurred purely by chance and cannot be duplicated. Therefore, before accepting a hypothesis, researchers repeat the experiment several times to guarantee that the results are valid. Another scientist working separately must be able to repeat the same experiments and get essentially the same results for a hypothesis to be valid and accepted. Alternative experiments should also be conducted to ensure that other variables have not been overlooked. Only if many different approaches fail to disprove a hypothesis will it be considered accurate; even then, the acceptance of the hypothesis is subject to change if new information comes to light. Thus, the aim of a scientist is not to prove something but to test it many times to achieve a more accurate explanation of the phenomenon being investigated.

① Use of the Scientific Method to Design Experiments
② Observation: A Prerequisite of Hypothesis Formation
③ Science: Repeating Experiments to Test a Hypothesis
④ A Decisive Experiment Makes a Hypothesis a Theory
⑤ Science Is Not about Process, but about Conclusion

25 다음 도표의 내용과 일치하지 않는 것은?

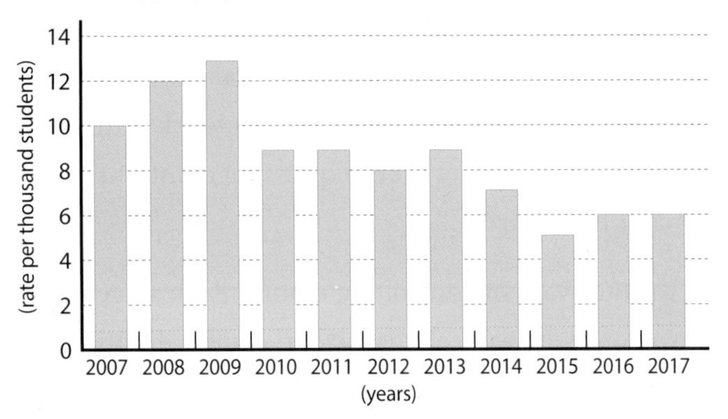

This graph shows the violent crime rate per thousand students in schools across the United States. The data covers the years 2007 to 2017 and includes students between the ages of 12 and 18. ① From 2007 to 2009 the violent crime rate increased steadily, from 10 to 13 student victims per thousand. ② However, contrary to popular belief, violent crime in schools has declined dramatically overall since 2009, despite two minor increases. ③ The lowered crime rate remained at the same level for four consecutive years after 2009. ④ The rate went on to drop to its lowest point in 2015, but rose a little again in 2016. ⑤ The rate of violent crime in 2017 did not even reach half that of 2009.

26 musk ox에 관한 다음 글의 내용과 일치하지 않는 것은?

The musk ox gets its name from the musk-like perfume the male gives off, which is produced by glands beneath the bull's eyes. Both males and females have horns which can reach up to two feet. Musk oxen don't mind the Arctic climate, because their outfit comes with an "all weatherproof" warranty. Musk oxen travel in herds of 20 to 30 to find adequate food. When attacked, the adults will form a circle with the young safe inside. The adults will face the outside and use their sharp horns as weapons against their enemy. Musk oxen eat large quantities of food to increase their internal heat production and feed on grasses, lichens and willow trees. Bulls will compete for breeding rights by violently ramming their heads together until one bull walks away. It is no wonder that bulls generally have a shorter life span than cows!

*musk: 사향(麝香) **ram: 들이받다

① 수컷에게만 사향 냄새가 난다.
② 추위를 피해 무리 지어 이동한다.
③ 무리 지어 뿔로 적의 공격을 방어한다.
④ 체온을 높이기 위해 많은 양의 풀을 먹는다.
⑤ 암컷이 수컷보다 수명이 더 길다.

27 Modern Photo Arts Center의 행사에 관한 다음 안내문의 내용과 일치하지 않는 것은?

Modern Photo Arts Center

Artist Lecture & Book Signing

Who: Joyce Evans
When: Tuesday, November 18, 6:00 P.M.−7:30 P.M.
Where: The White Space in MPAC (Modern Photo Arts Center)
Admission: Free

Patron Party

When: Tuesday, November 18, 8:00 P.M.−9:30 P.M.
Admission: $75 per person or $125 for two

Joyce Evans will discuss her career and work as a fine artist and editorial photographer as well as introduce her most recent book, *Love*. *Love* shows nine years of intensely intimate photographs of her motherhood/childhood project with her children. The lecture will be followed by a book signing, and copies of *Love* will be sold at the event. Please complete an application form to reserve a seat.

① 강연 및 책 사인회는 1시간 30분 동안 열린다.
② 후원 파티에 두 사람이 참석하려면 125달러를 내야 한다.
③ Joyce Evans가 자신의 경력과 작품에 대해 강연할 것이다.
④ *Love*는 Evans가 9년간 작업한 사진들을 담고 있다.
⑤ *Love*는 현장 참석자들에게 무료로 배부된다.

28 Valley Music Festival에 관한 다음 안내문의 내용과 일치하는 것은?

Valley Music Festival

Valley Music Festival takes place at Centennial Field, located approximately 45 minutes north of Vancouver and 30 minutes south of Whistler.

FESTIVAL PASSES

Festival passes are non-refundable, and the full price, including taxes and fees, will be displayed before you make a purchase.

CAMPING

Campsites are available, and one camping ticket gets you one 10′×12′ plot and 4 camping wristbands.

BOX OFFICE HOURS

Friday, August 8, 2−10 p.m.
Saturday, August 9, noon−10 p.m.
Sunday, August 10, noon−10 p.m.

GATES OPEN

Friday 5 p.m.−The music will begin a few hours after the gates open each day. Exact times will be posted in the weeks prior to the festival.

① 개최지는 Vancouver 남쪽과 Whistler 북쪽 사이에 있다.
② 음악 축제 입장권은 환불이 가능하다.
③ 캠핑 입장권 한 장으로 네 명까지 들어갈 수 있다.
④ 금요일에는 주말보다 매표소를 두 시간 빨리 연다.
⑤ 음악 축제는 금요일 오후 5시 정각에 시작된다.

29 다음 글의 밑줄 친 부분 중, 어법상 틀린 것은? [3점]

In one study, participants were asked to create a video lesson. An "expert" gave the participants detailed feedback on ① their performance. Participants performed alongside a partner who performed the same task. The question being ② investigated was how the feedback would affect participants' moods. For happy people, whether they heard or didn't hear the feedback given to their partners ③ making no difference. Unhappy people, in contrast, were very much affected. If a participant got positive feedback, but her partner got better feedback, the participant's mood worsened. Thus, it seemed as though the only thing ④ that mattered to the unhappy people was how they did in comparison to their partners. Better to be told that you're a pretty bad teacher but that others are ⑤ even worse than to be told that you're a pretty good teacher but that others are better.

30 (A), (B), (C)의 각 네모 안에서 문맥에 맞는 낱말로 가장 적절한 것은? [3점]

We know that we have some bad habits. We know that we would be better off without them. We have all tried to change many times with various degrees of success. But the changes have never been deep enough or lasting. The problem is that our approach to attacking this problem is (A) [faulty / desirable]. We tend to take a bad habit and just try hard to stop doing it. We gather all of our will to not do something. This creates a sense of (B) [deprivation / satisfaction] in our mind. We did whatever the wrong behavior was because we enjoyed it. So we are actually removing something that provided pleasure and are creating a void in our lives. Naturally, this type of change is not (C) [sustainable / temporary]. Sooner or later we will have to fill that void again, and we will inevitably return to those old behaviors because that's the only way we can fill that void.

*void: 상실감

	(A)		(B)		(C)
①	faulty	……	deprivation	……	sustainable
②	faulty	……	satisfaction	……	sustainable
③	faulty	……	deprivation	……	temporary
④	desirable	……	satisfaction	……	temporary
⑤	desirable	……	deprivation	……	sustainable

[31~34] 다음 빈칸에 들어갈 말로 가장 적절한 것을 고르시오.

31 A key requirement for negative emotions is __________. This means that you take things personally. You interpret what has happened as a personal attack on you. If you cannot personally associate yourself with a negative situation, you will have difficulty generating any emotion, positive or negative, about it. If you read in the paper that a thousand people—men, women, and children—had been washed away and drowned by a flood in northern China, you would feel some sorrow and then probably flip the page to the next subject with little or no emotion. Because you do not know any of the people affected or even know much about that part of the world, you do not equate with the tragedy. As a result, you experience no negative emotions about it. This does not mean you can't feel compassion for someone else's experience or hurt, but you do not become emotionally involved. [3점]

① denial
② deception
③ reflection
④ identification
⑤ rationalization

32 Most of us don't have any memories from the first three to four years of our lives. The phenomenon, known as "childhood amnesia," has been puzzling psychologists for more than a century—and we still don't fully understand it. But research is starting to suggest an answer: autobiographical memory might begin with the stories we tell each other. It is true to some extent that a child's ability to verbalize about an event at the time that it happened predicts how well they remember it months or years later. One lab group conducted this work by interviewing toddlers brought to accident and emergency departments for common childhood injuries. Toddlers over 26 months, who could talk about the event at the time, recalled it up to five years later—whereas those under 26 months, who could not talk about it, recalled little or nothing. This suggests that preverbal memories are lost if they are not ____________________.

*amnesia: 기억상실

① shared with peers
② associated with trauma
③ translated into language
④ recorded on a regular basis
⑤ encoded into long-term ones

33 Retail, advertising, and marketing strategies rely a great deal on ______________. It's one of the reasons why pop-up ads and infomercials, to name but a few strategies, work so effectively on us. Merchandisers have complete power over us, and they know the psychology of shoppers and that willpower stands no chance. To this end, tempting snacks are placed within easy reach at checkout counters; websites instantly suggest other products at discounted prices as soon as you place a single product in your shopping cart; mannequins are styled in clothes and accessories that look so good together you simply have to buy the whole look. Retailers know that you're not likely to think twice about buying items which are complementary to the ones you are already buying when you have your wallet in hand at the checkout stand, so it is here that you are given "special offers" by sales clerks and asked if you also want this or that. [3점]

① our weakness for spending on impulse
② our desire to make shopping convenient
③ our appetite to compare shops for better prices
④ research to understand the needs of consumers
⑤ the timing of placing the right ads in the right media

34 Mood transfer via facial expressions and body language is so powerful that people doing it on a daily basis literally start to look alike. This has been tested with portraits of longtime couples: One set of pictures was taken on their wedding day and another set twenty-five years later. Presented with separate portraits of these men and women, human subjects were asked to match them on similarity. For the set taken at an older age, they had no trouble deciding who was married to whom. But for the pictures taken at a younger age, subjects failed the task. Married couples resemble each other, therefore, not because they pick partners who look like them, but because their features converge over the years. The similarity was strongest for couples in the study who reported the greatest happiness. Daily sharing of emotions apparently leads one partner to "internalize" the other, and vice versa, to the point that ______________. [3점]

*converge: 하나로 모이다, 점점 비슷해지다

① physical appearance is not a concern to them
② anyone can see how much they belong together
③ negative health outcomes are expected to improve
④ it enables them to know what the other is thinking
⑤ they always prevent each other's feelings from being hurt

35 다음 글에서 전체 흐름과 관계 없는 문장은?

How fast would you have to travel to stay in sunlight while circling the globe? Assuming for argument's sake that you want to try this trick at the Equator, we use the following calculations. Earth's diameter is 12,756 km and its circumference is 40,074 km. ① The whole circumference of Earth passes under the sun in one day. ② If the sun were an empty sphere, about one million Earths could fit inside it. ③ One day consists of almost exactly twenty-four hours. ④ Thus, the speed you would have to travel over the surface of Earth at the Equator is the circumference divided by the number of hours in the day. ⑤ That comes to 1,670 km/h, which is about 1.33 times the speed of sound, or more than five times faster than the top speed of a Formula One race car.

*circumference: 원주, 원둘레

[36~37] 주어진 글 다음에 이어질 글의 순서로 가장 적절한 것을 고르시오.

36

Richard Dawkins argued that genes are selfish because it is in their natural interest to replicate themselves, but they may act altruistically for their own preservation.

(A) It is the same in organizations. Typically, employees who work at the same level for the same company will all desire the same job openings, the same control of projects, and the same special benefits.

(B) But they come together and work as a team every day because it makes them happier and more productive, and increases their chances of earning a promotion or getting an end-of-year bonus. All of us are selfish, but the smartest ones understand that cooperation is good for self-interest.

(C) Thousands of genes, for instance, work together to create organs, including 1,195 genes for the human heart and 3,195 genes for the human brain. These individual genes must have figured out that it doesn't pay to be alone in the harsh environment of the gene pool.

① (A) — (C) — (B)
② (B) — (A) — (C)
③ (B) — (C) — (A)
④ (C) — (A) — (B)
⑤ (C) — (B) — (A)

37

Although not as popular as other art therapy methods, family sculpting is unique in its more tactile approach to art therapy. This method was first developed by psychotherapist Virginia Satir and seeks to unlock the inner feelings a patient has toward his/her family that the patient is otherwise unwilling or unable to express.

(A) This can identify issues between certain individuals; for example, if the patient placed the sculpture of the mother far away from the rest of the family, it might indicate the mother is distant.

(B) The patient is provided with several lumps of clay and is then instructed to mold the clay into representations of each individual family member. The way the patient creates each figure can provide the therapist with vital information.

(C) For example, a patient who is fearful of his or her father might sculpt that figure as large and menacing in comparison to another figure. Some therapists might take the process one step further and ask the patient to then situate the sculptures in relation to each other.

① (A) — (C) — (B)
② (B) — (A) — (C)
③ (B) — (C) — (A)
④ (C) — (A) — (B)
⑤ (C) — (B) — (A)

[38~39] 글의 흐름으로 보아, 주어진 문장이 들어가기에 가장 적절한 곳을 고르시오.

38

A lot of this land has been made available by clearing vast areas of forest, yet forests are absolutely vital in removing CO_2 from the atmosphere.

Our growing appetite for meat and dairy products is a recipe for environmental disaster, especially in the area of climate change. (①) Livestock farming now takes up a full 30 percent of the entire land surface on Earth, and most of it is permanent pasture for grazing sheep and cattle. (②) This includes 33 percent of the world's fertile agricultural land, which is used to grow grain to feed the livestock. (③) CO_2 emissions from livestock farming represent 9 percent of the world's total human-related CO_2 emissions. (④) But nitrous oxide and methane are far more powerful in their warming of the atmosphere than CO_2 is. (⑤) And 65 percent of the world's nitrous oxide emissions and 37 percent of its methane emissions come from livestock.

*nitrous oxide: 아산화질소 **methane: 메탄가스

39

Researchers complain, however, that boys are still very seldom shown doing nontraditional things like caring for younger children or doing housework.

Gender studies scholars examined children's picture books in the 1970s and found that it was rare for girls to be leading characters. (①) When pictured at all, girls tended to be represented as passive and doll-like, whereas boys were active and adventurous. (②) They were shown doing things that required independence and self-confidence, while girls were shown as helpers. (③) Feminists protested these stereotypes and began publishing children's books with strong girl characters, to fix the imbalance. (④) As a result, children's books today have roughly equal numbers of boys and girls as the main characters. (⑤) As gender roles continue to evolve, it's fair to assume that this, too, will change.

40 다음 글의 내용을 한 문장으로 요약하고자 한다. 빈칸 (A), (B)에 들어갈 말로 가장 적절한 것은? [3점]

Belonging to social groups and associating with other people do much more than help us create a meaningful life; reflecting on ourselves through the eyes of others also serves important identity functions. It is only through social comparisons that we may engage in self-evaluation. Think about a time when your grades were posted after an exam. Did you simply check to see how you had done, or did you compare your score against others? Why? Of course, it's because a score is only seen as good or bad in relation to others. But other people may serve as more than points of comparison. Other people may also be internalized to become a part of the self. As we seek groups of others to associate with and join for companionship and social bonding, these groups of others come to be seen as part of ourselves. We develop a social component to the sense of self; that is, our self-concept and self-esteem are linked to the social groups to which we belong.

↓

Groups of others serve as not only social ____(A)____ to evaluate our performance against but also as social components of our ____(B)____.

(A)		(B)
① approval	……	identity
② approval	……	hierarchy
③ authorities	……	existence
④ comparisons	……	identity
⑤ comparisons	……	hierarchy

[41~42] 다음 글을 읽고, 물음에 답하시오.

How the brain responds to poetry is one thing. But why it responds in this way is another. Scientists have been attempting to find an answer for quite some time. Revelations like the discovery that full-term fetuses increase their heart rates when they hear their mothers reciting poetry suggest that perhaps there's something (a) <u>inherent</u> in the human brain that responds to poetic sounds. Scientists also reveal that brains respond to poetry in a way similar to when they reflect on the past and introspect. This means that reading poetry also provides space for (b) <u>self-reflection</u>. And a 2017 study indicates that even if we haven't been taught about poetry, we seem to respond (c) <u>positively</u> to it. There's a traditional form of Welsh-language poetry called *cynghanedd* that has very strict rules about verse form and rhyming in single lines. Researchers collected volunteers who spoke Welsh but had no knowledge of *cynghanedd* and presented them with sentences, some of which obeyed the rules of *cynghanedd* and others of which violated them in some way. When the sentences fit the rules perfectly, the volunteers' brains showed pleasure, and when they somehow departed from the mold, their brains were less keen on the words. What exactly this proves is clear. Human love for (d) <u>randomness</u> may show through in our reactions to language, even if we ourselves don't have any background in understanding the specifics of poetry. This is also likely why we respond so (e) <u>strongly</u> to lyric and rap.

*fetus: (임신 9주 후의) 태아

41 윗글의 제목으로 가장 적절한 것은?

① Can Poetry Change Your Life?
② Poetry, Music, and the Link Between Them
③ Why Is Poetry Important to Our World Today?
④ What Happens to Your Brain When You Read Poetry
⑤ Reading Poetry Influences Our Memories and Language

42 밑줄 친 (a)~(e) 중에서 문맥상 낱말의 쓰임이 적절하지 <u>않은</u> 것은? [3점]

① (a) ② (b) ③ (c) ④ (d) ⑤ (e)

[43~45] 다음 글을 읽고, 물음에 답하시오.

(A)

Bob's father, a car salesman, owned a 1958 Cadillac that was his pride and joy. It was the kind of car that looked more like a boat; it was huge and had tail fins on it that curved up high. (a) It was cared for like a baby, never left outside overnight, and faithfully washed and waxed every Saturday. It was a shining example of a man's treasured wheels.

(B)

After carefully parking the car, he went in with his head bowed, and spoke to his father. They came back out together to survey the damage — and (b) it was considerable. They stood there for what seemed like an eternity, his father saying nothing. Finally, Bob said in a trembling voice, "Dad, what do you want me to do?" Slowly his father took out two dollars from his pocket. Handing it to Bob and looking him straight in the eye, he said, "Son, I think you'd better go back and fill (c) it with some more gas."

(C)

Then, the unthinkable happened. As he pulled out of the station, Bob cut the corner too sharply and scraped the side of (d) the car along a concrete pillar. He felt sick. For a moment, he thought of running away. The idea of facing his father, who would be angry and disappointed, was awful. Slowly, he turned the car toward home.

(D)

Bob was sixteen, had just gotten his driver's license, and was practically bursting with desire to get behind the wheel of (e) that Cadillac, so his kind father gave him three dollars and sent him to get gasoline. Full of pride and youthful enthusiasm, Bob drove to the station and sat in the car with a great big smile on his face as the station attendant filled the car with gas and washed the windows.

43 주어진 글 (A)에 이어질 내용을 순서에 맞게 배열한 것으로 가장 적절한 것은?

① (B) — (D) — (C) ② (C) — (B) — (D)
③ (C) — (D) — (B) ④ (D) — (B) — (C)
⑤ (D) — (C) — (B)

44 밑줄 친 (a)~(e) 중에서 가리키는 대상이 나머지 넷과 다른 것은?

① (a) ② (b) ③ (c) ④ (d) ⑤ (e)

45 윗글의 Bob에 관한 내용으로 적절하지 않은 것은?

① 아버지의 직업은 자동차 판매원이었다.
② 파손 부분이 생각보다 크지 않아 안도했다.
③ 차를 몰다가 기둥에 차 옆면을 긁었다.
④ 운전면허를 취득한 지 얼마 되지 않았다.
⑤ 아버지의 자동차를 몰고 주유소에 갔다.

: AFTER TESTING

⏱ 종료 시 분

⌛ 소요시간 분

학습 마무리

1 채점하기 | 정답 및 해설 p.82

주의 틀린 문제를 다시 풀 수 있도록 정답을 본문에 표기하지 마세요.

2 등급 확인

3 틀린 유형 확인 후 전략 적용 복습 및 해설지 확인

How to Review

1 틀린 문제와 ✓ 표시한 문제는 다시 풀고 해설 확인하기

2 내가 표시한 정답 근거가 해설과 일치하는지 확인하기

3 잘 모르는 부분으로 표시한 내용은 해설을 통해 완전히 이해하기

4 어휘 외우기 (어휘 목록 다운로드 www.cedubook.com)

5 다음 회에 개선할 점 정리하기 (시간 엄수, 취약 유형 보완 등)

POWER UP!

실전 모의고사

12

: BEFORE TESTING

시작 시 분

학습 목표

1 **제한시간** (OMR 마킹시간 포함) ☐ 40분 ☐ 45분
2 **어휘예습** ☐ 해당 없음 ☐ 완료
3 **문제풀이순서** ☐ 순서대로 ☐ 2점 → 3점 ☐ 기타 ....
4 **기타 목표** ....

Check Point

1 **정답 근거** *e.g.* 밑줄 긋기
2 **잘 모르는 부분** *e.g.* 〈 〉 또는 ? 표시
3 **자신 없는 문제** *e.g.* 문제 번호에 ✓표시

18 다음 글의 목적으로 가장 적절한 것은?

To Whom It May Concern,

To begin, let me just say that I have nothing but respect for the efforts of everyone working for the Spring Clean Donation Drive. After the tragic flooding which affected so many homes in the Sandy City community, it seemed that something had to be done to help. By collecting unwanted household items and reselling them, thousands of dollars have been raised to help flood victims. My only wish is that collection trucks could be sent further into rural communities. There are many of us living outside the Sandy City limit who would love to donate items to your charity. Please consider this as a way to increase donations and keep the good efforts going!

Sincerely,
Heather Nandall

① 기부 운동 단체의 설립을 촉구하려고
② 기부 운동에 동참하는 방법을 설명하려고
③ 홍수 피해자들이 처한 상황을 알려주려고
④ 기부 가능 지역을 확대하는 방안을 제안하려고
⑤ 홍수 피해자들을 돕는 기부 운동에 감사하려고

19 다음 글에 드러난 Edward의 심경 변화로 가장 적절한 것은?

Edward couldn't stay in bed any longer. Reviews of his play would surely be online by now, and he was eager to read them. After all, the play had seemed successful. No longer able to wait, he jumped out of bed, switched on his laptop, and sat down to read the good news. The first review, however, wasn't what he'd expected. Slightly let down by the author's negative tone, Edward quickly searched for another review. This one was even worse! Edward's face started to turn a light shade of red as the words "uninspired," "lazy," and "tired" met his eyes. He wanted to respond in the comments, but then he realized that would look even worse. So he closed his laptop, shut the blinds, crawled back into bed, and tried to think of how to avoid any phone calls.

① dissatisfied → relieved
② hopeful → embarrassed
③ excited → envious
④ gloomy → grateful
⑤ frustrated → joyful

20 다음 글에서 필자가 주장하는 바로 가장 적절한 것은?

When psychologists study frozen thinking, they call it "dogmatic cognition." In the psychologist's definition, it is "the tendency to process information in a manner that reinforces the individual's prior opinion or expectation." Zen Buddhism has a concept for a style of thought completely opposed to dogmatic cognition. It is called "beginner's mind." It refers to an approach in which you have a lack of preconceptions and perceive even routine situations as if you are encountering them for the first time, without automatically making assumptions based on your past experience. That doesn't mean you discard your expertise, but that you remain open to new experience despite it. Most of us have a cognitive style that falls somewhere between the extremes of a beginner's mind and dogmatic cognition. The ideal expert in any field is one who has a great breadth and depth of knowledge and yet maintains, to a large extent, a beginner's mind.

① 전문 지식에 대한 지나친 과신을 경계하라.
② 성공에 급급하지 말고 넓은 시야를 가져라.
③ 눈앞의 이익 때문에 초심을 잃지 않도록 하라.
④ 전문성을 가지고 있더라도 열린 마음을 유지하라.
⑤ 선입견을 깨기 위해 먼저 자신의 생각을 들여다보라.

21 다음 글의 요지로 가장 적절한 것은?

In England in the early 20th century, many infants died from a condition that was then called *marasmus*, which means "wasting away" in Greek. Some orphanages in very poor districts had infant mortality rates as high as 100 percent, but even the most advanced homes and institutions also had babies suffering from marasmus. Eventually, it was found that the infants were actually suffering from lack of physical contact. They hadn't been held or stroked, and as a result, they weakened and died. After this discovery, nurses in one hospital ensured that they picked babies up, carried them around, and otherwise physically interacted with them throughout the day. Soon, the infant mortality rate at this hospital fell from 65 percent to below 10 percent, confirming that what the nurses were doing is vital for babies.

*marasmus: (유아의) 쇠약(증)

① 신체 접촉을 하는 것이 아이들의 건강에 좋다.
② 아동 건강을 위해 보호시설의 환경 개선이 필요하다.
③ 유아기에는 신체 접촉을 통한 감염을 주의해야 한다.
④ 20세기 초반까지 위생상의 문제로 많은 아이가 사망했다.
⑤ 의료 기술의 발달이 신생아 사망률 감소에 영향을 주었다.

22 다음 글의 주제로 가장 적절한 것은? [3점]

Many people feel that power should be withheld from those who most actively seek it. Because of this general antipathy toward power and power seekers, writes Rosabeth Moss Kanter, "People who have it deny it; people who want it do not want to appear to hunger for it; people who engage in its machinations do so secretly." Given our feeling toward power and those who hold it, it is no surprise that democratic political systems contain checks on power. These systems also specify measures to distribute power in ways that prevent it from becoming absolute or concentrated in too few hands. The founders of the United States clashed over this issue. Their constitutional solution? Establish mechanisms that prevent the concentration of power in one branch of government and that protect the interests of minorities against the power of the majority. The U.S. Constitution's Bill of Rights checks power by specifying individual rights that government cannot abridge, no matter how powerful it is.

*machination: 음모, 모략 **abridge: 축소하다

① necessity of peaceful and democratic power shifts
② history of political efforts to solve power struggles
③ consequences of people's hunger for power in society
④ importance of exercising political power in a democracy
⑤ reasons and ways to prevent power abuse in democracy

23 다음 글의 제목으로 가장 적절한 것은?

It is quite simply wrong to believe that therapeutic cloning will allow us to create, for example, a soccer team of David Beckhams, or a peace movement of Martin Luther Kings, or a publishing house of J. K. Rowlings. The thing is, even if we can copy the complete genetic makeup of an individual, we still cannot predict that individual's future. We only need look at the many thousands of identical twins who, although raised in the same home and schools as their twin, are still very different in talents and likes and dislikes, and we can see that identical genes do not make identical lives. Increasingly sophisticated research is showing that the better we understand gene function, the more obvious the impossibility of producing a made-to-order human being.

① How Humans Can Be Cloned
② Advantages of Human Cloning
③ Identical Twins and Human Cloning
④ Reasons for Banning Human Cloning
⑤ A Misconception about Human Cloning

24 다음 도표의 내용과 일치하지 않는 것은?

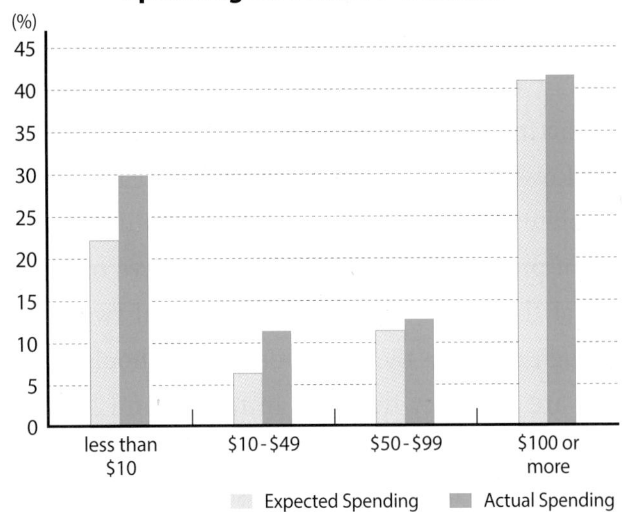

The above chart compares expected spending and actual spending on online purchases, as reported by a sample of shoppers. ① The overall trend is that people spent more than they had expected to. ② According to the chart, the largest percentage of people spent more than $100 online, while the smallest percentage of people spent between $10 and $49. ③ People who spent less than $10 accounted for the second largest percentage in the chart. ④ The narrowest difference between expected and actual spending was in the $50 to $99 category. ⑤ On the contrary, the gap between expected spending and actual spending was the greatest when people spent less than $10.

25 United States Military Academy에 관한 다음 글의 내용과 일치하지 않는 것은?

The United States Military Academy, also known as West Point, is located approximately 50 miles north of New York City in the scenic Hudson Valley. Established by Thomas Jefferson in 1802, it is the oldest military academy in the United States. During the American War of Independence, George Washington realized an academy to train army officers was urgently needed, which led to the establishment of the academy. Jefferson Finis Davis, the leader of the Confederate side, and Ulysses S. Grant, the leading general on the Union side of the American Civil War, were both graduates of West Point. To be accepted into the academy, candidates must be aged between 17 and 23, score highly on the Scholastic Aptitude Test (SAT), and be of good moral character.

*the Confederate side: (남북전쟁 때의) 남부 연합 측
**the Union side: (남북전쟁 때의) 북부 연합 측

① West Point라 불리기도 한다.
② 미국에서 가장 오래된 사관학교이다.
③ 졸업생들이 미국 독립전쟁에서 큰 업적을 남겼다.
④ 남북전쟁 시 양측 지휘관이 이 학교 졸업생이었다.
⑤ 입학 시 SAT 점수와 인성을 모두 평가한다.

26 Max Fitness Center의 회원 혜택에 관한 다음 안내문의 내용과 일치하지 않는 것은?

Max Fitness Center

April is Relaxation Month!

Join the April Fitness Challenge at Max Fitness Center and enjoy free enrollment through April 14! Orientations are a free service recommended for all new members. The orientation only takes 30 minutes and will review fitness center rules, regulations, programs and promotions.

Benefits of Membership

- Work with our fitness specialists to determine your workout goal, whether it is flexibility, aerobic ability, strength or weight loss.
- A complimentary fitness assessment is designed to assess overall health and includes a body composition test and flexibility measurement.
- A 60-minute-long one-on-one training will help you address your goals.

① 4월 14일까지 등록비가 면제된다.
② 신입 회원들은 무료로 오리엔테이션을 받는다.
③ 전문가와 상담하여 운동 목표를 설정할 수 있다.
④ 종합 건강 평가는 유료로 신청 가능하다.
⑤ 개인 트레이닝을 한 시간 동안 받을 수 있다.

27 Biofin에 관한 다음 안내문의 내용과 일치하는 것은?

How to Use Biofin

Wash your hands before applying this medication. Gently clean the affected skin with a mild or soapless cleanser and pat dry. Apply a thin layer of this medication usually once daily or as directed by your doctor.

Warnings

- Do not apply to the inner lip area or inside the nose/mouth.
- Do not apply to cut, scraped, or sunburned skin.
- Avoid getting this medication in your eyes. If this medication gets into your eyes, flush with large amounts of water.
- Do not share this medication with others.

Tell your doctor if your condition does not improve or if it worsens.

① 감염 부위를 따로 씻지 않아도 된다.
② 가능하면 수시로 얇게 펴 발라야 한다.
③ 햇볕에 탄 화상 치료에 사용할 수 있다.
④ 눈에 닿지 않도록 해야 한다.
⑤ 다른 사람과 같이 사용할 수 있다.

28 다음 글의 밑줄 친 부분 중, 어법상 틀린 것은?

One of the fastest ways for you to overcome any shyness and social anxieties you may feel ① is to ask questions of the other person and then try to understand their true feelings and concerns. While they speak, listen closely to their answers. Ask follow-up questions and check for understanding. Repeat back in your own words what they have said ② to be sure you understand. As coach Lou Holtz says, "Everyone's first question is: Do you care about me?" Listening shows ③ that you do care. Most people are so preoccupied with themselves and the details of their lives ④ which they pay little attention to others. When you do the opposite and empathize with them by trying to understand their concerns, by asking them questions and ⑤ listening to them when they talk, they will like you and want to cooperate with you.

29 다음 글의 밑줄 친 부분 중, 문맥상 낱말의 쓰임이 적절하지 않은 것은? [3점]

Wrapped up in the idea of embracing failure is the related notion of breaking things to make them better—particularly complex things. Often the only way to improve a complex system is to examine its ① limits by forcing it to fail in various ways. Software, among the most complex things we make, is usually tested for quality by employing engineers to systematically find ways to ② crash it. Similarly, one way to troubleshoot a complicated device that's broken is to deliberately force negative results (temporary breaks) in its multiple functions in order to ③ locate the actual dysfunction. Great engineers have a respect for breaking things that sometimes surprises nonengineers, just as scientists have a ④ patience with failures that often puzzles outsiders. But the habit of ⑤ preventing negative results is one of the most essential tricks to gaining success.

*troubleshoot: (고장을) 수리하다 **dysfunction: 기능 장애

30 밑줄 친 it이 가리키는 대상이 나머지 넷과 다른 것은?

Why, in general, do people feel better in sunlight? Perhaps the most obvious answer is that everyone knows that we would be dead without ① it. At the most basic psychological level, ② it makes people feel safer, more confident, and more alive. Another, more technical, answer lies in the amazing discoveries that neuroscientists are revealing about our brains. In the absence of ③ it, our brains start producing melatonin, a hormone that helps to lower body temperature and reduce activity in the brain. This helps us to sleep. Too much of ④ it, however, is thought to play a part in depression, so it's a good thing that sunlight shuts off its production. What's more, ⑤ it appears to raise the levels of serotonin and noradrenalin in the brain, and these are the hormones that make us feel really good. That's why a long, dark winter can be such a drag.

[31~34] 다음 빈칸에 들어갈 말로 가장 적절한 것을 고르시오.

31 While researching animal behavior for her book *Mongoose Watch*, British ethologist Anne Rasa was surprised to discover that when a dwarf mongoose became ill with chronic kidney disease, he was treated differently by his peers. The other mongooses permitted the ill animal to eat much earlier than he normally would have, considering his rank in the mongoose social order. To Rasa's astonishment, the sick mongoose was even allowed to have a bite of the same piece of food that the dominant male was eating—something that would never occur normally. When the ill mongoose lost his ability to climb, the entire group of mongooses gave up their decided preference for sleeping on elevated objects such as boxes. Instead, they all opted to sleep on the floor with their sick friend. These examples show that a 'community' of mongooses has ______________. [3점]

*ethologist: 동물 행동학자

① creativity
② self-control
③ interest
④ respect
⑤ compassion

32 A good memorial should be designed in a way that best helps observers to actually feel what was experienced during the memorialized event. Creating a good memorial, however, does not necessarily ________________________. A good example of such a memorial is "The Soldier and the Nurse." The memorial shows a battlefield ward, but does not include a surgical table or other medical facilities. This conveys a greater sense of the soldier's vulnerability; it better enables viewers to feel the soldier's pain when so little could be done to help him. And just the hint of sympathy in the eyes of the nurse is enough to make the memorial a powerful one. The memorial makes viewers never want to be in the same situation. [3점]

① reflect the spirit of the era
② express the artist's intention
③ have to depict everything in detail
④ require public awareness of its goal
⑤ get favorable comments from observers

33 The first step toward more effective reading is to look quickly at the entirety of the written information before you actually read it. This prepares your mind to take in the information and to think about the particular topic. This is similar to taking a step back and looking at a mountain before you begin to climb it, so that you can choose the best path available. It is also like looking at a map before you get on the highway or start out on your trip. Understanding the whole purpose and flow of the material helps you to piece together and correctly understand each part as you come to it. Naturally, a piece of a jigsaw puzzle makes more sense and fits more easily into place when ______________________.

① you have already seen the whole picture
② you finally finish the border of the puzzle
③ you sort each piece according to its color
④ you see that it has a very distinctive shape
⑤ you face each difficulty with more confidence

34 Contemporary artists have presented their views in lectures, interviews, essays, and a variety of novel formats. E-mails, text and voice messages, and other virtual public forums have all but replaced letters and journals. Many artists have sophisticated websites with blogs, chats and, nowadays, some social media accounts. These new possibilities allow the audience, not just specialists, to be informed and to engage in meaningful dialogues with artists. But there is a potential problem with these exciting electronic platforms. Unlike tangible documents, e-mails and other electronic textual, visual, and audio materials may be, and often are, deleted. Even when they are saved, digital media's endurance over time is still unknown. This raises important questions about ______________________. [3점]

① difficulties in agreeing on a true definition of art
② when contemporary art turns into conventional art
③ whether art should be obligated to provide meaning
④ availability of contemporary art records in the future
⑤ why it is that art and life are consciously linked together

35 다음 글에서 전체 흐름과 관계 없는 문장은?

Events experienced in a state of high emotion are easier to remember. ① A girl involved in a fire may have a vivid memory of something small, such as the pattern on the dress she was wearing at the time. ② Heightened memory is not caused by the emotion of the event itself but by the fact that the brain goes through chemical changes when the shocking event occurs. ③ The relaxation technique helps the brain neutralize the extreme emotions and treat the fearful stimulus just like details at the scene. ④ While people are in a state of extremely high emotion, the brain releases special hormones, which make the nerves exceptionally receptive, enabling the most insignificant details to be recorded. ⑤ The unusual amount of detail included in memories of emotionally intense experiences may account for the feeling that time passes slowly every time the experiences are recalled.

[36~37] 주어진 글 다음에 이어질 글의 순서로 가장 적절한 것을 고르시오.

36

All new parents watch with joy and pride their baby's display of mastery of each new skill — the first words spoken, the first steps taken, the first signs of his or her ability to read or write.

(A) Because of the pleasure they take in the progress, parents may be tempted to hurry their baby into learning too much too soon. But rushing development can cause children to become overly anxious and performance-oriented.

(B) On the other hand, if children are denied plenty of age-appropriate guided activities combined with praise from a parent, they may lose their natural curiosity and courage.

(C) If parents actively encourage a baby to write or draw too soon, for example, the baby may try very hard to please them and then suffer feelings of failure when unable even to hold the pencil properly.

① (A) — (C) — (B) ② (B) — (A) — (C)
③ (B) — (C) — (A) ④ (C) — (A) — (B)
⑤ (C) — (B) — (A)

37

Plants whose tender parts would be killed by extreme cold often survive if they are insulated from a severe climate by an air-filled snow blanket.

(A) Besides, a snow cover protects untold numbers of insects, worms, snails and many other small creatures in the soil. Winter air temperatures can easily plunge low enough to kill many of the organisms living just below the soil's surface.

(B) Snow, however, prevents this. The layer of air that is preserved between the surface of the soil and the base of the snowfall acts as an insulator, preserving enough warmth to stop the creatures beneath from freezing.

(C) If snowfall covers a boxwood plant, for example, a gardener may be tempted to knock it off. However, it's wiser to leave a blanket of snow on boxwood; otherwise, the extreme temperatures of the air and wind can easily kill it.

*boxwood: 회양목(상록 활엽 관목의 일종)

① (A) — (C) — (B) ② (B) — (A) — (C)
③ (B) — (C) — (A) ④ (C) — (A) — (B)
⑤ (C) — (B) — (A)

[38~39] 글의 흐름으로 보아, 주어진 문장이 들어가기에 가장 적절한 곳을 고르시오.

38

Unfortunately, people and nature united to take precious water away from the Everglades.

The Everglades region is a subtropical wetland featuring vast sawgrass marshlands found only in southern Florida. Water is vital to this unique environment. (①) The region was formed over thousands of years of flooding from Lake Okeechobee. (②) These annual floods always provided the marsh with the fresh water needed to support its wide variety of plants and animals. (③) For example, the Miami, Little, and New rivers all remove a lot of water from the area. (④) But worse are the dams and canals that were built last century, as they prevent annual flooding. Without this flooding, the Everglades cannot survive. (⑤) Reclamation and restoration projects have begun in the hope of saving this unique ecosystem.

*sawgrass: (식물) 참억새류 **reclamation: 개간

39

This was such a severe restriction that it became common for the athlete who drew the inside lane for the final (by being the slowest qualifier on times) not to take part in the final in indoor championships.

Have you ever wondered whether it's best to have an inside or an outside lane in track races like the 200 m where you have to sprint around the bend? (①) Athletes have strong preferences. (②) Tall runners find it harder to get round the tighter curve of the inside lane than that of the gentle outer lanes. (③) The situation is even more extreme when sprinters race indoors where the track is only 200 m around, so the bends are far tighter and the lanes are reduced in width from 1.22 m to 1 m. (④) This was because there was so much less chance of winning from the inside and a considerable risk of injury. (⑤) As a result, this event has largely disappeared from the indoor championship list.

*qualifier: 예선 통과자

40 다음 글의 내용을 한 문장으로 요약하고자 한다. 빈칸 (A), (B)에 들어갈 말로 가장 적절한 것은? [3점]

One study examined how rats respond to food and location. First, researchers tested the preference of the chamber among rats. The rats were free to choose their locale, and there was no food in either chamber. And then, the rats, which were not hungry at the time of the experiments, were divided into two groups. The first was given high-sweetened cereals in its less-favored chamber. The second group was fed standard food in the chamber it preferred. Next, the second group was offered a high-calorie, high-fat snack in its less-preferred chamber, while the first group got standard food in its preferred locale. Then the initial chamber preference test was repeated. Again the rats were free to choose their locale, and again there was no food in either chamber. The findings were clear: Regardless of their previous choices, both groups of rats had learned to choose the chamber where they had eaten either sweetened cereals or high-fat snacks.

↓

The exposure to foods high in sugar or fat conditioned rats in the experiment to ____(A)____ foods with location and ____(B)____ the place where that exposure had occurred.

	(A)		(B)
①	confuse	……	prefer
②	confuse	……	avoid
③	compare	……	remember
④	associate	……	prefer
⑤	associate	……	avoid

[41~42] 다음 글을 읽고, 물음에 답하시오.

There is a famous joke on dieting, "If I just see food, I gain weight." A well-respected teacher of weight control said that there is actually some truth to this statement. She explained that the emotion of fear leads to a chemical reaction in the body which activates the ____________ process. One of the byproducts of this reaction is to build fat, which is a food reserve. Fat is used by the body for survival if it does not have another source of nutrition. People who are worried about gaining weight often become anxious when surrounded by mouthwatering food, as they feel guilt about breaking their diet and fear failing. This anxiety stimulates the bodily process that builds fat. That is why it seems that some people can never lose weight — worrying about losing weight is precisely the trigger that keeps the weight on!

In our natural state, we will not view food as a threat, but if we have been on many diets that haven't worked, we'll see it as a symbol of temptation, testing, and failure. There are many people who eat plenty of enjoyable food, including an occasional rich delicacy, and are in perfect health and look good. The secret is to not let food become a bugaboo, a dark monster that runs our life.

41 윗글의 제목으로 가장 적절한 것은?

① Eat Less and Move More Each Day
② Remember to Stop Before You're Full
③ A Dieting Secret: Let Food Be Your Friend!
④ Persistence: A Keyword of Successful Dieting
⑤ Eat with Your Intellect, Not with Your Senses

42 윗글의 빈칸에 들어갈 말로 가장 적절한 것은? [3점]

① anti-aging
② stress-driven
③ diet-centered
④ self-protecting
⑤ weight-losing

[43~45] 다음 글을 읽고, 물음에 답하시오.

(A)

Old Joe was a farmer with a neighbor who lived across from him for years and years. Joe and his neighbor had only each other. Often the words they spoke would be the only words they said all day, until one afternoon when they spied a calf outside the window. The neighbor said "Hey, look at my calf out there." Joe replied "Any fool can see from the markings that the calf is mine." They began to argue until cruel words ended in silence.

(B)

The carpenter replied, "I think I can do a job that will make you happy." (a) He and Joe agreed that the next day, the carpenter would take the wood and build a fence while Joe spent the day in town. The next day when Joe came back home, he saw what the carpenter had done. Instead of a fence, (b) he had built a bridge across the creek. Furious, Joe started to climb down to give the carpenter a piece of his mind.

(C)

But before he could meet the carpenter, the neighbor crossed the bridge and gave him a big hug. "Joe, you are a bigger man than I am. I'd never have had the courage to build a bridge. Can you forgive me?" Joe hugged him back and whispered, "Nothing to forgive," and glanced at the carpenter, who winked and smiled at (c) him. Joe asked the carpenter to stay around, but he said (d) he had other work to do.

(D)

Months turned into years, but words were never spoken. One day a traveling carpenter knocked on Joe's door. He needed work so Joe invited him in. Joe said, "See that creek over there? My damned fool neighbor built it.—He took a plow, dug a ditch and flooded it, just to upset me." (e) He nodded. Joe said, "I want you to build fence—a really high one—so I never have to look at this fool again."

43 주어진 글 (A)에 이어질 내용을 순서에 맞게 배열한 것으로 가장 적절한 것은?

① (B) — (D) — (C)　② (C) — (B) — (D)
③ (C) — (D) — (B)　④ (D) — (B) — (C)
⑤ (D) — (C) — (B)

44 밑줄 친 (a)~(e) 중에서 가리키는 대상이 나머지 넷과 다른 것은?

① (a)　② (b)　③ (c)　④ (d)　⑤ (e)

45 윗글에 관한 내용으로 적절하지 않은 것은?

① Joe는 유일한 이웃과 송아지 때문에 싸웠다.
② 목수는 Joe가 외출한 동안 울타리를 만들기로 했다.
③ 목수는 Joe와 이웃이 먼저 사과하자 받아들였다.
④ Joe와 이웃은 몇 년 동안 서로 말을 하지 않았다.
⑤ Joe는 이웃과의 사이에 높은 울타리를 세우려고 했다.

: AFTER TESTING

종료 시 분
소요시간 분

학습 마무리

1 채점하기 | 정답 및 해설 p.90
주의 틀린 문제를 다시 풀 수 있도록 정답을 본문에 표기하지 마세요.
2 등급 확인
3 틀린 유형 확인 후 전략 적용 복습 및 해설지 확인

How to Review

1 틀린 문제와 ✓ 표시한 문제는 다시 풀고 해설 확인하기
2 내가 표시한 정답 근거가 해설과 일치하는지 확인하기
3 잘 모르는 부분으로 표시한 내용은 해설을 통해 완전히 이해하기
4 어휘 외우기 (어휘 목록 다운로드 www.cedubook.com)
5 다음 회에 개선할 점 정리하기 (시간 엄수, 취약 유형 보완 등)

POWER UP!

고난도 모의고사 13

: BEFORE TESTING

시작 시 분

학습 목표

1 **제한시간** (OMR 마킹시간 포함) ☐ 40분 ☐ 45분
2 **어휘예습** ☐ 해당 없음 ☐ 완료
3 **문제풀이순서** ☐ 순서대로 ☐ 2점 → 3점 ☐ 기타 ....
4 **기타 목표** ....

Check Point

1 **정답 근거** *e.g.* 밑줄 긋기
2 **잘 모르는 부분** *e.g.* 〈 〉 또는 ? 표시
3 **자신 없는 문제** *e.g.* 문제 번호에 ✓표시

18 다음 글의 목적으로 가장 적절한 것은?

Dear Samantha Park,

Thank you for your submission to the Eco Festival's Sustainable Art Contest. Each year, we receive hundreds of submissions from amateur artists and professionals alike, but few display the talent and care that your piece clearly shows. Unfortunately, in the interest of promoting sustainability and environment awareness, we must remain strict in our enforcement of the contest guidelines. One of these states that entries must use at least 90% recycled content, whether that be metals, plastic, glass, or another type of material. After careful consideration, our judges have ruled that your submission does not meet this qualification requirement. Your piece will be returned to you by mail sometime during the next week. Thank you for your participation, and we wish you the best of luck in your career as an artist.

Sincerely,
Kate Ling, Festival Organizer

① 대회에 참가해준 데 대해 감사하려고
② 대회 출품작의 일괄 반환을 요청하려고
③ 대회 출품작이 접수되었는지 확인하려고
④ 대회 참가를 위한 주요 규정을 설명하려고
⑤ 출품작이 자격 기준에 미치지 못함을 통보하려고

19 다음 글에 드러난 Jennifer의 심경 변화로 가장 적절한 것은?

Jennifer stopped writing and listened to a dull, scraping noise that came from somewhere deep inside the house. "Hello," she called. "Is anybody there?" No one answered her. Slowly, quietly, she stood and started down the steps. A pool of black swirled in front of her. Bam! The basement door slammed shut and a rush of cool air swept past her. She felt her hands shaking. Jennifer tiptoed down the last few steps, and darted into her father's bedroom. She grabbed his heavy flashlight, turned it on, and inched toward the kitchen doorway. "Oh! You scared me," said her dad, jumping back as he turned on the lights. "I scared you?!" said Jennifer, her hands shaking. "Sorry honey. My key wouldn't work tonight. And since the front of the house was dark, I thought that you weren't home. I forced a basement window open and crawled in." "Next time," said Jennifer with a sigh of relief. "Just ring the doorbell."

① frightened → relieved
② angry → ashamed
③ anxious → pleased
④ furious → satisfied
⑤ worried → confident

20 다음 글에서 필자가 주장하는 바로 가장 적절한 것은?

Companies that take an outcome-driven approach to innovation recognize that once an outcome is satisfied, it no longer represents a chance for improvement. Messages that continue to advertise one strength of a product will lose their impact on customers. This means that a company's messaging must adapt over time to remain effective. Being "stronger than dirt" may be a good message for a laundry detergent when that feature represents a unique advantage, but once all available products are "stronger than dirt," the message becomes meaningless. It fails to connect any other advantages the product may have with other outcomes and, therefore, no longer communicates the true value of the product. Because value changes, innovation must be dynamic—and so must messaging. Holding on to a message that is no longer relevant will only slow sales and growth.

① 제품 홍보 메시지는 계속해서 바뀌어야 한다.
② 고객이 원하는 것이 무엇인지 꾸준히 조사해야 한다.
③ 고객 유출을 막기 위해 끊임없이 품질을 개선해야 한다.
④ 상업 광고는 소비자의 이성보다 감성에 호소해야 한다.
⑤ 홍보 메시지는 타사 제품과의 차별점을 보여줘야 한다.

21 밑줄 친 a nutritional catch-22가 다음 글에서 의미하는 바로 가장 적절한 것은?

Highly-motivated dieters often are trapped in a nutritional catch-22. In recent lab studies, college students who performed self-control tasks found themselves having higher desires for sweet foods. When allowed to snack during the next task, those who had previously exerted self-control ate more sweet snacks, but not other (salty) snacks. If you've ever been on a diet and found yourself unable to escape those intrusive cravings for chocolate or ice cream, this is more than a matter of repressed desires coming back to haunt you. Sweet food becomes especially hard to resist because self-control depletes the glucose in the bloodstream. In order not to eat, you need willpower, but to have willpower, you need to eat. There is a sound physiological basis. The body "knows" that it has depleted the glucose in its bloodstream by exerting self-control, and it also seems to know that sweet-tasting foods are typically the fastest way to get an infusion of energy-rich glucose.

① going on a diet without losing weight
② using willpower in order to quit a diet
③ resisting the temptation to eat and diet
④ having to crave sweet food in order not to eat
⑤ maintaining a diet with proper intake of nutrition

22 다음 글의 요지로 가장 적절한 것은?

We easily slip into the idea that the things around us were discovered, or at least basically adapted, by our own society. Yet if you think for a moment, you will find that almost everything was invented in other civilizations. England is a particularly obvious example of this because, being part of a small island near a great continent, and being a trading and imperial nation, it has sucked in almost all of its culture from abroad. There is scarcely anything, in music, painting, architecture, science and knowledge, up to the eighteenth century at least, that was not largely the result of borrowings. The same would be true if we went to any other part of the world, where many of the characteristically 'local' things were imported from elsewhere. One civilization is a basket of foreign imports. We borrow, imitate, trade and steal and then conveniently forget.

① 경제적 토대 없이 문명의 발전은 불가능하다.
② 모든 문명은 서로 영향을 주고받으며 형성된다.
③ 근대의 활발한 문명 교류가 세계화를 이루어냈다.
④ 지리적 환경의 차이가 문명 간의 차이를 결정짓는다.
⑤ 한 문명은 다른 문명과의 경쟁과 협력 속에서 존속한다.

23 다음 글의 주제로 가장 적절한 것은?

Some argue that expenditures on education generate no direct increase in productivity or growth, but this ignores the many immediate returns to education spending that do occur in society. Especially at the higher education level but also through agricultural institutes, vocational education, and other connections to lower levels of education, spending potentially contributes to relatively rapid returns from the generation and diffusion of knowledge throughout society. Education spending can also improve a country's economic performance fairly quickly by targeting lifelong learning, an element of attainment not generally captured by average years of education. In addition, much education investment replaces workers who retire or die with new workers; the new workers may not add years of experience to the population, but they do embody more recent knowledge and technology, which can translate into a higher GDP.

① transition from elite education to mass education
② impact of education spending on economic growth
③ limitations of traditional education in modern society
④ ways to reduce unemployment rates through education
⑤ necessity of encouraging lifelong education for retirees

24 다음 글의 제목으로 가장 적절한 것은?

Traditionally, forgetting has been regarded as a passive decay over time of the information recorded and stored in the brain. But while some memories may simply fade away like ink on paper exposed to sunlight, recent research suggests that forgetting is often more intentional, with erasure arranged by elaborate cellular and molecular mechanisms. And forgetfulness is not necessarily a sign of a faulty memory. In fact, it's been shown over and over in computational models and also in animal work that an intelligent memory system needs forgetting. Far from signifying failure, forgetting may be the brain's frontline strategy in processing incoming information. Forgetting is essential, because the biological goal of the brain's memory system is not preserving information, but rather helping the brain make sound decisions.

① Forgetting Relaxes the Mind More
② What Can Forgetfulness Be a Sign of?
③ To Remember Is the Mother of All Wisdom
④ Forgetting: Proper Functioning of the Brain
⑤ Science Behind Forgetting and How to Overcome It

25 다음 도표의 내용과 일치하지 않는 것은?

Water Consumption in Britain, USA, and Australia, 2020

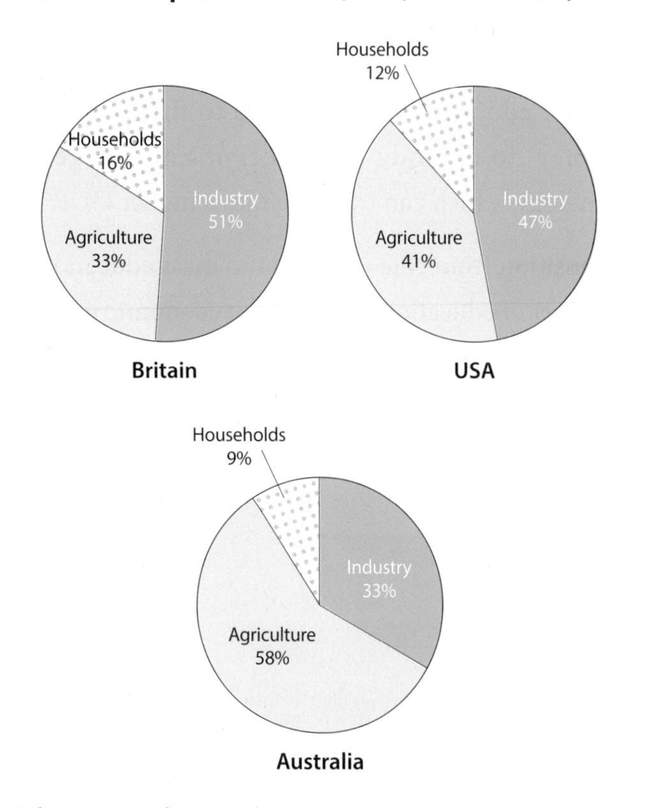

These pie charts compare water usage in Britain, the USA, and Australia in the year 2020. ① In both the USA and Britain, about 50% of total water was consumed by the industrial sector, the biggest consumer of water by a substantial margin over other sectors in those countries. ② In Australia, on the other hand, the biggest water consumer was agriculture, which took more than 50% of the total share. ③ Agriculture was the second biggest consumer in the USA, taking about two fifths of the total, while in Britain the same sector took just about a third. ④ In Australia, a third was consumed by industry. ⑤ Households consumed the least water in all three countries; 16% in Britain was 4%p less than that in the USA and 7%p more than in Australia.

26 Marin Marais에 관한 다음 글의 내용과 일치하지 않는 것은?

Marin Marais was the top bass viol player in turn-of-the-seventeenth-century France. Marais spent his entire life in Paris. Little is known of his childhood other than his having studied with Sainte-Colombe, the most prominent violist and teacher at the time. In 1679, he became the "Regular Violist for the King," a position he held until his retirement in 1725. Marais also studied composition with Lully and subsequently worked with him throughout his career as a violist in his ensemble. Lully probably encouraged Marais to compose his four operas, *Alcide* (1693), *Ariane et Bacchus* (1696), *Alcione* (1706), and *Sémélé* (1709). All four are rather typical five-act tragedies very much in Lully's style, and were considerably successful, *Alcione* being staged as late as 1771. It is as the greatest and most important composer for the bass viol, however, that Marais is remembered today.

*viol: 비올(바이올린과 비슷한 초기 현악기)

① 17세기 전환기의 프랑스 음악가이다.
② 어릴 때 Sainte-Colombe의 지도를 받았다.
③ Lully의 합주단에서 작곡가로 일했다.
④ 그가 작곡한 오페라는 모두 비극이었다.
⑤ 베이스 비올 음악의 최고의 작곡가였다.

27 공항 분실물 보관소 이용에 관한 다음 안내문의 내용과 일치하지 않는 것은?

Lost and Found

The Tucson International Airport Lost and Found Office is located in the Main Terminal on the baggage claim level.

- Items found in the airport terminal, parking garage or airport parking lots are stored securely for 30 days before disposition.
- For items lost or left on an airplane, please contact your airline.

How Are Found Items Claimed and Returned?

You may arrange for the return of items by:

- On-site pickup: If you properly identify items, you may pick them up during normal business hours, Monday through Friday, 9 a.m. – 4 p.m. You may pre-arrange after-hours pickup by calling (520) 573-8156 during business hours.
- U.S. mail: The Lost and Found Office can return small items via U.S. mail if you pay for the shipping cost.

① 공항 터미널에서 발견된 분실물은 30일간 보관된다.
② 기내에서 분실한 물품은 해당 항공사에 연락해야 한다.
③ 보관소의 근무시간은 평일 오전 9시부터 오후 4시까지이다.
④ 보관소 근무 시간 외에는 분실물을 직접 찾아갈 수 없다.
⑤ 배송료를 부담하면 우편으로 물건을 돌려받을 수 있다.

28 자원봉사자 모집에 관한 다음 안내문의 내용과 일치하는 것은?

Volunteers Needed

We have a number of ways for you to partner with us in caring for those we serve at CHS (Children's Home Society).

How to volunteer at CHS:

FOR GROUPS:

- Landscaping, painting, etc. – keep our facility safe and beautiful

FOR INDIVIDUALS:

- Cooking: help with meal preparation and clean-up
- Flea market: tag, sort, and sell at events
- Special events: register to be contacted for specific needs as they arise

For tutoring:

Please fill out the application form and mail it to us. Once your application has been processed, you will be asked to attend a required orientation and training.

Thank you for your interest in helping us change lives at CHS!

① 개인 봉사자는 환경미화 작업에 참여한다.
② 단체 봉사자는 식사 준비와 정리를 돕는다.
③ 벼룩시장에서 판매할 물품을 수집하는 일을 돕는다.
④ 특별 행사를 위한 봉사는 전화로 신청이 가능하다.
⑤ 개인교사 업무를 위해서는 별도의 교육을 받아야 한다.

29 다음 글의 밑줄 친 부분 중, 어법상 틀린 것은? [3점]

There is a rather large difference between the concepts of empathy and sympathy, with the latter ① being a rather well-known word that people use. ② Similar as they may appear, they have a very distinct meaning and usage. According to Chloe Chong, a social media expert, the feeling of sympathy emerges from the recognition that another person is suffering, in contrast to empathy, ③ where the other person's pain or suffering is felt. Sympathy requires giving unasked advice or being told what to do. Empathy requires active listening. In this case, empathy means the ability to feel what it's ④ likely to be in someone else's shoes. Sympathy's favorite expression is "poor you." It creates a sense of pity over the plight of the person. Empathy's favorite expression is "I can understand how it feels. It must be really hard." This helps a person to feel ⑤ heard.

30 다음 글의 밑줄 친 부분 중, 문맥상 낱말의 쓰임이 적절하지 않은 것은? [3점]

Certain types of news are significantly overreported, and others are significantly underreported. This ① imbalance leads to major problems such as distortion of rational public policy. But it is reason to be ② optimistic. Once you realize you're being brainwashed to believe that things are worse than they are, you can, with a little courage, step out into the sunshine. How does the deception take place? The problem starts with a deep human ③ psychological response. We're wired to react more strongly to ④ dramatic stories than to abstract facts. One can readily imagine possible historical and evolutionary reasons why this might be so. The news that an invader has just set fire to a hut in your village demands immediate response. Genes promoting ⑤ agitation in such circumstances would have burned up long ago. Although our village is now global, we still instinctively react the same way.

*brainwash: 세뇌하다

[31~34] 다음 빈칸에 들어갈 말로 가장 적절한 것을 고르시오.

31 Today most of us believe that artistic creativity is spontaneous, not overly planned or organized. We like to think of our artists as strong individualists, working in isolation, not influenced by the prevailing ideas taught in art schools or by old-fashioned museum curators. But like so much about our contemporary creativity myths, this idea only emerged in the 19th century. In the second half of the 20th century, the idea that the artist is a person who rejects convention took an even stronger hold on the popular consciousness. Ironically, at the same time, artists were entering art schools in increasingly large numbers to be trained in the conventions of the art world. In the United States today, a greater proportion of artists have an MFA degree than at any other time in history. Yet few of us are aware of the growing influence of formal schooling in fine art. In general, when the facts clash with our creativity myths, the facts are ______________. [3점]

*curator: 큐레이터(박물관 · 미술관 등의 전시 책임자)
**MFA: 예술 석사(Master of Fine Arts)

① revealed
② ignored
③ transformed
④ preserved
⑤ acknowledged

32 Whether we think of ourselves as ______________ ______________ is important in understanding consumer choice. In Western cultures, consumer choice is viewed as an act of self-expression: uniqueness is desirable and consumption is a way to represent yourself to the outside world, so we vary our purchases in an attempt to gain a sense of "specialness." In behavioral economics, this is called diversification bias. When this choice is an act of self-expression, it becomes extremely important for the individual, and the psychological impact of either lack of choice or failed choice is larger, which leads to strategies such as variety-seeking. However, in cultures that emphasize groups over individuals, consumer choice is often an interpersonal task, which means the success or failure of making a decision that portrays oneself in the most favorable light is not as big a concern. Subsequently, recent research has shown that the diversification bias is weaker in these cultural contexts. [3점]

① entirely rational beings or not
② fashion-conscious or unconscious
③ aware of the impacts of marketing
④ a member of the upper class or lower class
⑤ separate individuals or connected with others

33
The urge to ______________________ is as old as music itself. Plato's concern with the potential moral damage to be found in types of music marks one of the earliest recorded examples. "The overseers," Plato is recorded as saying, "must constantly be watchful against innovation in music counter to the established order, and to the best of their power guard against it." In seventeenth-century England, the performance of unlicensed ballads could lead to fines or imprisonment, while in nineteenth-century Italy the scripts of all operas were subject to a review process. Throughout human history, music has been the source of terror and the object of repression. Every century on every continent has seen those in authority—whether as church or as state—use their powers to silence certain sounds or performers.

① use music to manipulate others
② censor music for fear of its effects
③ surprise people with unheard-of melodies
④ control those with unusual musical ability
⑤ soothe ourselves with music when depressed

34 Philosophers have for centuries debated the nature of "reality," and whether the world we experience is real or an illusion. But modern neuroscience teaches us that all our perceptions must be considered illusions. That's because we perceive the world only indirectly, by processing and interpreting the raw data of our senses. Our unconscious processing creates a model of the world. For example, when you look around, you have the feeling that you are looking into a three-dimensional space. But you don't directly sense those three dimensions. Instead, your brain reads a flat, two-dimensional array of data from your retinas and creates the sensation of three dimensions. Your unconscious mind is so good at processing images that if you were fitted with glasses that turn the images in your eyes upside down, after a short while you would see things right side up again. If the glasses were then removed, you would see the world upside down again, but just for a while. Therefore, when we say, "I see a chair," what we really mean is that ______________________.
[3점]

① there is a physical object of a chair before us
② our brain has created a mental model of a chair
③ all we can see is the light reflected from the chair
④ we can only see what's visible from where we're standing
⑤ the chair is the objective reference, and 'I' is the observer

35 다음 글에서 전체 흐름과 관계 없는 문장은?

Linguistics makes a distinction between the surface structure of a sentence (the way the sentence is spoken or written) and the deep structure of a sentence (the way the sentence is to be understood). ① For instance, the surface structure of the sentence "Jane talked to the doctor on Tuesday" has one clear meaning, or deep structure. ② But the sentence "Jane hit the man with a bat" can either mean that Jane hit a man who was holding a bat, or that she used a bat to hit a man. ③ Good writers know that if the same idea can be expressed in a simple way or a complex way, the simple way is better, to avoid ambiguity. ④ The sentence has two deep structures, but you probably automatically understood the sentence to mean just one or the other. ⑤ Because you automatically processed that particular meaning, you probably didn't even consider the other meaning until we showed it to you.

[36~37] 주어진 글 다음에 이어질 글의 순서로 가장 적절한 것을 고르시오.

36

Since animals lose body heat through surfaces, a higher surface-to-volume ratio could result in greater loss of body heat. This is why smaller animals lose more body heat.

(A) Their faster metabolic rate means that they do not live as long. Small animals tend to have shorter lives than large animals, and warm-blooded animals shorter lives than cold-blooded animals.

(B) Conversely, large animals can maintain warm bodies with less effort, which allows them to live longer lives. Heart failure will occur much later for the slower-beating heart of the larger animal.

(C) As a result, a mouse or a hummingbird must burn a lot of calories to maintain a constant body temperature. This is the main reason that, among warm-blooded animals, metabolic rate declines with increasing body size. Small mammals have evolved to produce relatively more body heat.

*surface-to-volume ratio: 표면적 대 부피의 비율
**metabolic: 물질대사의

① (A) — (C) — (B)
② (B) — (A) — (C)
③ (B) — (C) — (A)
④ (C) — (A) — (B)
⑤ (C) — (B) — (A)

37

> Evaporation occurs anywhere there is water, from lakes and rivers to storm drains and birdbaths. All of this warm water vapor begins to rise, joining billions of other water molecules in a dizzying ascent into the troposphere.

(A) Not all the precipitation reaches the ground, however; some of it evaporates directly back into the atmosphere on its way down. What's left finally reaches the ground in the form of rain, snow, hail, or sleet, sometimes ruining picnics or closing schools in the process.

(B) Eventually the vapor reaches cooler layers and condenses around small particles of dust, pollen, or pollution. As the condensation process continues, the droplets become too big for the wind to support, and they begin a plunge toward the surface.

(C) If the precipitation falls in the ocean, the cycle is ready to begin again right away, and that's exactly what happens to the majority of raindrops and snowflakes. After all, oceans cover more than 70 percent of the earth's surface, making them a big target.

*troposphere: 대류권

① (A) — (C) — (B)　② (B) — (A) — (C)
③ (B) — (C) — (A)　④ (C) — (A) — (B)
⑤ (C) — (B) — (A)

[38~39] 글의 흐름으로 보아, 주어진 문장이 들어가기에 가장 적절한 곳을 고르시오.

38

> The plants, as a precaution, took certain steps to protect their seeds from the greed of their consumers.

Sweetness has proved to be a force in evolution. (①) By covering their seeds in sugar and nutritious flesh, fruiting plants such as the apple hit on an ingenious way of exploiting the mammalian sweet tooth. (②) In exchange for fructose, the animals provide the seeds with transportation, allowing the plant to expand its range. (③) As parties to this grand co-evolutionary bargain, animals with the strongest inclination for sweetness and plants offering the biggest, sweetest fruits prospered together and multiplied, evolving into the species we see, and are, today. (④) They held off on developing sweetness and color until the seeds had matured completely; before then, fruits tend to be inconspicuously green and unpalatable. (⑤) In some cases, like the apple's, the plants developed poisons in their seeds to ensure that only the sweet flesh is consumed. [3점]

*fructose: 과당

39

The smallpox vaccine was a special case and later vaccines worked in a different way, which meant other scientists could not use the same method as Jenner.

Edward Jenner's discovery of a smallpox vaccination in 1796 was very important for the prevention of smallpox. (①) Before this, some people had tried the method of inoculation—exposing themselves to mild cases of smallpox to avoid the disease, but nobody had made the link between milder forms of pox and a resistance to smallpox. (②) Jenner's discovery was picked up by the British government who offered the vaccination to everybody for free and eventually made it compulsory, and many lives were saved as a result. (③) Jenner's work also showed that vaccination could succeed, which inspired other scientists. (④) However, it was not especially important for preventing diseases other than smallpox. (⑤) This is because Jenner did not understand how the vaccine worked, and therefore the theory could not be applied to other diseases.

*smallpox: 천연두 **inoculation: (예방) 접종

40 다음 글의 내용을 한 문장으로 요약하고자 한다. 빈칸 (A), (B)에 들어갈 말로 가장 적절한 것은?

In 1990, Elizabeth Newton at Stanford University invited her peers in college to participate in a study. Each student was assigned one of two roles: "tapper" or "listener." The tappers were given a list of twenty-five popular tunes, such as "Happy Birthday to You" and "Jingle Bells." They had to tap out the tune with their fingers on a table, and the listeners had to guess the song. They were then asked to guess what percentage of listeners would be able to guess the song they had tapped. The tappers estimated that on average 50 percent of the listeners would guess the song they were listening to. In reality, participants who listened to their tapping could only guess 2.5 percent of the songs. Why? When they were tapping, they were hearing the song in their head. But they couldn't know that all the listeners were hearing was a bunch of disconnected taps.

According to the experiment, once tappers had been given the knowledge of a song, they couldn't ___(A)___ that the listeners would ___(B)___ that knowledge.

	(A)		(B)
①	imagine	……	utilize
②	imagine	……	lack
③	believe	……	expand
④	ignore	……	utilize
⑤	ignore	……	lack

[41~42] 다음 글을 읽고, 물음에 답하시오.

In the wider sense, a gift is not just a present but can be many things done to please or impress another. Whatever the gift, it has several elements. There is the (a) <u>external</u> 'material' element — anything from food to a poem, from a victorious battle to a new theory in mathematics. Then behind this there is the 'spirit' of the gift, which is the symbolic relationship it represents. The way of giving and receiving and the appreciation expressed in the counter-gift all express a (b) <u>social</u> relation. They allow the individual to show respect, express his or her personality, and win esteem.

The pursuit of scientific knowledge can be seen as a giant gift-giving network. What is presented to others in the network is more than mere material things. A scientist may discover a new fact or theory that she presents to her colleagues. Part of the scientist's spirit is invested in the theory. Furthermore, the gift tends to set up the obligation to reciprocate, with new knowledge building on earlier findings. Hence each scientific discovery is (c) <u>accidental</u>, not merely because it opens up diverse new understandings, but because it puts an obligation on others to give something back.

The gift should not be too (d) <u>calculating</u>. If scientists are constantly thinking of what would 'pay off' quickly, the kind of fundamental science which requires real risks and long-term effort would never be undertaken. Most significant science is fairly crazy, following hunches for years, struggling for very small rewards and forgoing shortcuts and short-term gains. For whom does the scientist do such (e) <u>unprofitable</u> work? For others — a small group of friends and colleagues, teachers and pupils, a society which will honor his name — for posterity, but always as a gift to the other.

*hunch: 예감 **forgo: 포기하다

41 윗글의 제목으로 가장 적절한 것은?

① The Ethics of Gift-Giving: Give Without Rewards
② Our Pursuit of Scientific Knowledge Will Never End
③ The Consequences of Taking Shortcuts in Gift-giving
④ Why Benefits of Science Are Important in the Modern World
⑤ The Principle of Gift-Giving in the Quest for Scientific Knowledge

42 밑줄 친 (a)~(e) 중에서 문맥상 낱말의 쓰임이 적절하지 <u>않은</u> 것은? [3점]

① (a) ② (b) ③ (c) ④ (d) ⑤ (e)

[43~45] 다음 글을 읽고, 물음에 답하시오.

(A)

In November 1995, Emily the Cow stood in a line of a New England slaughterhouse, awaiting her turn to pass through the doors to the kill floor. When workers at the slaughter facility went on a break, Emily managed to jump over a five-foot fence and ran for her life. She fled through the woods and a group of surprised slaughterhouse workers chased her, but to no avail. "This is one of the quickest cows I have ever seen," one employee told a reporter.

(B)

Meg brought her to live in a sanctuary at Peace Abbey on Christmas Eve. Soon the news of Emily the Cow spread across the country and the globe. (a) She became a national celebrity and folk hero, and visitors from all over the world who admired her bravery came to see her. (b) She inspired many to embark on the road to vegetarianism and soon became a representative of animal rights and vegetarianism.

(C)

When Meg Randa read the story in a local newspaper, she brainstormed on how she could save Emily from being caught. Meg decided to place a call to the owner of the slaughterhouse and said she wanted to resolve the situation and to provide a place for (c) her to live. The owner, Frank Arena, at first offered her the cow for $350. At the urging of his granddaughter Angela, however, he agreed to sell the $500 cow for just one dollar to (d) her.

(D)

For forty frigid days and nights, Emily hid from her pursuers in the wooded areas of Hopkinton, Massachusetts, a small rural town. And though the owner of the slaughterhouse from which Emily escaped was determined to capture her, the locals were determined to aid (e) her in her flight to freedom. People hid her in their backyards and fed her. In a short period, Emily gained popularity, and her story made the headlines in local newspapers.

43 주어진 글 (A)에 이어질 내용을 순서에 맞게 배열한 것으로 가장 적절한 것은?

① (B) — (D) — (C)
② (C) — (B) — (D)
③ (C) — (D) — (B)
④ (D) — (B) — (C)
⑤ (D) — (C) — (B)

44 밑줄 친 (a)~(e) 중에서 가리키는 대상이 나머지 넷과 다른 것은?

① (a) ② (b) ③ (c) ④ (d) ⑤ (e)

45 윗글에 관한 내용으로 적절하지 않은 것은?

① Emily는 도축장 직원들이 쉬고 있는 시간에 도망쳤다.
② 도축장 직원들은 Emily를 쫓아갔지만 잡지 못했다.
③ Emily는 채식주의의 상징적 존재가 되었다.
④ Meg은 Emily를 시세보다 150달러 싸게 샀다.
⑤ Emily의 도주 기사가 지역 신문에 실렸다.

: AFTER TESTING

종료 시 분

소요시간 분

학습 마무리

1 채점하기 | 정답 및 해설 p.98
주의 틀린 문제를 다시 풀 수 있도록 정답을 본문에 표기하지 마세요.
2 등급 확인
3 틀린 유형 확인 후 전략 적용 복습 및 해설지 확인

How to Review

1 틀린 문제와 ✓ 표시한 문제는 다시 풀고 해설 확인하기
2 내가 표시한 정답 근거가 해설과 일치하는지 확인하기
3 잘 모르는 부분으로 표시한 내용은 해설을 통해 완전히 이해하기
4 어휘 외우기 (어휘 목록 다운로드 www.cedubook.com)
5 다음 회에 개선할 점 정리하기 (시간 엄수, 취약 유형 보완 등)

고난도 모의고사

14

: BEFORE TESTING

시작 시 분

학습 목표

1 **제한시간** (OMR 마킹시간 포함) ☐ 40분 ☐ 45분
2 **어휘예습** ☐ 해당 없음 ☐ 완료
3 **문제풀이순서** ☐ 순서대로 ☐ 2점 → 3점 ☐ 기타
4 **기타 목표**

Check Point

1 **정답 근거** *e.g.* 밑줄 긋기
2 **잘 모르는 부분** *e.g.* 〈 〉 또는 ? 표시
3 **자신 없는 문제** *e.g.* 문제 번호에 ✓표시

18 다음 글의 목적으로 가장 적절한 것은?

To Whom It May Concern,

Let me begin by praising the efforts of the Pathway and River Cleanup Committee. By organizing a yearly cleanup event, your organization has removed loads of garbage and waste from our city's river banks. As a long-time resident, I can confidently say that the difference you have made is huge. That being said, I have some concerns about the safety of the volunteers, especially the younger ones. As a first-time volunteer, I was quite shocked to see a number of potentially dangerous activities. Volunteers as young as ten or eleven were picking up broken glass and other dangerous objects with bare hands, while older members carried heavy items up steep slopes on unstable ground. It seems like only a matter of time until someone gets seriously injured. Please take this into consideration when organizing next year's cleanup.

Sincerely,
Brian Spencer

① 효율적인 대청소 계획을 제안하려고
② 하천 제방 대청소 노력에 감사하려고
③ 자원봉사자가 해야 할 봉사 내용을 문의하려고
④ 지역 주민에게 제방 대청소 참여를 호소하려고
⑤ 자원봉사자의 안전에 유의해 줄 것을 당부하려고

19 다음 글의 상황에 나타난 분위기로 가장 적절한 것은?

It's always difficult to turn a car around. I live in a remote area up in the hills outside San Rafael, California, surrounded by forests full of giant trees. You have to drive up the mountain in low gear to get to our driveway, which is barely wide enough for one car and ends at a steep drop-off. I twisted around and backed up slowly. Just then, a flash of sunlight blinded me. I put my hand up to cover my eyes. I felt a shock as the left rear section of the SUV dropped. The car slipped in the soft soil, and rolled. I hadn't put on my seat belt yet; I was waiting to finish turning around. Now I tumbled inside the car as it rolled down the mountainside.

① urgent ② peaceful
③ dreary ④ exciting
⑤ monotonous

20 다음 글에서 필자가 주장하는 바로 가장 적절한 것은?

People have suggested that we would be better protected against our rulers and the tyranny of the majority through a written constitution. Certainly the American Constitution was a noble document, guaranteeing individual liberties and freedom of conscience. But it has worked because the principles it preserved were very vague and general truisms, a statement of the obvious ideas transferred from the unwritten British political system. It could be, and has been, interpreted in entirely different ways by different people. By its silences and omissions it may destroy rather than increase liberty. Written constitutions, in themselves, are no guarantee of liberty. The French, Italians, and Germans have had many written constitutions over the last two hundred years, but this has not protected them against tyranny.

① 법을 해석하는 과정에서 다양한 견해를 수렴해야 한다.
② 헌법의 기본 가치인 개인의 자유가 침해되어서는 안 된다.
③ 헌법은 시대와 국가를 뛰어넘는 보편적 가치를 담아야 한다.
④ 불문 헌법을 성문화할 때는 사례별로 구체화할 필요가 있다.
⑤ 성문 헌법만으로 자유를 보장할 수 있다고 생각해서는 안 된다.

21 밑줄 친 our ego is like a black hole이 다음 글에서 의미하는 바로 가장 적절한 것은?

When asked to judge their ability to get along with others, 60 percent of high school seniors rated themselves in the top 10 percent, and 25 percent considered themselves in the top 1 percent. And when asked about their leadership skills, only 2 percent assessed themselves as below average. Teachers aren't any more realistic: 94 percent of college professors say they do above-average work. In one study, employees in the workplace gave themselves too much credit for their skill, making it difficult to give meaningful feedback. CEOs also displayed confidence in their judgments, particularly when stepping into new markets or novel projects—for example, proposing takeovers that hurt, rather than helped, the price of their company's stock. Similarly, people are unrealistically optimistic about their own health risks compared with those of other people. These examples show our ego is like a black hole.

① we tend to focus on success and ignore failures
② our memories can be manipulated by our expectations
③ our self-perception gets distorted by our superiority bias
④ we overestimate the likelihood of events with greater availability
⑤ our consciousness rejects new evidence that contradicts our belief

22 다음 글의 요지로 가장 적절한 것은?

Researchers have learned that children cannot be divided into sociable kids who meet face to face and isolated loners who chat to strangers online. The latter, a minority, does exist, deserving attention insofar as their Internet use may make their problems worse. But early assumptions that teenagers interact with strangers for reasons of lonely curiosity are being challenged. In other words, it appears that the Internet fosters rather than undermines existing social contacts. In today's media-rich environment, the sociable teenager who does not communicate online as well as offline is a rarity, and online, they communicate mainly with already established, often local friends, the strongest ties being centered on pre-existing local contexts. The 'rich get richer' hypothesis works especially for instant messaging as the self-disclosure provided by one-to-one online communication encourages intimacy and thus strengthens relationships.

① 온라인상의 인간관계는 친밀감과 유대감이 부족하다.
② 아이들은 오프라인상의 인간관계를 강화시켜야 한다.
③ 십 대들은 성인보다 인터넷의 영향을 더 많이 받는다.
④ 인터넷은 인간관계의 폭을 넓혀주는 역할을 할 수 있다.
⑤ 온라인 소통은 기존 오프라인상의 인간관계를 강화한다.

23 다음 글의 주제로 가장 적절한 것은?

From the earliest days of agriculture, humans have been transporting seeds, plants, and animals from one location on earth to another. Very often the introduction of new species into a new region has been intentional, as when potatoes were brought to Europe from the Andes. Sometimes the introduction of species is unintentional, as when hyacinths invaded Lake Victoria and nearly choked the lake by depriving it of vast areas of sunlight. Humans have long been rearranging the Earth's ecology with little understanding of side effects and unintended consequences. Some introduced species act as devastating weeds, taking over an ecosystem that lacks proper defenses. Pests and pathogens easily cross from one location to another. In general, the consequences of such introduced species are complex, typically unpredictable, and occasionally devastating to native species and to the functioning of the local ecosystems.

*hyacinth: 히아신스(백합과의 화초) **pathogen: 병원균

① reason why invasive species spread rapidly
② unexpected negative impacts of exotic species
③ ways to introduce alien species to a new region
④ necessity of protecting species native to an area
⑤ intentional introduction of exotic invasive species

24 다음 글의 제목으로 가장 적절한 것은?

In most traditional societies, people tended to look to the past. They admired their ancestors, tried to retain the traditions, and lived in a remembered world. In contrast, increasingly for us, the past is a foreign country where strangers lived. Most people, especially in rapidly changing societies like America or China, tend to think much more about the future than the past. Technology plays a part. The great inventions of printing, the compass and gunpowder meant that the seventeenth-century philosophers felt that they were no longer the same as the Ancients. Now we often feel that those who lived before electricity, cars, photography and modern medicine must have been very different. Technological change is so rapid that a world before the Internet, mobile phone, genetic engineering and the latest generation of weapons seems a different one, with little to teach us.

① Does the Past Determine the Future?
② The Past is the Present and the Future
③ Technology Cuts Us Off from the Past
④ Why Technological Change Has Taken Place
⑤ Technological Change: Enhancing the Benefits

25 다음 도표의 내용과 일치하지 않는 것은?

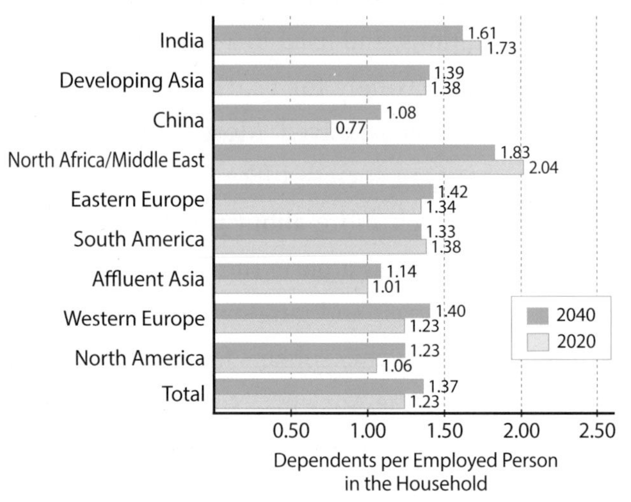

The graph above shows the number of people supported by each employed person in the household for each region in 2020 and as predicted for 2040. ① The total average number of dependents per employed person in the household was 1.23 in 2020 and, it is expected to increase to 1.37 in 2040. ② Overall, many regions are expected to have more dependents per worker in 2040 than in 2020 except three regions—India, North Africa/Middle East, and North America. ③ China shows the lowest number of dependents both in 2020 and in 2040, although the margin of increase between 2020 and 2040 is the largest of all the regions. ④ On the other hand, the workers in North Africa/Middle East had the greatest support burden of 2.04 dependents in 2020. ⑤ Although their burden is expected to decline to 1.83 dependents in 2040, North Africa/Middle East will still stand as the region whose average number of dependents per employed person is the greatest of all the regions.

26 northern mockingbird에 관한 다음 글의 내용과 일치하지 않는 것은?

If you've been hearing an endless string of 10 or 15 different birds singing outside your house, you might have a northern mockingbird in your yard. The northern mockingbird is the only mockingbird commonly found in North America. The mockingbirds can imitate animal sounds, such as those made by squirrels and frogs. The birds may move south during harsh weather. They sing all through the day and often into the night, with nighttime singing occurring more during a full moon. Most of the singing is done by males who use their large repertoire to impress females during the mating season. The female northern mockingbird sings too, although usually more quietly than the male does. She rarely sings in the summer and usually only when the male is away from the territory.

① 15종 이하의 다른 새소리를 낼 수 있다.
② 북아메리카에서 쉽게 볼 수 있는 새이다.
③ 다람쥐나 개구리 소리도 흉내 낼 수 있다.
④ 낮보다 밤에 더 많이 소리를 낸다.
⑤ 암컷은 수컷이 곁에 없을 때에만 지저귄다.

27 College Access Days에 관한 다음 안내문의 내용과 일치하지 않는 것은?

College Access Days

What It Is

College Access Days provides the opportunity for high school students to visit the University of Nebraska-Lincoln campus for a day. It is designed to accommodate groups of all sizes.

Session Topics Covered

Academics:

The academics session is a hands-on learning experience. They'll spend time in a classroom with UNL faculty and students. They are allowed to attend a lecture related to any major they are interested in.

Student Life:

Students can learn about:

- the student government
- clubs/organizations
- residence halls: take a tour of a typical room
- dining halls: experience the cuisine and atmosphere

① 일일 대학 체험 프로그램이다.
② 참여하는 학생 수에는 제한이 없다.
③ 강의실에서 직접 대학 강의를 들을 수 있다.
④ 들을 수 있는 전공 수업이 한정되어 있다.
⑤ 기숙사의 일반실을 둘러볼 수 있다.

28 Artisans Asylum에 관한 다음 안내문의 내용과 일치하는 것은?

Rock Climbing Gym Partnership

Artisans Asylum is a non-profit community craft studio located in Somerville, Massachusetts. We're thrilled to announce our partnership with our new neighbor, Brooklyn Boulders (BKB)!

More than just a rock climbing gym, Brooklyn Boulders offers a new type of community space. In honor of their grand opening and our partnership, BKB is extending the following limited-time-only offers to the Artisans Asylum community:

- Free climbing for all current Artisans Asylum members and volunteers this week, July 29–August 4.
- 10% off annual membership for current members who sign up by December 31.
- 15% off annual membership for dedicated Artisans Asylum volunteers who sign up by December 31.

Join us at the grand opening later this week!

① 영리 단체가 설립한 공방이다.
② 암벽 클라이밍 체육관을 인수했다.
③ 회원은 한 달간 무료 클라이밍의 특전을 누린다.
④ 회원은 연말까지 BKB의 연간 회원권을 10% 할인받는다.
⑤ 자원봉사자는 회원과 동일한 혜택을 받을 수 있다.

29 다음 글의 밑줄 친 부분 중, 어법상 틀린 것은? [3점]

An older guy I know told me a story of the first pizza place ① that moved into his little town. The pizza was lousy and the owner was rude, but he had the only game in town. So he made a ton of money and retired early. He left the pizza place to his two sons, who made the same bad pizza and were just as ② rude as their father. But now that time had passed, other competitors had come into the local marketplace and this was no longer the only pizza place in town. The place closed its doors in no time. The original owner was lucky because he was the first to do something ③ where it had never been done before. But he never learned what his mistakes were, nor ④ did his sons. If they ⑤ did, they would have improved the quality of their product as well as their customer service. I can imagine those two sons are just moping around today, wondering what on earth went wrong.

*the only game in town: 유일하게 이용 가능한 것
**mope around: 침울하게 서성거리다

30 다음 글의 밑줄 친 부분 중, 문맥상 낱말의 쓰임이 적절하지 않은 것은? [3점]

Human energy ① resembles the energy of light. When it is released, as in the average light bulb, it gets work done in an average way. But when that same energy is focused on a single target, as with a laser beam, it has the power to ② penetrate any kind of obstacle. In the same way, the average person ③ gathers his/her energy into a wide range of pursuits. In contrast, the person of "genius" is able to harness his or her energy, direct it toward one single pursuit at a time, and ④ accomplish much more than others. This principle of ⑤ concentration of energy also applies when you are considering the efforts of a large group of people — an organization. The success of that organization is directly related to the amount of energy its people are willing to invest, and to its ability to harness and direct those energies toward a single, burning purpose.

*harness: 이용하다

[31~34] 다음 빈칸에 들어갈 말로 가장 적절한 것을 고르시오.

31 We all know that life is a mixture of pleasure and pain, of comfort and hardship. Probably, you tend to cling to pleasure, hoping that it will never leave you, and you are overwhelmed by pain, fearing that it will never end. But when you start practicing ____________, you will be able to endure difficult moments with even a certain sense of humor, knowing that — as a wise saying goes — this too shall pass. All this doesn't mean that you need to live in constant insecurity, fearing that everything you rely upon could crumble at any given moment. Quite the opposite; keeping distance from success and failure, from pleasure and pain, will bring you back into connection with the only thing that is invariably present, stable, and safe: your center of pure awareness and pure love. In the same way, you will enjoy the beautiful moments of life without being tainted by the fear that they will end — as they undoubtedly will. [3점]

① detachment
② vision
③ flexibility
④ observation
⑤ optimism

32 We see the effects of lack of knowledge on creative performance every day, when people come up with ideas that are original for them but that nevertheless have been thought of before. A strikingly pitiful case of this phenomenon is that of the Indian mathematician Srinivasa Ramanujan, considered one of the most brilliant mathematical thinkers ever. Because of his lack of contact with the outside world, he unknowingly spent much of his lifetime independently "rediscovering" much of what was already known in Western mathematics. Had he first ________________________, he could have avoided this amazing yet useless career and instead turned his considerable talents to advancing, not reworking, the mathematical knowledge base. [3점]

① gotten ahead in his career
② overcome his lack of creativity
③ built confidence in his abilities
④ gained a broad perspective of his field
⑤ calmed his mind and increased creativity

33 Elephants have been found to ________________________. "The social complexity of the elephant, its well-known altruistic behavior and, of course, its huge brain, made the elephant a logical candidate species for testing in front of a mirror," said Joshua Plotnik, a psychologist at Emory University in Atlanta. In the past, only a few apes (including humans) and bottlenose dolphins were thought to possess this faculty. As with previous research carried out in this area on apes and dolphins, it was measured by putting a paint mark on a place the subject would normally be unable to see, and then observing his reaction to a mirror-image — touching himself indicates that the animal identifies the mirror-image as himself, whereas touching the mirror shows social behavior suggesting the subject is investigating another individual. The tested elephant looked in the mirror and then touched the paint mark on his head.

① have complex social systems
② develop a positive self-image
③ communicate with other animals
④ operate in a self-conscious manner
⑤ have the capacity for self-awareness

34 London taxi drivers famously navigate one of the most complex cities in the world. British neurologist Eleanor Maguire and her colleagues conducted MRI scans on their brains and compared them with the brain scans of others. In contrast with non-taxi drivers, experienced taxi drivers had a greatly enlarged posterior hippocampus — that part of the brain that specializes in recalling spatial representations. What's more, the size of taxi drivers' hippocampi correlated directly with each driver's experience: the longer the driving career, the larger the posterior hippocampus. That strongly suggested that spatial tasks were actively changing taxi drivers' brains. This was perfectly consistent with studies of violinists, Braille readers, meditation practitioners, and recovering stroke victims. Our brains ________________________. [3점]

*posterior hippocampus: (두뇌에서) 해마의 뒤쪽

① identify patterns by connecting some information
② adapt in response to the demands we put on them
③ prefer traveling down familiar pathways to new ones
④ produce a reward signal for discomfort we experience
⑤ have the capacity to control unexpected events quickly

35 다음 글에서 전체 흐름과 관계 없는 문장은?

The people who inhabit the world's harshest environment, the land above the Arctic Circle, are diverse in culture and language and, by necessity, extremely tough and resourceful. ① Scarcity is the word that best describes the Arctic ecosystem, where life-giving solar energy is not the only resource that is in short supply. ② Even during the summer months when it is light for 20 hours per day, the sun's rays are not strong enough to thaw the frozen subsurface soil. ③ But more than the severe cold, a lack of resources defines the kind of life led by the people of the Arctic. ④ Changes in the food web not only threaten life in the Arctic region, they also could have impacts on Earth's climate. ⑤ Very few plants can grow here, and there are no trees, no wood, no shops, no cars, nothing that we in the developed world take for granted every day.

[36~37] 주어진 글 다음에 이어질 글의 순서로 가장 적절한 것을 고르시오.

36

Every statistics book ever written contains the phrase "correlation is not causation." It's actually a simple concept: A correlation between two pieces of information means that they are related.

(A) This does not mean that one is causing the other, however. A frequent need to urinate is correlated with diabetes, but needing to use the bathroom many times a day does not cause diabetes (nor does it mean you already have it).

(B) If the correlation in the measurement of two phenomena is positive, when the measure of one goes up, so too does the other. If the correlation is negative, their measures move in opposite directions.

(C) Causation takes a step further than correlation. It says any change in the value of one variable (exercising) will cause a change in the value of another variable (calories burned), which means one variable makes the other happen. [3점]

① (A) — (C) — (B)
② (B) — (A) — (C)
③ (B) — (C) — (A)
④ (C) — (A) — (B)
⑤ (C) — (B) — (A)

37

The "natural" monopoly conferred on music rights owners is limited in its operation. This is a reflection of the pressures exerted by the economic interests of music users (broadcasters and others) on the legislature. For example, this property right has a time limit.

(A) This is, of course, a considerable period of time. If Paul McCartney lives until 2030, not only his own compositions but also those he composed with the late John Lennon will remain in copyright until at least the end of the twenty-first century.

(B) In contrast, the earliest recordings by the Beatles, issued in 1962, entered the public domain in 2012. The disparity between these two periods of property rights discloses the idea that the residual aura of authorship guarantees that this will be more highly rewarded than the "industrial" connotation of recording.

(C) After fifty years, copyright in a sound recording comes to an end, and anyone may issue copies of it to the public. Where a musical composition is concerned, the copyright expires seventy years after the death of the author.

*confer: 부여하다 **disparity: 차이, 불평등

① (A) — (C) — (B)
② (B) — (A) — (C)
③ (B) — (C) — (A)
④ (C) — (A) — (B)
⑤ (C) — (B) — (A)

[38~39] 글의 흐름으로 보아, 주어진 문장이 들어가기에 가장 적절한 곳을 고르시오.

38

But the expansion of the universe has stretched the wavelengths of that light, and we see it today as microwave radiation.

Gravitational lenses are tools for exploring the distant universe. (①) They act on light from across the electromagnetic spectrum, so they can be used to study the last faint tremors of light from the Big Bang, called the cosmic microwave background. (②) This is a dispersed background of light that began its journey across space some 370,000 years after the creation of the universe. (③) It was once very energetic, hot, and possibly as bright as the surface of a star. (④) It's faint and difficult to study. (⑤) Gravitational lensing offers a way to observe changes and fluctuations in this remnant radiation that contains the last echoes of the Big Bang. [3점]

39

> Radiocarbon also reveals that the paintings may have been completed over the course of 20,000 years, as opposed to in a single session.

The first major discovery of cave paintings came in 1876 when archaeologist Marcelino de Sautuola stumbled upon Spain's Altamira cave. (①) The subject matter consisted mostly of large animals including deer, horses, and herds of bison, and those were created using paint made from charcoal and ochre. (②) The paintings were so detailed and elaborate that Sautuola's contemporaries accused him of forgery. (③) They refused to believe that ancient humans were capable of such extraordinary works of art. (④) As it turned out, the paintings were quite authentic and we now know they were painted as many as 35,000 years ago. (⑤) If the dating is accurate, this would mean that hundreds of generations of early humans retouched the drawings and added their own figures over the course of millennia.

*radiocarbon: 방사성 탄소 (연대 측정에 사용) **ochre: 황토(색)

40 다음 글의 내용을 한 문장으로 요약하고자 한다. 빈칸 (A), (B)에 들어갈 말로 가장 적절한 것은?

> Artistic works are often created to produce certain experiences in viewers, but this intention of the artist is sometimes secondary to the intention to express the artistic imagination creatively. Consider actions generally for the moment. Think, for example, of people watching their favorite sports team. Whether it is at an actual match or in a bar, at crucial periods in a game, people tend to gesture in anticipation, or cheer in exhortation. Depending on the situation, these actions may be performed to communicate a sense of urgency to the team or a feeling of disgust to others at the bar. But people typically express themselves in this manner without any thought for what others think or how they may respond. Actions we perform through which we intend to express our feelings, thoughts, and attitudes need not have thought for how others may respond. At least some works should be understood as the embodiment of just this kind of action.
>
> *exhortation: 권고, 충고

↓

> Sometimes an artist's creation is not intended to ___(A)___ some meaning or draw viewers' responses but is intended to be an exercise of his or her ___(B)___.

	(A)		(B)
①	convey	……	creativity
②	interpret	……	influence
③	represent	……	principle
④	conceal	……	ability
⑤	distort	……	enthusiasm

[41~42] 다음 글을 읽고, 물음에 답하시오.

Conventional wisdom has it that one of our mightiest competitive motivators is social (a) comparison: we begin competing with others as soon as we compare ourselves to them. New research published in the journal *Psychological Science*, however, shows that the (b) number of people we're competing against has a direct effect on our motivation to compete. Here's an illustration: Jessica takes a seat in a classroom with ten other students. She looks around, evaluates the competitive landscape, and determines that her odds of doing well against this small group are good. The instructor passes out the particle physics exam, and Jessica is off and running, motivated to score among the best in this class. Jason arrives at a different room to take his exam, and it's a lot bigger than Jessica's. In fact, it's ten times as big, and Jason has to find a seat in a crowd of one hundred students. The instructor passes out the exam and Jason begins without feeling a competitive edge.

The (c) lack of motivation that Jason feels, in comparison to Jessica's resolve, is what psychologists refer to as the N-Effect. The effect occurs when an increase in total competitors results in (d) increased motivation for individual competitors. Researchers assessed this effect through a series of five studies: the first examined SAT and CRT (Cognitive Reflective Test) scores in light of how many people took the tests in given venues over multiple years. Even when controlling for other variables, researchers found a significant inverse correlation between the number of test takers and scores: the more people taking the test, the (e) worse the scores.

41 윗글의 제목으로 가장 적절한 것은?

① Competition: The Best Motivator
② Competition Is Motivation with Rewards
③ Competition Motivates Some, but Not All
④ Competition Goes Up, Motivation Goes Down
⑤ The Better the Mood, the More Competitive the Mindset

42 밑줄 친 (a)~(e) 중에서 문맥상 낱말의 쓰임이 적절하지 않은 것은?

① (a) ② (b) ③ (c) ④ (d) ⑤ (e)

[43~45] 다음 글을 읽고, 물음에 답하시오.

(A)

Winning is a wonderful thing. It can be helpful to a career and often leads to success. Even so, it is how we handle good fortune that counts in the long run. That is what the journalist Ellen Singer learned in a move to avoid working a night shift. Her newspaper editor, Linda Wells, gave her what was, for (a) her, a nightmare assignment—a month of working the night shift.

(B)

In addition, (b) she would be allotted a month of writing about anything she wanted to. The quiz topic turned out to be the television series, *Bewitched*, and Singer easily won. Now came the bigger challenge: She had to deal with the tricky situation of having beaten her boss. To begin with, Singer used her month-at-liberty to write excellent articles which won praise for (c) her and the paper.

(C)

Instead of celebrating her victory, she told everyone who would listen that her editor had let her win on purpose in order to inspire her. The editor was understandably delighted to be given some credit for a positive outcome; also (d) she did not forget the gracious manner in which Singer had behaved following her "win." Singer wisely passed up the short-term prize of winning. She invested her "win" in a long-term professional relationship which continues to create "wins" for her and for others.

(D)

By nature a "day person," she first tried to argue her way out of the assignment rationally. It did not work. Desperate, she then tried to turn her knowledge of entertainment to her advantage. Singer bet her editor that if Wells could beat her at a quiz, (e) she would work not one but six months on the night shift. On the other hand, if Wells won, she would be exempt from night work for a year.

43 주어진 글 (A)에 이어질 내용을 순서에 맞게 배열한 것으로 가장 적절한 것은?

① (B) — (D) — (C)　② (C) — (B) — (D)
③ (C) — (D) — (B)　④ (D) — (B) — (C)
⑤ (D) — (C) — (B)

44 밑줄 친 (a)~(e) 중에서 가리키는 대상이 나머지 넷과 다른 것은?

① (a)　② (b)　③ (c)　④ (d)　⑤ (e)

45 윗글에 관한 내용으로 적절하지 않은 것은?

① Wells는 Singer에게 한 달간 야근을 하라고 했다.
② Singer는 내기에서 Wells를 이겼다.
③ Singer는 한 달간 훌륭한 기사를 써서 칭찬받았다.
④ Wells는 내기에서 Singer에게 일부러 져주었다.
⑤ Singer는 야근을 힘들어하는 사람이었다.

: AFTER TESTING

종료 시 분
소요시간 분

학습 마무리

1 채점하기 | 정답 및 해설 p.106
주의 틀린 문제를 다시 풀 수 있도록 정답을 본문에 표기하지 마세요.
2 등급 확인
3 틀린 유형 확인 후 전략 적용 복습 및 해설지 확인

How to Review

1 틀린 문제와 ✓ 표시한 문제는 다시 풀고 해설 확인하기
2 내가 표시한 정답 근거가 해설과 일치하는지 확인하기
3 잘 모르는 부분으로 표시한 내용은 해설을 통해 완전히 이해하기
4 어휘 외우기 (어휘 목록 다운로드 www.cedubook.com)
5 다음 회에 개선할 점 정리하기 (시간 엄수, 취약 유형 보완 등)

고난도 모의고사

15

: BEFORE TESTING

시작 시 분

학습 목표

1 **제한시간** (OMR 마킹시간 포함) ☐ 40분 ☐ 45분
2 **어휘예습** ☐ 해당 없음 ☐ 완료
3 **문제풀이순서** ☐ 순서대로 ☐ 2점 → 3점 ☐ 기타
4 **기타 목표**

Check Point

1 **정답 근거** *e.g.* 밑줄 긋기
2 **잘 모르는 부분** *e.g.* 〈 〉 또는 ? 표시
3 **자신 없는 문제** *e.g.* 문제 번호에 ✓표시

18 다음 글의 목적으로 가장 적절한 것은?

Attention Staff,

As you may already be aware, the city of Newport has put in place new laws related to waste disposal. Many of these are aimed specifically at the recycling of businesses. Over the years, we here at Dunbar Electronics have done our best to be environmentally responsible, but we are far from perfect. In order to meet the new legal requirements, we will need to update many of our practices. The first step is for everyone to get a better understanding of recycling and waste reduction. To accomplish this, there will be a mandatory training session this Thursday. I apologize for the inconvenience, but I'm sure everyone can recognize the importance of this issue. Please check the announcement board in the lunchroom for details, and please arrive on time. Thank you.

Andy Spade, General Manager

① 환경 보호 운동에 동참해줄 것을 호소하려고
② 쓰레기 처리에 관련된 의무 훈련 시행을 공지하려고
③ 새롭게 시행되는 쓰레기 처리 법안에 대해 설명하려고
④ 쓰레기 수집 및 재활용 촉진을 위한 법 개정을 촉구하려고
⑤ 새로운 쓰레기 처리 규정 논의를 위한 회의 개최를 안내하려고

19 다음 글에 드러난 필자의 심경 변화로 가장 적절한 것은?

I applied to some law schools that award financial aid, and that process was flooded with rejection. One day while driving back from the mall with two friends, I got a call from an admissions officer at the University of California, Berkeley. She asked if it was a good time to talk and I told her no because I was driving. She said, "Okay, but call me back as soon as you can. I have some great news." I got off the phone and told my friends about the call. One of them said, "Maybe she's calling to offer you a scholarship." I said, "I hope you're right." And I imagined my school life at Berkeley for a while. As soon as I got back to the dorm, I called her back and she said, "Congratulations! You have been accepted to Berkeley." I politely thanked her for the call and after I got off the phone, I went back to lamenting over my situation. I thought to myself, "So what? It's not like I'll be able to go anyway. I can't afford law school. What I want is a scholarship."

① nervous → angry
② anxious → relieved
③ doubtful → confident
④ depressed → satisfied
⑤ anticipating → disappointed

20 다음 글에서 필자가 주장하는 바로 가장 적절한 것은?

Man is socially the most highly developed of all creatures. Interaction with other human beings is an environmental necessity to him. No man can survive as an island entirely by himself. No man wants to be an island. But every human being wants and needs to replenish his resources for being social by having a room of his own, as it were, a sanctuary to which he can retire and in which he can be alone with himself, undisturbed by the rumors and alarms of the outside world. I am going to suggest that the increasing loss of privacy from which Western man is suffering, particularly in the United States of America, serves, among other things, to reduce rather than to increase the chances of the individual being able to discover what those things are that are right and healthy for him, as a human being, to do. And that from this fact spring certain serious psychological consequences.

*replenish: 보충하다 **sanctuary: 보호 구역

① 공익을 위한 개인의 희생이 항상 합리적인 것은 아니다.
② 사생활 침해를 막을 수 있는 법적 보호 장치가 필요하다.
③ 개인적인 삶과 사회적인 삶 사이의 균형을 유지해야 한다.
④ 개인의 고립을 막기 위한 다양한 프로그램을 개발해야 한다.
⑤ 건강한 개인생활과 사회생활을 위해 사생활 보호가 필요하다.

21 밑줄 친 political cargo enthusiasts가 다음 글에서 의미하는 바로 가장 적절한 것은?

People living in parts of New Guinea noticed that when the white people arrived, they often built airfields. Planes would then arrive to spill out huge quantities of desirable things or "cargo." It seemed clear that the airfields were the key. They attracted the planes. So people hopefully built airfields and then waited for the cargo to arrive. They were disappointed. We have become the same with "democracy." We have observed that democracy is often associated with consumer success and some forms of freedom. Democracies, we feel, deliver the goods. We conclude that if we set out and "build democracies" around the world, the benefits linked to democracy will automatically follow. If we put out the voting boxes, the rest will soon occur. But we have become political cargo enthusiasts. We will be equally disappointed. We have forgotten that "democracy" is the result of many other things. It is as much the consequence as the cause of things we appreciate.

① people who confuse democracy with capitalism
② people who argue democracy guarantees equality
③ people who believe democracy delivers prosperity
④ people who regard democracy as equaling freedom
⑤ people who think democracy is the best form of government

22 다음 글의 요지로 가장 적절한 것은?

Each language has its own peculiarities about color naming. Cultural groups throughout the world talk about color differently—some don't even have a word for color. Among the people I work with in Nepal there is only one word, *pingya*, which means both blue and green. Can they see the difference if they cannot speak it? A clue to the answer is given by the fact that in Russian there are two words for 'blue' which roughly mean light and dark blue. A Russian anthropologist studying us might come to the logical, but incorrect, conclusion that because we cannot differentiate the two blues, the Oxford and Cambridge boat race teams could not tell each other apart. When I asked my Nepalese friends, they said that of course they could see the difference between the green grass and the blue sky.

① 색상을 구분하는 어휘가 풍부할수록 색상을 빨리 인지한다.
② 우리가 사용하는 언어가 우리의 인식을 제한하고 지배한다.
③ 색상을 표현하는 단어의 유무와 색상의 인지는 별개의 문제이다.
④ 언어권의 자연환경에 따라 색상을 표현하는 단어 수가 달라진다.
⑤ 미묘한 차이를 표현하는 단어가 많을수록 그 언어권의 문화 수준이 높다.

23 다음 글의 주제로 가장 적절한 것은?

Many people's plates tend to be beige and brown with meats and refined grains. A diet rich in these foods provides high fat and cholesterol, with little nutritional quality. The National Cancer Institute has launched a campaign called "Savor the Spectrum." They are encouraging people to eat fruits and vegetables that consist of the primary color groups: red, yellow, orange, green, blue, purple, and white. Why? A diet rich in the most colorful fruits gives you the beneficial compounds that you need to help prevent a heart attack and diabetes. Also, colorful vegetables control your blood pressure, prevent some types of cancers, and guard against vision loss. The more colors you see, the better. Loreli Disogra, director of the National Cancer Institute program says, "When you see colors on your plate you know you are doing good for yourself. Think of your dinner plate as an artist's canvas."

① harmful effects of junk food on health
② tips for selecting and trying colorful foods
③ health benefits of eating more colorful foods
④ reasons why colorful foods appeal to our senses
⑤ methods to choose healthy foods that suit your body

24 다음 글의 제목으로 가장 적절한 것은?

Just a few decades ago, many scholars believed in the myth of the peaceful savage, which depicts war as a by-product of modern civilization that did not exist in pre-state societies. The anthropologist Steven LeBlanc disproves this myth, pointing out that the vast majority of primitive, pre-state societies engaged in at least occasional warfare. Mortality rates from violence in some societies reached as high as 50 percent. In fact civilization, far from creating the problem of warfare, is apparently helping us to solve it. In the blood-soaked 20th century, 100 million men, women, and children died from war-related causes. The total would have been 2 billion if our rates of violence had been as high as in the average primitive society. Moreover, conventional wars between the armies of two or more nations, and even civil wars, have become much less common in recent decades. We are now dealing primarily with guerrilla wars, insurgencies, terrorism—or what the political scientist John Mueller calls "the remnants of war."

*insurgency: 폭동 **remnant: 잔재

① How Does War Affect Crime?
② Humans Are Less Violent Than Ever
③ Is It Natural for Humans to Start Wars?
④ Modern Age: A New Era of Conflict and Violence
⑤ Why Human Society Is More Violent Than in the Past

25 다음 도표의 내용과 일치하지 않는 것은?

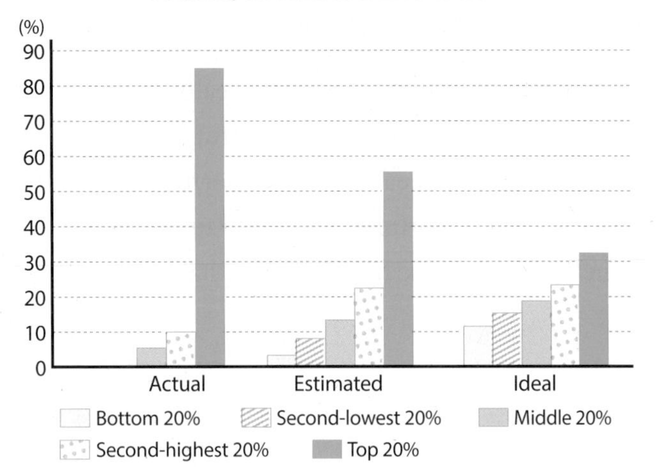

NOTE: In the "Actual" bar, the bottom 20% and the Second-lowest 20% are invisible, because they together hold just 0.3% of all wealth.

The graph above shows the results of a survey asking people in the US about their estimation of US wealth distribution and their ideal distribution, as well as the actual distribution in the US. ① The actual numbers paint a striking picture, with the wealthiest Americans holding 85% of all wealth and the bottom 40% of Americans sharing less than 1% of all wealth. ② However, when asked for their estimation, Americans guessed that the richest held just over half of all wealth while the middle 20% had a little over 10%. ③ In fact, the survey participants underestimated the share of wealth held by the second-highest 20% by nearly 12 percentage points. ④ Furthermore, those surveyed guessed that the second-poorest group had less than 10% of wealth while the bottom 20% had around 3-4% of wealth. ⑤ Still, the survey respondents said their ideal was a much more even country, where the bottom had access to a little over 10% of wealth and the top around three times this amount.

26 Horace Greeley에 관한 다음 글의 내용과 일치하지 않는 것은?

Born on February 3, 1811, Horace Greeley was an American politician from a poor family in Amherst, New Hampshire. At the age of 20, he moved to New York, where he made his living writing and editing political news stories. In 1841, he founded the *Tribune*, one of the great newspapers of its time. He was also interested in politics and was eventually elected to Congress in 1848 as a representative of New York State. In 1854, he helped to found the Republican Party, which was considered quite progressive. He was a strong supporter of Abraham Lincoln during the American Civil War, and campaigned against Andrew Jackson afterward. In 1872, Greeley himself would run for president, though he was eventually defeated by a wide margin. His wife died just five days before the election, and Greeley passed away three weeks later.

① New York에서 정치 관련 기사를 썼다.
② *Tribune* 신문사를 창립했다.
③ New York 주(州)의 의원으로 선출되었다.
④ 남북전쟁 당시 Lincoln의 강력한 지지자였다.
⑤ 대통령 선거에 출마하여 근소한 차이로 패배했다.

27 HG Magazine 구독에 관한 다음 안내문의 내용과 일치하지 않는 것은?

Subscribe to HG Magazine!

E-book Subscription (1 year/12 issues) $15
It includes:
- monthly e-mails with the latest issue in digital format
- 2 biannual collections, each containing 18 stories and 6 spotlight interviews

Print Subscription (1 year/12 issues) $30
(US ADDRESSES ONLY)
It includes:
- paperback editions of the magazine

This is IN ADDITION to everything in the e-book subscription!

Subscription Renewal

If you are already a subscriber and wish to renew your subscription, please purchase a subscription here. If you're using a different e-mail address from the one your previous subscription was under, you should include the old e-mail address as well.

① e-book 구독료는 1년에 15달러이다.
② 연 2회 발행하는 모음집에는 주요 인터뷰가 실려 있다.
③ 인쇄본은 미국 내 거주자만 신청할 수 있다.
④ 인쇄본을 구독 신청하면 e-book 구독료가 할인된다.
⑤ 이메일 주소 변경 시 예전 주소도 함께 첨부해야 한다.

28 Internship for Project-E에 관한 다음 안내문의 내용과 일치하는 것은?

Internship for Project-E

Project-E provides market-oriented vocational education for orphans in Ethiopia.

I. Offer
- Inspiring work atmosphere in a young and motivated team
- Financial support for travel and accommodation

II. Tasks
- Networking with Ethiopian and international businesses, governments and NGOs
- Selecting new students, negotiating business partnerships, and organizing workshops

III. Requirements
- Students need to have completed 2 years of study at university
- Excellent English speaking and writing skills, good IT knowledge
- Experience in developing countries
- High level of communication skills and ability to work in a team

IV. Application
Please send an e-mail with your résumé and cover letter to jasper@email.com.

① 해외 취업을 위한 프로젝트이다.
② 일체의 비용과 보수가 지급된다.
③ 교사를 선발하는 일이 포함된다.
④ 대학 졸업자를 대상으로 한다.
⑤ 개발도상국에서의 경험이 있어야 한다.

29 다음 글의 밑줄 친 부분 중, 어법상 틀린 것은? [3점]

Suppose you went to a party with your camera, and you sat in one corner, focused on a group of people who were arguing. How would that party be represented? It would be pictured as an unpleasant, frustrating party ① where no one had a good time and everyone was fighting. This is why there is so much trouble over "unauthorized" biographies: they are only one person's perception of another's life. And often, this view is offered by people ② their jealousy gives them a vested interest in distorting things. The problem is, the biography's view is limited only to the author's "camera angle," and we all know that cameras distort reality — that a close-up can make things look bigger than they really ③ are. And when ④ manipulated expertly, a camera can minimize or blur important parts of the reality. As Ralph Waldo Emerson says, each of us sees in others ⑤ what we carry in our own hearts.

30 다음 글의 밑줄 친 부분 중, 문맥상 낱말의 쓰임이 적절하지 않은 것은? [3점]

For human beings, children are linked to optimism in a way that runs deeper than just the biological continuation of the species. Optimism isn't essentially a matter of the ① rational assessment of the future — it's an attitude rather than a judgment. And it's the most characteristically human attitude, the one that's built into our DNA. The greatest human evolutionary advantage is our ② innate ability to imagine possible universes that could exist in the future and to figure out how to make them real. It's the ability to find better ③ alternatives to the current world, and we can see it in the fantastic pretend play of even the youngest children. This ability to change the physical and social world in unprecedented and unpredictable ways is deeply bound up with our characteristically ④ extended human childhood — that long period of protected immaturity. We change the world bit by bit, generation by generation. The ⑤ gradual changes have never transformed human lives for the better. We pass on our own innovations and the new worlds they create to our children — who imagine new ideas.

[31~34] 다음 빈칸에 들어갈 말로 가장 적절한 것을 고르시오.

31 Henry Ward Beecher, a renowned clergyman, said that the apple is the true ________________ fruit. Happy to grow just about anywhere, whether neglected, abused or abandoned, it is able to take care of itself, and to be fruitful of excellence. The Horatio Alger apple that emerged from a nineteenth-century seedling orchard was also in some sense "self-made," something that can't be said about many other plants. The great rose, for example, is the result of careful breeding, the deliberate crossing of aristocratic parents — "elite lines," in the breeder's speech. Not so the great apple, which distinguishes itself from "the hosts of unoriginal men" without reference to ancestry or breeding. The American orchard, or at least Johnny Appleseed's orchard, is a blooming, fruiting meritocracy, in which every apple seed roots in the same soil and any seedling has an equal chance at greatness, regardless of origin or heritage. [3점]

*meritocracy: 능력[실력]사회

① independent
② generous
③ democratic
④ profitable
⑤ multi-purpose

32 As human history demonstrates, ____________ is a very useful survival strategy, a type of risk management. It is an ancient technique. Without it, humanity — and countless species of animals — would be long extinct. We see it in all species whose food supplies are subject to change in availability. Imagine you are a hunter-gatherer. One day you are fortunate and kill a deer. You can't possibly eat all of it in a day, and refrigerators are still a few centuries away. You decide to share the deer with the group, which ensures that you will benefit from others' success when your luck is less impressive. The bellies of your friends serve as your refrigerator. It is a necessary ingredient for economic growth and wealth creation. There would be no global economy without it — there would be no economy at all. [3점]

① cooperative interchange
② cultural adaptability
③ competitive rivalry
④ novel invention
⑤ staying alert

33 The current consensus in child development research is that children as young as two or three have an elementary ability ______________________.
I've seen it in my own twins. When they were around eighteen months old, if my son was crying, his sister would try to comfort him by giving him her toy dog. But once they reached twenty-four months, if he was crying she would no longer offer him her own little dog, but realized he would be much happier if she passed him his favorite toy cat. This is what cognitive empathy or perspective-taking is all about. It involves making an imaginative leap and recognizing that other people have different tastes, experiences and worldviews than our own. The very fact that cognitive empathy develops naturally in early childhood — just at the time when the distinction between self and other begins to emerge — tells us that human beings are inherently social creatures that are wired for empathy.

① to explore external stimuli on their own
② to make their untold intentions understood
③ to mimic emotions and expressions of others
④ to imagine perspectives other than their own
⑤ to be immersed in activities that interest them

34 Green consumer behavior has come to function as a prism for disputes among environmentalists and social scientists. One debate, as simple as it is straightforward, sets "liberal consumerists" against "counter-consumerists." For the former, the roots of environmental crisis lie in the nature of mass consumption. They emphasize the ability of consumers to make a difference. As the awareness of environmental crisis spreads, and as individual consumers respond by opting for environmentally-friendly products and services, the purchasing power of the mass market will come to force businesses to "green" their products and their manufacturing and distribution processes for fear of being avoided in the marketplace by green-leaning consumers. In contrast, for ascetically inclined "deep greens," the crisis results less from the quality than from the quantity of consumption. For them, the primary aim ______________________________. [3점]

*ascetically: 금욕적으로

① is to let consumers buy as much as possible
② might be to apply techniques from social scientists
③ is to share knowledge regarding eco-friendly goods
④ would be eco-friendly and also enhance their self-image
⑤ doesn't mean consuming discerningly but consuming less

35 **다음 글에서 전체 흐름과 관계 없는 문장은?**

Objectivity is authority in disguise: "objective" facts always support particular points of view, and their "objectivity" can exist only as part of a display of power. ① More importantly, objective facts cannot be challenged: objectivity discourages audience activity and participation. ② Objectivity cannot exist when some individuals insist on arguing over facts that have long been established. ③ Rather than being "objective," therefore, TV news should present multiple perspectives that, like those of a soap opera, have as unclear a hierarchy as possible. ④ The more complex the events it describes, the more the contradictions among the different social positions from which to make sense of them should be left open and raw. ⑤ The anchors and reporters should be less concerned about telling the final truth of what has happened and should present, instead, different ways of understanding it and the different points of view inscribed in those different ways. [3점]

[36~37] 주어진 글 다음에 이어질 글의 순서로 가장 적절한 것을 고르시오.

36

We think of the word *normal* in many different ways — usual, expected, average, mean, common, regular, optimal. *Operating normally* usually means "without a problem." The trouble starts when we associate "normal" with common or expected, as in the case of age-related changes.

(A) This is often seen as normal simply because it is so common. Doctors often perpetuate the misconception by explaining diagnoses as: "It's just part of aging, the price we pay for living so long." We expect older folks to have these diseases.

(B) However, by definition, disease is not normal in the sense that it represents a disconnect from "proper" functioning. *Normal* may actually be worse than *aging* in how it is used.

(C) Many of the negative changes associated with increasing age, for example, are considered "normal" because they are so common. The same is true for a chronic disease at older ages. Most elderly people have multiple diagnoses and are on several prescriptions.

*perpetuate: 영속시키다

① (A) — (C) — (B)
② (B) — (A) — (C)
③ (B) — (C) — (A)
④ (C) — (A) — (B)
⑤ (C) — (B) — (A)

37

In this century, Earth's northern axis points toward Polaris, the North Star. It won't always, though, because Earth's axis moves very slowly, about a half a degree per century, like a top just before it stops and falls over.

(A) When the angle is smaller, there will be less seasonal variation at middle latitudes; with a larger angle, the variations will be amplified. It's thought that this change in tilt angle is one of the main factors that causes the periodic ice ages that sweep across our planet.

(B) Further complicating the picture is the fact that Earth's 23.5-degree tilt changes over time too, taking about 41,000 years to run through a full cycle that varies from about 21.5 to 24.5 degrees.

(C) This motion, called precession, causes the planet's axis to make a giant narrow circle in the sky that takes nearly 26,000 years to complete. So, in about 11,000 years, Earth will be closer to the Sun in July and farther away in December — the opposite of today's situation. In 26,000 years, things will be back to the way they are now. [3점]

*precession: 세차(歲差)운동

① (A) — (C) — (B)
② (B) — (A) — (C)
③ (B) — (C) — (A)
④ (C) — (A) — (B)
⑤ (C) — (B) — (A)

[38~39] 글의 흐름으로 보아, 주어진 문장이 들어가기에 가장 적절한 곳을 고르시오.

38

Art also had an impact because it helped to create more realistic and lifelike images of the human body.

Printing helped doctors and medical professors to share their discoveries and research more efficiently with each other during the Renaissance. (①) Printing made it easier and cheaper to mass-produce copies of medical research, therefore improving communication among doctors from across Europe. (②) For example, the development of printing made it possible for Vesalius's collection of books *On the Fabric of the Human Body* to be sold widely among medical professionals. (③) Vesalius's books had over 200 illustrations which were drawn by artists from dissections he had carried out on the human body. (④) The books were different from the past ones, when artists had drawn in a more two-dimensional style and rarely from life. (⑤) This meant that there were a lot more accurate portrayals of the human body available to doctors, who used this to improve their understanding of anatomy.

*dissection: 해부

39

Many cultures have offered sacrificial animals to the gods, perhaps as a way to convince themselves that it was the gods' desires that demanded the slaughter, not their own.

The idea that only in modern times have people become uneasy about killing animals is a flattering one. Taking a life is momentous, and people have been attempting to justify it for thousands of years. Religion and ritual have played a crucial part in helping us evaluate the moral costs. (①) Native Americans and other hunter-gatherers would give thanks to their prey for giving up its life so the eater might live. (②) For example, in ancient Greece, the priests responsible for the slaughter would sprinkle holy water on the sacrificial animal's brow. (③) The beast would promptly shake its head, and this was accepted as a sign of assent. (④) Slaughter doesn't necessarily preclude respect. (⑤) For all these people, ceremony allowed them to accept what they ate.

*preclude: ~을 못하게 하다, 불가능하게 하다

40 다음 글의 내용을 한 문장으로 요약하고자 한다. 빈칸 (A), (B)에 들어갈 말로 가장 적절한 것은?

Psychologist Ellen Langer designed a few experiments to see how self-induced dependence develops. She conducted the experiments at the airport, on the assumption that people who travel are likely to be somewhat independent and self-assured. In the first phase of one of these experiments, the subjects were given arithmetic problems which they could solve with ease. In phase two, she put the subjects in a position likely to lead them to question their competence. Ellen Langer gave some the title of "assistant" and others "boss," and had them all perform tasks in a manner appropriate to their roles. In the third phase, all the subjects returned to the same kind of easy arithmetic problems they had successfully completed in phase one. Those who had been made "assistants" now solved the problems only half as well as they had originally.

↓

The experiments suggest that, although the subjects began participating with ___(A)___ competence, the ___(B)___ that they had assumed influenced their performance.

	(A)		(B)
①	equal	……	labels
②	equal	……	tasks
③	high	……	attitudes
④	different	……	labels
⑤	different	……	tasks

[41~42] 다음 글을 읽고, 물음에 답하시오.

In one study, social psychologists placed flyers on 139 cars in a large hospital parking lot. They were curious about whether the cars' drivers would throw the flyers in the trash, or whether they would instead litter by leaving them in the parking lot. Before some of the cars' drivers emerged from the parking lot elevator, the researchers scattered discarded flyers, candy wrappers, and coffee cups throughout the parking lot. At other times, they removed every last cigarette butt and piece of trash from the parking lot floor, conveying the idea that littering was (a) inappropriate. Nearly half of all drivers littered when the parking lot was already covered in litter — what's one more piece of trash atop a foundation of garbage? — but only one in ten drivers littered when the parking lot was spotless. This experiment showed that an orderly environment (b) reduces the sense of responsibility.

The researchers added another twist to see whether environmental cues (c) shape people's actions. They asked an assistant to conspicuously drop an unwanted flyer on the ground just as some of the drivers were exiting the elevator. This (d) intentional act drew the drivers' attention to the existing state of the parking lot, either emphasizing that it was already full of litter, or highlighting how neat it was before the assistant indifferently cast aside his discarded flyer. When the assistant drew the drivers' attention to the state of the parking lot, only 6 percent littered in the clean parking lot, whereas a dramatically higher 54 percent littered in the already cluttered parking lot. The drivers (e) adopted the behavior that seemed most appropriate given their understanding of the area's prevailing norms.

41 윗글의 제목으로 가장 적절한 것은?

① Criminal Acts: Context and Consequences
② Signs of Disorder Undermine Social Norms
③ Sensible Living Creates an Orderly Environment
④ How Can We Reduce Crime in Our Community?
⑤ What Happens When You Violate Social Norms?

42 밑줄 친 (a)~(e) 중에서 문맥상 낱말의 쓰임이 적절하지 않은 것은?

① (a) ② (b) ③ (c) ④ (d) ⑤ (e)

[43~45] 다음 글을 읽고, 물음에 답하시오.

(A)

Willie was the kind of guy who got along with everyone. He was a great student with a promising future—until his head collided with the dashboard when his car accidentally hit a guard rail. Although Willie felt dazed, he seemed to be okay. But three months later he got into another accident when he turned sharply to avoid hitting a dog while driving, and this time he had to be sent to an emergency room. After examining Willie, the doctor told him that he had nothing to worry about; (a) he had only a minor head injury.

(B)

The next step was clear. Willie was prescribed medication to relieve his symptoms: special medication for the brain abnormality and an antidepressant to help him get unstuck from negative thoughts. After several weeks of treatment, the results were dramatic. Willie began to regain his sense of humor and to reconnect with his friends and family. (b) He has been on medication to control the trauma-induced brain problems ever since, and he is now one of the nicest human beings you will ever meet.

*antidepressant: 항우울제

(C)

In the months that followed, however, Willie found that it was causing trouble in his life. His whole attitude and demeanor began to change. (c) He now had a short fuse and was always angry. His irritability and constant flares of temper began to alienate his friends and family. He knew that he was out of control and that he had to stop himself before it was too late. He called a friend, who gave (d) him a specialist's telephone number, and the immediate crisis was averted.

(D)

Willie described for the doctor his two accidents and the severity of his mood swings. (e) He immediately ordered a brain study, which revealed abnormalities. Two areas were working too hard: One was in the left side of the brain, where dysfunction is often associated with paranoia and violence. The second was the top, middle section of the front part of the brain, which allows a person to shift attention freely from one thing to another. The brain study clearly explained the changes: paranoia, fiery temper, and negative thoughts.

*paranoia: 편집증

43 **주어진 글 (A)에 이어질 내용을 순서에 맞게 배열한 것으로 가장 적절한 것은?**

① (B) — (D) — (C)
② (C) — (B) — (D)
③ (C) — (D) — (B)
④ (D) — (B) — (C)
⑤ (D) — (C) — (B)

44 **밑줄 친 (a)~(e) 중에서 가리키는 대상이 나머지 넷과 다른 것은?**

① (a) ② (b) ③ (c) ④ (d) ⑤ (e)

45 **윗글의 Willie에 관한 내용으로 적절하지 않은 것은?**

① 운전 중 개를 피하려다 사고가 나서 응급실에 갔다.
② 상태가 호전된 후에 약물 치료를 중단했다.
③ 사고 이후 성급해지고 항상 화를 냈다.
④ 친구에게 전화하여 전문의의 연락처를 받았다.
⑤ 뇌 검사 결과 이상이 발견되었다.

: AFTER TESTING

종료 시 분
소요시간 분

학습 마무리

1 채점하기 | 정답 및 해설 p.114
주의 틀린 문제를 다시 풀 수 있도록 정답을 본문에 표기하지 마세요.
2 등급 확인
3 틀린 유형 확인 후 전략 적용 복습 및 해설지 확인

How to Review

1 틀린 문제와 ✓ 표시한 문제는 다시 풀고 해설 확인하기
2 내가 표시한 정답 근거가 해설과 일치하는지 확인하기
3 잘 모르는 부분으로 표시한 내용은 해설을 통해 완전히 이해하기
4 어휘 외우기 (어휘 목록 다운로드 www.cedubook.com)
5 다음 회에 개선할 점 정리하기 (시간 엄수, 취약 유형 보완 등)

ANSWERS

01

18 ④ 19 ③ 20 ⑤ 21 ② 22 ③ 23 ④ 24 ② 25 ⑤ 26 ② 27 ③ 28 ② 29 ③ 30 ② 31 ③
32 ① 33 ③ 34 ③ 35 ② 36 ④ 37 ⑤ 38 ⑤ 39 ⑤ 40 ② 41 ⑤ 42 ④ 43 ⑤ 44 ① 45 ④

02

18 ④ 19 ⑤ 20 ② 21 ④ 22 ④ 23 ④ 24 ① 25 ④ 26 ② 27 ⑤ 28 ③ 29 ⑤ 30 ④ 31 ①
32 ④ 33 ③ 34 ② 35 ② 36 ⑤ 37 ④ 38 ④ 39 ④ 40 ② 41 ⑤ 42 ③ 43 ③ 44 ④ 45 ④

03

18 ② 19 ① 20 ④ 21 ① 22 ④ 23 ⑤ 24 ③ 25 ③ 26 ③ 27 ④ 28 ⑤ 29 ③ 30 ① 31 ④
32 ① 33 ③ 34 ③ 35 ③ 36 ④ 37 ③ 38 ④ 39 ④ 40 ② 41 ③ 42 ⑤ 43 ③ 44 ③ 45 ③

04

18 ② 19 ⑤ 20 ③ 21 ⑤ 22 ④ 23 ④ 24 ② 25 ⑤ 26 ⑤ 27 ⑤ 28 ② 29 ⑤ 30 ⑤ 31 ⑤
32 ① 33 ① 34 ④ 35 ⑤ 36 ② 37 ⑤ 38 ⑤ 39 ④ 40 ③ 41 ④ 42 ⑤ 43 ④ 44 ③ 45 ⑤

05

18 ① 19 ② 20 ③ 21 ④ 22 ② 23 ④ 24 ③ 25 ⑤ 26 ④ 27 ⑤ 28 ② 29 ⑤ 30 ④ 31 ②
32 ⑤ 33 ⑤ 34 ⑤ 35 ③ 36 ① 37 ③ 38 ④ 39 ④ 40 ④ 41 ③ 42 ② 43 ③ 44 ① 45 ③

06

18 ⑤ 19 ④ 20 ② 21 ② 22 ① 23 ② 24 ④ 25 ⑤ 26 ⑤ 27 ⑤ 28 ⑤ 29 ③ 30 ③ 31 ②
32 ⑤ 33 ② 34 ① 35 ③ 36 ① 37 ⑤ 38 ② 39 ④ 40 ① 41 ② 42 ⑤ 43 ⑤ 44 ② 45 ③

07

18 ⑤ 19 ④ 20 ④ 21 ⑤ 22 ⑤ 23 ① 24 ① 25 ② 26 ③ 27 ④ 28 ③ 29 ④ 30 ① 31 ④
32 ④ 33 ① 34 ⑤ 35 ③ 36 ① 37 ② 38 ⑤ 39 ③ 40 ④ 41 ⑤ 42 ④ 43 ③ 44 ④ 45 ⑤

08

18 ④ 19 ⑤ 20 ④ 21 ② 22 ② 23 ① 24 ① 25 ⑤ 26 ⑤ 27 ⑤ 28 ④ 29 ③ 30 ⑤ 31 ②
32 ③ 33 ① 34 ② 35 ③ 36 ③ 37 ② 38 ③ 39 ④ 40 ③ 41 ④ 42 ③ 43 ④ 44 ④ 45 ②

09

18 ② 19 ⑤ 20 ① 21 ① 22 ⑤ 23 ② 24 ② 25 ⑤ 26 ③ 27 ⑤ 28 ③ 29 ④ 30 ① 31 ③
32 ④ 33 ① 34 ⑤ 35 ③ 36 ② 37 ① 38 ④ 39 ⑤ 40 ② 41 ③ 42 ④ 43 ③ 44 ② 45 ④

10

18 ⑤ 19 ① 20 ② 21 ② 22 ③ 23 ③ 24 ③ 25 ④ 26 ④ 27 ④ 28 ③ 29 ③ 30 ④ 31 ③
32 ⑤ 33 ② 34 ① 35 ④ 36 ③ 37 ④ 38 ③ 39 ③ 40 ② 41 ⑤ 42 ② 43 ① 44 ⑤ 45 ③

11

18 ⑤ 19 ④ 20 ② 21 ② 22 ② 23 ⑤ 24 ③ 25 ③ 26 ② 27 ⑤ 28 ③ 29 ③ 30 ① 31 ④
32 ③ 33 ① 34 ② 35 ② 36 ④ 37 ③ 38 ③ 39 ⑤ 40 ④ 41 ④ 42 ④ 43 ⑤ 44 ② 45 ②

12

18 ④ 19 ② 20 ④ 21 ① 22 ⑤ 23 ⑤ 24 ④ 25 ③ 26 ④ 27 ④ 28 ④ 29 ⑤ 30 ④ 31 ⑤
32 ③ 33 ① 34 ④ 35 ③ 36 ① 37 ④ 38 ③ 39 ④ 40 ④ 41 ③ 42 ④ 43 ④ 44 ③ 45 ③

13

18 ⑤ 19 ① 20 ① 21 ④ 22 ② 23 ② 24 ④ 25 ⑤ 26 ③ 27 ④ 28 ⑤ 29 ④ 30 ⑤ 31 ②
32 ⑤ 33 ② 34 ② 35 ③ 36 ④ 37 ② 38 ④ 39 ⑤ 40 ② 41 ⑤ 42 ③ 43 ⑤ 44 ④ 45 ④

14

18 ⑤ 19 ① 20 ⑤ 21 ③ 22 ⑤ 23 ② 24 ③ 25 ② 26 ④ 27 ④ 28 ④ 29 ⑤ 30 ③ 31 ①
32 ④ 33 ⑤ 34 ② 35 ④ 36 ② 37 ④ 38 ④ 39 ⑤ 40 ① 41 ④ 42 ④ 43 ④ 44 ④ 45 ④

15

18 ② 19 ⑤ 20 ⑤ 21 ③ 22 ③ 23 ③ 24 ② 25 ③ 26 ⑤ 27 ④ 28 ⑤ 29 ② 30 ⑤ 31 ③
32 ① 33 ④ 34 ⑤ 35 ② 36 ④ 37 ⑤ 38 ③ 39 ② 40 ① 41 ② 42 ② 43 ③ 44 ⑤ 45 ②

파워업 독해실전편 모의고사 15회 답안지

③ 교시 영어 영역

※ 답안지 작성(표기)은 반드시 컴퓨터용 사인펜만을 사용하고, 연필 또는 샤프펜을 절대 사용하지 마십시오.
※ 뒷면의 〈수험생이 지켜야 할 일〉을 꼭 읽어 보십시오.

※ 결시자 확인 (수험생은 표기하지 말것.)

컴퓨터용 사인펜을 사용하여 수험번호란과 옆란을 표기	○

※ 아래 '필적확인란'에 "○○○○○○○○○○ ○○○"를 정자로 반드시 기재하여야 합니다.

필 적 확인란	

성 명								
수 험 번 호								
				—				
	0	0	0		0	0	0	0
1	1	1	1		1	1	1	1
2	2	2	2		2	2	2	2
3	3	3	3		3	3	3	3
4	4	4	4		4	4		4
5	5	5	5		5	5		5
6	6		6		6	6		6
7	7		7		7	7		7
8	8		8		8	8		8
	9		9		9	9		9

문 형
홀수형 ○
짝수형 ○

※ 문제의 문형을 확인후 표기

※ 감독관 확인 (수험생은 표기하지 말것.)

본인여부, 수험번호 및 문형의 표기가 정확한지 확인, 옆란에 서명 또는 날인	서 명 또는 날 인

문번	답 란
1	① ② ③ ④ ⑤
2	① ② ③ ④ ⑤
3	① ② ③ ④ ⑤
4	① ② ③ ④ ⑤
5	① ② ③ ④ ⑤
6	① ② ③ ④ ⑤
7	① ② ③ ④ ⑤
8	① ② ③ ④ ⑤
9	① ② ③ ④ ⑤
10	① ② ③ ④ ⑤
11	① ② ③ ④ ⑤
12	① ② ③ ④ ⑤
13	① ② ③ ④ ⑤
14	① ② ③ ④ ⑤
15	① ② ③ ④ ⑤
16	① ② ③ ④ ⑤
17	① ② ③ ④ ⑤
18	① ② ③ ④ ⑤
19	① ② ③ ④ ⑤
20	① ② ③ ④ ⑤

문번	답 란
21	① ② ③ ④ ⑤
22	① ② ③ ④ ⑤
23	① ② ③ ④ ⑤
24	① ② ③ ④ ⑤
25	① ② ③ ④ ⑤
26	① ② ③ ④ ⑤
27	① ② ③ ④ ⑤
28	① ② ③ ④ ⑤
29	① ② ③ ④ ⑤
30	① ② ③ ④ ⑤
31	① ② ③ ④ ⑤
32	① ② ③ ④ ⑤
33	① ② ③ ④ ⑤
34	① ② ③ ④ ⑤
35	① ② ③ ④ ⑤
36	① ② ③ ④ ⑤
37	① ② ③ ④ ⑤
38	① ② ③ ④ ⑤
39	① ② ③ ④ ⑤
40	① ② ③ ④ ⑤

문번	답 란
41	① ② ③ ④ ⑤
42	① ② ③ ④ ⑤
43	① ② ③ ④ ⑤
44	① ② ③ ④ ⑤
45	① ② ③ ④ ⑤

〈수험생이 지켜야 할 일〉

> 답안지 작성(표기)은 반드시 컴퓨터용 사인펜만을 사용하여야 합니다.
> (연필, 샤프펜 사용 시 불이익을 받을 수 있습니다.)

1. 성명란에는 수험생의 성명을 바르게 기재하여야 합니다.
2. 수험번호란에는 아라비아 숫자로 기재하고 해당란에 "●"와 같이 완전하게 표기하여야 합니다.
3. 문형란에는 배부받은 시험 문제지의 문형을 정확히 확인하고 해당란에 "●"와 같이 표기하여야 합니다.
   - 답안지의 '문형'란에 표기가 되어있지 않거나 이중으로 표기된 경우 불이익을 받을 수 있습니다.
   - 시험특별관리대상자의 문제지 문형은 홀수형 입니다.
4. 답란은 "●"와 같이 완전하게 표기하여야 하며, 바르지 못한 표기(ⓥ ⦶ ⊙ ◑ ▨ 등)를 하였을 경우는 불이익을 받을 수 있습니다.
5. 답란 수정을 원할 경우에는 수정테이프만을 사용하여 완전하게 수정하여야 합니다. 불완전한 수정처리로 인해 발생하는 불이익은 수험생에게 있습니다.
   - 수정테이프는 감독관이 소지하고 있습니다.
   - 수정액이나 스티커 등은 절대로 사용할 수 없습니다.
   - 답란 수정 후 수정테이프가 떨어지지 않게 손으로 눌러 주십시오.
   - 답안지 교체를 원할 경우 교체 가능합니다.
6. 답안지에 낙서를 하거나 불필요한 표기를 하였을 경우 불이익을 받을 수 있으므로 답안지를 최대한 깨끗한 상태로 제출하여야 합니다.

파워업 독해실전편 모의고사 15회 답안지

③ 교시 영어 영역

※ 결시자 확인 (수험생은 표기하지 말것.)

컴퓨터용 사인펜을 사용하여 수험번호란과 옆란을 표기	○

※ 아래 '필적확인란'에 "○○○○○○○○○○○○○"를 정자로 반드시 기재하여야 합니다.

필 적 확인란	

성 명								
수 험 번 호								
				—				
	⓪	⓪	⓪		⓪	⓪	⓪	⓪
①	①	①	①		①	①	①	①
②	②	②	②		②	②	②	②
③	③	③	③		③	③	③	③
④	④	④	④		④	④		④
⑤	⑤	⑤	⑤		⑤	⑤		⑤
⑥	⑥		⑥		⑥	⑥		⑥
⑦	⑦		⑦		⑦	⑦		⑦
⑧	⑧		⑧		⑧	⑧		⑧
	⑨		⑨		⑨	⑨		⑨

문 형
홀수형 ○
짝수형 ○

※ 문제의 문형을 확인 후 표기

※ 감독관 확인 (수험생은 표기하지 말것.)

본인여부, 수험번호 및 문형의 표기가 정확한지 확인, 옆란에 서명 또는 날인	서 명 또는 날 인

※ 답안지 작성(표기)은 반드시 컴퓨터용 사인펜만을 사용하고, 연필 또는 샤프펜을 절대 사용하지 마십시오.
※ 뒷면의 〈수험생이 지켜야 할 일〉을 꼭 읽어 보십시오.

문번	답 란	문번	답 란	문번	답 란
1	① ② ③ ④ ⑤	21	① ② ③ ④ ⑤	41	① ② ③ ④ ⑤
2	① ② ③ ④ ⑤	22	① ② ③ ④ ⑤	42	① ② ③ ④ ⑤
3	① ② ③ ④ ⑤	23	① ② ③ ④ ⑤	43	① ② ③ ④ ⑤
4	① ② ③ ④ ⑤	24	① ② ③ ④ ⑤	44	① ② ③ ④ ⑤
5	① ② ③ ④ ⑤	25	① ② ③ ④ ⑤	45	① ② ③ ④ ⑤
6	① ② ③ ④ ⑤	26	① ② ③ ④ ⑤		
7	① ② ③ ④ ⑤	27	① ② ③ ④ ⑤		
8	① ② ③ ④ ⑤	28	① ② ③ ④ ⑤		
9	① ② ③ ④ ⑤	29	① ② ③ ④ ⑤		
10	① ② ③ ④ ⑤	30	① ② ③ ④ ⑤		
11	① ② ③ ④ ⑤	31	① ② ③ ④ ⑤		
12	① ② ③ ④ ⑤	32	① ② ③ ④ ⑤		
13	① ② ③ ④ ⑤	33	① ② ③ ④ ⑤		
14	① ② ③ ④ ⑤	34	① ② ③ ④ ⑤		
15	① ② ③ ④ ⑤	35	① ② ③ ④ ⑤		
16	① ② ③ ④ ⑤	36	① ② ③ ④ ⑤		
17	① ② ③ ④ ⑤	37	① ② ③ ④ ⑤		
18	① ② ③ ④ ⑤	38	① ② ③ ④ ⑤		
19	① ② ③ ④ ⑤	39	① ② ③ ④ ⑤		
20	① ② ③ ④ ⑤	40	① ② ③ ④ ⑤		

〈수험생이 지켜야 할 일〉

답안지 작성(표기)은 반드시 컴퓨터용 사인펜만을 사용하여야 합니다.
(연필, 샤프펜 사용 시 불이익을 받을 수 있습니다.)

1. 성명란에는 수험생의 성명을 바르게 기재하여야 합니다.
2. 수험번호란에는 아라비아 숫자로 기재하고 해당란에 "●"와 같이 완전하게 표기하여야 합니다.
3. 문형란에는 배부받은 시험 문제지의 문형을 정확히 확인하고 해당란에 "●"와 같이 표기하여야 합니다.
   – 답안지의 '문형'란에 표기가 되어있지 않거나 이중으로 표기된 경우 불이익을 받을 수 있습니다.
   – 시험특별관리대상자의 문제지 문형은 홀수형 입니다.
4. 답란은 "●"와 같이 완전하게 표기하여야 하며, 바르지 못한 표기(◌ ◌ ◌ ◌ ◌ 등)를 하였을 경우는 불이익을 받을 수 있습니다.
5. 답란 수정을 원할 경우에는 수정테이프만을 사용하여 완전하게 수정하여야 합니다. 불완전한 수정처리로 인해 발생하는 불이익은 수험생에게 있습니다.
   – 수정테이프는 감독관이 소지하고 있습니다.
   – 수정액이나 스티커 등은 절대로 사용할 수 없습니다.
   – 답란 수정 후 수정테이프가 떨어지지 않게 손으로 눌러 주십시오.
   – 답안지 교체를 원할 경우 교체 가능합니다.
6. 답안지에 낙서를 하거나 불필요한 표기를 하였을 경우 불이익을 받을 수 있으므로 답안지를 최대한 깨끗한 상태로 제출하여야 합니다.

파워업 독해실전편 모의고사 15회 답안지

※ 답안지 작성(표기)은 반드시 컴퓨터용 사인펜만을 사용하고, 연필 또는 샤프펜을 절대 사용하지 마십시오.
※ 뒷면의 〈수험생이 지켜야 할 일〉을 꼭 읽어 보십시오.

③ 교시 영어 영역

※ 결시자 확인 (수험생은 표기하지 말것.)

컴퓨터용 사인펜을 사용하여 수험번호란과 옆란을 표기	○

※ 아래 '필적확인란'에 "○○○○○○○○○○ ○○○"를 정자로 반드시 기재하여야 합니다.

필 적 확인란	

성 명								
수 험 번 호								
				—				
	0	0	0		0	0	0	0
1	1	1	1		1	1	1	1
2	2	2	2		2	2	2	2
3	3	3	3		3	3	3	3
4	4	4	4		4	4		4
5	5	5	5		5	5		5
6	6		6		6	6		6
7	7		7		7	7		7
8	8		8		8	8		8
	9		9		9	9		9

문 형
홀수형 ○
짝수형 ○

※ 문제의 문형을 확인 후 표기

※ 감독관 확인 (수험생은 표기하지 말것.)

본인여부, 수험번호 및 문형의 표기가 정확한지 확인, 옆란에 서명 또는 날인	(서 명 또는 날 인)

문번	답 란	문번	답 란	문번	답 란
1	① ② ③ ④ ⑤	21	① ② ③ ④ ⑤	41	① ② ③ ④ ⑤
2	① ② ③ ④ ⑤	22	① ② ③ ④ ⑤	42	① ② ③ ④ ⑤
3	① ② ③ ④ ⑤	23	① ② ③ ④ ⑤	43	① ② ③ ④ ⑤
4	① ② ③ ④ ⑤	24	① ② ③ ④ ⑤	44	① ② ③ ④ ⑤
5	① ② ③ ④ ⑤	25	① ② ③ ④ ⑤	45	① ② ③ ④ ⑤
6	① ② ③ ④ ⑤	26	① ② ③ ④ ⑤		
7	① ② ③ ④ ⑤	27	① ② ③ ④ ⑤		
8	① ② ③ ④ ⑤	28	① ② ③ ④ ⑤		
9	① ② ③ ④ ⑤	29	① ② ③ ④ ⑤		
10	① ② ③ ④ ⑤	30	① ② ③ ④ ⑤		
11	① ② ③ ④ ⑤	31	① ② ③ ④ ⑤		
12	① ② ③ ④ ⑤	32	① ② ③ ④ ⑤		
13	① ② ③ ④ ⑤	33	① ② ③ ④ ⑤		
14	① ② ③ ④ ⑤	34	① ② ③ ④ ⑤		
15	① ② ③ ④ ⑤	35	① ② ③ ④ ⑤		
16	① ② ③ ④ ⑤	36	① ② ③ ④ ⑤		
17	① ② ③ ④ ⑤	37	① ② ③ ④ ⑤		
18	① ② ③ ④ ⑤	38	① ② ③ ④ ⑤		
19	① ② ③ ④ ⑤	39	① ② ③ ④ ⑤		
20	① ② ③ ④ ⑤	40	① ② ③ ④ ⑤		

〈수험생이 지켜야 할 일〉

> 답안지 작성(표기)은 반드시 컴퓨터용 사인펜만을 사용하여야 합니다.
> (연필, 샤프펜 사용 시 불이익을 받을 수 있습니다.)

1. 성명란에는 수험생의 성명을 바르게 기재하여야 합니다.
2. 수험번호란에는 아라비아 숫자로 기재하고 해당란에 "●"와 같이 완전하게 표기하여야 합니다.
3. 문형란에는 배부받은 시험 문제지의 문형을 정확히 확인하고 해당란에 "●"와 같이 표기하여야 합니다.
   - 답안지의 '문형'란에 표기가 되어있지 않거나 이중으로 표기된 경우 불이익을 받을 수 있습니다.
   - 시험특별관리대상자의 문제지 문형은 홀수형 입니다.
4. 답란은 "●"와 같이 완전하게 표기하여야 하며, 바르지 못한 표기(☑ ⦶ ⊙ ◑ ▨ 등)를 하였을 경우는 불이익을 받을 수 있습니다.
5. 답란 수정을 원할 경우에는 수정테이프만을 사용하여 완전하게 수정하여야 합니다. 불완전한 수정처리로 인해 발생하는 불이익은 수험생에게 있습니다.
   - 수정테이프는 감독관이 소지하고 있습니다.
   - 수정액이나 스티커 등은 절대로 사용할 수 없습니다.
   - 답란 수정 후 수정테이프가 떨어지지 않게 손으로 눌러 주십시오.
   - 답안지 교체를 원할 경우 교체 가능합니다.
6. 답안지에 낙서를 하거나 불필요한 표기를 하였을 경우 불이익을 받을 수 있으므로 답안지를 최대한 깨끗한 상태로 제출하여야 합니다.

파워업 독해실전편 모의고사 15회 답안지

③ 교시 영어 영역

※ 결시자 확인 (수험생은 표기하지 말것.)

컴퓨터용 사인펜을 사용하여 수험번호란과 옆란을 표기 ○

※ 아래 '필적확인란'에 "○○○○○○○○○○○○○"를 정자로 반드시 기재하여야 합니다.

필 적 확인란	

성 명								
수 험 번 호								
				—				
	0	0	0		0	0	0	0
1	1	1	1		1	1	1	1
2	2	2	2		2	2	2	2
3	3	3	3		3	3	3	3
4	4	4	4		4	4		4
5	5	5	5		5	5		5
6	6		6		6	6		6
7	7		7		7	7		7
8	8		8		8	8		8
	9		9		9	9		9

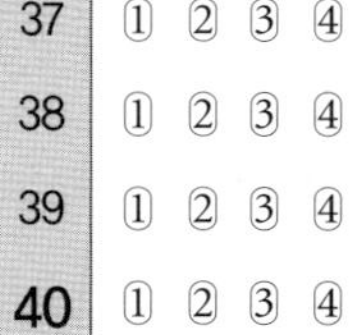

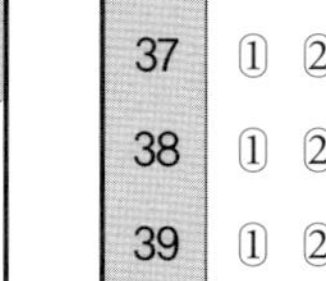

※ 감독관 확인 (수험생은 표기하지 말것.)

본인여부, 수험번호 및 문형의 표기가 정확한지 확인, 옆란에 서명 또는 날인 (서 명 또는 날 인)

※ 답안지 작성(표기)은 반드시 컴퓨터용 사인펜만을 사용하고, 연필 또는 샤프펜을 절대 사용하지 마십시오.
※ 뒷면의 〈수험생이 지켜야 할 일〉을 꼭 읽어 보십시오.

문번	답 란	문번	답 란	문번	답 란
1	① ② ③ ④ ⑤	21	① ② ③ ④ ⑤	41	① ② ③ ④ ⑤
2	① ② ③ ④ ⑤	22	① ② ③ ④ ⑤	42	① ② ③ ④ ⑤
3	① ② ③ ④ ⑤	23	① ② ③ ④ ⑤	43	① ② ③ ④ ⑤
4	① ② ③ ④ ⑤	24	① ② ③ ④ ⑤	44	① ② ③ ④ ⑤
5	① ② ③ ④ ⑤	25	① ② ③ ④ ⑤	45	① ② ③ ④ ⑤
6	① ② ③ ④ ⑤	26	① ② ③ ④ ⑤		
7	① ② ③ ④ ⑤	27	① ② ③ ④ ⑤		
8	① ② ③ ④ ⑤	28	① ② ③ ④ ⑤		
9	① ② ③ ④ ⑤	29	① ② ③ ④ ⑤		
10	① ② ③ ④ ⑤	30	① ② ③ ④ ⑤		
11	① ② ③ ④ ⑤	31	① ② ③ ④ ⑤		
12	① ② ③ ④ ⑤	32	① ② ③ ④ ⑤		
13	① ② ③ ④ ⑤	33	① ② ③ ④ ⑤		
14	① ② ③ ④ ⑤	34	① ② ③ ④ ⑤		
15	① ② ③ ④ ⑤	35	① ② ③ ④ ⑤		
16	① ② ③ ④ ⑤	36	① ② ③ ④ ⑤		
17	① ② ③ ④ ⑤	37	① ② ③ ④ ⑤		
18	① ② ③ ④ ⑤	38	① ② ③ ④ ⑤		
19	① ② ③ ④ ⑤	39	① ② ③ ④ ⑤		
20	① ② ③ ④ ⑤	40	① ② ③ ④ ⑤		

〈수험생이 지켜야 할 일〉

답안지 작성(표기)은 반드시 컴퓨터용 사인펜만을 사용하여야 합니다. (연필, 샤프펜 사용 시 불이익을 받을 수 있습니다.)

1. 성명란에는 수험생의 성명을 바르게 기재하여야 합니다.
2. 수험번호란에는 아라비아 숫자로 기재하고 해당란에 "●"와 같이 완전하게 표기하여야 합니다.
3. 문형란에는 배부받은 시험 문제지의 문형을 정확히 확인하고 해당란에 "●"와 같이 표기하여야 합니다.
   – 답안지의 '문형'란에 표기가 되어있지 않거나 이중으로 표기된 경우 불이익을 받을 수 있습니다.
   – 시험특별관리대상자의 문제지 문형은 홀수형 입니다.
4. 답란은 "●"와 같이 완전하게 표기하여야 하며, 바르지 못한 표기(⊘ ⦶ ⊙ ◑ ▨ 등)를 하였을 경우는 불이익을 받을 수 있습니다.
5. 답란 수정을 원할 경우에는 수정테이프만을 사용하여 완전하게 수정하여야 합니다. 불완전한 수정처리로 인해 발생하는 불이익은 수험생에게 있습니다.
   – 수정테이프는 감독관이 소지하고 있습니다.
   – 수정액이나 스티커 등은 절대로 사용할 수 없습니다.
   – 답란 수정 후 수정테이프가 떨어지지 않게 손으로 눌러 주십시오.
   – 답안지 교체를 원할 경우 교체 가능합니다.
6. 답안지에 낙서를 하거나 불필요한 표기를 하였을 경우 불이익을 받을 수 있으므로 답안지를 최대한 깨끗한 상태로 제출하여야 합니다.

파워업 독해실전편 모의고사 15회 답안지

③ 교시 영어 영역

※ 결시자 확인 (수험생은 표기하지 말것.)

컴퓨터용 사인펜을 사용하여 수험번호란과 옆란을 표기 ○

※ 아래 '필적확인란'에 "○○○○○○○○○○○○○"를 정자로 반드시 기재하여야 합니다.

필 적 확인란	

성 명	

수 험 번 호								
				—				
	0	0	0		0	0	0	0
1	1	1	1		1	1	1	1
2	2	2	2		2	2	2	2
3	3	3	3		3	3	3	3
4	4	4	4		4	4		4
5	5	5	5		5	5		5
6	6		6		6	6		6
7	7		7		7	7		7
8	8		8		8	8		8
	9		9		9	9		9

문 형
홀수형 ○
짝수형 ○

※ 문제의 문형을 확인 후 표기

※ 감독관 확인 (수험생은 표기하지 말것.)

본인여부, 수험번호 및 문형의 표기가 정확한지 확인, 옆란에 서명 또는 날인 (서 명 또는 날 인)

※ 답안지 작성(표기)은 반드시 컴퓨터용 사인펜만을 사용하고, 연필 또는 샤프펜을 절대 사용하지 마십시오.
※ 뒷면의 〈수험생이 지켜야 할 일〉을 꼭 읽어 보십시오.

문번	답 란
1	① ② ③ ④ ⑤
2	① ② ③ ④ ⑤
3	① ② ③ ④ ⑤
4	① ② ③ ④ ⑤
5	① ② ③ ④ ⑤
6	① ② ③ ④ ⑤
7	① ② ③ ④ ⑤
8	① ② ③ ④ ⑤
9	① ② ③ ④ ⑤
10	① ② ③ ④ ⑤
11	① ② ③ ④ ⑤
12	① ② ③ ④ ⑤
13	① ② ③ ④ ⑤
14	① ② ③ ④ ⑤
15	① ② ③ ④ ⑤
16	① ② ③ ④ ⑤
17	① ② ③ ④ ⑤
18	① ② ③ ④ ⑤
19	① ② ③ ④ ⑤
20	① ② ③ ④ ⑤

문번	답 란
21	① ② ③ ④ ⑤
22	① ② ③ ④ ⑤
23	① ② ③ ④ ⑤
24	① ② ③ ④ ⑤
25	① ② ③ ④ ⑤
26	① ② ③ ④ ⑤
27	① ② ③ ④ ⑤
28	① ② ③ ④ ⑤
29	① ② ③ ④ ⑤
30	① ② ③ ④ ⑤
31	① ② ③ ④ ⑤
32	① ② ③ ④ ⑤
33	① ② ③ ④ ⑤
34	① ② ③ ④ ⑤
35	① ② ③ ④ ⑤
36	① ② ③ ④ ⑤
37	① ② ③ ④ ⑤
38	① ② ③ ④ ⑤
39	① ② ③ ④ ⑤
40	① ② ③ ④ ⑤

문번	답 란
41	① ② ③ ④ ⑤
42	① ② ③ ④ ⑤
43	① ② ③ ④ ⑤
44	① ② ③ ④ ⑤
45	① ② ③ ④ ⑤

〈수험생이 지켜야 할 일〉

답안지 작성(표기)은 반드시 컴퓨터용 사인펜만을 사용하여야 합니다. (연필, 샤프펜 사용 시 불이익을 받을 수 있습니다.)

1. 성명란에는 수험생의 성명을 바르게 기재하여야 합니다.
2. 수험번호란에는 아라비아 숫자로 기재하고 해당란에 "●"와 같이 완전하게 표기하여야 합니다.
3. 문형란에는 배부받은 시험 문제지의 문형을 정확히 확인하고 해당란에 "●"와 같이 표기하여야 합니다.
   - 답안지의 '문형'란에 표기가 되어있지 않거나 이중으로 표기된 경우 불이익을 받을 수 있습니다.
   - 시험특별관리대상자의 문제지 문형은 홀수형 입니다.
4. 답란은 "●"와 같이 완전하게 표기하여야 하며, 바르지 못한 표기(⊘ ◯ ⊙ ◑ ◍ 등)를 하였을 경우는 불이익을 받을 수 있습니다.
5. 답란 수정을 원할 경우에는 수정테이프만을 사용하여 완전하게 수정하여야 합니다. 불완전한 수정처리로 인해 발생하는 불이익은 수험생에게 있습니다.
   - 수정테이프는 감독관이 소지하고 있습니다.
   - 수정액이나 스티커 등은 절대로 사용할 수 없습니다.
   - 답란 수정 후 수정테이프가 떨어지지 않게 손으로 눌러 주십시오.
   - 답안지 교체를 원할 경우 교체 가능합니다.
6. 답안지에 낙서를 하거나 불필요한 표기를 하였을 경우 불이익을 받을 수 있으므로 답안지를 최대한 깨끗한 상태로 제출하여야 합니다.

파워업 독해실전편 모의고사 15회 답안지

※ 답안지 작성(표기)은 반드시 컴퓨터용 사인펜만을 사용하고, 연필 또는 샤프펜을 절대 사용하지 마십시오.
※ 뒷면의 〈수험생이 지켜야 할 일〉을 꼭 읽어 보십시오.

③ 교시 영어 영역

※ 결시자 확인 (수험생은 표기하지 말것.)	
컴퓨터용 사인펜을 사용하여 수험번호란과 옆란을 표기	○

※ 아래 '필적확인란'에 "○○○○○○○○○○○○○"를 정자로 반드시 기재하여야 합니다.

필 적 확인란	

성 명								
수 험 번 호								
				—				
	⓪	⓪	⓪		⓪	⓪	⓪	⓪
①	①	①	①		①	①	①	①
②	②	②	②		②	②	②	②
③	③	③	③		③	③	③	③
④	④	④	④		④	④		④
⑤	⑤	⑤	⑤		⑤	⑤		⑤
⑥	⑥		⑥		⑥	⑥		⑥
⑦	⑦		⑦		⑦	⑦		⑦
⑧	⑧		⑧		⑧	⑧		⑧
	⑨		⑨		⑨	⑨		⑨

문 형
홀수형 ○
짝수형 ○

※ 문제의 문형을 확인후 표기

※ 감독관 확인 (수험생은 표기하지 말것.)	
본인여부, 수험번호 및 문형의 표기가 정확한지 확인, 옆란에 서명 또는 날인	(서 명 또는 날 인)

문번	답 란
1	① ② ③ ④ ⑤
2	① ② ③ ④ ⑤
3	① ② ③ ④ ⑤
4	① ② ③ ④ ⑤
5	① ② ③ ④ ⑤
6	① ② ③ ④ ⑤
7	① ② ③ ④ ⑤
8	① ② ③ ④ ⑤
9	① ② ③ ④ ⑤
10	① ② ③ ④ ⑤
11	① ② ③ ④ ⑤
12	① ② ③ ④ ⑤
13	① ② ③ ④ ⑤
14	① ② ③ ④ ⑤
15	① ② ③ ④ ⑤
16	① ② ③ ④ ⑤
17	① ② ③ ④ ⑤
18	① ② ③ ④ ⑤
19	① ② ③ ④ ⑤
20	① ② ③ ④ ⑤

문번	답 란
21	① ② ③ ④ ⑤
22	① ② ③ ④ ⑤
23	① ② ③ ④ ⑤
24	① ② ③ ④ ⑤
25	① ② ③ ④ ⑤
26	① ② ③ ④ ⑤
27	① ② ③ ④ ⑤
28	① ② ③ ④ ⑤
29	① ② ③ ④ ⑤
30	① ② ③ ④ ⑤
31	① ② ③ ④ ⑤
32	① ② ③ ④ ⑤
33	① ② ③ ④ ⑤
34	① ② ③ ④ ⑤
35	① ② ③ ④ ⑤
36	① ② ③ ④ ⑤
37	① ② ③ ④ ⑤
38	① ② ③ ④ ⑤
39	① ② ③ ④ ⑤
40	① ② ③ ④ ⑤

문번	답 란
41	① ② ③ ④ ⑤
42	① ② ③ ④ ⑤
43	① ② ③ ④ ⑤
44	① ② ③ ④ ⑤
45	① ② ③ ④ ⑤

〈수험생이 지켜야 할 일〉

답안지 작성(표기)은 반드시 컴퓨터용 사인펜만을 사용하여야 합니다.
(연필, 샤프펜 사용 시 불이익을 받을 수 있습니다.)

1. 성명란에는 수험생의 성명을 바르게 기재하여야 합니다.
2. 수험번호란에는 아라비아 숫자로 기재하고 해당란에 "●"와 같이 완전하게 표기하여야 합니다.
3. 문형란에는 배부받은 시험 문제지의 문형을 정확히 확인하고 해당란에 "●"와 같이 표기하여야 합니다.
   - 답안지의 '문형'란에 표기가 되어있지 않거나 이중으로 표기된 경우 불이익을 받을 수 있습니다.
   - 시험특별관리대상자의 문제지 문형은 홀수형 입니다.
4. 답란은 "●"와 같이 완전하게 표기하여야 하며, 바르지 못한 표기(⊘ ⊖ ⊙ ◑ ▨ 등)를 하였을 경우는 불이익을 받을 수 있습니다.
5. 답란 수정을 원할 경우에는 수정테이프만을 사용하여 완전하게 수정하여야 합니다. 불완전한 수정처리로 인해 발생하는 불이익은 수험생에게 있습니다.
   - 수정테이프는 감독관이 소지하고 있습니다.
   - 수정액이나 스티커 등은 절대로 사용할 수 없습니다.
   - 답란 수정 후 수정테이프가 떨어지지 않게 손으로 눌러 주십시오.
   - 답안지 교체를 원할 경우 교체 가능합니다.
6. 답안지에 낙서를 하거나 불필요한 표기를 하였을 경우 불이익을 받을 수 있으므로 답안지를 최대한 깨끗한 상태로 제출하여야 합니다.

파워업 독해실전편 모의고사 15회 답안지

③ 교시 영어 영역

※ 결시자 확인 (수험생은 표기하지 말것.)

컴퓨터용 사인펜을 사용하여 수험번호란과 옆란을 표기 ○

※ 아래 '필적확인란'에 "○○○○○○○○○○○○○"를 정자로 반드시 기재하여야 합니다.

필 적 확인란	

성 명								
수 험 번 호								
				—				
	⓪	⓪	⓪		⓪	⓪	⓪	⓪
①	①	①	①		①	①	①	①
②	②	②	②		②	②	②	②
③	③	③	③		③	③	③	③
④	④	④	④		④	④		④
⑤	⑤	⑤	⑤		⑤	⑤		⑤
⑥	⑥		⑥		⑥	⑥		⑥
⑦	⑦		⑦		⑦	⑦		⑦
⑧	⑧		⑧		⑧	⑧		⑧
	⑨		⑨		⑨	⑨		⑨

문 형

홀수형 ○

짝수형 ○

※ 문제의 문형을 확인 후 표기

※ 감독관 확인 (수험생은 표기하지 말것.)

본인여부, 수험번호 및 문형의 표기가 정확한지 확인, 옆란에 서명 또는 날인 (서 명 또는 날 인)

※ 답안지 작성(표기)은 반드시 컴퓨터용 사인펜만을 사용하고, 연필 또는 샤프펜을 절대 사용하지 마십시오.
※ 뒷면의 〈수험생이 지켜야 할 일〉을 꼭 읽어 보십시오.

문번	답 란	문번	답 란	문번	답 란
1	① ② ③ ④ ⑤	21	① ② ③ ④ ⑤	41	① ② ③ ④ ⑤
2	① ② ③ ④ ⑤	22	① ② ③ ④ ⑤	42	① ② ③ ④ ⑤
3	① ② ③ ④ ⑤	23	① ② ③ ④ ⑤	43	① ② ③ ④ ⑤
4	① ② ③ ④ ⑤	24	① ② ③ ④ ⑤	44	① ② ③ ④ ⑤
5	① ② ③ ④ ⑤	25	① ② ③ ④ ⑤	45	① ② ③ ④ ⑤
6	① ② ③ ④ ⑤	26	① ② ③ ④ ⑤		
7	① ② ③ ④ ⑤	27	① ② ③ ④ ⑤		
8	① ② ③ ④ ⑤	28	① ② ③ ④ ⑤		
9	① ② ③ ④ ⑤	29	① ② ③ ④ ⑤		
10	① ② ③ ④ ⑤	30	① ② ③ ④ ⑤		
11	① ② ③ ④ ⑤	31	① ② ③ ④ ⑤		
12	① ② ③ ④ ⑤	32	① ② ③ ④ ⑤		
13	① ② ③ ④ ⑤	33	① ② ③ ④ ⑤		
14	① ② ③ ④ ⑤	34	① ② ③ ④ ⑤		
15	① ② ③ ④ ⑤	35	① ② ③ ④ ⑤		
16	① ② ③ ④ ⑤	36	① ② ③ ④ ⑤		
17	① ② ③ ④ ⑤	37	① ② ③ ④ ⑤		
18	① ② ③ ④ ⑤	38	① ② ③ ④ ⑤		
19	① ② ③ ④ ⑤	39	① ② ③ ④ ⑤		
20	① ② ③ ④ ⑤	40	① ② ③ ④ ⑤		

〈수험생이 지켜야 할 일〉

답안지 작성(표기)은 반드시 컴퓨터용 사인펜만을 사용하여야 합니다. (연필, 샤프펜 사용 시 불이익을 받을 수 있습니다.)

1. 성명란에는 수험생의 성명을 바르게 기재하여야 합니다.
2. 수험번호란에는 아라비아 숫자로 기재하고 해당란에 "⬮"와 같이 완전하게 표기하여야 합니다.
3. 문형란에는 배부받은 시험 문제지의 문형을 정확히 확인하고 해당란에 "⬮"와 같이 표기하여야 합니다.
   – 답안지의 '문형'란에 표기가 되어있지 않거나 이중으로 표기된 경우 불이익을 받을 수 있습니다.
   – 시험특별관리대상자의 문제지 문형은 홀수형 입니다.
4. 답란은 "⬮"와 같이 완전하게 표기하여야 하며, 바르지 못한 표기(⊘ ⦶ ⊙ ◑ ▨ 등)를 하였을 경우는 불이익을 받을 수 있습니다.
5. 답란 수정을 원할 경우에는 수정테이프만을 사용하여 완전하게 수정하여야 합니다. 불완전한 수정처리로 인해 발생하는 불이익은 수험생에게 있습니다.
   – 수정테이프는 감독관이 소지하고 있습니다.
   – 수정액이나 스티커 등은 절대로 사용할 수 없습니다.
   – 답란 수정 후 수정테이프가 떨어지지 않게 손으로 눌러 주십시오.
   – 답안지 교체를 원할 경우 교체 가능합니다.
6. 답안지에 낙서를 하거나 불필요한 표기를 하였을 경우 불이익을 받을 수 있으므로 답안지를 최대한 깨끗한 상태로 제출하여야 합니다.

파워업 독해실전편 모의고사 15회 답안지

③ 교시 영어 영역

※ 결시자 확인 (수험생은 표기하지 말것.)

컴퓨터용 사인펜을 사용하여 수험번호란과 옆란을 표기

※ 아래 '필적확인란'에 "○○○○○○○○○○○○○"를 정자로 반드시 기재하여야 합니다.

필 적 확인란

성 명

수 험 번 호

				—				
	0	0	0		0	0	0	0
1	1	1	1		1	1	1	1
2	2	2	2		2	2	2	2
3	3	3	3		3	3	3	3
4	4	4	4		4	4		4
5	5	5	5		5	5		5
6	6		6		6	6		6
7	7		7		7	7		7
8	8		8		8	8		8
	9		9		9	9		9

문 형

홀수형 ○

짝수형 ○

※ 문제의 문형을 확인 후 표기

※ 감독관 확인 (수험생은 표기하지 말것.)

본인여부, 수험번호 및 문형의 표기가 정확한지 확인, 옆란에 서명 또는 날인

(서 명 또는 날 인)

※ 답안지 작성(표기)은 반드시 컴퓨터용 사인펜만을 사용하고, 연필 또는 샤프펜을 절대 사용하지 마십시오.

※ 뒷면의 〈수험생이 지켜야 할 일〉을 꼭 읽어 보십시오.

문번	답				란
1	1	2	3	4	5
2	1	2	3	4	5
3	1	2	3	4	5
4	1	2	3	4	5
5	1	2	3	4	5
6	1	2	3	4	5
7	1	2	3	4	5
8	1	2	3	4	5
9	1	2	3	4	5
10	1	2	3	4	5
11	1	2	3	4	5
12	1	2	3	4	5
13	1	2	3	4	5
14	1	2	3	4	5
15	1	2	3	4	5
16	1	2	3	4	5
17	1	2	3	4	5
18	1	2	3	4	5
19	1	2	3	4	5
20	1	2	3	4	5

문번	답				란
21	1	2	3	4	5
22	1	2	3	4	5
23	1	2	3	4	5
24	1	2	3	4	5
25	1	2	3	4	5
26	1	2	3	4	5
27	1	2	3	4	5
28	1	2	3	4	5
29	1	2	3	4	5
30	1	2	3	4	5
31	1	2	3	4	5
32	1	2	3	4	5
33	1	2	3	4	5
34	1	2	3	4	5
35	1	2	3	4	5
36	1	2	3	4	5
37	1	2	3	4	5
38	1	2	3	4	5
39	1	2	3	4	5
40	1	2	3	4	5

문번	답				란
41	1	2	3	4	5
42	1	2	3	4	5
43	1	2	3	4	5
44	1	2	3	4	5
45	1	2	3	4	5

〈수험생이 지켜야 할 일〉

답안지 작성(표기)은 반드시 컴퓨터용 사인펜만을 사용하여야 합니다. (연필, 샤프펜 사용 시 불이익을 받을 수 있습니다.)

1. 성명란에는 수험생의 성명을 바르게 기재하여야 합니다.
2. 수험번호란에는 아라비아 숫자로 기재하고 해당란에 "●"와 같이 완전하게 표기하여야 합니다.
3. 문형란에는 배부받은 시험 문제지의 문형을 정확히 확인하고 해당란에 "●"와 같이 표기하여야 합니다.
   - 답안지의 '문형'란에 표기가 되어있지 않거나 이중으로 표기된 경우 불이익을 받을 수 있습니다.
   - 시험특별관리대상자의 문제지 문형은 홀수형 입니다.
4. 답란은 "●"와 같이 완전하게 표기하여야 하며, 바르지 못한 표기(✓ ⦶ ⊙ ◐ ▨ 등)를 하였을 경우는 불이익을 받을 수 있습니다.
5. 답란 수정을 원할 경우에는 수정테이프만을 사용하여 완전하게 수정하여야 합니다. 불완전한 수정처리로 인해 발생하는 불이익은 수험생에게 있습니다.
   - 수정테이프는 감독관이 소지하고 있습니다.
   - 수정액이나 스티커 등은 절대로 사용할 수 없습니다.
   - 답란 수정 후 수정테이프가 떨어지지 않게 손으로 눌러 주십시오.
   - 답안지 교체를 원할 경우 교체 가능합니다.
6. 답안지에 낙서를 하거나 불필요한 표기를 하였을 경우 불이익을 받을 수 있으므로 답안지를 최대한 깨끗한 상태로 제출하여야 합니다.

파워업 독해실전편 모의고사 15회 답안지

③ 교시 영어 영역

※ 결시자 확인 (수험생은 표기하지 말것.)

컴퓨터용 사인펜을 사용하여 수험번호란과 옆란을 표기 ○

※ 아래 '필적확인란'에 "○○○○○○○○○○○○○"를 정자로 반드시 기재하여야 합니다.

필 적 확인란	

성 명								
수 험 번 호								
				—				
	⓪	⓪	⓪		⓪	⓪	⓪	⓪
①	①	①	①		①	①	①	①
②	②	②	②		②	②	②	②
③	③	③	③		③	③	③	③
④	④	④	④		④	④		④
⑤	⑤	⑤	⑤		⑤	⑤		⑤
⑥	⑥		⑥		⑥	⑥		⑥
⑦	⑦		⑦		⑦	⑦		⑦
⑧	⑧		⑧		⑧	⑧		⑧
	⑨		⑨		⑨	⑨		⑨

문 형

홀수형 ○

짝수형 ○

※ 문제의 문형을 확인 후 표기

※ 감독관 확인 (수험생은 표기하지 말것.)

본인여부, 수험번호 및 문형의 표기가 정확한지 확인, 옆란에 서명 또는 날인 (서 명 또는 날 인)

※ 답안지 작성(표기)은 반드시 컴퓨터용 사인펜만을 사용하고, 연필 또는 샤프펜을 절대 사용하지 마십시오.

※ 뒷면의 〈수험생이 지켜야 할 일〉을 꼭 읽어 보십시오.

문번	답 란	문번	답 란	문번	답 란
1	① ② ③ ④ ⑤	21	① ② ③ ④ ⑤	41	① ② ③ ④ ⑤
2	① ② ③ ④ ⑤	22	① ② ③ ④ ⑤	42	① ② ③ ④ ⑤
3	① ② ③ ④ ⑤	23	① ② ③ ④ ⑤	43	① ② ③ ④ ⑤
4	① ② ③ ④ ⑤	24	① ② ③ ④ ⑤	44	① ② ③ ④ ⑤
5	① ② ③ ④ ⑤	25	① ② ③ ④ ⑤	45	① ② ③ ④ ⑤
6	① ② ③ ④ ⑤	26	① ② ③ ④ ⑤		
7	① ② ③ ④ ⑤	27	① ② ③ ④ ⑤		
8	① ② ③ ④ ⑤	28	① ② ③ ④ ⑤		
9	① ② ③ ④ ⑤	29	① ② ③ ④ ⑤		
10	① ② ③ ④ ⑤	30	① ② ③ ④ ⑤		
11	① ② ③ ④ ⑤	31	① ② ③ ④ ⑤		
12	① ② ③ ④ ⑤	32	① ② ③ ④ ⑤		
13	① ② ③ ④ ⑤	33	① ② ③ ④ ⑤		
14	① ② ③ ④ ⑤	34	① ② ③ ④ ⑤		
15	① ② ③ ④ ⑤	35	① ② ③ ④ ⑤		
16	① ② ③ ④ ⑤	36	① ② ③ ④ ⑤		
17	① ② ③ ④ ⑤	37	① ② ③ ④ ⑤		
18	① ② ③ ④ ⑤	38	① ② ③ ④ ⑤		
19	① ② ③ ④ ⑤	39	① ② ③ ④ ⑤		
20	① ② ③ ④ ⑤	40	① ② ③ ④ ⑤		

〈수험생이 지켜야 할 일〉

답안지 작성(표기)은 반드시 컴퓨터용 사인펜만을 사용하여야 합니다.
(연필, 샤프펜 사용 시 불이익을 받을 수 있습니다.)

1. 성명란에는 수험생의 성명을 바르게 기재하여야 합니다.
2. 수험번호란에는 아라비아 숫자로 기재하고 해당란에 "●"와 같이 완전하게 표기하여야 합니다.
3. 문형란에는 배부받은 시험 문제지의 문형을 정확히 확인하고 해당란에 "●"와 같이 표기하여야 합니다.
   - 답안지의 '문형'란에 표기가 되어있지 않거나 이중으로 표기된 경우 불이익을 받을 수 있습니다.
   - 시험특별관리대상자의 문제지 문형은 홀수형 입니다.
4. 답란은 "●"와 같이 완전하게 표기하여야 하며, 바르지 못한 표기(⊘ ⦶ ⊙ ◑ ▨ 등)를 하였을 경우는 불이익을 받을 수 있습니다.
5. 답란 수정을 원할 경우에는 수정테이프만을 사용하여 완전하게 수정하여야 합니다. 불완전한 수정처리로 인해 발생하는 불이익은 수험생에게 있습니다.
   - 수정테이프는 감독관이 소지하고 있습니다.
   - 수정액이나 스티커 등은 절대로 사용할 수 없습니다.
   - 답란 수정 후 수정테이프가 떨어지지 않게 손으로 눌러 주십시오.
   - 답안지 교체를 원할 경우 교체 가능합니다.
6. 답안지에 낙서를 하거나 불필요한 표기를 하였을 경우 불이익을 받을 수 있으므로 답안지를 최대한 깨끗한 상태로 제출하여야 합니다.

파워업 독해실전편 모의고사 15회 답안지

③ 교시 영어 영역

※ 결시자 확인 (수험생은 표기하지 말것.)

컴퓨터용 사인펜을 사용하여 수험번호란과 옆란을 표기	⬯

※ 아래 '필적확인란'에 "○○○○○○○○○○○○○"를 정자로 반드시 기재하여야 합니다.

필 적 확인란	

성 명								
수 험 번 호								
				—				
	⓪	⓪	⓪		⓪	⓪	⓪	⓪
①	①	①	①		①	①	①	①
②	②	②	②		②	②	②	②
③	③	③	③		③	③	③	③
④	④	④	④		④	④		④
⑤	⑤	⑤	⑤		⑤	⑤		⑤
⑥	⑥		⑥		⑥	⑥		⑥
⑦	⑦		⑦		⑦	⑦		⑦
⑧	⑧		⑧		⑧	⑧		⑧
	⑨		⑨		⑨	⑨		⑨

문 형
홀수형 ⬯
짝수형 ⬯

※ 문제의 문형을 확인 후 표기

※ 감독관 확인 (수험생은 표기하지 말것.)

본인여부, 수험번호 및 문형의 표기가 정확한지 확인, 옆란에 서명 또는 날인	(서 명 또는 날 인)

※ 답안지 작성(표기)은 반드시 컴퓨터용 사인펜만을 사용하고, 연필 또는 샤프펜을 절대 사용하지 마십시오.
※ 뒷면의 〈수험생이 지켜야 할 일〉을 꼭 읽어 보십시오.

문번	답 란	문번	답 란	문번	답 란
1	① ② ③ ④ ⑤	21	① ② ③ ④ ⑤	41	① ② ③ ④ ⑤
2	① ② ③ ④ ⑤	22	① ② ③ ④ ⑤	42	① ② ③ ④ ⑤
3	① ② ③ ④ ⑤	23	① ② ③ ④ ⑤	43	① ② ③ ④ ⑤
4	① ② ③ ④ ⑤	24	① ② ③ ④ ⑤	44	① ② ③ ④ ⑤
5	① ② ③ ④ ⑤	25	① ② ③ ④ ⑤	45	① ② ③ ④ ⑤
6	① ② ③ ④ ⑤	26	① ② ③ ④ ⑤		
7	① ② ③ ④ ⑤	27	① ② ③ ④ ⑤		
8	① ② ③ ④ ⑤	28	① ② ③ ④ ⑤		
9	① ② ③ ④ ⑤	29	① ② ③ ④ ⑤		
10	① ② ③ ④ ⑤	30	① ② ③ ④ ⑤		
11	① ② ③ ④ ⑤	31	① ② ③ ④ ⑤		
12	① ② ③ ④ ⑤	32	① ② ③ ④ ⑤		
13	① ② ③ ④ ⑤	33	① ② ③ ④ ⑤		
14	① ② ③ ④ ⑤	34	① ② ③ ④ ⑤		
15	① ② ③ ④ ⑤	35	① ② ③ ④ ⑤		
16	① ② ③ ④ ⑤	36	① ② ③ ④ ⑤		
17	① ② ③ ④ ⑤	37	① ② ③ ④ ⑤		
18	① ② ③ ④ ⑤	38	① ② ③ ④ ⑤		
19	① ② ③ ④ ⑤	39	① ② ③ ④ ⑤		
20	① ② ③ ④ ⑤	40	① ② ③ ④ ⑤		

〈수험생이 지켜야 할 일〉

> 답안지 작성(표기)은 반드시 컴퓨터용 사인펜만을 사용하여야 합니다.
> (연필, 샤프펜 사용 시 불이익을 받을 수 있습니다.)

1. 성명란에는 수험생의 성명을 바르게 기재하여야 합니다.
2. 수험번호란에는 아라비아 숫자로 기재하고 해당란에 "●"와 같이 완전하게 표기하여야 합니다.
3. 문형란에는 배부받은 시험 문제지의 문형을 정확히 확인하고 해당란에 "●"와 같이 표기하여야 합니다.
   - 답안지의 '문형'란에 표기가 되어있지 않거나 이중으로 표기된 경우 불이익을 받을 수 있습니다.
   - 시험특별관리대상자의 문제지 문형은 홀수형 입니다.
4. 답란은 "●"와 같이 완전하게 표기하여야 하며, 바르지 못한 표기(✓ ⦶ ⊙ ◑ ▨ 등)를 하였을 경우는 불이익을 받을 수 있습니다.
5. 답란 수정을 원할 경우에는 수정테이프만을 사용하여 완전하게 수정하여야 합니다. 불완전한 수정처리로 인해 발생하는 불이익은 수험생에게 있습니다.
   - 수정테이프는 감독관이 소지하고 있습니다.
   - 수정액이나 스티커 등은 절대로 사용할 수 없습니다.
   - 답란 수정 후 수정테이프가 떨어지지 않게 손으로 눌러 주십시오.
   - 답안지 교체를 원할 경우 교체 가능합니다.
6. 답안지에 낙서를 하거나 불필요한 표기를 하였을 경우 불이익을 받을 수 있으므로 답안지를 최대한 깨끗한 상태로 제출하여야 합니다.

파워업 독해실전편 모의고사 15회 답안지

※ 답안지 작성(표기)은 반드시 컴퓨터용 사인펜만을 사용하고, 연필 또는 샤프펜을 절대 사용하지 마십시오.
※ 뒷면의 〈수험생이 지켜야 할 일〉을 꼭 읽어 보십시오.

③ 교시 영어 영역

※ 결시자 확인 (수험생은 표기하지 말것.)

컴퓨터용 사인펜을 사용하여 수험번호란과 옆란을 표기 ⓪

※ 아래 '필적확인란'에 "○○○○○○○○○○○○○"를 정자로 반드시 기재하여야 합니다.

필 적 확인란

성 명

수 험 번 호

				—				
	⓪	⓪	⓪		⓪	⓪	⓪	⓪
①	①	①	①		①	①	①	①
②	②	②	②		②	②	②	②
③	③	③	③		③	③	③	③
④	④	④	④		④	④		④
⑤	⑤	⑤	⑤		⑤	⑤		⑤
⑥	⑥		⑥		⑥	⑥		⑥
⑦	⑦		⑦		⑦	⑦		⑦
⑧	⑧		⑧		⑧	⑧		⑧
	⑨		⑨		⑨	⑨		⑨

문 형

홀수형 ⓪
짝수형 ⓪

※ 문제의 문형을 확인후 표기

※ 감독관 확인 (수험생은 표기하지 말것.)

본인여부, 수험번호 및 문형의 표기가 정확한지 확인, 옆란에 서명 또는 날인

(서 명 또는 날 인)

문번	답 란
1	① ② ③ ④ ⑤
2	① ② ③ ④ ⑤
3	① ② ③ ④ ⑤
4	① ② ③ ④ ⑤
5	① ② ③ ④ ⑤
6	① ② ③ ④ ⑤
7	① ② ③ ④ ⑤
8	① ② ③ ④ ⑤
9	① ② ③ ④ ⑤
10	① ② ③ ④ ⑤
11	① ② ③ ④ ⑤
12	① ② ③ ④ ⑤
13	① ② ③ ④ ⑤
14	① ② ③ ④ ⑤
15	① ② ③ ④ ⑤
16	① ② ③ ④ ⑤
17	① ② ③ ④ ⑤
18	① ② ③ ④ ⑤
19	① ② ③ ④ ⑤
20	① ② ③ ④ ⑤

문번	답 란
21	① ② ③ ④ ⑤
22	① ② ③ ④ ⑤
23	① ② ③ ④ ⑤
24	① ② ③ ④ ⑤
25	① ② ③ ④ ⑤
26	① ② ③ ④ ⑤
27	① ② ③ ④ ⑤
28	① ② ③ ④ ⑤
29	① ② ③ ④ ⑤
30	① ② ③ ④ ⑤
31	① ② ③ ④ ⑤
32	① ② ③ ④ ⑤
33	① ② ③ ④ ⑤
34	① ② ③ ④ ⑤
35	① ② ③ ④ ⑤
36	① ② ③ ④ ⑤
37	① ② ③ ④ ⑤
38	① ② ③ ④ ⑤
39	① ② ③ ④ ⑤
40	① ② ③ ④ ⑤

문번	답 란
41	① ② ③ ④ ⑤
42	① ② ③ ④ ⑤
43	① ② ③ ④ ⑤
44	① ② ③ ④ ⑤
45	① ② ③ ④ ⑤

〈수험생이 지켜야 할 일〉

답안지 작성(표기)은 반드시 컴퓨터용 사인펜만을 사용하여야 합니다. (연필, 샤프펜 사용 시 불이익을 받을 수 있습니다.)

1. 성명란에는 수험생의 성명을 바르게 기재하여야 합니다.
2. 수험번호란에는 아라비아 숫자로 기재하고 해당란에 "●"와 같이 완전하게 표기하여야 합니다.
3. 문형란에는 배부받은 시험 문제지의 문형을 정확히 확인하고 해당란에 "●"와 같이 표기하여야 합니다.
   – 답안지의 '문형'란에 표기가 되어있지 않거나 이중으로 표기된 경우 불이익을 받을 수 있습니다.
   – 시험특별관리대상자의 문제지 문형은 홀수형 입니다.
4. 답란은 "●"와 같이 완전하게 표기하여야 하며, 바르지 못한 표기(◌ ◌ ◌ ◌ ◌ 등)를 하였을 경우는 불이익을 받을 수 있습니다.
5. 답란 수정을 원할 경우에는 수정테이프만을 사용하여 완전하게 수정하여야 합니다. 불완전한 수정처리로 인해 발생하는 불이익은 수험생에게 있습니다.
   – 수정테이프는 감독관이 소지하고 있습니다.
   – 수정액이나 스티커 등은 절대로 사용할 수 없습니다.
   – 답란 수정 후 수정테이프가 떨어지지 않게 손으로 눌러 주십시오.
   – 답안지 교체를 원할 경우 교체 가능합니다.
6. 답안지에 낙서를 하거나 불필요한 표기를 하였을 경우 불이익을 받을 수 있으므로 답안지를 최대한 깨끗한 상태로 제출하여야 합니다.

파워업 독해실전편 모의고사 15회 답안지

③ 교시 영어 영역

※ 결시자 확인 (수험생은 표기하지 말것.)

컴퓨터용 사인펜을 사용하여 수험번호란과 옆란을 표기

※ 아래 '필적확인란'에 "○○○○○○○○○○ ○○○"를 정자로 반드시 기재하여야 합니다.

필 적 확인란

성 명

수 험 번 호

				—				
	0	0	0		0	0	0	0
1	1	1	1		1	1	1	1
2	2	2	2		2	2	2	2
3	3	3	3		3	3	3	3
4	4	4	4		4	4		4
5	5	5	5		5	5		5
6	6		6		6	6		6
7	7		7		7	7		7
8	8		8		8	8		8
	9		9		9	9		9

문 형

홀수형

짝수형

※ 문제의 문형을 확인후 표기

※ 감독관 확인 (수험생은 표기하지 말것.)

본인여부, 수험번호 및 문형의 표기가 정확한지 확인, 옆란에 서명 또는 날인

서 명 또는 날 인

※ 답안지 작성(표기)은 반드시 컴퓨터용 사인펜만을 사용하고, 연필 또는 샤프펜을 절대 사용하지 마십시오.
※ 뒷면의 〈수험생이 지켜야 할 일〉을 꼭 읽어 보십시오.

문번	답 란	문번	답 란	문번	답 란
1	① ② ③ ④ ⑤	21	① ② ③ ④ ⑤	41	① ② ③ ④ ⑤
2	① ② ③ ④ ⑤	22	① ② ③ ④ ⑤	42	① ② ③ ④ ⑤
3	① ② ③ ④ ⑤	23	① ② ③ ④ ⑤	43	① ② ③ ④ ⑤
4	① ② ③ ④ ⑤	24	① ② ③ ④ ⑤	44	① ② ③ ④ ⑤
5	① ② ③ ④ ⑤	25	① ② ③ ④ ⑤	45	① ② ③ ④ ⑤
6	① ② ③ ④ ⑤	26	① ② ③ ④ ⑤		
7	① ② ③ ④ ⑤	27	① ② ③ ④ ⑤		
8	① ② ③ ④ ⑤	28	① ② ③ ④ ⑤		
9	① ② ③ ④ ⑤	29	① ② ③ ④ ⑤		
10	① ② ③ ④ ⑤	30	① ② ③ ④ ⑤		
11	① ② ③ ④ ⑤	31	① ② ③ ④ ⑤		
12	① ② ③ ④ ⑤	32	① ② ③ ④ ⑤		
13	① ② ③ ④ ⑤	33	① ② ③ ④ ⑤		
14	① ② ③ ④ ⑤	34	① ② ③ ④ ⑤		
15	① ② ③ ④ ⑤	35	① ② ③ ④ ⑤		
16	① ② ③ ④ ⑤	36	① ② ③ ④ ⑤		
17	① ② ③ ④ ⑤	37	① ② ③ ④ ⑤		
18	① ② ③ ④ ⑤	38	① ② ③ ④ ⑤		
19	① ② ③ ④ ⑤	39	① ② ③ ④ ⑤		
20	① ② ③ ④ ⑤	40	① ② ③ ④ ⑤		

〈수험생이 지켜야 할 일〉

> 답안지 작성(표기)은 반드시 컴퓨터용 사인펜만을 사용하여야 합니다.
> (연필, 샤프펜 사용 시 불이익을 받을 수 있습니다.)

1. 성명란에는 수험생의 성명을 바르게 기재하여야 합니다.
2. 수험번호란에는 아라비아 숫자로 기재하고 해당란에 "●"와 같이 완전하게 표기하여야 합니다.
3. 문형란에는 배부받은 시험 문제지의 문형을 정확히 확인하고 해당란에 "●"와 같이 표기하여야 합니다.
   - 답안지의 '문형'란에 표기가 되어있지 않거나 이중으로 표기된 경우 불이익을 받을 수 있습니다.
   - 시험특별관리대상자의 문제지 문형은 홀수형 입니다.
4. 답란은 "●"와 같이 완전하게 표기하여야 하며, 바르지 못한 표기(ⓥ ⓞ ⊙ ◑ ▨ 등)를 하였을 경우는 불이익을 받을 수 있습니다.
5. 답란 수정을 원할 경우에는 수정테이프만을 사용하여 완전하게 수정하여야 합니다. 불완전한 수정처리로 인해 발생하는 불이익은 수험생에게 있습니다.
   - 수정테이프는 감독관이 소지하고 있습니다.
   - 수정액이나 스티커 등은 절대로 사용할 수 없습니다.
   - 답란 수정 후 수정테이프가 떨어지지 않게 손으로 눌러 주십시오.
   - 답안지 교체를 원할 경우 교체 가능합니다.
6. 답안지에 낙서를 하거나 불필요한 표기를 하였을 경우 불이익을 받을 수 있으므로 답안지를 최대한 깨끗한 상태로 제출하여야 합니다.

파워업 독해실전편 모의고사 15회 답안지

③ 교시 영어 영역

※ 결시자 확인 (수험생은 표기하지 말것.)

컴퓨터용 사인펜을 사용하여 수험번호란과 옆란을 표기	○

※ 아래 '필적확인란'에 "○○○○○○○○○○○○○"를 정자로 반드시 기재하여야 합니다.

필 적 확인란	

성 명								
수 험 번 호								
				–				
	⓪	⓪	⓪		⓪	⓪	⓪	⓪
①	①	①	①		①	①	①	①
②	②	②	②		②	②	②	②
③	③	③	③		③	③	③	③
④	④	④	④		④	④		④
⑤	⑤	⑤	⑤		⑤	⑤		⑤
⑥	⑥		⑥		⑥	⑥		⑥
⑦	⑦		⑦		⑦	⑦		⑦
⑧	⑧		⑧		⑧	⑧		⑧
	⑨		⑨		⑨	⑨		⑨

문 형
홀수형 ○
짝수형 ○

※ 문제의 문형을 확인후 표기

※ 감독관 확인 (수험생은 표기하지 말것.)

본인여부, 수험번호 및 문형의 표기가 정확한지 확인, 옆란에 서명 또는 날인	서 명 또는 날 인

※ 답안지 작성(표기)은 반드시 컴퓨터용 사인펜만을 사용하고, 연필 또는 샤프펜을 절대 사용하지 마십시오.
※ 뒷면의 〈수험생이 지켜야 할 일〉을 꼭 읽어 보십시오.

문번	답 란	문번	답 란	문번	답 란
1	① ② ③ ④ ⑤	21	① ② ③ ④ ⑤	41	① ② ③ ④ ⑤
2	① ② ③ ④ ⑤	22	① ② ③ ④ ⑤	42	① ② ③ ④ ⑤
3	① ② ③ ④ ⑤	23	① ② ③ ④ ⑤	43	① ② ③ ④ ⑤
4	① ② ③ ④ ⑤	24	① ② ③ ④ ⑤	44	① ② ③ ④ ⑤
5	① ② ③ ④ ⑤	25	① ② ③ ④ ⑤	45	① ② ③ ④ ⑤
6	① ② ③ ④ ⑤	26	① ② ③ ④ ⑤		
7	① ② ③ ④ ⑤	27	① ② ③ ④ ⑤		
8	① ② ③ ④ ⑤	28	① ② ③ ④ ⑤		
9	① ② ③ ④ ⑤	29	① ② ③ ④ ⑤		
10	① ② ③ ④ ⑤	30	① ② ③ ④ ⑤		
11	① ② ③ ④ ⑤	31	① ② ③ ④ ⑤		
12	① ② ③ ④ ⑤	32	① ② ③ ④ ⑤		
13	① ② ③ ④ ⑤	33	① ② ③ ④ ⑤		
14	① ② ③ ④ ⑤	34	① ② ③ ④ ⑤		
15	① ② ③ ④ ⑤	35	① ② ③ ④ ⑤		
16	① ② ③ ④ ⑤	36	① ② ③ ④ ⑤		
17	① ② ③ ④ ⑤	37	① ② ③ ④ ⑤		
18	① ② ③ ④ ⑤	38	① ② ③ ④ ⑤		
19	① ② ③ ④ ⑤	39	① ② ③ ④ ⑤		
20	① ② ③ ④ ⑤	40	① ② ③ ④ ⑤		

〈수험생이 지켜야 할 일〉

답안지 작성(표기)은 반드시 컴퓨터용 사인펜만을 사용하여야 합니다. (연필, 샤프펜 사용 시 불이익을 받을 수 있습니다.)

1. 성명란에는 수험생의 성명을 바르게 기재하여야 합니다.
2. 수험번호란에는 아라비아 숫자로 기재하고 해당란에 "●"와 같이 완전하게 표기하여야 합니다.
3. 문형란에는 배부받은 시험 문제지의 문형을 정확히 확인하고 해당란에 "●"와 같이 표기하여야 합니다.
   - 답안지의 '문형'란에 표기가 되어있지 않거나 이중으로 표기된 경우 불이익을 받을 수 있습니다.
   - 시험특별관리대상자의 문제지 문형은 홀수형 입니다.
4. 답란은 "●"와 같이 완전하게 표기하여야 하며, 바르지 못한 표기(✓ ⦶ ⊙ ◑ ▨ 등)를 하였을 경우는 불이익을 받을 수 있습니다.
5. 답란 수정을 원할 경우에는 수정테이프만을 사용하여 완전하게 수정하여야 합니다. 불완전한 수정처리로 인해 발생하는 불이익은 수험생에게 있습니다.
   - 수정테이프는 감독관이 소지하고 있습니다.
   - 수정액이나 스티커 등은 절대로 사용할 수 없습니다.
   - 답란 수정 후 수정테이프가 떨어지지 않게 손으로 눌러 주십시오.
   - 답안지 교체를 원할 경우 교체 가능합니다.
6. 답안지에 낙서를 하거나 불필요한 표기를 하였을 경우 불이익을 받을 수 있으므로 답안지를 최대한 깨끗한 상태로 제출하여야 합니다.

파워업 독해실전편 모의고사 15회 답안지

③ 교시 영어 영역

※ 결시자 확인 (수험생은 표기하지 말것.)

컴퓨터용 사인펜을 사용하여 수험번호란과 옆란을 표기	0

※ 아래 '필적확인란'에 "○○○○○○○○○○○○○"를 정자로 반드시 기재하여야 합니다.

필 적 확인란	

성 명								
수 험 번 호								
				—				
	0	0	0		0	0	0	0
1	1	1	1		1	1	1	1
2	2	2	2		2	2	2	2
3	3	3	3		3	3	3	3
4	4	4	4		4	4		4
5	5	5	5		5	5		5
6	6		6		6	6		6
7	7		7		7	7		7
8	8		8		8	8		8
	9		9		9	9		9

문 형
홀수형 0
짝수형 0

※ 문제의 문형을 확인후 표기

※ 감독관 확인 (수험생은 표기하지 말것.)

본인여부, 수험번호 및 문형의 표기가 정확한지 확인, 옆란에 서명 또는 날인	서 명 또는 날 인

※ 답안지 작성(표기)은 반드시 컴퓨터용 사인펜만을 사용하고, 연필 또는 샤프펜을 절대 사용하지 마십시오.
※ 뒷면의 〈수험생이 지켜야 할 일〉을 꼭 읽어 보십시오.

문번	답 란	문번	답 란	문번	답 란
1	① ② ③ ④ ⑤	21	① ② ③ ④ ⑤	41	① ② ③ ④ ⑤
2	① ② ③ ④ ⑤	22	① ② ③ ④ ⑤	42	① ② ③ ④ ⑤
3	① ② ③ ④ ⑤	23	① ② ③ ④ ⑤	43	① ② ③ ④ ⑤
4	① ② ③ ④ ⑤	24	① ② ③ ④ ⑤	44	① ② ③ ④ ⑤
5	① ② ③ ④ ⑤	25	① ② ③ ④ ⑤	45	① ② ③ ④ ⑤
6	① ② ③ ④ ⑤	26	① ② ③ ④ ⑤		
7	① ② ③ ④ ⑤	27	① ② ③ ④ ⑤		
8	① ② ③ ④ ⑤	28	① ② ③ ④ ⑤		
9	① ② ③ ④ ⑤	29	① ② ③ ④ ⑤		
10	① ② ③ ④ ⑤	30	① ② ③ ④ ⑤		
11	① ② ③ ④ ⑤	31	① ② ③ ④ ⑤		
12	① ② ③ ④ ⑤	32	① ② ③ ④ ⑤		
13	① ② ③ ④ ⑤	33	① ② ③ ④ ⑤		
14	① ② ③ ④ ⑤	34	① ② ③ ④ ⑤		
15	① ② ③ ④ ⑤	35	① ② ③ ④ ⑤		
16	① ② ③ ④ ⑤	36	① ② ③ ④ ⑤		
17	① ② ③ ④ ⑤	37	① ② ③ ④ ⑤		
18	① ② ③ ④ ⑤	38	① ② ③ ④ ⑤		
19	① ② ③ ④ ⑤	39	① ② ③ ④ ⑤		
20	① ② ③ ④ ⑤	40	① ② ③ ④ ⑤		

〈수험생이 지켜야 할 일〉

답안지 작성(표기)은 반드시 컴퓨터용 사인펜만을 사용하여야 합니다.
(연필, 샤프펜 사용 시 불이익을 받을 수 있습니다.)

1. 성명란에는 수험생의 성명을 바르게 기재하여야 합니다.
2. 수험번호란에는 아라비아 숫자로 기재하고 해당란에 "●"와 같이 완전하게 표기하여야 합니다.
3. 문형란에는 배부받은 시험 문제지의 문형을 정확히 확인하고 해당란에 "●"와 같이 표기하여야 합니다.
   – 답안지의 '문형'란에 표기가 되어있지 않거나 이중으로 표기된 경우 불이익을 받을 수 있습니다.
   – 시험특별관리대상자의 문제지 문형은 홀수형 입니다.
4. 답란은 "●"와 같이 완전하게 표기하여야 하며, 바르지 못한 표기(⊘ ⦶ ⊙ ◑ ▨ 등)를 하였을 경우는 불이익을 받을 수 있습니다.
5. 답란 수정을 원할 경우에는 수정테이프만을 사용하여 완전하게 수정하여야 합니다. 불완전한 수정처리로 인해 발생하는 불이익은 수험생에게 있습니다.
   – 수정테이프는 감독관이 소지하고 있습니다.
   – 수정액이나 스티커 등은 절대로 사용할 수 없습니다.
   – 답란 수정 후 수정테이프가 떨어지지 않게 손으로 눌러 주십시오.
   – 답안지 교체를 원할 경우 교체 가능합니다.
6. 답안지에 낙서를 하거나 불필요한 표기를 하였을 경우 불이익을 받을 수 있으므로 답안지를 최대한 깨끗한 상태로 제출하여야 합니다.

파워업 독해실전편 모의고사 15회 답안지

③ 교시 영어 영역

※ 결시자 확인 (수험생은 표기하지 말것.)

컴퓨터용 사인펜을 사용하여 수험번호란과 옆란을 표기

※ 아래 '필적확인란'에 "○○○○○○○○○○○○○"를 정자로 반드시 기재하여야 합니다.

필적 확인란

성 명

수 험 번 호

				—				
	0	0	0		0	0	0	0
1	1	1	1		1	1	1	1
2	2	2	2		2	2	2	2
3	3	3	3		3	3	3	3
4	4	4	4		4	4		4
5	5	5	5		5	5		5
6	6		6		6	6		6
7	7		7		7	7		7
8	8		8		8	8		8
	9		9		9	9		9

문 형

홀수형 ○

짝수형 ○

※ 문제의 문형을 확인후 표기

※ 감독관 확인 (수험생은 표기하지 말것.)

본인여부, 수험번호 및 문형의 표기가 정확한지 확인, 옆란에 서명 또는 날인

(서 명 또는 날 인)

※ 답안지 작성(표기)은 반드시 컴퓨터용 사인펜만을 사용하고, 연필 또는 샤프펜을 절대 사용하지 마십시오.

※ 뒷면의 〈수험생이 지켜야 할 일〉을 꼭 읽어 보십시오.

문번	답 란
1	① ② ③ ④ ⑤
2	① ② ③ ④ ⑤
3	① ② ③ ④ ⑤
4	① ② ③ ④ ⑤
5	① ② ③ ④ ⑤
6	① ② ③ ④ ⑤
7	① ② ③ ④ ⑤
8	① ② ③ ④ ⑤
9	① ② ③ ④ ⑤
10	① ② ③ ④ ⑤
11	① ② ③ ④ ⑤
12	① ② ③ ④ ⑤
13	① ② ③ ④ ⑤
14	① ② ③ ④ ⑤
15	① ② ③ ④ ⑤
16	① ② ③ ④ ⑤
17	① ② ③ ④ ⑤
18	① ② ③ ④ ⑤
19	① ② ③ ④ ⑤
20	① ② ③ ④ ⑤

문번	답 란
21	① ② ③ ④ ⑤
22	① ② ③ ④ ⑤
23	① ② ③ ④ ⑤
24	① ② ③ ④ ⑤
25	① ② ③ ④ ⑤
26	① ② ③ ④ ⑤
27	① ② ③ ④ ⑤
28	① ② ③ ④ ⑤
29	① ② ③ ④ ⑤
30	① ② ③ ④ ⑤
31	① ② ③ ④ ⑤
32	① ② ③ ④ ⑤
33	① ② ③ ④ ⑤
34	① ② ③ ④ ⑤
35	① ② ③ ④ ⑤
36	① ② ③ ④ ⑤
37	① ② ③ ④ ⑤
38	① ② ③ ④ ⑤
39	① ② ③ ④ ⑤
40	① ② ③ ④ ⑤

문번	답 란
41	① ② ③ ④ ⑤
42	① ② ③ ④ ⑤
43	① ② ③ ④ ⑤
44	① ② ③ ④ ⑤
45	① ② ③ ④ ⑤

〈수험생이 지켜야 할 일〉

답안지 작성(표기)은 반드시 컴퓨터용 사인펜만을 사용하여야 합니다.
(연필, 샤프펜 사용 시 불이익을 받을 수 있습니다.)

1. 성명란에는 수험생의 성명을 바르게 기재하여야 합니다.
2. 수험번호란에는 아라비아 숫자로 기재하고 해당란에 "●"와 같이 완전하게 표기하여야 합니다.
3. 문형란에는 배부받은 시험 문제지의 문형을 정확히 확인하고 해당란에 "●"와 같이 표기하여야 합니다.
   - 답안지의 '문형'란에 표기가 되어있지 않거나 이중으로 표기된 경우 불이익을 받을 수 있습니다.
   - 시험특별관리대상자의 문제지 문형은 홀수형 입니다.
4. 답란은 "●"와 같이 완전하게 표기하여야 하며, 바르지 못한 표기(◌ ◌ ⊙ ◐ ◌ 등)를 하였을 경우는 불이익을 받을 수 있습니다.
5. 답란 수정을 원할 경우에는 수정테이프만을 사용하여 완전하게 수정하여야 합니다. 불완전한 수정처리로 인해 발생하는 불이익은 수험생에게 있습니다.
   - 수정테이프는 감독관이 소지하고 있습니다.
   - 수정액이나 스티커 등은 절대로 사용할 수 없습니다.
   - 답란 수정 후 수정테이프가 떨어지지 않게 손으로 눌러 주십시오.
   - 답안지 교체를 원할 경우 교체 가능합니다.
6. 답안지에 낙서를 하거나 불필요한 표기를 하였을 경우 불이익을 받을 수 있으므로 답안지를 최대한 깨끗한 상태로 제출하여야 합니다.

천일문·어법끝 온라인 복습테스트를 찾는다면?

POWER

절대평가 대비 수능 영어 실력 충전

파워업 독해실전편

모의고사 15회

정답 및 해설

쎄듀

파워업

독해실전편

모의고사 15회

정답 및 해설

POWER Up

실전 모의고사 01

본문 p.13

18 ④	19 ③	20 ⑤	21 ②	22 ③	23 ④	24 ②	25 ⑤	26 ②	27 ③
28 ②	29 ③	30 ②	31 ③	32 ①	33 ③	34 ③	35 ②	36 ④	37 ⑤
38 ⑤	39 ⑤	40 ②	41 ⑤	42 ④	43 ⑤	44 ①	45 ④		

18 글의 목적 ④

소재 수업 장소 변경 요청

해설 강의실 간의 거리가 멀어서 겪는 어려움을 먼저 설명한 뒤, Therefore 뒤에서 수업을 한 건물에서 받을 수 있도록 수업 장소를 재배치해줄 것을 요구하고 있으므로 글의 목적으로 가장 적절한 것은 ④이다.

해석 행정관분께,
넓은 캠퍼스에 자리 잡은 아름다운 건물들과 정원이 있는 우리의 새 학교에 대해 저희 신입생들은 매우 자랑스럽게 생각합니다. 저희에게는 이 대학교의 일류 시설들과 풍부한 학문적 자원을 이용할 수 있는 특권이 있습니다. 하지만 저희는 서로 멀리 떨어진 곳에 위치한 다른 건물들에서 듣는 수업이 너무 많이 포함되어 있는 매우 꽉 찬 시간표로 인해 걱정스럽습니다. 어학 실습실은 캠퍼스의 북쪽 끝에 있고 주 강당은 그 반대편 끝에 있는데, 이것은 강의실들이 걸어서 최소한 15분 거리에 있는 셈입니다. 눈이 내리면 강의실 사이를 이동하는 데 30분이 걸릴지도 모릅니다. 주제문 따라서 저희는 대학 당국이 저희 수업을 한 건물로 재배치해주실 것을 촉구합니다. 그렇게 되면 수업 시간 사이에 바쁘게 질주하는 데 드는 시간을 줄이고, 공부를 하는 것과 교수님 및 동료 학생들과 교류하는 데 더 많은 시간을 쓰게 될 것입니다.
신입생 대표 드림

구문 [9행~12행] *The language lab is at the north end ~ at the opposite end*, // **which** means // (that) our classrooms are at least a 15 minutes' walk / from each other.
which는 앞의 절 전체를 받는 관계대명사의 계속적 용법으로 사용되었으며, and it으로 해석하면 된다. 동사 means의 목적어절에 접속사 that이 생략되었다.

[15행~18행] That way, we will **spend** less time *rushing* ~ and more time *studying* and *interacting* ~.
「spend+O+v-ing」는 'v하는 데 O를 소비하다'란 뜻이며, spend의 목적어 less time과 more time이 등위접속사 and로 연결된 병렬구조이다.

어휘 **administrator** 행정관, 관리자 *cf.* **administration** (대학 등의) 당국 행정기관 **freshman** 신입생, 1학년생 **vast** 광대한, 광활한 **privileged** 특권이 있는 **have access to A** A를 이용할 수 있다, A에 접근할 수 있다 **first-class** 일류의, 최상의 **facility** (복수형) 편의시설, 설비 **troubled** 걱정스러운, 불안해하는 **language lab** 어학 실습실 **auditorium** 강당, 대강의실 **urge** 촉구하다 **relocate** 재배치하다 **interact with** ~와 상호작용하다; ~와 어울리다

19 심경 변화 ③

소재 아픈 엄마를 위하는 딸의 예쁜 마음

해설 Jane은 아파서 침대에 누워 딸 Becky에게 집을 어지르지 말라고 했지만, 잠에서 깨 보니 집안이 엉망진창이어서 화가 났다(furious). 하지만 잠든 딸 옆에서 딸이 빨리 나으라는 메시지를 담아 자신을 위해 만든 카드를 발견하고 감동을 받았으므로(touched) 정답은 ③이다.

해석 어느 날 저녁 Jane은 독감에 걸려 침대에 누워있었고 5살 딸 Becky에게 자신이 자는 동안 어지르지 말라고 부탁했다. 한 시간 후에 Jane은 부엌으로 걸어가서 크레용이 바닥 전체에 펼쳐져 있고, 가위는 쓰레기통에, 그리고 절반을 마신 우유 잔이 냉장고 옆 조리대 위에 있는 것을 보았다. 주제문 Jane은 혼잣말했다. "엉망진창이네! 내가 아프다고 얘기했는데." Jane은 그녀를 참을 수 없었다. Jane은 Becky를 찾아 나섰고 그녀가 거실 텔레비전 앞에서 곤히 잠든 것을 발견했다. Becky의 머리 근처에 놓인 쿠션에는 "사랑해요, 엄마! 빨리 나으세요!"라고 적혀있는, 하트로 뒤덮인 밝은색의 커다란 카드가 있었다. 주제문 갑자기 목이 메는 것 같았다. Jane은 천천히 고개를 저으며 미소지었다. 그녀는 Becky의 어깨를 담요로 덮어주고 이마에 키스했다.
① 자랑스러운 → 질투하는 ② 무서운 → 편안한
④ 의심하는 → 확신하는 ⑤ 실망한 → 희망찬

구문 [10행~12행] On the cushion near Becky's head (부사구) was (V) *a large, brightly colored card* (S), (covered in hearts), [that **read**, "I love you, Mom! Please get well soon!"]
장소 부사구가 앞으로 나오면서 주어, 동사 도치가 일어난 「부사구+V+S」 구문이다. covered in hearts는 수동의 의미의 분사구문으로 a large, brightly colored card를 수식한다. read는 '~라고 쓰여 있다'의 뜻이다.

어휘 **flu** 독감 **mess** 엉망인 상태 **spread** 펼치다 **stand** 참다, 견디다 **soundly** 깊이, 곤히 **all of a sudden** 갑자기 **lump** 덩어리 **throat** 목 **tuck** (따뜻하게) 덮어주다, 감싸다; 밀어[쑤셔]넣다

20 필자 주장 ⑤

소재 지속적인 도전의 중요성

해설 열린 마음을 가지고 끊임없이 도전하다 보면 뜻하지 않은 행운이 따르게 된다는 내용의 글이다. 마지막 문장에서 뜻밖의 행운이 기다리고 있을 수도 있으니 너무 빨리 포기해서는 안 된다고 했는데, 이는 바꿔 말하면 포기하지 말고 계속해서 도전해야 한다는 의미이다. 따라서 필자의 주장으로 가장 적절한 것은 ⑤이다.

해석 'serendipity'라는 단어는 보통 어떤 이가 완전히 다른 것을 찾고 있던 와중에 뜻하지 않게 운 좋은 무언가를 발견하게 되는 멋진 상황을 묘사한다. 역사상 가장 위대한 과학적 발견 중 다수는 이 serendipity(뜻밖의 행운)에서 기인했는데, 순전히 그런 상황이 모험가들이나 뭔가를 추구하는 사람들에게 가장 자주 일어나기 때문이다. 우리의 모험이 신체적인 것이든 지적인 것이든 정신적인 것이든 간에, 우리가 열린 자세로 우리가 하는 모든 일에 접근하면 우리의 진정한 통찰력이 우리에게 더 잘 드러날 수 있다. 반면에, 우리가 마음을 닫는다면, 우리는 우리가 찾고 있던 것보다 더 가치 있거나 더 좋은 멋진 무언가를 아마도 놓치게 될 것이다. 주제문 당신이 찾고 있는 것이 아직 세상에 존재하지 않더라도 너무 빨리 포기해서는 안 된다. 행복한 우연이 바로 당신을 기다리고 있을지도 모르니 말이다.

구문 [7행~9행] **Whether** our adventures are physical, intellectual, **or** spiritual, // if we approach *all* [that we do] with an attitude of openness, ~.
「Whether A, B, or C」는 'A이든 B이든 C이든'의 의미이다. that we do는 선행사 all을 수식하는 목적격 관계대명사절이고, 밑줄 친 with an attitude of openness는 동사 approach를 수식하는 부사구이다.

어휘 **serendipity** 뜻밖의 행운; 기대하지 않았던 것을 뜻밖에 찾아내는 재능 **circumstance** 상황; 환경 **accidentally** 뜻하지 않게, 우연히 *cf.* **accident** 우연; 사고 **fortunate** 운이 좋은 **entirely** 완전히, 전적으로 **intellectual** 지적인, 지성의 **spiritual** 정신적인; 영혼의 **approach** 접근하다, 다가가다;

접근(법) **openness** 열려 있음; 숨김없음, 솔직함 **vision** 통찰력, 선견지명; 시력, 시각 **reveal** 드러내다; 누설하다 **pursue** 추구하다, 얻으려고 애쓰다 **exist** 존재하다; 생존하다

21 밑줄 함의 ②

소재 미술품 감정

해설 미술 감정가는 은행 금고에서 꺼내온 그림들이 진품인지 감정한 후 의뢰인에게 그것들을 금고에 다시 넣어두실 필요가 없다고 했는데, 그 이유는 그림이 진품이 아니었기 때문일 것이다. 따라서 밑줄 친 부분이 의미하는 것은 ② '그림들은 진짜가 아닌 것으로 밝혀졌다.'이다.

해석 미술상으로서 내 파트너 Sidney와 나는 많은 감정을 한다. 미술 감정은 대단히 전문화된 기술이다. 미술 감정가에게 부과되는 가장 힘든 과제 중 하나는 그 예술 작품의 작가일 수 있다고 여겨지는 예술가의 진품임을 입증하는 일이다. 얼마 전에 Sidney는 큰 재산의 일부인 그림 몇 점을 조사하도록 은행에 불려갔다. 그는 예술 작품이 금고에서 하나씩 꺼내지자 유명 예술가의 작품을 검토했고, 그동안 은행 임원은 기대에 차서 그것들의 가치에 대한 확인과 가장 수익성이 좋은 판매 방법을 논할 기회를 기다렸다. "자," 은행 임원은 검토 후에 물었다. "제가 뭘 해야 하죠?" "할 필요가 없는 일을 말씀드릴게요." Sidney가 대답했다. "그것들을 금고에 다시 넣어두실 필요가 없습니다."

① 그림들이 팔렸다.
③ 그림들은 추가적인 분석과 검토가 필요하다.
④ 그림들은 금고 외의 다른 곳에 보관되어야 한다.
⑤ 그림들은 상태가 안 좋으며 복원될 필요가 있다.

구문 [3행~5행] **One** (of *the most challenging tasks* (imposed upon the fine art appraiser)) / is **that** of authenticating *the artist* [**to whom** the art may have been attributed].
(S: One, V: is)

주어의 핵심어구가 One이므로 단수동사 is가 왔다. is 다음의 that은 the task를 지칭한다. to whom에서 to는 be attributed to(~의 것으로 여겨지다)의 to가 관계대명사 앞으로 온 것이다.

[9행~11행] ~ while the bank officer waited expectantly for confirmation of their value and to discuss the most profitable method of sale.

밑줄 친 부분은 and로 연결되어 병렬구조를 이루며 둘 다 waited에 연결된다.

어휘 **fine art** 미술 **specialize** 전문화하다; 전공하다 **impose** 부과하다 **authenticate** 진짜임을 증명하다 **attribute** (작품을) ~의 것이라고 보다 **call in** 불러들이다 **estate** 재산; 부동산 **vault** 금고 **officer** (회사의) 임원, 간부 **confirmation** 확인 **profitable** 수익성이 있는 **inspection** 검토, 조사 **vault** (은행의) 금고, 귀중품 보관실 [선택지 어휘] **genuine** 진짜의 **analysis** 분석 **examination** 검토, 조사 **restore** 복원[복구]하다

22 글의 요지 ③

소재 비판적으로 여론조사를 바라볼 필요성

해설 전반부에서 사람들이 여론조사 결과를 맹신하는 세태를 언급하고, 중반부에 내용을 전환시키는 역접의 접속사 However가 나오면서 이를 반박하는 주제문(Understand that ~)이 이어진다. 이어서 주제를 뒷받침하기 위해 여론조사 결과를 신뢰할 수 없는 여러 이유를 질문 형식으로 나열하고 있으므로 글의 요지로 가장 적절한 것은 ③이다.

해석 대중매체는 지속적으로 여론조사 결과를 보도하고, 많은 사람들이 이에 관심을 기울인다. 사람들은 여론조사에 과학적 권위가 있다는 느낌이 들기 때문에 (그 결과에) 깊은 인상을 받고, 그 결과는 엄청나게 정확한 것처럼 보도된다. 또한, 사람들은 신문이나 라디오, 또는 텔레비전 방송국 등이 공평하고, 권위가 있으며, 지적이라고 믿는 경향이 있다. 하지만 우리는 모두 더 비판적이 되는 것을 배울 필요가 있다. 주제문 본질적으로 여론조사는 신뢰할 수 없을 가능성이 있다는 점을 이해하라. 당신이 여론조사 결과를 읽을 때 이렇게 질문하라. "특정한 답을 하도록 응답자가 기만당한 방식으로 여론조사 질문이 쓰였다면 어찌 되겠는가?", "여론조사에 참여한 사람들의 표본이 일반 사람들을 공정하게 대표하지 못한다면 어찌 되겠는가?", "여론조사를 만든 사람과 그 결과를 보도하는 대중매체가 사적인 목적이 있다면 어찌 되겠는가?" (그에 대한) 답변들은 당신이 여론조사 결과를 매우 다른 관점으로 볼 수 있도록 도와줄 것이다.

구문 [16행~17행] The answers **should help** you **see** opinion polls in a very different light.
(S: The answers, V: should help, O: you, C: see ~)

여기서 should는 문맥상 추측의 의미인 '~할 것이다'라고 해석하는 것이 자연스럽다. help는 목적격보어로 원형부정사나 to부정사를 쓸 수 있다.

어휘 **poll** 여론조사 **have an air of** ~한 느낌이 들다, ~한 분위기가 있다 **authority** 권위, 권력 *cf.* **authoritative** 권위 있는 **precision** 정확(성), 정밀(성) **or whatever** 그 밖에 무엇이든지; 기타 등등 **unbiased** 공평한, 치우치지 않은 **intelligent** 지적인 **critical** 비판적인; 중대한; 위기의 **unreliable** 신뢰할 수 없는 **in such a way that** ~와 같은 방법으로 **respondent** 응답자 **fool A into v-ing** A가 v하도록 속이다 **representation** 대표; 설명; 표현 **light** 관점, 견해; 빛

23 글의 주제 ④

소재 눈 결정체가 대칭인 이유

해설 Thus 이하가 결론으로, 눈 결정체 줄기의 변화는 다른 줄기에서도 거울에 비친 것처럼 동일하게 발생하며 이것이 눈 결정체의 구조가 대칭적인 이유라고 설명하고 있다. 따라서 글의 주제로 가장 적절한 것은 ④ '눈 결정체의 줄기가 똑같은 이유'이다.

해석 이상하게 들릴지 모르지만, 매우 떨어져 있는 눈 결정체의 줄기들은 서로 신호를 보낼 수 있다. 눈 결정체들은 독특한 진동 구조를 갖고 있다. 이 진동은 결정체의 반대편에서 똑같은 자리에 위치해 있는 다른 원자와 박자를 맞춰 움직이는 원자에 의해 형성된다. 원자들이 대형을 이뤄 움직일 때, 한 부분에서의 변화는 그 대형에 있는 다른 부분에까지 고르게 퍼져 가는데, 이것은 마치 행군 대열에서 걷는 속도를 바꾼 어느 한 병사가 대개 대열 전체의 걷는 속도에 지속적인 변화를 일으키는 것과 유사하다. 주제문 그러므로 생성되는 눈 결정 줄기들은 서로 직접 닿아 있지 않더라도 여전히 서로의 변화에 영향을 받는 것이다. 거울에서처럼 어떤 줄기에서의 변화가 반대쪽에서도 발생할 수 있으며, 이것이 모든 눈 결정체의 구조들이 대칭적인 이유이다.

① 눈 결정체 모양의 다양성
② 눈 결정체가 만들어지는 조건
③ 눈 결정체의 유형에 영향을 미치는 요소
⑤ 눈 결정체에서 우리가 배울 수 있는 교훈

구문 [1행] Strange **as** it may sound, ~.

「형용사+as[though]+S´+V´」 구문은 양보의 부사절을 만든다. 여기서 as는 '~이지만[~이건만]'이라는 의미이다.

[13행] **As** (what happens) in a mirror, ~.

여기서 As는 '~처럼[~하듯이]'이라는 의미의 접속사이며, 주어와 동사는 어떤 내용인지 명확하여 생략된 것이다.

어휘 **arm** 줄기, 가지; 팔; 무장하다 **crystal** 결정체 **distinctive** 독특한, 뚜렷이 구별되는 **vibration** 진동 **form** 형성하다 *cf.* **formation** 대형; 형성 **atom** 원자 **in time** 박자에 맞추어; 시간에 맞춰 (늦지 않게) **located** ~에 위치한 **matching** (색·모양 등이) 같은; 어울리는 **evenly** 고르게 **alter** 바꾸다; 달라지다 **march** 행진하다 **set off** (반응을) 일으키다; 시작하게 하다; 점화하다 **affect** 영향을 미치다 **symmetrical** 대칭적인(↔ **asymmetrical** 비대칭적인) [선택지 어휘] **diversity** 다양성 **condition** 조건; 상황; 상태

24 글의 제목 ②

소재 인식에 영향을 주는 기존 정보

해설 첫 문장에서 '인식(perception)'에 대한 정의를 내리고 두 번째 문장에서 인식이 '뇌에 들어있는 정보'에 영향을 받는다는 주제문을 서술한 뒤, 이어서 이를 뒷받침하는 예

시를 제시하고 있다. 또한 글의 후반부에서 인식에 영향을 주는 것이 기존의 지식임을 다시 한번 언급하고 있다. 따라서 이러한 내용을 가장 잘 반영한 제목은 ② '우리의 인식에 영향을 미치는 요소들'이다.

해석 인식은 우리의 감각기관에 의해 정보가 수용될 때 우리가 그 정보에 부여하는 의미를 나타낸다. 주제문 우리의 눈이 카메라처럼 작동할지도 모르지만, 우리가 보는 것(또는 인식하는 것)은 우리의 뇌에 들어있는 정보에 영향을 받는다. 예를 들어, 다음의 I3을 보라. 이것이 무슨 '숫자'인지 질문을 받는다면, 여러분은 아마 '13'이라고 말할 것이다. 하지만 그 '글자'의 명칭을 대라는 요청을 받으면 여러분은 아마 'B'라고 답할 것이다. 형상은 하나밖에 없지만, 여러분이 받는 질문과 여러분이 이미 지니고 있는 숫자와 글자에 관한 지식에 근거해서 여러분의 인식이 바뀌는 것이다. 숫자나 글자 어느 것에 관해서도 저장된 정보가 없는 어린아이에게 이런 것들은 종이 위에 새겨진 무의미한 표시일 것이다. 주제문 따라서 들어오는 자극에 의미를 부여하는 것은 기존의 지식과 우리가 보고자 기대하는 것에 달려 있다. 어떤 의미에서 뇌는 항상 새로운 정보를 이전에 접했던 것들과 대조하고 있는 것이다.

① 인식에서 감각의 역할

③ 일반적으로 오해되고 있는 상징들

④ 뇌는 어떻게 감각을 속일 수 있는가

⑤ 우리는 왜 정보에 의미를 부여하는가

구문 [8행~10행] ~, but your perception changes / based **on** what you are asked and your existing knowledge of numbers and letters.
전치사 on의 목적어 역할을 하는 what ~ asked와 your existing ~ letters가 and로 병렬연결되었다.

어휘 **perception** 인식; 지각; 통찰력 *cf.* **perceive** 인지[감지]하다 **assign** (일 등을) 부여하다, 할당하다; (사람을 직책에) 임명하다 *cf.* **assignment** 할당; (임명된) 직위; 숙제 **contain** 담고 있다, 포함하다 **figure** 형상; 모습; 도형; 숫자 **based on** ~에 근거하여 **existing** 기존의, 현재 있는 **store** 저장하다; 보관하다 **meaningless** 무의미한 **incoming** 들어오는 **stimuli** (**stimulus**의 복수형) 자극(제); 자극이 되는 것 **prior** 사전의, 먼저의 **check A against B** A를 B와 대조하다 **encounter** 접하다, 마주치다; (반갑지 않은 일에) 맞닥뜨리다 [선택지 어휘] **trick** 속이다

25 도표 이해 ⑤

소재 뉴스 출처의 중요성 평가 결과

해설 전국 뉴스 부문에서 중요도가 가장 높게 평가된 뉴스 출처는 online newspapers이다. non-commercial online sources는 두 번째로 중요하다고 평가된 출처이므로 ⑤가 도표와 일치하지 않는 설명이다.

해석 〈지역/전국 뉴스 출처의 중요도 평가〉

주제문 위의 도표는 우리 독자들이 지역 뉴스 및 전국 뉴스를 제공하는 6개의 다양한 출처의 중요성을 어떻게 평가했는지를 보여준다. ① 6개 중, 지역 뉴스의 단 두 개의 출처만이 텔레비전보다 덜 중요하다고 인식되었다. ② 뜻밖은 아니겠지만, 잡지나 뉴스레터를 포함하는 '기타 인쇄매체' 범주가 모든 뉴스 출처 중 가장 덜 중요한 것으로 평가되었다. ③ 전국 뉴스보다 지역 뉴스 면에서 더 중요하다고 여겨진 유일한 뉴스 출처는 종이신문이었다. ④ 독자들은 전국 뉴스 출처로 종이신문보다 온라인신문을 더 선호했다. ⑤ 비영리적인 온라인 출처가 가장 중요한 전국 뉴스 출처로 평가되었다는 점을 보는 것 또한 흥미롭다.

구문 [8행~10행] *The only news source* (considered **more important** for local news **than** for national news) was print newspapers.
S: The only news source / V: was / C: print newspapers

considered ~ national news는 The only news source를 수식하는 분사구이며 분사구 내에 for local news와 for national news를 비교하는 비교급 구문이 쓰였다.

어휘 **rate** 평가하다 **source** 출처, 정보원; 근원 **local** 지역의(↔ **national** 전국적인; 국가적인) **unsurprisingly** 뜻밖은 아니지만, 놀랄 것 없이 **category** 범주 **newsletter** (특별 구독자에게 우송하는) 시사 통신[해설]; (회사·단체 등의) 사보, 회보 **prefer A to B** B보다 A를 선호하다 **note** 주의[주목]하다; 적어 두다

26 내용 불일치 ②

소재 미국의 천재 수학자 John Nash

해설 두 번째 문장에서 약물 치료를 중단한 후 점차 회복되었다(he stopped taking antipsychotic medication, and gradually began to recover)고 했으므로 ②가 글의 내용과 일치하지 않는다.

해석 ① 천재적인 미국의 수학자 John Nash는 28세에 편집증적 조현병 진단을 받고, 이후 30년간 정신병원을 드나들며 보냈다. ② 그러나 1970년 그는 항정신병 약물 치료를 중단하고 차츰 회복하기 시작했다. ③ 그는 Princeton 대학원생일 때 게임 이론에서 그가 했던 연구를 인정받아 1994년 노벨 경제학상을 수상했다. 그는 게임에서 한 개인의 성공이 다른 참여자들의 선택에 의해 결정된다는 것을 이론화했다. Princeton 대학의 전설적 이야기에서 Nash는 'Fine Hall의 유령'이었는데, ④ Princeton 대학 수학과의 중앙 강당인 Fine Hall에서 한밤중에 방정식을 칠판에 갈겨쓰곤 했던 유령 같은 인물이었다. ⑤ Nash는 오스카상을 수상한 할리우드 영화 〈뷰티풀 마인드〉의 주인공이기도 했다.

구문 [9행~11행] He **had theorized** // that an individual's success in a game **depends** on the choices of the other players.
노벨상을 받기(He was awarded ~.) 전에 이론을 정립한 것이므로 주절에는 과거보다 이전의 일을 나타내는 과거완료(had p.p.)가 쓰였다. 목적어인 that절은 John Nash가 정립한 이론을 설명하는 내용이며, 이는 과거의 한 시점에 국한하지 않는 '일반적 진리'에 해당하므로 depends는 현재시제로 쓰였다.

어휘 **mathematician** 수학자 **diagnose A with B** A에게 B를 진단하다 **mental** 정신의 **antipsychotic** 항정신병의 **medication** 약물 치료 **gradually** 차츰, 서서히 **recover** 회복하다 **award** 상을 주다; 상 **in recognition of** ~을 인정하여 **theory** 이론 *cf.* **theorize** 이론화하다 **graduate** 대학원의; (대학) 졸업생 **phantom** 유령 **figure** 인물; 모습; 숫자 **scribble** 갈겨쓰다, 낙서하다 **equation** (수학) 방정식; 등식 **subject** 대상; 주제; 과목; 피실험자

27 안내문 불일치 ③

소재 대학 졸업식 안내

해설 졸업식 초대 손님은 4명까지 가능하며 추가로 온 손님은 별도의 장소에 자리가 마련되어 있다고 했으므로 4명 이상도 올 수 있다는 것을 알 수 있다. 따라서 정답은 ③이다.

해석

Pattison 대학 졸업식

날짜: 2020년 9월 18일 금요일

시간: ① 오후 2시~3시 30분 (② 학생들은 졸업 가운과 졸업식 지도를 받기 위해 오후 12시 30분에서 1시 사이에 도착해야 합니다.)

장소: Pattison 강당

초대 손님: ③ 졸업생 1명당 4명까지 가능합니다. (추가 손님들은 별도의 장소에 자리가 마련됩니다.)

④ 본인 참석 여부와 초대 손님 수를 알려주시기 바랍니다.
졸업 가운을 위해 신장(에 대한 정보)도 필요합니다.

모든 졸업생 여러분 — 전화 604-580-1770 또는 이메일 admin@pattison.com을 통해 회신해 주시기 바랍니다. ⑤ 3~11세 어린이를 위한 무료 아동보호소가 운영됩니다. 세부사항을 좀 더 알고 싶으시면 전화 604-580-2772 또는 msa@pattison.com을 통해 Mahsa에게 연락하시기 바랍니다.

어휘 **graduation** 졸업 **instruction** 지도, 지시; 설명 **auditorium** 강당; 객석 **additional** 추가의, 부가적인 **RSVP** 회신 바랍니다(**"Reply, if you please."**에 해당하는 프랑스어 표현의 줄임말) **complimentary** 무료의; 칭찬의 **childcare** 탁아소 **detail** 세부사항, 정보

28 안내문 일치 ②

소재 지구의 날 재활용 행사 안내

해설 재활용을 위한 중고품 수집 행사를 안내하는 글로, 교육 워크숍도 제공한다고(offering educational workshops) 했으므로 ②가 안내문의 내용과 일치한다.

해석

지구의 날 재활용 행사!
① 모든 Blain County 주민들에게 개방합니다

여러분의 가족이 재활용과 쓰레기 감소에 대해 더 잘 이해하도록 돕고 싶다면, DHS ReStore에서 열리는 '지구의 날 재활용 행사'에 오세요. ② 교육 워크숍을 제공할 뿐만 아니라 재사용과 재활용을 위한 각양각색의 중고품을 모을 것입니다.

③ **날짜와 시간:** 4월 22일 토요일, 오전 11시부터 오후 4시까지
장소: 430 N. Front Ave., Sturgeon Bay

가져와야 할 것
- 책과 DVD
- 안경과 선글라스
- ④ 전자기기 (핸드폰은 삼가 주세요)
- 많이 착용하지 않은 옷과 신발

*⑤ 무료입장에는 점심이 포함되지 않습니다. 햄버거는 3달러에 그리고 핫도그는 2달러에 구입 가능할 것입니다.

어떤 것을 재활용할지에 대한 추가적인 정보를 위해서는 온라인으로 저희 blaincountyhabitat.org에 방문해 주세요.

구문 [6행~8행] We will be collecting a variety of used goods for reuse and recycling (A) **as well as** offering educational workshops (B).

「A as well as B」는 'B뿐만 아니라 A도'의 뜻이다. A와 B 자리에 공통적으로 will be에 이어지는 현재분사구가 쓰여 병렬구조를 이룬다.

어휘 **resident** 주민, 거주자 **waste** 쓰레기; 낭비(하다) **reduction** 감소 **used goods** 중고품 **electronics** 전자기기 **entry** 입장 **available** 구입 가능한; 이용 가능한

29 밑줄 어법 ③

소재 수익 변화가 법률 제정에 미치는 영향

해설 ③ 주어의 핵심어구가 all other attempts이므로 fails를 복수동사 fail로 고쳐야 한다. 주어를 수식하는 to부정사구(to explain ~ a law)가 주어와 동사 사이에 삽입된 형태이므로 바로 앞의 a law나 the reason을 주어로 착각하지 않도록 주의한다.

오답 분석 ① 앞의 절과 겹치는 어구를 생략한 형태로, but why isn't it legal to drive를 대신한다. ② 핸드폰의 사용이 정신을 '분산시키는' 것(능동)이므로 현재분사형을 쓴 것은 옳다. ④ if절에 동사의 과거형 banned가 쓰였고, 현재 상황의 반대를 가정하는 문맥이므로 가정법 과거임을 알 수 있다. 가정법 과거의 기본 형태는 「If+주어+동사의 과거형 ~, 주어+조동사 과거형+동사원형 ...」이다. ⑤ 부사 even은 비교급을 강조하는 수식어로 사용되었다. 비교급을 강조하는 다른 부사로는 much, far, still, a lot 등이 있다.

해석 왜 먹거나 마시면서 운전하는 것은 합법적이고, 핸드폰으로 통화하면서 운전하는 것은 그렇지 않은가? 핸드폰 사용이 그런 다른 활동들보다 정신을 더 산만하게 한다고 주장하는 것은 충분한 설득력이 없다. 주제문 어떤 법의 근거를 설명하려는 모든 시도가 실패할 때는, 법이 그 법의 영향을 받는 자들의 수입을 어떻게 변화시킬지 묻는 것이 좋은 전략이다. 입법자들이 운전 중에 커피, 탄산음료, 햄버거의 섭취를 금지한다면, 패스트푸드점의 매출은 급락할 것이다. 하지만 운전 중 핸드폰 사용 금지에는 헤드셋이라는 예외를 허용함으로써, 입법자들은 그런 위험을 감수하지 않게 된다. 게다가, 이동전화 업체들은 부가적인 헤드셋 판매를 통해 훨씬 더 높은 수익을 벌어들일 수도 있다.

어휘 **legal** 합법의; 법률(상)의 **convincing** 설득력이 있는, 납득이 가는 **argue** 주장하다, 논하다 **distracting** 정신을 산만하게 하는, 집중을 방해하는 **income** 수입, 소득 **affect** 영향을 미치다 **legislator** 입법자, 국회의원 **ban** 금지(하다) **consumption** 섭취; 소비 **decline** 감소하다 **exception to A** A에 대한 예외 **run a risk** 위험을 감수하다 **stand to-v** v할 것 같다, v한 형세에 있다

30 밑줄 어휘 ②

소재 효과적으로 글의 내용을 파악하는 방법

해설 신문이나 잡지를 읽을 때, 미리 훑어보고 나서 자세한 내용을 파악하는 것이 효과적이라는 내용의 글이다. 신문의 머리기사를 먼저 읽으면 '세세한' 내용이 아닌 '전반적인' 내용을 알 수 있게 될 것이므로, ②는 overall 등으로 고쳐야 한다.

해석 주제문 글로 쓰인 정보를 더욱 효과적으로 다루는 한 가지 방법은 그 정보를 실제로 읽기 전에 전체를 빠르게 ① 훑어보는 것이다. 신문을 읽을 때, 이야기의 머리기사를 먼저 읽어라. 그러면 그 이야기가 다루는 것에 대한 ② 세세한(→ 전반적인) 생각을 이해하게 될 것이다. 그런 다음 이야기를 읽으면 그것을 좀 더 설명해주는 정보를 더 많이 찾게 된다. 기본 정보부터 읽으며 그것에 살을 붙인다면 (읽고 있는) 자료가 당신에게 ③ 낯설지 않다. 사실, 당신이 신문 가판대에서 잡지를 집어 들어 내용을 ④ 미리 보지도 않고 사는 일은 없을 것이다. 이렇게 할 때(= 내용을 미리 볼 때), 당신은 그것(= 잡지)에 돈을 쓰기 전에 잡지 전체를 훑어보고 그것이 무엇에 관한 것인지 그리고 어떤 내용을 담고 있는지를 알게 되는 것이다. 이런 식으로 하면, 당신은 더욱 ⑤ 합리적인 구매와 (합리적인) 돈의 사용을 보장하게 된다.

구문 [3행~5행] When you read the newspaper, // **read** the headline of a story first, // **and** you will get the overall idea **of** what it concerns.

「명령문, and ...」는 '~해라. 그러면 …할 것이다'란 의미이다. 밑줄 친 what it concerns는 전치사 of의 목적어 역할을 하는 명사절이다.

[11행~13행] When doing this (= When you do this), / you look over (V1) the whole magazine and get (V2) an idea **of** what it is about and what it contains / before spending your money on it (= before you spend your money on it).

When doing this와 before spending ~ money on it은 의미를 명확히 하기 위해 접속사를 남겨둔 분사구문이다. 두 개의 what절은 of의 목적어 역할을 한다.

어휘 **effective** 효과적인 **handling** 처리; 조작 **scan** 훑어보다 **headline** 머리기사, 표제 **detailed** 상세한 **concern** ~에 관해 다루다; ~에 관여하다; 관심(사); 우려 **material** 자료; 재료; 물질 **unfamiliar** 낯선, 익숙하지 않은 **newsstand** 신문가판대 **preview** 미리 보다 **content** 내용(물); 목차; 함유량 **look over** ~을 살펴보다[검토하다] **contain** 포함하다, 담고 있다 **ensure** 보장하다; 확실하게 하다 **sensible** 합리적인; 분별 있는

31 빈칸 추론 ③

소재 여객기 이용이 감소시킨 선박 이동

해설 초대형 여객기는 사람들을 빠르게 이동시키고 국경을 연결시켰지만, 상대적으로 선박 여행은 감소시켜서 가까운 섬 사회들 간의 교류를 막게 되었으므로 그들의 '고립(isolation)'을 증가시켰다는 문맥이 알맞다. 따라서 정답은 ③이다.

해석 초대형 여객기는 한국의 컴퓨터 컨설턴트들이 마치 옆집에 잠깐 가는 것처럼 실리콘 밸리로 날아갈 수 있게 해주었고, 싱가포르의 기업가들은 이제 하루 만에 시애틀에 도착할 수 있다. 세계 최대 대양(= 태평양)의 경계들이 전례 없이 연결되었다. 하지만 초대형 여객기가 5마일 상공 위를 날아가는 섬 주민들은 어떠한가? 이 엄청난 초대형 여객기가 그들에게 똑같은 바닷물이 해안을 적시는 섬사람들과의 더 많은 교류를 가져다주었는가? 물론, 그렇지 않다. 주제문 비행기 여행은 여행자들이 바다를 건너 바쁘게 돌아다닐 수 있게 해주었을지 모르나, 동시에 선박 여행의 감소는 많은 섬 사회들의 고립을 오히려 증가

태평양의 많은 다른 섬들처럼 피트케언 섬도 지금까지 한 번도 이웃들에게서 이렇게 멀리 떨어져 있다고 느껴본 적이 없었다.
① 정체성 ② 세력 ④ 단결 ⑤ 경쟁

구문 [1행~3행] Jumbo jets have **enabled** *Korean computer consultants* **to fly** to Silicon Valley // **as if** (they were) popping next door, ~.
「enable+O+C(to-v) (O가 v하게 하다)」의 구조이다. as if가 이끄는 부사절은 「주어+be동사」가 생략되었으며, 여기에서 생략된 they는 앞의 Korean computer consultants를 가리킨다.

어휘 **jumbo jet** 초대형 여객기, 점보제트기 **pop** 잠깐 가다[들르다]; 펑 하고 소리 나다 **Singaporean** 싱가포르 사람; 싱가포르의 **entrepreneur** 기업가, 전문 경영인 **border** 국경, 경계 **mighty** 엄청난, 대단한; 강력한 **communion** 교류, 친교 **shore** 해안, 바닷가 **buzz** 바쁘게 돌아다니다; 윙윙거리다 **Pacific** 태평양의

32 빈칸 추론 ①

소재 시행착오를 통한 문제 해결

해설 아이였을 때 사용했던 문제 해결 전략이 '무엇'이었을지는 이어지는 예시를 통해 파악한다. 아이가 장난감을 가져오기 위해 어떤 방법을 시도해보고, 실패하면 다른 방법을 고안하여 실행해보는 과정을 반복하며, 여러 번의 ① '시행착오'를 통해 문제를 해결했다는 것을 알 수 있다.

해석 주제문 어렸을 때 우리가 사용했던 가장 일반적인 문제 해결 전략은 아마 시행착오였을 것이다. 예를 들어 한 어린이가 직면한 문제가 아이의 어머니가 선반에 올려둔 장난감을 어떻게 회수할 것인지에 관한 것이라고 해보자. 어린이는 장난감에 닿으려고 팔을 뻗으려 애쓸 수 있다. 그것은 효과가 없다. 다음으로 그 아이는 장난감에 닿기 위해 선반에 올라가려고 노력한다. 그는 떨어진다. 그것은 효과가 없다. 혼자 힘으로 그것을 얻을 수 없을 때, 그는 어머니에게 장난감을 달라고 부탁한다. 그녀는 안 된다고 말한다. 그것은 효과가 없다. 여전히 단념하지 않고 아이는 장난감을 달라고 약간 울어본다. 어머니는 울음을 무시한다. 그것은 효과가 없다. 마지막으로 그는 비명, 발차기와 눈물로 완성되는 완전한 성질을 부린다. 몹시 짜증이 나서 어머니는 아이를 달래기 위해 장난감을 준다. 빙고. 성질부리기는 효과가 있었다.
② 복제와 모방
③ 추론과 분석
④ 보상과 처벌
⑤ 연상과 시각화

구문 [3행~4행] For instance, let's say *the problem* [(that[which]) a child faces ●] is how to retrieve *a toy* [(that[which]) his mother has put up ● on a shelf].
[ ] 부분은 목적격 관계대명사 that[which]가 생략된 관계사절로 각각 the problem과 a toy를 수식한다.

어휘 **employ** 사용하다; 고용하다 **likely** 아마 **retrieve** 회수하다, 되찾다 **on one's own** 혼자서, 혼자 힘으로 **undeterred** 단념하지 않는 *cf.* **deter** 단념시키다 **full-blown** (~의) 모든 특성을 갖춘, 만개한 **tantrum** 성질을 부림, 짜증을 냄 **exasperate** 몹시 화[짜증]를 내다 **appease** 달래다

33 빈칸 추론 ③

소재 라이브 공연에서의 공동 상호작용

해설 빈칸이 글의 첫 한두 문장에 있는 경우 주제문일 가능성이 크므로, 이어지는 글의 구체적인 예시나 상술에서 빈칸에 들어갈 말의 추론 근거를 찾도록 한다. 빈칸이 포함된 문장은 라이브 공연 경험이 '무엇'인지 정의하고 있고, 뒤에 이어지는 예시는 공연장 안에서 극작가와 감독, 배우, 관객이 서로에게 영향을 주고받으며 라이브 공연을 경험한다는 내용이므로, 정답은 ③ '(그것과) 관계된 사람들의 공동 경험'이다.

해석 주제문 라이브 공연의 경험은 (그것과) 관계된 사람들의 공동 경험이다. 예를 들어, 라이브 공연장의 공연과 세 부류의 주요 관계자들을 보자. 이들은 극작가 또는 감독, 배우, 관객이다. 극작가는 각본이 어떤 생각을 표현하도록 의도하고, 이런 의도는 배우의 연기나 관객의 반응 모두에 의해 영향을 받는다. 배우는 자신의 역할에 가져오는 개인적인 경험들로 극작가의 대사에 여러 의미를 덧붙이고, 다음에는 그들의 연기가 관객의 반응에 영향을 받는다. 관객은 배우를 통해서 뿐만 아니라 극장에 와 있는 신체적인 경험을 통해 극작가의 생각에 반응한다. 어떤 공연 중에든 무언가 놀라운 일이 일어난다. 각각의 관계자들은 자신의 관점에서뿐 아니라 다른 두 관계된 사람들의 관점에서도 공연을 경험하는 것이다.
① 어떤 관객들에게는 종종 도전적인 일
② 가장 창의적인 사람들의 엉뚱한 모임
④ 모두가 기억할 깜짝 파티와 같은 것
⑤ 그 의미가 개별적으로 가장 잘 해석되는 것

구문 [11행~13행] Audiences respond to the playwright's ideas / **not only** through the actors (A) / **but also** through the physical experience of being in the theater (B).
「not only A but also B」는 'A뿐만 아니라 B도'라는 뜻으로 A와 B는 문법적으로 성격이 대등해야 한다. 여기에서 A와 B는 모두 through가 이끄는 전명구가 쓰였다.

어휘 **performance** 공연; 연기, 연주; 실행; 성과 **party** 관계자, 당사자; 모임; 일행; 정당 **playwright** 극작가 **director** 감독; 책임자 **audience** 관객 **affect** 영향을 끼치다 **add A to B** A를 B에 더하다 **layer** 층(層), 겹 **in turn** 다음에는; 차례로, 교대로 **reaction** 반응 **physical** 신체의; 물리적인 **perspective** 관점, 견해; 원근법 [선택지 어휘] **gathering** 모임; 집단 **mutual** 공동의, 상호 간의 **interpret** 해석하다; 설명하다 **individually** 개별적으로, 개인적으로

34 빈칸 추론 ③

소재 인간이 공격성을 보이는 이유

해설 빈칸에는 인간이 공격성을 보이는 이유가 '무엇'인지가 들어가야 한다. 빈칸 뒤에 이어지는 두 가지 예시 모두 인간은 개인 공간을 침해당했을 때(your comfort zone had been violated) 공격성을 보인다는 내용이므로 정답은 ③ '개인 공간 침해와 관련해'이다.

해석 공격성, 즉 어떤 사람이 다른 사람에 대해 보이는 적대적 행동은 어디에서나 볼 수 있는 것이다. 주제문 실제로, 공격성은 우리가 동물계의 다른 생물 종(種)들과 함께 공통적으로 지니고 있는 분명한 특징 중 하나이다. 동물들에 있어서 공격성의 원인이 주로 부족한 식량 자원과 영토 세력권에 관한 것인 반면, 인간은 보통 개인 공간 침해와 관련해 공격적인 행동을 보인다. 어린 남동생과 십 대인 누나를 생각해보라. 이들은 서로 끊임없이 말다툼을 하는데, 동생이 이런저런 것에 대한 질문으로 누나를 성가시게 하거나 누나의 어깨너머로 (누나가 하는 일을) 끊임없이 훔쳐보면서 십 대인 누나를 가만 내버려 두지 않을 것이기 때문이다. 또는 어떤 지인(知人)이 대화 중 당신에게 너무 바짝 다가온 상황을 떠올려보자. 그 상황에서 당신은 당신이 안락함을 느끼는 영역을 침해당했다고 느꼈고, 그래서 당신은 몇 걸음 물러나야 했거나 그 사람을 당신에게서 밀쳐냈을지도 모른다.
① 형편없이 대우받는 것에 대해 대응할 때
② 체구가 더 작고 힘이 더 약한 타인에게
④ 자신의 가족과 재산을 보호할 필요가 있을 때
⑤ 낯선 사람이나 자신이 속한 사회에 새로 온 사람에 대해

구문 [8행~13행] Think of *a little brother and his teenage sister*, // **who** are constantly arguing with each other // because the younger sibling won't leave the teenage sibling alone, / **bothering** her with questions about this or that and constantly **looking** over her shoulder.
who는 앞의 a little brother and his teenage sister를 가리키는 계속적 용법의 관계대명사이다. bothering ~ and constantly looking ...은 부대상황을 나타내는 분사구문으로 '~하면서'로 해석한다. 분사구문의 의미상 주어는 the younger sibling이다.

[13행~17행] Or recall *a situation* [**where** an acquaintance ~ during a conversation], // **in which** you felt (that) your comfort zone had been violated so you had to take a few steps back or you **might have pushed** the person away from you.
관계부사 where가 이끄는 절이 a situation을 수식하고 in which는 계속적 용법으로 쓰여 앞의 a situation ~ a conversation을 가리킨다. in which 이하의 관계대명사절은 접속사 so로 대등하게 연결되어 있으며, so 앞의 절은 원인, so 이후의 절은 그에 따른 결과를 나타낸다. 「might have p.p.」는 '어쩌면 ~했을지도 모른다'란 뜻으로 과거에 대한 불확실한 추측을 나타낸다.

어휘 **aggression** 공격(성) *cf.* **aggressive** 공격적인 **hostility** 적대감, 적개심 **defining** 분명한; 결정적인 **have A in common with** ~와 A를 공통적으로 지니다 **species** 《생물》 종(種) **scarce** 부족한; 드문, 희귀한 **territory** 세력권; 영역; 영토 **constantly** 끊임없이 **sibling** 형제자매 **leave A alone** A를 내버려 두다[건드리지 않다] **look over A's shoulder** A의 어깨너머로 보다[훔쳐보다] **recall** 기억해 내다, 상기하다 **acquaintance** 지인(知人), 아는 사람 **comfort** 안락; 위안 **violate** 침해하다; 위반하다 *cf.* **violation** 침해; 위반 **take a step back** 한 걸음 물러서다 **push A away** A를 밀쳐내다 [선택지 어휘] **in[with] regard to A** A와 관련하여, A에 대해 **react to** ~에 반응하다 **property** 재산; 부동산; 특성

35 무관한 문장 ②

소재 지렁이의 겨울나기

해설 지렁이는 추운 겨울을 보내기 위해 토양이 얼지 않는 땅속 깊은 곳으로 이동한다는 내용의 글이다. 지렁이가 눈이 없어서 피부에 닿는 빛에 반응하고, 피부가 민감해서 화학물질이 닿으면 쉽게 죽는다는 내용은 지렁이가 겨울을 나는 방법과는 무관하므로 정답은 ②이다.

해석 주제문 매해 가을, 햇빛이 비추는 시간이 점점 짧아지고 기온이 떨어질 때, 동물들은 다가오는 추위에 대비하여 조치를 취한다. 많은 종(種)이 더 따뜻한 남쪽 땅이나 대양에서 겨울을 보내려고 수천 킬로미터를 여행한다. 지렁이는 영하의 기온에서는 생존할 수 없어서 지표면에서 더 아래 깊숙한 땅속까지 수직 이동을 시작한다. 지렁이는 눈이 없어서 피부를 통해 빛의 변화에 반응하는데, 지렁이의 피부는 너무나 민감해서 화학물질은 지렁이를 쉽게 죽일 수 있다. 지표에서 수 미터 아래에서는, 기온이 지렁이에게 편안한 상태로 유지된다. 지렁이는 흙을 붙잡으려고 몸에서 삐져나온 작은 수염을 이용하며, 토양이 얼지 않는 곳까지 아래로 깊숙이 파고 들어간다. 안전한 장소에 다다르면, 지렁이는 공처럼 몸을 말아서 겨우내 활동하지 않고 따뜻한 상태로 보낸다.

구문 [5행~8행] Earthworms(S), [which cannot survive in freezing temperatures], start(V) on a vertical migration **from** *soil* (at the surface of the earth) **to** *soil* (deeper underground).
문장 전체의 주어는 Earthworms, 동사는 start이며 주어를 부연 설명하는 관계대명사절이 삽입되었다. migration 뒤에 방향을 나타내는 부사구 「from A to B (A에서 B까지)」가 쓰였다. at the surface of the earth와 deeper underground는 각각 앞의 soil이 어떤 토양을 지칭하는지 구체적으로 설명해준다.

[15행~16행] When they reach the safe area, // they curl up(V1) into a ball and spend(V2) the entire winter (being) **inactive and warm**.
inactive and warm은 앞에 being이 생략된 분사구문으로, '~한 채로, ~하면서'의 의미로 해석한다.

어휘 **autumn** 가을 **daylight** 일광, 빛; 낮 **earthworm** 지렁이 **freezing** 영하의; (얼어붙을 듯이) 몹시 추운 *cf.* **freeze** 얼어붙다 **vertical** 수직의, 세로의 **migration** 이주, 이동 **surface** 표면 **sensitive** 민감한, 예민한 **chemical** (보통 복수형) 화학물질 **stick out** 튀어나오다 **grasp** 붙잡다; (요점·의미 등을) 파악하다 **curl up** 동그랗게 말다; 몸을 웅크리다 **dig deep** 깊이 파고들다 **inactive** 활동하지 않는, 움직이지 않는

36 글의 순서 ④

소재 적색 신호를 대하는 바람직한 운전자의 태도

해설 주어진 글은 바람직한 운전자에 대한 묘사인데, (A), (B), (C)의 주어는 모두 주어진 글과 상반되는 운전자를 지칭한다. 따라서 역접의 연결사(however)와 함께 Intelligent drivers와 대조적인 운전자를 처음 소개하는 Other drivers가 주어로 쓰인 (C)가 주어진 글 바로 다음에 온다. (A)에는 (C)에서 언급한 운전자의 행동을 묘사하는 내용이 이어지며, (B)는 (C)와 (A)에 언급된 운전자가 취해야 할 올바른 태도를 제시하며 글을 마무리한다. 따라서 올바른 글의 순서는 ④ '(C)-(A)-(B)'이다.

해석 분별 있는 운전자들은 교통 신호가 삶의 현실이며, 시간이 지날수록 대략 같은 수의 적색등과 녹색등을 만날 것이라는 것을 안다. 그들은 앞의 신호가 빨간색으로 바뀌더라도 그것을 감정적으로 받아들이지 않는다. 그들은 그저 멈추고 그들의 여정에 있어 짧은 방해를 견딘다.

(C) 그러나 다른 운전자들은 단연코 좋지 않은 태도를 가지고 있다. 그들은 적색 신호를 물리쳐야 할 적으로 보며, 적색 신호로 인해 멈추는 것을 나약함의 신호로 본다.

(A) 그래서 그들은 어리석게 운전하는데, 황색 신호에 속도를 높여서 다른 차량과 보행자들이 건너지 못하도록 교차로를 막는다. 아니면 더 나쁘게는 충돌 사고를 일으킨다.

(B) 주제문 이런 운전자들은 그들의 인식을 바꾸어 적색 신호등을 반가운 모습으로 봐야 한다. 만약 그들이 적색등을 잠시 동안 편히 쉴 신호로 본다면, 운전은 더 즐거운 경험이 되고, 도로는 모든 이에게 더 안전해질 것이다.

구문 [4행~5행] They don't take it personally // **if** a light ahead turns red; ~.
여기서 if는 '~하더라도'란 뜻으로, '양보'의 부사절을 이끄는 접속사이다.

[12행~15행] **If** they **saw** red lights as a signal to relax for a moment, // driving **would be** a more pleasant experience, and the roads **would be** safer for everyone.
「If+S'+동사의 과거형 ~, S+조동사 과거형+동사원형 ...」 구조의 가정법 과거 문장으로, 주절에 두 개의 절이 접속사 and로 병렬 연결되었다.

[17행~19행] ~; they **see** red lights / **as** *enemies* [that have to be beaten] and (**see**) getting stopped by **one** / **as** a sign of weakness.
they를 공통 주어로 하는 두 개의 「see A as B (A를 B로 보다)」 구문이 and로 연결되었으며 반복되는 두 번째 see가 생략되었다. 부정대명사 one은 a red light를 의미한다.

어휘 **a fact of life** 삶의 (피할 수 없는) 사실, 현실 **encounter** (우연히) 만나다, 맞닥뜨리다 **roughly** 대략 **take A personally** A를 감정적으로[기분 나쁘게] 대하다 **put up with** ~을 참다 **interruption** 방해; 중단 **intersection** 교차로 **pedestrian** 보행자 **collision** 충돌 (사고) **perception** 인식 **decidedly** 단연코, 확실히

37 글의 순서 ⑤

소재 뱅크런(bank run)의 원인

해설 많은 사람들이 일시에 돈을 인출하려 하면 은행이 요구에 부응할 수 없다는 주어진 글 다음에는, 그 원인이 은행의 재정 건전성에 대한 루머나 추측 때문이며, 그 루머를 믿는 사람들은 은행에서 돈을 인출하려 한다는 (C)가 나온다. 이로 인해 은행 문 밖에 긴 줄이 생기면, 은행에 대한 나쁜 소문이 더욱 더 증폭된다는 (B)가 나오며, 나쁜 소문이 너무나 만연하면 은행이 다른 은행에서 돈을 빌릴 수조차 없고, 전체 금융 시스템이 무너지는 결과를 초래할 수 있다는 (A)가 마지막에 나온다. 따라서 정답은 ⑤ '(C)-(B)-(A)'이다.

해석 뱅크런(= 사람들이 예금을 찾으러 은행에 몰려드는 현상) 혹은 은행 공황은 미국 역사 전체에 걸쳐 여러 번 일어났다. 은행은 100퍼센트에 훨씬 못 미치는 법정준비금을 가지고 영업하기 때문에, 충분한 수의 고객들이 단 하루에 그들의 잔고를 요구한다면 은행이 그 요구를 맞춰줄 수 없게 되는 일이 있을 수 있다.

(C) 주제문 많은 은행 공황은 은행의 재정 건전성에 대한 루머나 추측으로 인해 발생했다. 충분한 수의 사람들이 그 루머를 믿는다면, 논리적으로 그들은 자신의 자금을 인출하

여 그것을 다른 금융 기관으로 옮기거나 매트리스 아래에 채워 넣고 싶을 것이다.

(B) 일단 은행 문에 줄이 생기기 시작하면, 다른 고객들도 알아차리고 루머가 확산될 것이다. 은행은 다른 은행에서 차입하여 자기 고객의 잔고를 내어줄 수 있다면 뱅크런을 피할 수 있다.

(A) 그러나 추측이나 루머가 만연하면, 은행은 그때 서로에게 대출해주기를 꺼리게 될 수 있다. 이런 일이 발생할 때, 그것은 훨씬 더 많은 추측을 촉발시키고, 전체 금융 시스템에 뱅크런을 일으킬 수 있다.

구문 [2행~6행] Because banks operate with **far** *less* than 100% required reserves, // it is possible that if enough customers demand their account balances on a single day, / the bank will not be able to meet the demand.

far는 비교급을 강조하는 부사이다. it은 가주어이고 that절이 진주어이며, that절은 「if절+주절」로 이루어져 있다.

어휘 **multiple** 다수의 **operate** 운용되다, 영업하다 **required reserve** 법정준비금(회사나 은행 등이 손실 보충에 대비하여 적립해 놓는 준비금) **balances** 잔고, 잔액 **speculation** 추측, 억측; 심사숙고; 투기 **pervasive** 만연하는, 널리 퍼지는 **unwilling** 꺼리는 **spark** 촉발시키다; 불꽃을 일으키다 **financial** 금융의, 재정의 **avert** 방지하다, 피하다 **withdraw** (돈을) 인출하다; (군대를) 철수시키다 **fund** 기금, 자금 **institution** 기관 **stuff** 채워 넣다

38 문장 넣기 ⑤

소재 아침형 인간이 저녁형 인간보다 건강한 이유

해설 주어진 문장에 역접을 나타내는 however가 있고 저녁형 인간(night owls)의 생활상이 소개되고 있으므로, 아침형 인간(early birds)의 생활상과 그에 따른 건강상의 이점에 대한 소개가 끝나는 ⑤에 주어진 문장이 들어가는 것이 적절하다. ⑤ 뒤에는 저녁형 인간의 불규칙한 일상을 규칙적으로 고치는 데 도움이 될 조언이 주어지고 있으므로 흐름이 자연스럽게 이어진다.

해석 주제문 건강에 관해서는 아침형 사람들이 저녁형 사람들보다 유리하다. 한 연구에 의하면 일찍 일어나는 사람들은 습관이 일관된 경향이 있고, 이러한 규칙성은 더 좋은 건강으로 이어진다. 그 연구는 아침형 사람들이 매일 비슷한 시간에 먹고 운동하고 잘 가능성이 더 크다는 것에 주목했다. 그 연구는 또한 그들의 규칙적인 일상이 잠을 더 잘 자게 해준다는 것도 주목했다. 잠을 더 잘 잔다는 것은 그들이 낮 동안 에너지를 더 많이 가졌다는 것을 의미했다. 하지만 저녁형 사람들은 매일 불규칙하게 먹고 잤으며, 그 결과 '약한 시차' 증상을 겪었다. 그들은 매일 밤 11시 취침 시간에 이르게 될 때까지 15분 일찍 잠자리에 들고, 잠자기 전에 운동이나 음식 섭취를 하지 않으며, 주말에 늦잠 자는 것을 피함으로써 그들의 불규칙한 일상을 고치도록 권고 받았다.

구문 [5행~7행] A study has found // **that** early risers tend to be consistent in their habits, and **that** this regularity leads to better health.
(has found: V, that early risers ~ habits: O1, that this regularity ~ health: O2)

동사 has found의 목적어 역할을 하는 명사절 두 개가 병렬구조를 이루고 있다.

[12행~16행] They were advised to fix their irregular routines / **by** going to bed 15 minutes earlier ~, / (by) not exercising or (not) eating before sleep, and (by) avoiding sleeping in on weekends.

전치사 by 뒤에 동명사 going, not exercising, (not) eating, avoiding이 대등하게 연결된 형태이다.

어휘 **night owl** 밤늦은 시간에 깨어 있는 사람(↔ **early bird[riser]** 아침에 일찍 일어나는 사람) **inconsistently** 변덕스럽게, 일관성 없게 *cf.* **consistent** 일관된 **jet lag** 시차로 인한 피로 **symptom** 증상, 징후 **when it comes to A** A에 관해서는, A의 문제라면 **A have the advantage over B** A가 B보다 유리하다 **tend to-v** v하는 경향이 있다 **regularity** 규칙성 *cf.* **regular** 규칙적인 **note** 주목하다, 유념하다 **be likely to-v** v할 가능성이 많다, v할 것 같다 **routine** 일과 **promote** 증진[촉진]하다; 홍보하다; 승진시키다 **sleep in** 늦잠을 자다

39 문장 넣기 ⑤

소재 경험재로서 관광 산업의 특징

해설 주어진 문장은 관광 산업이 지닌 '어떤 특징'이 관광 서비스 공급자에게 도전 과제를 제시한다는 내용이므로 관광 산업이 지닌 특징을 설명하는 내용 다음에 오는 것이 자연스럽다. 따라서 구매 전에 직접 경험해 볼 수 없어서 소비자가 구매 결정을 할 때 평판, 조언, 경험 등에 의존한다는 내용 뒤인 ⑤에 주어진 문장이 들어가는 것이 적절하다.

해석 구매하기 전에 제품을 비교해보는 것은 항상 지혜로운 일이다. 소비자는 그것을 사기로 결정하기 전에 제품을 보고, 만지고, 어쩌면 냄새를 맡거나 맛을 볼 수도 있다. 반면에, 서비스는 소비자들이 구매 전에 먼저 살펴볼 수 없으므로 비교하기 어렵다. 예를 들어, 호텔, 기념품 가게, 관광명소 같은 관광 산업은 주로 서비스로 이루어져 있다. 구매 후에야 특징이 결정될 수 있는 이런 상품들은 경험재로 불린다. 경험재를 구매할 때, 소비자는 구매 결정을 하는 데 있어 판매자의 평판, 전문 조언자, 친구나 친지의 경험, 그리고 자신의 과거 경험에 자주 의존해야 한다. 관광 산업의 이런 특징은 잠재 고객들에게 자신의 상품을 광고하는 법을 생각해 내야 하는 관광 서비스 공급자들에게 중요한 도전 과제를 제시한다. 주제문 요컨대, 관광 산업은 서비스의 실제 판매 이전과 실제 판매하는 과정의 많은 부분에서 정보 산업이다.

구문 [13행~14행] *Those products* [**whose** attributes can be determined only after purchase] are called experience goods.
(Those products: S, are called: V, experience goods: C)

소유격 관계대명사 whose가 이끄는 관계대명사절이 주어 Those products를 수식하고 있다. 「call A B (A를 B로 부르다)」 구문이 수동태로 바뀐 문장으로 목적어는 주어가 되고 목적격보어는 동사 뒤에 남았다.

어휘 **attribute** 특징, 속성 **significant** 중요한; 상당한 **supplier** 공급자 **figure out** 알아내다, 생각해 내다 **potential** 잠재적인; 잠재력 **compare** 비교하다 **consumer** 소비자 **inspect** 검사하다, 면밀하게 살피다 **souvenir** 기념품 **tourist attraction** 관광명소 *cf.* **attraction** (사람을 끄는) 명소, 명물; 매력(적인 요소) **be composed of** ~로 구성되다 **experience goods** 경험재(직접 구입해서 체험을 해봐야 품질을 알 수 있는 상품) **reputation** 평판, 명성 **advisor** 조언자, 고문 **relative** 친척; 관계있는

40 요약문 완성 ②

소재 자세가 자기평가에 미치는 영향

해설 실험에서 자세가 바른 피실험자들은 자신에 대한 긍정적인 특성을 잘 생각해내고 강하게 믿을 수 있었던 반면, 자세를 수그린 피실험자들은 자기평가 자체에 어려움을 겪었다. 즉, 자신을 '평가하는(rated)' 방식이 '자세(posture)'의 영향을 받았음을 알 수 있다.

해석 주제문 Madrid 자치대학교의 심리학 교수인 Pablo Briñol은 신체와 정신 간의 관계에 대한 연구를 수행했다. 그는 자신의 피실험자들에게 똑바로 앉아서 가슴을 내밀거나 얼굴이 무릎을 보는 상태로 앞으로 구부정하게 앉아있도록 지정했다. 그들이 이러한 자세를 몇 분 동안 지속했을 때, 그들은 미래의 직업인으로서의 삶에서 그들에게 도움이 되거나 해가 될 것 같은 세 가지 긍정적인 특성 혹은 세 가지 부정적인 특성을 가지고 스스로를 묘사해보라는 요청을 받았다. 똑바른 자세로 있던 사람들은 자신에 대하여 긍정적이고 할 수 있다는 생각을 하는 것이 더 쉽다는 점을 깨달았을 뿐만 아니라, 자신이 나열한 특성을 더욱 강하게 믿었다. 반면에 구부정한 사람들은 자신의 긍정적인 혹은 부정적인 특성을 확신하지 못했다. 그들은 심지어 자기가 누구인지를 알기 위해 고군분투했다.

⬇

위 실험에 따르면, 피실험자들이 자신의 특성을 묘사할 때, 그들이 자신을 (A) 평가하는 방식은 자신의 (B) 자세의 영향을 받았다.

구문 [4행~7행] He assigned their subjects to **either** sit up straight and push out their chests **or** sit slouched forward **with** *their faces* **looking** at their knees.
(sit up ~ chests: A, sit slouched ~ knees: B)

「either A or B」는 'A나 B 둘 중 하나'의 뜻이다. A, B 자리는 공통적으로 to 다음에 이어지는 동사원형으로 시작된다. 「with+O+v-ing」는 'O가 v한 채로'라는 뜻의 분사구문이다.

[11행~14행] **Not only** did *those* (in the upright position) find **it** easier **to think** positive, empowering thoughts about themselves, // they **also** believed more strongly in *the traits* [(which[that]) they listed].

「not only A but also B」는 'A뿐만 아니라 B도'의 뜻이다. 이 문장에서는 but이 생략되었다. not only와 같은 부정 표현이 문두로 나아가면 「Not only+조동사+주어+동사원형」의 어순으로 도치가 일어난다. find 다음의 it은 가목적어이고 to think ~ themselves가 진목적어이며, 「find it+형용사+to-v」는 'v하는 것이 …하다는 것을 알게 되다'의 뜻이다. [ ]는 앞에 목적격 관계대명사 which[that]가 생략되어 the traits를 수식한다.

어휘 **autonomous** 자치의, 자율의 **assign** 지정하다, 배정하다 **subject** 피실험자; 대상; 주제 **slouch** 구부정하게 앉다[서다] **pose** 자세 **trait** 특성, 특질 **upright** 똑바른, 꼿꼿한 **empower** ~할 수 있도록 하다; 권한을 부여하다 **be convinced of** ~을 확신하다 **struggle** 고군분투하다 [선택지 어휘] **mentality** 정신력; 지력(知力)

41~42 장문

41 ⑤ 42 ④

소재 비난 본능

해설 41. 어떤 문제가 발생했을 때 이를 단 한 사람이나 하나의 단순한 이유 탓으로 돌려버리면, 문제의 전체적이고 복잡한 측면에 대해 눈을 감아버리게 되어 문제로부터 배우는 것도 없고, 향후 비슷한 문제가 발생했을 때에도 제대로 대처할 수 없다는 내용의 글이다. 따라서 제목으로 가장 적절한 것은 ⑤ '비난 본능은 문제해결 능력을 약화한다'이다.

① 비난 본능은 양날의 검

② 우리는 어떻게 비난 본능을 통제할 수 있는가?

③ 당신의 관계에서 비난 게임을 멈추어라

④ 우리는 왜 다른 견해들을 조율해야 하는가

42. 우리는 나쁜 일이 발생했을 때 문제의 원인을 한 개인 혹은 하나의 단순한 이유로 축소하는데, 현실은 대부분 더 복잡하며 개인 탓만 하고 문제를 덮어두는 것은 미래를 대비하는 데 아무런 도움이 되지 않는 자세이므로, 우리는 문제를 이해하기 위해 개인이 아닌 시스템에 주목해야 한다. 따라서 (d)의 individual을 system으로 바꿔 써야 한다.

해석 비난 본능은 왜 나쁜 일이 발생했는지에 대해 분명하고 단순한 이유를 찾으려는 본능이다. 일이 잘못될 때는 그것이 어떤 나쁜 의도를 가진 나쁜 사람 때문인 것이 틀림없다고 우리가 결정하는 것은 자연스러운 것처럼 보인다. 우리는 누군가가 바랐기 때문에 일이 일어난 거라고, 개인에게 권력과 힘이 있다고 믿고 싶어 하는데, 그렇지 않으면 세상은 예측 불가능하고 혼란스럽고 두렵게 느껴지기 때문이다. 비난 본능은 우리가 개인이나 특정 집단의 중요성을 (a) 과장하게 한다. 주제문 (b) 죄가 있는 당사자를 찾아내려는 이러한 본능은 세상에 대해 진실하고 사실에 기반을 둔 이해를 발달시키는 우리의 능력을 저해한다. 일단 누구의 얼굴에 주먹을 날릴지를 결정하면, 우리는 다른 곳에서 설명을 찾는 것을 멈추기 때문에 그것은 우리의 배움을 (c) 막는다. 예를 들어 졸음 비행을 한 기장에게 비행기 추락 문제를 탓하는 것은 미래의 추락을 막는 데 도움이 되지 않을 것이다. 그렇게 하기 위해(= 미래의 추락을 막기 위해) 우리는 물어야 한다. 그는 왜 졸렸을까? 미래에는 졸음 비행을 하는 조종사들을 어떻게 규제할 수 있을까? 우리가 졸음 비행을 하는 기장을 찾게 되었을 때 생각하기를 멈춘다면, 어떠한 발전도 이루지 못한다. 세상 대부분의 중요한 문제를 이해하기 위해 우리는 (d) 개인(→ 시스템)에 시선을 돌려야 한다. 일이 잘될 때도 같은 본능이 촉발된다. 어떤 일이 잘될 때 우리는 재빨리 공(功)을 한 개인이나 하나의 단순한 원인에 돌리지만, 그때에도 그것은 보통은 더 복잡한 일이다. 정말로 세상을 바꾸고 싶다면 당신은 세상을 이해해야 한다. 당신의 비난 본능을 (e) 따르는 것은 도움이 되지 않을 것이다.

구문 [3행~5행] It seems that it comes very naturally *for us* **to decide** O that when things go wrong, it must be because of some bad individual with bad intentions.

it은 가주어, to decide 이하가 진주어이고, for us는 to decide에 대한 의미상 주어이다. that절은 decide에 대한 목적어이다.

[16행~17행] ~, **blaming** *an airplane crash* **on** *a sleepy pilot* will not help to stop future crashes.

「blame A on B」는 'A를 B의 탓으로 돌리다, A를 B에게 책임지게 하다'의 뜻이다.

어휘 **blame** 비난; 책임 **come naturally** 자연스럽다, 아주 쉽다 **agency** 힘, 작용; 기관, 단체 **unpredictable** 예측할 수 없는 **exaggerate** 과장하다 **party** 당사자 **hinder** 방해[저해]하다 **regulate** 규제하다 **look to** ~에 시선을 돌리다; ~을 생각해 보다 **trigger** 촉발하다 **credit** 공, 칭찬, 인정 [선택지 어휘] **undermine** 약화하다

43~45 장문

43 ⑤ 44 ① 45 ④

소재 부모님의 첫 만남과 운명적인 재회

해설 43. (A)는 Joe와 Nicole이 뉴욕의 어느 카페에서 우연히 만나 서로에게 끌렸고, Nicole이 읽던 책에 전화번호를 적어 Joe에게 주고 헤어졌다는 내용이다. 이어서 Joe가 지하철에서 그 책을 넣어 둔 코트를 잃어버렸다는 내용의 (D)가 오고, Joe의 연락을 기다렸던 Nicole이 영국으로 공부를 하러 갔다가 잠시 파리로 여행을 떠났다는 내용인 (C)가 이어진다. 그리고 마지막으로, 두 사람이 파리의 카페에서 다시 만나게 되는 내용인 (B)로 마무리된다. 따라서 정답은 ⑤ '(D)-(C)-(B)'이다.

44. (a)는 Joe와 Nicole이 재회한 카페의 종업원을 가리키고 나머지는 필자의 아버지인 Joe를 가리킨다.

45. (C)에서 Nicole은 학업을 위해 영국에 머무르고 있었고, 파리에는 3일간의 방학을 즐기기 위해 방문한 것임을 알 수 있으므로 ④가 글의 내용과 일치하지 않는다.

해석 (A) ① 나의 부모님 Nicole과 Joe는 뉴욕에서 처음 만났다. Nicole은 카페에 혼자 앉아 Charles Dickens의 〈위대한 유산〉을 읽고 있었다. 카페는 꽉 차 있었기 때문에 Joe는 그녀의 테이블에 함께 앉아도 되는지 물었다. 그들은 서로에게 단번에 이끌렸고 몇 시간 동안 이야기를 나누었다. ② Nicole이 떠나야 했을 때, 그녀는 그 책에 전화번호를 적어 Joe에게 주었다.

(D) 그녀가 떠난 후, Joe는 그녀에 대한 생각을 멈출 수가 없었다. 잠을 설친 다음날, (d) 내 아버지(= Joe)는 그의 부모님을 만나기 위해 브루클린으로 떠났고 지하철에서 읽기 위해 그 책을 가지고 갔다. 그는 피곤했기 때문에 코트 주머니에 책을 살짝 넣고 코트를 (e) 그(= Joe)의 옆자리에 놓아둔 채 눈을 감았다. 아버지가 눈을 떴을 때, 그는 이미 브루클린을 지나버렸고 그의 코트도 사라졌다. ⑤ 누군가 그 코트는 물론 그것과 함께 책도 훔쳐 간 것이다. 어머니의 전화번호가 사라져 버렸다.

(C) Joe는 깜박하고 나의 어머니의 성(姓)을 묻지 않았었다. 책에 있는 전화번호가 그녀와 연결될 수 있는 유일한 고리였다. Nicole이 그토록 바랐던, 뉴욕에서 만난 (b) 젊은 남자(= Joe)로부터 전화는 결국 오지 않았다. Joe는 카페에 계속해서 다시 가봤지만, (c) 그(= Joe)는 Nicole을 찾을 수는 없었다. ④ 세 번의 여름이 지나고 어머니는 문학 과정을 이수하기 위해 영국에 갔다. 학업 중 3일의 방학 기간에 72시간 동안의 관광을 하기 위해 비행기를 타고 파리로 갔다.

(B) 그녀는 새로 산 〈위대한 유산〉을 가지고 갔다. 하루 종일 관광을 한 후, ③ 어느 카페의 테이블에 앉아 책의 첫 페이지를 펼치며 뉴욕에서 만났던 그 남자를 다시 생각하기 시작했다. 음식이 담긴 쟁반을 들고 와 테이블을 같이 쓸 수 있는지 불어로 물어보는 (a) 어떤 젊은 남자(= 종업원) 때문에 그녀는 책 읽는 것을 잠시 중단했다. 그녀는 고개를 끄덕이고는 다시 책을 읽기 시작했다. 잠시 후에 그녀는 그의 목소리를 들었다. "그 책을 잃어버리지 말았어야 했어요."라는 말이었다. 다시 고개를 들어 바라보니 그녀를 향해 웃고 있는 Joe가 있었다.

어휘 **(A) share** 함께 쓰다, 공유하다; 몫, 지분 **instantly** 즉시 **be attracted to A** A에게 끌리다 **one another** 서로 **(B) copy** (책의) 부, 권 **interrupt** 중단하다; 방해하다 **tray** 쟁반 **nod** 고개를 끄덕이다 **(C) link** 연결; (사슬의) 고리 **long for** ~을 간절히 기다리다[열망하다] **literature** 문학 **(D) sleepless** 잠 못 이루는, 불면증의 **slip A into B** A를 B에 살짝 넣다[끼우다] **lay (laid-laid)** 놓다[두다] **steal (stole-stolen)** 훔치다

실전 모의고사 02

본문 p.27

18 ④	19 ⑤	20 ②	21 ④	22 ④	23 ④	24 ①	25 ④	26 ②	27 ⑤
28 ③	29 ⑤	30 ④	31 ①	32 ④	33 ③	34 ②	35 ②	36 ⑤	37 ④
38 ④	39 ④	40 ②	41 ⑤	42 ③	43 ③	44 ④	45 ④		

18 글의 목적 ④

소재 결혼식에서 찍은 사진 요청

해설 글 후반부의 I would be most grateful if ~ by guests.에 편지를 쓴 목적이 드러나 있다. 공식적으로 찍은 사진이 별로라서 하객들이 찍은 사진들로 결혼식 앨범을 꾸미려 한다고 한 뒤, 가지고 있는 결혼식 사진을 보내달라는 부탁을 하고 있으므로 글의 목적으로 가장 적절한 것은 ④이다.

해석 Ellen 씨께,
당신이 저희 딸의 결혼식에 오셔서 무척 즐거운 시간을 보내셨다니 저희도 매우 기쁘군요. Victoria와 저희 새 사위는 곧 신혼여행에서 돌아올 테지만 그 아이들의 결혼식 앨범은 아직 준비되지 않았어요. 이렇게 된 이유는 공식 사진들이 형편없었기 때문이에요. 대부분 초점이 맞지 않았고 다른 것들은 구도가 나빴던 데다가, 몇몇 사진에서는 사진사의 손가락이 사진을 덮고 있었다니까요! 그래서 저희는 그에게 돈을 지불하지 않겠다고 알려줬죠. 저희는 당신이 결혼식에 카메라를 가져온 것을 알았어요. 주제문 당신이 찍은 사진들을 제게 이메일로 보내주셔서 저희가 하객들이 찍은 사진들로 결혼식 앨범을 정리할 수 있게 해주신다면 정말 감사하겠습니다. 곧 연락해 주시길 기대할게요.
Janet Miller 드림

구문 [12행~15행] **I would be most grateful** // **if you could** email me *any pictures* [(that) you have] // **so that** we can assemble a wedding album of *photographs* (taken by guests).
「I would be grateful if you could[would] ~」는 '~해주시면 감사하겠습니다'란 뜻의 관용 표현이다. you have는 any pictures를 수식하는 관계대명사절로서 목적격 관계대명사가 생략되었다. so that은 '~하기 위해, ~하도록'이란 뜻으로 '목적'을 나타내는 접속사이다. 과거분사구 taken by guests는 앞의 명사 photographs를 후치수식하고 있다.

어휘 **enjoy oneself** 즐겁게 보내다 **son-in-law** 사위 **useless** 쓸모없는; 헛된 **out of focus** 초점이 벗어난 **compose** 구도를 짜다; 구성하다 **grateful** 고맙게 생각하는, 감사하는 **assemble** (모아) 정리하다; 모으다; 조립하다 **look forward to v-ing** v할 것을 기대[고대]하다

19 심경 변화 ⑤

소재 Keenan의 유치원 생활 시작

해설 처음에 아버지가 Keenan을 유치원에 데려가서 여러 이야기를 해줘도 Keenan은 관심을 보이지 않았지만(indifferent), 수업 첫날이 되자 아버지를 앞질러 유치원으로 뛰어 들어가는 Keenan의 모습에서 그가 들떠있음(excited)을 알 수 있다. 따라서 정답은 ⑤ '무관심한 → 신이 난'이다.

해석 John Assaraf의 아들 Keenan이 유치원에 입학하기 2주 전에, John은 Keenan을 유치원 건물까지 데려가서 그와 함께 창문으로 들여다봤다. 주제문 Keenan은 아무런 감정도 보이지 않았고 아무 말도 하지 않았다. 그는 그저 자신이 가져온 장난감을 가지고 놀았다. John은 아들에게 유치원에 대한 다양한 이야기와 Keenan이 얼마나 멋진 시간을 보낼 것인지에 대한 얘기를 해줬다. 그러나 그의 아들은 귀 기울이지 않았다. 걱정되었지만 무엇을 해야 할지 몰라서 John은 유치원에 대해 다시 언급하지 않기로 했다. 주제문 놀랍게도 수업 첫날이 되자 Keenan은 완전히 바뀌어 있었다. John과 Keenan이 건물로 들어가기 위해 함께 계단을 걸어 올라갈 때, John은 Keenan이 자신을 앞질러 안으로 뛰어 들어가는 것을 좀처럼 막을 수 없었다. 그것은 아주 새로운 경험이었지만, Keenan은 완전히 준비되어 있었다. 들떠있는 것처럼 그의 얼굴은 밝았다. John은 Keenan이 준비되는 데 단지 좀 더 시간이 필요했었다는 것을 깨달았다.

① 지루한 → 실망한 ② 기쁜 → 겁먹은
③ 초조한 → 창피한 ④ 겁에 질린 → 자랑스러운

구문 [13행~14행] ~ John could *hardly* **keep** him **from running** in ahead of him.
hardly는 '좀처럼 ~않는'의 뜻으로 부정의 의미를 갖는 부사이고, 「keep+O+from+v-ing」는 'O가 v하지 못하게 막다'라는 뜻이다.

어휘 **kindergarten** 유치원 **mention** 언급하다 **completely** 완전히, 전적으로 **brand-new** 아주 새로운, 신상품의 **brighten (up)** 반짝이다; 밝아지다 **float on air** 들떠있다

20 필자 주장 ②

소재 식물 질병의 문제를 해결해야 하는 이유

해설 식물이 질병에 걸리기 쉬운데다가, 주요 곡물이 질병에 걸릴 경우 기근을 초래할 수 있기 때문에 이를 해결하기 위한 연구가 진행되고 있다는 내용의 글이다. 특히 마지막 문장(In order to ~ plant diseases.)에 식물 질병의 피해를 해결할 방안을 강구해야 한다는 필자의 주장이 잘 드러나 있으므로 정답은 ②이다.

해석 동물과 같이 식물도 여러 병에 걸리기 쉽다. 3만 종의 서로 다른 질병이 식물에 침범하는 것으로 추정되어 왔다. 예를 들어, 40종의 질병이 옥수수를 침범하며 밀에도 그만큼의 질병이 엄습하는 것으로 알려져 있다. 전 세계 사람들이 식량으로 이러한 곡물에 의존하기 때문에 확인되지 않은 식물의 질병이 일으키는 결과는 끔찍할 수 있다. 만약 주요 곡물 중 하나라도 질병에 걸려 없어지면, 이에 따른 기근이 수백만 명의 사람들을 죽일 수 있다. 현재로서는, 주요 곡물에서 감염을 일으키는 흔한 질병이 완전히 박멸될 수 없고, 식물은 물리적으로 질병으로부터 완전히 격리될 수가 없다. 따라서 많은 식물학자들은 식물이 자체 면역력을 기를 수 있도록 돕는 유전자 변형을 연구하고 있다. 주제문 세계 인구에 충분한 식량 공급을 유지하기 위해서는 식물의 성장과 관리에 관련된 인력이 식물 질병에 맞서 싸울 수 있는 방법을 찾는 것이 필요하다.

구문 [7행~9행] **If** just *one* (of the major crops) **were attacked and destroyed** by disease, // the resulting famines **could kill** millions of people.
「If+S'+동사의 과거형 ~, S+조동사 과거형+동사원형 ...」의 구조인 가정법 과거 구문이다. be동사의 경우, 가정법 구문에서는 주어의 수에 상관없이 종종 were를 쓴다. 이 문장은 문맥상 미래의 일에 대한 가정을 나타낸다.

[16행~18행] ~, it is necessary **for *those*** (involved in plant growth and management) to find *ways* (to combat plant diseases).
(it: 가주어, to find ~: 진주어)
가주어 it은 진주어인 to부정사구(to find ~ diseases)를 대신한다. for those는 to부정사구의 의미상 주어이며 those는 뒤에 오는 과거분사구의 수식을 받는다.

어휘 **be subject to A** A의 영향을 받기 쉽다; A의 대상이다 **estimate** 추정하다, 어림잡다 **wheat** 밀 **crop** 곡물, 작물 **unchecked** 확인되지 않은 **disastrous** 끔찍한, 피해가 막심한 **famine** 기근, 기아 **presently** 현재; 곧,

머지않아 **lead to A** A를 일으키다; A를 이끌다 **infection** (병의) 감염; 전염(병) **eliminate** 제거하다 **physically** 물리적으로; 육체적으로 **work on** ~에 대해 연구하다; ~에 착수하다 **genetic** 유전의 **modification** 변형 **built-in** 본래 갖춰진; 붙박이의 **immunity** 면역력 **sufficient** 충분한 **involved in** ~에 관련된 **combat** 싸우다; 전투

21 밑줄 함의 ④

소재 포기하면 성공할 수 없다

해설 꿈을 이루는 사람들은 어려움 속에서도 포기하지 않고 한 걸음 더 나아가고 견디는 사람들이라는 내용의 글이다. 코치가 말한 "물론 (Elmer McAllister에 대해) 못 들어봤겠지. 그는 그만뒀으니까."라는 말은 '그만두는 사람은 이름을 남길 만큼 위대한 일을 이루지 못한다'는 의미이다. 따라서 밑줄 친 부분의 의미는 ④ '포기하고서 위대해진 사람은 아무도 없다.'가 된다.

해석 주제문 자신의 꿈에 대해 패배를 인정하는 사람들과 자신의 꿈을 유지하기 위해 애쓰는 사람들 간의 차이는 무엇인가? 그것은 다시 일어나서 그저 조금 더 앞으로 한 걸음 나아가는 것이다. 나는 예전에 선수들이 힘든 시즌을 인내하고 나아가게 하려고 시도한 고등학교 농구 코치의 멋진 이야기를 들었다. 몇 번의 길고 성공적이지 못했던 경기 후에, 그는 자신의 팀 앞에 서서 말했다. "Michael Jordan이 그만둔 적 있었나?" 팀은 "아니요!"라고 대답했다. 그는 외쳤다. "Wright 형제는 어떻지? 그들이 포기했나?" "아니요!" 팀은 대답했다. "Walt Disney가 그만둔 적 있었나?" 다시 팀은 대답했다. "아니요!" "Elmer McAllister가 그만둔 적 있었나?" 오랫동안 침묵만 흘렀다. 마침내 한 선수가 "Elmer McAllister가 누구예요? 그 사람에 대해서 들어본 적이 없어요."라고 물을 정도로 충분한 용기를 냈다. 코치는 날카롭게 맞받아 대답했다. "물론 못 들어봤겠지. 그는 그만뒀으니까."

① 누구든지 더 열심히 노력하면 유명해질 수 있다.
② 모든 사람들은 재능을 갖고 있으며 그것을 향상시킬 의무가 있다.
③ 미래는 그것을 오늘 대비하는 사람들의 것이다.
⑤ 유명해지는 것은 타고난 능력과 끊임없는 노력을 요구한다.

구문 [1행~3행] What is *the difference* (**between** *those* [who throw in the towel on their dreams] **and** *those* [who struggle to maintain their dreams])?
(A, B)
「between A and B (A와 B 사이의)」 구조의 전명구가 the difference를 수식한다.
[ ]는 각각 바로 앞의 those를 수식한다. those who는 '~하는 사람들'로 해석한다.

[4행~7행] I once heard a great story of *a high school basketball coach* [who was attempting to **get** his players **to persevere** through a difficult season].
[ ]는 a ~ coach를 수식한다. 「get+O+C(to-v)」는 'O가 v하게 하다'의 뜻이다.

어휘 **throw in the towel** 패배를 인정하다 **struggle** 애쓰다, 고군분투하다 **get back up** 다시 일어서다 **persevere** 인내하다 **quit** 그만두다(= **give up**) **yell** 외치다 **bold** 대담한, 용감한 **snap back** (날카롭게) 말대꾸하다; (용수철 등이) 튀어 돌아오다 [선택지 어휘] **belong to** ~에 속하다, ~의 소유이다 **constant** 끊임없는

22 글의 요지 ④

소재 무지의 깨달음을 통한 발견

해설 인간은 새로운 발견을 통해 최종적인 해답이 아니라 더 많은 의문을 갖게 되고 오히려 무지의 영역이 드러나게 되며, 이러한 무지함을 인정하는 용기가 새로운 발견의 첫 단계라는 내용의 글이다. 따라서 글의 요지로 가장 적절한 것은 ④이다.

해석 발견의 역사에서 우리가 배울 교훈이 있다면, 그것은 과학에 대한 우리의 지식과 숭배가 엄청나게 성장한 것이 우리를 속여서 우리가 실제보다 덜 무지하다고 생각하게 만들 수도 있다는 것이다. 우리는 발견이 최종적인 해답을 준다고 생각하고 싶어 하지만, 그 대신 우리가 대체로 얻는 것은 더 많은 의문들이다. 주제문 모든 위대한 발견은 상상도 하지 못했던 무지의 영역을 드러낸다. 진보의 거대한 장애물은 무지가 아니라 오히려 확실하다는 착각이란 것은 분명하다. 발견자들은 항상 우리는 우리가 생각하는 것만큼 많이 알지 못한다고 말하는 사람들이었다. 우리가 무언가를 알지 못한다고 믿는 용기야말로 발견의 첫 단계이다. 바로 이것이 과거나 현재 할 것 없이 Charles Darwin(찰스 다윈), Albert Einstein(알버트 아인슈타인), Stephen Hawking(스티븐 호킹)과 같은 위인들의 용기이다.

어휘 **reverence** 숭배, 존경 **trick A into v-ing** A를 속여서 v하게 하다 **ignorant** 무지한 *cf.* **ignorance** 무지 **disclose** 드러내다, 밝히다 **realm** 영역, 범위 **obstacle** 장애(물), 방해 **illusion** 착각; 환상, 환영 **certainty** 확실(성), 확신 **courage** 용기 *cf.* **courageousness** 용감함

23 글의 주제 ④

소재 미디어로 인해 심화되는 공포

해설 공포감을 조장하면 사람들의 주의를 사로잡을 수 있다는 사실을 이용하여, 현대의 광고와 언론계 종사자들이 우리가 살고 있는 세상을 위험이 만연한 환경으로 묘사하여 사람들의 불안감을 가중시키고 있다는 내용의 글이므로, 이 글의 주제로 가장 적절한 것은 ④ '미디어로 인한 현대의 심화된 불안'이다.

해석 공포감을 이용하여 이야기와 호소를 표현하면 우리의 주의를 끌 수 있다는 것을 광고와 언론에 종사하는 사람들이 발견하는 결정적인 순간이 19세기에 발생했다. 주제문 그것(= 공포감)은 우리가 저항하거나 조절하기 어렵다고 여기는 감정이고, 그래서 그들은 새로이 생길 수 있는 근심거리 쪽으로 우리의 초점을 끊임없이 이동시켰다. 그들은 가장 최근의 건강에 대한 불안, 새로운 범죄의 급증, 우리가 저지르고 있을지도 모르는 사회적 무례, 그리고 우리가 인식하지 못했던, 환경에 존재하는 끝없는 위험을 이용했다. 미디어가 점점 더 고도로 발전되는 것과 영상이 가진 막강한 특성을 이용하여, 비록 우리가 우리의 선조들이 알았던 것보다 훨씬 더 안전하고 더욱 예측이 가능한 세계에 살고 있음에도, 그들(= 미디어)은 우리에게 우리가 위험으로 가득 찬 환경 속의 연약한 존재라는 느낌을 계속 줄 수 있었다. 주제문 그들(= 미디어) 덕분에 우리의 불안은 증가해오기만 했다.

① 비현실적인 공포와 불안에 대처하는 방법
② 광고에 이용된 과거와 현재의 전략
③ 소비자의 권리를 보호하는 데 있어서 미디어의 역할
⑤ 미디어의 여론 조작 양상

구문 [1행~4행] *A decisive moment* (S) occurred (V) in the nineteenth century [**when** *those* (in advertising and journalism) (S′) discovered (V′) // that if they framed their stories and appeals with fear, // they could capture our attention (O′)].
when 이하는 주어를 수식하는 관계부사절로, 주어 뒤에 쓰면 주어가 너무 길어지므로 술어 뒤로 보냈다.

어휘 **decisive** 결정적인 **frame** (특정한 방식으로) 표현하다; 틀에 넣다; 틀, 뼈대 **appeal** 호소(하다); 간청(하다) **take advantage of** ~을 이용하다 **wave** (특정 활동의) 급증; 파도 **commit** (범죄 등을) 저지르다; 약속하다; 전념[헌신]하다 **sophistication** (기계 등의) 복잡화, 정교화; 교양, 세련 **overpowering** 아주 강한[심한] **imagery** 이미지, 형상 **fragile** 취약한, 허약한; 부서지기 쉬운 **infinitely** 대단히, 몹시; 무한히 **multiply** 크게 증가하다; 곱하다 [선택지 어휘] **intensify** (정도 · 강도가) 심해지다 **aspect** 양상; 측면 **manipulation** 조작, 속임수

24 글의 제목 ①

소재 소유 효과로 인한 가치 상승

해설 인간은 자신이 소유한 물건에 특별한 가치를 두어서, 다른 물건과 교환할 상황이 있을 때 새 물건으로 얻을 이득보다 현재 가지고 있는 물건을 잃는 손실을 더 높게 평가하며, 이에 따라 물건을 교환하지 않고 지금 가지고 있는 것을 그대로 소유하려는 성향을 보인다는 내용의 글이다. 이를 제목으로 가장 잘 표현한 것은 ① '소유권은 우리의 가치 평가에 영향을 미친다'이다.

해석 여러분이 어떤 연구에서 대규모 참가자 집단의 일원이고, 여러분의 시간에 대한 보상으로 커피 머그잔이나 멋진 펜 둘 중의 하나를 받는다고 가정해 보자. 그 두 개의 선물은 비슷한 가치를 지니고 있고 무작위로 배부된다. 당신과 동료 참가자들에게 그 후 (선물을) 바꿀 기회가 주어진다. 무작위 배부를 감안한다면, 당신은 사람들 중 절반가량은 바꾸는 데에 만족할 것으로 생각할 것이다. 하지만 실제로 교환은 거의 이루어지지 않는다. 이 현상은 '소유 효과'라고 불린다. 주제문 일단 어떤 것이 당신에게 주어지면, 그것은 당신의 것이다. 심지어 고작 몇 분 후라 해도, 그것을 포기하는 것은 손실을 수반할 것이다. 이익이 좋은 것보다도 손실은 더 안 좋기 때문에, 당신에게 '선사되었던' 머그잔이나 펜은 잠재적인 교환 상대에게보다 당신에게 더 가치가 있다. 그리고 펜을 '잃는 것은' (포기하는 것은) 머그잔을 '얻는 것이' (교환하는 것이) 주는 기쁨보다 당신의 마음을 더 심하게 아프게 할 것이다. 그러므로 당신은 교환하기를 거부한다.
② 이익은 손실보다 강력하다
③ 무역 규제에 대한 찬반양론
④ 불확실한 세상에서의 이성적 선택
⑤ 원하는 것 말고 마땅히 받아야 할 것을 얻어라

구문 [8행] But in fact there are very **few** trades.
few는 가산명사 앞에 쓰여 '거의 없는'이라는 부정적 의미를 나타낸다. 반면, a few는 '조금 있는, 다소의'란 긍정적 의미로 해석한다.

[12행~14행] ~, *the mug or pen* [**with which** you have been "endowed"] is worth more to you / than it is (worth) to a potential trading partner.
with which는 원래 절인 which you have been "endowed" with에서 with가 관계대명사 앞으로 이동한 것이다.

어휘 **value** 가치; 소중히 하다; 평가하다 *cf.* **valuation** 가치 평가 **randomly** 임의로 *cf.* **random** 무작위의, 닥치는 대로 하는 **distribute** 나누어주다, 분배하다 *cf.* **distribution** 분배(방식); 분포 **assume** 당연한 것으로 생각하다; 추측하다; (책임을) 맡다 **swap** (어떤 것을 주고 그 대신 다른 것으로) 바꾸다 **phenomenon** (복수형 **phenomena**) 현상 **endowment** 기증, 기부(금) *cf.* **endow** 주다, 부여하다; 기부하다 *cf.* **endowment effect** 소유 효과(자기가 갖게 된 대상의 가치를 갖기 전보다 높게 인식하는 것) **entail** 수반하다 [선택지 어휘] **ownership** 소유(권) **pros and cons** 찬반양론 **restriction** 제한, 규제 **rational** 이성적인, 합리적인 **deserve** ~을 받을 만하다

25 도표 이해 ④

소재 주간 음주 소비량에 대한 정부 지침을 초과하는 비율

해설 도표를 보면 여자들 중 주당 권장 단위 이상의 음주를 가장 많이 하는 집단은 가장 나이 많은 집단이 아니라 가장 젊은 집단(20~28세)이다. 따라서 ④의 most senior를 youngest로 바꿔야 올바른 설명이 된다.

해석 〈주간 음주 소비량에 대한 정부 지침을 초과하는 비율〉
주제문 이 도표는 남자와 여자의 연령 집단에 따른 평균적인 주간 음주 습관을 보여준다. 알코올 1단위는 맥주 250밀리리터 한 잔이나 와인 125밀리리터 한 잔과 같다. ① 남자는 여자보다 모든 연령대에서 더 많은 양의 술을 마시며, 그 차이는 56~64세 연령대에서 가장 크다. ② 남자들 중에 주당 21단위를 초과하는 비율은 56~64세 범주까지 대략 30퍼센트에서 꽤 일정한 상태를 유지한다. ③ 그보다 더 나이 든 남성 집단에서는 그 비율이 65~73세의 사람들은 22퍼센트, 74세 이상의 사람들은 15퍼센트로 떨어진다. ④ 여자들 중에서는, 정부의 주당 권장량인 14단위 이상의 음주자 비율이 가장 높은 것은 가장 나이가 많은 집단이다. ⑤ 47~55세 집단이 두 번째로 많이 초과 음주를 하는 여성 집단이며, 그다음이 29~37세 집단이다.

구문 [10행~13행] Among women, / **it's** *the most senior age group* **that** has the highest percentage of *drinkers* (exceeding the government's 14 recommended units per week).
「it is[was] ~ that ...」 강조구문으로 주어인 the most senior age group을 강조하고 있다. exceeding 이하는 drinkers를 수식하는 현재분사구이다.

어휘 **proportion** 비율 **exceed** 초과하다 **guideline** 지침; 유도 지표 **consumption** 소비 **equivalent** 같은, 동등한 **uniform** 동일한; 획일적인 **senior** 연장자; 상위의 **excessive** 과도한, 지나친

26 내용 불일치 ②

소재 Somerset Maugham의 작품

해설 신체장애가 있었던 것은 〈인간의 굴레〉의 주인공인 Philip이다. Maugham에게는 언어장애가 있었고 이를 반영한 것이 소설 속 Philip의 신체장애라고 했으므로 둘을 혼동하지 않도록 주의한다. 따라서 정답은 ②이다.

해석 ① Somerset Maugham(서머셋 모옴)의 대표작이 〈인간의 굴레〉라는 것에는 일반적으로 견해가 일치하는데, 이는 Maugham이 그랬듯이 고아이면서 삼촌에 의해 양육되는 주인공 Philip Carey가 나오는 준(準)자전적인 소설이다. Philip은 스스로 고통스럽게 남의 시선을 의식하고 창피해하는 만곡족(굽은 발)이 있었는데, ② 이는 Maugham 자신이 언어장애로 고군분투한 것을 반영하고 있다. ③ 그의 다른 성공작들 또한 실재하는 인물들을 기초로 하는데, 그중에는 화가 Paul Gauguin(폴 고갱)의 삶을 소설화한 〈달과 6펜스〉가 있다. Maugham의 마지막 주요 소설인 〈면도날〉은 많은 면에서 그에게 새로운 출발점이 되었다. 그 소설 중 많은 부분이 유럽에서 벌어지지만, ④ 주인공은 1차 세계대전에 참전한 미국 군인으로, 깨달음을 얻기 위해 인도를 여행한다. ⑤ 전쟁의 피폐함을 다룬 그 이야기의 주제는 많은 독자들에게 감명을 주었다.

구문 [4행~7행] Philip has a *clubfoot* [of **which** he is painfully self-conscious and embarrassed], / **echoing** Maugham's own struggles with a speech disability.
관계대명사 which는 a clubfoot을 선행사로 취하며 전치사 of의 목적어 역할을 하고 있다. He is painfully self-conscious and embarrassed of it (= a clubfoot).의 의미와 같다. echoing 이하는 부대상황을 나타내는 분사구문으로, and it(= Philip has a clubfoot ~ embarrassed) echoes ~의 의미이다.

어휘 **masterpiece** 대표작; 걸작, 명작 **bondage** 굴레, 속박; 노예의 신분 **semi-autobiographical novel** 준(準)자전적 소설 **main character** 주인공 **orphan** 고아 **raise** 키우다; (들어) 올리다 **self-conscious** 남의 시선을 의식하는; 자기 존재를 의식하는 **embarrassed** 창피한, 당황스러운 **echo** 반영하다; 흉내 내다; (소리 등이) 메아리치다 **struggle** 분투, 노력; 투쟁 **disability** 장애; 무능 **fictionalize** 소설화하다 **razor** 면도칼 **enlightenment** 깨달음, 지혜; 계몽, 계발 **war weariness** 전쟁의 피폐함, 전쟁으로 지침

27 안내문 불일치 ⑤

소재 공연 장소 공지

해설 문화 포럼은 광범위한 학문 분야에 걸친 성과를 보여주고, 문화 및 정치 관련 문제들에 대해서도 토론과 강연을 한다고 했으므로 ⑤가 안내문과 일치하지 않는다.

해석

공연 장소 공지

① Schubert(슈베르트)의 Goethe(괴테) 가곡 무대 공연이 5월 20일 금요일 밤 8시에 오스트리아 대사관에서 오스트리아 문화 포럼에 의해 주최될 예정입니다. 저희는 이번 특별 공연을 대사관과 공동으로 제작하는 것이 기대됩니다!

작품에 관하여:
② 두 명의 성악가와 한 명의 피아노 연주자가 대사관의 아트리움에서 원작인 독일어로 공연할 것입니다. ③ 가곡을 중심으로 선정된 곡들은 현 시대에서의 Schubert의 예술 가곡이 주는 울림을 탐구해보는 90분의 극적인 서사로 구성될 것입니다.
일반 입장료: 25달러
④ 학생 및 연장자(65세 이상): 20달러

문화 포럼에 관하여:
문화 포럼은 광범위한 학문 분야에 걸쳐 혁신적인 현대 예술 및 과학의 성과를 보여주고, ⑤ 문화, 정치 관련 문제들에 관한 토론과 강연을 위한 포럼으로 활동하는 것을 목적으로 합니다.

구문 [18행~22행] The Cultural Forum aims **to present** innovative ~ disciplines [and] **to act** as a forum ~ politics.

동사 aims의 목적어로 두 개의 to부정사구가 and로 연결되어 있다.

어휘 **venue** (콘서트 · 경기 등의) 장소 **host** 주최하다; 접대하다 **embassy** 대사관 **collaborate** 공동으로 작업하다 **production** 연출; 상연; 생산 **atrium** (건축) 아트리움, 안마당 **selection** 선정(된 것들) **weave into** ~로 짜다[구성하다] **narrative** 서사, 이야기 **contemporary** 현대의; 동시대의 **innovative** 혁신적인 **discipline** 학문 (분야); 훈련, 단련 **relevant** 관련된

28 안내문 일치 ③

소재 장학금 안내

해설 Number of Recipients(수여자 수)가 매해 대략 20~40명이라고 했으므로 ③이 안내문의 내용과 일치한다.

해석

장학 프로그램

다음 사항은 학부생 지원자에게 제공되는 장학 프로그램입니다. ① 학생들은 입학 신청 기간 동안이나 그 이전에 이 프로그램에 신청할 수 있습니다.

자격 요건

ANU 대학교의 4년제 대학 교과과정에 신청하고자 하는 국제 대학생 지원자

* ② *의학과, 수의학과, 약학과, 건축과 등 4년 이상인 교과 과정에서 공부하려는 사람들은 이 장학금을 신청할 수 없습니다.*

③ 수여자 수

매년 약 20~40명

학업 보조금

- ④ 전체 수업료: 8학기 동안 수업료 면제
- 항공료: 1회 이코노미 왕복 티켓
- 한국어 교육비: 1년

  * ⑤ *한국어 교육은 의무적입니다.*

신청 기간: 2021년 7월 1일 ~ 2021년 8월 20일

연락처: ANU 담당 직원: 82-2-820-6000, anuadmit@anu.ac.kr

구문 [9행~13행] *Those* [**who** wish to study in *the programs* [**that** are longer than 4 years]] — such as medicine, ~ and architecture — cannot apply for this scholarship.
(S: Those, V: cannot apply)

주어는 Those who ~ 4 years이고 동사는 cannot apply이다. who 이하의 관계사절이 주어 Those를 수식하며 '~한 사람들'로 해석한다.

어휘 **scholarship** 장학금 **applicant** 지원자, 신청자 *cf.* **application** 지원 **admission** 입학 **eligibility** 자격; 적임 **undergraduate** 대학 학부 재학생 *cf.* **graduate student** 대학원생 **medicine** 의학 **veterinary medicine** 수의학 **recipient** 수령인, 수상자 **subsidy** 보조금, 장려금 **exemption** 면제 **mandatory** 의무적인 **in charge** ~의 담당인, ~을 맡은

29 밑줄 어법 ⑤

소재 호주 여행 중 가장 기억에 남은 여정

해설 ⑤ 선행사 a century-old steam locomotive와 engineers는 '100년 된 증기 기관차의 기관사들'이라는 소유의 관계이므로 whom을 소유격 관계대명사 whose로 바꾸어야 한다.

오답 분석 ① 「anything but+동사원형」은 '~이외에는 무엇이든'이라는 뜻이다. ② 여기서 that은 형용사 early를 수식하는 지시부사로 '그렇게'란 뜻이다. ③ the time ~ Dandenong Ranges를 강조하는 「It was ~ that ...」 강조구문의 that이다. ④ 명사구 densely forested hills와 locate(~을 위치시키다)의 관계는 수동이므로 과거분사가 알맞게 쓰였다.

해석 새벽에 눈을 뜨자마자, 휴식을 취하는 것 외에는 어떤 것도 할 마음이 들지 않던 날이었다. 호주 멜버른에서의 세 번째 날이었다. 그날의 일정이었던 단데농 산맥 국립공원으로의 여행은 그렇게 이른 시간에는 그다지 매력적이지 않았다. 하지만 아주 흥미롭게도 비행기를 타고 집으로 돌아오는 날, 내 기억 속에 계속 맴돌던 것은 바로 단데농 산맥에서 보냈던 시간이었다. 단데농 산맥은 멜버른 동쪽에 위치한 빽빽하게 숲이 우거진 언덕으로, 하늘 높이 자란 유칼립투스 나무가 장엄한 분위기를 만들어내는 곳이다. 이 지역은 또한 길고 하얀 턱수염이 난 기관사들이 전 세계에서 온 관광객들을 실어 나르는 100년 된 증기 기관차 Puffing Billy의 고향이기도 하다.

구문 [1행~2행] It was *a day* [when, **upon opening** my eyes at dawn, I had *no desire* (to do anything but get some rest)].

when이 이끄는 관계부사절이 a day를 제한하고 있다. 「upon[on]+v-ing」는 'v하자마자'란 뜻이다. to부정사구는 앞의 no desire를 수식하는 형용사적 용법으로 쓰였다.

어휘 **dawn** 새벽 **range** 산맥; 다양성; 범위 **appeal** 매력; 호소; 간청; 관심을 끌다 **hover** 맴돌다 **densely** 빽빽하게 **forested** 숲이 우거진 **eucalyptus** 유칼립투스(호주산 나무) **majestic** 장엄한 **atmosphere** 분위기; 대기 **steam** (수)증기 **locomotive** 기관차 **transport** 수송하다

30 밑줄 어휘 ④

소재 연구의 가변성

해설 키 크는 약을 먹은 집단과 먹지 않은 집단 각각에서 일부 사람들의 키가 컸는데 다만 약을 먹은 집단이 평균적으로 상대 집단보다 약간 더 키가 컸다면, 이 효과가 오로지 약 때문인지 아니면 다른 변수 때문인지를 분간하는 것은 쉽지 않을 것이며, 약의 효과에 대해 '의심할 여지가 없는' 게 아니라 '의심스럽다'는 생각이 들 것이다. 따라서 ④의 unquestionable을 questionable로 바꿔 써야 한다.

해석 주제문 연구자에게 가변성은 일반적으로 ① 저주이다. 그것은 출간할 수 있는 연구와 파일 캐비닛으로 직행하는 연구 간의 차이를 의미할 수 있다. 본질적으로 연구자들은 우연히 혹은 '자연적인' 가변성으로 발생하는 것을 ② 넘어서는 차이를 알아차리도록 가설이 조건을 충분히 개선할 수 있는지를 보고 그들의 가설을 검증한다. 내가 사람들의 키를 더 크게 하는 약을 시험해서 약을 먹은 모든 사람들은 키가 커지고, 약을 먹지 않은 사람들은 누구도 키가 커지지 않는다면, 처치의 효과성을 알아보기란 어렵지 않을 것이다. 그러나 그렇게 간단한 것은 좀처럼 없다. 실험 조건에서 다양성이 많으면 많을수록, 약이 효과가 있는지를 알아보는 것은 ③ 더 힘들다. 양쪽 집단의 일부 사람들이 자라지만 평균적으로 약을 먹은 집단의 키가 약간 더 크다면, 약의 효과는 ④ 의심할 여지가 없다(→ 의심스럽다). 약은 통계적으로 유의미한 차이를 초래했을 수도 있고 그렇지 않았을 수도 있다. 그렇지(= 약이 유의미한 결과를 초래하지) 않았다면, 논문은 출간되지 않으며 약을 진행시키는 것은 ⑤ 쉽지 않을 것이다.

구문 [10행~11행] **Rarely**, however, are things so straightforward.
(V: are, S: things)

Rarely(좀처럼 ~않다)와 같은 부정어가 문두로 나오면 「동사+주어」 순서로 도치가 일어난다. are가 동사이고 things가 주어이다.

[11행~13행] **The more** variety there is in the conditions of the experiment, **the harder** it is to see **if** the drug is effective.

「The 비교급, the 비교급」은 '…하면 할수록 더 ~하다'의 뜻이다. the harder 다음의 it은 가주어이고 to see 이하가 진주어이며, 접속사 if는 '~인지'의 뜻이다.

어휘 **variability** 가변성; 다양성 **hypothesis** 가설 **by chance** 우연히 **treatment** 처치; 치료 **straightforward** 간단한 **unquestionable** 의심할 여지가 없는 **statistically** 통계상으로 **promote** 촉진하다, 진행[진척]시키다

31 빈칸 추론 ①

소재 오랜 친구가 될 수 없는 사람들의 특징

해설 That is 이하에 오래가는 우정을 쌓지 못하는 사람들의 한 가지 약점이 잘 나타나 있다. 그들은 상대방에게 전혀 관심을 갖지 않고 자기 자신의 생각에만 몰두해 있다고 했으므로 타인에게 ① '무관심한' 사람들임을 알 수 있다.

해석 오래가는 우정을 쌓지 못하는 사람들이 있다. 그들은 어떤 사람들일까? 좋은 친구가 될 수 없는 사람들이다. 아마도 문제는 이해력 부족이나 좋은 천성이 부족한 것이 아닐 것이다. 또한 남을 즐겁게 해주거나 유익한 자질이 부족해서도 아니다. 반대로 그들은 매력적인 면을 많이 가지고 있을 수도 있다. 그러나 그들은 대체로 이 모든 좋은 특징을 망쳐버리는 한 가지 약점이 틀림없이 있을 것이다. 주제문 즉, 그들은 당신에 대해 조금도 개의치 않고, 당신이 그들을 어떻게 생각하는지에 전혀 영향을 받지 않는다는 것이다. 그들은 당신이 다가가도 조금도 기쁜 빛을 보이지 않고 당신이 그들을 떠날 때도, 당신 없이도 똑같이 잘 지낼 수 있다는 느낌을 가질 뿐이다. 이것은 기분이 뿌루퉁하거나 멍하게 있다는 게 아니다. 그들은 단지 타인에게 무관심하고 온전히 자기 자신의 생각에만 몰두해 있을 뿐이다.

② 거만한 ③ 무례한 ④ 책임감 없는 ⑤ 무자비한

구문 [3행~4행] **It is** *probably* **not** *their lack of understanding* **nor** *lack of good nature* **that** is at fault; ~.
(A: their lack of understanding, B: lack of good nature)

「It is[was] ~ that ...」 강조구문이 쓰여 probably not ~ good nature를 강조하고 있다. 「not[neither] A nor B」는 'A도 B도 아니다'란 뜻으로 A와 B에 동일한 문법 형태를 써서 병렬구조를 이룬다.

[4행~5행] ~; **neither** is it *their lack* (of entertaining or useful qualities).
(V: is, S: it)

부정어(neither)가 문장 앞에 위치해서 주어와 동사가 도치되었다.

[11행~12행] ~, it is with a feeling that they can get along just as well without you.
(a feeling = that they can get along just as well without you)

a feeling 뒤에 이를 설명하는 동격의 that절이 수반된 형태이다.

어휘 **lasting** 오래가는, 지속적인 **lack of** ~의 부족[결핍] **nature** 천성, 본성; 자연 **at fault** (~에 대해) 잘못[책임]이 있는 **entertain** 즐겁게 하다 **aspect** 측면, 양상 **spoil** 망치다, 못 쓰게 만들다 **characteristic** 특성, 특질 **that is (to say)** 바꿔 말하면, 즉 **get along** 지내다, 살아가다 **sullenness** 뿌루퉁함, 기분이 언짢음 **absent-mindedness** 멍한 상태, 방심 **concentrate on** ~에 주의를 집중하다 **solely** 단지, 오로지

32 빈칸 추론 ④

소재 건물 설계 시 소음 차단에 대한 인식 변화

해설 빈칸 포함 문장 앞에는 건축가들이 예전에는 소음을 제거하는 데 관심을 기울여 건물을 설계했다는 내용이 나오고, 뒤에는 이제 필요한 소리는 보존하고 불필요한 소음은 줄여 건물을 설계한다는 내용이 나온다. 따라서 이러한 변화의 원인에 해당하는 빈칸 문장은 사람들이 ④ '소리의 부족'에 부정적인 반응을 보였다는 내용이 되어야 한다.

해석 20세기에는 유럽 주요 도시의 건축가들이 소음을 줄이면서도 가능한 한 쾌적하게 생활할 수 있는 방식으로 건물을 설계했다. 그들은 벽체(벽을 이루는 구조 부분)를 비우고 그 공간에 소음을 흡수하는 자재를 채우는 것과 같은 기법을 사용했다. 두꺼운 카펫과 무거운 커튼을 이용하여 바닥과 창을 덮었다. 에어컨과 벽난로는 방음재를 통해 공기를 걸러낼 수 있도록 고안되었다. 주제문 그러나 건물을 덜 시끄럽게 만들기 위해 많은 시간과 노력을 들인 후에, 사람들이 소리의 부족에도 부정적으로 반응한다는 것이 밝혀졌다. 이제 건축가들은 원치 않는 소음을 줄이면서도 사람들이 필요로 할 것 같은 소리는 보존하는 건물을 설계하고 있다.

① 형편없는 디자인 ② 극심한 소음 ③ 질 낮은 자재 ⑤ 과도한 세간

구문 [12행~14행] Now, architects are designing *structures* [**that** reduce undesirable noise but retain the kind of *noise* [**that** people seem to need ●]].
(V'1: reduce, V'2: retain)

첫 번째 that은 structures를 받는 주격 관계대명사이고, 두 번째 that은 need의 목적어인 noise를 받는 목적격 관계대명사이다.

어휘 **architect** 건축가 **design** 설계하다; 고안하다 **structure** 건물; 구조 **hollow** 속이 빈; 공허한 **material** 자재, 재료; 물질 **absorb** 흡수하다 **filter** 거르다, 여과하다 **soundproofing** 방음이 되게 하는 **undesirable** 원하지 않는; 바람직하지 않은 **retain** 보유[유지]하다 [선택지 어휘] **extreme** 극도의, 극심한 **excessive** 과도한, 지나친 **furnishings** (가구, 카펫, 커튼 등의) 세간, 비품

33 빈칸 추론 ③

소재 시간 관리에 대한 조언

해설 빈칸 문장 이전에 해결하지 못한 할 일 목록이 불행의 원천이 된다는 문제를 제기한 후, 빈칸 문장에서 '무엇'을 위해 일상을 계획해야 할지 생각해야 한다고 제안하고 있다. 이어지는 내용에서 우리가 하는 일은 우리 자신에게 달려 있다(what we do is actually up to us)고 생각함으로써 업무 일정에 휘둘리기보다 자신의 통제하에 업무 계획을 세우라는 의미를 전달하고 있으므로, 빈칸에 가장 적절한 것은 ③ '시간 계획을 우리의 통제하에 있는 실질적인 도구로 만들기'이다.

해석 우리가 계획을 세우고 하루를 준비하게 도와주는 도구인 할 일 목록은 약속을 기록하는 달력이나 일정 관리표, 또는 많은 전자기기로 작성될 수 있다. 우리가 이러한 '할 일' 목록들을 만들 때 꼼꼼할지라도, 불가피하게 한쪽으로 미뤄둘 수 없는 다른 일이 생겨서 하루가 저물 때면 다 끝마치지 못한 '할 일' 목록이 남게 되는데, 이것은 엄청난 불안과 불행의 원천이 된다. 주제문 이제는 시간 계획을 우리의 통제하에 있는 실질적인 도구로 만들기 위해 일상을 어떻게 계획할지 다시 생각해야 할 때이다. 핵심은 "이 중요한 업무는 오늘 처리해야 해."라고 말하는 것이 아니라, 오히려 "이 중요한 업무를 할 만한 적절한 날을 찾아야겠다."라고 말하는 것이다. 이것은 우리가 하는 일이 사실 우리 자신에게 달려 있으며, 절대로 끝내지 못할 일을 정말로 끝마치려는 데 감정적으로 얽매이지 않는 것을 의미할 것이다.

① 집안일을 할 수 있는 여유 시간을 더 많이 갖기
② 목록을 작성하기에 알맞은 형식의 도구를 선택하기
④ 필요할 때는 언제든 우리의 감정을 통제할 수 있기
⑤ 하루가 저물 때까지 '할 일' 목록을 완벽하게 마치기

구문 [4행~8행] **Even though** we are thorough when making these 'to-do' lists, // inevitably *something else*, **which** cannot be pushed to the side, comes up // and at the end of the day / we're left with *an unfinished 'to-do' list*, // **which** becomes *a source* (of great tension and unhappiness).
(S1: something else, V1: comes up, S2: we, V2: 're)

「even though 부사절+주절」 구조의 문장이다. 주격 관계대명사 which의 선행사는 각각 something else와 an unfinished 'to-do' list이다.

[9행~10행] **It's time to rethink** [O' how we plan our days **so that** we make time planning *a real tool* [that is under our control]].
(S": we, V": make, O": time planning, C": a real tool ~)

「it is time to-v」는 'v해야 할 때이다'란 뜻이다. how ~ control은 rethink의 목적어인 의문사절이며, 「so that ~」은 '~하기 위하여'란 뜻으로 '목적'을 나타낸다.

어휘 **a host of** 많은 **electronic** 전자의 **device** 기구, 장치 **thorough** 꼼꼼한, 빈틈없는 **inevitably** 불가피하게 **push A to the[one] side** A를 한쪽으로 미뤄두다 **come up** 발생하다, 생기다 **tension** 긴장, 불안 **deal with** ~을 처리하다[다루다] **up to A** A에 달려 있는, A가 해야 할 **be committed to A** A에 전념[헌신]하다 [선택지 어휘] **household** 가정의, 가사의 **chore** 잡일, 허드렛일 **be under one's control** ~의 통제하에 있다

34 빈칸 추론 ②

소재 전기 에너지의 비효율성

해설 빈칸 이후 내용을 보면, 전력 발전소 구축에 상당한 에너지가 소비되고 전기 에너지의 송전 과정에서도 에너지 손실이 크다고 했다. 또한, 수요량에 맞춰 생산하지 못하면 막대한 금전적 손실도 발생한다고 했다. 이러한 설명은 모두 전기 에너지의 비효율성을 보여주므로, 빈칸에 가장 적절한 것은 ② '세계에 전력을 공급하는 대단히 비효율적인 방식'이다.

해석 주제문 전기 에너지는 다용도로 사용되는 매우 깨끗하고 편리한 형태의 에너지이지만, 그것은 세계에 전력을 공급하는 대단히 비효율적인 방식이다. 발전소가 지어지고 가동되어야 하며 고전압의 송전선이 구축되어야 하는데, 이 모든 것들은 상당한 양의 에너지를 소비한다. 초기의 발전소들에서는 생산한 에너지의 4퍼센트를 제외한 모든 에너지를 손실했고, 이것은 1920년대 중반에 약 13퍼센트로 올랐으며, 이후 1950년대에 이르러 약 25퍼센트로 향상되었다. 하지만 그 이후로는 (효율성에서) 더 이상의 발전이 거의 없었다. 이것은 세계 에너지의 3분의 1이 전기를 생산하는 데 사용되지만, 적어도 그것의 3분의 2는 발전과 송전 과정에서 낭비되고 있다는 것을 의미한다. 게다가, 전기는 저장이 매우 어려워서 보통 수요에 맞춰 생산된다. 수요가 예측과 맞지 않을 경우, 그 결과는 수천 명의 사람에게 영향을 미치고 수백만 달러의 손실을 입힐 수 있는 블랙아웃(대규모 정전 사태)이다.

① 시대에 뒤떨어진 송전 방식
③ 오늘날 세계 에너지 위기의 주원인
④ 수요와 공급 법칙을 오용한 것
⑤ 예측이 불가능한 원자재의 완벽한 예

어휘 **exceptionally** 매우, 대단히(= **exceedingly, highly**); 예외적으로 **a wide array[range] of** 다양한, 광범위한 **generating station** 발전소 *cf.* **generate** 만들어내다; (전기 등을) 발생시키다 *cf.* **generation** (전기 · 열 등의) 발생; 세대 **high-voltage** 고전압의 **transmission line** 송전선 *cf.* **transmission** 전송; (열 · 전기 등의) 전도; 전염 *cf.* **transmit** 전송하다; 전도하다; 전염시키다 **substantial** (양 · 가치 등이) 상당한; 견고한 **blackout** 정전(停電); 소등(消燈) [선택지 어휘] **outdated** 구식의, 시대에 뒤처진 **leading** 주요한; 선두의 **misapplication** 오용, 악용 **commodity** 원자재; 상품

35 무관한 문장 ②

소재 투표 의무화의 필요성

해설 낮은 선거 참여율은 민주주의에 위기를 초래할 수 있으므로, 사회 전체의 이익을 위해 개인의 자유를 일부 제한하는 것이 불가피하다고 주장하는 내용의 글이다. 반면에 ②는 지방 선거와 총선을 동시에 실시하면 투표율을 높일 수 있다는 내용으로, ①의 a lack of participation in elections와 ③의 Low participation rates가 연결되는 글의 흐름을 방해하는 문장이다.

해석 호주에서 투표하지 않는 것은 벌금이나 심지어 징역으로 처벌받을 수 있다. 우리 중 일부는 이것이 권력의 남용이라고 생각하는 반면, 다른 많은 사람들은 주민의 민주적 참여를 더 많이 확보하기 위해 우리 정부가 그와 같은 체제를 도입하는 것을 고려해야 한다고 주장한다. 현재 우리 민주주의는 선거 참여 부족으로 몹시 위기에 처해 있다. 지방 선거를 총선과 동시에 실시한다면, 일반적으로 더 높은 투표율이 얻어진다. 낮은 참여율은 우리 정치인들이 주민 전체를 대표하지 않는다는 것을 의미한다. 빈곤층과 사회적 약자들은 다른 사회 경제 집단보다 투표할 가능성이 훨씬 더 낮으므로, 이들은 주류 정치인들에게서 별문제 없이 도외시될 수 있다. 주제문 자유민주주의는 권리의 균형을 필요로 하고, 따라서 그러한 민주주의의 위기에 대한 해결이 작게는 개인의 자유를 일부 제한할 수도 있지만, 그것은 사회 전체를 위한 것이다.

구문 [3행~6행] ~, while many others **insist** // that our government (should) **consider** adopting the same system / to secure greater democratic involvement of the population.

요구, 주장, 제안 등을 나타내는 동사(insist, recommend, suggest 등)의 목적어인 that절이 '당위성'을 나타낼 경우 「(should) 동사원형」을 쓴다.

cf. that절의 내용이 '당위'가 아닌 '사실'을 나타내는 경우에는 직설법을 쓴다.

e.g. She **insisted** that she **was** acting out of compassion.
(그녀는 자신이 동정에서 나온 행동을 하고 있었다고 주장했다.)
The symptoms **suggested** that he **had** a minor heart attack.
(그 증상들은 그가 경미한 심장마비를 겪었음을 시사했다.)

어휘 **punishable** 처벌할 수 있는 **imprisonment** 투옥; 감금 **abusive** 남용하는; 모욕적인; 학대하는 **adopt** 채택하다; 입양하다 **democratic** 민주주의의 *cf.* **democracy** 민주주의 **involvement** 참여, 관여; 몰두 **simultaneously** 동시에 **turnout** 투표율; 동원, 소집 **representative** 대표(자); 대리인; 대표하는 **the disadvantaged** 사회적 약자들 **socio-economic** 사회 경제적인 **mainstream** (사상 · 견해 등의) 주류, 대세 **liberal** 자유민주적인; 진보주의의 **resolution** 해결; 결정; 결단 **restrict** 제한[한정]하다 **in the interest(s) of** ~을 (도모하기) 위하여

36 글의 순서 ⑤

소재 패러다임

해설 패러다임(사물을 바라보는 방식)을 안경에 비유하여 설명하는 글이다. (A), (B)가 연결사 Then으로 시작하므로 그 문장의 내용보다 시간상 또는 논리적인 정황상 앞선 문장을 찾는 것이 좋은 해결 방법이다. 즉, (A) 앞에는 필자가 새 안경을 쓰기 이전의 상황인 (B)가 오고, (B)의 앞에는 어리석은 행동을 하게 된 이유가 드러난 (C)가 와야 한다. 따라서 글의 순서는 ⑤ '(C)-(B)-(A)'가 자연스럽다.

해석 패러다임은 신념, 가정, 가치의 체계이다. 그것은 안경을 쓰는 것처럼, 당신이 실재를 판단하거나 사물을 보는 방법이다.

(C) 당신이 자신이나 세상과 관련하여 일반적으로 결함이 있는 패러다임을 가진다면, 이는 잘못 처방된 안경을 끼는 것과 같다. 왜냐하면, 당신이 보는 것이 당신이 얻는 것이기 때문이다. 예를 들어, 당신의 패러다임에 따라 당신이 스스로를 어리석게 본다고 가정해보자.

(B) 그러면 당신은 아마도 어리석은 방식으로 행동할 것이다. 당신이 해야 하는 것은 당신의 처방을 바꾸는 것이다! 나는 시력을 검사받을 때까지 내 시력이 아주 좋다고 생각했고 시력이 실제로 꽤 나쁘다는 것을 알고 충격받았다.

(A) 그 후, 새 안경을 끼자 모든 것이 얼마나 놀랍도록 분명하고 상세하게 보이는지에 나는 깜짝 놀랐다. 종종 그렇다. 주제문 잘못된 패러다임을 고쳐야 비로소 우리는 얼마나 많은 것을 놓치고 있는지를 알게 된다.

구문 [4행~6행] Then I got new glasses and was astonished at **how** wonderfully clear and detailed everything now looked.

전치사 at의 목적어로 감탄문이 왔으며, 감탄문의 어순은 「how+형용사[부사]+S+V」이다. 두 개의 형용사 clear와 detailed가 and로 연결되어 있다.

어휘 **paradigm** 패러다임, 사고의 틀; 전형적인 양식 **assumption** 가정, 추측 **astonished** 깜짝 놀란 **detailed** 상세한 **prescription** 처방(전) **faulty** 결점이 있는, 불완전한 **regarding** ~에 관하여 **in general** 일반적으로, 대개 **let's say (that)** ~라고 가정해보자

37 글의 순서 ④

소재 천문학의 시작

해설 수렵 채집인의 생활 모습을 가정하며 천문학이 어떻게 시작되었는지를 설명하는 글이다. 동굴인이 밤에 잠깐 밖에 나간다는 내용의 주어진 글 다음에는, 해가 진 후 밤하늘의 반짝이는 별들을 보게 되는 (C)가 이어지는 것이 알맞다. 동굴인은 별의 경로가 해마다 동일하다는 것을 관찰하게 된다는 (A)가 그 뒤에 오고, 관찰한 것을 기록하여 그 지식을 다른 사람들에게 전해준다는 내용인 (B)가 마지막에 이어지는 것이 자연스럽다. 따라서 정답은 ④ '(C)-(A)-(B)'이다.

해석 주제문 천문학은 어떻게 시작되었는가? 날마다 수렵 채집 일을 하며 멀리서 노동한 후 어두워진 후에는 밤의 동물들이 당신과 당신 가족을 잡아먹지 못하도록 당신의 바위로 된 집에 숨는 동굴인이 되었다고 상상해보라. 당신이 정말로 위험을 무릅쓰고 밤에 나간다면, 그것은 동굴에서 멀지 않은 곳으로 잠깐 다녀오기 위해서일 것이다.

(C) 그래서 하늘의 밝은 물체(= 태양)가 지평선 아래로 떨어진 후의 어느 밤에, 당신은 이제 막 동굴로 돌아가려던 참에 우연히 고개를 들어 절정에 달한 밤하늘을 정말로 주목하게 된다. 빛의 작고 밝은 점들(= 별들)이 당신에게 반짝인다.

(A) 당신은 이 모든 것으로 뭘 할지 거의 알지 못한다. 당신이 보는 모든 것에는 당신의 힘이 미치지 않지만, 당신은 그것들을 관찰해오던 세월 동안 하늘의 빛들이 해마다 같은 경로를 따른다는 것을 알아차렸다.

(B) 아마 당신은 당신이 본 것을 기록하기로 결심할 것이다. 동굴 벽이나 동물 가죽에 그림으로 말이다. 그러한 방식으로 당신은 다른 사람들에게 그것을 가르쳐주고 당신과 당신의 일족이 생존하는 데 필요한 정보에 그 지식을 추가할 수 있다.

구문 [8행~11행] ~ but you've noticed over *the years* [(when[that] you've been watching them] // that *the lights* (in the sky) follow the same paths / year after year.
(S: you / V: 've noticed / O: that ~ year)

[ ]는 앞에 관계부사 when[that]이 생략되어 the years를 수식한다. that절은 have noticed의 목적어인 명사절이다.

[14행~16행] That way you can teach others about it and **add** that knowledge **to** *the information* [(which[that]) you and your clan need ● to survive].

동사 teach와 add가 병렬구조를 이루어 can에 연결된다. 「add A to B」는 'A를 B에 더하다[첨가하다]'의 뜻이다. [ ]는 앞에 목적격 관계대명사 which[that]가 생략되었으며 the information을 수식한다. ●는 need의 목적어인 the information의 자리이다.

어휘 **astronomy** 천문학 **cave** 동굴 **venture** 위험을 무릅쓰고 ~하다 **beyond one's reach** 손이 닿지 않는, 힘이 미치지 않는 **hide** (큰 짐승의) 가죽 **clan** 씨족, 일족 **horizon** 지평선, 수평선 **be about to-v** 이제 막 v하려 하다 **in all one's glory** 절정의, 전성기의 **twinkle** 반짝반짝 빛나다

38 문장 넣기 ④

소재 해적의 선원 모집

해설 주어진 문장은 해적이 항상 포로들에게 자신들과 한패가 되도록 강요한 것은 아니라는 내용이고 역접의 연결어 However가 있으므로, 앞에는 이와 반대되는 내용, 즉 해적이 선원들을 강제로 자신들에게 합류시킨다는 내용이 나와야 한다. 또한 뒤에는 한패가 되도록 강요하지 않은 이유(This is because ~ plunder.)가 이어지는 것이 흐름상 자연스럽다. 따라서 정답은 ④이다.

해석 해적질이 있던 옛날에, 포획된 배의 선원들은 때때로 해적 선원에 자발적으로 합류했다. 해적들이 추가적인 일손이 필요하면, 자원자들은 받아들여지고 합의 조항, 즉 해적 법전에 서명하도록 허락되었을 것이다. 해적들이 일손이 많이 필요한 경우에는 원하지 않는 선원들을 강제로 해적질에 합류시켰을 것이다. 목수, 항해사 그리고 유용한 기술을 지닌 사람들이 특히 해적 선원에 합류하도록 강요당했을 가능성이 있었다. 주제문 하지만 일반적인 믿음과는 반대로, 해적들은 일상적으로 수많은 포로들에게 그들과 한패가 되도록 강요한 것은 아니다. 이는 너무 많은 신입 선원을 추가하는 것이 해적이 현재 가지고 있는 비축물자에 지나친 부담을 가하고, 약탈품에서 각 선원이 나눠 갖는 할당 몫의 가치를 줄이기 때문이다. 그래서 자원하는 사람들조차도 필요가 없을 땐 거부당할 수 있었을 것이다.

어휘 **pirate** 해적 *cf.* **piracy** 해적질 **routinely** 일상적으로 **compel A to-v** A가 v하도록 시키다[강요하다] **classical** 고전주의의; 전형적인 **capture** 포획하다, 잡다 **voluntarily** 자발적으로 **crew** 선원; 승무원 **article** 조항, 항목; 기사 **code** 법규, 규정; 암호 **unwilling** 마음이 내키지 않는, 꺼리는 (↔ **willing** 기꺼이 하는, 자진해서 하는) **carpenter** 목수 **navigator** 항해사 **overburden** 과중한 부담을 주다 **existing** 현존하는, 기존의 **supply** 비축물자; 공급 **turn A away** A를 거부하다[쫓아버리다]

39 문장 넣기 ④

소재 직접적인 질문을 받는 소비자의 심리 왜곡

해설 주어진 문장은 응답자가 조사원이 단순히 선호도에 관해서만 묻는다고 생각하지 않을 수 있다는 내용이다. 문장이 Therefore로 시작하므로 앞에는 이에 대한 원인이 나올 것임을 짐작할 수 있다. 따라서 무슨 상표의 음료를 좋아하느냐는 질문이 사실상 응답자가 어떤 사람인지를 묻는 것과 같음을 설명한 문장 다음인 ④에 오는 것이 적절하다. 또한, 뒤에는 응답자가 질문을 실제로 어떻게 듣는지에(Rather, he or she hears ~) 관한 부연 설명이 이어지는 것이 자연스럽다.

해석 주제문 사람들은 자신의 의견에 대해 질문을 받거나 자신이 좋아하는 제품에 관한 설문조사를 받을 때 인터뷰 담당자에게 자기 자신을 잘못 표현할 수도 있다. 이와 같은 왜곡의 잠재적 요소 때문에 몇몇 소비자 심리학자들은 사람들에게 그들의 의견이나 선호하는 것을 직접 묻는 것은 생산적이지 못하다고 믿는다. 그들(= 소비자 심리학자들)은 (응답자들이) 받고 있던 직접적인 질문은 그 응답자들이 실제로 들은 것과는 다를 수 있다고 주장한다. 예를 들어, 어떤 사람에게 무슨 상표의 음료를 좋아하느냐고 물음으로써, 우리는 본질적으로 그 사람이 어떤 종류의 사람인가를 묻고 있게 된다. 그래서 응답자는 소비자 조사원이 단순히 선호도에 관해서만 묻고 있다고 느끼지 않을 수도 있다. 오히려 그 사람(=응답자)은 그 질문을 "당신은 싼 것을 마시나요, 아니면 비싸고 품격 높은 상표의 제품을 마시나요?"라고 묻는 것으로 듣는다. 주제문 설문조사 방법을 비판하는 사람들은 응답자가 자신의 감정을 왜곡하게 하는 직접적인 질문을 통해서는 우리가 진정한 인간의 동기와 감정을 밝혀낼 수 없다고 주장한다.

구문 [4행~6행] People may misrepresent themselves to interviewers // **when** (they are) **questioned** about their opinions or (when (they are)) **surveyed** about the products they prefer.

when questioned는 부사절에서 「주어+be동사」가 생략된 형태이며, 접속사 or 뒤에도 when (they are)가 반복을 피해 생략되었다.

어휘 **respondent** (특히 조사에서) 응답자 **merely** 단지, 그저 **preference** 선호(도) *cf.* **prefer** 좋아하다, 선호하다 **misrepresent** 잘못 표현하다, 부정확하게 말하다 **potential** 잠재적인; 잠재력 **distortion** 왜곡; 찌그러뜨림 *cf.* **distort** (사실을) 왜곡하다; 비틀다 **productive** 생산적인, 결실 있는 **claim** 주장하다; 요구하다 **beverage** (물 이외의) 음료, 마실 것 **essentially** 본질적으로, 근본적으로 **high-status** 높은 지위의 **critic** 비판하는 사람; 평론가 **motivation** 동기 (부여); 자극

40 요약문 완성 ②

소재 정기적인 스트레스 노출이 주는 이점

해설 두려움을 주는 낯선 장소를 정기적으로 드나들었던 다람쥐원숭이들이 어미 곁에만 머물렀던 원숭이들보다 훨씬 더 용감하고 호기심이 많았고, 그런 경험이 스트레스에 대한 예방접종으로 작용했다는 연구 결과를 소개하는 내용이다. 이는 원숭이뿐만 아니라 사람에게도 적용될 수 있다고 했으므로, 감당할 수 있는 스트레스에 '반복적으로(repeatedly)' 또는 '정기적으로(regularly)' 노출되는 것이 이후 스트레스에 더 잘 '적응할 수(adaptable)' 있게 한다는 내용으로 요약문을 완성할 수 있다. 따라서 정답은 ②이다.

해석 (위험하지 않게) 두려움을 느낄 정도로만 겁을 먹는 것의 이점에 대한 가장 설득력 있는 신경과학 데이터의 일부는 다람쥐원숭이에 관한 연구에서 나온다. 겨우 17주밖에 되지 않았을 때, 원숭이들은 10주 동안 일주일에 한 번씩 자신들의 안락한 우리에서 꺼내졌다. 그 원숭이들은 자신들이 모르는 어른 원숭이들과 함께 한 시간 동안 다른 우리에 넣어졌는데, 이는 다람쥐원숭이 새끼들에게는 무서운 일이었다. 그 후 막 젖을 떼었을 때, 그 동일한 원숭이들은 자신들의 어미와 함께 낯선 우리에 넣어졌다. 앞서 스트레스를 받게 하는 우리에 노출되었던 원숭이들은 한 번도 어미 곁을 떠난 적이 없었던 같은 나이의 다른 원숭이들보다 새로운 환경이라는 어려움을 잘 대처할 수 있었고 훨씬 더 용감하고 호기심이 많다는 것이 드러났다. 무서운 장소를 정기적으로 드나들었던 것이 스트레스에 대한 예방접종으로 작용했다. 주제문 신경과학자들은 원숭이뿐만 아니라 사람도 그들이 다스리는 법을 배운 스트레스에 노출되면, 이러한 숙달이 신경 회로에 새겨져 스트레스에 대한 예방접종으로 작용하게 된다고 결론을 내린다.

⬇

연구는 사람들이 자신이 감당할 수 있는 스트레스에 (A) 반복적으로 노출되면, 나중에 스트레스에 직면할 때 더 잘 (B) 적응할 수 있게 될 것임을 시사한다.

구문 [10행~14행] *Those monkeys* [**who had** earlier **been exposed** to the stressful cages] were able to meet the challenge ~ and proved **far** braver and more curious / than *others their age* [**who had** never **left** their mothers' side].
(S: Those monkeys ~ cages / V1: were able to meet / V2: proved)

who가 이끄는 관계대명사절이 Those monkeys와 others their age를 각각 수식하고 있다. 과거 시제(were, proved)인 문장의 시제보다 관계대명사절의 시제가 시간상 먼저이므로 과거완료 시제(had been exposed, had left)가 쓰였다. far는 비교급을 강조하는 부사이다.

어휘 **convincing** 설득력 있는; (승리 등이) 확실한 **neuroscience** 신경과학 *cf.* **neural** 신경(계통)의 **terrifying** 무서운, 겁나게 하는 **youngster** 아이, 청소년 **be exposed to A** A에 노출되다 **meet the challenge** 어려움에 잘 대처하다 **circumstance** 환경 **vaccination** 예방[백신]접종 **mastery** 숙달, 통달; 지배력 **imprint** 새기다; 각인시키다; 자국; 각인 **circuitry** (전기 · 신경) 회로 [선택지 어휘] **reluctant** 꺼리는, 마음 내키지 않는 **accidentally** 우연히 **resistant** 저항력 있는; 잘 견디는; 저항[반대]하는 **adjustable** 조절[조정] 가능한 **vulnerable (to)** (~에) 취약한[연약한]

41~42 장문

41 ⑤ 42 ③

소재 전망 이론

해설 41. 선택의 폭이 넓고 선택지가 매력적일수록 결정을 주저하게 되는 현상인 '전망 이론(prospect theory)'에 근거하여 다양한 의사결정을 설명하는 글이다. 따라서 제목으로 가장 적절한 것은 ⑤ '전망 이론: 의사결정에 대한 생각들'이다.

① 당신의 유일한 최고의 선택
② 빠른 결정을 하는 법
③ 아무것도 하지 않는 것이 최고의 결정이다
④ 당신의 결정이 당신의 삶을 더 좋게 만든다

42. 빈칸 문장의 바람직하지 않은 것이 '무엇'인지 추론해야 한다. 빈칸 앞 문장에서 선택의 폭이 넓으면 선택을 주저하게 되고 무능해진다고 했으므로, 이와 같은 맥락에서 ③ '더 넓은 범위의 선택권'이 항상 더 바람직한 것은 아니라는 내용이 되어야 한다. 빈칸 뒤 단락에서는 선택의 폭이 넓어서 바람직하지 않은 결과를 낳는 경우에 대한 예시가 이어져 내용이 자연스럽게 이어진다.

① 금전적 보상
② 계획에 대한 마감일
④ 삶의 너무 많은 자유
⑤ 결정에 대한 시간제한

해석 주제문 '전망 이론'은 우리가 행동해야 할 때 왜 행동하지 않는지를 설명해준다. 그 이론은 사람들에게 매우 많은 선택권(또는 '가능성')이 제시되었을 때, 선택권이 거의 없을 때보다 빨리 결정을 할 가능성이 더 적다는 것이다. 또한, 그 선택사항이 매우 매력적이라면 결정을 하기는 더 어려워진다. 게다가 결정하는 데 시간을 오래 끌면 끌수록 사람들이 주저하지 않을 가능성은 더 적어진다(=사람들이 더 주저하게 된다). 근본적으로, 선택의 너무 많은 자유로 인해 (결정을 못하고) 마비되는 것이다. 확실히, 더 넓은 범위의 선택권이 항상 더 바람직한 것은 아니다.

한 연구는 사람들에게 보상을 지급하는 대가로 설문지를 작성하게 했는데, 어떤 사람들은 완료된 설문지를 제출하는 데 5일의 여유가 있다고 듣고, 또 다른 사람들은 21일이 있다고 들었으며, 세 번째 집단은 마감기한이 없었다. 그 결과, 마감기한이 5일인 사람들의 66퍼센트가 설문지를 돌려주었고, 마감기한이 21일인 사람들의 40퍼센트가 설문지를 돌려주었으며, 시간제한이 없는 사람들은 25퍼센트만이 설문지를 돌려주었다. 결정 마비를 겪는 사람들에게 심리학자들은 아무것도 하지 않는 것 자체가 바로 결정이며, 그것이 바로 우리가 할 수 있는 가장 최악의 결정이라는 것을 기억하라고 조언한다. 그보다는 무엇이든 그냥 해버려라!

구문 [7행~9행] Further, **the longer** it takes them to make a decision, **the less likely** it is that they will stop hesitating.

「the+비교급 ~, the+비교급 ....」은 '~할수록 더욱 더 …한'이란 뜻이다. 「it takes A to-v」는 'A가 v하는 데 (얼마의) 시간이 걸리다'로 해석한다.

어휘 **prospect** 전망, 가능성 **option** 선택(권), 선택사항 **attractive** 매력적인 **hesitate** 망설이다, 주저하다 **essentially** 근본적으로 **paralyze** 마비시키다 *cf.* **paralysis** 마비 **preferable** 바람직한, 선호하는 **complete** (서류 등을 빠짐없이) 작성하다; 완성하다 **questionnaire** 설문지 **in return for** ~의 대가로 **reward** 보상; 보답 **submit** 제출하다 **deadline** 마감 기한

43~45 장문

43 ③ 44 ④ 45 ④

소재 인내심과 끈기에 관한 일화

해설 43. 학업에 어려움을 겪은 Bopdeb이 학교를 그만두고 비참한 기분으로 공원에 가는 내용인 (A) 이후에, 마을의 연못 옆에서 한 청년이 주전자에 물을 채워 돌계단 위에 놓는 것을 관찰하게 되는 내용인 (C)가 이어져야 한다. 그 청년의 반복된 행위로 인해 마모된 돌계단을 보고 끈기와 인내라는 교훈을 얻게 되는 (D)에 이어, 꾸준히 노력해서 위대한 학자가 되었다는 내용의 (B)가 마지막에 와야 한다. 따라서 정답은 ③ '(C)-(D)-(B)'이다.

44. (d)는 물 주전자를 채우러 연못에 온 한 청년을 가리키고, 나머지는 모두 Bopdeb을 나타낸다.

45. 연못 근처에서 물 주전자를 돌계단에 내려놓고 목욕하는 청년을 관찰한 것이지 그와 대화한 것은 아니므로 ④가 글의 내용과 일치하지 않는다.

해석 (A) 주제문 Sri Chinmoy는 그의 책 〈기쁨의 날개〉에서 끈기와 자기 훈련에 대한 흥미로운 이야기를 해준다. 한때, 성적이 가장 뒤떨어지던 Bopdeb이라는 이름의 어린 인도 소년이 있었다. ① 결국, 그의 선생님은 그를 포기하고 퇴학시켰다. 그의 아버지는 (a) 그(=Bopdeb)를 더는 보고 싶지 않다고 했다. 그래서 Bopdeb은 비참한 기분으로 집을 떠나 마을에 있는 공원으로 갔다.

(C) 좌절하고 혼란스러운 상태로 Bopdeb은 나무 아래에 앉아 혼잣말했다. "나는 쓸모없어." Bopdeb은 매일 마을의 커다란 연못 옆 나무 아래에 앉아 있었다. ④ 그곳에서 (c) 그(=Bopdeb)는 빈 물 주전자를 들고 연못에 와서 물을 채우는 한 청년을 보았다. Bopdeb은 그가 주전자들에 물을 채우고 그것들을 돌계단 위에 두고 연못에 목욕하러 가는 것을 주시했다. 깨끗하게 씻은 뒤에, (d) 그(=a young man)는 물이 든 주전자들을 가지고 집으로 돌아갔다.

(D) 어느 날, 아무도 거기에 없을 때 Bopdeb은 청년이 자신의 주전자를 놓아두던 계단의 일부가 나머지 부분과 같이 더 이상 평평하지 않았다는 것을 알아챘다. (e) 그(=Bopdeb)는 혼잣말을 했다. ⑤ "그 남자가 주전자를 여기 반복해서 놓았기 때문에 돌이 마모되었구나. 돌조차도 마모될 수 있다면 내 머리는 뭐가 잘못된 걸까?" 이 경험으로부터 Bopdeb은 인내심과 끈기를 이해하기 시작했다.

(B) 며칠 후, 그는 자신의 오래된 산스크리트어 문법책을 다시 읽기 시작했다. 그는 산스크리트어를 정말 못했지만, 이제 그는 읽은 것을 기억할 수 있었다. 그는 아버지에게 '덜 엄한' 가정교사를 구해달라고 부탁했고, 그 가정교사는 그에게 산스크리트어 쓰는 법을 차근차근 가르쳤다. 각 단계는 그로 하여금 (b) 그(=Bopdeb)의 목표를 달성하는 데 더 가까이 가도록 했고, ② 그 과정 중에 그는 다른 목표들, 즉 자신감과 자부심도 함께 성취했다. 가정교사의 도움으로 ③ 그는 인도의 가장 위대한 산스크리트어 학자가 되었다.

구문 [(C) 1행~2행] (Being) **Frustrated and confused**, / Bopdeb sat under a tree and said to himself, "I am useless."

Frustrated and confused는 Because Bopdep was frustrated and confused의 의미로, Being이 생략된 분사구문이다.

[(C) 4행~6행] From there, / he **watched**(V) a young man(O) **carrying**(C1) empty pitchers / to the pond [and] **filling**(C2) them.

지각동사 watched의 목적어로 a young man이, 목적격보어로 carrying과 filling이 쓰였다.

어휘 (A) **perseverance** 인내, 끈기(= **patience**) **self-discipline** 자기훈련, 수양 **throw out of** ~에서 쫓아내다 **miserable** 비참한, 괴로운 **village** 마을 (B) **Sanskrit** 산스크리트어 **harsh** 엄한, 가혹한 **achieve** 이루다, 달성하다(= **accomplish**) **objective** 목표; 객관적인 **confidence** 자신(감) **self-esteem** 자부심 **scholar** 학자 (C) **frustrated** 좌절한, 실망한 **useless** 쓸모없는, 소용없는 **day after day** 매일같이, 날마다 **pitcher** 물 주전자 **observe** 관찰하다, 주시하다; 준수하다 (D) **flat** 평평한; 납작한 **repeatedly** 반복해서 **wear down** 마모되다, 마모시키다

실전 모의고사 03

본문 p.41

18 ②	19 ①	20 ④	21 ①	22 ④	23 ⑤	24 ③	25 ③	26 ③	27 ④
28 ⑤	29 ③	30 ①	31 ④	32 ①	33 ③	34 ③	35 ③	36 ④	37 ③
38 ④	39 ④	40 ②	41 ③	42 ⑤	43 ③	44 ③	45 ③		

18 글의 목적 ②

소재 상품 환불 규정 및 절차 안내

해설 구매한 제품을 환불하고 싶다면 30일 이내에 제품을 반송하고, 30일 이후에 반품하고 싶다면 고객센터로 전화하라는 환불 규정을 안내하고 있으므로, 글의 목적으로 가장 적절한 것은 ②이다.

해석 고객님께,
Office Wares사(社)의 온라인 판매 제품을 구매해 주셔서 감사드립니다. 저희는 고객님이 저희의 고품질 제품에 만족하시리라 자부합니다. 이 배달의 내용물을 주의 깊게 살펴보셔서 귀하의 모든 물품이 손상되지 않은 상태로 도착했는지 확인해 주시기 바랍니다. 주제문 어떤 이유로든, 구매하신 것에 완전히 만족하지 못하실 경우에는 30일 안에 저희에게 돌려보내 주시면 전액을 무조건 환불해 드립니다. 다만, 고객님께 배달되었던 똑같은 상자에 다시 포장하시고 동봉된 반송 표를 상자 밖에 부착해 주시기 바랍니다. 반송 요금은 고객님께서 지불하시게 됩니다. 주제문 만약 구매일로부터 30일이 지난 후 상품을 반환하고 싶으신 경우에는 800-232-1002로 고객 서비스 사무실에 전화해 주시면, 구매 주문 담당자가 도와드릴 것입니다.
감사합니다.

구문 [7행~10행] **In the event that** you are not totally satisfied ~, // you can return it to us within 30 days for a full refund, / no questions asked.
In the event that은 '만약 ~할 경우에'라는 뜻으로 If로 바꿔 쓸 수 있다.

어휘 **goods** 상품(= merchandise, product) **inspect** 검사하다, 조사하다 **content** 내용; 함유량; 목차 **ensure** 확인하다, 확실히 하다 **undamaged** 손상되지 않은 **full refund** 전액 환불 **no questions asked** 무조건, 이의 없이 **repack** 다시 포장하다 **enclosed** (상자 · 봉투에) 동봉된 **shipping** 배송; 선적 **representative** 담당자, 대표자

19 심경 변화 ①

소재 폭풍 피해 지역에 사는 가족의 안부

해설 글의 앞부분은 폭풍 피해 지역에 사는 필자의 작은할머니, 할아버지와 연락이 되지 않아 걱정하는(worried) 상황이다. 뒷부분은 인터넷을 통해 그 지역 부동산업자와 연락이 되어 할머니와 통화하게 됨으로써 두 분이 무사하신 것을 알고 안도하는(relieved) 상황이다. 따라서 정답은 ① '걱정하는 → 안도하는'이다.

해석 주제문 폭풍이 남긴 피해 영상을 뉴스로 보고 있자니 걱정이 생겼다. 대재앙적인 홍수로 인해 수많은 사람들이 절박하게 피난처를 찾고 있었다. 허리케인 카트리나가 멕시코만 해안을 휩쓸고 간 지 며칠 지나지 않았을 때였는데, 뉴올리언스 근교 리버리지에 사는 작은할머니 Iva와 작은할아버지 Bob에게 연락이 닿지 않았었다. 나는 인터넷을 검색했다. 그때 부동산 중개사무소로 연결되는 링크가 눈에 들어왔다. '저 사람들은 그 지역 소식을 알지도 몰라.'라고 나는 생각했다. 나는 그 페이지를 클릭해 보았다. 전화번호가 있기에 전화를 걸었다. 드디어 어떤 남자가 전화를 받아서 내가 말을 꺼냈다. "저 좀 도와주셨으면 해서요. 리버릿지 상황이 얼마나 안 좋은가요?" "홍수 피해가 미미해서 나무 몇 그루 쓰러지는 정도였어요."하고 남자가 말했다. "오, 다행이네요." 내가 말했다. "누구를 찾고 계신가 봐요?" 그가 궁금하다는 듯이 물었다. 나는 대답했다. "작은할아버지 내외분을 찾고 있어요. 혹시 루럴가 상황은 아시는지 모르겠네요?" 그가 말했다. "알고 말고요, 제가 거기 사는 걸요." 두 시간 후 Iva 할머니로부터 전화가 왔다. "길 아래 사는 남자 말이, 네가 우리를 찾고 있었다는구나." 주제문 할머니와 Bob 할아버지 모두 무사하셨고, 집도 경미한 피해만 있었다.
② 흥분한 → 실망한
③ 호기심이 있는 → 지루해하는
④ 부끄러운 → 자랑스러운
⑤ 편안한 → 겁이 난

어휘 **trouble** 걱정시키다; 괴롭히다 **catastrophic** 대재앙의 **desperately** 필사적으로; 자포자기하여 **shelter** 피난처, 대피소; 거처 **Gulf Coast** 멕시코 연안 지역 **great-aunt** 종조할머니 *cf.* **great-uncle** 종조할아버지 **suburb** 교외, 근교 **real estate** 부동산 **minor** 작은, 가벼운; 미성년의

20 필자 주장 ④

소재 운동 경기 관람을 즐기는 방법

해설 필자는 운동 경기를 볼 때 지는 팀을 응원하게 되는 위험을 감수하지 않으려고 어느 쪽도 응원하지 않으면 승자의 즐거움 또한 누릴 수 없다고 하였다. 즉, 필자는 한 팀을 선택해서 응원하는 능동적인 관중이 되어 경기를 관람하라고 충고하고 있으므로 정답은 ④이다.

해석 우리 중 수백만 명은 소파의 안락함을 떠나지 않고도 모든 종류의 경쟁적인 시합을 즐긴다. 어떤 점이 매력인가? 나의 경우, 우리 팀을 응원하고 상대 팀에게 악담을 하는 것에서 재미가 생긴다. 하지만 어떤 사람들은 실은 어떤 쪽도 응원하지 않고 경기를 본다. 그들은 지는 쪽이 되는 위험을 감수하지 않으려 한다. 그들은 회색의 중립 지대에 앉아서, 승자를 고른 것에서 오는 기쁨을 한 번도 느껴본 적이 없다. 그들처럼 되지 마라. 주제문 열심히 응원할 쪽을 선택하라. 응원하고 야유하라. 웃고 한숨을 쉬어라. 다채로움과 동작뿐 아니라 격렬한 싸움을 즐겨라. 물론 당신 팀이 질 수도 있다. 하지만 또 한편으로는 그들이 이길 수도 있다. 어느 쪽이든지 관중으로서의 당신의 경험은 풍부하고 생생할 것이며, 맥없고 소극적이며 빈약하지 않을 것이다.

구문 [6행~8행] They sit in their grey-colored neutral zone, / **never tasting** *the joy* [that comes from picking a winner].
never tasting 이하는 부대상황을 나타내는 분사구문이다. 부정형 분사구문에서 부정어는 분사 앞에 둔다.

어휘 **competitive** 경쟁적인; 경쟁력 있는 **comfort** 안락(함); 위로, 위안 **attraction** 매력; 끌림; 명소 **curse** 악담하다, 욕하다; 저주하다 **opposition** 상대 팀; 반대 **root for** ~을 응원[성원]하다 **neutral** 중립인 **pull for** ~을 열심히 지원하다[편들다] **boo** 야유를 보내다 **intense** 격렬한; 강렬한 **spectator** (특히 운동 경기의) 관중; 구경꾼 **pale** 맥없는, 활기 없는; (얼굴이) 창백한 **passive** 소극적인, 수동적인

21 밑줄 함의 ①

소재 스위스 치즈 기법

해설 부담스러운 과제가 생겼을 때 일주일 동안 하루에 10~15분 정도만 그 일을 하는 데 투자하면 일에 대한 부담이 줄고 흥미를 느끼며 일을 더 많이 하고 싶도록 동기부여를

받을 수도 있다는 전략을 소개하는 글인데, 이를 '스위스 치즈 기법'이라고 칭했으므로 이는 ① '큰 과제를 작은 부분으로 나누기' 기법이라고 할 수 있다. 스위스 치즈는 구멍이 많은 것이 특징인데, 큰 치즈 덩어리가 부담스러운 과제를 비유한다면, 여기에 구멍을 하나씩 내서 큰 덩어리를 부담스럽지 않게 만드는 것, 즉 한 번에 조금씩 일을 나누어 하는 것이 스위스 치즈 기법이다.

해석 일이 어렵거나 불쾌하거나 압도적인 것처럼 보일 때, 당신은 그것을 미루기 쉽다. 일을 더 많이 미룰수록 그것을 시작하는 것이 더 어려워진다. 주제문 당신이 압도적인 일의 존재로 고통받고 있다면, 스위스 치즈 기법을 시도해보아라. 큰 과제를 받자마자 그것을 작업하기 위해 일주일 동안 하루에 10분이나 15분만 따로 떼어두어라. 첫 번째 주가 끝날 때까지 당신은 그 일에 적어도 한 시간은 썼을 것이며, 그것이 당신이 생각했을 만큼 그렇게 나쁘지는 않다는 것을 발견했을지도 모른다. 매일 몇 분만 써서 당신은 작은, 따라서 덜 위협적인 일을 성취하고 있다. 당신이 일단 그 일에 관여하고 아마 심지어 흥미마저 느낀다면, 당신은 그 일에 더 많은 시간을 쓸 마음이 생길지도 모른다.
② 일하는 동안 정기적인 휴식을 갖기
③ 각각의 일에 우선순위 확립하기
④ 상세한 계획을 미리 세우기
⑤ 일터에서 주의 산만을 피하기

구문 [7행~10행] By the end of the first week, / you**'ll have spent** at least an hour on the task, // and you **may have found** // that it's not quite as bad as you **may have thought**.
「will have p.p.」는 '~하게 될 것이다'의 뜻으로 미래의 어느 시점에 완료될 일을 나타내는 미래완료 시제이다. 「may have p.p.」는 '~했을지도 모른다'의 뜻으로 과거 사실에 대한 불확실한 추측을 나타낸다.

어휘 **overwhelming** 압도적인 **put off** 미루다, 연기하다 **presence** 존재; 출석 **assignment** 과제 **set aside** 따로 떼어두다 **accomplish** 성취하다, 달성하다 **intimidating** 위협적인 **involved** 관련된, 관여하는 **motivated** 동기 부여된, ~할 의욕이 있는 [선택지 어휘] **regular** 정기적인, 규칙적인; 보통의 **establish** 확립하다; 설립하다 **priority** 우선순위 **detailed** 상세한 **in advance** 미리, 앞서 **distraction** 주의 산만; 기분 전환

22 글의 요지 ④

소재 완벽주의를 버리고 마음의 평안을 얻는 방법

해설 모든 것을 완벽하게 고치려 하지 말고 인생이 있는 그대로도 괜찮다고 생각함으로써 마음의 평안함을 찾을 수 있다는 내용이므로, 글의 요지로 가장 적절한 것은 ④이다.

해석 나는 완벽주의자이면서 마음도 평화로 가득 찬 이를 아직 만나보지 못했다. 그것은 완벽해지려는 욕구와 만족해하는 능력이 서로 충돌하기 때문이다. 결함이 당신의 것이든 당신이 다른 사람에게서 감지하는 것이든 결함에 집중하는 바로 그 행동이 당신을 친절하고 만족하게 할 가능성에서 멀어지게 한다. 끊임없이 일들을 바로잡는 것은 더 나은 사람이 되는 것과 전혀 관계없으며, 부정적인 것에 과도하게 집착하고 집중하는 것과 많은 관계가 있다. 만약 당신에게 이런 문제가 있다면, 당신이 해야 할 것은 어떤 것이 지금 상태와 달라야 한다고 고집하고 있는 자신을 발견하기 시작하는 것이다. 그 즉시, 당신의 끈질긴 생각을 다음과 같은 생각으로 바꿔라. 주제문 "인생은 지금 이대로 괜찮다." 더 많은 것들을 그저 그대로 놓아두는 것을 배움에 따라, 당신은 인생 그 자체에서 더 완벽한 것을 발견하게 될 것이다.

구문 [7행~10행] Constantly fixing things **has nothing to do with** being a better person but (has) **much to do with** being overly attached to and focused on negatives.
has nothing to do with와 (has) much to do with는 접속사 but으로 연결되어 병렬구조를 이룬다. with 뒤에도 각각 being으로 시작하는 동명사구가 쓰여 대구를 이룬다.

[10행~12행] If you have this problem, // then **what** you need to do (S) **is** (V) to start catching yourself in the act of **insisting** / that a thing **should be** other than it is. (C)
what은 주어인 명사절을 이끌며 '~하는 것'의 의미로 해석한다. that 이하의 절은 insist의 목적어로 쓰인 명사절로, that절이 '~해야 한다'는 당위를 나타내므로 동사는 「(should) 동사원형」을 썼다.

어휘 **have yet to-v** 아직 v하지 못하다 **perfectionist** 완벽주의자; 완전론자 *cf.* **perfection** 완벽, 완전 **contented** 만족해하는 **be in conflict with** ~와 충돌하다; ~와 모순되다 **imperfection** 결함, 결점 **perceive** 감지하다, 인식하다 **pull A away from B** A를 B로부터 떠나게 하다 **have nothing to do with** ~와 아무 관계가 없다 *cf.* **have much to do with** ~와 많은 관계가 있다 **overly** 지나치게, 과도하게 **be attached to** ~에 집착하다; ~에 붙어 있다 **negative** 부정적인 말[태도]; 부정적인 **catch A in the act of v-ing** A가 v하고 있는 것을 발견하다 **insist** 고집하다; 주장하다

23 글의 주제 ⑤

소재 직장 여성과 낮은 출산율에 대한 오해

해설 더 많은 여성이 직업을 가지면 출산율이 더 낮아질 것이라는 통념과는 반대로, 여성의 노동 참여율이 높은 나라에서는 직장 여성에 대한 정책적인 뒷받침으로 인해 오히려 출산율이 낮지 않다는 내용이다. 따라서 글의 주제로 가장 적절한 것은 ⑤ '직장 여성과 낮은 출산율에 대한 오해'이다.

해석 더 많은 여성이 일자리로 나서면 출산율이 더 낮아질 것이라고들 해왔다. 부모 양쪽이 모두 전일제로 근무하게 되면 아이들을 양육하기 훨씬 더 어렵다는 것이 그 의견이다. 주제문 그러나 몇몇 나라에서는 사실이 그와 다름을 보여준다. 스웨덴과 같이 여성 노동 참여율이 높은 나라는 일하는 여성이 더 적은 이탈리아, 일본보다 출산율이 더 높은 경향이 있다. 실제로 출산율 저하는 여성 고용이 낮은 나라에서 가장 두드러졌다. 주제문 여성 노동력 참여가 적절한 정책으로 지원된다면, 출산율이 떨어질 필요가 없는 것으로 보인다. 일반적으로 집에 있는 여성이 더 많은 나라에서는 일하는 어머니들을 위한 지원이 더 적고, 이것은 출산율의 저하를 초래한다. 여성과 남성이 꽤 동등하게 노동에 참여하고 보육 서비스 비용이 부담 없으며 이를 폭넓게 이용할 수 있는 나라에서는 출산율이 평균보다 낮지 않은 경향이 있다.
① 보육 서비스에 대한 국가적 차원의 접근
② 높은 출산율을 보이는 국가의 이점
③ 엄마가 되는 것을 선택하는 여성들이 더 줄어드는 이유
④ 일하는 어머니들에 관한 관점의 변화

구문 [11행~14행] In general, / *countries* [**in which** more women have stayed at home] offer less support for working mothers, // **which** causes lower birth rates.
in which는 관계부사 where로 바꾸어 쓸 수 있으며, 두 번째 which는 앞의 절 내용 전체를 선행사로 하는 계속적 용법의 관계대명사로 and it으로 바꾸어 쓸 수 있다.

어휘 **birthrate** 출산율 **labor** 노동; 수고 **fertility** 출산, 생식력; 비옥함 *cf.* **fertile** 다산의; 비옥한 **decline** 감소, 하락 **policy** 정책, 방침 **fairly** 꽤, 상당히; 공평히 **workforce** 노동력; 노동자 **affordable** (가격이) 알맞은; 구입할 수 있는 **average** 평균; 보통의, 평균의 [선택지 어휘] **approach** 접근(법); 접근하다 **perspective** 관점, 시각; 전망 **misconception** 오해

24 글의 제목 ③

소재 질문 순서가 대답에 미치는 영향

해설 두 질문에 대한 대답의 상관관계를 조사한 실험에서 질문을 하는 순서에 따라 응답자들이 한 대답 간의 상관관계가 유의미하게 변화했음을 보여주고 있으므로, 제목으로 가장 적절한 것은 ③ '(질문) 순서가 질문에 대한 대답에 미치는 영향'이다.

해석 연구자들은 학생들이 '여러분은 삶 전반에 대해 얼마나 만족하는가?'와 '지난달에 얼마나 많은 데이트를 했는가?'와 같은 질문을 받은 실험에 대해 보고했다. 보통 사람의 경우, 이러한 질문에 대한 응답 간에 어떤 연관성이 있는데, 그렇게 강하지는 않다. 결국, 데이트하는 것은 완전한 삶의 한 부분에 불과하다. 주제문 그리고 실험에 참가한 학생들이 이 질문들을 이러한 순서로 받았을 때, 질문에 대한 응답 간의 상관관계는 통계적으로 0과 다르지 않았다. 그러나 또 다른 표본으로 추출된 학생들에게 그 (질문의) 순서를 반대

로 했을 때 그 상관관계는 0.66으로 증가했다. 응답자들이 그들의 행복에 관한 좀 더 일반적인 질문에 맞닥뜨렸을 때, (먼저 질문 받은) 데이트에 관한 질문이 분명 삶의 그러한 면(=행복)과 연관을 맺고, 그것의 중요성을 과장되게 한 것이다. 응답자들의 결혼이나 건강에 첫 번째로 주의가 환기되었을 때에도 비슷한 결과들이 나타났다.

① 삶에서 우리의 만족에 영향을 미치는 요소들

② 기쁨의 순간: 작은 것들에 감사하기

④ 데이트와 삶의 질 사이의 상관관계

⑤ 좋은 질문: 성공적인 실험의 비결

구문 [12행~14행] The dating question(S) evidently caused(V) that aspect of life(O1) to become relevant(C1) and its importance(O2) to be exaggerated(C2) ~.

「cause+O+C(to-v) (O가 v하게 하다)」의 구조로, 두 개의 「O+C(to-v)」가 and로 병렬연결되어 있다.

어휘 **experiment** 실험 **complete** 완전한; 완성하다 **order** 순서; 명령; 규칙; 주문 **correlation** 연관성, 상관관계 **statistically** 통계(학)상으로 **reverse** 뒤바꾸다; 반대(의), 뒷면(의) **evidently** 분명히, 명백하게 **aspect** 측면, 양상 **relevant** (주제·상황과) 관련 있는, 적절한 **exaggerate** 과장하다 **respondent** (특히 실태 조사에서) 응답자 **encounter** 맞닥뜨리다, 마주치다 **observe** 관찰하다; 목격하다 [선택지 어휘] **appreciate** 감사하다; 평가하다; 인정하다

25 도표 이해 ③

소재 미국 가정의 식료품 예산 지출

해설 sugars & sweets, vegetables의 지출 예산 비율은 각각 4퍼센트, 8퍼센트로, 합하면 12퍼센트이므로 dairy products의 11퍼센트보다 높다. 따라서 ③이 도표와 일치하지 않는다.

해석 〈미국인 식료품 예산〉

주제문 이 원그래프는 미국 가정의 식료품에 대한 지출을 보여준다. ① 종합적으로, 기타 식품, 시리얼과 빵, 그리고 육류, 가금류, 생선, 계란의 세 부문이 전체 지출의 절반 이상을 구성한다. ② 미국인들은 음료를 사는 데 쓰는 것과 거의 같은 비율로 채소를 사는 데 식료품 예산을 쓴다. ③ 설탕 및 단 음식과 채소에 소비한 총액은 유제품에 소비한 것보다 더 적다. ④ 유제품은 식료품 지출의 10분의 1이 조금 넘는 반면, 과일과 채소는 합쳐도 20퍼센트가 되지 않는다. ⑤ 가장 (지출이) 적은 부문은 유지류, 설탕 및 단 음식으로 둘 다 가정 식료품 예산의 5퍼센트 미만이다.

구문 [7행~9행] *The total amount* (spent on sugars & sweets plus vegetables) is less / than ***that*** (spent on dairy products).

앞에 나온 명사구 the total amount의 반복을 피하기 위해 지시대명사 that이 사용되었다.

[12행~14행] The smallest categories are *fats & oils*, *and sugars & sweets*, // **both of which** fall under 5 percent of household food budgets.

both of which는 관계대명사의 계속적 용법으로, and both of them(= fats ~ sweets)으로 바꿔 쓸 수 있다.

어휘 **budget** 예산 **miscellaneous** 잡다한, 갖가지의 **poultry** (닭 등의) 가금(家禽)류 **constitute** 구성하다(= comprise) **expenditure** 지출, 비용 **beverage** 음료 **dairy** 유제품의 **combined** 결합된 **account for** (전체 중 얼마를) 차지하다; 설명하다 **household** 가정의

26 내용 불일치 ③

소재 기생 식물인 Cuscuta pentagona의 특징

해설 Cuscuta pentagona는 엽록소가 없어서 광합성을 할 수 없고, 그래서 스스로 양분을 만들어내지 못하기 때문에 주변 식물에 붙어서 양분을 흡수하는 기생 식물이라고 했으므로 ③이 일치하지 않는 내용이다.

해석 Cuscuta pentagona는 당신이 생각하는 전형적인 식물이 아니다. ① 그것은 1미터 높이까지 자랄 수 있는 가늘고 긴 주황색 덩굴 식물이며, 다섯 개의 꽃잎으로 된 조그마한 하얀 꽃을 만들어내고, ② 북아메리카 전역에 걸쳐 발견된다. Cuscuta의 독특한 점은 그것이 잎이 없고 식물이 광합성을 통하여 빛을 당분과 산소로 전환하게 하는, 태양 에너지를 흡수하는 색소인 엽록소가 없기 때문에 녹색이 아니라는 점이다. ③ Cuscuta는 확실히 대부분의 식물들처럼 광합성을 수행할 수 없어서, 빛에서 자기 자신의 식량을 만들 수 없다. 이 모든 것을 염두에 두면 Cuscuta가 굶어 죽을 것 같지만, 대신에 그것은 번성한다. Cuscuta는 다른 방식으로 생존한다. 그것은 이웃들로부터 식량을 얻는다. 그것은 기생 식물이다. 살기 위하여 ④ Cuscuta는 자기 자신을 숙주 식물에 부착시켜 그것에 의해 제공되는 양분을 흡수한다. 놀라울 것도 없이 ⑤ Cuscuta는 농사일에 있어서 골칫거리이며 미국 농무부에 의해 심지어 '유해 잡초'로 분류된다.

구문 [1행~4행] It's *a tall and thin orange vine* [that can grow up to a meter high], produces tiny white flowers of five petals, and is found all over North America.

동사 is, produces, is found가 접속사 and로 연결되어 병렬구조를 이루고 있다.

어휘 **typical** 전형적인, 일반적인 **vine** 덩굴 식물 **petal** 꽃잎 **unique** 독특한; 유일한 **lack** ~이 없다; 부족, 결핍 **pigment** 색소 **absorb** 흡수하다 **starve** 굶어 죽다 **thrive** 번성하다 **parasitic** 기생하는 **host** (기생 동식물의) 숙주 **nutrient** 영양소 **agricultural** 농업의 **nuisance** 성가신 것, 골칫거리 **harmful** 유해한 **weed** 잡초

27 안내문 불일치 ④

소재 학교 방문 발레 공연 안내

해설 공연은 춤과 대화, 학생이 참여하는 악절 등으로 구성되어 있다고 했으므로 ④가 안내문과 일치하지 않는다.

해석

전문 무용수들이 여러분 학교를 방문하는 그곳에서의 특별한 경험

① 매년 리치몬드 발레단의 전문 무용수들이 초등학교를 돌아다니며 강의 시범공연을 보여줍니다. 이 시연은 고전 발레 이야기를 기반으로 한 테마를 특별 상연합니다. ② 이번 공연의 테마는 신데렐라이며, Carpenter 극장에서 2021년 2월에 전체 이야기를 담은 발레 공연이 있을 예정입니다.

공연

③ 45분간의 공연은 극단의 다섯 명의 무용수들에 의해 상연됩니다. ④ 몇 개의 댄스 작품과 테마에 관한 대화, 학생과의 상호작용/학생이 참여하는 악절로 구성됩니다.

질의응답 시간

⑤ 상연에 이어서 질의응답 시간에는 무용수들이 학생들의 질문에 답할 것입니다.

더 많은 정보를 알고 싶으시면, (802) 310-0900로 전화하거나 tdolphin@richmondb.com으로 이메일을 보내서 교육 책임자인 Tanya Dolphin에게 문의하세요.

어휘 **demonstration** 시연, 공개 수업; 논증 **feature** 특징[특색]을 이루다; 특별히 포함하다 **consist of** ~로 이루어지다[구성되다] **dialogue** 대화, 문답; 토론 **interaction** 상호작용 **section** (음악) 악절; 부분, 부문 **coordinator** 책임자, 진행자

28 안내문 일치 ⑤

소재 크랜베리 수확일 행사 안내

해설 안내문 마지막에서 CDC가 크랜베리 재배 전통을 사람들에게 교육하는 비영리기관이라고 소개하고 있으므로 ⑤가 안내문의 내용과 일치한다.

해석

크랜베리 수확일

① 매년 10월 첫째 주의 토요일에 열리는 이 행사는 크랜베리 디스커버리 센터(CDC)와 워런 지역 기업 연합에서 후원합니다.

② 이곳에는 허리까지 오는 장화가 몇 켤레가 있어서 여러분은 크랜베리가 떠다니는 웅덩이에 걸어 들어갈 수 있습니다.

③ 무료 습지 투어가 오전 10시부터 11시까지 제공됩니다. 습지 투어를 마치고나면 ④ CDC는 무료 크랜베리 와인 시음회와 고급 크랜베리 음식 시식회를 제공합니다.

일시: 2020년 10월 3일
개최 장소: 크랜베리 디스커버리 센터
전화: 608-300-2800
주소: 위스콘신 주 워런 Main Street 202

CDC에 관해:
⑤ 비영리센터인 CDC는 우리 주의 크랜베리 재배 전통을 대중들에게 교육시키는 전용 공간입니다.

구문 [6행~8행] We'll have several pairs of hip boots available // **so** (that) you can walk out into a pool of floating cranberries.
여기에서 so (that)은 목적의 부사절을 이끈다.

어휘 **annually** 해마다; 일 년에 한 번 **sponsor** 후원하다 **association** 연합; 협회 **hip boots** 허리까지 오는 장화 **floating** 떠있는 **gourmet** (미식가용) 고급의; 미식가의 **sampling** 시음, 시식; (시험·분석 등을 위한) 표본 추출 **venue** 개최 장소 **nonprofit** 비영리적인 **dedicated** 특정한 목적을 위한, 전용의 **heritage** 전통, 전승; 유산

29 밑줄 어법 ③

소재 새 깃털의 다양한 기능

해설 ③ '깃털이 정확하게 해석될 때'라는 문맥이므로 interpreted가 되어야 한다. when they(= feathers) are interpreted에서 부사절의 「주어+be동사」가 생략된 형태이다.

오답 분석 ① 문장의 주어는 관계대명사 that절의 수식을 받는 Those이므로 동사 역시 복수동사인 provide가 적절히 쓰였다. ② flight's를 대신하므로 3인칭 단수 소유격인 its가 바르게 사용되었다. ④ 여기서 tell은 '구별하다'의 뜻으로 쓰인 동사로, 새의 성별이 조류 관찰자에 의해서 '구별되는' 것이므로 수동태 be told는 올바르다. ⑤ '~인지 아닌지'의 뜻으로 문장의 주어인 명사절을 이끄는 접속사이다.

해석 주제문 새의 깃털은 새들의 일상생활에서 여러 가지 기능을 제공하고, 몸의 각기 다른 부위에 난 깃털들은 다양한 목적을 위해 발달해왔다. 몸의 대부분을 덮고 있는 그것들(= 깃털들)은 추위로부터 필요한 단열 효과와 정도의 차이는 있지만, 방수 처리 효과도 제공한다. 그리고 물론 모든 형태의 비행이 이루어질 수 있도록 해주는 날개 위에 난 깃털도 있다. 조류 관찰자의 관점에서 볼 때, 깃털은 경탄의 대상이 되기 위해 존재하지만, 정확하게 해석될 때 깃털은 논의되고 있는(= 관찰되고 있는) 새에 대한 풍부한 정보 또한 제공해 줄 수 있다. 예를 들어, 흔히 어떤 새의 성별은 한눈에 구별될 수 있다. 그뿐만 아니라, 많은 경우에 그 새의 나이와 번식깃이 나 있는지 혹은 비번식 깃이 나 있는지도 파악될 수 있다. 그러한 세부 정보는 그 자체만으로도 흥미롭지만, 더 근본적으로 그 정보는 조류 관찰자들에게 식별과 관련하여 단서들을 제공한다.

구문 [6행~8행] ~, there are *the feathers* (on the wing) [that **enable** flight in all its forms **to take place**].
주격 관계대명사 that의 선행사는 전명구의 수식을 받는 the feathers이므로 관계사절의 동사도 선행사의 수에 맞추어 복수동사 enable이 쓰였다. that절에는 「enable+O+C(to-v) (O가 v할 수 있게 하다)」 구조가 쓰였다.

어휘 **serve** 제공하다; 도움이 되다; 일[봉사]하다 **evolve** 발달하다; 진화하다 **a range of** 다양한 *cf.* **range** 다양성; 범위[폭] **insulation** 단열[방음] (재료); 절연체 **waterproofing** 방수 처리[가공] **birdwatcher** (야생) 조류 관찰자 **admire** 감탄하다; 존경하다 **interpret** 해석[설명]하다; 통역하다 **a wealth of** 풍부한 **in question** 논의가 되고 있는; 의심스러운 **at a glance** 한눈에, 즉시 **breeding** 번식 **discern** 파악하다, 포착하다; 분별하다 **in one's own right** 혼자만의 힘[능력]으로 **fundamentally** 근본적으로 **clue** 단서 **with regards to** ~와 관련하여, ~에 대하여 **identification** 식별; 신원 확인; 동일시

30 네모 어휘 ①

소재 에어컨이 생활방식에 미친 영향

해설 (A) 에어컨이 발명되기 전에는 베란다가 있는 집을 지었으나, 에어컨의 사용 증가로 베란다가 있는 집이 '드물어졌다'는 문맥이 되어야 하므로 scarce가 적절하다. scarce는 '드문, 부족한'의 뜻이며 abundant는 '풍부한, 많은'의 뜻이다.
(B) 에어컨의 등장으로 사람들이 집안에 머무르는 경향이 증가해서 사회로부터 '물러나게' 되었다는 문맥이므로 withdrawn이 적절하다. outgoing은 '사교성이 풍부한, 외향적인'의 뜻이고 withdrawn은 '집안에 틀어박힌, 수줍어하는'의 의미이다.
(C) 에어컨이 발명되기 전에는 더위 때문에 '갇힌' 공간을 피했다는 문맥이 되어야 하므로 confined가 와야 한다. confined는 '갇힌'의 뜻이고 wide-open은 '완전히 열린'의 뜻이다.

해석 주제문 에어컨의 발명은 남쪽 지역의 생활방식에 급진적인 영향을 미쳤다. 아마 가장 눈에 띄게, 그리고 특히 시각적으로, 이것은 남쪽 지역의 건축 양식을 변화시켰다. 이것의 발명 이전에는 남쪽 지역 사람들은 지붕이 덮인 베란다가 있는 집을 지었지만, 가정환경에서 에어컨의 사용이 증가하면서 베란다는 점점 (A) 드물어졌다. 둘째, 에어컨은 (사람들 사이의) 사회적 상호작용에서의 우연한 기회를 감소시켰다. 일단 그것이 등장하자 사람들은 자신의 집안에 머무르려 했고, 따라서 공동체로부터 더욱 (B) 물러나게 되었다. 셋째, 그것은 여름철 여가 활동에 사실상 혁명을 일으켰다. 에어컨이 생기기 전에 사람들은 해변과 수영장에 모여들었고, 덥고 (C) 갇힌 공간을 피했다. 그러나 에어컨의 등장으로 사람들은 찌는 듯한 더위에 대한 걱정 없이 연주회, 영화, 연극을 자유로이 관람할 수 있게 되었다.

어휘 **invention** 발명(품) **radical** 급진적인; 근본적인 **manner** 방식, 방법; 태도 **notably** 눈에 띄게 **alter** 바꾸다, 변경하다 **architecture** 건축 양식; 건축술 **prior to** ~에 앞서, ~보다 먼저 **construct** 건설하다 **domestic** 가정의; 국내의 **casual** 우연한; 격식을 차리지 않은, 평상시의 **arrive on the scene** 등장하다, 나타나다 **virtually** 사실상; (컴퓨터를 이용하여) 가상으로 **revolutionize** 혁명을 일으키다 **gather** 모이다; 모으다 **at liberty** 자유로이 **stifling** 숨 막힐 듯한, 답답한

31 빈칸 추론 ④

소재 간지럽히면 웃는 이유

해설 빈칸에는 간지럼과 웃음 사이에 무슨 관련이 있는지에 관한 내용이 필요하다. 웃음이 불안(anxiety)에 의해 야기되고, 신체가 공격당하는 것을 위협적으로 느낀다(it feels threatening ~ are attacked)는 내용이 이어지므로, 웃음은 간지럽힘으로 인해 생긴 불안을 해소하려는 일종의 ④ '자기 방어'임을 추론할 수 있다.

해석 대부분의 사람들은 조금씩은 다 간지럼을 타는데, 특히 겨드랑이, 복부, 발바닥처럼 부드러운 부분에서 그렇다. 몇몇 다른 이론들은 왜 사람들이 간지럼힘을 당하면 웃게 되는지 설명하고자 한다. 주제문 일부 과학자들은 그것이 자기 방어와 어느 정도 관련이 있다고 말한다. 우리는 간지럽힘을 당할 때 웃지만, 그것을 재미있다고 여겨서는 아니다. 간지러울 때 나오는 웃음은 불안에서 야기된다. 우리는 약간 겁을 먹는데, 우리 신체의 부드러운 부분이 공격당할 때 그것이 위협적이라고 느끼기 때문이다. 이렇게 겁을 먹는 것은 놀라기도 하고, 다음에 어디를 간지럽힘 당할지 모른다는 요인에서 생긴다. 그래서 보통은 더 불안할수록 더 간지럼을 타는 경향이 있다. 이것이 바로 누군가 당신을 간지럽힐 때 당신이 그렇게 반응하는 이유다.

① 문화 ② 유전 ③ 만족 ⑤ 건강

구문 [3행~4행] A few different theories seek to explain why ^{S}being tickled ^{V}makes ^{O}some people ^{C}laugh.
why가 이끄는 절은 explain의 목적어로 쓰였다. 사역동사로 쓰인 makes가 SVOC 구조를 취하여 목적격보어 자리에는 원형부정사 laugh가 쓰였다.

[12행~14행] Therefore, **the more anxious** you normally are, **the more ticklish** you tend to be.
「the+비교급 ~, the+비교급 ....」은 '~하면 할수록 더욱 …하다'란 뜻이다.

어휘 **more or less** 다소, 어느 정도 **ticklish** 간지럼을 타는 *cf.* **tickle** 간지럽게 하다 **tender** 부드러운 **armpit** 겨드랑이 **belly** 복부, 배 **sole (of the feet)** 발바닥 **have something to do with** ~와 관련이 있다 **anxiety** 불안 *cf.* **anxious** 불안한, 걱정하는 **panic** 겁[공포]에 질리다 **threatening** 위협적인 **arise from** (일 등이) ~에서 생기다[일어나다] **element** (주요) 요소 **react** 반응하다

32 빈칸 추론 ①

소재 창의성을 발전시키는 방법

해설 빈칸 문장은 창의적인 사람이 되는 가장 좋은 '방법'을 설명하는 내용이다. 창의성은 전염되므로(Creativity is contagious.) 창의적인 사람들과 많은 시간을 보내라(you ought to spend your time with other dreamers)고 했으므로 빈칸에 적절한 것은 ① '다른 창의적인 사람들과 상호 작용하는'이다.

해석 꿈은 세상을 넓혀 준다. 그런 이유로 James Allen은 '꿈꾸는 자들이 세상의 구세주'라고 말했다. 우리가 자유로운 꿈을 펼치려 한다면, 다른 무엇보다도 창의적인 환경이 필요하다. 하지만 당신이 일하거나 공부하는 장소가 창의성에 적대적인 환경이고 당신이 그 환경을 바꿀 만한 능력이 거의 없다면 어찌할 것인가? 주제문 당신이 선택할 수 있는 최선은 다른 창의적인 사람들과 상호 작용하는 것이다. 창의성은 전염된다. 제대로 된 브레인스토밍 시간에 어떤 일이 일어나는지 주목해 본 적이 있는가? 한 사람이 아이디어를 던지면 다른 사람이 그것을 발판으로 이용하여 결국 또 다른 아이디어를 발견하고, 그 사람은 또 다른 누군가가 그에 더해 또 다르면서도 훨씬 더 좋은 방향으로 자신의 아이디어를 받아들인다는 것을 발견한다. 당신이 많은 시간을 함께 보내는 사람들처럼 생각하기 시작한다는 것은 사실이므로, 꿈꾸길 원한다면 당신은 완전히 새로운 수준의 아이디어를 이끌어내는 다른 꿈꾸는 사람들과 시간을 보내야 한다.
② 당신이 꿈꾼 것을 기억하는
③ 새로운 관점에서 사물을 바라보는
④ 당신의 직업을 더 창의적인 것으로 바꾸는
⑤ 하루의 매 순간에 창의적으로 사고하려고 노력하는

구문 [3행] If we **are to promote** the freedom to dream, ~.
「be to-v」는 여러 가지 의미가 있는데, 여기서는 '~하려면'의 의미로 '의도'를 나타낸다.

[10행~14행] One person throws out *an idea*, // **which** is used as a springboard / **to discover** another idea by *another person*, // **who** finds / that someone else has taken his idea / in **yet** another, even better direction.
계속적 용법의 관계대명사 which와 who는 각각 앞의 an idea와 another person을 대신한다. to discover ~는 '(결국) ~하게 되다'란 뜻의 '결과' 용법으로 해석하는 것이 자연스럽다. yet은 문맥상 '그에 더해서, 그 위에'란 뜻으로 증가를 강조한다.

어휘 **expand** 넓히다, 확장하다 **suggest** (넌지시) 말하다; 시사[암시]하다; 제안하다 **savior** 구원자, 구조자 **promote** 장려하다; 홍보하다; 승진시키다 **first and foremost** 다른 무엇보다도 더 **what if** ~라면 어찌할 것인가 **hostile** 적대적인; 강력히 반대하는 **possess** 소유하다 **contagious** 전염성의 **brainstorming** 브레인스토밍(어떤 주제에 대해 여러 사람이 자유롭게 생각을 제시하는 것) **session** 시간, 기간 **springboard** 발판, 출발점 **ought to-v** v해야 한다 [선택지 어휘] **perspective** 관점, 견해, 시각

33 빈칸 추론 ③

소재 악기 연주를 배우는 것이 두뇌에 미치는 영향

해설 악기 연주를 배우면 뇌에 주요한 이점으로 작용하여 학교 교육을 안정적으로 받는 데 도움이 될 것이라는 내용으로, 특히 아이의 언어 능력 발달에 긍정적 영향을 미친다는 연구 결과를 제시하고 있다. 이는 어릴 적 악기를 배운 것이 쓸모없지 않다는 내용과 일맥상통하므로 정답은 ③ '그것이 완전한 시간 낭비는 아니었을지 모른다'이다.

해석 선도적인 한 과학자에 따르면, 어릴 적 오랜 기간 악기를 배우다가 십 대에 이르러 결국 흥미를 잃는다 하더라도 그것이 완전한 시간 낭비는 아니었을지 모른다. 주제문 악기 연주를 배우는 것은 아이의 성장하는 두뇌에 주요한 이점으로 작용하여 학교 교육을 안정되게 받을 수 있는 요소가 될 것이라고 신경과학자인 Nina Kraus 교수가 말하는데, 그녀는 음악 수업이 아이들의 언어 능력을 향상시키는 데 도움이 된다는 것을 보여주는 강력한 증거가 있다고 지적한다. Kraus 교수는 악기 연주가 말소리에 대한 정상아의 두뇌 민감도뿐만 아니라 난독증이나 자폐증과 같은 발달 장애를 가진 아이들의 두뇌 민감도 또한 상당히 향상시킨다는 점을 입증한 연구를 실시했다.
① 왼쪽 두뇌가 발달할 것이다
② 당신의 가족은 많은 돈을 헛되이 낭비했다
④ 그것은 당신의 언어 능력 발달을 저해했을지도 모른다
⑤ 그것은 당신이 다른 과목에 흥미가 생겼기 때문이었을지도 모른다

구문 [1행~4행] **If** you spent hours learning a musical instrument as a child / **only to lose** interest when you reached your teens, // it **may** not **have been** a complete waste of your time, / according to a leading scientist.
여기서 if는 '비록 ~하더라도'란 뜻으로 쓰였으며, 「only to-v」는 '결국 ~하다'란 뜻으로 '결과'를 나타낸다. 「may have p.p.」는 '~했을지도 모른다'란 뜻으로 과거에 대한 불확실한 추측을 나타낸다.

[4행~9행] Learning to play an instrument(S'1) has(V'1) major advantages ~ and **should**(V'2) be a stable part ~, // says(V) *neuroscientist Professor Nina Kraus*(S), // **who** points out that there is *strong evidence* (to show that music lessons (V'')**help** (O'')children (C'')**improve** their language skills).
Learning ~ school education은 says의 목적어이며, 여기서 should는 '~일 것이다'란 뜻으로 추측을 나타낸다. who 이하는 neuroscientist Professor Nina Kraus를 부연설명하는 계속적 용법의 관계대명사절이다. 관계대명사절 내에서 밑줄 친 that절은 points out의 목적어절이다. help는 목적격보어로 원형부정사 또는 to부정사를 취할 수 있다.

[10행~14행] Prof. Kraus conducted *research* [**which** demonstrated // that (S')playing a musical instrument significantly (V')improves (O')not only *the sensitivity* (of a normal child's brain) to speech sounds / but also **that** (of children with developmental problems / such as dyslexia and autism)].
research는 주격 관계대명사 which가 이끄는 절의 수식을 받고 있다. 「not only A but also B」는 'A뿐만 아니라 B도'란 뜻이며, 여기서 that은 앞에 나온 명사(the sensitivity)의 반복을 피하기 위해 쓰였다.

어휘 **musical instrument** 악기 **leading** 선도적인 **advantage** 이점 **stable** 안정된 **neuroscientist** 신경과학자 **point out** 지적하다; 언급하다 **conduct** 수행하다 **demonstrate** 입증[증명]하다 **significantly** 상당히, 크게 **sensitivity to A** A에 대한 민감성 **developmental** 발달상의 [선택지 어휘] **in vain** 헛되이 **hinder** 방해하다, 저해하다

34 빈칸 추론 ③

소재 해충의 대륙 간 이동으로 인한 문제점

해설 대륙 간 장거리 여행이 보편화되면서 다른 대륙의 곤충이 유입되어 문제를 일으키는 경우에 관한 내용이다. 나무를 죽이는 곤충인 유리알락하늘소가 다른 지역으로 퍼지는 것을 막으려고 나무를 베어냈다고 했으므로, 현재는 이 곤충에 대항할 수 있는 다른 방어 수단이 없다는 것을 추론할 수 있다. 따라서 정답은 ③ '그것에 대한 알려진 화학적 또는 생물학적 방어 수단이 없어서'이다.

해석 장거리 여행이 더욱 빨라지고 쉬워지면서, 사람과 화물이 해마다 대륙을 넘나들며 더 많은 거리를 이동하고 있다. 그런데 그들은 새로운 땅으로 가는 그 여행에서, 종종 작

고 반갑지 않은 승객인 곤충들을 동반한다. 주제문 수하물과 화물 컨테이너에 숨어 있는 이 벌레들이 만약 빠져나와 증식한다면 큰 문제를 일으킬 수 있다. 예를 들어, 유리알락하늘소를 생각해보라. 이 해충의 애벌레는 나무에 구멍을 뚫어서 나무를 죽게 만든다. 화물을 보호하려고 사용된 나무 상자, 화물 깔판, 기타 목재 포장 자재 속에 들어가 중국에서 미국으로 유입된 이 딱정벌레는 전국의 창고에서 발견되었다. 현재 그것에 대한 알려진 화학적 또는 생물학적 방어 수단이 없어서, 뉴욕 시와 시카고는 그 곤충이 다른 지역으로 퍼져 나가는 것을 막고자 5,500그루 이상의 나무를 베어야 했다.

① 미국 내 숲에 매우 다양한 곤충이 있어서
② 곤충이 먹을 오래된 목재나 뿌리가 충분하지 않아서
④ 종(種)의 멸종에 대한 죄책감이 커지고 있어서
⑤ 독성이 가장 적은 농작물 보호 방법에 대한 요구가 있어서

구문 [1행~2행] **With** *long-distance travel* **becoming** ever faster and easier, ~.
「with+(대)명사+분사」 형태의 분사구문으로 '~가 …한 채로, ~가 …하며'로 해석한다.

어휘 **cargo** 짐, 화물 **intercontinental** 대륙 간의, 대륙을 잇는 **be accompanied by[with]** ~을 동반하다 **passenger** 승객 **multiply** 증식하다; 크게 증가시키다; 곱하다 **larva** (복수형 **larvae**) 애벌레, 유충 **pest** 해충 **tunnel** 터널[굴]을 파다 **crate** (포장 운송용의) 나무 상자 **pallet** 화물 깔판 **material** 재료, 자재; 물질 **warehouse** 창고, 저장소 [선택지 어휘] **chemical** 화학의 **sense of guilt** 죄책감 **destruction** 멸망, 파멸; 파괴(행위) **species** (생물) 종(種) **toxic** 유독성의 **crop** (농)작물

35 무관한 문장 ③

소재 개별 소비자를 고려한 상품 기획의 필요성

해설 일반적인 사용자들에게 초점이 맞춰진 시장 조사를 기반으로 상품이 제작된다면 다양한 개별 소비자를 충분히 만족시키지 못하게 되며, 그에 따라 고객의 수는 줄어들 것이라는 내용의 글이다. 반면에 ③은 일반적인 소비자 연구가 마케팅 전략 향상에 도움이 된다는 내용으로 글의 전체 흐름과 반대되는 내용이다.

해석 주제문 시장 조사는 지나치게 자주 일반적인 사용자에 초점이 맞추어진다. 사업가로서, 우리는 일을 단순화하기 위해 이런 패러다임에 의존하는 경향이 있지만, 그것은 우리가 개별 소비자에게 적절한 것이 무엇인지에 대한 핵심을 놓치고 있다는 의미이다. 지나치게 많은 경우에, 선택된 계층의 전체를 대표한다고 여겨지는 소비자 유형을 염두에 두고 상품이 제작된다. 그러면 다음과 같은 핵심을 놓치기 쉽다. 즉, 각각의 개별 소비자는 상품이나 서비스를 이용하는 동안 만족스러운 경험을 하고 싶어 한다는 것이다. 일반적인 소비자에 대한 연구는 기업과 기관들이 마케팅 전략을 향상시키는 데 도움을 준다. 잠시 멈추고 당신 회사가 소비자들의 체격, 나이, 지적 능력, 시각적 능력, 종교적 신념, 가족 유형, 성별 등에 상관없이 소비자들을 충분히 만족시키는지 생각해보라. 만약 그렇지 않다면, 당신의 회사는 가질 수 있는 고객보다 더 적은 수의 고객을 갖게 된다.

구문 [5행~7행] ~, products are designed with *a user type* in mind [**which** is believed to represent *the whole* (of a chosen segment)].
관계대명사 which의 선행사는 a user type이다.

[15행~17행] If it **does** not, // your company has fewer consumers than it could have.
does는 앞 문장에서 나왔던 fully satisfies its consumers를 받는다.

어휘 **average** 일반적인, 보통의; 평균의 **paradigm** 패러다임, 이론적 틀; 전형적인 예[양식] **simplify** 단순화하다 **essence** 핵심, 본질 **relevant** 적절한; 관련 있는 **represent** 대표하다; 표현하다, 나타내다 **segment** 부분; 조각; 계층 **regardless of** ~에 상관없이 **build** (남성의) 체격; 건축하다

36 글의 순서 ④

소재 의식적인 인지에 필요한 주의 집중

해설 주어진 글은 무언가에 주의를 기울여야 인지할 수 있다는 내용이다. (C)는 앞서 설명한 내용(just that), 즉 주어진 글의 내용보다 더 많은 설명이 있어야 한다고 하면서, 한 가지 자극에 집중하고 있을 때 또 다른 자극을 받는 경우를 가정하고 있다. (A)는 도서관에서 책 읽는(한 가지 자극) 데 집중하고 있을 때 누군가 소리 지르는 것(또 다른 자극)을 인지한다는 내용으로 (C)에 대한 예시이다. (B)는 집중하고 있지 않은 자극도 인지할 수 있어야 하는 당위성을 강조하기 위해 (A)에서 예로 든 상황을 들어 설명하고 있으므로, ④ '(C)-(A)-(B)'의 순서가 가장 자연스럽다.

해석 주제문 주의 집중은 의식적인 인지를 위한 필수 전제 조건이다. 사실, 당신이 무언가에 주의를 기울이고 있지 않다면, 당신의 바로 앞에 있는 것을 인지하지 못할 수도 있다.
(C) 하지만 단지 그것보다 많은 설명이 있어야 한다. 당신이 한 자극에 완전히 집중해 있는데 환경 속의 다른 자극이 당신의 주의를 필요로 한다면 어떻게 될까?
(A) 예를 들어, 당신이 도서관에 앉아 책을 읽고 있는데 누군가가 "저기 불 난 거야?"라고 소리친다고 상상해보라. 당신이 책에 집중하고 있다 할지라도 당신은 그 외침을 여전히 감지할 것이다.
(B) 실제로, 주제문 배경에 있는 자극이 전혀 처리되지 않는다면, 당신은 무언가 중요한 일이 일어나고 있는지 확인하기 위해 주변 환경을 훑어보는 의식적인 결정을 주기적으로 할 필요가 있을 것이다. 어디 보자, '불이야'라고 외치는 사람이라도 있나?

구문 [10행~13행] it(가주어) would be necessary / to periodically make *a conscious decision*(진주어) (to scan your surroundings / to ^{V}see // ^{O}**if** anything important was happening):
it은 to periodically make 이하를 대신하는 가주어이다. if는 '~인지 아닌지'의 뜻으로, see의 목적어인 명사절을 이끈다.

어휘 **conscious** 의식[자각]하는; 지각 있는; 의도적인 **perception** 지각, 자각; 인식 *cf.* **perceive** 감지[인지]하다 **process** 처리하다; 진행; 과정 **stimulus** (복수형 **stimuli**) 자극(제), 격려 **periodically** 정기[주기]적으로

37 글의 순서 ③

소재 Wikipedia의 한계

해설 (B)의 this는 주어진 글의 내용(집단 지성에 직접 호소)을 받으며, 그 증거로 Wikipedia의 예를 들어 그 장점을 말하고 있으므로 주어진 글 다음에 (B)가 와야 한다. 그 다음 However로 시작하여 (B)의 내용과 반대되는 Wikipedia의 한계점에 대해 설명하는 (C)가 이어진다. (A)의 맨 앞에 있는 This는 (C)에 나와 있는 Wikipedia에 대한 부정적 언급을 가리키므로 (C) 다음에 (A)가 와야 한다. 따라서 적절한 글의 순서는 ③ '(B)-(C)-(A)'이다.

해석 어떤 사람들은 인터넷에 의해 가능해진 '지식의 민주화'는 우리가 더 이상 전문가들에게 의존할 필요가 없으며, 아마추어들의 집단 지성에 직접 의뢰할 수 있음을 의미한다고 생각한다.
(B) 이것의 증거로서, 그들은 온라인 백과사전인 Wikipedia를 가리키는데, 그것은 주로 아마추어들에 의해 집필된다. 특히 그것의 과학 기사는 대단히 정확하다고 알려져 있다.
(C) 하지만 Wikipedia는 내용을 창조하는 일을 하는 것이 아니라, 주로 전문가에 의해 다른 곳에서 만들어진 내용을 요약하는 일을 한다는 것에 주목하는 것이 중요하다. 더구나 대단히 칭찬을 받는 그 기사의 정확성 자체는 전문가들에 의해서만 판단될 수 있다.
(A) 이것은 Wikipedia를 비판하려는 것이 아니라 전문가들에게 의뢰하는 것에서 벗어날 수 없다는 것을 지적하는 것이다. 주제문 Wikipedia가 다루는 넓은 범위의 주제는 많은 방식으로 환영받을 수 있으며, 그것은 때때로 여러분의 연구를 시작하기에 좋은 장소이다. 하지만 그것은 연구를 끝내는 장소로는 나쁘다.

구문 [1행~5행] Some people(S) think(V) // that(O) ^{S}*the "democratization of knowledge"* (made possible by the Internet) ^{V}means // ^{O}that we no longer need to rely on experts ~.
( ) 부분은 the "democratization of knowledge"를 수식하는 과거분사구이다. 문장의 주어는 Some people이고 동사는 think이며 that절 이하가 think의 목적어로 쓰인 구조이다.

[16행~19행] However, it is important / to note // that Wikipedia is not in the business of content creation, / but (in the business) of summarizing *content* [**that** has been created elsewhere — usually by experts].

it은 진주어인 to note 이하를 받는 가주어이며, 진주어 부분에 「not A but B (A가 아니라 B)」 구문이 사용되었다. [ ] 부분은 주격 관계대명사 that이 이끄는 관계대명사절로 content를 수식한다.

어휘 **rely on** ~에 의존[의지]하다; ~을 믿다 **collective** 집단적인, 집단의; 공동의 **intelligence** 지성; 지능 **criticize** 비판[비평]하다; 비난하다 **spectrum** 범위, 영역; 스펙트럼 **evidence** 증거 **encyclopedia** 백과사전 **article** (신문·잡지의) 기사; 논문; 조항; 물품 **remarkably** 대단히, 매우 **accurate** 정확한 *cf.* **accuracy** 정확성 **content** 내용(물); 함유량; 만족하는 **summarize** 요약하다

38 문장 넣기 ④

소재 태양 흑점과 지구 온난화의 관계

해설 주어진 문장은 역접의 접속사 However 뒤에 태양 흑점 수가 변하지 않았는데도 지구의 기온이 올라갔다는 내용이므로, 앞에는 이와 반대로 흑점 수의 변화에 따라 기온이 상승했다는 내용이 와야 한다. 따라서 ④가 정답이다. ④를 기준으로 앞에는 태양의 활동, 즉 흑점 수의 증가에 따른 지구 온난화가, 뒤에는 인간의 활동이 빚어낸 온실 효과로 인한 지구 온난화가 등장한다.

해석 태양 흑점은 1610년 이래로 태양 위에서 관측되어 그 수가 기록되어 왔다. 지난 수백 년간의 기록은 태양 흑점의 수가 꾸준히 증가해 왔음을 보여준다. 이러한 경향은 20세기에 빨라졌는데, 이는 지구가 현저하게 따뜻해지기 시작한 시기와 일치한다. 이는 변화하는 태양의 활동이 어찌됐든 지구 온난화에 영향을 끼치고 있음을 시사해주는 듯하다. 그러나 지난 20년 동안은 태양 흑점 수에 실제 변화가 없었는데도 지구의 온도가 계속해서 상승했다. 우리는 이것을 농업과 인간의 화석 연료 연소로 인해 초래된 온실 효과 때문이라고 볼 수 있다. 주제문 이러한 최근의 분석은 과거에 태양이 지구의 기후에 간접적인 영향을 상당히 끼쳤으며, 인간의 활동이 지구를 덥히는 태양의 최근 움직임을 더욱 확대하고 있다는 것을 보여준다.

구문 [4행~5행] Sunspots **have been** observed on the Sun and their numbers (have been) recorded since 1610.

중복되는 have been이 생략된 형태이다.

[12행~13행] ~ *the greenhouse effect* (caused by farming and *human* burning of fossil fuels).

the greenhouse effect 뒤에 이를 수식하는 분사구가 수반된 형태이며, human은 동명사구 burning ~ fuels의 의미상 주어이다.

어휘 **sunspot** 태양 흑점(태양 표면에 보이는 검은 반점) **observe** 관측[관찰]하다; (규칙 등을) 준수하다 **steadily** 꾸준히 **accelerate** 빨라지다, 가속하다 **coincide with** ~와 일치[부합]하다 **noticeably** 현저히, 두드러지게 **solar** 태양의 **somehow** 어떻게 해서든지, 아무튼 **attribute A to B** A를 B의 탓[덕분]으로 돌리다 **greenhouse effect** 온실 효과 **fossil fuel** 화석 연료 **analysis** 분석 **considerable** 상당한, 많은 **magnify** 확대하다 **attempt** 시도

39 문장 넣기 ④

소재 민감한 이야기를 시작하는 방법

해설 주어진 문장에서 This가 가리키는 어떤 행위가 상대방에게 대화 시작의 어려움을 암시한다고 했으므로, 그 행위가 나오는 문장(문자 메시지를 보내는 내용)과 그 이후의 변화(대화를 시작할 준비가 된 상태)가 등장하는 문장 사이에 주어진 문장이 들어가는 것이 알맞다. 따라서 정답은 ④이다.

해석 누군가와 민감한 문제에 관해 이야기를 나눌 필요가 있을 때, 그 사람에게 다가가는 것에 대한 당신의 두려움은 논의 그 자체보다 언제나 더 심하다. 아마 당신은 '완벽한 기회'를 기다리고 있다고 자신에게 말하며 그 곤란한 문제를 꺼내길 미루고 있는 자신을 발견할 것이다. 그러나 실제 삶에서는 적당한 때가 거의 찾아오지 않으므로, 당신은 어쨌든 대화가 일어나게 해야 한다. 이런 상황에서는 '민감한' 것(=사안)에 관해 이야기할 시간을 요청하는 문자 메시지같이, 주제문 간접적인 방법으로 시작하는 것이 최선이다. 이는 상대방에게 당신이 대화하고 싶지만 대화를 시작하는 것을 다소 어려워한다는 신호를 보낸다. 일단 문자 메시지를 보냈다면, 당신은 문자 수신자가 당신과 이야기를 나눌 준비가 되어, 대화가 이미 시작되었음을 알게 될 것이다. 물론 당신은 여전히 불안한 채로 있다가 (상대와) 실제로 자리를 같이 하게 되겠지만, 그래도 괜찮다. 해야 했던 대화를 당신이 시작한 것이니까.

구문 [1행~3행] This signals / to the other person // **that** you need to talk, / but you're finding **it** a bit difficult **to start the discussion**.

문장의 목적어는 that절이며, 목적어가 길어서 전명구(to the other person) 뒤에 위치했다. 「find+O+C」 구문은 'O가 C임을 알다'라는 의미이다. to부정사구는 SVOC구조에서 목적어 자리에 오지 못하므로 대신 가목적어 it이 사용되었다.

[16행~17행] ~, **with** *the recipient* **preparing** to talk with you.

「with+O+분사」는 'O가 ~인 상태로'란 뜻으로 부대상황을 나타낸다.

어휘 **signal** 신호를 보내다; 신호 **invariably** 언제나, 변함없이 **bring up** (화제를) 꺼내다 **come along** (기회 등이) 나타나다; 함께 가다 **regardless** 개의치 않고, 어쨌든 **circumstance** (주로 복수형) 상황, 환경 **delicate** 민감한, 예민한; 섬세한 **put A in motion** A를 추진하다, A를 움직이게 하다 **recipient** 수신인, 수령인

40 요약문 완성 ②

소재 익숙한 것에 긍정적으로 반응하는 경향

해설 요약문을 보면, 우리에게 '어떠한' 얼굴을 가진 사람에게 우리가 '어떻게' 반응하는지를 글에서 찾아내야 한다. 우리가 알고 있는 누군가와 닮은 사람이나, 비록 의식하지는 못하지만 화면에 잠깐 등장한 사람들은 '익숙함'을 만들어내고, 그런 사람들에게 '우호적'으로 반응한다는 내용이므로, (A)에는 positively(긍정적으로)나 agreeably(호의적으로)가 알맞고, (B)에는 빈칸 앞에 not이 있으므로 familiar와 반대 의미인 strange가 알맞다. 따라서 정답은 ②이다.

해석 주제문 반복적인 노출은 우리로 하여금 단지 우연히 익숙해 보이는 낯선 사람들에게 긍정적으로 반응하게 한다. 어떤 사람이 우리 삼촌 Harry, 우리의 오랜 친구 Mary, 혹은 우리 동네 식료품 가게의 계산원처럼 생겼다는 단순한 사실은 그들을 낯익고, 그렇기 때문에 덜 위협적으로 보이게 하기에 충분하다. 이것은 우리가 특정한 얼굴에 노출되었다는 것을 의식적으로 인식하지 않을 때조차도 발생한다. 이것을 증명한 한 연구에서, 실험 대상자들은 어떤 중립적인 주제에 관해 실험자의 공모자인 두 사람과 이야기하도록 요청받았다. 대화를 하기 전에, 공모자 중의 한 사람의 사진이 스크린에 잠깐 비쳤는데 너무나 빨라서 실험 대상자들은 그것을 인식하지 못했다. 부지불식간에 영향을 미치는 이 노출에 대한 인식이 없었음에도 불구하고, 실험 대상자들은 사진이 비치지 않았던 사람에게 자신들이 반응한 것보다 그 낯익은 사람에게 여전히 더 호의적으로 반응했다.

⬇

> 의식하든 그렇지 않든 간에, 우리는 우리에게 (B) 낯설지 않은 얼굴을 가진 사람에게 (A) 호의적으로 반응하는 경향이 있다.

구문 [3행~6행] The mere fact that a person looks like our uncle Harry, ~ grocery store / is enough to **make** him or her seem familiar and thus less threatening.

주어인 The mere fact와 어어지는 that절이 동격을 이루고 있다. make는 '~하게 하다'란 사역의 의미로 「make+O+C」의 형태로 쓰였고, 목적어와 목적격보어가 능동 관계이므로 목적격보어로 원형부정사(seem)를 썼다. seem의 보어인 familiar와 less threatening은 병렬구조를 이룬다.

[14행~18행] Despite their lack of awareness of this subliminal exposure, / the subjects still responded more favorably toward the familiar person / than they **did** toward *the person* [**whose** photograph was not flashed].

비교구문이 쓰인 문장이며, than 뒤의 did는 앞에 나온 responded favorably를 대신한다. whose ~ flashed는 the person을 수식하며, 선행사인 the person과 관계대명사 뒤에 오는 photograph는 소유 관계가 성립하므로 소유격 관계대명사 whose가 쓰였다.

어휘 **exposure** 노출; 폭로 *cf.* **expose** 노출시키다; 폭로하다 **positively** 긍정적으로 **happen to-v** 우연히 v하다 **mere** 단순한; 단지 ~에 불과한 **threatening** 위협적인, 협박하는 **consciously** 의식적으로 **aware** 인식하는, 알고 있는 *cf.* **awareness** 인식, 자각 **demonstrate** 증명[입증]하다; 보여주다 **subject** (실험) 대상(자); 주제; 과목 **neutral** 중립적인 **experimenter** 실험자, 실험을 하는 사람 *cf.* **experiment** 실험(하다) **flash** (잠깐) 비치다[번쩍이다]; 비추다 **favorably** 호의적으로 **be inclined to-v** v하는 경향이 있다 [선택지 어휘] **promptly** 즉시, 신속히

41~42 장문

41 ③ 42 ⑤

소재 해외 학생 유치에 대한 통념

해설 41. 대학원생의 유학이 학생의 본국과 유학하는 국가 모두에 손해라는 통념은 잘못된 것이며 오히려 양국에 이익이 된다는 내용의 글이므로 제목으로 가장 적절한 것은 ③ '고등 교육 세계화: 통념과 현실'이다.

① 우리는 고등 교육에 대한 통념을 떨쳐버려야 한다
② 세계화는 고등 교육에 어떻게 영향을 미치는가?
④ 고등 교육 세계화의 부정적 영향들
⑤ 교육 세계화와 국경을 넘는 학생 이동성

42. 세계화 시대에 유학을 장려하는 고등 교육이 하는 순기능 중 하나는 시민과 지도자들이 '개인화된' 문화가 아닌 '뒤섞인' 문화의 시대에 잘 대비할 수 있게 해준다는 점이므로 (e)의 individualized를 interwoven(뒤섞여있는) 등으로 바꿔 써야 한다.

해석 주제문 어떠한 국가에 대해서도 해외에서 학생을 모집하는 것은 혼합된 감정을 불러일으킨다. 국제 학생의 쇄도에 대한 두 가지 통념이 있다. 하나는 두뇌 유출에 대한 통념인데, 이에 따르면 본국이 인재들을 (a) 강탈당하고 있다는 것이다. 대개 과학과 공학에서 지난 30년 정도에 걸쳐 인도에서 모집된 다수 대학원생들의 경우를 예로 들어보자. 두뇌 유출에 관한 심각한 경고는 (b) 잘못된 것으로 판명됐다. 학생들은 인도와 미국 두 나라에 안정적인 정치적 관계와 더불어 새로운 경제적 기회를 제공하는 양국 간의 다리를 놓았다. 국제적으로 인재를 기회와 연결해주는 것은 과학과 공학에만 (c) 국한된 것은 아니다. 훌륭한 미국의 음악 학교들은 우리의 콘서트홀 무대처럼 일본계, 중국계, 한국계 학생들로 채워져 있다.
국경을 넘어서는 학생들의 이동에 대한 두 번째 통념은 초청국이 순 비용을 부담한다는 것이다. 과학과 공학에서 인도인 대학원생을 모집하는 미국 대학들의 예를 다시 들어보면, 진실은 초청국이 이 투자로 (d) 이익을 얻고 있다는 것이다. 미국의 과학과 공학 대학원 프로그램은 미국의 과학자와 공학자 수요를 맞추기 위해 인도 공과대학의 졸업반에 오랫동안 의존해왔다. 지식은 국경을 알지 못하며 배움 또한 그래선 안 된다. 고등 학습 기관은 문화가 그 어느 때보다 더욱 (e) 개인화된(→ 뒤섞여있는) 세상에 시민과 지도자들이 대비하게 해주기 위해 국가를 넘어서서 손을 내미는 일에 솔선수범하고 있다.

구문 [3행~5행] One is *the brain-drain myth*, / **according to which** the countries of origin are being robbed of talent.
according to which는 according to the brain-drain myth를 나타낸다.

[14행~17행] The great American conservatories of music are filled with students of Japanese, Chinese, and Korean descent, **as** are(V') the stages of our concert halls(S').
여기에서 접속사 as는 '~처럼'의 뜻이다. as 다음에 「동사+주어」로 어순이 도치되어 있다. 대동사 are는 are filled with students of Japanese, Chinese, and Korean descent를 나타낸다.

어휘 **recruit** 모집하다, 뽑다 **evoke** 떠올려 주다, 환기시키다 **be robbed of** ~을 강탈당하다 **graduate student** 대학원생 **mostly** 대개 **dire** 심각한, 지독한 **descent** 혈통, 가계 **border** 국경, 경계 **bear a net cost** 순 비용을 부담하다 **return** 수익 **institution** 기관 **take the lead** 선두에 서다, 솔선수범하다 [선택지 어휘] **dispel** 떨쳐 버리다, 없애다 **higher education** 고등[대학] 교육 **cross-border** 국경을 넘는

43~45 장문

43 ③ 44 ③ 45 ③

소재 가짜 거인 석상이 만들어진 이야기

해설 43. (A)는 농부가 가짜 석상을 만들 계획을 세운 뒤 조각가를 고용한 내용으로, 뒤에는 석상을 만들어 땅에 묻은 후 계획적으로 발굴해낸 내용의 (C)가 이어지는 것이 자연스럽다. 그 다음에는 가짜 석상으로 돈을 벌었다는 내용의 (D)가 오고, 그 석상이 가짜임이 드러났음에도 불구하고 사람들이 여전히 그 석상을 보러 온다는 내용의 (B)가 이어지는 것이 자연스럽다. 따라서 정답은 ③ '(C)-(D)-(B)'이다.

44. (c)는 석상을 조각한 조각가를 가리키고, 나머지는 모두 가짜 거인 석상을 계획한 농부(George Hull)를 가리킨다.

45. 거인 석상은 우물을 파다가 우연히 발견된 것이 아니라, 농부가 계획적으로 일꾼들을 시켜 파낸 것이므로 ③이 글의 내용과 일치하지 않는다.

해석 (A) George Hull이라는 한 농부가 돈을 벌고 싶어서 별난 생각을 해냈다. 그것은 바로 돌로 거대한 인간 형체를 만들어 그것이 무덤 속에서 수 세기 동안 돌로 굳어진 거인의 시체라고 광고하는 것이었다. (a) 그(= 농부)는 5톤짜리 돌덩어리를 사들이고 조각가를 고용하여 조각상을 만들게 했다.
(C) (c) 그(= 조각가)가 조각상을 완성하는 데 3개월간의 힘든 작업 시간이 걸렸다. 그리고 George는 그 석상의 외관이 오래되고 석화된 피부처럼 보이도록 하려고 화학 약품을 부어 마무리 손질을 했다. 그다음에 그 거인은 나무 상자 안에 넣어져서 뉴욕 주의 카디프에 있는 한 농장으로 옮겨졌다. 그곳에서 그 거인은 헛간 옆에 묻혔고, 1년 동안 계속 그곳에 있었다. ③ 그러고 나서 농부는 일꾼들을 고용해서 헛간 옆에 우물을 파도록 했고, 일꾼들은 (d) 그(= 농부)가 오랫동안 계획해 온 '발견'을 이루어냈다.
(D) 그 거인이 발견되고 이틀 후, ④ (e) 그(= 농부)는 그것을 보려는 관광객들에게 각각 50센트씩을 부과하기 시작했다. 하루에 300명에서 500명의 사람들이 방문했고, 주말에는 2,000명을 넘었다. ⑤ 곧 그는 그 거인을 5,000달러에 팔았다. 그 거인의 새 주인이 그것을 뉴욕 주의 시러큐스로 옮겨서 전시했지만, 그것의 출처에 대한 의혹은 이미 커지고 있었다.
(B) ① 커가는 의심 속에서 한 전문가가 그 석상을 조사했고, 그것이 매우 최근에 만들어졌다는 사실을 발표했다. 결국, (b) 그(= 농부)는 자신의 거인이 가짜였다는 것을 하는 수 없이 인정하게 되었다. 진실이 드러났음에도 불구하고 사람들은 여전히 그 거인을 보려고 모여들었다. 그 석상은 수년 동안 주인이 여러 번 바뀌다가 결국에는 뉴욕 주에 있는 Cooperstown Farmers' Museum에 팔렸고, ② 그곳에서 그 석상은 오늘날에도 계속 전시되고 있다.

구문 [(A) 1행~4행] George Hull, a farmer, had an unusual idea to make money — **by having** *a huge human figure* (made from stone) and (by) **advertising** it / as *the body of a giant*, (petrified by centuries in the grave).
전치사 by의 목적어로 두 개의 동명사구가 and로 연결되어 있는 구조이며, 두 개의 과거분사구가 각각 앞의 명사구를 수식하고 있다.

[(C) 2행~4행] And George(S) gave(V) it(IO) a final touch(DO) / by pouring a chemical over it / **to** make(V') its exterior(O') look like old, petrified skin(C').
동사 give의 목적어가 두 개인 SVOO 구조이다. 목적을 나타내는 to부정사로 쓰인 to make는 목적어로 its exterior를, 목적격보어로 look like old, petrified skin을 취하고 있다. make는 사역동사로 쓰여 원형부정사를 목적격보어로 취할 수 있다.

어휘 (A) **unusual** 별난, 기이한 **figure** 인물상; 형상 **hire A to-v** A를 고용해서 v하게 하다 **sculptor** 조각가 **carve** 조각하다, 새기다 **statue** 조각상 (B) **amid** ~이 한창일 때 **suspicion** 의심, 혐의 **expert** 전문가 **examine** 조사하다; 면밀히 살펴보다 **declare** 발표하다; 선언하다 **recent** 최근의 **origin** 기원, 원천 **fake** 가짜 **come out** (본성 · 비밀 등이) 드러나다 **flock** 모여들다 **remain** 계속[여전히] ~이다; 남다, 머무르다 (C) **chemical** 화학 약품; 화학의 **exterior** 외관; 외부 **crate** 나무 상자 **barn** 헛간 **well** 우물 (D) **uncover** 덮개를 벗기다; 적발하다; 폭로하다 **charge** 청구하다

실전 모의고사 04

본문 p.55

18 ②	19 ⑤	20 ③	21 ⑤	22 ④	23 ④	24 ②	25 ⑤	26 ⑤	27 ⑤
28 ②	29 ⑤	30 ⑤	31 ⑤	32 ①	33 ①	34 ④	35 ⑤	36 ②	37 ⑤
38 ⑤	39 ④	40 ③	41 ④	42 ⑤	43 ④	44 ③	45 ⑤		

18 글의 목적 ②

소재 취업 제의 거절

해설 글 중반부의 This week the Ministry of Environment ~ accept the offer.에 글쓴이의 주된 의도가 드러나 있다. 면접 기회를 주고 일자리를 제안해 준 것에는 감사하지만, 자신의 목표에 더 부합하는 환경부의 제안을 받아들이기로 했다는 내용이므로, 글의 목적으로 가장 적절한 것은 ②이다.

해석 Hayes 씨께,
제게 그 자리를 제안해 주셔서 감사합니다. 면접 과정은 대단히 도전적이었고, 제가 귀하의 첫 번째 선택이 된 것에 매우 자부심을 느낍니다. 또 제게 제안을 고려할 시간을 주시고 세부사항에 대해 솔직하게 논의해주신 것도 감사드립니다. 기억하시겠지만, 저는 몇 가지 다른 취업 기회도 알아보고 있다는 것을 말씀드렸습니다. 주제문 이번 주에 환경부가 제 경력의 현 단계에서의 목표와 이상적으로 맞아떨어지는 제안을 해왔습니다. 심사숙고 끝에 저는 그 제안을 받아들이기로 결정했습니다. 저를 신뢰해주신 데 대해 진심으로 감사드리고 싶습니다. 귀하를 뵙고 올해 학교가 시행하고 있는 혁신적인 지역사회 프로그램에 대해 알게 된 것은 정말 흥미로웠습니다. 귀하와 귀하의 직원들의 모든 일이 잘 되기를 기원합니다.
Lindsay Jones 올림

구문 [4행~6행] I also appreciate(V) *your* **having given** me time to consider the offer(O1) [and] your frank discussion of the details(O2).

동사 appreciate의 두 개의 목적어가 and로 연결된 형태이다. your는 동명사구 having given ~ the offer의 의미상 주어이며, 제안을 고려할 시간을 준 시점이 감사하는 시점보다 시간상 더 이전이므로 완료형 동명사(having p.p.)가 쓰였다.

어휘 **incredibly** 대단히, 믿을 수 없을 만큼 **challenging** 도전적인; 힘든, 까다로운 **appreciate** 고맙게 여기다; 진가를 인정하다; 감상하다 **consider** 고려하다; 생각하다 *cf.* **consideration** 고려; 숙고 **frank** 솔직한, 숨김없는 **recall** 상기하다, 생각해내다 **state** 말하다, 진술하다; 사정, 형편 **explore** 알아보다; 탐구하다; 탐험하다 **ministry** (정부의 각) 부처; 목사, 성직자 **ideal** 이상적인; 이상 **sincerely** 진심으로, 진정으로 **confidence** 신임, 신뢰 **innovative** 혁신적인 **implement** 실행[이행]하다

19 심경 변화 ⑤

소재 발표 내용을 잊어버린 발표자

해설 Kevin은 강연 연습을 많이 했기 때문에 처음에는 자신감 있게(confident) 강의를 잘 진행했다. 그러나 갑자기 할 말을 잊어버리고 당황하여(embarrassed) 땀이 폭포처럼 흐르고, 사라져버리고 싶은 심정이었으므로 정답은 ⑤ '자신감 있는 → 당황한'이다.

해석 마침내 Kevin은 한 무리의 고객들에게 금융 상품에 대한 강연을 할 준비가 되었다. 강연 전 주말에 그는 연설을 반복해서 연습했다. 주제문 그는 자부심을 갖고 세미나실에 들어갔는데, 몇 번이나 연설을 연습했기 때문이었다. Kevin은 자신이 할 말을 틀림없이 알고 있었다. 그는 청중 앞에서 일어나 미소를 지으며 말하기 시작했다. 그는 심지어 농담을 했을 때 청중들로부터 웃음도 얻어냈다. 그런 후… 그는 자신이 할 말을 잊어버렸다. 그는 다음에 무슨 말을 할 예정이었는지 알지 못했다. 주제문 갑자기 구슬 같은 땀이 나기 시작했다. 땀방울이 그의 이마 아래로 흘러내렸고 곧 그것은 마치 나이아가라 폭포 같았다. 그는 마치 아무런 사전 리허설 없이 'America's Got Talent'에 나간 것 같았다. 그 순간 그는 사라질 수 있으면 좋겠다고 생각했다.

① 희망찬 → 걱정하는
② 분노한 → 만족한
③ 불안한 → 안도한
④ 수치스러운 → 기쁜

구문 [12행~13행] He felt **as if** he **had gone** into *America's Got Talent* without any prior rehearsal.
「as if+S+had p.p.」는 가정법 과거완료 표현으로 '마치 ~했던 것처럼'의 뜻이다.

[13행~14행] He **wished** // that he **could disappear** at the moment.
「S+wish+S'+(조)동사 과거형+동사원형」은 가정법 과거 표현으로 '~할 수 있다면 좋을 텐데[좋을 거라고 생각하다]'의 뜻이다.

어휘 **set** (~할) 준비가 된 **deliver a talk** 강연을 하다 **financial** 재정의, 금융의 **rehearse** (예행) 연습을 하다 **line** 말, (글자의) 행; 선[줄] **without fault** 틀림없이(= without fail) **break out in** (갑자기) ~이 잔뜩 나다 **bead** 구슬 **sweat** 땀 **prior** 사전의, 이전의

20 필자 주장 ③

소재 진실한 조언을 해줄 수 있는 인간관계 확립

해설 인간은 상호의존을 바탕으로 발전하게 되어 있는 존재이므로 자신에 대해 진실을 말해줄 수 있는 신뢰할 만한 사람들과의 인간관계를 확립해 놓으라는 내용이다. 따라서 필자가 주장하는 바로 가장 적절한 것은 ③이다.

해석 우리는 상호의존하게 되어 있으므로, 최선을 다하기 위해서는 다른 사람들로부터의 도움을 필요로 한다. 자기주도 학습 이론에는 '당신의 이상적 자아를 확인하거나 진정한 자아를 발견하기 위해, 당신의 강점과 격차를 알아내기 위해, 미래를 위한 안건을 개발하기 위해, 그리고 실험하고 실천하기 위해 당신은 다른 사람들을 필요로 한다'는 발견이 있다. 모든 사람들은 자신의 목표에 대한 진심어린 마음을 유지하는 데 도움이 되어줄 신뢰할 수 있는 친구들과 동료들의 지지를 필요로 한다. 주제문 당신이 듣고 싶지 않을 수 있을 때조차도 당신 자신에 대해 진실을 말해줄 사람들과 적어도 소수의 관계를 반드시 확립하라. 당신의 가치와 목표를 알며 당신이 그것들(= 당신의 가치와 목표)에 따라 살지 못하고 있을 때 당신에게 알려줄 신뢰받는 사람들을 찾아라. 당신이 행동을 바꾸려고 시도하고 있을 때, 당신이 어떤 변화를 이루고자 애쓰고 있는지 그들에게 알리고, 당신이 머뭇거리는 모습을 그들이 보면 말해달라고 부탁하라.

구문 [2행~6행] Within the theory of self-directed learning(부사구) is(V) the discovery(S) that "you need others **to identify** your ideal self or **find** your real self, / **to discover** your strengths and gaps, / **to develop** an agenda for the future, [and] **to experiment and practice**."

동사는 is이고 주어는 the discovery로, 부사구가 문두에 위치하면서 주어와 동사의 도치가 일어났다. that 이하는 the discovery와 동격을 이룬다. '목적'을 나타내는 to부정사구가 콤마와 and로 연결되어 병렬구조를 이룬다.

[11행~13행] Find *trusted people* [**who** know your values and goals **and** will let you know // when you are not living up to them].
(know: V'1, will let: V'2)
주격 관계대명사 who는 trusted people을 받으며, 관계사대명사절 내의 동사 know와 will let이 접속사 and에 의해 병렬구조로 연결된다.

어휘 **wired** (사전에) 내정된; 컴퓨터 시스템에 연결된 **interdependence** 상호 의존 **self-directed learning** 자기주도 학습 **identify** 확인하다; 동일시하다 **agenda** 의제, 안건 **experiment** 실험(하다) **trustworthy** 신뢰할 수 있는 **colleague** 동료 **establish** 확립하다; 설립하다 **live up to** ~에 부끄럽지 않게 살다; (기대에) 부응하다 **attempt** 애써 해보다, 시도하다 **hesitate** 머뭇거리다, 주저하다

21 밑줄 함의 ⑤

소재 창의성을 높여주는 환경

해설 어떤 사람은 시끄럽고 부산한 환경에서 일을 잘하는 반면, 외부 자극에 극도로 예민한 사람도 있음을 보여주는 내용의 글이다. 즉, 인간의 정신에 관한 한 '두루 적용되는 한 가지 설명 같은 건 없다'는 말의 의미는 ⑤ '창의적 활동에 대한 최적의 환경은 사람마다 다르다'로 풀이될 수 있다.

해석 주제문 인간의 정신에 관한 한 두루 적용되는 한 가지 설명 같은 건 없다. 나는 80권이 넘는 책의 저자인 Deepak Chopra가 기차역이나 비행기의 소음과 북적거림에 둘러싸여 책 작업을 하는 것을 본 적이 있다. 물리학자 Richard Feynman은 패서디나의 시끄럽고 붐비는 바에서 세븐업을 홀짝이며 아이디어를 얻는 것을 좋아했다. 반면에 만화 〈가필드〉의 창작자인 Jim Davis는 그 개념을 만들기 위해 필요한, 중단되지 않는 마음의 평화를 얻기 위해 호텔 방에 4일 동안 스스로 고립되어야 한다고 나에게 말했다. 소설가이자 수필가인 Jonathan Franzen은 산타크루즈의 California 대학 사무실에서 혼자 일하는데, 많은 경우 너무나 깨지기 쉬운 주문에 걸려서, 복도 아래에서 전자레인지에 카레를 데우는 인도인 교수의 향으로 인해 그것이 깨져버린다. 나 자신도 내가 멈춰야 하는 고정된 시간이 있다고 느끼면 상상력 넘치는 일을 할 수 없다.
① 작가들은 자신의 창의력을 신장시켜주는 방법을 찾기 위해 노력한다
② 높은 민감성이라는 성격 특질이 작가를 더 창의적으로 만든다
③ 창의력과 시간 관리 사이에 어떤 관계가 있다
④ 글을 쓸 최고의 장소는 작가의 매일의 생체 주기와 많은 관계가 있다

구문 [2행~5행] I've **seen** Deepak Chopra, the author of more than eighty books, **work** on a book / **surrounded** by the noise and bustle of a train station, and on an airplane.
(seen: V, Deepak Chopra: O, the author of more than eighty books: = O, work ~ airplane: C)
지각동사 see의 목적격보어로 원형부정사(work)를 썼다. Deepak Chopra와 the author of more than eighty books는 동격 관계이다. surrounded 이하는 수동 의미의 분사구문이다.

[11행~15행] Jonathan Franzen, a novelist and essayist, works alone ~, / often under *a spell* (**so** fragile **that** it is broken by the fragrance of *an Indian professor* down the hall (heating curry in a microwave)).
(Jonathan Franzen: S, a novelist and essayist: = S, works: V)
첫 번째 ( )는 a spell을 수식하며 「so ~ that ... (너무 ~해서 …하다)」 구문이 쓰였다. 두 번째 ( )는 능동의 의미로 an Indian professor를 수식한다.

어휘 **when it comes to A** A에 관한 한 **one size fits all** 널리 적용되는 것, 범용 **bustle** 부산함, 북적거림 **physicist** 물리학자 **sip** 홀짝이다 **comic strip** (연재) 만화 **uninterrupted** 중단되지 않는, 연속된 **under a spell** 주문에 걸려 **fragile** 깨지기 쉬운 **fragrance** 향(香) [선택지 어휘] **boost** 신장시키다, 밀어 올리다 **creativity** 창의성 **trait** 특질, 특성 **sensitivity** 민감함; 감수성 **time management** 시간 관리 **biological cycle** 생체 주기 **optimal** 최적의, 최고의

22 글의 요지 ④

소재 유기농 식품의 환경 유해성

해설 글 앞부분에서 유기농 식품의 좋은 점에 대해 언급한 뒤, However 이후부터는 유기농 식품의 이동 거리가 길수록 환경을 더 오염시킬 수 있다는 내용으로 전환되고 있다. 일반적인 통념에 이어 반론을 제시하는 형태의 구조로, However 이후가 실질적인 글의 요지에 해당하므로 정답은 ④이다.

해석 유기농 식품은 전통적인 살충제나 호르몬, 인공 화학제품을 사용하지 않고 생산되며, 산업 폐기물에 의해 오염되지 않으며, 지속 가능한 지구를 위해 매우 중요하고 우리 건강에 더 좋은 것으로서 홍보된다. 주제문 그러나 다른 학설은 모든 유기농 식품이 항상 좋다는 생각에 이의를 제기한다. 이 학설에 따르면, 유기농 식품 구매의 이득을 계산할 때, 우리는 산지에서 식료품점까지 식품이 이동한 거리로 정의되는 '식품 이동 거리'를 계산해야 한다. 주제문 어떤 농산물의 식품 이동 거리가 길수록 그것이 환경에 주는 피해도 더 크다. 근방에서 재배한 평범한 사과 대신에 트럭과 비행기로 아주 먼 거리를 이동한 유기농 사과를 선택하면 당신은 과도하고 불필요한 오염, 화석 연료 소비, 그리고 탄소 배출을 몸소 장려하는 것이다.

구문 [10행~12행] **The more** food miles any product has, **the greater** damage it does to the environment.
「the+비교급 ~, the+비교급 ... (~하면 할수록 더 …하다)」 구문이 사용되었다.

어휘 **organic** 유기농법의; 유기체의 **conventional** 전통적인, 관습적인; 틀에 박힌 **pesticide** 살충제 **artificial** 인공적인 **contamination** 오염 **industrial** 산업의, 공업의 **vital** 중요한, 필수적인; 활기 있는 **sustainable** (환경 파괴 없이) 지속 가능한 **school** 학파; 학교; (물고기) 떼 *cf.* **school of thought** 학설, 신조 **locally** 근처에; 지방적으로 **excessive** 과도한, 지나친 **fossil fuel** 화석 연료 **consumption** 소비 **carbon** 탄소 **emission** (빛 · 열 · 가스 등의) 배출(물), 배기가스

23 글의 주제 ④

소재 공포로 인한 비이성적인 행동

해설 사람이든 개미든 공포에 빠지게 되면 이성적 사고가 불가해지고 군중을 따르게 된다는 내용으로, 위급한 상황에서 사람과 개미가 대피할 때 공통적으로 보이는 행동을 예로 들어 설명하고 있다. 따라서 글의 주제로 적절한 것은 ④ '사람과 개미의 공통된 어리석은 행동'이다.

해석 주제문 개미 떼는 우르르 몰려가는 축구 팬만큼 이성을 잃을 수 있다. 공포에 빠진 개미들은 제정신을 잃은 사람들처럼 무리를 따라가는데, 심지어 그 무리가 어리석은 결정을 하는 순간에도 그렇다. 우르르 몰려가는 것은 치명적일 수 있고, 특히 운동 경기장, 댄스 클럽, 백화점과 같은 폐쇄된 공간에서 더욱 그렇다. 불이 나거나 공포를 유발하는 다른 원인이 발생하면, 사람들은 빈번히 그리고 비논리적으로 단 하나의 문으로만 탈출하려고 하고 그곳에 밀집하는 반면, 다른 출구들은 텅텅 비워 둔다. 주제문 공포에 빠진 사람들은 이성적인 전략은 잊어버리고 군중만을 따라가면서 마치 개미처럼 행동한다. Havana 대학의 한 연구에서 연구원들은 동그란 방에 개미를 가둔 후 똑같이 생긴 문 두 개를 열어주었다. 침착한 개미들은 두 개의 문을 똑같은 비율로 사용했다. 그러나 방충제로 인해 공포에 휩싸인 개미들은 다른 문은 무시한 채 하나의 문에만 몰려들었다.
① 우르르 몰려가는 행동을 피하는 방법
② 군중 속에서 공포에 빠지는 사람들의 경향
③ 비이성적인 축구 팬들로 인한 문제점
⑤ 공포에 빠졌을 때 서로 다른 개미 그룹이 보이는 반응

구문 [7행~9행] ~, people frequently — and illogically — try to escape / through just one door, / **jamming** it(=one door) up, / **while leaving** other exits free.
jamming it up은 부대상황의 분사구문으로 and they jam it up으로 바꿔 쓸 수 있다. while leaving은 접속사를 생략하지 않은 분사구문으로, while은 '~인 반면에'의 뜻으로 쓰였다.

어휘 **irrational** 이성을 잃은, 분별이 없는 **panic** 공포에 휩싸이다, 당황하다; 공포, 당황 **herd** 무리, (가축의) 떼 **fatal** 치명적인 **enclosed** 폐쇄된

illogically 비논리적으로 **jam up** 밀집하다; 혼잡하게 하다 **reasonable** 이성적인; 타당한; (가격이) 적정한 **trap** 가두다; 함정에 빠뜨리다; 덫 **circular** 원형의 **chamber** 방; 회의실 **identical** (모양이) 똑같은 **insect repellent** 방충제 *cf.* **repellent** 다가오지 못하게 하는 것; 쫓아버리는 [선택지 어휘] **tendency** 경향, 추세

24 글의 제목 ②

소재 할인 판매 이외의 다양한 마케팅 전략 수립의 필요성

해설 구매자들은 점점 더 높은 할인을 바라기 때문에 할인 판매 전략만으로는 성공할 수 없으므로, 소매업자는 구매자의 구매 의욕을 높일 다른 대안들을 모색해야 한다는 내용이다. 이를 가장 함축적으로 잘 표현한 제목은 ② '가격 할인이 최선의 마케팅 전략인가?'이다.

해석 대다수의 구매자는 세일 전망에 아주 강력하게 반응한다. 그러나 구매자가 소매업자들의 가격 인하 전략에 대해 더 많이 알게 되면서 점점 더 큰 할인을 기대하게 된다. 전에는 10에서 20퍼센트의 할인이 구매자에게 설렘을 주었던 곳에서 이제 그들은 50이나 심지어 60퍼센트의 할인을 원하고 있다. 주제문 소매업자들은 지나치게 단순한 50퍼센트 할인 접근법을 넘어서는, 구매자들을 자극할 다른 방법을 탐구해야 한다. 불가피하게, 소매업자와 제조업자는 재고가 넘쳐나는 매장과 지나친 할인에 대한 대가를 치르게 된다. 그들은 다른 감정적 추진 요인을 이용할 필요가 있으며, 단지 할인을 제공하는 것 외에 구매자의 관심을 불러일으키고 그들이 돈을 쓸 기분이 되게 만드는 많은 것들이 있다.

① 소매업자의 마지막 수단인 특가 판매
③ 고객의 호기심을 어떻게 일깨울 것인가?
④ 고객과의 상호작용 시스템을 구축하는 방법
⑤ 소매업자의 가격 인하 전략 이해하기

구문 [4행~6행] Where 10 or 20 percent off **might have given** shoppers a thrill before, // today they want 50 or even 60 percent off.
「might have p.p. (~이었을지도 모른다)」는 과거 사실에 대한 불확실한 추정을 나타낸다.

어휘 **prospect** 전망; 가망; 예상 **markdown** 가격 인하 **retailer** 소매업자 **thrill** 설렘, 흥분 **stimulate** 자극하다, 관심을 불러일으키다 **beyond** ~을 넘어서는, ~ 이상 **simplistic** 지나치게 단순화한 **inevitably** 불가피하게, 필연적으로 **pay the price for** ~의 대가를 치르다 **overstocked** 재고[공급] 과잉의 **floor** 매장, (공장 · 소매점 등) 제조소 **make use of** ~을 활용[이용]하다 **driver** 추진 요인; 운전자 [선택지 어휘] **last resort** 마지막 수단 **evoke** 일깨우다, 환기시키다

25 도표 이해 ⑤

소재 한국인 남녀 기대 수명 변화 추이

해설 한국인 남녀 기대 수명의 차이는 1983년 이후 계속 감소하고 있으므로 ⑤가 잘못된 설명이다.

해석 〈기대 수명〉

주제문 이 도표는 1973년, 1983년, 1993년, 2003년, 2013년의 한국 남녀의 기대 수명을 나타낸 것이다. 이 도표는 한국 남녀 모두의 기대 수명이 이 기간에 꾸준하고도 극적으로 증가해왔음을 분명하게 보여준다. ① 한국 남성은 기대 수명이 40년간 18.9년 증가했다. ② 동시에, 한국 여성의 기대 수명은 18.1년 증가했다. ③ 한국 여성의 기대 수명이 2003년 이후 80세를 넘어섰다는 것에 주목하는 것은 흥미롭다. ④ 한편, 남성과 여성의 기대 수명의 차이는 평균 약 6년에서 8년이었다. ⑤ 그러나 남녀 기대 수명 간의 그 차이는 1983년 이후 꾸준히 증가했는데, 그 당시 그것(= 차이)은 8.3년에 달했다.

구문 [12행~14행] ~, *the gap* (between male and female life expectancies) has been steadily increasing / since *1983*. // **when** it(= the gap) reached 8.3 years.
when은 1983을 선행사로 하는 계속적 용법의 관계부사이다.

어휘 **life expectancy** 기대 수명 *cf.* **life span** 수명 **indicate** 나타내다; 가리키다 **steadily** 꾸준히 **dramatically** 극적으로; 급격히 **as for[to]** ~는 어떤가 하면, ~에 관해서는 **note** 주목하다, 특별히 언급하다 **meanwhile** 한편; 그동안에 **average** 평균 ~이 되다; 평균(의) **reach** ~에 이르다[닿다]

26 내용 불일치 ⑤

소재 영국의 환경 운동가 Norman Myers

해설 마지막 문장에서 Myers가 발견한 지역은 매우 많은 수의 다양한 종이 사는 지역임을 알 수 있으므로, 이와 반대되는 내용인 ⑤는 글의 내용과 일치하지 않는다.

해석 1934년 8월 24일에 태어난 Norman Myers는 ① 생물의 다양성 연구를 전문으로 하는 영국의 환경운동가이다. Myers는 현재 영국 옥스퍼드의 헤딩턴에서 살고 있다. ② 그는 UN, 세계은행, 그리고 전 세계의 수많은 과학 학술원을 포함한 기관들의 고문을 맡아왔다. 1970년대에 그의 연구는 주로 열대림의 손실에 초점을 맞추었다. 그 이후 10년 동안, 그는 ③ 목축으로 인한 환경 훼손에 주목하기 시작했다. ④ 그의 저서 〈궁극적 안보: 정치적 안정의 환경적 기초〉는 국내외 정치에 큰 영향을 미쳐 왔다. 1991년에 그는 Blue Planet 상을 수상했고, 1994년에는 미국 국립 과학 학술원의 외국인 회원으로 선출되었다. 2007년에 그는 ⑤ 매우 많은 수의 다양한 종이 사는 지역들을 발견한 연구로 〈타임〉지의 '환경 영웅'으로 선정되었다.

구문 [15행~17행] In 2007, he was named *Time* magazine's "Hero of the Environment" / for *his work* (discovering regions with very high numbers of different species).
discovering이 이끄는 현재분사구가 앞에 있는 명사구 his work를 수식한다.

어휘 **environmentalist** 환경운동가, 환경(보호)론자 *cf.* **environmental** 환경의, 환경과 관련된 **specialize in** ~을 전문으로 하다; ~을 전공하다 **advisor** 고문; 조언자 **organization** 기관, 조직(체); 구성 **tropical forest** 열대림 **decade** 10년 **cattle** (집합적) 소; 가축 **local** 지역의, 현지의 **politics** 정치(학) **award** (상을) 주다, 수여하다; 상 **elect** 선출[선거]하다 **associate** 회원; 동료; 연상하다, 연관 짓다 **region** 지역, 지방; 분야 **species** (생물) 종(種)

27 안내문 불일치 ⑤

소재 Akron 마라톤 안내

해설 마라톤용품은 경주 하루 전날인 24일에 엑스포에서 받아 갈 수 있고 경주 당일에는 받을 수 없다고 했으므로 ⑤가 안내문과 일치하지 않는다.

해석

> **Akron 마라톤 (2021.9.25)**
>
> Akron 마라톤은 굉장한 경품을 나누어주는 것으로 유명하며, ① 모든 풀코스 마라토너(26.2마일 풀코스 경주 참가자)에게 드리는 올해의 공식 경주용 재킷도 예외가 아닙니다! ② K Sports에서 후원받은 이 가벼운 육상 재킷은 65달러의 가치가 있으며, 선선한 아침 달리기를 위해 여러분이 찾게 되는 재킷이 될 것입니다.
>
> **행사 정보**
> - ③ 출발 시간: 오전 7시
> - ③ 종료 시간: 오후 1시 (이 코스는 1마일당 13분 44초의 속도를 계속 유지하는 것을 기준으로 종료됩니다.)
> - ④ (참가) 최소 연령: 경주 당일 기준으로 16세
>
> **용품 수령**
> 주자는 자신의 마라톤용 용품을 2021년 9월 24일 금요일 오전 11시부터 오후 9시 사이에 엑스포에서 가져가셔야 합니다. 이곳은 여러분의 등번호, 재킷, 선물 주머니를 가져갈 수 있는 유일한 장소입니다. ⑤ 경주 당일에는 (용품을) 받을 수 없습니다.

구문 [8행~11행] **Sponsored** by K Sports, / this lightweight track jacket is a $65 value / and will be your go-to jacket / for those cool morning runs.

Sponsored ~는 수동 분사구문으로 의미상의 주어는 this ~ jacket이다.

어휘 **giveaway** (손님을 끌기 위한) 경품, 무료 증정품 **official** 공식의 **exception** 예외 **sponsor** 후원하다 **lightweight** 무게가 가벼운 **go-to** 늘 찾는 **continuous** 지속적인 **package** 꾸러미; 포장한 상품 **goodie bag** 선물 주머니

28 안내문 일치 ②

소재 시애틀 국제영화제 안내

해설 두 번째 문장에서 SIFF를 미국에서 가장 큰 규모의 영화제로 소개하고 있으므로 ②가 안내문의 내용과 일치한다.

해석

SIFF 2021 출품작 요청

시애틀 국제영화제는 47번째의 연례 축제를 맞아 ① 장편영화, 다큐멘터리, 단편영화, 애니메이션 영화 등을 찾고 있습니다. ② SIFF는 미국에서 가장 큰 규모이자 가장 많이 참석하는 영화제입니다. ③ 게다가 매년 15만 명이 넘는 관객이 찾고 있습니다.

올해 SIFF는 자랑스럽게도 다음 부문에서 8,000달러의 상금을 현금으로 지급합니다. 2,500달러 신인 영화감독 경선 / 2,500달러 다큐멘터리 경선 / ④ 1,000달러 단편영화: 실사 촬영 / 1,000달러 단편영화: 애니메이션 / 1,000달러 단편영화: 다큐멘터리

이 국제적인 상은 영화 제작 기법, 형식, 내용에서 우수한 작품들에 주어집니다.

제출 기한
일반 제출 기한: 2020년 11월 4일
⑤ 최종 제출 기한: 2021년 1월 3일
연장 – 온라인(에 한정) 제출 기한: 2021년 2월 3일

어휘 **call for** 요청하다 **entry** 출품작; 참가; 입장 **full-length movie** 장편 영화 **annual** 1년에 한 번의, 연례의; 1년의 *cf.* **annually** 매년 **attend** 참석하다; 주목하다 **director** 감독 **live action** 실사 촬영(영화에서 그림 · 모형 · 컴퓨터를 이용하지 않고 실제 인물과 동물을 이용해서 찍은 것) **excellence** 우수성, 탁월함 **content** 내용 **submission** 제출 **extension** 연장

29 밑줄 어법 ⑤

소재 글쓰기의 개인적인 성격

해설 ⑤ that절의 주어인 the personal element의 동사가 접속사 but에 의해 병렬구조로 연결된 형태이므로 varying은 varies가 되어야 한다.

오답 분석 ① '가장 ~한 것들 중 하나'를 나타내는 표현은 「one of the+최상급+복수명사」이므로 알맞게 쓰였다. ② show의 직접목적어인 간접의문문으로 「의문사+주어+동사」의 어순이 바르게 쓰였다. ③ 주어와 동사의 위치가 바뀐 도치구문으로, 주어 the writer's choice ~ shaped에 맞춰 복수동사인 are를 쓴 것은 적절하다. ④ 사람들에 의해 어떤 글이 '개인적'이라고 '불리는 것'이므로 수동태를 쓴 것은 옳다. 조동사가 포함된 수동태는 「조동사+be+p.p.」의 형태가 된다.

해석 주제문 모든 글쓰기는 어느 정도 개인적이다. 쇼핑 목록조차도 우리에게 그걸 쓴 사람에 대해 꽤 많이 알려준다. 장교를 가장 높은 계급 중 하나로 진급시키기 전에 그 장교의 작문 견본을 보겠다고 요구했다는 점에서 Napoleon(나폴레옹)은 이 점을 잘 알았던 것 같다. 설명문, 논설문, 기술문, 서사문은 모두 서서히 그렇지만 확실하게 그 글쓴이가 어떤 사람인지를 우리에게 보여준다. 그 작가의 주제 선택과 드러나는 지식의 깊이, 소재를 다듬는 기술은 똑같이 흥미로운 사실을 보여준다. 이 모든 것이 사실이라면, 당신이 왜 어떤 특정한 종류의 글쓰기만 '개인적'이라고 불려야 하는지 묻는 것도 당연한 일이다. 그 해답은, 개인적인 요소는 산문에 늘 존재하지만, 그것이 부각되는 정도는 많이 다르다는 데 있다.

구문 [8행~10행] Equally revealing(C) are(V) the writer's choice of topic(S), / *the depth of knowledge* (**displayed**), / and *the skill* [with **which** the material is shaped].

보어를 강조하기 위해 문장 앞에 위치시키고 주어와 동사의 자리를 바꾼 도치구문이다. displayed와 with ~ shaped는 각각 앞의 명사(구)를 수식하는 과거분사와 관계대명사절이다.

어휘 **more or less** 어느 정도, 다소 **be aware of** ~을 알다[알아차리다] **given that** ~라는 점에서, ~을 고려[가정]하면 **promote** 진급[승진]시키다; 촉진하다 **rank** 계급, 지위 **revealing** 흥미로운 사실을 보여주는; 노출이 심한 **material** 소재; 재료; 물질 **label** ~이라고 부르다; 라벨을 붙이다; 표, 라벨 **element** 구성 요소, 성분 **prominence** 부각, 두드러짐; 중요성

30 밑줄 어휘 ⑤

소재 행동의 동력이 되는 감정

해설 감정이 행동에 변화를 일으키는 동력이 될 수 있다는 내용의 글이다. 통제된 분노를 세상을 움직이는 힘으로 바꾼 Gandhi의 경우처럼, 충동적인 반응을 자제하고 적절한 순간에 그 감정적 에너지를 '발산하라'는 내용이 되어야 하므로 ⑤의 conceal(감추다)은 반대 의미인 release(발산하다) 등으로 바꿔야 한다.

해석 주제문 감정은 행동에 ① 연료를 공급하는 매우 중요한 기능을 한다. 감정은 우리를 휩쓸어 유혹에 빠지게 할 수 있는 반면, 용기와 결단을 주어서 적절한 행동을 취하게 할 수도 있다. 이 ② 후자의 변화 과정을 Mahatma Gandhi(마하트마 간디)보다 더 잘 설명해준 사람은 없는데, 그는 무기 하나 없이, 수세기에 걸친 대영제국의 인도 식민 지배를 종식시키는 데 성공했다. 그는 자신의 비결을 다음과 같이 설명했다. "저는 분노를 ③ 보존하는 최고의 교훈 한 가지를 쓰라린 경험을 통해 배웠습니다. 그리고 열이 에너지로 바뀌듯, 통제된 분노조차도 세상을 움직일 수 있는 힘으로 바뀔 수 있습니다." Gandhi가 제안했듯 ④ 충동적인 반응을 자제하라. 이는(=충동적인 반응은) 당신의 소중한 에너지를 쓸데없이 낭비할 뿐이다. 마지막으로 적절한 순간에, 목적의식을 갖고 결단을 내리듯 감정적 에너지를 ⑤ 감춰라(→ 발산하라).

구문 [5행~7행] **No one**(S) demonstrated(V) this latter process of transformation(O) **better than** *Mahatma Gandhi*, // who(S'), / without a single weapon, / succeeded(V') in putting an end ~.

「No ~ 비교급+than」은 최상급의 의미를 나타낸다. 계속적 용법으로 쓰인 who는 Mahatma Gandhi를 가리킨다.

[11행~14행] And **as** heat is transmitted into energy, // even **so** *our anger* (controlled)(S) can be transformed(V) / into *a power* [**which** can move the world].

「as ~, so ...」는 '~처럼, …도 그렇다'의 의미이다. which ~ world는 a power를 수식하는 주격 관계대명사절이다.

어휘 **critical** 매우 중요한, 결정적인 **sweep over** ~을 휩쓸다[압도하다] **lead A into B** A를 B로 이끌다 **temptation** 유혹 **compel A to-v** A가 v하게 하다 **resolve** 결심, 의지; 해결하다 **demonstrate** 입증하다; 설명하다 **latter** 후자의(↔ **former** 전자의) **transformation** 변화, 변신 *cf.* **transform[transmit] A into B** A를 B로 바꾸다 **put an end to A** A를 끝내다[종식시키다] **colonial** 식민(지)의 **domination** 지배, 통치; 우세 **as follows** 다음과 같이 **supreme** 최고의 **conserve** 보존하다; 아끼다 **refrain from** ~을 자제하다[삼가다] **impulsive** 충동적인 **reckless** 무모한, 신중치 못한 **waste** 낭비; 쓰레기; 낭비하다 **purposively** 목적의식을 가지고, 목표가 분명하게

31 빈칸 추론 ⑤

소재 자기표현 수단으로서의 자동차

해설 빈칸 뒤에 젊은이들이 세상에 자신을 보여주려고 자동차를 이용하고, 자동차를 자신의 신체나 성격의 연장으로 여긴다는 내용이 나오므로, 자동차 운전이 ⑤ '자기표현(self-expression)'의 기회가 된다는 것을 추론할 수 있다.

해석 자동차 사고에 대해 연구하는 사람들은 사고의 원인을 더 잘 이해하고 규명하기를 바라며 운전자의 평균 반응 시간, 시력, 속도와 거리를 추정하는 능력을 조사하는 데 많은 시간을 할애해 왔다. 주제문 그러나 위험한 운전은 아마도 자동차가 제공하는 자기표현의 기회들과 더 많은 관련이 있을지도 모른다. 사실, 어떤 사람들, 특히 젊은이들은 운전석에 앉으면 자신이 얼마나 빠르고, 얼마나 영리한지, 얼마나 강하고, 또는 얼마나 화가 나 있는지를 (자신을 제외한) 나머지 세상에 보여주려고 자신의 자동차의 힘을 이용한다. 그들은 자신의 자동차를 자신의 신체나 성격의 연장이라고 보는데, 이것은 그들이 무모해지면 문제가 된다.

① 지위 ② 편리함 ③ 즐거움 ④ 경쟁

구문 [8행~11행] The thing is, // **when** some people — and young men in particular — get behind the wheel, // (that) they use the power of their car / **to show** IO the rest of the world DO how fast, clever, strong, or angry they are.

주어는 The thing, 동사는 is이며, 접속사 that이 생략된 절이 보어 역할을 하고 있다. 보어절의 to show는 '목적'을 나타내는 부사적 용법으로 쓰였다. when이 이끄는 부사절이 중간에 삽입되었다.

어휘 **motor vehicle** 자동차 *cf.* **vehicle** 차량, 탈것 **a great deal of** 많은 **investigate** 조사하다 **visual acuity** 시력 **estimate** 추정하다; 평가하다 **in the hope of** ~을 기대하여, ~을 바라며 **have more[less] to do with** ~와 더[덜] 관련이 있다 **get behind the wheel** 운전하다

32 빈칸 추론 ①

소재 관료주의의 단점

해설 이 글에서 제시된 관료주의의 해로운 영향은 직급이 오를수록 실무는 줄고 행정 업무가 늘어서, 잘 가르치는 교수나 수술을 잘하는 의사가 자신이 잘하는 일을 더 이상 하지 못하고 행정 업무를 하게 된다는 것이므로, 이러한 단점을 정리하면 ① '재능을 딴 데로 돌린다'가 된다.

해석 일정량의 관료주의, 책임과 조직은 우리가 사는 세상에서 필수적이다. 관료주의의 이점은 재촉을 필요로 하지 않는다. 그러나 숨겨진 비용이 상당히 많다. 주제문 과도한 관료주의의 해로운 영향은 그것이 재능을 딴 데로 돌린다는 점이다. 거의 모든 조직에서 급료가 높아지고 지위가 오를수록, 실무는 줄고 행정은 늘어난다. 아마 뛰어난 전달자였을 교장은 더 이상 가르치지 않는다. 뛰어난 외과 의사는 결국 병원 원장으로서 서류 업무를 한다. 훌륭한 교수는 결국 대학의 행정 책임자가 된다. 그들 중 누구도 자신이 가장 즐기는 혹은 잘하는 것을 더 이상 하지 않는다. 그들은 기금 모금자, 인사 사무관, 위원회 의장으로 시간을 보낸다. 그것은 널리 퍼진 경향이다. 어떤 일을 정말로 잘할 수 있다면, 그 일을 멈추고 행정가가 되라는 것 말이다.

② 예산을 낭비한다 ③ 불의를 정당화한다
④ 부패를 유발한다 ⑤ 불평등을 강화한다

구문 [6행~8행] ~, **the higher** the pay and **the higher** the status, **the less** practical work and **the more** administration.

「the 비교급 ~, the 비교급 ...」은 '~하면 할수록 더 …하다'의 뜻이다.

어휘 **bureaucracy** 관료주의 **accountability** 책임, 의무 **urge** 재촉하다 **considerable** 상당한 **over-active** 과도한 **administration** 관리, 행정 *cf.* **administrative** 관리의, 행정상의 *cf.* **administrator** 관리자, 행정인 **head teacher** 교장 **surgeon** 외과 의사 **end up v-ing** 결국 v하게 되다 **paperwork** 서류 작업 **academic** 교수 **fundraiser** 기금 모금자 **personnel officer** 인사 사무관 **chair** 의장 [선택지 어휘] **divert** 딴 데로 돌리다, 전환하다 **provoke** 유발하다 **reinforce** 강화하다

33 빈칸 추론 ①

소재 영어 사용 범위의 변화

해설 빈칸 앞부분은 지금은 영어가 전 세계적인 언어가 되었다는 내용이고, 빈칸 뒷부분은 400년 전만 해도 일부 지역을 제외하고는 영어가 널리 사용되지 않았다는 내용이다. 현재와 달리 과거에는 영어가 보편적인 언어가 아니었다는 내용이 되어야 하므로, 빈칸에는 ① '그것이 항상 지금 같았던 것은 아니라는 것을'이 가장 적절하다.

해석 현대의 영어는 외교, 의사소통, 항공, 무선 통신, 사업, 과학, 관광, 오락에 있어서 주요 국제 언어이며 전 세계적으로 18억 인구가 사용한다. 주제문 따라서 그것(=영어)이 항상 지금 같았던 것은 아니라는 것을 이해하는 데는 상당한 노력의 상상력이 필요하다. 예를 들어 William Shakespeare(윌리엄 셰익스피어)가 희곡을 집필하고 제작했던 4세기 전만 해도, 이 언어는 거의 완전하게 잉글랜드와 남부 스코틀랜드 지방에만 국한되었고 사실상 전 세계 다른 누구에게도 알려지지 않았다. 심지어 바로 이웃하고 있는 아일랜드와 웨일즈 지방에도 깊숙이 스며들지 못했다. 그때 당시, Shakespeare 희곡에 사용된 언어를 이해했을 것으로 예상되는 사람의 전체 수는 기껏해야 약 5백만 명이었다.

② 이것이 스코틀랜드에는 좋은 소식이 아니라는 것을
③ Shakespeare가 영어의 성공에 책임이 있다는 것을
④ 어떻게 고대 영어가 현대 영어로 변했는지를
⑤ 왜 다른 유럽의 언어들은 그렇게 널리 퍼지지 않는지를

구문 [12행~15행] Back then, the total number (of *people*) [who **could have been expected** to understand the language of a Shakespeare play] / was, at most, around five million.

S: the total number, V: was

주어의 핵은 the total number이고 동사는 was이다. who가 이끄는 관계사절이 people을 수식하여 주부가 길어진 구조이다. 「could have p.p.」는 '~였을 것이다'란 뜻으로 과거 사실에 대한 추측을 나타내며 '예상되다'라는 수동의 의미가 더해져 「could have been p.p.」의 형태로 쓰였다.

어휘 **dominant** 주요한; 지배적인; 우위의 **diplomacy** 외교; 외교적 수완 **aviation** 항공(술) **be confined to A** A에 한정되다[제한되다] **virtually** 사실상, 거의 **penetrate into** ~에 스며들다[침투하다] **neighboring** 이웃의, 근처의 **at most** 기껏해야, 많아야 [선택지 어휘] **widespread** 널리 퍼진

34 빈칸 추론 ④

소재 새로운 것 배우기를 꺼리는 이유

해설 무언가를 가르치는 것을 여행을 권유하는 것에 비유한 글이다. 새로운 여행지가 위험하다고 들었던 적이 있는 곳이라면 가길 꺼려하는 것과 같이 새로운 것을 배울 때에도 사람들에게 두려움이 있다고 하였으므로, 사람들에게 가르칠 때 그것이 불쾌한 것이 아닌 좋은 것임을 알려줘서 두려움을 낮춰야 한다는 내용이 되어야 한다. 따라서 빈칸에는 ④ '목적지는 우리 모두가 가고 싶어 하는 곳이라는'이 가장 적절하다.

해석 나는 컴퓨터를 사용하지 않는 사람들에게 컴퓨터로 어떻게 일을 더 쉽게 할 수 있는지를 설명하려고 때때로 노력한다. 그들의 태도는 "고맙지만 괜찮아."란 말로 완벽하게 표현될 때가 꽤 자주 있다. 주제문 왜 어떤 사람들은 일을 더 잘, 또는 더 쉽게 할 수 있게 하는 것을 배우기를 거부할까? 대부분의 경우에 그 이유는 두려움이다. 기술에 대해 잘 알지 못하는 사람들은 컴퓨터가 그들을 대신하거나 컴퓨터가 그들을 무능력하게 보이게 할 것이라고 걱정할지 모른다. 이것이 바로 가르치는 것이 다른 사람에게 여행을 가도록 요구하는 것과 같다고 보아도 좋은 이유다. 위험하거나 유쾌하지 않다고 들은 장소에 가는 초대에 누구도 응하지 않는 것과 마찬가지로, 사람들은 그들이 생각하기에 자신을 더욱 더 궁색하게 할 것들을 배우길 꺼린다. 누군가에게 새로운 것을 가르치려고 할 때, 목적지는 우리 모두가 가고 싶어 하는 곳이라는 것을 처음부터 분명히 해야 한다.

① 모든 직업은 컴퓨터에 의해 바뀔 것이라는
② 즐거운 여행은 우리의 삶에 에너지를 줄 수 있다는
③ 그 사람이 일을 더 쉽게 할 수 있게 하겠다고 약속하는
⑤ 변화는 정보화 시대에는 의무라는

구문 [1행~3행] I sometimes try to explain to *people* [who don't use a computer] how a computer could make their job easier.
how ~ easier는 explain의 목적어인 의문사절이며, to people ~ a computer는 대상을 나타내는 부사구이다.

[7행~10행] *People* [who don't know much about technology] may worry // **that** computers will replace them, / or **that** a computer will **make** them **look** incompetent.
(S: People, V: may worry, O1: that computers will replace them, O2: that a computer will make them look incompetent)
목적어인 두 개의 that절이 접속사 or에 의해 병렬구조로 연결된 구조이다. make가 사역동사로 쓰이면 목적격보어로 원형부정사가 온다.

[11행~15행] Just as nobody would accept *an invitation* (to go to *a place* [**that** (they've heard) is dangerous or unpleasant]), // people are reluctant to learn *things* [**that** (they think) will make them worse off].
to go 이하의 to부정사구는 an invitation을 수식하는 형용사적 용법이다. 두 개의 that은 모두 주격 관계대명사로 각각 앞의 a place와 things를 받으며, 관계대명사절 내에 they've heard와 they think가 삽입된 형태이다.

어휘 **resist** 꺼리다; 저항하다 **replace** 대체하다, 교체하다 **incompetent** 무능한, 기술이 부족한 **unpleasant** 유쾌하지 않은, 불쾌한 **reluctant to-v** v하기를 꺼리는 **worse off** 더욱 더 궁색한, 더 나빠지는 [선택지 어휘] **destination** 목적지 **obligation** 의무

35 무관한 문장 ⑤

소재 논쟁에서 역지사지(易地思之)의 중요성

해설 논쟁을 할 때 반대편의 입장에서 상황을 바라보는 것은 중요한 기술이며, 이를 위해서 상대방의 감정에 대한 공감과 자신의 의견을 보류하는 자세가 필요하다는 내용의 글이다. 반면에 ⑤는 설득력 있는 논증이 승리의 열쇠라는 내용으로 이 글의 주제에서 벗어난 문장이다.

해석 주제문 논쟁을 할 때, 반대편의 입장에서 상황을 바라보는 능력은, 어렵겠지만, 당신이 지닐 수 있는 가장 중요한 기술 중의 하나이다. 다른 사람이 사물을 다르게 본다는 것을 아는 것만으로는 충분하지 않다. 사람들에게 영향을 끼치고 싶다면, 그들의 견해와 그들이 그 견해를 믿는 데 사용되는 감정적인 힘에 대한 진정한 공감 또한 필요하다. 현미경 아래에 있는 벌레처럼 그들을 연구하는 것으로는 충분하지 않다. 즉, 그 벌레가 되는 것이 어떤 것인지 알아야 한다. 이것을 이루기 위해서는 다른 사람의 관점을 이해하려고 하는 동안 잠시 당신의 판단을 보류할 준비가 되어야 한다. 논쟁은 목소리가 큰 사람이 이기는 것이 아니고, 가장 설득력 있는 논증을 펼치는 사람이 이긴다.

구문 [1행~3행] ~, *the ability* (to see the situation // as the other side sees it), (as difficult as it may be), / is one of *the most important skills* [(that) you can possess].
(S: the ability, V: is, C: one of the most important skills)
as difficult as it may be는 '어렵겠지만'이라는 의미를 추가하기 위해 삽입된 구이다.

[5행~7행] ~, you also need to feel real empathy / for their point of view and *the emotional force* [**with which** they believe in it(= their point of view)].
「전치사+관계대명사」가 이끄는 절이 앞의 명사구 the emotional force를 수식하고 있다. 원래의 절인 they believe in it with the emotional force에서 with가 관계대명사 앞으로 이동한 것이다.

어휘 **argument** 논쟁, 논의, 토론 **empathy** 공감, 감정이입 **point of view** 관점, 견해 **microscope** 현미경 **accomplish** 이루다, 달성하다 **withhold** 보류하다; 억누르다 **compelling** 설득력 있는; 강제적인

36 글의 순서 ②

소재 '중력 렌즈' 현상의 발견

해설 공간과 시간이 물질의 영향을 받는다는 주어진 글 다음에는, 이것이 아인슈타인의 연구의 기반이었으며, 이를 바탕으로 아인슈타인이 먼 곳에서 온 빛이 태양 옆에서 휘어질 거라고 예측했다는 (B)가 나온다. 일식은 아인슈타인의 가설을 확인하기에 좋은 기회였으며, 관찰자들은 실제로 빛의 휘어짐을 관찰했다는 내용의 (A)가 그다음에 나오며, 이러한 관찰(This observation)을 바탕으로 아인슈타인이 연구 결과물을 출간했다는 내용의 (C)가 마지막에 이어진다. 지시어와 관사를 통해 파악해 본다면, (B)의 This는 주어진 글의 '공간과 시간이 물질의 영향을 받는다'는 내용이며, (A)의 The eclipse는 (B)의 a solar eclipse that occurred in 1919를 지칭한다.

해석 주제문 공간과 시간은 흥미로운 것이다. 그것은 둘 다 물질(특히 강력한 중력의 영향력을 가지는 대량의 물질)의 영향을 받는다.
(B) 이것이 Albert Einstein(알버트 아인슈타인)이 했던 연구의 기반이며, 1919년에 일어난 일식이 이에 자극이 되었다. 그는 먼 곳의 별에서 나온 빛의 광선은 태양의 중력의 영향으로 인해 태양 옆을 지날 때 휘어질 거라고 예측했다.
(A) 일식은 햇빛을 차단하여 관찰자들이 보통은 보지 못했을 별을 보게 해 주었고, 그들은 중력 렌즈(= 무거운 중력장 내에서 빛이 굴절하는 현상)로 인한 빛의 작은 이동을 측정하는 데 성공했다.
(C) 이러한 관찰은 Einstein이 물체의 질량이 어떻게 지역적인 시공간을 휘게 하여, 빛의 광선이 아주 조금 휘어지게 하는지를 기술하는 연구를 출간하게 했다. 1919년의 일식은 중력 렌즈에 대한 최초의 실험적 확인을 제공했다.

구문 [14행~17행] This observation **led** Einstein **to publish** *work* (**describing** how the mass of an object curves local space-time, / thus **forcing** light rays **to bend** ever so slightly).
「lead+O+C(to-v)」는 'O가 v하도록 이끌다[유도하다]'의 뜻이다. ( )는 능동의 의미로 work를 수식하는 현재분사구이며, thus 이하는 분사구문이다. 「force+O+C(to-v)」는 'O가 (억지로) v하게 하다'의 뜻이다.

어휘 **gravitational** 중력의 **eclipse** (일식 · 월식 등의) 식 **gravitational lensing** 중력 렌즈(무거운 중력장 내에서 빛이 굴절하는 현상) **basis** 근거, 기반 **spur on** 자극하다; 격려하다; 채찍질하다 **mass** 질량 **ever so** 매우, 몹시 **confirmation** 확인

37 글의 순서 ⑤

소재 사회적 고립에 대한 이해

해설 사회적 고립을 이해하기 위해서는 그 사람의 상황에 대한 인식이 필요하다는 내용의 글로, 각 글의 앞부분에 나온 연결어와 지칭어구를 통해 글의 순서를 파악할 수 있다. 먼저 주어진 글의 On one hand(한편으로는)에 이어 (C)의 On the other hand(다른 한편으로는, 반면에)가 자연스럽게 연결된다. (C)의 마지막 문장과 (B)의 That's why ~ 문장은 인과관계로 연결된다. 끝으로 (A)의 For example ~ 문장은 (B)의 마지막 문장을 부연 설명하는 예시이다. 따라서 글의 순서는 ⑤ '(C)-(B)-(A)'가 자연스럽다.

해석 어떤 사람이 사회적으로 고립되는 상황을 해석하는 데에는 여러 방법이 있다. 한편으로는, 사람들이 때때로 홀로 있는 것을 추구하는 것은 건강한 일이다.
(C) 반면에, 사람들이 사회적이고 감정적인 상호작용이 없어서 고립되고 불행하며 괴롭다고 느낄 때는 분명히 문제가 된다. 선택에 의한 고립은 즐거운 고독이지만 선택이 없다면 그것은 암울한 외로움이다.
(B) 주제문 그것이 바로 고립된 사람의 상황에 대한 인식이 사회적 고립을 이해하는 데 핵심이 되는 이유이다. 단순히 어떤 사람의 사회적 상호작용의 수와 빈도를 세는 것은 그 사람이 괜찮은지를 판단하는 데 충분하지 않다.
(A) 예를 들어, 집에 틀어박힌 노인은 그의 딸이 매일 찾아와도 여전히 고립되고 우울하다고 느낄 수 있다. 만족스러운 사회적 삶은 사람의 사회적 상호작용의 수와 빈도에 의해 결정되는 것이 아니라 그것(= 상호작용)의 질과 공유된 감정 교환에 의해 결정된다.

구문 [13행~15행] Simply counting *the number and frequency* (of someone's social interactions) / is not enough to decide **whether** he or she is okay.
(S: Simply counting ~ interactions, V: is)
counting이 이끄는 동명사구가 주어이므로 단수동사 is를 썼다. whether는 decide의 목적어인 명사절을 이끄는 접속사로 '~인지 아닌지'로 해석한다.

어휘 **interpret** 해석하다 **isolated** 고립된, 격리된 *cf.* **isolation** 고립, 격리 **homebound** 집에 틀어박힌 **depressed** 우울한; 침체된 **give-and-take** (공평한 조건에서의) 교환 **frequency** 빈도; 진동, 주파수 **interaction** 상호작용 **perception** 인식, 지각 **distressed** 괴로운, 고민하는 **solitude** 고독, 외로움(=**loneliness**)

38 문장 넣기 ⑤

소재 감자 개량을 통한 병충해 예방 노력

해설 주어진 문장이 감자의 끈적이는 털의 문제점을 설명하고 있고, Unfortunately(불행히도)로 시작하므로 이 문장 앞에 끈적이는 털의 긍정적인 사례가 언급되어야 한다. 또한 마지막 문장에 나온 this problem은 끈적이는 털이 이로운 곤충을 죽이는 문제점을 가리킨다. 따라서 주어진 문장은 ⑤에 들어가는 것이 가장 적절하다.

해석 영양가 많고 맛있는 감자는 중요한 식용 작물로, 전 세계적으로 수백만 명을 먹여 살리고 있다. 하지만 감자는 작물 전체를 파괴시킬 수 있는 해충의 피해를 당하기 쉽다. 주제문 그래서 식물 연구가들은 곤충을 잡아서 죽일 수 있는, 끈적이는 독특한 털이 난 새로운 감자 종을 개발했다. 끈적이는 털이 난 이 감자는 보통 감자와 볼리비아산 야생 변종을 교배한 것이다. 그것은 가장 해로운 감자 해충 중의 하나인 콜로라도 감자 풍뎅이를 포함하여 일반적인 해충들의 수를 40~60퍼센트 줄이는 것으로 나타났다. 불행히도, 그 잡종 감자의 끈적이는 털들은 이로운 곤충들도 잡아서 죽인다. 식물 연구가들은 이 끈적이는 털의 밀도를 줄이려는 노력을 하며 이 문제를 연구하고 있다.

어휘 **hybrid** 교배종, 잡종 **sticky** 끈적거리는 **trap** 덫으로 잡다; 올가미, 덫 **beneficial** 유익한, 유용한 **nutritious** 영양분이 풍부한 **feed** 먹이다 **vulnerable** 피해를 입기 쉬운; 상처받기 쉬운 **pest** 해충 **species** 《생물》 종(種) **cross** 《생물》 이종교배, 잡종 **variety** 《생물》 변종; 다양(성) **beetle** 풍뎅이, 딱정벌레 **destructive** 해로운; 파괴적인 **work on** ~을 연구하다; ~에 착수하다 **density** 밀도, 밀집

39 문장 넣기 ④

소재 최고 경영자가 젊은 직원들과 상호작용해야 하는 이유

해설 주어진 문장의 this cabinet은 ③ 뒤의 문장에서 언급된 a "shadow cabinet"을 가리키는 것이므로 ④에 내각을 만나야 한다는 내용의 주어진 문장이 오는 것이 자연스럽다.

해석 젊은 사람들은 흔히 사회의 중요한 풍조에 대한 예리하고 빠른 이해력을 가진다. 그들은 기술, 패션, 건강 생활, 그리고 환경과 같은 분야의 최신 아이디어와 제품에 큰 친숙함을 가지고 있는 경향이 있다. 주제문 그런 이유로, Gary Hamel은 최고 경영자들이 그들의 조직 속에 있는 가장 어리고 가장 똑똑한 사람들과의 관계를 유지하기 위해 특별한 노력을 해야 한다고 주장한다. 그는 최고 경영자들에게 이십 대와 삼십 대의 매우 유능한 직원으로 구성된 '예비 내각'을 구성할 것을 권한다. 그런 다음에 최고 경영자들은 핵심적인 전략 쟁점에 관한 그들의 시각이 상급 관리팀의 구성원들로부터 자신들이 듣고 있는 것과 어떻게 다른지 보기 위해 정기적으로 이 내각을 만나야 한다. Hamel은 젊은 사람들과의 상호 작용이 최고 경영자들로 하여금 상급 임원들이 인지하지 못할 수 있는 기회와 위협을 보도록 도울 것이라고 믿는다. 더욱이, Hamel은 이 젊은 사람들의 시각이 조직 계층의 전형적인 교묘한 술책에 맡겨진다면 흔히 걸러지고 만다는 것을 알고 있다.

구문 [1행~4행] CEOs should then meet with this cabinet periodically / to see **how** *its perspective* (on key strategic issues) differs from **what** they are hearing from *the members* (of the senior management team).

how ~ team은 see의 목적어로 쓰인 간접의문문으로, 「의문사(how)+주어(its ~ issues)+동사(differs)」의 어순으로 쓰였다. what ~ team은 전치사 from의 목적어로 쓰인 명사절이다.

[17행~20행] Moreover, Hamel recognizes // that *the perspectives* (of these young people) are often filtered out // if (they are) left to *the normal machinations* (of the organizational hierarchy).
조건을 나타내는 접속사 if 다음에는 they(=the perspectives of these young people) are가 생략되어 있다.

어휘 **periodically** 주기적으로 **perspective** 시각, 관점 **strategic** 전략적인 **keen** 예리한, 날카로운 **societal** 사회의 **familiarity** 친숙함, 익숙함 **latest** 최신의 **go out of one's way** 비상한 노력을 하다; 굳이[일부러] ~하다 **capable** 유능한 **threat** 위협 **perceive** 인식하다 **filter out** (원치 않는 것을) 걸러내다 **hierarchy** 계급, 계층

40 요약문 완성 ③

소재 '거절'을 이용하여 '승낙'을 받아내는 방법

해설 처음에 큰 것을 요청하고 그것이 '거절'되었을 때 그보다 작은 요청을 하면 승낙할 확률이 '높아진다'는 것을 일화와 실험을 통해 설명하는 글이다. 그러므로 요약문의 빈칸에는 'refusal(거절)'과 'increases(증가시킨다)'가 들어가는 것이 적절하다.

해석 한 소녀의 쿠키를 파는 비결을 아는가? 그녀는 이웃들에게 아프리카에 자전거를 기부할 수 있는지 묻는다. 만일 이웃들이 그녀(의 요청)를 거절한다면 그때 그녀는 그들에게 5달러에 쿠키 한 상자를 구입함으로써 아프리카 어린이를 도울 수는 있는지 묻는다. 그러면 이웃들은 그들이 자전거를 기부하지 않은 것을 만회할 수 있어서 기뻐한다. 이 방법은 심리학자 Robert Cialdini가 실험을 통해 밝혀냈던 것이다. Cialdini는 자신의 조수들을 자원봉사자로 위장하도록 했다. 그들은 대학생들에게 접근해 적어도 2년 동안 매주 2시간씩 기꺼이 봉사해줄 수 있는지 물어보라고 지시받았다. 예상했다시피 이 요청들이 거절되었을 때, 좀 더 적당한 요청이 덧붙여졌는데, 그것은 비행 청소년 한 집단이 동물원에 가는 2시간짜리 소풍을 인솔하는 것이었다. 그들의 요청 중 거의 85%가 받아들여졌다.

⬇

처음의 더 큰 요청의 (A) 거절은 두 번째 더 작은 요청의 승낙을 (B) 증가시킨다.

어휘 **donate** 기부하다, 기증하다 **turn A down** A를 거절[거부]하다 **make up for** (잘못된 상황을 바로잡도록) 만회하다; 보상하다 **assistant** 조수, 보조원 **disguise** 변장하다, 가장하다; 위장하다, 숨기다 **be willing to-v** 기꺼이 v하다 **follow up with A** A를 덧붙이다 **reasonable** 적당한; 타당한, 합리적인 **compliance** 승낙; 준수; 따름 [선택지 어휘] **target** 목표 **hesitance** 머뭇거림, 주저

41~42 장문 41 ④ 42 ⑤

소재 정황 변화와 피로

해설 41. 실험에서 완전히 지쳐서 더 이상 과제를 수행할 수 없다고 느낀 피실험자들이 실험자가 정황을 바꿔 과제 수행의 목표를 새롭게 제시하자 에너지를 새롭게 얻어서 계속 과제를 수행할 수 있었으므로, 제목으로 가장 적절한 것은 ④ '정황의 변화가 새로워진 에너지를 가져다준다'이다.
① 지루함이 피로를 일으키는가?
② 두뇌의 원기를 즉시 회복하는 방법
③ 정신적 탈진: 원인과 치료
⑤ 피로: 심리적 이상의 증상

42. 그림을 더 이상 그릴 수 없을 정도로 지친 피실험자들은 과제 목표가 '그림 그리기'에서 '그림 그리는 속도 측정'으로 넘어가자 새로운 에너지로 그림을 그릴 수 있었다. 단순한 문자를 반복적으로 쓰는 일에 지쳐서 한 글자도 더 못 쓰게 된 피실험자들은 이름과 주소를 써달라고 했을 때 이를 문제없이 수행했다. 마찬가지로 짧은 시를 반복해서 읽고 목이

쉰 피실험자들이 이를 불평하느라 목소리를 내었을 때는 정황 전환으로 인해 새로운 에너지를 얻어 목소리에 아무 문제도 없이 의견을 낼 수 있었을 것이다. 따라서 쉰 목소리는 나타나는 것이 아니라 사라졌을 것이므로 ⑤의 appeared를 disappeared로 바꿔 써야 한다.

해석 주제문 피로가 반드시 고정점에서 발생하는 것은 아니다. 대개 정신적, 육체적 탈진은 의심할 여지없는 예상에 의해 결정될지도 모른다. 심리학자 Anita Karsten은 처음에는 좋은 느낌이지만 (a) 반복되면 이도저도 아니거나 불편하게 되는 상황들을 연구했다. 그녀는 피실험자들이 수행할 과제를 부여받지만 피곤할 때면 언제든지 일을 그만둘 수 있다는 지시를 받은 '(b) 반 자유 상황'에 그들을 투입했다. 그들은 일을 즐겁게 하는 한에서만 수행하라는 말을 들었다. 과제는 두 종류로서, 그리기나 쓰기 같은 연속적인 활동과, 짧은 시를 반복하여 읽는 것과 같은 빠르게 끝나지만 반복되는 과제였다. 각 종류의 과제에 대해 피실험자들은 지칠 때까지 활동했다.
그 후 연구자는 정황을 바꿨다. 예를 들어 피실험자들이 완전히 지칠 때까지 그린 후에, 연구자는 그들에게 페이지를 넘겨서 그들이 그렸던 마지막 그림을 얼마나 빨리 그릴 수 있는지 실험자에게 보여주기 위해 다시 그려달라고 요청했다. '완전히 지쳐버린' 피실험자들은 새로운 정황에서 그림을 다시 그리는 데 아무런 어려움도 없었다. 다른 피실험자는 진절머리가 날 때까지 ababab...를 쓰는 과제를 받았다. 그는 정신적으로 그리고 육체적으로 (c) 지칠 때까지 계속했다. 그의 손은 심지어 표시를 하나 더 하기 위해 움직일 수조차 없는 것처럼 무감각했다. 그때 연구자가 그에게 다른 용도로 그의 이름과 주소를 서명해 달라고 요청했다. 새로운 요청으로 생성된 정황이 그에게 새로운 (d) 자극으로 작용하는 것처럼 보였다. 그는 꽤 수월하게 그 일을 수행했다. 마찬가지로 다른 피실험자들은 짧은 시를 반복해서 읽고 마찬가지 일을 해냈다. Karsten이 피실험자들에게 큰 소리로 시를 읽게 했을 때, 잠시 후 그들의 목이 쉬었다. 그러나 그들이 그녀에게 그 일이 얼마나 싫은지를 불평할 때, 쉰 목소리는 (e) 나타났다(→ 사라졌다).

구문 [4행~6행] Psychologist Anita Karsten studied *situations* [that at first feel good, but with repetition become neutral or uncomfortable].
[ ]는 situations를 수식하며, [ ] 절에서 동사 feel과 become이 병렬구조를 이룬다. 「with+명사」는 부사적인 의미를 가진다.

[17행~19행] For instance, after the subjects had drawn until (they were) exhausted, the investigator **asked** *them* **to turn** the page over ~.
until exhausted는 부사절의 「주어+동사」가 생략된 형태이다. 주절에는 「ask+O(them)+C(to turn ~)」의 5문형이 쓰였다.

어휘 **fatigue** 피로 **fixed point** 정점(定點) **to a large extent** 대부분, 크게 **exhaustion** 탈진, 고갈, 소진 **unquestioned** (아주 분명하여) 의심할 수 없는 **neutral** 이도저도 아닌; 중립적인 **come to an end** 끝나다 **weary** 지친 **turn ~ over** 뒤집다, 넘기다 **have no difficulty v-ing** v하는 데 전혀 어려움이 없다 **have had enough** 진절머리가 나다 **numb** 감각이 없는 **stimulus** 자극 **hoarse** 목이 쉰 *cf.* **hoarseness** 쉰 목소리

43~45 장문 43 ④ 44 ③ 45 ⑤

소재 양심을 지키고 동아리 회장에 당선된 Kevin

해설 43. Kevin이 작년에 투표에 진 다음 올해 다시 동아리 회장에 선출되기를 바라는 주어진 글에 이어 선거의 시작 부분에 관한 내용으로 시작하는 (D)가 이어지는 것이 적절하다. Kevin이 투표용지에 후보자의 이름을 적으면서 갈등하는 (B)가 다음에 오고, 마지막으로 신임 회장을 발표하는 (C)가 오는 것이 자연스럽다.

44. (c)는 전임 회장인 Dave Hamilton을 가리키고, 나머지는 모두 Kevin을 가리킨다.

45. (D)에서 선거 전에 친구들은 Kevin이 이길 거라고 말했지만 Kevin은 알 수 없었고, (B)에서 투표용지에 자기 이름을 쓸지 말지 고민했으므로 승리를 확신하지 못했음을 알 수 있다. 따라서 ⑤가 글의 내용과 일치하지 않는다.

해석 (A) 10학년 때에 Kevin은 다니던 고등학교 음악 동아리에 가입했고 ① 거기서 제1트럼펫을 연주했다. 그는 음악 동아리 회원들과 함께 하는 5월 축제 공연을 위해 열심히 연습했고, 동아리를 위한 많은 아이디어를 냈다. Kevin은 회원들 사이에서 인기가 많아졌고 작년에 동아리 회장에 입후보했다. 그는 첫 투표에서 Dave Hamilton과 동점이 되었지만 최종 투표에서 졌다. Kevin은 올해에는 ② 음악 동아리의 회장으로 선출되기를 다시 바라고 있었다.
(D) 이제 또 다른 선거를 할 시간이었다. ⑤ 그의 친구들은 올해에는 그가 선거에서 이길 것이라고 말했지만 Kevin은 알 수 없었다. 그는 작년에 Dave와 동점이 되었다가 진 것을 잊을 수 없었다. 만일 (e) 그(=Kevin)가 그때 자신에게 투표했다면 좋았을 텐데! 물론 동아리 전통은 각각의 후보자가 상대에게 투표하는 것이었다. 하지만 아주 많은 회원들이 투표를 하는데 누가 알 것인가? 어쨌든 투표는 비밀이었다.
(B) 서기가 투표용지를 나누어 주고 있었다. Kevin은 초조하게 연필을 깨물었다. "나는 내 이름을 쓸 수도 있어."라고 그는 생각했다. "아무도 내가 나한테 투표했다는 걸 모를 거야." Kevin은 자신에게 투표할 뻔 했지만 그의 양심이 (a) 그(=Kevin)를 멈추게 했다. "내가 동아리 전통을 존중하지 않는다면, 난 회장이 될 자격이 정말 없는 거야."라고 그는 혼잣말을 했다. 그래서 (b) 그(=Kevin)는 ③ 투표용지에 Bill Cummings를 썼고 그것을 제출했다.
(C) 서기가 투표용지를 모았고 말없이 그것의 수를 세었다. 그리고 그는 투표용지와 총계를 퇴임하는 회장인 Dave Hamilton에게 건넸다. (c) 그(=Dave Hamilton)는 미소 지으며 말했다. "이건 아주 놀랄 만한데. 한 명만 빼고 모든 회원들이 우리의 다음 동아리 회장인 Kevin Moore에게 투표했어. ④ 축하해, Kevin." Kevin은 행복하게 미소 지었다. (d) 그(=Kevin)는 자기가 양심에 귀 기울였던 것이 기뻤다.

구문 [(C) 5행~6행] All members **but** one / have voted for Kevin Moore, our next club president.
주어는 All members but one이다. 여기서 but은 전치사로 except(~을 제외하고)의 의미이다. 콤마(,)를 사이에 두고 Kevin Moore와 our next club president는 동격 관계를 나타낸다.

[(D) 4행~5행] **If only** he **had voted** for himself then!
'~ 했다면 좋았을 텐데'의 뜻을 지닌 「if only+가정법 과거완료」 구문이다.
e.g. **If only** I **had met** her then. (그때 내가 그녀를 만났다면 좋았을 텐데.)

어휘 **(A) rehearse** 예행연습하다 **run for** 입후보하다 **tie** 동점이 되다 **(B) secretary** 서기; 비서 **give out** 나눠 주다 **bite (bit-bitten)** (이빨로) 물다 **nervously** 초조하게; 신경질적으로 **print** (글씨를) 인쇄체로 쓰다; 인쇄하다 **conscience** 양심 **deserve** ~을 누릴 자격이 있다 **pass in** 제출하다, 건네다 **(C) retiring** 퇴임하는 **remarkable** 놀랄 만한, 주목할 만한 **(D) election** 선거 **candidate** 후보자 **opponent** 상대(방); 반대자, 적

실전 모의고사 05

본문 p.69

18 ① 19 ② 20 ③ 21 ④ 22 ② 23 ④ 24 ③ 25 ⑤ 26 ④ 27 ⑤
28 ② 29 ⑤ 30 ④ 31 ② 32 ⑤ 33 ⑤ 34 ⑤ 35 ③ 36 ① 37 ③
38 ④ 39 ④ 40 ④ 41 ③ 42 ② 43 ③ 44 ① 45 ③

18 글의 목적 ①

소재 동반 가족 여행 제안

해설 도입에서 가족 여행을 제안하게 된 배경을 밝힌 후, 두 가족이 함께 야구 명예의 전당으로 휴가를 가자는 제안을 하면서 해당 여행 패키지에 대해 자세하게 설명하고 있으므로, 글의 목적으로 가장 적절한 것은 ①이다.

해석 Brianna에게,
네가 보낸 지난번 이메일을 읽는 건 아주 좋았어. 난 특히 해변에서의 네 가족사진을 즐겁게 보았지. 그것은 즐거운 시간처럼 보였고, 내게 우리 두 가족이 함께 만난 지 그저 얼마나 오래됐는지를 상기시켜줬어. 주제문 그걸 바로잡기 위해서 난 내셔널 야구 명예의 전당으로의 여행을 제안하고 싶어. Brad는 이것에 대해 쉬지 않고 이야기해왔고, 아이들 역시 매우 신이 나 있어. 거기엔 아이들이 직접 해보는 활동뿐만 아니라 가족들이 과거 선수들의 물건 사이에서 잘 수 있게 해주는, 7~12세 아이들을 위한 하룻밤짜리 패키지도 있어. 나는 네 가족 중에도 야구팬이 몇 명 있다는 것을 알고 있기 때문에, 이건 우리들이 즐겁게 무언가를 같이 할 수 있는 훌륭한 기회인 것 같아. 조기 등록 할인이 있으니 관심 있으면 내게 빨리 알려줘.
친구, Sarah

구문 [4행~6행] ~ it **reminded** me(A) **of** just how long it's been // since our two families got together(B).
「remind A of B」는 'A에게 B를 상기시키다'의 뜻이다. B의 자리에 간접의문문이 쓰였다.
[9행~12행] They have *overnight packages* (for children ages 7-12) [that **let** *families* **sleep** / among the artifacts of past players], **as well as** *hands-on activities* (for the kids).
[ ] 부분은 overnight packages를 수식하며, 「사역동사(let)+O+원형부정사(O가 ~하게 하다)」 구문이 사용되었다. 「A as well as B」는 'B뿐만 아니라 A도'의 뜻이다.

어휘 **get together** 만나다 **in the interest of** ~을 위하여 **correct** 바로잡다; 수정하다 **suggest** 제안하다; 시사[암시]하다 **the Hall of Fame** 명예의 전당 **overnight** 하룻밤 동안의 **artifact** 공예품, 인공물 **hands-on** 직접 해보는 **registration** 등록

19 심경 변화 ②

소재 노숙자를 오해한 일화

해설 필자는 항상 자신을 이상하게 쳐다보던 노숙자가 다가오자 공격을 당하진 않을지 겁을 먹었지만(scared), 그 노숙자의 죽은 동생이 자신과 닮아서 쳐다보았다는 것을 알게 된 후 터무니없는 오해를 했다는 죄책감(guilty)에 가슴이 내려앉았던 상황이다. 따라서 정답은 ② '겁먹은 → 죄책감이 드는'이다.

해석 시장에 가는 길에 나는 전에 수십 번 본 적이 있는 여자 노숙자를 보았다. 주제문 그녀는 자신이 항상 하는 그 이상한 방식으로 나를 쳐다보고 있어서 나는 속도를 내기 시작했다. 항상 그녀가 나에게서 무언가를 원하는 것처럼 보였다. 그때 그녀가 나를 향해 걸어오기 시작했다. 나는 재빠르게 머리를 굴리기 시작했다. 그녀가 날 공격하진 않을 거야, 그렇지? 그녀가 충분히 가까이 왔을 때, 그녀는 "이봐요, 미안해요, 당신을 당황하게 하려는 건 아니었어요."라고 말했다. 그리고 나서 나와 닮은 한 여자의 오래된 사진을 꺼냈다. 그녀는 "제 동생 Claire에요. 그 애는 10년 전에 죽었어요. 당신은 그 애와 꼭 닮았어요. 전 동생이 정말 그리워요."라고 설명했다. 괴로움 속에 있는 사람에 대해 내가 그런 끔찍한 일들을 생각했다는 것을 깨달았을 때, 주제문 나는 가슴이 내려앉았다. 집에서조차도 그녀의 슬퍼 보이는 눈을 잊을 수 없었다.
① 당황한 → 들뜬 ③ 행복한 → 겁에 질린
④ 차분한 → 놀란 ⑤ 걱정스러운 → 안도한

구문 [2행~4행] She was looking at me in *that odd way* [(that) she always did], // so I started to speed up.
생략된 관계부사 that이 이끄는 절이 that odd way를 수식한다.

어휘 **on one's way to A** A로 가는 길에 **homeless** 노숙자(의) **dozens of** 수십 번의; 많은 **odd** 이상한, 특이한 **toward** ~쪽으로, ~을 향하여 **sink** 내려앉다, 가라앉다; 싱크대 **horrible** 끔찍한, 소름 끼치는

20 필자 주장 ③

소재 상황에 따라 상대적인 사람의 장단점

해설 사람의 장점과 단점은 절대적인 것이 아니라 상황에 따라 다르게 이해될 수 있으므로 사람을 단정 짓지 말고 그 이면을 보아야 한다는 내용으로, 마지막에서 두 번째 문장(So it is important ~ and assets.)에 필자의 주장이 잘 나타나 있다. 따라서 정답은 ③이다.

해석 모든 상황에 완벽하게 딱 맞는 사람은 없을 것이다. 주제문 어떤 상황에서는 장점인 성격적 특성이 또 다른 상황에서는 단점으로 여겨질 수 있고 또 그 반대일 수도 있다. 예를 들어, 한 일터에서 신중하고 꼼꼼한 일 처리로 칭찬받는 사람들이 다른 일터에서는 따분하고 모험심이 없다고 비난받는 그들 자신을 발견할 수도 있다. 또는 많은 평범한 상황에서 지나치게 저돌적이라고 여겨지는 친구가 위급 상황에서는 영웅이 될 수도 있다. 모든 사람은 자신만의 강점과 약점을 가지고 있는데 이것은 절대적인 것이 아니다. 대신 그것들은 상황과 관련이 있다. 주제문 그러므로 모든 사람의 약점과 강점의 이면을 보는 것이 중요하다. 항상 다른 사람들의 약점을 찾아내어 (그것에만) 초점을 맞추는 사람들은 친구나 추종자가 거의 없을 것이다.

구문 [4행~8행] *Those*(S) [**who** are admired for their deliberate and careful handling of things / in one workplace], for example, / may find(V) *themselves*(O) **criticized**(C) as boring and unadventurous / in another workplace.
who가 이끄는 관계대명사절이 Those를 제한하여 주어가 길어지고, 동사인 find가 목적어와 목적격보어를 취한 SVOC 구조이다. '그들 자신이 비난 받는 것'이므로 목적어와 목적격보어의 수동 관계를 나타내기 위해 목적격보어로 과거분사가 쓰였다.

어휘 **fit in** 꼭 맞다, 적합하다 **personality** 성격, 개성 **trait** 특성 **merit** 장점, 강점(= **strong point, asset**) **circumstance** 상황, 환경 **shortcoming** 단점, 결점(= **weak point, drawback**) **vice versa** 반대도 또한 같음 **admire** 칭찬하다; 감탄하다 *cf.* **admirer** 추종자; 숭배자 **deliberate** 신중한, 사려 깊은; 계획[의도]적인 **handling** 처리; 취급 **unadventurous** 모험심이 없는 **aggressive** 저돌적인, 적극적인; 공격적인 **ordinary** 평범한, 일반적인 **absolute** 절대적인 것; 절대적인, 완전한 **relative to A** A와 관계있는[관련된] **dig out** ~을 찾아내다; ~을 파내다

21 글의 요지 ④

소재 온라인 소비자 상품평의 기능

해설 소비자가 상품평을 통해 적극적으로 의견을 개진하기 때문에 기업들이 소비자들의 불만을 사지 않도록 더 좋은 제품과 서비스를 제공하려고 노력한다는 내용이므로 글의 요지로 적절한 것은 ④이다.

해석 중요한 구매를 하기 전에는, 소비자들이 판매 중인 상품에 대한 개인적인 상품평을 올릴 수 있게 하는 웹사이트들을 이용하라. 요즘 점점 더 많은 사람들이 피자에서 호화로운 차에 이르기까지 어떤 것에 대해서든지 상품평을 올리고 있다. 이 상품평들은 독립적이기 때문에 우호적이든 부정적이든 넓은 범위의 의견을 반영한다. 인터넷상에서 특정 회사나 제품에 대한 보편적인 의견을 얻을 수 있는 곳을 쉽게 찾을 수 있다. 주제문 이런 소비자 포럼(=토론회)은 실제로 제품이나 회사의 평판과 매출에 강력한 영향을 미칠 수 있다. 회사들은 이제 소비자는 늘 옳다는 말이 정말로 무엇을 의미하는지를 이해하고 있다. 그들은 온라인상에 불만이 올라올 가능성을 줄이기 위해 더 좋은 제품을 만들고 더 좋은 서비스를 제공하려고 노력한다.

구문 [7행~10행] It's easy to find *places* (on the Internet) [***where*** you can get *an idea* (of the general opinion about a particular company or product)].
가주어 진주어

It은 가주어이며 to find 이하가 진주어이다. where ~ product는 places를 수식하는 관계부사절이다.

[12행~13행] Companies now understand / **what** it really means to say // **that** the customer is always right.
가주어 진주어

what 이하는 understand의 목적어 역할을 하는 명사절이며, 명사절 내에 「가주어(it)-진주어(to say ~)」 구문이 쓰였다. that은 say의 목적어인 명사절을 이끄는 접속사이다.

어휘 **significant** 중요한, 중대한 **take advantage of** ~을 이용[활용]하다 **post** (인터넷상에 정보 · 메시지 등을) 게시하다 **review** 비평, 평론 **luxurious** 호화로운, 사치스러운 **whether A or B** A이든지 B이든지 **favorable** 우호적인, 호의적인(↔ **unfavorable** 비우호적인) **particular** 특정한 **forum** 포럼, 공개 토론(회) **have an effect on** ~에 영향을 미치다 **reputation** 평판, 명성

22 글의 주제 ②

소재 새롭게 밝혀진 맹장의 역할

해설 유익한 박테리아를 보호해주는 맹장의 새로운 역할이 밝혀졌음을 알리고 그에 대해 상술하고 있으므로, 이 글의 주제로 가장 적절한 것은 ② '맹장에 대해 밝혀진 새로운 발견'이다.

해석 작은 벌레처럼 대장에 붙어 있는 맹장은 소화에는 아무런 영향도 미치지 않는 것처럼 보인다. 사실, 오랫동안 과학자들은 맹장이 왜 만들어졌는지 설명할 수 없었다. 주제문 하지만 Duke 대학의 Parker 박사와 그의 팀은 맹장이 우리의 장기를 보호하는 막을 만드는 중요하고 유익한 박테리아의 '안전 가옥'이라고 주장한다. 그에 의하면, 인간의 맹장은 좋은 박테리아를 위한 대체 저장소로서 역할을 한다. 맹장의 모양은 박테리아를 위한 안전한 장소로서 더할 나위 없이 적합하다. 그래서 장에 심한 통증을 유발하는, (유익한) 박테리아를 죽이는 질병에 걸린 경우에는, 아주 많은 박테리아의 부대가 맹장에 피해 있다가 나중에 다시 장을 채운다. Parker 박사는 "이러한 종류의 질병이 흔한 곳에서 무해한 박테리아를 보유할 맹장이 없다면, 당신은 생존에 유리한 점을 덜 가지고 있다는 것이다."라고 말한다.

① 맹장에 존재하는 박테리아의 다양한 역할
③ 맹장의 정확한 모양과 위치
④ 맹장의 순기능과 역기능
⑤ 맹장의 기능에 대한 논란

구문 [14행] "**Where** this kind of disease is common," ~.
여기서 where는 장소의 부사절을 이끄는 접속사로 사용되어 '~하는 곳에서'로 해석한다.

어휘 **attached** 부착된, 첨부된 **intestine** 장, 창자 **digestion** 소화(력) **claim** 주장하다; 요구[요청]하다 **beneficial** 유익한, 이로운 **film** (얇은) 막 **back-up** 대체의, 예비의 **suited** 적합한, 알맞은 **in the event of** 만일 ~의 경우에는 **severe** 심각한, 극심한 **concentration** 집단; 집중; 농도 **shelter** 피하다; 피난처 [선택지 어휘] **reveal** 밝히다, 드러내다 **accurate** 정확한 **adverse** 역(逆)의, 거스르는 **controversy** 논란; 논쟁

23 글의 제목 ④

소재 도시의 진보성과 미래성

해설 도시는 시골보다 수십 년 앞서 있으며 더 많은 기회, 자유, 선택권을 제공하므로, '타임머신을 타지 않고' 미래 여행을 하는 최선의 방법은 진보적인 도시로 이주하는 것이라는 내용의 글이다. 도시의 진보성과 미래성을 제시한 글이므로 제목으로 가장 적절한 것은 ④ '도시는 미래가 일어나는 곳이다'이다.

해석 내가 아는 사람 중에 아직 미래를 사는 방법을 찾은 이는 없다. 아마 언젠가 우리는 100년 후의 미래로 휴가를 떠날 수 있게 해주는 비싸지 않은 타임머신을 발명할지도 모른다. 주제문 바로 지금 우리가 '내일'(오늘보다 단지 약간 더 나은 곳)을 살고자 한다면 우리가 할 수 있는 최선은 지구상의 가장 진취적인 도시에서 사는 것이다. 증대된 기회와 가능성이 있는 도시에서 말이다. 매일 백만 명의 사람들이 시골을 떠나 도시로 이동하는데, 이는 공간(여행)이라기보다는 시간여행인 여정이다. 이러한 이주자들은 정말로 수십 년 앞으로 이동하고 있으며, 옛 마을에서 21세기의 제멋대로 뻗어나가는 도시 지역으로 이전한다. 빈민가의 해악은 대단히 눈에 띄지만 (사람들의) 도래를 멈추지는 못한다. 그들은 우리 모두가 그러하듯이, 전에는 가져본 적 없는 더 많은 자유와 선택을 찾아 계속해서 온다. 이것이 우리가 사는 곳에서 우리가 사는 방식으로 살아가는 이유이다. 더 많은 선택을 갖기 위해서 말이다.

① 우리는 미래에 어떻게 살 것인가
② 시간 여행: 새로운 관점
③ 우리가 사는 매일이 미래다
⑤ 인구, 도시화, 그리고 삶의 질

구문 [4행~7행] Right now, if we want to live in 'tomorrow'—*that place* [which is just a little better than today]—// *the best* [(that) we can do] is **live** in the most forward-looking city on Earth.
the best we can do와 같이 do로 끝나는 주어 다음에 is가 오면 그다음에 to부정사보다는 원형부정사를 사용하는 경향이 있기 때문에 보어 자리에 to live를 쓰지 않고 live를 썼다.

[8행~10행] Every day, a million people move from the countryside into cities, *a journey* [that is **less** a trip in space **than** in time].
[ ] 부분은 a journey를 수식하는 관계사절이며, 「less A than B」는 'A라기보다는 B'의 의미이다.

어휘 **forward-looking** 진취적인, 진보적인 **migrant** 이주자 **decades of** 수십의 **relocate** 이전[이동]하다 **sprawling** 제멋대로 뻗어나가는 **urban** 도시의 **ill** 문제, 해악 **slum** 빈민가 **arrival** 도래, 도착 **option** 선택(권), 선택의 자유

24 도표 이해 ③

소재 고객 집단에 따른 대학 서점 서적 판매량

해설 논픽션 서적을 가장 적게 구입한 것은 대학생이 아니라 대학 교직원이므로 ③이 도표와 일치하지 않는다.

해석 〈고객 집단에 따른 대학 서점 판매량〉

주제문 이 표는 한 달 동안 대학 서점에서 서로 다른 집단의 고객들에 의해 팔린 품목의 종류를 보여준다. 이 그래프에 따르면, 각 집단은 뚜렷하게 다른 선호도를 갖는다. ① 북 클럽 회원들과 비회원들은 대략 비슷한 수의 소설을 구입했다. ② 그러나 논픽션 서적의 판매량은 고객 집단에 따라 상당히 달랐다. ③ 북 클럽 회원들은 논픽션 도서를 가장 많이 구입했고, 대학생들은 가장 적게 구입했다. ④ 세 개 부문의 품목 중에서 잡지가 가장 많이 팔렸고, 대부분은 대학생에 의해 구입되었다. ⑤ 전반적으로 가장 많이 구입한 사람들은 대학생이었고, 두 번째로 북 클럽 회원들, 그리고 대학 교직원이 뒤를 이었다.

어휘 **distinctively** (뚜렷이) 다른 것과 달리; 독특하게 **roughly** 개략적으로, 대충 **non-fiction** (집합적) 논픽션(소설이나 허구의 이야기가 아닌 전기, 역사, 기행문, 수필 등) **significantly** 상당히, 두드러지게 **followed by** 뒤이어, 잇달아

25 내용 불일치 ⑤

소재 멕시코의 Dia de Muertos(죽은 자의 날) 축제

해설 마지막 문장을 보면 죽은 이들이 입었던 옷을 입고 행진하는 것이 아니라, 죽음의 분위기가 나는 인물로 분장하고 행진하는 것이므로 ⑤가 글의 내용과 일치하지 않는다.

해석 주제문 *Dia de Muertos*('죽은 자의 날')는 멕시코의 가장 중요한 축제 중 하나이다. ① 가족들은 고인이 되어 버린 사랑하는 사람들에 대한 추억을 기리고, 고인은 가족들을 다시 보기 위해 영혼으로 지상에 돌아오는 날이다. ② 어린아이로 죽은 이들은 첫 날에, 성인의 영혼은 둘째 날에 방문한다. 그들을 환영하기 위해 가족들은 집안을 치우고 꽃, 양초, 사탕, 사진, 고인이 좋아했던 음식을 담은 접시 등을 준비한다. ③ 심지어 어떤 가족들은 영혼 방문객이 먹기 전에 씻을 수 있도록 수건과 비누를 진열해둔다. 이는 또한 멕시코인들이 ④ 가족묘에 찾아가 묘를 정돈하고 꾸미고, 종종 남아 밤새 묘를 지키기도 하는 때이다. 낮이 되면 음악과 춤, 그리고 ⑤ 유령, 악마, 다른 죽음의 분위기가 나는 인물들처럼 옷을 입은 사람들의 행진이 있는 시끌벅적한 길거리 파티가 열린다.

구문 [5행~6행] *Those* [who died as children] visit on the first day, / the spirits of adults (visit) on the second.
the spirits of adults와 on the second 사이에는 반복되는 동사 visit가 생략되었다.

[9행~11행] Some families even set out towels and soap // **so that** a spirit visitor can wash / before eating.
여기서 so that은 '목적'을 나타내는 부사절을 이끌어 '~하기 위해, ~하도록'이란 뜻으로 해석한다.

어휘 **deceased** 사망한; (the ~) 고인(故人) **grave** 무덤, 묘 **throughout** ~ 동안 내내 **uproarious** 시끌벅적한 **themed** 특정한 테마[시대]의 분위기를 살린

26 안내문 불일치 ④

소재 요리 잡지 구독 안내

해설 Regional Favorites에서 지방의 잘 알려지지 않은 요리를 소개한다고 했으므로 ④가 안내문과 일치하지 않는다.

해석

Cooking Country
여러분의 무료 증정본을 요청하세요!

① 〈Cooking Country〉 무료 증정본을 받아보세요. 마음에 드시면 ② 1년 동안 (증정본을 포함하여 6권) 19달러만 지불하시게 되는데, 그러면 가판대에서 사는 가격인 35달러의 45퍼센트가 절약됩니다.

모든 발행 호에
- **보장된 간편한 요리:** 손쉬운 평일 저녁 식사를 준비하세요.
- **사라졌던 요리법:** ③ 이제는 영원히 사라졌다고 생각했던 요리법을 찾으세요. 현대 요리사가 더 쉽게 만들 수 있게 되어 있습니다.
- **지방의 맛있는 요리:** ④ 전국에 있는 잘 알려지지 않은 지방의 특별 요리를 소개받으세요.
- ⑤ **객관적인 요리 기구 평가와 등급:** 어떤 브랜드나 모델을 사야 할지, 그리고 어떤 것을 피해야 할지에 관한 정보를 찾아보세요.

여기를 클릭해서 여러분의 구독 정보와 함께 성명과 주소를 입력하세요.

구문 [11행~13행] **Lost Recipes:** Find *recipes* [(that[which]) (you thought) were gone forever], // **which** have been made easier for the modern cook
recipes를 수식하는 관계사절에 주격 관계대명사가 생략되었다. think, hope 등의 동사를 포함한 삽입절 앞에 오는 주격 관계대명사는 종종 생략된다. which가 이끄는 계속적 용법의 관계대명사 절이 recipes를 부연 설명한다.

어휘 **trial** 시험적인; 견본의 **issue** (잡지 등의) 발간 호 **newsstand** 신문 가판대 **guarantee** 보장하다, 보증하다 **regional** 지방의, 지역적인 **specialty** 특산품; 자랑할 만한 물건; 전문, 전공 **objective** 객관적인 **equipment** 장비, 기기 **rating** 등급; 평가 **subscription** 구독(료)

27 안내문 일치 ⑤

소재 햇볕으로 인한 화상 치료법

해설 911에 전화해야 하는 두 가지 경우 중 첫 번째가 치료에 반응이 없는 경우이므로 ⑤가 안내문의 내용과 일치한다.

해석

햇볕으로 인한 화상 치료

1. 수분을 보충하세요
- ① 물, 주스, 스포츠 음료로 신체 수분을 보충하세요.

2. 증상을 치료하세요
- ② 알로에나 처방전 없이 살 수 있는 보습 로션을 지시에 따라 피부에 바르세요.
- 피부를 진정시키고 열을 내리기 위해서 ③ 미지근한 물로 씻거나 (화상) 부위에 시원한 습포를 두르세요.

다음의 경우에는 의료인에게 전화하세요:
- 화상으로 물집이 생기거나 ④ 피부가 마비되거나 하얗게 보이면, 이것들은 더 심각한 햇볕에 의한 화상 증상들입니다.
- 햇볕으로 인한 화상을 입은 사람이 한 살 이하의 어린이일 때.

환자가 다음과 같은 경우에는 911에 전화하세요:
- ⑤ 치료에 적절하게 반응하지 못하는 것처럼 보일 때
- 발작, 시력 변화 또는 다른 신경계 증상이 있는 경우

어휘 **sunburn** 햇볕으로 인한 화상 **treatment** 치료 *cf.* **treat** 치료하다 **rehydrate** 다시 수분을 보충하다 **body fluids** 체액 **symptom** 증상 **apply** (연고를) 바르다; 지원하다 **over-the-counter** 처방전 없이 살 수 있는 **moisturizing** 보습의 **as directed** 지시대로 **soothe** 진정시키다, 달래다 **lukewarm** 미지근한 **compress** 습포, 압박붕대 **numb** 마비된, 감각을 잃은 **seizure** 발작 **neurological** 신경계의

28 네모 어법 ②

소재 판소리

해설 (A) 문장의 주어는 *Pansori*, 동사는 is이다. 접속사 없이 문장의 동사가 또 나올 수 없으므로 분사구문을 이끄는 과거분사 referred가 적절하다.
(B) 문맥상 네모 안의 대명사는 pansori를 의미하므로 단수형(it)을 사용해야 한다.
(C) 네모 안의 관계대명사는 문맥상 앞 절 전체(These people were looked down on by the Joseon gentry)를 의미하므로 앞부분의 전체 내용을 받을 수 있는 계속적 용법의 관계대명사 which가 적절하다.

해석 때로 '한국의 오페라'라고도 불리는 판소리는, 조선시대(1392~1910) 중기에 처음 탄생한 음악적 이야기 서술 방식인 한국의 민속 전통이다. 공연은 무대 위에서 함께 서사적 서술 기법의 이야기를 들려주는 한 명의 창자(唱者)와 한 명의 고수(鼓手)를 특징으로 한다. 판소리를 최초로 창작한 사람이 누구인지, 그리고 정확히 몇 년도에 판소리가 출현했는지는 알려져 있지 않다. 그것(= 판소리)은 전문 예능인에 의해 채택된 구전(口傳)에서 시작되었다. 이들은 조선의 양반 계층에게 멸시를 받았는데, 아마도 이것이 판소리가 오랫동안 농민들의 전유물로 남아 있던 이유를 설명해줄 것이다. 조선 후기 양반 계층에서 예술 형식에 보인 (판소리에 대한) 관심 증대로 판소리의 청중은 확대되었으며, 2003년 유네스코는 판소리를 세계 무형 문화유산의 뛰어난 본보기로 공식 인정했다.

어휘 **folk** 민속의; 민중의 **refer to A as B** A를 B라고 부르다 **emerge** 등장하다, 나타나다 *cf.* **emergence** 출현, 발생 **dynasty** 왕조; 시대 **epic** 서사시의, 서사시적인 **identity** 신원, 정체; 독자성; 유사성 **oral** 구전의, 구두의; 입의 **adopt** 채택하다; 입양하다 **look down on** ~을 멸시[경멸]하다 **preserve** 전유물; 저장 식품; 보존하다 **peasant** 농부, 소작농 **recognize A as B** A를 B로 인정[공인]하다 **outstanding** 뛰어난, 두드러진 **intangible** 무형의; 손으로 만질 수 없는(↔ **tangible** 유형의; 손으로 만질 수 있는) **heritage** 유산

29 밑줄 어휘 ⑤

소재 문화마다 다른 대화와 침묵의 의미

해설 말을 통해서 감정과 생각을 표현하는 문화와는 대조적으로, 무언의 방식으로 의사소통하는 문화에서는 많은 말이 필요하지 않으므로 ⑤는 unnecessary로 바꾸어야 한다.

해석 주제문 대화와 침묵의 의미는 문화마다 ① 다르다. 나는 언젠가 방콕에서 현지 직원들에게 발표한 적이 있다. 나는 발표가 성공적일 거라 확신했지만, 어떤 이유에서인지 그렇지 않았다. 직원들은 나를 ② 멍하니 응시하며 그저 미소지었다. 아무도 질문하지 않았다. 나는 내 발표가 활발한 토론을 일으킬 거라 예상했었지만, 대신에 ③ 어색한 침묵이 흘렀다. 타이(= 태국)의 방식을 조금 더 알아간 후에, 나는 직원들이 내가 말을 너무 많이 했다고 생각했다는 것을 깨달았다. 우리나라 문화에서, 우리는 주로 말을 통해 의미를 표현한다. 우리는 우리가 느끼고 생각하는 것을 표현하기 위해 상당히 말을 많이 하며, 침묵은 우리를 ④ 긴장하게 만든다. 몇몇 다른 문화의 사람들은 맥락을 통해 무슨 일이 일어나고 있는지를 상당히 이해하고, 보통 말을 많이 하는 것이 ⑤ 필요하다(→ 불필요하다)고 느낀다. 사람들은 무언의 방식으로 의사소통한다.

구문 [8행~9행] **After getting** to know Thai ways better, / I realized // (= After I got ~)
that the staff thought // O′(**that**) I had talked too much.
O

After getting 이하는 의미를 명확히 하기 위해 접속사를 남겨둔 분사구문이다. that이 이끄는 절들이 각각 realized와 thought의 목적어로 쓰였다.

어휘 **silence** 침묵; 고요 **vary** 각기 다르다, 달라지다 **local** 현지의, 지역의 **stare at** ~을 응시하다[쳐다보다] **blankly** 멍하니 **lively** 활발한, 활기 넘치는 **mainly** 주로, 대부분 **a great deal** 상당히, 많이 **context** 맥락, 전후 사정 **unspoken** 무언의, 말로 하지 않는

30 지칭 대상 ④

소재 무대 공포증

해설 ④는 대중 앞에서 말하는 것(public speaking)을 가리키고, 나머지는 모두 무대 공포증(stage fright)을 가리킨다.

해석 사람들 앞에서 말을 할 때 느끼는 두려움은 때로 '무대 공포증'이라 불린다. 주제문 ① 그것(=무대 공포증)은 전체 인구의 75퍼센트나 되는 사람들에게 영향을 미치는 것으로, 단일 공포증으로는 가장 흔한 것으로 생각된다. 심지어 ② 그것(=무대 공포증)은 죽음에 대한 공포보다도 더 높은 순위를 차지한다고들 한다. 미국의 유명 코미디언 Jerry Seinfeld는 ③ 그것(=무대 공포증)에 관해 다음과 같은 농담을 했다. "장례식에 참석한 일반인들은 추도문을 낭독하는 것보다는 차라리 관에 들어가 있길 바란다." 하지만 많은 직업이 고객이나 동료에게 발표하는 것과 같은 어느 정도의 연설 능력을 요구한다. 대중 앞에서 말을 하는 능력은 때때로 개인이 보유할 수 있는 가장 유용한 기술들 가운데 하나로 간주된다. 대부분의 위대한 연설가는 ④ 그것(=대중 앞에서 말하는 것)에 대해 타고난 능력을 갖고 있지만, 그렇다고 해서 그들이 무대 공포증도 겪지 않는다는 뜻은 아니며, 위대한 연설가와 형편없는 연설가의 차이점은 무대 공포증이 생길 때 ⑤ 그것(=무대 공포증)을 통제하는 방법을 아느냐에 있다.

어휘 **public speaking** (대중) 연설 **stage fright** 무대 공포증 *cf.* **fright** 두려움, 공포 **phobia** 공포증, 병적인 공포 **affect** 영향을 미치다 **rank** (순위를) 차지하다[매기다]; 등급; 계급 **average** 일반적인, 보통의; 평균의 **funeral** 장례식 **coffin** 관 **make[give] a presentation** 발표하다 **colleague** 동료 **valuable** 유용한, 가치 있는 **possess** 보유하다, 소유하다 **suffer** 겪다; 고통 받다

31 빈칸 추론 ②

소재 수준별 교육 정책의 결함

해설 빈칸 뒤에 이어지는 내용이 능력별로 학생들을 나누는 영국 총리의 교육 정책이 갖는 문제점을 지적하는 것이므로 ② '결함'이 빈칸에 가장 적절하다.

해석 주제문 Sussex 대학의 교육 전문가들은 영국 총리의 교육 정책에 중대한 결함이 있음을 발견하였다. 그 교육 정책은 주요 과목에서 능력별 그룹화를 기준으로 하는 것을 목표로 한다. 개별적으로 이루어진 두 가지 새로운 연구는 학생들을 그룹화하여 조직하는 것은 불공평하고 능력을 평가하는 정확한 수단도 아니라는 것을 보여주었다. Sussex 대학의 교육학 교수인 Jo Boaler가 행한 연구는 능력별 그룹에 속한 학생들보다 능력이 혼재된 수학 교실의 학생들의 수행 능력이 더 좋았다는 것을 밝혀냈다. Sussex의 연구원들에 의한 다른 새 연구는 아이들이 사회적 배경에 따라서 그룹에 배정되고 있다는 것을 보여주었다. 이전의 학업 성취와 상관없이, 중산층 가정의 학생들이 우등반에 배치될 가능성이 더 컸다.

① 이익 ③ 통찰력 ④ 변화 ⑤ 놀라움

어휘 **norm** 기준; 표준 **accurate** 정확한 **means** 수단, 방법 **assess** 평가하다 **reveal** 밝히다, 드러내다 **outperform** 능가하다, ~보다 성능이 낫다 **assign** 지정하다; 할당하다 **pupil** 학생, 제자; (눈의) 동공 **irrespective of** ~에 상관없이 **prior** 이전의 **scholastic** 학문적인, 학교의 **achievement** 성취; 업적

32 빈칸 추론 ⑤

소재 자신의 거울 이미지의 유무가 부정을 저지르는 데 미치는 영향

해설 본문의 실험에서 테스트를 수행하는 동안 자신의 모습을 봐야 했던 피실험자들은 부정을 저지르는 비율이 현저히 낮았으므로, 자기 자신의 모습인 거울 이미지는 그들에게 ⑤ '도덕 경찰이 된다'고 말할 수 있다.

해석 1970년대 중반에 두 명의 사회심리학자들이 어떤 큰 대학의 학생들에게 그들의 생각의 복잡성을 측정하도록 고안된 짧은 테스트를 완료하는 데 5분을 사용해줄 것을 요청했다. 학생들은 일련의 애너그램(철자 순서를 바꾼 어구)을 해독해야 했지만, 그들은 전체 시리즈를 할당된 5분의 시간 내에 끝마칠 방도가 없었다. 연구자는 학생들에게 5분이 지나면 벨이 울릴 것이며, 벨이 울린 다음에는 부정행위가 될 것이므로 작업을 계속해선 안 된다고 말했다. 일부 학생들은 큰 거울의 맞은편에서 테스트를 마친 반면 다른 학생들은 애너그램 작업을 하는 동안 자기 자신의 모습을 볼 수 없었다. 그 동안에 실험자는 일방 유리를 통해 지켜보며 몇 명의 학생들이 5분 종소리가 난 후에도 계속해서 작업하는지를 셌다. 결과는 놀라웠다. 자신의 모습을 거울을 통해 본 학생들 중 오직 7퍼센트만이 부정을 저지른 반면, 71퍼센트라는 대규모의 사람들이 정직하게 행동할지 결정할 때 자신의 모습을 보도록 강제되지 않았을 때 부정을 저질렀다. 주제문 사람들이 나쁜 행동을 할 것을 생각할 때, 그들의 거울 이미지는 도덕 경찰이 된다.

① 상호 역전된다
② 갈등을 일으키는 경향이 있다
③ 모든 방식으로 그들을 왜곡한다
④ 다른 페르소나를 반영한다

구문 [5행~7행] ~ but there was *no way* [they could finish the entire series / within the allotted five-minute period].

[ ]는 관계부사절로 앞에 의미상 how가 생략되어 no way를 수식한다. way와 how는 함께 쓸 수 없어 둘 중 하나가 생략되었다.

어휘 **unscramble** 해독하다, 순서를 맞추다 **allot** 할당하다 **across from** ~의 바로 맞은편에 **astonishing** 놀라운 **massive** 대규모의, 거대한 [선택지 어휘] **mutually** 상호간에, 서로 **reverse** 역전시키다, 뒤집다 **distort** 왜곡하다 **persona** (심리) 페르소나, 외적 인격 (가면을 쓴 인격) **moral** 도덕의

33 빈칸 추론 ⑤

소재 익명을 사용하는 이유

해설 빈칸이 포함된 문장 이후에, 세월이 흐르면서 인용문의 초기 저자에 관한 정보가 훼손되는 과정에서 익명성이 생겨나게 되었음을 설명하고 있다. 따라서 빈칸에 가장 적절한 것은 ⑤ '소유권에 대한 정보가 점차 훼손되면서'이다.

해석 주제문 사람들은 여러 가지 이유로 이름을 밝히지 않으려 노력한다. 그중 어떤 이유는 사람들이 투표할 때와 같이 합법적이다. 또 다른 이유는 범죄자들이 범죄를 저지르거나 체포를 면하려고 가명을 쓰는 경우처럼 불법적이고 비도덕적이다. 또 다른 종류의 익명성은 개인의 선택으로 인해서가 아닌 소유권에 대한 정보가 점차 훼손되면서 생겨난다. 이것은 특히 인용문에 발생한다. 많은 인용문들이 알려진 저자가 없어, '작자 불명의'라고 서명되어 있다. 이러한 인용문들은 모두 단 한 명의 저자가 있는 원문에서 시작했던 것이 분명하나, 수십 년 혹은 심지어 수백 년이 지나면서 저자의 이름이 잘못 표기되고 생략되고 변경되어서 결국에 모두 사라지게 된 것 같다. 또는 그 인용문 자체가 현대에 와서 원문의 글귀들이나 아이디어가 '자신의 것'이라고 주장할 수 없었던 여러 사람에 의해 약간 변형되었을 수도 있다. 이러한 과정을 거쳐 그 인용문은 '작자 불명의'라고 쓰이게 된 것이다.

① 듣거나 보지 않는 척하면서
② 판매를 위해 원본을 베끼면서
③ 지금에 와서 현대적으로 변형되면서
④ 관련 시민 단체의 노력에서

구문 [5행~7행] Another kind of anonymity is n't created by an individual's choices (A) but (is created) by a gradual eroding of ownership information (B).

「not A but B」는 'A가 아니라 B'라는 뜻의 상관접속사이다. 이때 A와 B는 문법적으로 같은 성격이 되어야 한다. 반복되는 is created가 생략되어 B의 자리에 by가 이끄는 전명구만 남은 형태이다.

[9행~13행] Each of these quotations **must have started** out / as an original with a single author, // but ~ the author's name **may have been misspelled**, **omitted**, **changed**, and then finally **lost** altogether.

「must have p.p.」는 '~했음에 틀림없다'란 뜻으로 과거에 대한 강한 추측을 나타내며, 「may have p.p.」 역시 과거에 대한 추측을 나타내나 '~했을[였을] 것이다'란 뜻으로 「must have p.p.」보다는 확신의 정도가 약하다. 「may have been p.p.」는 '수동'의 의미를 나타내며 4개의 과거분사가 and로 연결되어 있는 구조이다.

어휘 **anonymous** 익명의; 작자 불명의 *cf.* **anonymity** 익명성 **lawful** 합법적인(↔ **illegal** 불법의) **immoral** 비도덕적인 **criminal** 범죄자 **commit a crime** 범죄를 저지르다 **capture** 체포, 포획 **quotation** 인용(문) **decade** 10년간 **misspell** 철자를 잘못 쓰다 **omit** 생략하다, 빠뜨리다 **slightly** 약간, 조금 **modify** (일부) 변경하다, 수정하다 **claim** (~의 소유권을) 주장하다 **author** 책을 쓰다; 작가 [선택지 어휘] **current** 지금의, 현재의 **concerned** 관계가 있는; 관심을 가진; 걱정스러운 **gradual** 점차적인, 단계적인 **erode** 서서히 파괴하다; 침식하다 **ownership** 소유권

34 빈칸 추론 ⑤

소재 사교성과 전염병 감염률의 관계

해설 인기 있는 사람들이 질병 발생을 선도한다고 한 후, 이에 관한 연구 결과를 설명하는 글이다. 사교성이 좋은 집단이 일반적인 집단보다 2주 먼저 신종 인플루엔자에 걸렸다는 연구 결과를 통해 사교성 좋은 사람들이 ⑤ '여기저기 돌아다니는 전염균에 최초로 감염될' 가능성이 높다는 것을 추론할 수 있다.

해석 주제문 인기 있는 사람들은 사회의 유행을 선도하는데, 질병 발생에 관해 특히 그렇다. 신종 인플루엔자가 전 세계적으로 유행하는 동안 연구진들은 한 대학에서 (일반적인) 학생들과 보다 사교성이 좋은 학생 집단의 무작위 표본에서 그 질병의 확산을 추적하고 비교했다. 두 집단 모두 결국 비슷한 수로 독감에 걸리긴 했지만, 더 '인기 있는' 집단의 학생들이 사회적 관계를 덜 갖는 또래들보다 약 2주 먼저 병에 걸렸고, 이 사실은 앞으로 언제 그리고 어느 정도까지 독감 발생이 일어날 것인지에 대해 그들이 어쩌면 유용한 판단 기준이 될 수 있다. 사회적 관계 속에서 관계를 더 많이 맺는 사람들은 그 관계 속에 있는 사람들과 더 자주 접촉하기 때문에, 이런 사교성 좋은 나비들(=사교성 좋은 사람들)이 여기저기 돌아다니는 전염성 있는 벌레를 최초로 잡을(=전염균에 최초로 감염될) 가능성이 더 높다는 것 또한 일리가 있다.

① 다른 사람들로부터 자신을 고립시키기가 어렵다는 것을 알
② 자신의 광범위한 활동 때문에 지칠
③ 모든 전염병에서 보다 빠르게 회복할
④ 안 좋은 상황 속에서도 자신이 원하는 모든 것을 얻을

어휘 **trendsetter** 유행의 선도자 **when it comes to A** A에 관한 한 **outbreak** 발생, 발발 **pandemic** 전 세계적으로 유행하는 전염병 **random** 무작위의 **dominant** 우세한, 지배적인 **end up v-ing** 결국 v하게 되다 **come down with** (병에) 걸리다 **the flu** 독감(=**influenza**) **potentially** 잠재적으로, 어쩌면 **gauge** 판단 기준 **extent** 정도, 규모 **come into contact with** ~와 접촉하다, ~와 만나다 **logic** 논리 **social butterfly** 사교성이 좋은 사람 [선택지 어휘] **isolate A from B** A를 B로부터 고립시키다 **exhausted** 지친 **wide range of** 광범위한, 다양한 **recover from** (병에서) 회복되다 **contagious** 전염성의(=**communicable**)

35 무관한 문장 ③

소재 환경 보호가 우선시되지 않는 이유

해설 환경 보호가 뒷전이 될 수밖에 없는 이유로 정부나 기업이 경제 개발을 더 중요하게 여기거나, 일반적으로 사람들이 자신의 행동이 지구에 미칠 영향을 알지 못하고, 문제를 인식하더라도 행동을 바꾸려 하지 않는다는 점 등을 설명하는 글이다. 반면에 ③은 몇몇 회사가 환경 보호를 위한 노력으로 '친환경 건물'을 세운다는 내용으로 글의 흐름과 반대된다.

해석 환경은, 우리가 들이마시는 공기, 마시는 물, 먹는 음식을 포함해 지구상 생명체의 모든 면에 영향을 미친다. 주제문 당신은 환경 보호가 다른 모든 우선사항보다 우위에 있다고 생각할지 모르지만, 현실은 환경 보호 노력이 경제 개발 같은 다른 압력들에 비해 종종 부차적으로 취급된다는 것이다. 예를 들어, 어떤 정부나 기업은 공기 청정도와 수질을 유지하는 것이나 다른 천연자원을 보호하는 것보다 산업 육성이 더 중요하다고 결정할지 모른다. 몇몇 회사들은 자연 환경에 대한 전체적인 영향을 줄일 수 있도록 설계된 '친환경 건물'을 지으려고 노력하고 있다. 일반적으로 말하자면, 사람들은 자신의 행동이 지구에 미칠 수 있는 영향에 대해 교육받지 못했고, 문제를 알고 있는 사람들 중 많은 이들은 자신의 행동을 변화시키는 것을 회피할 뿐이다. 환경을 보호하는 데 있어서의 어려움은, 몇몇 사람들이 환경 보호를 반대한다는 점이 아니라 그들이 더 환경 친화적인 선택을 꺼리거나 혹은 할 수 없다는 점이다.

구문 [7행~10행] ~, a government or company might decide // that building up industry is **more** important / **than** maintaining air and water quality or protecting other natural resources.

that절은 「비교급+than」의 구조로, 비교하는 대상은 각각 building up industry와 maintaining ~ natural resources이다. 등위접속사 or로 than 이후의 동명사구가 병렬 연결되어 있다.

[17행~20행] ~, the challenge is n't that some people are against conservation but that they are unwilling or unable to make more Earth-friendly choices.

「not A but B」는 'A가 아니라 B'란 뜻이며, 두 개의 that절을 대등하게 연결하고 있다.

어휘 **aspect** 측면, 양상 **top** 능가하다, ~보다 더 낫다 **priority** 우선사항, 우선순위 **conservation** 보호, 보존 *cf.* **conservationist** 환경 운동가 **secondary to A** A에 비해 부차적인, A에 비해 뒷전인 **build up** 강화하다, 증강시키다 **natural resources** 천연자원 **generally speaking** 일반적으로 말하자면 **have an impact on** ~에 영향을 미치다 **be aware of** ~을 알다[알아차리다] **when it comes to A** A에 관해서라면 **Earth-friendly** 환경 친화적인

36 글의 순서 ①

소재 감정이 섞인 언어의 사용

해설 loaded language는 언어를 사용하는 사람의 감정이 담겨 있는 언어이다. 이 글은 loaded language를 통해 그 말을 한 사람의 견해를 알아낼 수 있다는 것을 두 가지 예시를 들어 설명하고 있다. 먼저 (A)의 This는 주어진 글 전체 내용을 가리킨다. (B)와 (C)는 낙태에 대해 서로 다른 견해를 가진 사람들이 쓰는 언어에 대한 예시인데, (B)의 However로 보아 그 앞에 반대되는 내용인 (C)가 나와야 함을 알 수 있다. 따라서 글의 순서는 ① '(A)-(C)-(B)'가 자연스럽다.

해석 주제문 (사람들의) 의견에 영향을 주고 어떤 특정한 방식으로 생각하는 데 동의하도록 듣는 사람이나 읽는 사람을 설득하려고 할 때, 사람들은 종종 논리 대신 감정을 자극하는 그것(= 단어)의 능력 때문에 신중하게 선택된 단어를 사용한다.

(A) 이것은 감정이 섞인 언의의 사용이라고 불린다. 예를 들어, 진보적인 기자는 보수주의자들이 사용할 만한 '국방'이라는 표현 대신에 정부가 '군대'에 돈을 지출하고 있다는 글을 쓸 것이다.

(C) 마찬가지로 필자가 낙태를 찬성한다면, 자신과 견해를 같이하는 사람들을 '선택 옹호론자'라고 부를 것인데, 이 표현이 강한 긍정의 의미를 내포하고 있기 때문이다. 그리고 그러한 표현과 관련된 사람들은 긍정적인 견해를 가진 것처럼 보일 것이다.

(B) 하지만 필자가 낙태를 반대한다면 같은 이유로 자신과 견해를 같이하는 사람들을 '생명 옹호론자'라고 부를 것이다. 그러므로 이렇게 감정이 섞인 언어를 알아내는 것은 (그 말을) 사용하는 사람의 견해에 대한 중요한 단서를 밝히는 것이다.

구문 [1행~5행] When **trying to influence** opinion [and] **(to) persuade** listeners or readers to agree with a certain way of thinking, // people often use *words* [that are carefully selected for *their ability* (to stir up emotions instead of logic)].

「try to-v」는 'v하려고 애쓰다'란 뜻으로 두 개의 to부정사가 and로 연결되어 있다. words는 that이 이끄는 절의 수식을 받으며 이 that절 내의 to부정사구는 their ability를 수식한다.

어휘 **stir up** (불러)일으키다; 휘젓다 **logic** 논리 **loaded** 감정이 섞인, 숨은 저의가 있는; (짐을) 실은 **liberal** 진보적인; 자유주의의 **conservative** 보수주의자; 보수적인 **anti-** …반대의 **abortion** 낙태, 유산 **pro-** …찬성의 **reveal** 드러내다, 밝히다 **favor** 찬성하다; 호의를 보이다 **connotation** 내포, 의미; 함축 **light** 견해, 관점

37 글의 순서 ③

소재 중앙집권화된 의사결정 체제의 발달 배경

해설 수렵 채집에서 농경으로 넘어가면서 조직화된 체계가 필요하게 되었다는 주어진 글 다음에는 이것(This: 조직화된 체계의 필요성)이 파종, 수확, 저장을 위해 과거보다 더 많은 체계를 요구했다는 내용의 (B)가 나온다. 이러한 사회에서 시간이 흐르면서 의사결정은 중앙집권화되고 소수 집단이 전유하게 되었다는 내용의 (C)가 나온다. 마지막으로 이러한 체제의 이점이 '빠른 의사결정'임을 제시한 (A)가 이어진다. (A)의 this type of system은 (C)의 '중앙집권화되고 소수 집단이 의사결정을 내리는 체제'를 지칭한다.

해석 수렵 채집 사회가 성장하여 결국 자연의 식량 공급을 소진했을 때, 어떤 사람들은 한 곳에 머물러 사는 농부가 되어서 살아남았다. 농경의 도래와 함께 작물 심기, 수확하기, 저장하기의 조직화된 체제에 대한 필요가 생겨났다.

(B) 이것은 전통적인 경제에서 존재하던 것보다 더 많은 체계를 요구했다. 사회의 생존을 보장하기 위하여 어떤 작물을 기르고 얼마나 많은 수확물을 저장할지에 대한 결정이 이루어져야 했다.

(C) 주제문 시간이 흐르며 의사결정은 중앙집권화되었고, 명령 경제 체제가 발달했다. 한 명의 지도자나 강력한 개인들로 구성된 한 집단이 전체 사회를 위한 핵심적인 경제적 결정을 내린다.

(A) 이러한 유형의 체제의 이점은 의사결정자들이 그들의 사회에서 빠른 변화를 일으킬 수 있다는 것이다. 예를 들어 소련의 독재자인 Josef Stalin(이오시프 스탈린)의 5개년 계획은 소련을 농노 기반의 농경사회에서 세계의 산업 초강대국 중 하나로 빠르게 탈바꿈시켰다.

구문 [3행~5행] With the advent of farming came *a need* (for an organized system of planting, harvesting, and storing crops).
(부사구 / V / S)

부사구가 문두에 오면서 「동사+주어」 어순으로 도치되었다.

[6행~8행] The advantage of this type of system is *the ability* (*for decision-makers* **to produce** rapid changes in their society).

( )는 the ability를 수식하는 형용사적 용법의 to부정사구이며, for decision-makers는 to produce의 의미상 주어이다.

어휘 **exhaust** 다 써버리다 **with the advent of** ~의 도래로 **dictator** 독재자 **transform** 변형시키다 **peasant** 농부, 소작농 **agricultural** 농업의, 농경의 **superpower** 초강대국 **centralize** 중앙집권화하다 **command** 명령, 지휘

38 문장 넣기 ④

소재 요청을 하는 효과적인 방법

해설 주어진 문장의 those steps는 원하는 것을 얻기 위해 취하는 행동의 단계들을 의미하며, 이 과정들이 효과적이지 않다는 내용 뒤에는 다른 효과적인 방법이 제시될 것임을 알 수 있다. 따라서 주어진 문장은 아무 말도 하지 않고 기다리다가 결국 신경질을 내며 요청하게 되는 단계들에 관한 내용과 정중하게 보이기보다는 문제를 해결하는 데 집중하는 것이 원하는 것을 얻는 효과적인 방법이라는 내용 사이인 ④에 들어가는 것이 적절하다.

해석 우리가 누군가로부터 진정 어떤 것을 원할 때, 우리 중 다수는 예상 가능한 조치를 취하는데, 각각의 조치는 그 이전의 것보다 우리를 더 화나게 할 뿐이다. 우리는 아무 말도 하지 않고 기다리는 것으로 시작할 것이다. 그다음에는 우리가 필요한 것을 '빙빙 돌려' 말하고 절대로 직접 언급하지는 않을 것이다. 이후에 우리는 신경질을 내며 요청하기 시작하거나 심지어 화를 내며 요구할 것이다. 우리는 그러한 조치들이 더 정중한 접근법이라고 생각하겠지만, 그것들은 효과적이지 않다. 주제문 우리는 정중하게 보이려는 욕망보다는 우리가 가진 문제를 해결하는 데 집중해야 한다. 우리가 해결책을 찾는 데 집중하면 단순한 요청이 취할 수 있는 가장 생산적인 접근법인 반면, 빙빙 돌려 이런저런 조치를 취하는 것은 그렇지 못하다는 것이 분명해진다.

구문 [4행~5행] ~, many of us take predictable steps, / **each one** making us more upset than **the last**.

each one은 making이 이끄는 분사구문의 주어로, and each one makes us more upset than the last로 바꿔 쓸 수 있다. 여기서 one은 a step을 the last는 the last step을 의미한다.

[9행~11행] We should focus on solving *the problem* [(that[which]) we have], / **rather than** on *our desire* (to seem polite).

「A rather than B」 구문이 쓰여 'B보다는 오히려[차라리] A'의 의미를 나타낸다. 두 개의 전명구가 rather than에 의해 대등하게 연결된 병렬구조이다. the problem과 our desire가 각각 관계대명사절과 to부정사구의 수식을 받고 있다.

어휘 **approach** 접근(법), 방법; 접근하다 **predictable** 예상할 수 있는 **talk around** 빙빙 돌려서 말하다 **irritated** 신경질이 난 **manner** 태도, 방식 **productive** 생산적인 **whereas** ~에 반하여 **winding** (길 등이) 꾸불꾸불한

39 문장 넣기 ④

소재 하지(夏至)에 가장 덥지 않은 이유

해설 ④의 앞 문장에서는 '하짓날 북회귀선에 서 있다면 태양이 머리 바로 위에 있을 것이다(= 하짓날 태양이 가장 높다)'고 했고, ④의 다음 문장은 '대양과 대륙이 데워지는 데에는 시간이 걸린다'는 내용으로, 두 문장 사이에 연관성이 없고, 역접의 연결사 But이 쓰일 이유도 없다. '태양이 가장 높고 낮이 가장 길면 기온도 가장 높을 것 같다'는 주어진 문장이 ④에 위치하면, '하짓날 태양이 가장 높다 → 그러면 기온도 가장 높을 것 같다 → 그러나 대양과 대륙이 뜨거워지는 데는 시간이 걸려서 하짓날 가장 뜨겁지는 않다'는 내용으로 글의 흐름이 자연스럽게 연결된다.

해석 주제문 왜 한 해 중 낮이 가장 긴 날이 가장 더운 날이기도 한 건 아닌 걸까? 열적 관성(온도가 같은 상태로 남아있으려는 경향)은 땅과 물이 즉각적으로 뜨거워지는 것을 막아준다. 하지(夏至: 일 년 중 낮이 가장 긴 날)로 알려진 6월 21일에 태양 광선은 북반구에 직접 내리쬔다. 지구는 23.5도 기울어져 있으므로, 태양은 북회귀선이라 불리는 지구 둘레의 가상의 선인 위도 23.5도 바로 위에서 빛난다. 당신이 여름의 첫 날에 이 선 위에 서 있다면, 태양은 바로 머리 위에 있을 것이며, 매일 하늘에서 더 낮은 곳으로 가라앉기 시작하기 전에 잠시 동안 정지한 것처럼 보일 것이다. 태양이 가장 높은 지점에 있고 낮이 가장 긴 상태에서, 상식적으로는 6월이 한 해 중 가장 뜨거운 달이 되어야 할 것 같다. 그러나 어떤 효과(= 열적 관성) 때문에 대양과 대륙은 데워지는 데 시간이 걸린다. 결과적으로 가장 뜨거운 날씨는 보통 하지에서 대략 6주 후에 당도한다.

구문 [1행~3행] **With** *the Sun* **at its highest point**, and (with) *the days* **at their longest**, / common sense would tell you // that June should be the hottest month of the year.
(O'1: the Sun, O'2: the days, S: common sense, V: would tell, IO: you, DO: that June ~ the year)

「with+O+전명구」는 'O가 ~한 상태에서'의 뜻이며, would tell의 직접목적어로 that절이 쓰였다.

[5행~7행] Thermal inertia—the tendency of temperatures to remain the same—**keeps** *the land and water* **from getting** instantly hot.

「keep+O+from v-ing」는 'O가 v하지 못하게 막다'의 뜻이다.

어휘 **common sense** 상식 **thermal inertia** 열적 관성 *cf.* **thermal** 열의; 뜨거운 *cf.* **inertia** (물리학) 관성 **beat down** (태양이) 강렬하게 빛나다 **the Northern Hemisphere** 북반구 **tilt** 기울이다 **latitude** 위도 **imaginary** 가상의 **seemingly** 겉보기에는, 외관상 **take time** 시간이 걸리다; 천천히 하다 **landmass** 대륙, 광대한 토지

40 요약문 완성 ④

소재 상황과 어조에 따른 말의 의미 변화

해설 '교훈을 주겠다'는 동일한 말을 상담자가 친절한 '어조(tone)'로 편안한 '상황[맥락](context)'에서 할 때와 상관이 단호한 어조로 경직된 분위기에서 할 때, 전달되는 메시지의 진정한 의미는 달라진다는 내용의 글이므로 정답은 ④이다.

해석 우리들 대부분은 사람들이 하는 말(구두 언어)에 주의를 기울이라고 배운다. 주제문 말은 정말로 우리에게 어떤 정보를 제공하지만, 의미는 너무나 많은 다른 원천으로부터 나온다. "내가 너에게 교훈을 주겠다."와 같은 간단한 구절을 예로 들어보자. 상담자가 고객에게 예의 바른 목소리로 "제가 교훈을 하나 드릴게요."라고 말한다면, 상담자는 자신의 개인 경험을 공유하여 그를 도울 수 있다고 암시하는 것일 수 있다. 그러나 병장이 목소리에 단호함을 담아서 같은 말을 이등병에게 한다면, 그는 이등병이 그의 범법 행위로 어떤 종류의 처벌을 받게 될 거라는 점을 암시할 것이다. 손님이 주인에게 목소리에 강조를 담아서 "여기는 약간 춥네요."라는 의견을 말한다면, 주인은 이것이 단지 관찰일 뿐만 아니라 정말로 창문을 닫아달라는 요청임을 이해한다.

⬇

메시지의 의미는 메시지가 수반하는 (A) 맥락과 화자가 사용하는 (B) 어조의 영향을 받는다.

구문 [14행~16행] ~ the host understands // that this is **not simply** an observation **but** really a request (to **have** the window **closed**).
(A: an observation, B: a request)

「not simply A but B」는 'A뿐만 아니라 B도'의 뜻이다. A, B자리 모두 명사구가 위치한다. ( )는 a request를 수식하며 「have+O+과거분사」는 'O가 ~되다[당하다]'의 뜻이다.

어휘 **verbal** 언어[말]의, 구두의 **be derived from** ~로부터 나오다 **phrase** 구[절] **counselor** 상담자, 고문 **imply** 암시하다, 함축하다 **firmness** 견고, 단호함 **wrongdoing** 범법 행위, 비행 **comment** 논평하다, 견해를 밝히다 **emphasis** 강조 **chilly** 쌀쌀한, 추운 **accompany** 동반하다

41~42 장문 41 ③ 42 ②

소재 부정적 생각을 적어서 불안을 감소시키는 방법

해설 41. 시험을 보기 전에 자신의 부정적 감정을 적는 것이 시험 불안을 누그러뜨리고 성적을 향상시킨다는 내용이므로 제목으로 가장 적절한 것은 ③ '감정에 관해 쓰는 것은 시험 불안을 이긴다'이다.

① 두뇌의 비밀은 무엇인가?
② 학생들이 시험 불안에 대해 공개적으로 말하다
④ 시험 불안: 주요한 교육 문제
⑤ 시험 중에 감시받는 것의 부정적 효과들

42. 부정적인 생각을 적는 것이 자신의 부정적 생각을 재고할 기회를 주고, 이로써 시험 중에 그러한 부정적 생각이 머릿속에 떠올라서 주의력이 흩뜨려지는 것을 줄여주었다고 하였다. 이는 다시 말해 부정적 생각이 머릿속에서 비워진 것이므로 정답은 ② '비웠다'이다.
① 무시했다 ③ 불안하게 했다 ④ 담험했다 ⑤ 강화했다

해석 시험 불안은 학생들이 경험하는 가장 흔한 문제 중 하나이다. 주제문 시험을 성공적으로 완수하기 위해 필요한 지적 능력이 걱정에 의해 강탈될 수 있다. Chicago 대학의 심리학 교수인 Sian Beilock과 그녀의 동료들은 스트레스로 가득 찬 상황에서 압박을 받아 숨이 막히는 것 같았고 기대만큼 일을 잘 수행하지 못한 학생들을 조사해 보았다. 그들은 20명의 대학생으로 이루어진 한 집단에게 일련의 수학 문제를 풀라고 요청하면서 그들에게 시험에서 가장 고득점을 받은 사람은 상으로 현금을 받게 될 것이라고 말했다. 그 압박을 정말 높이기 위해, 학생들에게 또한 시험 보는 중에 그들이 비디오로 촬영될 것이고 교수와 동료들 모두가 지켜보고 있을 것이라고 말했다.
학생들의 한 그룹은 시험이 시작되기 전 10분 동안 조용히 앉아 있으라는 지시를 받았고, 나머지 학생들은 다가오는 시험에 대한 그들의 생각과 느낌을 기록하면서 시간을 보냈다. 펜으로 기록한 학생들은 시험 성적에서 5퍼센트의 향상을 맛보며 다른 학생들보다 더 시험을 잘 보았다. 주제문 "이러한 부정적인 생각을 적는 것은 여러분이 종이에서 그것들을 바라볼 기회를 주고, 여러분의 부정적 성향을 재고하는 기회를 주었습니다. 그러자 그러한 생각이 시험을 보는 동안에 여러분의 머릿속에 떠올라서 주의력을 흩뜨리게 하는 것이 적어진 것 같습니다."라고 Sian Beilock은 말한다. "그것은 마치 여러분의 마음을 비웠다는 것과 같습니다. 이제 여러분은 최상의 상태에서 일을 수행할 인지적 힘을 갖는 것입니다." Beilock은 생물학 기말 시험을 치르는 9학년 학생들 50명 이상에게 유사한 실험들을 반복했다. 기말 시험 전에 그들의 걱정들을 적었던 학생들은 그 시험에서 B+를 받았고, 반면에 그 밖의 다른 것에 관해 썼던 학생들은 B−를 받았다.

구문 [4행~8행] Sian Beilock, a professor of psychology at the University of Chicago, and her colleagues / studied *students* [who seemed to choke under pressure and didn't perform **as well as** (they were) expected / in stress-filled situations].

Sian Beilock과 a professor ~ Chicago는 동격을 나타낸다. 동사는 studied이고 관계대명사절에서 동사구 seemed ~ pressure와 didn't perform ~ situations가 병렬구조를 이루고 있다. 여기에서 「~ as well as ...」는 '… 뿐만 아니라 ~도'의 뜻이 아니라, 부사 well의 원급 비교구문으로 '…만큼 잘'의 의미이다. 두 번째 as 뒤에는 they(=the students) were가 생략되었다.

어휘 **anxiety** 불안, 걱정 **hijack** 강탈하다; 강요하다 **colleague** 동료(=peer) **choke** 숨이 막히다; 질식시키다 **reward** 보상하다, 사례하다 **pile on** ~을 증가시키다, 쌓다 **outperform** 더 나은 결과를 내다, 능가하다 **boost** 증가; 밀어 올리다 **negativity** 부정적 성향; 소극성 **distract** (주의를) 딴 데로 돌리다 **cognitive** 인지[인식]의 [선택지 어휘] **speak out** ~을 공개적으로 말하다 **intensify** 강화하다; (정도 · 강도가) 심해지다

43~45 장문 43 ③ 44 ① 45 ③

소재 펜의 힘을 깨달은 청각장애인 아이

해설 43. Katherine을 초등학교에 등록시키기 위해 가족이 학교에 온 (A) 다음에는 부모님과 상담하는 동안 Katherine이 아무런 의사 표현을 하지 않는 모습을 보였으며, 글쓰기를 싫어했다는 (C)가 오는 것이 자연스럽다. 이후, 글쓰기의 위력을 실감한 사건이

나오는 (D)가 이어지고, 그 후로 글을 잘 쓰고 인생을 적극적으로 살게 되었다는 (B)로 마무리되는 것이 자연스럽다. 따라서 정답은 ③ '(C)-(D)-(B)'이다.

44. (a)는 Katherine에게 학업 면에서 희망을 갖지 말라는 말을 한 유치원 선생님을 가리키고, 나머지는 모두 Katherine을 가리킨다.

45. (B)의 마지막 문장, Katherine stays in touch ~에서 Katherine이 필자와 계속해서 연락하고 있음을 알 수 있으므로 ③이 일치하지 않는 내용이다.

해석 (A) 1990년대 말에 한 가족이 내가 청각장애 학생들을 가르치던 공립 초등학교에 왔다. 그들은 자신들의 청각장애가 있는 딸을 1학년에 입학시킬 계획이었다. 그들은 아이의 유치원 교사가 그들에게 ① 학업 면에서는 아이에게 높은 희망을 갖지 말라고 주의를 주어서 속상해했다. 평가 결과를 토대로, (a) 그녀(=유치원 선생님)는 그들의 작은 딸아이의 미래에 대해 비관적인 그림을 그렸던 것이다. 그들 뒤에는 그들의 딸인 Katherine이 있었다.

(C) 그녀의 부모님이 거기에 계신 동안 내내 그녀는 소리를 내지도 수어(手語)를 사용하지도 않았다. Katherine과 몇 주 지낸 후, 나는 그녀가 매우 똑똑하고 매우 의지가 강한 아이라는 것을 알게 되었다. 비록 가까스로 (d) 그녀(=Katherine)를 ④ 다양한 학습 활동에 참여시킬 수는 있었어도, 글쓰기는 계속 고생이었다. 연필이 나올 때마다 그녀는 하던 일을 멈추고 참여하기를 거부하곤 했다.

(D) 어느 날, Katherine이 버스에서 내린 뒤 큰소리로 울면서 학교 앞에 서 있었다. 수어를 모르던, 그곳에 있던 직원들은 (e) 그녀(=Katherine)에게 펜과 메모장을 가져다 주었다. Katherine은 'PAC BAK'이라고 썼다. 바로 사무실 직원들은 그녀가 가방(backpack)을 버스에 두고 왔다는 것을 알아차렸다. ⑤ 그들은 버스를 학교로 다시 불러왔고 Katherine은 곧 자신의 가방과 재회했다. 그날 Katherine은 마침내 펜의 힘을 알게 되었다.

(B) 그때부터 계속 그녀는 글쓰기에 대한 새로운 평가를 내리게 되었다. (b) 그녀(=Katherine)는 이제 젊은 여성이 되었고 뛰어난 작가, 대중 연설가이자 학생 지도자로 성장했다. ② 그녀는 선생님이 되려는 생각으로 Northern Colorado 대학교에 등록했다. ③ Katherine은 계속 연락하고 있고 나는 학기말 보고서가 첨부된 (c) 그녀(=Katherine)의 이메일을 특별히 소중히 여긴다. 이 젊은 여성은 매우 강력한 펜으로 무장하고 있다!

구문 [(A) 8행~9행] Standing behind them (C) was (V) their daughter (S), Katherine (=).

동사는 was이고 뒤의 their daughter가 주어인 도치구문이며, their daughter와 Katherine은 동격 관계이다.

어휘 (A) **deaf** 청각장애가 있는 **enroll** 입학시키다; 등록하다 **academically** 학업[학문]적으로 **assessment** 평가 (B) **appreciation** 평가; 감탄, 감상; 감사 **intent on** ~에 열중하고 있는 **treasure** 대단히 소중히 여기다; 보물 **term paper** 학기말 보고서 **attached** 첨부된 (C) **sign language** 수어(手語) **strong-willed** 의지가 강한 **engage** 참여하게 하다; (주의를) 사로잡다 **constant** 끊임없는; 계속되는 **struggle** 고군분투; 애쓰다 (D) **notepad** 메모장 **summon** 호출하다; 소환하다 **reunite** 재회하다

실전 모의고사 06

본문 p.83

18 ⑤	19 ④	20 ②	21 ②	22 ①	23 ②	24 ④	25 ⑤	26 ⑤	27 ⑤
28 ⑤	29 ③	30 ③	31 ②	32 ⑤	33 ②	34 ①	35 ③	36 ①	37 ⑤
38 ②	39 ④	40 ①	41 ②	42 ⑤	43 ⑤	44 ②	45 ③		

18 글의 목적 ⑤

소재 테니스 강습 프로그램에 대한 불만

해설 글쓴이는 프로 선수에게서 테니스를 배울 수 있다는 광고를 보고 강습에 참여했다가 기대 이하의 기본적인 강습에 그치자 크게 실망하여 항의하고 있으므로 정답은 ⑤이다. I was beyond disappointed ~ hold a racket.과 It was a complete waste of time and money.에 글의 목적이 잘 드러나 있다.

해석 관계자 분께,
저는 최근에 Orange County 헬스클럽이 제공하는 테니스 프로그램들 중 하나에 참가했습니다. 그것은 공인된 프로가 가르치는, 전 연령의 학생을 대상으로 한 4주 강습이라고 광고되었습니다. 지금, 저는 아마추어 수준에서 시합을 뛰어온 오랜 테니스 팬으로서 일반적인 학생이 아닐지도 모르겠습니다. 하지만 저는 프로 수준과는 거리가 멀어 분명히 프로로부터 배울 것이 많습니다. 주제문 그래서 제 60달러의 참가비로 라켓을 잡는 법에 대한 기본적인 조언밖에 얻지 못했을 때 저는 실망 이상이었습니다. 그것은 완전히 시간과 돈 낭비였습니다. 장차 어떤 상급 수준의 학생이 이 프로그램에 대해 제 의견을 묻는다면 저는 그들에게 그냥 제 자신이 그들을 가르쳐 주겠다고 제안하겠습니다.
David Blain 드림

구문 [10행~12행] So, I was beyond disappointed // when my $60 entry fee (S′) **got** (V′) me (IO′) nothing more than *basic advice* (**on** how to hold a racket) (DO′).
when 이하의 절에서 got은 두 개의 목적어 me와 nothing ~ a racket을 취하고 있다. how to hold a racket은 전치사 on의 목적어이다.

어휘 **to whom it may concern** (불특정 상대에 대한 편지 등의 첫머리에 써서) 관계자 분(들)께 **certified** 공인된, 보증된 **pro** (비격식) 프로 (선수) *cf.* **professional** 직업[프로] 선수; 전문적인, 프로의(↔ **amateur** 아마추어 선수; 아마추어의) **enthusiast** 열광자, 팬 **compete** (시합 등에) 참가하다; (시합에서) (~와) 겨루다 **nowhere near** 도저히 미치지 못하는, 거리가 먼 **beyond** 그 너머에; 그 이상으로 **entry fee** 참가비 **nothing more than** ~에 불과한, ~에 지나지 않는 **advanced** 고급[상급]의; 선진의

19 심경 변화 ④

소재 눈보라에 갇힌 형제

해설 필자는 동생과 단둘이 국유림에서 야영하며 평화로운 밤을 보냈으므로 '위안을 받은(comforted)' 기분이었을 것이다. 그러나 다음날에는 폭설이 심하게 내려서 두 사람이 위험에 처해 '걱정하는(worried)' 상황이 되었으므로 정답은 ④이다.

해석 내 동생 Ethan과 나는 한번은 몬태나 주 남부의 갤러틴 산으로 엘크를 사냥하러 나가 있었다. 밤에 우리는 국유림에 있는 우리가 가장 좋아하는 자유 지점에서 야영했다. 주제문 우리 둘을 위한 조용하고 평화로운 밤이었다. 나는 도시생활의 북새통에서 벗어나 상쾌한 기분을 느꼈다. 다음 날 아침에 우리가 사냥을 시작했을 때, 폭설이 내리기 시작했다. 매우 짧은 시간 내에 눈 상태가 극도로 위험해졌음이 분명했다. 동생과 내 주변의 쌓인 눈이 저 무시무시한 쿵 소리를 내며 무너졌다. 주제문 Ethan은 얼굴에 걱정하는 표정을 띤 채로 나를 보았다. 나는 억지로 미소를 지으려 애썼지만 그다지 성공하지는 못했다. 나는 뭘 해야 할지 몰랐다. 설상가상으로, 바람이 너무 강해서 나는 똑바로 서서 정상적인 방식으로 걸을 수도 없었다.

① 기쁜 → 외로운 ② 차분한 → 짜증 난
③ 수치스러운 → 부러운 ⑤ 희망찬 → 실망한

구문 [13행~15행] To make matters worse, the wind was **so** strong **that** I couldn't stand upright [and] walk in a normal fashion.
「so ~ that ...」 구문은 '너무 ~해서 …하다'의 뜻이다. couldn't 다음의 동사원형 stand와 walk가 and로 연결되어 병렬구조를 이룬다.

어휘 **elk** 엘크(북유럽 · 아시아 · 북아메리카산의 큰 사슴) **spot** 지점, 장소 **national forest** 국유림 **refreshed** 상쾌한 **hustle and bustle** 부산함, 북적거림 **apparent** 분명한 **perilous** 위험한 **layer** 층 **whump** 쿵쿵거리다 **concerned** 걱정하는 **to make matters worse** 설상가상으로 **upright** 똑바로 **fashion** 방식

20 필자 주장 ②

소재 유아의 수영 강습 시기

해설 부모들이 아이에게 너무 빨리 수영 강습을 억지로 시키려 하는데, 그보다는 우선 아이가 물을 좋아하도록 해주고 수영에는 천천히 접근하는 것이 좋다는 내용의 글이다. 따라서 필자 주장으로 가장 적절한 것은 ②이다.

해석 좋은 뜻에서 부모들은 자녀의 안전에 대해 걱정하여, 유아와 걸음마 단계 아이들을 수영 강습에 서둘러 예약한다. 수년 간 나는 수영 강습에서 완전히 통제 불능인 많은 아이들을 목격했다. 두세 살의 걸음마 단계 아이들이 심지어 발가락 하나라도 물에 닿는 것을 겁내기 때문에 흐느껴 울고 소리를 지르고 부모에게 매달려 있는 것 말이다. 다른 걸음마 단계 아이들은 부모에게 딱 달라붙어 머리를 (수영장 물) 속에 넣으려 하지 않거나 수영장 가장자리 부분을 놓는 것을 두려워한다. 주제문 부모들이 나에게 어떻게 해야 할지 물으면, 나는 그들에게 한동안 강습은 잊어버리라고, 아이들에게 강요하는 것은 단지 그들이 물에 대해 더 불안감을 느끼게 만들 뿐이라고 말해준다. "아이에게 목욕할 때 물을 튀겨주거나, 큰 플라스틱 물통에 물과 많은 장난감을 채워 주세요. 아니면 그냥 가족이 수영장에 가세요. 물을 싫은 일이 아니라 재미난 것으로 만들어 보세요. 그리고 혹시 모르니 12개월 후에 다시 시도해 보세요." 여러분의 아이가 초등학교나 심지어 그 이후까지 수영하는 법을 모른다 하더라도 그것이 세상의 종말은 아니다.

구문 [6행~7행] ~ because they are terrified **of** *even one toe* **touching** the water.
touching은 전치사 of의 목적어이며 even one toe는 동명사의 의미상 주어이다.
[16행~18행] It's not the end of the world // **if** your child doesn't learn to swim / until primary school or even later.
여기서 if는 '~하더라도'의 의미로 양보의 부사절을 이끈다.

어휘 **well-meaning** 좋은 뜻에서, 선의의 **rush** (너무 급히) 서두르다; 갑자기 덤벼들다 **infant** 유아, 갓난아기 **toddler** 걸음마를 배우는 아이 **witness** 목격하다 **out of control** 통제[조종] 불능의 **sob** 흐느끼다 **cling to** ~에 매달리다 **be terrified of** ~을 무서워하다 **be glued to** ~에 붙어서 떨어지지 않다; ~에 열중하다 **let go of** ~을 놓다[놓아주다] **force** 강요하다, 억지로 시키다 **splash** 물을 튀김, 물장구 침 **bucket** 양동이 **chore** 하기 싫은[따분한] 일, (정기적으로 하는) 일 **primary school** 초등학교

21 밑줄 함의 ②

소재 피라항족이 준 교훈

해설 피라항족은 필자가 알려준 경쟁에 입각한 게임의 성격을 모든 사람들이 함께 즐길 수 있고 낙오되는 사람이 없도록 바꾸었다. 이로부터 필자가 얻은 교훈은 ② '당신은 즐거운 시간을 보내고 모든 사람이 이기게 할 수 있다.'가 가장 적절할 것이다.

해석 주제문 아마존 열대우림의 피라항족과 함께 일한 30년의 세월은 나에게 많은 것을 가르쳐주었다. 나는 한때 피라항족에게 서구의 게임에 대해 가르쳐주는 것이 재밌을 거라고 생각해서, 다른 여러 가지 것들 중에서 도보 경주, 포대 뛰기, 그리고 줄다리기가 있는 운동회를 조직했다. 도보 경주에서는 한 친구가 다른 모든 사람들 앞으로 나왔다. 그는 그러고 나서 멈추고 다른 사람들이 결승선을 함께 넘을 수 있도록 그들이 따라잡기를 기다렸다. 이긴다는 생각은 새로울 뿐만 아니라 매력 없는 것이었다. 우리가 함께 선을 넘지 않으면 나는 넘지 않겠어. 마찬가지가 포대 뛰기에도 해당되었다. 줄다리기는 코미디였다. 사람들은 그저 밧줄을 느슨한 상태로 두고 이야기를 나누었다. 그들은 그 모든 걸 좋아했고, 하루 종일 웃고 떠들며 나에게 얼마나 즐거운 시간을 보냈는지 얘기해주었다. 그들은 나에게 잊지 못할 교훈을 가르쳐주었다. 그것은 나쁜 교훈이 아니었다. 그것은 좋은 교훈이었다.

① 때때로 당신은 단지 다시 이기기 위해 져야 한다.
③ 게임의 결과는 예측할 수 없고 가변적이다.
④ 당신의 가장 큰 고통 중 일부가 당신의 가장 큰 강점이 된다.
⑤ 게임의 주된 목적은 가르치는 것이 아니라 즐겁게 하는 것이다.

구문 [2행~4행] I once thought // (that) it might be fun to teach the Pirahã about Western games, ~
(it: 가주어, to teach ~: 진주어)
thought의 목적어인 that절에서 접속사 that이 생략되었으며, that절에서 it은 가주어이고 to부정사구가 진주어이다.

[7행~8행] He then stopped and waited *for the others* **to catch up** / **so** they could cross the finish line together.
for the others는 to catch up에 대한 의미상 주어이다. 접속사 so (that)은 '~하도록, ~하기 위하여'의 뜻이다.

어휘 **rainforest** 열대우림 **field day** 운동회; 야외 행사 **foot race** 도보 경주 **sack race** 포대 뛰기 **tug-of-war** 줄다리기 **catch up** 따라잡다 **finish line** 결승선 **novel** 새로운; 소설 **unappealing** 매력 없는 **go for** ~에 해당되다 **slack** 느슨한[처진] 부분 [선택지 어휘] **outcome** 결과 **unpredictable** 예측할 수 없는 **changeable** 가변적인; 변하기 쉬운 **primary** 주요한 **entertain** 즐겁게 하다

22 글의 요지 ①

소재 유전자 조작을 이용한 식물 개량

해설 식물 개량에 있어 이종 교배를 사용할 때의 단점을 언급한 뒤, 이 문제를 유전자 조작으로 해결할 수 있다는 것을 나팔수선화의 유전자를 이용한 벼의 개량을 예로 들어 설명하고 있다. 따라서 글의 요지로 가장 적절한 것은 ①이다.

해석 수천 년 동안, 농부들은 좋은 특성을 가지고 있는 식물들을 이종 교배함으로써 작물을 개량해왔다. 그들은 자기들이 원하는 특성을 가진 식물을 생산하기 위해 한 식물에서 꽃가루를 채취해 다른 식물의 꽃에 묻힌다. 주제문 그러나 이종 교배는 느리고 신뢰할 수 없다. 이제 놀라운 지름길이 있다. 과학자들은 한 생물에서 유전자를 채취해 다른 식물에 그것을 직접 집어넣을 수 있다. 그 방법으로, 변화가 훨씬 더 짧은 시간에 더 정확하게 생길 수 있게 되었다. 이 새로운 기술이 해충에 강하고, 질병에 저항력이 있으며, 더 영양분이 많은 작물들을 만들어 낼 수 있다. 예를 들어, 나팔수선화의 유전자로부터 비타민 A를 추가적으로 생산할 수 있도록 벼가 (유전자) 조작되었다. 그 벼는 식단에서 충분한 비타민 A를 얻을 수 없는 사람들을 위해 만들어졌다.

구문 [3행~5행] They take pollen from one plant / and add it to the flowers of another plant / to produce *a plant* (with *the traits* [(which [that]) they want]).
(take: V1, add: V2)
with ~ want 부분은 전명구로 a plant를 수식하고, 전명구 내 [ ] 부분은 목적격 관계대명사 which 또는 that이 생략된 관계사절로 앞에 나온 명사 the traits를 수식한다.

어휘 **crop** (농)작물; 수확량 **trait** 특성, 성질 **pollen** 꽃가루 **unreliable** 신뢰할 수 없는 **shortcut** 지름길 **gene** 유전자 **precisely** 정확하게; 엄밀히 **pest-proof** 해충에 강한 **disease-resistant** 질병에 저항력이 있는, 질병에 강한 **nutritious** 영양분이 많은; 영양의 **modify** 조작하다; 수정하다, 바꾸다 **boost** 증가, 증대; 밀어 올림; 증대시키다; 밀어 올리다

23 글의 주제 ②

소재 다양한 형태의 직업을 고려해야 할 필요성

해설 오늘날 전일제 고용은 줄어들고 시간제나 계약직과 같은 다양한 형태의 고용이 증가하고 있으므로 더 이상 전통적인 정규직에 얽매이지 말고 다양한 형태의 일을 추구하는 유연함을 가지라는 내용의 글이다. 따라서 글의 주제로 가장 적절한 것은 ② '일자리에 대한 인식 전환의 필요성'이다.

해석 분야나 산업에 따라 다르지만, 대개 25~40퍼센트의 노동자들이 임시 고용직이거나 시간제 근로자, 혹은 계약직 노동자이며, 이러한 비전통적 역할에서의 고용은 증가하고 있는 반면, 전일제 고용은 감소하고 있다. 주제문 분명히 오늘날의 현명한 구직자라면 옛날 방식의 전일제 직업이 아닌 다양한 형태의 유급 직업을 구해야 한다. 그렇지만 전일제 직업이 여전히 가장 이상적인 것으로 생각되고 있어서, 수많은 구직자들이 이러한 보다 유연한 전략을 제대로 활용하지 않고 있다. 많은 사람들이 전통적인 직업 모델 외에는 어떠한 합리적인 선택도 받아들이기를 거부한다. 그러나 이런 편협한 사람들은 감소하고 있는 '전통적인' 영구직의 공급을 두고 경쟁해야 할 것이다. 주제문 그보다 그들은 오늘날 생계를 제대로 유지하기 위해서는 좀 더 유연해야 하며 여러 형태의 일을 추구해야 한다는 것을 알아야 한다.

① 인기 있는 직장에 채용되는 방법
③ 전통적 정규 직장을 추구하는 이유
④ 가장 원하는 직책을 얻는 전략들
⑤ 일자리 부족으로 인해 심화되는 사회 문제들

어휘 **temporarily** 임시로 **contract** 계약(하다); (병에) 걸리다; 수축하다 **shrink** (수량 · 가치 등이) 감소하다; (물건이) 줄어들다 **ideal** 이상적인 것 **make use of** ~을 활용[이용]하다 **flexible** 유연한 **legitimacy** 합리성, 타당성; 합법(성) **narrow-minded** 편협한, 속이 좁은 **compete** 경쟁하다 **supply** 공급(하다) **conventional** 전통적인; 관습적인 **permanent** 영구적인 [선택지 어휘] **perception** 인식, 지각 **deepen** 악화되다; 깊어지다

24 글의 제목 ④

소재 뇌의 노화에 대한 잘못된 통념

해설 나이가 들면 뇌 기능이 저하된다는 통념과는 달리, 노년에도 새로운 뇌세포와 신경세포가 생성되고, 이로써 손상을 입은 뇌 부위도 재생될 수 있다는 내용의 글이다. 따라서 제목으로 가장 적절한 것은 ④ '새로운 뇌세포는 평생 만들어진다'이다.

해석 주제문 우리는 나이가 들면서 뇌세포 구조와 기능에 점진적인 저하가 발생한다고 생각했었다. 그러나 그러한 널리 퍼진 가정은 틀린 것으로 판명됐다. 새로운 신경세포가 나이 든 동물의 뇌에서 생성된다는 점이 밝혀졌으며, 우리는 나이 든 뇌의 이러한 놀라운 특성이 어떻게 조작될 수 있는지에 대해 점점 더 많이 알아가고 있다. 예를 들어, 낮은 수준의 규칙적인 운동은 기억을 처리하는 뇌 구조인 해마의 새로운 신경세포를 상당히 생성해주는 것으로 밝혀졌다. 게다가 새로운 연구에서는 나이 든 사람의 눈의 특정 신경세포가 새로운 과정을 생장시킬 수 있음이 밝혀졌다. 우리는 평생 동안 닳거나 손상을 입은 뇌의 부위를 재생시킬 수 있을 것이며, 이는 현재 노인이라고 여겨지는 사람들에게 새로워진 능력을 제공할 것이다.

① 항노화에 관한 통념과 사실
② 당신의 신경세포가 당신이 얼마나 잘 나이 들지를 결정한다
③ 당신의 인지 기능이 나이가 들면서 쇠퇴하는 이유
⑤ 노화를 긍정적인 성장 경험으로 생각하라

구문 [5행~7행] ~ we're learning **more and more** how this amazing property of the aged brain can be manipulated.
(S: we / V: 're learning / O: how this amazing property of the aged brain can be manipulated)

「비교급 and 비교급」은 '점점 더 ~한[하게]'의 뜻이다. how ~ manipulated는 are learning의 목적어 역할을 하는 간접의문문이며, 「의문사(how)+주어(this ~ brain)+동사(can be manipulated)」의 어순으로 쓰였다.

[12행~16행] We will be able to regenerate *parts of the brain* [**that** have worn out or been damaged in the course of a lifetime], / **providing** renewed capabilities to *those* [**who** are currently considered old folks].

that은 parts of the brain을 받는 주격 관계대명사이다. 완료시제의 과거분사 부분인 worn out과 been damaged는 병렬구조로 have에 연결된다. providing 이하는 분사구문이며, who는 those를 수식하는 관계사절을 이끈다.

어휘 **progressive** 점진적인; 진보적인 **deterioration** 저하, 퇴보; 악화 **assumption** 가정, 추정 **generate** 생성하다; 발생시키다 *cf.* **regenerate** 재생하다 **property** 특성, 속성 **manipulate** (능숙하게) 조작하다[처리하다] **significantly** 상당히, 크게; 중요하게 **be capable of** ~할 수 있다 **wear out** 닳다, 낡다, 해지다 **in the course of** ~ 동안 **renew** 새롭게 하다; 갱신하다; 재개하다 **currently** 현재 **folks** 사람들 [선택지 어휘] **myth** 사회적 통념; 신화 **cognitive** 인지의, 인식의 **decline** 쇠퇴[감소]하다; (아래로) 기울다

25 도표 이해 ⑤

소재 빅토리아의 화석 연료 수요와 공급

해설 화석 연료 수요와 공급 사이의 차이가 큰 해는 2005년과 2015년이다. 2005년에는 공급이 5 유닛 더 많았고, 2015년에는 수요가 4.5 유닛 더 많았으므로 차이가 가장 큰 해는 2005년이다. 따라서 ⑤가 잘못된 설명이다.

해석 〈빅토리아의 에너지 수요와 이용 가능성(공급)〉

주제문 이 도표는 1995년부터 2015년까지 빅토리아의 화석 연료의 에너지 수요와 이용 가능한 에너지(=화석 연료의 수요과 공급) 사이의 관계를 나타낸 것이다. 1 에너지 유닛은 1000억 메가줄을 나타낸다. ① 1995년과 2000년 사이에 에너지 수요는 5 유닛에서 약 2 유닛으로 꾸준히 감소했다. ② 그 후 5년간 에너지 수요는 일정하게 머물러 있었고, 이후 2005년부터 에너지 수요는 급격하게 올라서 2015년 7 유닛에 이르렀다. ③ 이와 반대로, 화석 연료 에너지 공급량은 1995년 약 3.5 유닛에서 2005년 최고치인 7 유닛에 이르기까지 꾸준히 증가하였다. ④ 최고치를 기록한 이후 에너지 공급량은 2010년 이후 마침내 약 2.5 유닛 정도의 수준을 계속 유지할 때까지 급격히 감소했다. ⑤ 에너지의 수요와 이용 가능성(=공급) 사이의 차이에 관해서는 2015년에 가장 컸으며, (차이가) 4.5 유닛에 이르렀다.

어휘 **demand** 수요 **availability** 이용할 수 있음, 유효성 *cf.* **available** 이용 가능한 **fossil fuel** 화석 연료 **represent** 나타내다; 대표하다 **billion** 10억 **steadily** 꾸준히, 점차 **approximately** 대략 **constant** 일정한, 변함없는 **onwards** 계속해서 **steeply** 급격하게; 가파르게 **peak** 절정, 최고점, 꼭대기 **sharply** 급격하게 **level out** ~한 수준을 유지하다; 편평하다

26 내용 불일치 ⑤

소재 James McNeill Whistler의 생애

해설 마지막 문장에서 Whistler가 Oscar Wilde의 소설 〈Dorian Gray의 초상〉에 영감을 주었다고 했으므로 ⑤는 글의 내용과 반대된다.

해석 James McNeill Whistler는 19세기 후반에 대단히 영향력이 컸던 ① 미국 태생의 영국인 화가였다. 그는 매사추세츠 주(州)의 로웰에서 1834년 7월 11일에 태어났다. 그는 러시아의 상트페테르부르크에서 교육을 받고 나서 웨스트포인트 미 육군사관학교에 다녔다. ② 파리와 런던에서 화가로 자리 잡은 뒤, Whistler는 부드러운 색조와 단순한 형태를 사용해서 자신 특유의 양식을 개발하였다. 그의 걸작은 'Whistler의 어머니(회색과 검정색의 배열 제1번)'로 널리 알려져 있다. ③ 지금은 파리에 있는 그것은 미국 밖에서 널리 알려진 소수의 미국 그림 중 하나이며, 종종 빅토리아 시대의 '모나리자'로 언급된다. ④ Whistler는 이어서 1898년에 미술 학교 설립을 시작했지만, 그것은 Whistler가 아프게 된 후 곧 문을 닫을 수밖에 없었다. 그는 1903년에 런던에서 사망했다. ⑤ 그의 작품은 나중에 Oscar Wilde의 소설 〈Dorian Gray의 초상〉(1890년)에 영감을 주었다.

구문 [6행~9행] **Establishing** himself as a painter in Paris and London, / Whistler developed his distinctive style, / **utilizing** soft colors and simple forms.
(S: Whistler / V: developed / O: his distinctive style)

주절의 앞과 뒤에 분사구문이 쓰인 형태로, Establishing ~ London은 After Whistler established ~ London의 의미이고, utilizing ~ forms는 부대상황을 나타내어 '~하면서'로 해석한다.

어휘 **influential** 영향력 있는 **establish oneself as** ~로서 자리를 잡다 **distinctive** 특유의, 독특한 **utilize** 활용[이용]하다 **masterpiece** 걸작, 명작 **credit A as B** A를 B로 여기다 **arrangement** 배열, 배치; 조정; 준비 **be referred to as** ~로 언급되다 **found** 설립하다, 세우다 **inspiration** (특히 예술적 창조를 가능하게 하는) 영감

27 안내문 불일치 ⑤

소재 국립 수족관 자원봉사 프로그램

해설 참가자에게는 정규직이 아닌 시간제 직원 채용 기회가 있을 수 있다고 했으므로 ⑤가 안내문의 내용과 일치하지 않는다.

해석

학생 여름 프로그램

① 이 학생 여름 프로그램은 고등학생들에게 국립 수족관에서 자원봉사하면서 수족관의 일과 매력을 나누며 여름을 보낼 독특한 기회를 제공합니다.

자격

지원자는

- ② 9학년과 최소 하나의 고등학교 생물학 과정을 성공적으로 마쳐야 하며
- 환경에 관한 의식이 있어야 하고
- ③ 해양 생물학에 대해 관심이 있으며
- 미소 짓고 사람들에게 이야기하는 것을 좋아해야 합니다.

혜택

전시실의 안내원으로 일하면서 누리게 될 혜택은 다음과 같습니다.

- 직업으로서 해양 생물학을 사실적으로 바라보게 됨
- ④ 학교의 사회 봉사활동 조건을 달성할 기회
- 직원 할인과 특전
- ⑤ 시간제 직원으로의 채용 가능성

지원 방법

작성된 지원서를 recruit@nationalaquarium.org로 보내주시기 바랍니다.

어휘 **unique** 독특한; 유일한 **aquarium** 수족관 **mission** 임무, 사명; 전도 **requirement** 필요조건, 요건 **applicant** 지원자 *cf.* **apply** 지원하다 *cf.* **application** 지원(서) **complete** 완료하다; 작성하다; 완전한 **biology** 생물학 **marine** 바다의, 해양의 **community service** 사회 봉사활동 **privilege** 특권, 특전 **part-time** 시간제의 **position** 직책

28 안내문 일치 ⑤

소재 Bedford 다리 공원 입장권 구매 안내

해설 거래약관 마지막에 가격과 조건이 변할 수 있다고 했으므로 ⑤가 안내문의 내용과 일치한다.

해석

Bedford 다리 공원

입장권 온라인 구입
① Bedford 다리 공원 입장권을 온라인으로 구입하셔서 매표소의 긴 줄을 지나쳐 가세요!

② Bedford 주민: 입장권과 함께 사진이 있는 신분증을 가져 오시면 1년 무료입장권을 받으실 수 있습니다!

거래 약관:
1. ③ 입장권은 환불되지 않습니다. 예외는 없습니다.
2. ④ 입장권은 구입한 날짜로부터 1년 동안 유효하며 언제라도 사용할 수 있습니다.
* ⑤ 가격과 약관은 사정에 따라 변할 수 있습니다. 입장권 배송에 문제가 있을 경우에는 help@bedfordpark.au로 이메일을 보내주시기 바랍니다.

어휘 **bypass** (정해진 절차 · 순서를 거치지 않고) 건너뛰다; 우회하다 **lineup** 줄; 줄을 서다 **resident** 주민 **complimentary** 무료의; 칭찬하는 **annual** 한 해의, 연간의; 매년의 **Terms and Conditions** 거래 약관 **refundable** 환불 가능한 **exception** 예외 **valid** 유효한 **rate** 요금; 비율; 속도 **be subject to** ~의 대상이다; ~을 당하기 쉽다

29 밑줄 어법 ③

소재 업무 압박감에 의한 건강 악화

해설 ③ 주어는 feeling으로 시작하는 동명사구이고 동명사 주어는 단수 취급하므로 동사 hold를 holds로 고쳐야 한다.

오답 분석 ① surprise는 '~를 놀라게 하다'라는 타동사로, statistics(통계)가 사람들을 놀라게 하는 것이므로, 능동 관계를 나타내는 현재분사 surprising이 알맞다. ② 앞에 나온 복수명사인 Workers를 받는 대명사이므로 복수형인 those가 적절히 쓰였다. ④ volunteers(지원자들)가 감기 바이러스에 '노출되는' 것이므로 수동태가 알맞다. ⑤ 문장의 주어 역할을 하는 동명사이므로 적절하다.

해석 런던에 있는 7,400명의 공무원에 관한 한 연구에서 놀라운 통계가 나왔다. 주제문 자신의 업무를 거의 통제할 수 없다고 느끼는 직원들은 업무 유연성이 더 많은 사람들보다 심장 질환 증상을 일으킬 위험이 50퍼센트 더 높았다. 다시 말해서, 해야 할 업무에 대한 요구와 압박감을 (자신이) 거의 통제할 수 없다고 느끼는 것은 고혈압과 같은 위험 요인만큼이나 심장 질환의 큰 위험을 갖고 있다. 그것이, 우리가 직장에서 가지는 모든 관계 중에서, 사장 혹은 상사와의 관계가 우리의 신체 건강에 가장 큰 영향을 미치는 이유이다. 한 영국의 감기 연구소에서 참가자들은 감기 바이러스에 노출되었고 누가 감기에 걸리는지 알아보기 위해 5일 동안 관찰되었는데, 사회적 긴장에 얽혀 있는 사람들이 가장 감염되기 쉬운 것으로 밝혀졌다. 사무실에서의 단 하루의 힘든 날은 문제가 되지 않았다. 하지만 상사와 지속적인 문제가 있는 것은 면역력을 약화시키기 충분한 스트레스였다.

구문 [2행~5행] *Workers* [who felt they had little control / over their work] had *a 50 percent higher risk* (of developing symptoms of heart disease) / than **those** (with more job flexibility).
(S: Workers, V: had, O: a 50 percent higher risk)
Workers가 관계대명사절의 수식을 받아 주어가 길어졌다. those는 앞에 쓰인 Workers의 반복을 피하기 위해 쓰였다.

[5행~8행] In other words, / feeling little control / over *the demands and pressures* (of *the work* [we have to do]) / holds **as** great a risk of heart disease **as** risk factors like hypertension.
(S: feeling little control ..., V: holds)
원급 비교인 「as ... as ~ (~만큼 …하다)」 구문이 쓰였다. 명사를 수식하는 형용사에 as가 붙을 때는 「as+형용사+a(n)+명사」의 어순이 된다.

어휘 **civil service worker** 공무원 **yield** (결과를) 내다, 생산하다; 항복하다; 양보하다 **statistic** 통계 **flexibility** 유연성; 융통성 **hypertension** 고혈압 **superior** 상관, 윗사람; 상급의; 우수한 **expose** 노출시키다; 폭로하다 **susceptible** 감염되기 쉬운; 영향을 받기 쉬운; 민감한 **persistent** 끊임없이 지속되는; 끈질긴 **immune system** 면역체계

30 네모 어휘 ③

소재 산악인 Edmund Hillary

해설 (A) 경쟁자들을 완전히 제압하려고 에베레스트를 정복한다는 말은 '대단히 적극적인' 태도를 드러내므로 aggressive가 알맞다. passive는 '수동적인'이란 뜻이다.
(B) Hillary가 네팔인들을 돕기 위해 수도관을 '설치하는' 것이 문맥상 적절하므로 install이 들어가야 한다. remove는 '제거하다'란 의미이다.
(C) 문맥상 Hillary가 '책임지고 맡은' 일의 양을 의미하므로 undertook이 적합하다. avoid는 '피하다'란 뜻이다.

해석 주제문 유명한 산악인 Edmund Hillary는 극도의 자신감과 진솔한 겸손함이 기묘하게 조화를 이룬 사람이었다. (A) 대단히 적극적인 태도로, 그는 경쟁자들을 완전히 제압하고자 하는 생각 때문에 에베레스트 산 정복에 끌리게 되었다고 말한 바 있다. 그러나 역사상 가장 위대한 정복 중의 하나인 그 산 정상에 이른 후에, 그는 그를 매우 자주 도왔던 가난한 네팔 국적의 셰르파들을 돕는 일에 인생의 대부분을 바쳤다. 자신이 만든 히말라야 트러스트(=기업 합동)를 통해 기금을 모은 Hillary는 수도관을 (B) 설치하는 것을 도왔으며 30개의 학교, 2개의 병원, 12개의 진료소, 여러 개의 다리 등을 세웠다. 그가 (C) 맡은 일의 양은 열 명의 사람을 바쁘게 할 수 있을 정도였지만, Hillary는 결코 속도를 늦추지 않았다. 1996년 87세의 나이에 그는 "나 자신이 네팔에 그렇게 자주 가지 않게 되는 것을 보고 싶습니다. 하지만 현재 나의 책무는 그곳에 있습니다. 그 일은 마무리되어야 합니다."라고 말했다.

구문 [3행~5행] With an aggressive manner, / he once said // (that) he **was drawn** to conquer Mt. Everest / **by** the idea [of] smashing his rivals into the ground.
(the idea = smashing ...)
he was drawn 이하는 the idea of smashing his rivals into the ground drew him to conquer Mt. Everest를 수동태로 전환한 것이다.

어휘 **mountaineer** 산악인, 등산가 **possess** 소유하다 **genuine** 진실한; 진짜의, 진품의 **modesty** 겸손, 겸허 **conquer** 정복하다 *cf.* **conquest** 정복 **smash** 철저하게 격파하다; 산산이 부수다 **devote A to B** A를 B에 바치다[헌신하다] **Sherpa** 셰르파족(티베트 또는 네팔 출신으로 히말라야 등반 때 길 안내자로 고용되는 사람) **raise** (돈을) 모으다, 모금하다 **fund** 기금, 자금 **trust** (상업) 트러스트, 기업 합동

31 빈칸 추론 ②

소재 의사소통 시 눈 맞춤과 신체 접촉의 문화별 차이

해설 영국과 같은 앵글로색슨계 문화에서는 신체 접촉을 자제하고 눈 맞춤에 의존한다고 한 후, 다른 문화권의 경우를 설명하고 있다. 지중해 문화권에서는 신체 접촉이 충분히 예상되는 것이라고 했으므로 신체 접촉이 영국의 눈 맞춤만큼이나 ② '일상적이다'라고 해야 알맞다.

해석 눈 맞춤은 특히 앵글로색슨계 백인 문화에서 중요한 것처럼 보인다. 예를 들어, 타인과 거리를 유지해야 하고, 다른 사람과의 신체 접촉은 아주 친밀한 상황이 아니고서는 피해야 하는 것은 영국 전통 문화의 일부이다. 타인과 거리를 두고 대해야 하는 이 사회적 관습 때문에, 영국 및 앵글로색슨계 백인 문화는 개인적인 커뮤니케이션을 위해 많은 부분을 눈에 의존한다. 그러나 다른 여러 문화에서는 사람들이 서로 가까이 다가서며, 사회생활에서의 친밀한 신체 접촉이 영국에서의 눈 맞춤만큼이나 일상적이다. 예를 들어, 지중해 문화에서 사람들과 어울리는 동안에는 타인의 접촉이나 체취가 모두 예상되는 일이다.
① 흥미진진한 ③ 냉담한 ④ 강렬한 ⑤ 무례한

구문 [2행~6행] **It** is part of traditional British culture, / for example, / **that** others should be kept at a distance, [and] **that** *contact* (with another person's body) should be avoided / in **all but** the most intimate situations.
It은 가주어이고 and로 연결된 두 개의 that절이 진주어이다. all but은 '~외에는 모두, 거의'란 뜻이다.

어휘 **at a distance** 거리를 두고, 좀 떨어져서 **intimate** 친밀한, 친숙한 **convention** (사회의) 관습, 풍습 **deal with** ~을 (상)대하다, 다루다 **rely on** ~에 의존[의지]하다 **interaction** 상호 작용 *cf.* **interact** 상호 작용하다 **Mediterranean** 지중해의

32 빈칸 추론 ⑤

소재 대학생들의 물질주의적 경향

해설 오늘날 대학생들이 '어떤' 특징을 가지는지를 빈칸 뒤에 이어지는 설명에서 추론할 수 있다. 요즘 대학생들에게 중요한 것은 인생철학이 아니라 돈을 많이 버는 것이며, 인문학보다 돈벌이에 도움이 되는 회계, 경영, 공학을 전공으로 훨씬 더 많이 선택한다는 내용에서 대학생들의 ⑤ '더 물질주의적이고 덜 비실용적'인 경향을 알 수 있다.

해석 17년의 기간에 걸쳐 매년 시행되어 188,000명이 넘는 학생들의 응답을 모은 한 조사에 따르면, 주제문 오늘날의 대학 신입생들은 이 조사가 행해진 17년 중 어느 때보다도 더 물질주의적이고 덜 비실용적이다. 오늘날 경제가 매우 불황인 것을 고려하면, 대부분의 학생들이 진술한 주요 목표가 '돈을 가능한 한 많이 버는 것'이라는 점은 별로 놀랍지 않다. 의미 있는 인생철학을 발전시키는 것이 자신에게 중요하다고 한 학생들은 여느 때보다 적었다. 그리고 요즘 가장 인기 있는 강좌는 문학이나 역사가 아니라 회계라는 사실이 뒤따른다. 교육이나 사회 복지 사업 분야에 관한 관심은 사상 최저이지만, 또한 놀랄 것도 없이, 경영 과정, 공학, 컴퓨터 공학 등록은 훨씬 더 높다.

① 더 인색하고 덜 낭비적
② 더 공정하고 덜 편파적
③ 더 본능적이고 덜 이성적인
④ 더 내성적이고 덜 야심적인

구문 [1행~3행] According to *a survey* (**conducted** annually over a period of 17 years), // and [**which** gathered responses from ~ students], ~.
conducted가 이끄는 분사구와 which가 이끄는 관계대명사절 모두 a survey를 수식하고 있다.

[5행~8행] **Given that** the economy is in such bad shape today, / it's hardly surprising // that the stated ~ money as possible."
「Given (that)+S+V」는 '~을 고려하면'이란 뜻이다. it은 진주어인 that the stated ~ possible을 대신하는 가주어이다.

어휘 **conduct** 실시하다; 행동하다; 지휘하다 **over a period of** (일정 시간의) 기간에 걸쳐 **in bad shape** 불황인 **objective** 목표, 목적; 객관적인 **indicate** 내비치다, 시사하다; 나타내다 **philosophy** 철학 **accounting** 회계(학) **social service** 사회 복지 사업 **an all-time low[high]** 사상 최저[최고] 수준 **enrollment** 등록; 입학 **way** (부사 · 전치사를 강조하여) 훨씬; 아주 멀리 [선택지 어휘] **stingy** 인색한, 구두쇠의 **impartial** 공정한, 편견 없는 **biased** 편파적인, 편향된 **instinctive** 본능적인; 직관적인 **rational** 이성적인; 합리적인 **introverted** 내성적인 **materialistic** 물질주의(자)의 **impractical** 비실용적인; 비현실적인

33 빈칸 추론 ②

소재 시장 연계성

해설 미국의 휘발유 가격을 억제하기 위해 옥수수를 이용한 대체 에너지로 수요를 돌렸더니, 옥수수를 더 많이 재배하느라 밀을 덜 재배하게 되었고, 밀의 공급이 떨어짐에 따라 밀과 함께 쌀의 가격이 상승했으며, 이로 인해 아시아 지역의 식량 공급이 타격을 입게 되었다는 상황을 정리하면 ② '시장이 서로 대화한다'라고 표현할 수 있다.

해석 몇 년 전에 휘발유 가격이 갑자기 오르기 시작했다. 그 결과 많은 미국인들의 경제 사정에 자리 잡은 (재정) 압박을 완화하라는 상당한 정치적 압력이 생겼다. 운전을 덜 하는 대신에 많은 사람들은 더 높은 가격을 지불할 필요 없이 차량을 운전하는 자신의 삶의 방식을 지속하기를 원했다. 그래서 무슨 일이 일어났는지는 다음과 같다. 휘발유 가격이 상승함에 따라, 대체 연료에 대한 수요가 증가했다. 이러한 대체 연료에 대한 수요 증가는 에탄올이라 불리는 제품을 가지고 있던 옥수수 재배자들 사이에서 인기 있었다. 에탄올을 더 낮은 비용으로 공급하기 위해, 옥수수 재배자들은 더 많은 보조금을 얻으려고 의회에 로비를 했다. 이는 더 많은 땅이 다른 작물, 즉 밀을 희생하고 옥수수 생산에 배치되는 결과를 가져왔다. 밀 공급이 감소하고 밀 가격이 오름에 따라, 대체 작물인 쌀의 가격도 올랐는데, 이제 쌀에 대한 수요가 더 많아졌기 때문이었다. 이는 쌀 가격이 남아시아와 동남아시아 사람들이 자신의 기본 주식(主食)을 공급할 수 없는 지점까지 상승하는 것으로 이어졌다. 기아가 재빨리 뒤따랐다. 주제문 사람들은 시장이 서로 대화한다는 사실을 간과했다.

① 판매자들이 가격을 통제할 수 있다
③ 기아가 예상치 못하게 발생한다
④ 기업들이 수익으로 동기를 부여받는다
⑤ 노동 이동이 공급 충격을 만든다

구문 [12행~14행] This resulted in *more land* being placed into corn production / at the expense of other crops, namely wheat.
resulted in 다음에 이어지는 목적어는 동명사 being placed ~이며, more land는 being placed에 대한 의미상 주어이다.

어휘 **alleviate** 완화하다 **squeeze** 압박, 긴축 **pocketbook** 경제 사정; 지갑 **vehicle** 차량, 탈것 **alternative** 대체 가능한; 대안 **lobby** 로비를 하다; 로비 **Congress** 의회 **at the expense of** ~을 희생하여 **namely** 즉, 다시 말해 **substitute** 대용품, 대체물 **afford** 제공하다; 여유[형편]가 되다 **staple** 주식; 주요한 **starvation** 기아 **overlook** 간과하다 [선택지 어휘] **mobility** 이동성

34 빈칸 추론 ①

소재 부모가 자녀의 성취를 과소평가하는 이유

해설 부모가 자녀의 성취를 과소평가하는 이유에 대한 내용이다. 자녀에 대해 부모의 칭찬이 인색한 이유 중 하나는, 칭찬을 많이 하면 자녀가 스스로를 과대평가하여 기고만장해질(big-headed) 수 있기 때문이라고 했다. 따라서 부모는 자녀가 다른 아이들보다 뛰어나길 바라면서도 ① '그들이 오만하고 잘난 척하는 사람이 되기를 바라지는 않는다'는 내용이 들어가는 것이 문맥상 적절하다.

해석 상식적으로 어떤 사람이 스스로 발전하게 하는 가장 좋은 방법은 그에게 긍정적인 피드백을 주고 그가 잘하는 것들에 대해 칭찬해 준 다음, 비판적이기보다는 건설적인 방법으로 실수를 지적해주는 것이다. 주제문 그러나 많은 부모들이 자녀의 약점에 대해서는 단호하게 꾸짖는 반면, 동시에 자녀들이 성취한 것의 중요성은 일부러 과소평가한다. 이에 대한 한 가지 보편적인 이유는, 부모는 흔히 자녀가 성장해서 자기 자신을 과대평가하고 그 결과 흔히 말하는 '기고만장한' 사람이 되지 않도록 못 박고 싶어 한다는 것이다. 많은 부모는 자녀가 자만하거나 자기만족감에 빠질까봐 염려한다. 부모들은 자녀가 이웃의 아이들보다 더 낫기를 바라지만, 그들이 오만하고 잘난 척하는 사람이 되기를 바라지는 않는다.

② 그들이 인기 있으면서 동시에 붙임성 있기를 바란다
③ 그들이 이미 충분히 활발하게 학교생활을 한다고 믿는다
④ 그들이 스스로 세상을 탐구하고 발견하길 바란다
⑤ 그들에게 문화의 전통과 가치를 가르치지는 않는다

구문 [1행~4행] Common sense suggests // **that** *the best way* (to get O′ somebody C′ **to improve** himself) is **to give** him positive feedback and **(to) praise** about *the things* [(that) he does ● well] / **before** pointing out mistakes ~.
(S′: the best way, V′: is, C′1: to give ~, C′2: (to) praise ~)
that절은 to부정사구가 보어인 SVC 구조이다. 「get+O+C」는 'O가 C하게 하다'란 뜻으로 get은 목적어와 목적격보어의 관계가 능동일 때 목적격보어로 to부정사를 취할 수 있다. before 이하는 의미를 분명히 하기 위해 접속사를 남긴 분사구문으로 볼 수 있다. 문맥상 앞에서부터 차례로 '~하고 나서 …하다'로 해석하는 것이 자연스럽다.

[8행~12행] One common reason for this is **that** often parents are eager to ensure // (that) their children don't **grow up** / **to have** too good an opinion of themselves, / **becoming** C′ what is commonly known as "big-headed."
(S: One common reason for this, V: is, C: that ~)
=and they become what is ~.

that절이 보어인 SVC 구조이다. ensure 뒤에 목적어 역할을 하는 또 다른 (that)절이 이어지고 있다. 「grow up to-v」는 '성장해서 v가 되다'의 의미로 to부정사는 '결과'를 나타낸다. becoming 이하 또한 '결과'를 나타내는 분사구문으로 쓰였다.

어휘 **common sense** 상식 **feedback** 피드백, 개선 의견 **point out** 지적하다; 가리키다 **constructive** 건설적인 **A rather than B** B라기보다는 오히려 A **forcefully** 단호하게; 강압적으로 **rebuke** 꾸짖다, 질책하다 **purposely** 일부러, 고의로 **underrate** 과소평가하다 **significance** 중요성, 의의 **achievement** 성취, 업적 **be eager to-v** 몹시 v하고 싶어 하다 **ensure** 반드시 ~하게 하다 **big-headed** 자만심이 많은 **conceited** 자만하는 **complacent** 자기만족적인; 현실에 안주하는 **keen** ~을 열망하는; 열렬한; 예리한 [선택지 어휘] **arrogant** 오만한 **boastful** 뽐내는, 자랑하는 **sociable** 사교적인 **sufficiently** 충분히

35 무관한 문장 ③

소재 신용카드 사용의 이점

해설 직불카드와 신용카드의 사용이 증가하고 있다고 말한 뒤, 신용카드 사용 시 금융적인 이득과 보안상의 안전성이라는 두 가지 이점을 설명하고 있다. 반면에 ③은 무분별한 신용카드 사용으로 인해 생길 수 있는 문제점에 관한 내용이므로 글의 흐름에서 벗어난다.

해석 점점 더 많은 사람들이 직불카드와 신용카드를 사용해 상품 대금을 지불함에 따라, 우리 사회는 빠르게 현금이 불필요해지고 있다. 사람들은 한 달 후 신용카드 청구서가 올 때까지 상품 값을 지불하지 않아도 되기 때문에 한 달 가까이 이자 없이 돈을 빌려 쓸 수 있다. 이로 인해 사람들은 엄밀히 말하면 이미 써 버린 은행 예금에 대한 이자를 벌게 된다. 사람들이 불필요한 물건들을 사는데 신용카드를 사용하는 경우, 그들은 보통 자신이 얼마나 쓰는지도 모르고 소비하게 된다. 또한, 어떤 사람이 카드를 잃어버리거나 도난당하면 습득한 사람이나 절도범이 그 카드를 사용할 수 없도록 은행에 연락해 카드를 취소할 수 있다. 주제문 신용카드는 소비자들에게 유리할 수 있는데, 이는 신용카드가 금융과 보안상의 이점을 모두 제공해 준다는 점에서 본질적으로 유용하기 때문이다.

구문 [5행~7행] **This** allows people to earn interest / on *the savings* (in the bank) [**that** have technically already been spent].
This는 앞 문장 전체(=People ~ later)를 받으며 that의 선행사는 the savings in the bank이다.

[9행~12행] Also, if a person loses his or her card or it is stolen, // he or she can contact the bank / and **have** *the card* **canceled** // **so** the finder or thief **cannot** use the card.
이 문장에서 「have+O+C(p.p.)」는 'O가 C되도록 하다'란 의미를 갖는다. 「so (that) S+cannot ~」은 'S가 ~할 수 없도록'의 뜻으로 '목적'을 나타낸다.

어휘 **cashless** 현금이 불필요한 **goods** 상품 **loan** 대출(금) **interest** 이자; 관심 **saving** (복수형) 저축액, 저금 **technically** 엄밀히 따지면; (과학)기술적으로 **nonessential** 불필요한, 중요하지 않은 **lose track of** ~의 흐름을 놓치다 **inherently** 본질적으로; 선천적으로 **in a respect that** ~라는 점에서

36 글의 순서 ①

소재 사업에서 '보라색 눈송이'의 중요성

해설 주어진 글에서 '보라색 눈송이'의 의미를 설명한 뒤, 사업에서 제품이나 서비스가 주목받는 것이 중요하다고 하였다. (A)에서 주목을 받는 방법을 부연 설명하면서, 잡지 편집장에게 초대장을 보내는 예시를 들고 있다. (A)의 마지막에 나온 the finest stationery, ~ elegant handwriting에 대한 내용이 (C)의 후반에 a lovely handwritten one으로 이어진다. (B)는 글의 전체 내용을 다시 한번 정리하며 마무리하는 부분이다. 따라서 글의 순서로는 ① '(A)-(C)-(B)'가 자연스럽다.

해석 '보라색 눈송이'는 군중 속에서 두드러진 것을 뜻하는 은유이다. 주제문 사업에서 사람들이 당신, 당신의 제품 혹은 당신이 제공하는 서비스에 주목하게 하는 것이 어느 때보다 더 중요하다.

(A) 당신과 당신의 경쟁자들이 거의 모든 것에서 동일할 때 이러한 주목을 받기 위해서는 독특한 것을 할 필요가 있다. 예를 들어, 나는 바쁜 잡지 편집장이 내가 보낸 초대장을 열어보길 원할 때, 가장 좋은 편지지와 가장 좋은 펜과 우아한 필체를 사용한다.

(C) 물론, 더 싸고 시간이 덜 드는 방법이 있다. 하지만 잡지 편집장이 예쁜 필체로 쓰여 있는 봉투보다 일반 상업용 봉투를 열어볼 가능성이 훨씬 낮고, 이런 경우 예쁜 필체로 쓴 봉투가 나의 보라색 눈송이인 것이다!

(B) 분명, 모든 보라색 눈송이가 당신이 원하는 주목을 받게 해주지는 않을 것이다. 하지만 포기하는 대신에 당신이 다른 보라색 눈송이를 만들 수 있는지를 보라. 옛말에도 있듯이, '처음에는 성공하지 못할지라도 노력하고 또 노력하라.'

구문 [2행~4행] In business, / **it**'s *more important than ever* // **that** people notice you, your products, or *the services* [(that) you offer].
it은 가주어이고 that 이하가 진주어이다. it's more important than ever는 일종의 최상급 표현으로 '지금까지 어느 때보다 더 중요하다'란 의미이다.

[17행~20행] But a magazine editor is **far less** likely to open an ordinary business envelope / **than** *a lovely handwritten one*, // **which** (in this case) is my purple snowflake!
「less A than B」는 'B보다 덜 A한'의 의미를 나타내며, far는 비교급을 강조하는 부사이다. 계속적 용법으로 쓰인 관계대명사 which는 앞의 a lovely handwritten one(=envelope)을 가리킨다. 부사구 in this case를 괄호로 묶으면 관계대명사절의 구조가 쉽게 파악된다.

어휘 **snowflake** 눈송이 **metaphor** 은유 **competitor** 경쟁자 **editor** 편집장 **elegant** 우아한 **handwriting** 필체 **obviously** 분명히 **time-consuming** 시간이 걸리는 **ordinary** 보통의, 평범한

37 글의 순서 ⑤

소재 목표 설정 전 고려 사항

해설 목표를 정할 때는 그 목표를 달성하기 위해 감수해야 하는 희생과 얻게 되는 이득을 반드시 따져 봐야 한다는 내용의 글이다. (C)의 It은 주어진 글의 내용으로, 목표를 정했지만 포기하게 된 경우를 말한다. (B)의 Before you set it as your goal에 쓰인 it은 (C)에서 예로 든 an annual English prize를 지칭한다. (A)의 your potential losses는 (B)의 For instance ~에서 열거된 내용들이다. 따라서 글의 순서는 ⑤ '(C)-(B)-(A)'가 자연스럽다.

해석 목표를 정했지만 결국 그 목표를 위한 에너지를 다 써 버려서 목표를 포기해야만 한다는 것을 나중에서야 깨달은 적이 몇 번이나 있는가?

(C) 그것은 매우 흔한 경험인데, 많은 사람이 목표를 이루기 위해 그들이 감수해야만 하는 희생을 잠시라도 따져 보지 않기 때문이다. 학교에서 매년 영어대회 상을 수여한다고 해보자.

(B) 주제문 이 상을 목표로 정하기 전에 당신이 얼마나 많은 대가를 치러야 하는지 계산해 보라. 예를 들어, 당신은 에세이를 쓰고 연설을 연습하는 데 많은 시간을 보낼 수 있고, 그것은 곧 친구들과 어울릴 시간, 컴퓨터를 할 시간, 또는 TV를 볼 시간이 그만큼 없게 될 것임을 의미한다.

(A) 잠재적인 손실을 합산한 후에 그 상이 가져다 줄 이득을 계산해 보고, 그 이득이 손실보다 더 큰지를 판단하라. 만약 그렇지 않다면(= 이득이 손실보다 크지 않다면) (그 상을 타기 위해) 노력하지 마라. 비용과 이득을 계산하는 것은 당신이 목표를 정하려고 생각할 때, 언제나 어느 정도의 바람직한 현실성을 더해 준다.

구문 [13행~15행] ~, **which** means // you won't have as much *time* (to hang out with friends, (to) play on the computer, (to) watch TV).
which는 앞 문장 전체(you may ~ practicing speeches)를 가리키고, ( ) 안의 3개의 to부정사구는 형용사적 용법으로 time을 수식한다.

[16행~18행] ~, because many people don't pause / **to weigh up** *sacrifices* [(that) they'll have to make / **to achieve** their goals].
to weigh up과 to achieve는 '목적'을 나타내는 to부정사의 부사적 용법으로 쓰였다.

어휘 **potential** 잠재적인; 잠재력 **benefit** 이익, 혜택 **outweigh** ~보다 더 크다[대단하다] **commitment** 전념; 헌신; 약속 *cf.* **make a commitment** 노력하다, 헌신하다; 약속하다 **dose (of)** (어느 정도의) 양, 약간; (약의) 복용량, 투여량

hang out with ~와 어울려 놀다, ~와 시간을 보내다 **weigh up** (결정을 내리기 전에) ~을 따져보다, 저울질하다 **sacrifice** 희생; 제물 **annual** 매년의; 1년(간)의

38 문장 넣기 ②

소재 미국의 비만율 증가

해설 주어진 문장은 유전적 특징이 비만 증가의 원인이 아니라는 내용이므로, 지난 수십 년간 유전자 구성이 바뀌지 않았다는 ② 바로 뒤의 문장이 그 근거가 된다. 따라서 주어진 문장이 ②에 위치하고, 그 근거가 뒤따라 나오는 흐름이 되어야 자연스럽다.

해석 주제문 최근의 연구는 비만율이 미국의 모든 주(州)에서 성별, 연령, 인종 또는 교육 수준에 관계없이 증가하고 있음을 발견했다. 1991년에는 4개의 주(州)만 15퍼센트 이상의 비만율을 가지고 있었다. 하지만 오늘날에는 적어도 37개 주가 그러하다. 흥미로운 점은 비록 비만의 급증에 여러 원인이 있다 해도 유전적 특징은 그중 하나에 속하지 않는 것 같다는 점이다. 미국인의 유전자 구성과 구조는 지난 수십 년간 변하지 않았다. 변화한 것은 이 나라의 식단과 생활방식이다. 사람들은 더 많이 먹고 덜 움직일 때 살이 찐다. 미국에서는 사람들이 어디든 걸어가기보다는 운전해서 간다. 그들은 쉽게 걸어갈 수 있는 거리에 있는 곳조차도 운전해서 간다. 자동차에 대한 이런 중독이 지방과 열량이 매우 높은 일상의 음식과 결합되면, 비만이 널리 퍼지는 일이 일어나게 마련이다.

어휘 **upsurge** 급증, 쇄도 **obesity** 비만 **genetics** 유전적 특징; 유전학 *cf.* **gene** 유전자 **appear** ~인 것 같다; 나타나다 **regardless of** ~에 관계없이 **gender** 성(性), 성별 **makeup** 구성, 짜임새; 화장 **addiction** 중독 **be combined with** ~와 결합되다 **exceptionally** 유난히, 매우; 예외적으로 **widespread** 널리 퍼진, 광범위한 **be sure to-v** 반드시 v하다

39 문장 넣기 ④

소재 실용적 지식에 대한 편견

해설 ④ 이전까지는 이론적 지식에 비해 실용적 지식을 평가절하하는 편견에 대해 언급하고, ④ 이후에서는 실용적 지식이 이론적 지식보다 선행하며 더 근본적인 지식이라는 내용으로 글의 흐름이 전환되고 있다. 주어진 문장은 실용적 지식이 이론적 지식 못지않게 가치 있다는 내용이고, 역접의 연결어 However로 시작하므로 내용 전환이 이루어지는 ④에 들어가는 것이 적절하다.

해석 우리는 지식을 논할 때, 자주 이론적인 '머리의 지식'에 초점을 두고 실용적인 '손의 지식'은 간과한다. 정말로, 후자(=손의 지식)에 대한 편견이 약간 있는 듯하다. 예를 들어, 과학자의 추상적 지식은 자동차 정비공이나 수공예가의 실용적 지식보다 대체적으로 더 많은 존중을 받는다. 이런 편견은 이성에 대한 우리의 능력이 우리를 동물계의 나머지 들로부터 구별해주는 것이라는, 널리 퍼진 가정에서 나온 것일지도 모른다. 주제문 하지만 사물을 조작하는 우리의 능력은 똑같이 독특하며, 또한 유연한 엄지손가락을 지닌 손은 커다란 뇌를 가진 머리만큼 인간 지능의 상징으로 훌륭하다고 주장할 수 있을 것이다. 어떤 의미에서는 실용적 지식이 추상적 지식보다 앞서며 더 근본적임을 뜻한다. 결국, 우리는 어떤 종류의 지식이라도 습득할 수 있기 전에, 말을 하는 능력과 사물을 조작하는 능력 같은 기본적 기술을 필요로 한다.

구문 [1행~4행] However, **it** could be argued // **that** *our ability* (to manipulate things) is just **as** unique (**as** our capacity for reason), and **that** *the hand* (with its flexible thumb) is **as** good *a symbol* (of human intelligence) **as** *the head* (with its large brain).

it은 가주어이고 진주어인 두 개의 that절이 병렬구조로 연결되어 있다. that절에는 「as ~ as ...」 동등 비교 구문이 쓰였으며, just as unique 다음에는 앞문장의 as our capacity for reason이 생략되어 있는 것으로 볼 수 있다. 「as ~ as ...」 구문에서 형용사가 수식하는 명사가 있을 경우, as good a symbol of human intelligence에서와 같이 「as + 형용사 + a(n) + 명사 + as」의 어순이 된다.

[12행~15행] This prejudice may derive from the widespread assumption that our capacity for reason is / what distinguishes us from the rest of the animal kingdom.

that절은 the widespread assumption와 동격인 명사절이며, 명사절 내에서 what ~ kingdom은 is의 보어이다.

[15행~17행] There is *a sense* [in which practical knowledge is prior to, / and more fundamental than, / abstract knowledge].

[ ] 부분은 a sense를 수식한다. abstract knowledge는 (prior) to와 than의 공통 목적어이다.

어휘 **manipulate** (사물을 능숙하게) 조작하다, 다루다; (교묘하게) 조종하다 **flexible** 유연한 **theoretical** 이론상의 **overlook** 간과하다 **practical** 실용적인 **prejudice** 편견, 선입관 **the latter** (둘 중에서) 후자 **abstract** 추상적인; 이론적인 **esteem** 존중, 경의 **craftsman** (수)공예가 **derive from** ~에서 나오다[유래하다] **assumption** 가정, 추정 **distinguish A from B** A를 B와 구별하다 **reason** 이성, 사고력; 이유; 추론하다 **there is a sense in which** 어떤 의미에서는[말하자면] ~이 아닌가 **prior to** ~에 앞서, ~보다 먼저 **fundamental** 근본적인, 본질적인 **acquire** 습득하다, 얻다

40 요약문 완성 ①

소재 드라마 시청을 통한 감정 인지 능력 향상

해설 요약문을 먼저 읽어 보면, 텔레비전 드라마와 같은 양질의 '어떠한' 프로그램을 시청하는 것이 다른 사람들의 감정을 '무엇하는' 능력을 향상시켜 줄 수 있는지를 파악해야 함을 알 수 있다. 드라마를 보게 한 그룹과 다큐멘터리를 보게 한 그룹 중 드라마를 본 사람들이 감정을 더 정확하게 인지할 수 있었다는 실험 결과를 통해 (A)에는 '허구적(fictional)'이, (B)에는 '읽어내는(read)'이 가장 적절함을 알 수 있다.

해석 당신은 주변 사람들이 무슨 생각을 하고 어떤 감정을 느끼고 있는지, 심지어 그들이 공개하기를 꺼릴 때에도, 그것들을 잘 알아차릴 수 있는가? 그렇지 못하다면, 주제문 당신은 가상의 친구들과 귀중한 시간을 보냄으로써 이 소중한 능력을 향상시킬 수 있다. Jessica Black과 Jennifer Barnes는 한 연구를 수행했다. 그 연구는 상을 받은 텔레비전 드라마('Mad Men' 또는 'The West Wing') 혹은 다큐멘터리('How the Universe Works' 또는 'Shark Week: Jaws Strikes Back')의 긴 발췌물을 시청하도록 무작위로 배정된 100명의 대학생을 포함했다. 그리고 나서 참가자들은 36개의 눈 이미지 집합을 보고 jealous(질투하는), panicked(공황 상태인), arrogant(거만한), hateful(혐오스러운) 이 네 어휘 중 어떤 것이 사진 속의 사람을 가장 잘 묘사하는지 질문을 받았다. 놀라울 것도 없이, 연구자들은 정확한 감정을 선택하는 데 있어 여성이 남성보다 더 잘한다는 것을 발견했다. 그러나 남녀 모두에게 있어서, 드라마 중 하나를 시청한 사람들이 다큐멘터리를 본 사람들보다 평균적으로 더 높은 점수를 받았다.

⬇

텔레비전 드라마와 같은 양질의 (A) 허구적 프로그램을 시청하는 것이 다른 사람들의 감정을 (B) 읽어내는 우리의 능력을 향상시켜줄 수 있다.

구문 [6행~11행] It featured *100 college students* [who were randomly assigned / to watch *an extended excerpt* (from either an award-winning television drama (*Mad Men* or *The West Wing*), or a documentary (*How the Universe Works* or *Shark Week: Jaws Strikes Back*))].

관계사절 who ~ Back은 선행사 100 college students를 수식하며, 전명구 from ~ Back은 앞의 명사 an extended excerpt를 수식한다.

[11행~14행] Participants(S) were then shown(V1) *36 images* (of sets of eyes)(O1), / and (were) asked(V2) which of the four words best described *the person* (in the photograph): jealous, panicked, arrogant, or hateful(O2).

which ~ hateful은 의문사가 이끄는 명사절로 동사 asked의 목적어 역할을 한다.

어휘 **reluctant** 꺼리는, 주저하는 **quality time** (특히 퇴근 후의) 귀중한 시간 **imaginary** 가상의, 상상의 **conduct** 수행(하다); 행동(하다); 지휘하다 **randomly** 무작위로, 임의로 **assign** 배정하다, 할당하다; 임명하다 **extended** 길어진, 늘어난 **award-winning** 상을 받은 **participant** 참가자 **panic**

공황 상태에 빠지게 하다; 공황 (상태) **arrogant** 거만한, 오만한 **hateful** 혐오스러운 **not surprisingly** 놀랄 것 없이, 당연히 **on average** 평균적으로 [선택지 어휘] **internalize** 내면화하다 **instructive** 교육[교훈]적인, 유익한

vulnerable 취약한 **undermine** 손상[약화]시키다 **favorable** 호의적인 **interpretation** 해석 **simultaneously** 동시에 **rancher** 목장 주인 **sacred** 신성한 **molecular** 분자의 **cultivate** 함양하다, 육성하다; 재배하다

41~42 장문

41 ② 42 ⑤

소재 다양한 관점을 인식하는 것의 필요성

해설 41. 세상에는 사물을 관찰하는 사람들의 수만큼 다양한 관점들이 존재한다는 점을 깨달으면, '나도 옳을 수 있고 동시에 당신도 옳을 수 있다', 혹은 '어떤 대상이 단 하나의 개념으로 규정되는 것이 아니라 동시에 여러 가지 것의 성질을 지닐 수 있다'와 같은 태도를 갖게 되어 우리의 인식에 해방감을 준다는 내용의 글이므로 제목으로 가장 적절한 것은 ② '다른 관점들에 마음을 열어라'이다.

① 행복해지기 위하여 관점을 확장하라
③ 관점 전환이 차이를 만든다
④ 관점을 바꾸고, 인생을 바꿔라
⑤ 다른 관점에서 사물을 보는 방법

42. 하나의 대상이 동시에 여러 가지 성질을 가질 수 있다는 점을 깨달으면, 이것이 타인과의 교류 방식에 대해 정확한 계획을 세워주는 것은 아니지만, 적어도 대상에 대한 다양한 관점이 존재한다, 즉 다양한 관점이 결코 '소진되지 않는다'는 인식을 가지고 대상을 대할 수 있다. 따라서 (e)의 cultivated를 exhausted로 고쳐 써서 '다양한 관점들이 함양되지 않는' 것이 아닌, '다양한 관점들이 소진되지 않는' 인식 상태로 표현되어야 한다.

해석 오랫동안 사회심리학자들은 행위자의 관점과 관찰자의 관점 간의 차이에 관한 글을 써왔다. 예를 들어 우리는 우리 자신의 부정적인 행동에 대해서는 (a) 상황을 탓하기 쉽다. "난 지하철 때문에 항상 늦어." 그러나 바로 동일한 행동이 다른 사람에 의해 행해지면, 우리는 그 개인을 비난하는 경향이 있다. "저 사람은 만성적으로 일정보다 늦지."
주제문 우리가 일단 우리 자신의 것 외의 견해들을 유념하여 인식하게 되면, 우리는 각기 다른 관찰자들이 존재하는 만큼이나 각기 다른 견해들이 있다는 점을 깨닫기 시작한다. 그러한 인식은 잠재적으로 (b) 해방감을 준다. 예를 들어 누군가가 방금 당신보고 무례하다고 말했다고 상상해보자. 당신은 자신이 솔직하게 행동하고 있다고 생각했다. 오직 하나의 관점만이 존재한다면 둘 다 옳을 수 없다. 그러나 많은 관점에 대한 인식이 있으면, 당신은 둘 다 옳다는 점을 받아들일 수 있을 것이다. 우리가 우리 자신의 관점을 고수한다면, 우리가 다른 사람들에게 미치는 영향을 못 볼지도 모른다. 우리가 다른 사람들이 우리의 행동에 대해 내리는 정의에 지나치게 취약하다면, 우리는 (c) 손상을 입는다는 느낌을 받을 수 있는데, 왜냐하면 우리가 우리 자신에게 대하는 것보다 관찰자들이 일반적으로 우리에게 덜 호의적이기 때문이다.
우리가 말했던 대로, 잠재적으로 관찰자들이 존재하는 만큼이나 많은 (d) 해석들이 존재한다. 모든 생각, 모든 사람, 혹은 모든 대상은 그것을 보는 관점에 따라 잠재적으로 동시에 많은 것들이 된다. 소는 목장 주인에게는 스테이크이고, 힌두교인에게는 신성한 대상이고, 분자생물학자에게는 유전자와 단백질의 집합체이다. 유념한다는 것이 우리가 특정한 결과를 산출해 줄, 특정하게 규정된 타인과의 교류 방식을 계획할 수 있다는 것을 의미하지는 않는다. 오히려 그것은 우리가 가능한 다양한 관점들이 결코 (e) 함양되지(→ 소진되지) 않을 것임을 인식하는 상태로 있음을 의미한다. 우리는 웅대한 규모로 혹은 가장 일상적인 상황에서 이것을 볼 수 있다.

구문 [20행~22행] ~ we may feel undermined, for observers are generally **less** favorable to us **than** we are (favorable) of ourselves.
밑줄 친 for는 '~이므로'를 뜻하는 부사절 접속사이다. 「비교급+than」 구문이 쓰였으며 we are 뒤에는 favorable이 생략되어 있다.

[24행~27행] Every idea, person, or object (S) is (V) potentially simultaneously many things depending on *the perspective* [from which it is viewed].
every는 단수 취급하여 동사를 is로 썼다. [ ]는 「전치사+관계대명사」로 시작되는 관계사절로서 the perspective를 수식한다.

어휘 **perspective** 관점, 견해 **blame A for B** B에 대해서 A를 비난하다 **engage in** (활동[일]을) 하다 **chronically** 만성적으로 **behind schedule** 일정보다 늦게 **mindfully** 마음에 두고, 주의하여 **other than** ~ 외에 **liberate** 해방시키다 **cling to** ~을 고수하다 **blind** 못 보는, 깨닫지 못하는

43~45 장문

43 ⑤ 44 ② 45 ③

소재 눈에 보이는 것이 다가 아니다

해설 43. (A)는 두 명의 천사가 부자 가족에게 멸시를 당하며 지하실에서 밤을 지냈다는 내용이다. 그럼에도, 한 천사가 부잣집 지하실 벽에 있는 구멍을 수리했다는 내용의 (D)가 이어지고, 가난한 부부의 집에서는 환대를 받았다는 이야기 이후에 (C)의 그 다음 날 아침 가난한 부부의 소가 죽은 것을 알게 되는 내용이 이어지는 것이 적절하다. 마지막으로 (B)는 나이 많은 천사가 왜 이러한 일이 벌어졌는지 설명하며 글 전체의 교훈을 전하고 있으므로 마지막에 오는 것이 알맞다.

44. (b)는 농부와 그의 아내를 가리키며, 나머지는 모두 두 천사를 가리킨다.

45. (B)에서 천사는 가난한 농부의 아내를 죽음의 사자로부터 구하기 위해 소를 대신 데려가게 했으므로 ③이 글의 내용과 일치하지 않는다.

해석 (A) 두 명의 천사가 변장을 한 채 한 부자 가족에게 하룻밤 묵을 수 있는지를 물었다. 천사들은 그 가족에게 멸시를 당했고 침대에서 자는 것을 거절당했다. 대신에 ① (a) 그들(=천사들)은 춥고 어두운 지하실로 안내되었다.
(D) 젊은 천사가 춥고 딱딱한 바닥에서 잠을 청하고 있을 때, ④ 나이가 많은 천사가 벽에 난 구멍을 고치기 시작했다. 이는 젊은 천사를 어리둥절하게 했지만, 나이가 많은 천사는 "항상 눈에 보이는 것이 다가 아니란다."라고 말했다. 다음날 밤 (d) 그 둘(=천사들)은 매우 가난한 농부와 아내가 사는 집으로 갔다. 그들은 천사들과 모든 음식을 나누어 먹은 후, (e) 그들(=천사들)이 편안하고 환영받는 느낌을 받도록 ⑤ 그들의 침대를 천사들에게 내주었다.
(C) 다음날 아침 두 천사는 (b) 그들(=농부와 아내)이 슬피 우는 것을 발견했다. 그들이 지금까지 가졌던 유일한 재산인 소중한 젖소가 죽은 것이다. 젊은 천사는 매우 화가 났다. "어떻게 이런 일이 일어나도록 내버려 둘 수가 있습니까? 부자들은 우리에게 못되게 굴었지만, 당신은 그들을 도와줬어요!"라며 나이가 많은 천사를 비난했다. "그리고 이 가난한 사람들은 기꺼이 (c) 우리(=천사들)와 이 모든 것을 나누었는데, 당신은 그들의 소를 죽게 내버려뒀어요!" "항상 눈에 보이는 것이 다가 아니란다."라고 나이 많은 천사가 대답했다.
(B) "우리가 ② 대저택의 지하실에서 머물렀던 그 밤, 나는 벽 속의 구멍을 살펴보다가 금 무더기를 발견했단다. 주인이 우리에게 심술궂게 대했기 때문에 나는 그 금이 절대 발견되지 않도록 구멍을 막은 것이란다. 그리고 어젯밤, 우리가 농부 아내의 침대에서 자고 있을 때 ③ 죽음의 사자(使者)가 그녀에게 다가왔단다. 나는 그 사자가 농부의 소를 대신 데려가도록 했지. 주제문 항상 눈에 보이는 것이 다가 아니란다."

구문 [(C) 2행~3행] Their prized cow (S), *the only thing of value* [(that) they had ever owned], was (V) dead.
콤마로 연결된 두 개의 어구는 동격을 이룬다. [ ] 부분은 목적격 관계대명사가 생략된 관계사절로 the only thing of value를 수식한다.

어휘 (A) **in disguise** 변장을 한 채 **with contempt** 멸시하여, 경멸하여 **refuse** 거절하다 **basement** 지하실 (B) **mansion** 대저택 **inspect** 살피다, 조사하다 **a pile of** 한 무더기의, 산더미의 **mean** 심술궂은; 야비한 **seal** 막다, 봉하다 (C) **companion** 동료, 친구 **weep** 슬피 울다 **prized** 소중한, 가치 있는 **lose one's temper** 매우 화를 내다 **accuse** 비난하다; 고소하다 (D) **set to v-ing** v하기 시작하다 **puzzle** 어리둥절하게 하다, 당황하게 하다

실전 모의고사 07

본문 p.97

18 ⑤	19 ④	20 ④	21 ⑤	22 ⑤	23 ①	24 ①	25 ②	26 ③	27 ④
28 ③	29 ④	30 ①	31 ④	32 ④	33 ①	34 ⑤	35 ③	36 ①	37 ②
38 ⑤	39 ③	40 ④	41 ⑤	42 ④	43 ③	44 ④	45 ⑤		

18 글의 목적 ⑤

소재 학생 연주자 수를 늘리기 위한 조언 구하기

해설 글 중반부의 Do you have any advice for ~ 이하에 목적이 잘 나타나 있다. 악기를 연주하는 학생들의 수를 늘릴 방법에 대해 조언을 구하고 있으므로 정답은 ⑤이다.

해석 Palmer 선생님께,
저는 선생님의 학교 관현악단이 공연했던 음악 교사 학회에 참석했습니다. 선생님이 총 500명의 재적 인원 중 360명의 학생들을 기악 프로그램에 활발히 참여하게 한다는 것을 들었을 때, 저는 매우 감명을 받았습니다. 선생님께서도 분명히 아시겠지만, 그 숫자는 상당히 놀랄 만한 것입니다. 주제문 학교에서 학생 연주자의 수를 늘리려고 노력하는 신규 음악 교사들을 위한 조언이 있으신지요? 이 이메일에 회신할 시간이 없으시다면, 제가 전화를 드려도 되는 날짜와 시간을 알려주셔도 됩니다. 선생님이 가지고 계신 어떤 조언이라도 감사히 듣겠습니다.
Olivia Wright 드림

구문 [3행~6행] When I heard // that you **have**(V′) *360 students* (out of a total enrollment of 500)(O′) actively **participating** in ~.(C′)
that절은 SVOC 구조로, 여기서 have는 'O가 C하게 하다'란 뜻의 사역동사로 쓰였다. 진행의 의미를 강조할 때 목적격보어로 현재분사(participating)를 쓸 수 있다.

어휘 **present** 참석한; 현재의 **conference** 학회; 회의; 협의 **perform** (음악을) 연주하다; 공연하다; 수행하다 **enrollment** 등록 **instrumental** 악기(용)의 **impressed** 감명을 받은 **remarkable** 놀랄 만한, 주목할 만한 **indicate** 간단히 말하다; 나타내다; 가리키다 **appreciate** 감사하다; 진가를 인정하다; 감상하다

19 분위기 추론 ④

소재 은퇴 첫날의 아침 풍경

해설 은퇴 첫날 아침에 게으름을 피우며 여유 있게 아침을 맞이하는 주인공의 모습을 묘사하고 있다. 출근 준비로 분주했던 이전 아침과 달리 편안하고 느긋한 분위기를 느낄 수 있으므로 정답은 ④ '편안하고 느긋한'이다.

해석 시끄럽게 알람시계가 울려댔다. 나는 따뜻한 이불 아래에서 손을 뻗어 알람을 끄고 다시 침대로 파고들었다. 창문 밖은 침대 속에서 게으름을 부리며 꾸벅꾸벅 졸기에 딱 알맞게 춥고 비 내리는 흐린 날이었다. 지난 44년간 거의 매주 월요일 아침마다 나는 침대에서 벌떡 일어나 출근 준비를 하느라 분주하게 움직였다. 오늘은 아니다. 나는 집 안에서 나는 소리를 들으려고 귀를 기울였지만 곧 내 아내가 이른 월요일 아침마다 골프를 치는 것이 기억났다. 나는 게으름을 피우며 스트레칭을 하고 하품을 하며 아침식사에 대해 생각했다. 커피가 좋을 것 같았다. 나는 다리를 침대 밖으로 빼서 천천히 흔들어 슬리퍼를 신고는 목욕 가운으로 손을 뻗었다. 주제문 오늘은 나의 은퇴 첫날이었다.
① 분주하고 시끄러운
② 활기차고 즐거운
③ 지루하고 우울한
⑤ 긴박하고 무서운

어휘 **buzz** (기계 등이) 시끄럽게 울리다 *cf.* **buzzer** (알람시계·초인종 같은) 시끄럽게 울리는 물건 **switch off** ~을 끄다 **snuggle down** 침대 등에 편안히 눕다 *cf.* **snuggle** 바싹 파고들다, 달라붙다 **laze** 게으름을 피우다, 빈둥거리다 **doze** 깜빡 졸다; 낮잠을 자다 **leap out of** ~에서 뛰쳐나오다 **busy oneself** 분주히 움직이다 **listen for** ~을 들으려고 귀를 기울이다 **yawn** 하품하다 **swing (swung-swung)** 좌우로 흔들다 **bathrobe** 목욕 가운 **retirement** 은퇴, 퇴직

20 필자 주장 ④

소재 표준 영어의 쇠퇴

해설 엄격한 표준 영어 사용에 집착해서 스스로 스트레스 받지 말고, 표준 영어가 쇠퇴했다는 사실을 받아들이라는 내용이므로 필자의 주장으로 가장 적절한 것은 ④이다.

해석 구두법, 화법, 문법은 오늘날 많은 이에게 그리 중요하지 않은 듯하다. 예를 들어, 슈퍼마켓의 빠른 계산대 통로의 표지판은 '12 items or fewer'가 맞는데 항상 '12 items or less'로 표기되어 있다. 무관심과 전반적인 교육 수준의 하락이 표준 영어를 쇠퇴하게 만들었다. 어떤 이들은 이 문제에 몹시 신경을 쓴다. 그들은 모든 사람이 자기들이 하는 것만큼 표준 영어를 준수해야 한다고 생각하며, 영어가 오용되는 것을 볼 때마다 매우 화를 낸다. 슬프게도, 이들은 자신들이 평생 스트레스를 받도록 하고 있다. 주제문 그들은 기준이 쇠퇴했다는 사실을 받아들여야만 한다. 서툰 영어는 메뉴판, 거리 표지판, 광고, 신문, 심지어 학술 논문 등 어디에나 있다. 주제문 그것(= 서툰 영어)에 사로잡히거나 그것 때문에 화내지 마라.

구문 [1행~2행] It seems that punctuation, diction, and grammar are **of** little **importance** to many people these days.
「of+추상명사」는 형용사와 같다. (*e.g.* of importance=important / of courage=courageous / of no use=useless) 참고로, 「with+추상명사」는 부사로 바꿔 쓸 수 있다. (*e.g.* with ease=easily / with care=carefully)
[8행~10행] They(S) believe(V1) // (that) everybody should respect Standard English as much as they do, and are very angry(V2) // whenever (S)they (V)see (O)English (C)abused.
They를 공통된 주어로 하는 두 개의 절이 and로 연결된 구조이다. everybody should ~ they do는 명사절로 believe의 목적어 역할을 한다. whenever가 이끄는 절에서 see는 SVOC 구조를 취하며 목적어 English와 abuse가 수동 관계이므로 목적격보어 자리에 과거분사 abused가 왔다.

어휘 **punctuation** 구두법 **diction** 화법, 말투 **express** 고속의, 급행의 **checkout** (슈퍼마켓 등에서의) 계산(대) **aisle** (상점·열차 등의) 통로, 복도 **indifference** 무관심 **standard** (주로 복수형) 기준, 표준; 규범; 표준의 **go downhill** 쇠퇴하다, 질이 떨어지다 **terribly** 몹시, 굉장히 **respect** 준수하다; 존중하다 **abuse** 오용하다, 남용하다; 학대하다 **academic** 학문의 **be obsessed with[by]** ~에 사로잡히다

21 글의 요지 ⑤

소재 위험을 감수하지 않는 것의 위험성

해설 앞부분에서 미식축구 경기를 예로 들어 위험을 감수하지 않는 팀은 결국 지게 된

다고 하였고, 뒤이어 이것이 경력에도 똑같이 적용된다고 하였다. 마지막 부분에서 '위험을 감수하지 않는 것이 가장 큰 위험이다(Failing to take risks is the biggest risk of all)'라고 다시 한번 강조하고 있으므로 글의 요지로는 ⑤가 가장 적절하다.

해석 경기 중에 미식축구 해설자들의 말을 들어보아라. 그러면 그들이 위험에 대해 이야기하는 것을 듣게 되는데, 공을 아주 멀리 던지거나 대담하게 경기를 하는 것처럼 특히 득점하려는 것과 관련된 것들(=위험들)이다. 그러나 그들은 위험한 일을 '시도하지 않는' 위험에 대해서는 결코 이야기하지 않는다. 경기에서 실점이나 패배를 피하려고 하면 팀이 너무 신중해져서 어쨌든 경기에서 지게 되는데, 이는 필요한 위험을 감수하지 않았기 때문이다. 이와 똑같은 경우가 당신의 경력에도 적용된다. 도전적이고 새로운 직업을 얻으려고 노력할 때와 같은 경우에는, 목표를 높게 세우는 것과 관련된 위험을 만나기가 쉽다. 그러나 만약 당신이 위험을 감수하지 않으면 어디에도 갈 수 없을 것이다. 주제문 위험을 감수하지 않는 것이 가장 커다란 위험인데, 바로 그렇게 성공할 수 있는 당신의 모든 기회를 놓치게 되는 것이다.

구문 [1행~4행] **Listen** to football announcers during a game, / **and** you'll hear(V) them(O) talking about risks(C), / especially ***those*** (associated with trying to score — like throwing the ball too far [or] going for a big play).

「명령문+and ...」의 구조로 '~해라. 그러면 …할 것이다'란 뜻이다. and가 이끄는 절의 동사인 지각동사 hear는 SVOC 구조를 취하는데, 현재 진행 중인 행동을 강조할 때는 목적격보어로 현재분사를 쓸 수 있다. 반복을 피하기 위해 쓰인 대명사 those는 앞에 나온 명사 risks를 받으며, 과거분사구의 수식을 받고 있다.

어휘 **associated with** ~와 관련된 **go for** ~을 얻고자 노력하다; ~을 선택하다 **in the attempt to-v** v하려는 노력으로, v하기 위해 **setback** 패배; 후퇴 **conservative** 신중한, 조심스런; 보수적인 **take a risk** 위험을 감수하다 **apply** 적용하다 **career** 경력, 이력

22 글의 주제 ⑤

소재 수학적 연관성을 인과관계로 판단하는 오류

해설 수학적으로 연관성이 있다고 해서 인과관계가 성립한다고 판단하는 것은 잘못된 생각이라는 내용의 글이다. 공기 중 이산화탄소의 수치 증가와 범죄 발생 건수 증가 사이의 관계가 수치적으로 유의미하다고 해서 서로 인과관계가 있는 것으로 오판하게 되면 제대로 된 해결책이 나올 수 없다는 것을 예로 들어 설명하고 있다. 따라서 글의 주제로 가장 적절한 것은 ⑤ '수학적으로 연관성 있는 사건에 관한 잘못된 생각'이다.

해석 주제문 많은 사건들, 사실들, 관찰들, 변화들이 다른 것들과 수학적으로 상호 관련될 수 있지만, 그러한 상관관계가 어떤 인과관계를 증명하는 것은 전혀 아니다. 바로 이 그릇된 생각을 '증명하기' 위해서, 다음과 같은 어리석은 상관관계에 대해 생각해보라. 지난 100년 동안 지구상의 모든 국가들 상공의 공기 중에 들어 있는 이산화탄소의 수치가 증가해 왔다. 마찬가지로, 보고된 범죄의 발생 건수도 지난 100년 동안 전 세계에서 증가해 왔다. 그러므로 공기 중의 이산화탄소와 범죄 발생 건수 사이에는 인과관계가 존재한다는 결론이 내려진다. 물론 그것은 전혀 터무니없는 생각이다. 하지만 정치가들, 대중 매체의 보도 기자들, 그리고 일반 대중들은 모두 그러한 종류의 논리에 속는다. 그리고는, 이해했다고 생각되는 문제에 대한 '해결책'이 만들어지고, 그 해결책들은 흔히 세금을 올리고 후손으로부터 돈을 빌리는 것을 요구한다. 결국, 시간과 돈을 잃었는데 해결된 문제는 아무것도 없다.

① 대기오염이 범죄율에 미치는 영향
② 다수 의견을 따르는 것의 위험성
③ 현상의 원인을 알아내는 것의 필요성
④ 문제 해결 도구로서의 인과분석

어휘 **observation** 관찰 **mathematically** 수학적으로 **correlate A with B** A와 B를 연관시키다 *cf.* **correlation** 연관성, 상관관계 **cause-effect relationship** 인과관계 **fallacy** (많은 사람이 믿는) 그릇된 생각; 오류 **commit** (범죄를) 저지르다; 약속하다; 전념하다 **conclude** 결론을 내리다; 끝나다 **causative** 원인이 되는 **the public at large** 일반 대중 *cf.* **at large** (명사 뒤에 쓰여) 전체적인; 대체적인 **fall for** ~에 속아 넘어가다 **reasoning** 추리, 추론 [선택지 어휘] **phenomena** (**phenomenon**의 복수형) 현상 **misconception** (옳지 않은 정보에 근거한) 오해; 잘못된 통념(=**myth**)

23 글의 제목 ①

소재 냄새를 통해 전달될 수 있는 감정

해설 긍정적인 감정이 냄새를 통해 전달되는지를 알아보고자 한 실험에서, 행복감을 유발하는 영화를 본 남성들의 땀 냄새를 맡은 여성들이 더 많이 미소 짓는다는 결과를 얻었다. 즉, 행복감과 같은 긍정적인 감정이 냄새를 통해 전달될 수 있음을 보여주는 내용이므로 제목으로 가장 적절한 것은 ① '행복은 냄새를 통해 전염될 수 있다'이다.

해석 다른 누군가의 땀 냄새를 맡는 것은 불쾌할 수도 있지만, 여기 재미있는 사실이 하나 있다. 네덜란드 Utrecht 대학의 연구자들은 이전의 연구들로부터 부정적인 감정들이 '화학 신호'를 통해 냄새로 전달될 수 있다는 것을 알고 있어서, 그와 반대되는 감정(=긍정적인 감정)도 전달될 수 있는지 알고 싶어 했다. 그들은 12명의 남성을 모아서 그들에게 두려움이나 행복감을 유발하는 영화를 보여주었는데, 중립적인 장면들을 보게 된 통제 집단도 함께 있었다. 그들은 남성들의 팔 아래에 패드를 놓아서 각 남성으로부터 땀 샘플을 채취했다. 그런 다음 모든 땀 샘플은 36명의 여성 참가자들에게 냄새를 맡도록 주어졌고, 그러는 동안 그들의 얼굴 표정이 기록되었다. 주제문 연구자들은 여성들이 중립적인 클립을 본 사람들의 땀 냄새를 맡을 때보다 행복한 남성들의 땀 냄새를 맡을 때 더 많이 미소 짓는다는 결론을 내릴 수 있었다.

② 후각이 감정과 만나는 경우
③ 냄새가 사람들의 업무 수행에 영향을 미치는가?
④ 항상 좋은 냄새가 나는 사람들의 비결
⑤ 당신의 기분을 긍정적으로 변화시킬 수 있는 장면들

구문 [5행~6행] ~ so they wanted to know // **if** the opposite emotion could be conveyed, too.

if ~ too는 know의 목적어인 명사절이다. 여기서 if는 '~인지 (아닌지)'의 의미이다.

[13행~16행] The researchers were able to conclude // (that) the women smiled [more] when they smelled *the sweat* (of the happy men) [than] when they smelled *the sweat* (of *those* [who watched a neutral clip]).

전명구 of the happy men과 of those ~ neutral clip은 각각 앞의 명사 the sweat을 수식하고, 관계사절 who ~ clip은 선행사 those를 수식한다.

어휘 **unpleasant** 불쾌한, 불편한 **sweat** 땀; 땀을 흘리다 **previous** 이전의 **transfer** 전달하다; 옮기다, 나르다 **scent** 냄새, 향 **via** 통하여; 경유하여, 거쳐 **convey** 전달하다; 실어 나르다 **gather** 모으다, 모이다 **generate** 발생시키다 **along with** ~와 함께; ~와 마찬가지로 **neutral** 중립적인; 감정을 자제하는 **facial expression** 얼굴 표정 [선택지 어휘] **contagious** 전염성이 있는 **affect** 영향을 미치다

24 도표 이해 ①

소재 중동 6개국 석유 생산량 비교

해설 카타르(Qatar)의 석유 생산량 추정치를 1990년에 비해 2000년에는 증가했지만 2010년에는 2000년보다 줄어들었다. 따라서 모든 나라의 석유 생산량이 해마다 증가할 것으로 추정되었다는 ①의 내용은 도표와 일치하지 않는다.

해석 〈석유 생산량(추정)〉

주제문 이 그래프는 여섯 개 중동 국가의 석유 생산량 추정치를 비교한 것으로 몇 가지 주목할 만한 점이 있다. ① 가장 중요한 점은 석유 생산이 모든 나라에서 해마다 증가할 것으로 추정됐다는 것이다. ② 쿠웨이트와 이라크 모두 1990년과 2020년 사이에 생산량이 약 두 배가 될 것으로 예상됐다. ③ 아랍에미리트의 생산량은 1990년에서 2000년까지 하루 250만 배럴 수준에 머무르다가 2020년에는 400만 배럴에 달할 것으로 예상됐다. ④ 사우디아라비아의 1990년 생산량은 이란, 이라크, 쿠웨이트를 모두 합친 것을 넘어설 것으로 예상됐다. ⑤ 이 그래프는 또한 사우디아라비아가 2020년에 하루 1,450만 배럴을 생산할 것으로 예상되면서 생산량에서 선도자적인 위치를 계속 유지하고 강화할 것으로 예상한다.

구문 [11행~15행] The graph also **predicts** // that Saudi Arabia (S') would maintain and strengthen (V') its position as the leader in production capacity, (O') / **with** *14.5 million barrels per day* **expected** in 2020.
동사 predicts의 목적어인 that절은 SVO 구조를 갖는다. 「with+목적어+분사」는 부대상황을 나타내는 분사구문으로 '~한 채로, ~하면서'란 뜻이다. 목적어와 분사의 관계가 수동이어서 과거분사(expected)가 쓰였다.

어휘 **capacity** 용량, 용적; 능력 **estimate** 예상하다, 추정하다; 예상, 추정 **notable** 주목할 만한; 중요한 **year by year** 해마다 **roughly** 대략, 거의; 거칠게 **output** 생산량, 산출량 **steady** 안정된; 한결같은 **approach** (수준 등이) ~에 이르다; 다가가다 **exceed** 넘다, 능가하다 **combined** 합친, 결합된

25 내용 불일치 ②

소재 개썰매 경주 선수 Susan Butcher

해설 1985년 Iditarod 개썰매 경주에서 Susan은 사고로 경기를 포기하게 되었고, 그 경기에서는 Libby Riddles가 여성 최초로 우승을 차지했으므로 ②가 글의 내용과 일치하지 않는다.

해석 ① Susan Butcher는 20세 때 동물과 황야에 대한 애정을 쫓아 알래스카로 갔고, Iditarod 개썰매 경주에 참가하려고 훈련을 시작했다. 믿기지 않을 정도로 힘든 Iditarod는 1주일에서 2주일이 걸리는 1,100마일의 알래스카 황무지 코스를 통해 경주 참가자와 개의 인내력을 시험한다. ② 1985년 Iditarod에서 Susan은 사고 후 강제로 (경기를) 포기하게 되었고, 그 해 심한 눈보라에도 살아남은 Libby Riddles가 경주에서 우승한 최초의 여성이 되었다. 같은 해 얼마 후 Susan은 ③ 개썰매 경주 동료 선수인 David Monson과 결혼했고, 이 부부는 거의 모든 세계적인 주요 개썰매 경주에 계속해서 성공적으로 참가했다. ④ Susan은 1986, 1987, 1988, 1990년도 Iditarod에서 우승했다. ⑤ 그녀가 1989년 경주를 놓친 것은 단지 그녀가 첫 딸을 임신했기 때문이었다.

구문 [8행~10행] ~, and that year Libby Riddles survived a blizzard **to become** *the first woman* ever (**to win** the race).
to become ~은 생존해서 최초 여성 우승자가 되었다는 '결과'를 나타내는 부사적 용법의 to부정사이고, to win ~은 the first woman을 수식하는 형용사 역할을 한다.

어휘 **pursue** 쫓다; 추구하다 **wilderness** 황야, 황무지 **compete in** ~에 참가하다 **sled** 썰매 **endurance** 인내력, 지구력 **be forced to-v** (강제로) v하게 되다, v하도록 강요받다 **pull out of** ~에서 손 떼게 하다 **blizzard** 심한 눈보라 **fellow** 동료 **pregnant** 임신한

26 안내문 불일치 ③

소재 선거 운동 규칙

해설 5-a에서 후보자 연설은 수요일 수업 전에 녹화될 예정이라고 했으므로 ③이 안내문의 내용과 일치하지 않는다.

해석

선거 운동 규칙

1. 학생들은 포스터를 사용해서만 선거 운동을 할 수 있습니다. 모든 포스터는 Little 선생님의 승인을 받아야 합니다.
2. ① 학생들은 총 8장의 선거 운동 포스터를 만들 수 있습니다.
   a. 학생 사물함용 1장
   b. 일반 장소(식당, 복도)용 7장
3. 포스터는 긍정적인 내용이어야 하고 ② 다른 후보자를 언급할 수 없습니다.
4. 학생들은 사탕, 상품, 카드 등 어떤 것도 나눠줄 수 없습니다.
5. 직책을 맡기 위해 출마한 학생들은 연설을 준비해야 합니다.
   a. ③ 연설은 10월 9일 수요일에 수업 전에 녹화됩니다.
   b. ④ 연설은 최소 1분 이상이어야 하고 3분을 넘으면 안 됩니다.
6. ⑤ 부모님들은 선거 운동의 어떤 부분에도 참여할 수 없습니다.

어휘 **campaign** 선거 운동; (특별한 목적을 위한) 캠페인 **approve** 승인하다, 인정하다 **cafeteria** 학생식당, 구내식당 **candidate** 후보자 **hand out** 나눠주다 **run for office** 공직에 출마하다 *cf.* **office** 직무, 임무 **permit** 허용[허락]하다

27 안내문 일치 ④

소재 동창회 파티 안내

해설 연회비(annual membership fees)는 행사장 입구나 온라인으로 지불할 수 있다고 했으므로 ④가 안내문의 내용과 일치한다.

해석

휴일 파티

Franklin 연례 졸업생 및 교원 행사에 당신을 초대합니다.

① 12월 29일 오후 6시부터 10시까지, Oak 가(街) 8312번지 Chiba 식당

② 오셔서 우수한 과거와 현재의 교수님들을 축하해 주시고 동창들과도 대화하세요! Chiba의 요리, 특제 칵테일과 *The Courtyard Kings*의 라이브 재즈 음악뿐만 아니라, 전통 휴일 요리도 마음껏 즐기세요.

동창회

③ 동창회 회원은 입장료가 없으며, 회원은 초대 손님 한 분을 데려올 수 있습니다.
④ (파티)입구에서나 온라인 fafa.org를 통해 연회비를 지불하시기 바랍니다. 모든 회원들은 Chiba에서 특별히 우리를 위해 Franklin 대학의 뜻을 받들어 만든 특제 칵테일 'The Big Ben' 한 잔을 무료로 받게 됩니다.

기부금: ⑤ 권장 기부금은 30달러이지만 이것 때문에 참석하지 못하는 일은 없길 바랍니다. 어떤 수준의 기부금도 환영하며 감사히 받겠습니다.

이런 특별한 기회를 통해 여러분들을 만나 뵙기를 희망합니다!

구문 [15행~18행] All members receive one complimentary Franklin-inspired specialty cocktail, "*The Big Ben*," (created especially for us by Chiba).
one ~ specialty cocktail과 "The Big Ben"은 동격이며, "The Big Ben"은 과거분사구의 수식을 받는다.

어휘 **alumni** (**alumnus**의 복수형) 졸업생들 **faculty** 교수단, 교직원 **fellow** 동료의 **fare** 식사, 음식; (교통) 요금 **cuisine** (고급) 요리 **specialty** 특제품, 명물 **complimentary** 무료의; 칭찬하는 **inspired** ~의 영향을 (받았음을) 드러내는; 영감을 받은

28 밑줄 어법 ③

소재 인간의 뛰어난 장거리 달리기 능력

해설 ③ makes it(가목적어) 다음에 보어가 필요한 SVOC 구조이다. 보어 자리에 형용사는 사용 가능하지만 부사는 쓸 수 없으므로 easily를 easy로 바꿔 써야 한다.

오답 분석 ① compared to ~는 '~와 비교할 때'라는 의미의 분사구문이다. 인간이 '비교되는' 수동의 의미이기 때문에 과거분사를 사용한다. ② 관계대명사 what은 '~한 것'이라는 의미이며 문장에서 주어, 보어, 목적어 역할을 하는 명사절을 이끌 수 있다. 이 글에서는 are 뒤에서 보어 역할을 하는 명사절을 이끌고 있다. ④ do는 대동사로, 앞의 store energy long을 지칭한다. 일반 동사를 지칭하는 대동사 do가 옳게 쓰였다. ⑤ 수식어 so와 such를 비교해볼 때, so는 형용사, 부사 등을 수식하는 '부사'이고, such는 명사를 수식하는 '형용사'적 기능을 주로 수행한다. long distances(장거리)는 명사구이므로 형용사적인 such를 사용했다.

해석 주제문 우리 인간들은 다른 육지 포유류들과 비교하면 동물계에서 최고의 장거리 주자이다. 우리의 직립 자세와 열을 발산할 수 있는 능력은 사람들이 경주하는 동안 20마일보다 더 먼 거리를 달릴 수 있게 해주는 것들이다. 우리의 더 우수한 냉각 시스템은 우리가 더운 날에 장거리를 달리는 것을 쉽게 만들어준다. 우리는 또한 더 우수한 호흡계를

가지고 있으며, 이는 우리가 효율성을 잃지 않고 속도를 변환할 수 있게 해준다. 그리고 우리의 식단은 우리가 대부분의 다른 동물들보다 에너지를 더 오랫동안 저장할 수 있게 해준다. 특히 최고의 인간 선수가 수행하는 속도로 장거리를 달릴 수 있는 다른 동물들은 거의 없다. 이 모든 것이 더해져 하나의 단순한 사실이 된다. 우리는 달리도록, 특히 엄청난 장거리를 달리도록 태어났다는 사실이다.

구문 [5행~6행] Our superior cooling system **makes it** easy for us **to run long distances on hot days.**
「make+가목적어(it)+형용사+for 의미상 주어+to-v」는 '(의미상 주어)가 v하는 것을 (형용사)하게 만들다'의 뜻이다.

어휘 **mammal** 포유류 **distance runner** 장거리 주자 **animal kingdom** 동물계 **upright posture** 직립 자세 **shed (shed-shed)** 발산하다, 내뿜게 하다 **efficiency** 효율(성), 능률 **add up to** (합계 · 결과가) ~이 되다

29 밑줄 어휘 ④

소재 우주쓰레기 문제

해설 우주쓰레기 문제의 심각성과 이를 해결하려는 노력에 관한 글이다. 그 노력의 일환으로 우주왕복선이 지구 궤도를 돌며 '활동하지 않는' 우주선들을 수거하고 있다는 문맥이 되어야 하므로 ④는 nonfunctioning 등으로 바꿔야 한다.

해석 주제문 미래의 우주여행에 대해 너무 많이 기대하지 마라. 아름다운 별 대신 주위를 ① 떠다니는 많은 쓰레기를 발견하고 실망할지도 모른다. 1957년 이후 5천 개 이상의 인공위성이 우주로 발사되어 왔고, 그러한 모든 활동이 엄청난 양의 우주쓰레기를 야기해 왔다. 우주잔해라고도 불리는 우주쓰레기는 이제는 더 이상 유용한 목적을 수행하지 않는, 인공위성이나 ② 생산적인 활동을 하는 모든 단계의 인공위성을 보조했던 것과 같은 모든 인공적인 물체이다. 우주쓰레기의 심각성을 인식한 후, 국제연합(UN)은 잔해의 발생을 ③ 제한하는 지침을 고안해내는 데 주력하고 있다. 게다가, 우주왕복선은 수년 간 지구 궤도를 돌며 ④ 활동하는(→ 활동하지 않는) 우주선들을 수거하고 있다. 이러한 지속적인 노력이 없다면, 우주는 하나의 커다란 ⑤ 쓰레기장으로 변할 것이다.

구문 [6행~9행] Space trash, also called space debris, / is *any man-made object*, (**such as** a satellite or *anything* [**that** assisted *a satellite* (in any stage of its productive life)]), [**that** is now no longer serving a useful purpose].
any man-made object는 such as가 이끄는 구와 that이 이끄는 주격 관계대명사절(that is now ~)의 수식을 동시에 받고 있다. such as ~ 안에서는 that이 이끄는 관계대명사절이 anything을 수식한다.

어휘 **satellite** (인공)위성 **launch** (로켓 등을) 발사하다, 쏘아 올리다 **lead to A** A를 야기하다, A에 이르게 하다 **debris** 잔해, 쓰레기 **man-made** 사람이 만든, 인공의 **assist** 보조하다, 돕다 **productive** 생산적인 **seriousness** 심각성 **the United Nations (UN)** 국제연합 **work on** (~을 만들려고) 애쓰다, 공들이다 **guideline** 지침(서) **space shuttle** 우주 왕복선 *cf.* **spacecraft** 우주선 **function** 기능하다 **orbit** 궤도를 돌다; 궤도 **continuous** 계속되는, 지속적인 **turn into** ~로 변하다 **dump** (쓰레기를) 버리다; 쓰레기장

30 지칭 대상 ①

소재 프랑스의 언어 순화 노력

해설 나머지는 모두 '외래어들(foreign languages)'을 가리키지만, ①은 앞 절의 주어 '노력(efforts)'을 가리킨다.

해석 프랑스에서 때때로 자국어를 '순화하려는' 노력이 있어 왔고, 일부 민족주의 언어 권위자들이 ① 그것들(=노력들)을 이끌어 왔다. 그들은 어휘에서 외래어들을 추방하고, ② 그것들(=외래어들)을 경시되거나 몇몇 경우 잊혀지기까지 한 '순수 프랑스어' 단어들로 대체하려고 했다. 일부 언어 이론가들은 같은 의미의 자국어가 있을 때는 외국에서 유래된 어떤 단어도 사용해서는 안 된다는 원칙에 한결같은 입장이다. 주제문 그러나 프랑스어에서 ③ 그것들(=외래어들)의 사용을 금지하는 규칙을 만들려는 어떤 노력도 실패할 수밖에 없는 운명일 것이다. 오랫동안 프랑스어에서 흔히 사용되어 온 외래어는 마치 저명한 프랑스 작가이자 철학자인 Voltaire(볼테르)에 의해 ④ 그것들(=외래어들)이 만들어지기라도 한 것처럼 바로 그렇게 그 언어의 일부분이다. ⑤ 그것들(=외래어들)이 열등하다고 여겨지거나 버려져야 할 확실한 이유는 없다.

구문 [3행~7행] They **have attempted** to expel foreign words from the vocabulary [and] to replace them with *"pure French" words* [that **have become** neglected [and] in some cases even forgotten].
주절의 동사 have attempted에 to expel ~ vocabulary와 to replace ~ forgotten이 대등하게 연결되는 구조이다. "pure French" words를 수식하는 관계대명사절에는 형용사 neglected와 forgotten이 have become에 접속사 and로 병렬 연결되어 있다.

[11행~14행] *Foreign words* [that have long been in common use in French] are just **as much** part of the language // **as if** they **had been invented** by Voltaire, ~.
Foreign words는 주격 관계대명사 that이 이끄는 관계사절의 수식을 받는다. as much는 '(앞의 내용을 받아서) 그것처럼, 그럴 만큼'이라는 뜻을 나타낸다. 「as if+S´+had p.p.」는 주절이 나타내는 시제보다 '과거'를 나타내므로 '(과거에) 마치 ~한 것처럼' 이라고 해석한다.

어휘 **purify** (언어를) 순화하다; 깨끗이 하다 **nationalist** 민족주의(자)의; 민족주의자 **authority** 권위자; 권위, 권력 **attempt** 시도하다, 꾀하다; 시도, 노력 **expel** 내쫓다, 추방하다 **replace A with B** A를 B로 대체하다 **neglect** 무시[경시]하다 **theorist** 이론가 **even** (행동 · 품질 등이) 한결같은, 고른 **origin** 기원, 유래 **ban** 금지하다 **be doomed to A** A할 수밖에 없는 운명이다, 필히 A하게 되어 있다 **prominent** 저명한; 눈에 띄는 **sound** 확실한, 이론적으로 옳은; 건강한 **inferior** (~보다) 열등한; 2류의 **abandon** 버리다; 포기[단념]하다

31 빈칸 추론 ④

소재 자부심 표현의 보편성

해설 자부심의 표현(미소, 치켜든 팔 등)은 국적과 문화권에 관계없이 동일한 것으로 보이며, 심지어 시각장애인으로 태어나서 다른 사람들의 자부심 표현을 볼 기회가 없었던 사람들도 자신의 자부심을 표출할 때 다른 사람들과 마찬가지의 행동을 한다는 내용의 글이므로 자부심의 표현은 ④ '보편적(universal)'이라 할 수 있다.

해석 주제문 자연스럽게 나오는 자부심의 표현은 보편적인 것 같다. Tracy와 David Matsumoto는 2004년 올림픽과 패럴림픽의 유도 경기에서 승리하거나 패배한 후에 촬영된 30개가 넘는 국가 출신의 선수들의 사진을 분석했다. 전 세계에서 온 15명의 선수들이 승리 후(미소, 뒤로 젖힌 머리, V자로 들어 올린 팔, 내민 가슴)와 패배 후(축 처진 어깨, 내려간 턱, 그리고 좁아진 가슴)에 동일한 행동을 보이는 경향이 있었다. 이것은 몇몇 경우에 집산주의적 문화권 출신의 경쟁자들에게조차 해당했는데, 그 문화권에서는 자부심이 덜 인정되고 심지어는 저지된다. 그러나 아마 이러한 표현의 선천성에 대한 가장 강력한 증거는 시각장애인으로 태어난 선수들(다른 사람이 자부심이나 권능이나 승리를 표현하는 것을 한 번도 본 적 없는 선수들)조차 승리했을 때 자신의 몸으로 동일한 것(= 행동)을 했다는 사실이다.
① 기능적인 ② 예측의 ③ 전염되는 ⑤ 판독하기 어려운

구문 [12행~16행] But perhaps the strongest evidence of the innateness of these expressions is the fact that even *athletes* [who were born blind] — *athletes* [who had never **seen** *another person* **express** pride or power or victory] — did the same thing ~ when they won.
주어는 the strongest evidence이고 동사는 is이다. that ~ won은 the fact에 대한 동격절이다. 두 [ ] 부분은 각각 바로 앞의 athletes를 수식한다. 두 번째 [ ] 부분에서 지각동사 「see+O+원형부정사 (O가 ~하는 것을 보다)」 구문이 쓰였다.

어휘 **spontaneous** 자연 발생적인, 자발적인 **analyze** 분석하다 **tilt** 기울이다 **slump** 푹 쓰러지다 **chin** 턱 **collectivistic** 집산주의의 **appreciate** 진가를 인정하다; 평가하다 **discourage** 저지하다, 단념시키다 **innateness** 천부적임, 타고남

32 빈칸 추론 ④

소재 경험에 따라 달라지는 인간 본성

해설 인간의 본성을 엘리베이터에 비유한 글이다. 엘리베이터의 어떤 버튼을 누르는지에 따라 다른 층으로 이동하는 것처럼, 인간의 본성 역시 특정 경험에 따라 유전자가 반응한다는 내용이므로 빈칸에 가장 적절한 것은 ④ '유전자 단계에서 경험에 반응하도록'이다.

해석 주제문 당신의 본성은 유전자 단계에서 경험에 반응하도록 설계되어 있다. 다시 말하자면, 당신은 엘리베이터처럼 설계되어서 당신의 버튼이 눌러질 경우에 대비한다. 엘리베이터는 스위치라고 불리는 특수한 회로가 있는데, 그 회로는 어떤 버튼이 눌러졌는지와 그에 대해 반응하는 방법을 '기억하기' 위해 닫힌다. 몇몇 인간 유전자 역시 스위치로서 역할을 한다. 이 유전자들은 회로를 닫고, 복잡하면서 일방적인 발달 과정을 활성화하여 특정 경험에 반응하거나 그 경험을 '기억하는데', 그 이후에는 이전 상태로 돌아갈 방법이 없다. 이는 유전적으로는 동일한 쌍둥이가 완전히 똑같지 않은 한 가지 이유이다. 쌍둥이 중 한 명은 유전 스위치가 영원히 닫히게 하는 경험을 할 수도 있다. 만약 쌍둥이 중 다른 한 명이 똑같은 경험을 하지 않는다면 그 스위치는 열려 있다. 같은 방법으로, 두 개의 엘리베이터는 똑같이 설계될 수 있지만(본성), 다른 버튼이 눌러졌기 때문에 다른 층으로 간다(양육).

① 인생의 많은 흥망성쇠를 견뎌내도록
② 참을성도 있고 충동적이기도 하도록
③ 나쁜 일을 잊기 위한 호르몬을 만들어내도록
⑤ 어떤 경험에는 개방적이고 다른 경험에는 폐쇄적이도록

구문 [3행~6행] An elevator has *special circuitry*, (called a switch), // **which** closes to "remember" / which button was pushed and how to respond to it.
called a switch는 삽입구문이다. which 이하는 계속적 용법의 관계대명사절로 special circuitry를 보충 설명하고 있다. 관계대명사절 내에서 which ~ pushed와 how ~ to it은 remember의 목적어 역할을 하고 있다.

어휘 **circuitry** 회로 (설계) *cf.* **circuit** 회로; 순회 **gene** 유전자, 유전 인자 *cf.* **genetically** 유전학적으로 *cf.* **genetic** 유전자의 **activate** 활성화시키다, 작동시키다 **previous** 앞의, 이전의 **state** 상태 **identical** 동일한 **trigger** (일을) 일으키다, 유발하다; 방아쇠 **permanently** 영원히, 영구적으로 **nurture** 양육, 교육 [선택지 어휘] **tolerate** 견디다, 참다 **impulsive** 충동적인

33 빈칸 추론 ①

소재 생태학적 도미노 효과

해설 이 글은 해양 포유동물의 개체 수가 급감한 원인을 밝히고 있다. 빈칸 뒷부분은 고래잡이의 증가로 범고래의 먹이가 되는 큰 고래가 사라져 범고래가 다른 해양 포유동물을 차례로 잡아먹었다는 내용으로, 이 현상은 ① '생태학적 도미노 효과'로 지칭할 수 있다.

해석 주제문 생태계의 재앙이 알래스카에서 조금 떨어진 차가운 바다에서 펼쳐지고 있다. 1970년대 이후로 바다표범, 바다사자, 해달의 수는 급격히 줄어들어 왔다. 몇몇 과학자는 해류의 변화를 탓했고, 어떤 과학자들은 해양 포유동물의 식량을 마구 잡아대는 인간을 비난했다. 그러나 최근에 발표된 한 논문에서는 이러한 참상을 생태학적 도미노 효과의 탓으로 돌렸다. 제2차 세계대전의 여파로 상업적인 고래잡이가 빠르게 증가했고, 북태평양의 커다란 고래는 거의 전부 없어졌다. 이는 범고래의 먹이가 되는 주요 원천을 없애버린 것인데, 그러자 범고래는 먹이사슬 아래에 있는 먹잇감을 잡아먹기 시작했다. 점박이 바다표범을 시작으로(70년대 초에 개체 수가 급격히 줄었다), 다음에는 물개를, 이어서 바다사자, 마지막으로 해달을 계속 먹어치웠으며(현재), 차례대로 이들의 개체 수를 붕괴시켰다.

② 국제적인 무력 충돌
③ 해류에 대한 무지함
④ 범고래의 천적
⑤ 작은 해양 포유동물 사냥

구문 [11행~16행] This removed a major source of food for *killer whales*, / **who** then **began** to fish down the food web, / **beginning** with harbor seals ~, / then **moving on to** fur seals, ~, / **collapsing** these populations one after another.
who가 이끄는 관계사절은 계속적 용법으로 쓰여 killer whales를 부연 설명하고 있다. 여러 개의 분사구문(beginning ~, moving on to ~, collapsing ~)이 이어져 연속적으로 일어난 현상을 나타내고 있다.

어휘 **ecological** 생태학적 **unfold** 펼쳐지다, 일어나다 **seal** 바다표범 **sea lion** 바다사자 **sea otter** 해달 **blame** ~을 탓하다, 비난하다 **current** 해류; 흐름; 현재의 **point one's finger at** ~에게 손가락질하다[비난하다] **overfish** 물고기를 마구 잡다, 남획하다 **marine mammals** 해양 포유동물 **attribute A to B** A의 원인을 B에 돌리다 **devastation** 참상, 황폐 **aftermath** (전쟁·재해 등의) 여파, 영향 **commercial** 상업적인; 광고 (방송) **whaling** 고래잡이 **expand** 확장되다, 넓어지다 **North Pacific Ocean** 북태평양 **wipe out** ~을 없애다; 닦아내다 **food web** (생태) 먹이그물 **harbor seal** 점박이 바다표범 **collapse** 무너지다 **move on to A** A로 계속해서 넘어가다 **fur seal** 물개 [선택지 어휘] **domino effect** 도미노 효과(한 가지 사건이 연쇄적으로 다른 사건을 일으키는 현상) **armed** 무장한 **ignorance** 무지, 무식

34 빈칸 추론 ⑤

소재 직장에서 실수를 발전의 초석으로 삼는 방법

해설 실수가 개인적, 직업적 발전에 도움이 될 수 있다고 한 후, 그 결과가 어떻게 되든 배우고 있음을 보여주어야 한다고 했다. 이는 실수를 자산으로 바꿔야 한다는 것과 일맥상통하므로 빈칸에 가장 적절한 것은 ⑤ '실수를 결점에서 자산으로 바꿀'이다.

해석 실수는 개인적, 직업적 발전에 중요한 역할을 할 수 있다. 만약 그 실수가 서투른 결정의 결과였다면 앞으로는 어떻게 그와 똑같거나 비슷한 실수를 저지르지 않을지를 당신의 상사와 다른 이해 당사자들에게 설명하되, 사람들이 당신의 능력이나 전문성에 대해 판단을 내리기 전에 빨리 행동해야 한다는 것을 기억하라. 당신이 실수한 결과로 인해 변했음을 입증함으로써, 당신은 앞으로도 그와 똑같이 중요한 업무나 결정을 당신에게 믿고 맡길 수 있다는 것을 상사와 동료들에게 안심시킬 수 있다. 아마도 당신의 상사나 동료들은 당신에게 업무량을 더 많이 맡기거나 책임을 덜 지게 하는 식으로 (당신이) 실수한 데 대한 대가를 치르게 하겠지만, 결과가 어떻게 되든 당신은 배우고 있음을 보여주어야 한다. 이것은 성과 중심 문화에서보다 학습 중심 문화에서 훨씬 더 쉬운데, 성과 중심 문화에서는 실수가 종종 더 냉혹하게 판단되기 때문이다. 주제문 그러나 업무 환경에 상관없이, 당신은 실수를 결점에서 자산으로 바꿀 수 있는 방법을 알아야 한다.

① 다른 기업 문화에 스스로 적응할
② 당신이 저지른 실수를 받아들이고 그것을 대담하게 인정할
③ 당신이 똑같은 실수를 반복해서 저지르지 않을
④ 당신이 실수할지도 모르는 상황을 피할

구문 [2행~6행] If the error was a result of a poor decision, // **explain to** *your boss and other interested parties* [O]**how** you will avoid ~, but remember [O]**that** you have to act quickly // before people make judgments ~.
두 개의 명령문(explain ~, remember ~)이 but으로 대등하게 연결되어 있다. 「explain to A B」는 'A에게 B를 설명하다'의 뜻이며, B의 자리에 how가 이끄는 명사절이 쓰였다. that은 remember의 목적어인 명사절을 이끈다.

[11행~14행] Perhaps your boss or co-workers will **make** [O]*you* [C]**pay** *a price* (for making the mistake), / such as a higher workload or less responsibility, // but **whatever** the consequences (might be) / you need to show that you get it.
「make+O+C(O가 C하게 하다)」의 SVOC 구조이다. such as a higher ~ responsibility는 a price ~ mistake를 구체적으로 설명해주고 있다. whatever는 '무엇이 ~하더라도'의 의미로 no matter what으로 바꾸어 쓸 수 있다.

어휘 **play a role** 역할을 하다 **critical** 중요한; 비판적인 **professional** 직업적인; 전문적인 **an interested party** 이해 당사자 *cf.* **party** 당사자, 관계자 **misstep** 실수(= **mistake**) **make a judgment** 판단하다 **competence** 능력, 능숙함 **expertise** 전문 지식[기술] **demonstrate** 입증하다 **superior** 상사, 상급자; 더 우수한 **peer** 동료 **trust A with B** (신뢰

하여) A에게 B를 맡기다 **pay a price for** ~에 대한 대가를 치르다 **workload** 업무량, 작업량 **consequence** 결과 **performance** 성과 **harshly** 가혹하게 **regardless of** ~에 상관없이 **figure out** 알아내다, 이해하다 [선택지 어휘] **adapt A to B** A를 B에 적응시키다 **boldly** 대담하게 **admit** 인정하다, 시인하다 **translate** 바꾸다; 번역하다 **drawback** 결점, 문제점 **asset** 자산, 재산

35 무관한 문장 ③

소재 심리 위장 방법인 '인상 관리'와 '자기기만'

해설 사람들이 정직하지 않은 반응, 즉 '위장'을 하는 두 가지 방법인 '인상 관리'와 '자기기만'을 차례대로 설명하는 글이다. ③은 옷을 잘 차려입으면 낯선 사람에게 돈을 요구했을 때 받을 가능성이 더 높다는 실험 내용으로 글의 흐름과 무관하다.

해석 주제문 몇몇 사람들이 면담에서 거짓말을 하거나 설문지에 응답할 때 그리 정직하지 않다는 것은 인간 행동에 있어서 사실이다. 심리학자들은 이를 '위장'이라 하며, 이것은 뚜렷이 다른 두 가지 종류가 있다고 한다. 첫 번째는 '인상 관리'라고 하는데, 대체로 자신에 대한 어떤 사실을 '잊거나' 작은 거짓말을 함으로써 자기 자신을 긍정적인 시각으로 보여주려는 것이다. 두 번째는 '자기기만'이라고 하는데, 이것은 자신에 대해 사실이 아닌 것, 예를 들어 당신이 옷을 어떻게 입는지 아는 모든 사람은 당신이 패션 감각이 없다는 것을 알 수 있는데도 당신은 (패션 감각이) 있다고 믿는 것이다. 연구원들은 당신이 모르는 사람에게 돈을 요구하면, 당신이 더 잘 차려입을수록 그들이 당신에게 돈을 줄 가능성이 더 많다는 것을 발견했다. 자기기만은 또한 어떤 소녀가 못생기지 않은 게 분명한데도 자신이 그렇다고(=못생겼다고) 믿는 때처럼, 부정적이고 잘못된 생각에 근거할 수 있다. 어떤 경우에도 자기기만의 생각은 해롭지만, 전문적인 도움을 받으면 줄어들거나 치유되기까지 할 수 있다.

구문 [10행~11행] ~ even though *everyone* [**who** knows how you dress] can tell // (that) you are not (fashionable).
(S′: everyone, V′: can tell, O′: (that) you are not (fashionable))

who knows ~ dress는 관계사절로 everyone을 수식하고 있으며, not 뒤에는 fashionable이 생략되어 있다.

어휘 **questionnaire** 설문지 **psychologist** 심리학자 **distinct** 뚜렷이 다른, 별개의; 분명한 **variety** 종류, 품종; 다양성 **impression** 인상; 감명 **management** 관리 (능력); 경영 **present** 나타내다, 보여주다 **in a positive light** 긍정적인 시각으로 **self-deception** 자기기만 *cf.* **self-deceptive** 자기기만의, 자신을 속이는 **be based on** ~에 기초하다 **obviously** 명백히, 분명히

36 글의 순서 ①

소재 글쓰기에서 견고한 기본 구조의 중요성

해설 의자를 만들 때 디자인보다는 의자의 기본적인 기능을 우선 고려해야 하는 것처럼, 글도 세부적인 문법이나 표현보다는 기본 구조를 탄탄히 하는 것이 중요하다는 내용이다. 주어진 글과 (A) 전체, (C)의 첫 문장은 의자의 기본적인 기능에 대한 설명이고, (C)의 뒷부분과 (B)는 글의 기본 구조에 대한 내용이다. 의자에 대한 비유로 시작해서 글쓰기로 넘어가는 글의 흐름이므로 자연스런 글의 순서는 ① '(A)-(C)-(B)'이다.

해석 당신이 의자를 하나 만들고 있다고 상상해보라. 당신이 '대략적인 도안'에서 확인해야 할 우선적인 것은 그것이 의자의 필수적인 기능들을 수행하느냐이다. 가장 예술적인 의자조차도 앉을 자리와 몇 개의 다리가 있어야 한다.

(A) 다음에는 그 의자가 견고하게 조립되어 있는지를 시험해야 할 것이다. 누군가 앉자마자 그 의자가 쓰러진다면 멋진 새 의자를 가질 의미가 없다.

(C) 각 부품은 튼튼해야 하며 그 이음매는 견고해야 한다. 주제문 이는 당신의 글쓰기에 있어서도 마찬가지로 사실이다. 당신은 강한 연관성과 함께 견고한 기본 구조를 가져야 한다.

(B) 당신이 사소한 문법적인 문제나 독자에게 어휘로 인상을 심어주려 애쓰는 데 집중하다가 문장 사이와 문단 사이의 연계성이 약한 것을 알아채지 못한다면, 독자들은 당신의 요점을 오해할지도 모른다. 더 큰 그림을 마음에 담아두어라.

구문 [1행~3행] *The first thing* [(that) you will check on your "rough draft"] / is **whether** it performs the essential functions of a chair.
(S: The first thing, V: is, C: whether ~ chair)

목적격 관계대명사가 생략된 관계사절(you ~ "rough draft")이 The first thing을 수식하여 주어가 길어졌다. whether가 이끄는 명사절은 보어 역할을 하며, '~인지 아닌지'로 해석한다.

[8행~12행] If you concentrate on minor grammatical points [and] on trying to impress the reader with your vocabulary, // [but] you fail to notice *weak connections* (between sentences and paragraphs), // your readers may misunderstand your point.
(S′1: you, V′1: concentrate, S′2: you, V′2: fail; S: your readers, V: may misunderstand, O: your point)

If가 이끄는 조건의 부사절은 두 개의 절 you concentrate ~ vocabulary와 you fail ~ paragraphs가 등위접속사 but으로 연결된 병렬구조이다. you concentrate 뒤에는 on이 이끄는 두 개의 전명구가 and로 연결되어 concentrate에 이어진다.

어휘 **rough** (상세하지 않고) 대략적인; 거친 **draft** 도안; 초안 **solidly** 견고하게 *cf.* **solid** 견고한; 고체의 **put together** 짜 맞추다, 모으다 **chic** 멋있는, 세련된 **concentrate on** ~에 집중하다 **minor** 사소한; 작은; 미성년자 **impress** 깊이 감동시키다 **keep A in mind** A를 마음에 담아두다, A를 잊지 않고 있다 **joint** 이음매, 접합 부분 **stable** 견고한; 안정된

37 글의 순서 ②

소재 새로운 시도를 돕는 정신과 의사의 역할

해설 스스로에 대한 기존의 신념에서 벗어나 새로운 변화를 모색할 때 원하는 것을 이룰 수 있다는 내용이다. 주어진 글의 it's not because ~에 대한 대응어구인 (B) it's because ~가 이어지고, (B)에 설명된 잘못된 삶의 태도에 대한 진단 뒤에는 문제의 해결책을 제시하는 (A)가 나온 후, 그 해결책에 따른 긍정적인 결과인 (C)가 이어지는 것이 자연스럽다. 따라서 정답은 ② '(B)-(A)-(C)'이다.

해석 정신과 의사라는 나의 직업을 통해, 나는 많은 사람들이 그들의 인생에 '갇혀' 원하는 것을 충분히 이루지 못하는 것을 본다. 대부분의 경우에 이러한 이유가 돈이나 기회가 부족해서도, 또는 무능력하고 지능이 부족해서도 아니다.

(B) 그보다도, 그들이 뭔가 새로운 것을 시도하거나 색다른 곳을 가보거나 또는 스스로에게 조금의 변화도 주려고 하지 않기 때문이다. 그들이 되풀이해서 말하는 건, "난 항상 그런 식으로 해왔습니다."이거나 "나는 단지 그런 사람입니다."인데, 이것은 마치 그들의 생각이 돌에 새겨진 듯이, 또는 그 문제에 그들에게 선택의 여지가 없다는 듯이 말하는 것과 같다.

(A) 나의 일은 그들에게 스스로에 대한 신념이 어떻게 자신을 가두고 있는지 알려주고, 그들이 마음을 열어 새로운 것들을 시도하도록 도와주는 것이다.

(C) 주제문 그들이 작은 변화를 만들고 그들을 향해 열린 새로운 문에 들뜨게 될 때 진전이 있다. 그러면 머지않아 그들은 정말로 다시 움직이기 시작하고 진정으로 그 여행을 즐기기 시작한다.

구문 [2행~5행] In most cases, / it's **not** because of a lack of money or opportunity, // **neither** is it because of incompetence or a lack of intelligence.

「not A neither B」는 'A도 아니고 B도 아닌'이라는 뜻으로 A와 B는 문법적으로 성격이 대등해야 한다. 여기서 A와 B는 모두 because of가 이끄는 전명구가 쓰였다.

[6행~9행] My job is to show IO them DO how *their beliefs* (about themselves) are **keeping** them **trapped** [and] to **help** O them C **open** their minds and **try** new things.
(S: My job, V: is, C1: to show ~ trapped, C2: to help ~ new things)

전체 문장은 SVC 구조로 보어인 두 개의 to부정사구가 and로 연결되어 있다. 첫 번째 보어 부분에서 how가 이끄는 명사절이 show의 직접목적어이며, how절 안의 「keep+O+C」 구조에서 목적어와 목적격보어의 관계가 수동이므로 목적격보어 자리

에 과거분사가 왔다. 두 번째 보어 부분은 「help+O+C」의 구조로, help의 목적격보어 자리에는 원형부정사 또는 to부정사가 올 수 있다.

어휘 **psychiatrist** 정신과 의사 **stuck in** ~에 갇힌, ~에 끼어 움직이지 못하는 **unfulfilled** 원하는 것을 충분히 이루지 못하는, 실현되지 않은 **incompetence** 무능력; 부적격 **trap** 가두다; 덫을 놓다; 덫 **carve** (글씨를) 새기다[파다]; 조각하다 **it isn't long before** 머지않아, 곧

38 문장 넣기 ⑤

소재 교통 법규

해설 주어진 문장은 특정 상황이나 장소에서 경찰관에 의해 주어지는 지시 사항도 있다는 내용으로, also(또한)라는 부사로 보아 상시 적용되는 일반적인 규칙을 설명한 이후 추가 규정을 언급할 자리에 들어가야 하므로 ⑤가 가장 적절하다. 이는 마지막 문장에서 앞서 언급한 규칙들, 즉 일반적인 교통 규칙, 교통 표지, 경찰관에 의한 일시적인 통제를 통틀어 These rules라고 지칭하는 것과도 자연스럽게 연결된다.

해석 주제문 도로 법규는 자동차 운전자, 자전거를 타는 사람, 보행자를 포함한 모든 도로 이용자들에 의해 지켜져야 하는 일반적인 관습이자 절차다. 도로 법규는 다른 차량과 보행자 쌍방 간의 행동을 규제한다. 안전하게 운전하는 것은 운전자가 성문(成文) 및 불문(不文) 도로 규칙 모두에 익숙해진다면 대개는 쉬운 일이다. 일반적으로, 모든 운전자는 다른 차량, 보행자, 도로 근처의 어떤 것이라도 치어서는 안 되게 되어 있다. 언제나 적용되는 일반적인 규칙 외에도 신호등을 포함한 교통 표지가 있다. 또한, 통상적으로는 분주한 교차로에서, 또는 공사 현장이나 사고 현장 근처의 일시적인 도로 교통 통제로서 경찰관에 의해 지시 사항이 주어질 수도 있다. 이러한 규칙들은 차량을 운행하는 데 필요한 기계적인 작동 절차와는 구분되어야 한다.

구문 [1행~4행] And instructions may also be given by a police officer, / **either** routinely at busy intersections **or** as temporary road traffic control / around construction zones and accidents.
「either A or B」의 구조로 at과 as가 이끄는 두 개의 전명구가 연결되어 있다.

어휘 **routinely** 일상적으로 **intersection** (도로의) 교차로 **temporary** 일시적인, 임시의 **construction** 공사, 건설 **practice** 관습, 관례 **procedure** 절차, 순서 **pedestrian** 보행자 **govern** 규제하다, 통제하다; 지배하다 **interaction** 상호 작용 **adapt to A** A에 익숙해지다[적응하다] **as a general rule** 일반적으로, 대개 **distinguish** 구별하다 **mechanical** 기계(상)의 **procedure** 절차, 방법 **operate** 운전하다, 조종하다

39 문장 넣기 ③

소재 뮤지션 계약

해설 음반 회사와 뮤지션 사이의 계약 체결 과정에 있어서 각각의 입장 차이를 보여주는 내용이다. But으로 시작하는 주어진 문장은 뮤지션들의 태도를 설명하는 내용으로, ③ 앞부분까지 나와 있는 음반 회사의 입장과 대조를 이룬다. 또한 ③ 뒤의 They는 주어진 문장의 many musicians를 가리키므로 주어진 문장은 ③에 들어가는 것이 적절하다.

해석 나는 뮤지션들이 사업적인 관계가 정말로 빨리 발전한다고 생각하는 것에 종종 충격을 받는다. 뮤지션들과 함께 일해 온 평생 동안, 나는 신인 발굴 팀 직원이나 매니저가 뮤지션을 본 첫날에 생각을 밝히고, 그 사람과 계약을 하고 싶다고 말하는 것을 거의 본 적이 없다. 영화에서 본 적이 있을지 모르겠지만, 주제문 이것은 보통 그것이 진행되는 방식이 아니다. 서류 가방 안에는 서명되길 기다리는 계약서는 없다. 하지만 많은 뮤지션들은 잠재적인 팀 구성원을 만나는 날 밤에 자신들이 계약을 하지 못하면 그것이 마치 세상의 종말인 것처럼 행동한다. 그들은 이때가 관계의 시작이라는 것을 이해하지 못하고 있다. 누군가가 당신의 노래를 한 번 듣고 난 후 팬이 되지 않는 것처럼, 잠재적인 팀 구성원과 일하는 관계를 발전시키고 탐구하는 것 또한 시간이 걸린다. 첫날에 계약을 요구하는 것이 아니라, 누군가에게 함께 일하는 것이 얼마나 즐거운 것인지를 천천히 보여주는 것이 팀을 만드는 방법이다.

구문 [5행~8행] In all my years of working with musicians, / I've rarely **seen**(V) an A&R person or manager(O) **come** out on *the first day*(C1) [(when) they see a musician] **and** **say** (that) they want to sign them(C2).
지각동사 see의 목적격보어인 두 개의 원형부정사구(come ~, say ~)가 and로 병렬 연결된 형태이다. [ ]는 생략된 관계부사 when이 이끄는 관계부사절로 the first day를 수식한다. say 뒤에는 목적어절을 이끄는 접속사 that이 생략되어 있다.

[12행~15행] Just as someone isn't a fan after they hear your song one time, / **it** also takes time / **to develop and explore** a working relationship with potential team members.
it은 가주어, to develop 이하의 to부정사구가 진주어이다.

어휘 **contract** 계약(서); 계약하다 *cf.* **get a contract** 계약하다, 계약을 따내다 **potential** 잠재적인; 가능성 **rarely** 거의 ~하지 않는, 드물게 **briefcase** 서류 가방 **just as** ~처럼 **explore** 탐구하다; 탐험하다 **enjoyable** 즐거운

40 요약문 완성 ④

해설 호감도에 영향을 미치는 요소

해설 실험 참가자들은 어떤 사람이 유능하다고 생각하면 그가 실수를 했을 때 호감도가 높아졌고, 그가 유능하지 않다고 생각하면 실수를 했을 때 호감도도 같이 낮아졌다. 이를 정리하면, 어떤 사람이 '유능하다(competent)'고 생각할 때는 그의 인간적인 '약점(weakness)'이 그의 호감도를 상승시킨다고 할 수 있다.

해석 주제문 1966년에 사회심리학자인 Elliot Aronson은 개인에 대한 호감에 관한 실험을 수행했다. 실험에서 Minnesota 대학의 48명의 학생들로 이루어진 패널이 대학 퀴즈 볼(= 팀 퀴즈 대회) 팀에 지원하는 경쟁자들(실제로는 단지 한 명의 배우)의 테이프 녹음을 들었다. 테이프 중 하나에서 경쟁자가 우연히 자기 몸에 커피 한 잔을 쏟았고, 다른 테이프에서 그는 그러지 않았다. 학생 패널은 이 사람이 자기 몸에 커피 한 잔을 쏟지 않았을 때보다 그렇게 했을 때 그를 호감이 더 간다고 인식했다. 그러나 이러한 사실은 학생들이 이 경쟁자를 대단히 유능하다고 인식한 때에만 적용할 수 있었다. 이 예에서 경쟁자는 어려운 퀴즈 질문 중 92퍼센트를 맞게 대답했던 것이다. 그러나 퀴즈 문항의 30퍼센트만을 맞게 대답한 '보통의' 경쟁자를 소개하는 테이프에서는 커피를 쏟는 것이 패널에게 그 경쟁자를 호감이 덜 가는 것으로 보이게 만들었다.

⬇

위 실험에 따르면, 피실험자들은 경쟁자가 대단히 (B) 유능하다는 것을 전제로 하여, 그가 인간적인 (A) 약점을 보여줄 때 그를 더 좋아했다.

구문 [9행~11행] The panel of students **perceived** *this individual* **as** *more likeable* // when he spilled the cup of coffee on himself // than when he didn't (spill the cup of coffee on himself).
「perceive A as B」는 'A를 B로 인식하다'의 뜻이다. B 자리에 형용사를 쓰는 것도 가능하다. didn't 다음에는 spill the cup of coffee on himself가 생략되어 있다.

[15행~18행] Yet in *tapes* (showcasing *an "average" contestant*, **who** answered only 30 percent of quiz questions correctly), / spilling coffee(S) **made**(V) *that contestant*(O) **appear** less likeable to the panel(C).
( )는 능동의 의미로 tapes를 수식한다. who ~ correctly는 an "average" contestant에 대한 추가적인 설명을 제시한다. spilling coffee는 동명사구 주어이며, 「make+O+C(원형부정사) (O가 v하게 하다)」의 구조이다.

어휘 **likability** 호감 **panel** 패널, 전문가 집단, 토론 집단 **contestant** 경쟁자, 참가자 **try out for** ~에 지원하다 **Quiz Bowl** 퀴즈 볼(보통 4~5명으로 구성된 두 팀이 다양한 학문적 주제에 관해 겨루는 퀴즈 대회) **accidentally** 우연히 **spill** 쏟다 **likeable** 호감이 가는 **hold** 적용할 수 있다 **capable** 유능한 **showcase** 소개하다; 진열하다 **subject** 피실험자 **on the premise that** ~이라는 것을 전제로 하여

41~42 장문 41 ⑤ 42 ④

소재 전통적인 농업 관행의 한계

해설 41. 개발도상국의 농업은 노동 중심의 농업이어서 선진국의 전통 농업을 들여올 수 없고, 농업에 필요한 교육이나 규제, 연구가 부족한데다가, 선진국처럼 친환경 농업을 실시할 경제적 형편도 되지 못한다는 내용이다. 즉, 개발도상국이 처한 현대 농업의 문제점들을 열거한 글이므로 가장 적절한 제목은 ⑤ '개발도상국에서의 현대 농업의 현 과제'이다.
① 농업 관행의 역사
② 농업: 더 나은 삶에 대한 약속
③ 친환경 농업에 대한 반대
④ 부실 정책이 어떻게 농업 노동력을 해치고 있는가

42. 빈칸 이후에 선진국의 농업 관행이 개발도상국으로 옮겨졌을 때 발생하는 폐해가 서술되고 있다. 개발도상국의 척박한 토양이 더 악화되면 농부들은 그 땅이 황무지가 되게 내버려둔 채 다른 곳으로 옮겨 간다고 했고, 비료의 과용으로 지하수까지 오염시킬 수 있다고 했으므로 빈칸에는 ④ '충격적'이 오는 것이 적절하다.
① 지속 가능할 ② 유익할 ③ 간과될 ⑤ 경제적일

해석 개발도상국에서는 선진국과는 대조적으로 국민 대다수가 농업 활동에 종사한다. 선진국에서의 전통적인 농업 관행은 희소 자원인 노동력을 최소화하도록 계획된다. 이것은 개발도상국에서라면 육체노동이 사용될 곳에서 살충제, 화학비료, 중기계를 사용함으로써 이루어진다. 이러한 종류의 농업 체계가 부유한 국가에서 가난한 국가로 옮겨지면, 그 결과는 충격적일 수 있다. 예를 들어, 개발도상국은 경작이 가능한 공간이 흔히 제한되어 있고, 우선 많은 나라에서 토양이 별로 비옥하지 않다. 경작 기술이 토양의 질을 더 저하시키면, 토양은 경작용으로 유용성이 줄어든다. 농부들은 이러한 생산의 손실을 알아차리고 다른 곳으로 옮겨가서 자양분이 부족한 토양이 황무지로 변하게 내버려 둔다. 어떤 경우에는 비료를 과용하여 토양의 질 저하를 초래한다. 과도한 비료는 잔류 농약이 그러하듯이 지하수를 오염시킬 수 있다.
교육과 규제의 결여는 개발도상국에서 때때로 살충제가 남용된다는 것을 의미한다. 열악한 관개시설은 또한 연구와 교육의 결여를 나타낸다. 주제문 전통적인 농업은 선진국이나 개발도상국에서 장기적으로 지속할 수 있는 것이 아니라는 사실이 점점 더 분명해지고 있다. 선진국은 친환경 농업의 중요성을 인정하는 정책 결정을 내리기 시작했지만, 많은 개발도상국은 이런 호사를 누릴 여력이 없다. 친환경 농업 과정이 개발도상국에서 달성할 수 있는 계획인지 아닌지는 현재 많은 연구에서 다루고 있는 주제이다.

구문 [15행~17행] Farmers notice(V1) this loss of production [and] move(V2) to a different spot, **leaving** the nutrient-poor soil to turn into wasteland.
leaving 이하는 '결과'를 나타내는 분사구문으로 의미상의 주어는 Farmers이며 and they leave ~로 풀어 쓸 수 있다.
[19행~20행] The excess fertilizer can contaminate groundwater, // **as** does(V') pesticide residue(S').
as는 '~와 같이, ~처럼'을 뜻하는 접속사이다. as 뒤의 대동사 does는 앞 절의 contaminate groundwater를 대신하며, 주어와 동사가 도치되었다.
[31행~34행] **Whether** environmentally-friendly agricultural processes are an achievable proposition in developing countries(S) / **is**(V) *the subject* (of much current research)(C).
whether가 이끄는 명사절이 문장의 주어로 쓰였다. 명사 상당어구(to부정사, 동명사, 명사절)가 문장의 주어로 쓰인 경우 단수 취급하므로 단수동사 is를 썼다.

어휘 **as opposed to** ~와는 대조적으로 **a large proportion of** ~의 대부분 *cf.* **proportion** 부분; 비율; 균형 **be engaged in** ~에 종사하다; ~로 바쁘다 **conventional** 전통적인; 관습적인; 진부한 **scarce** 부족한 **pesticide** 농약 **fertilizer** 비료 **machinery** 기계(류) **manual labor** 육체노동; 수(手)작업 **cultivation** 경작, 재배 **fertile** (토양이) 비옥한; 다산(多産)의(= **fruitful**) **degrade** (질적으로) 저하시키다; 분해되다; 비하하다 *cf.* **degradation** 저하, 악화; 비하 **wasteland** 황무지, 불모지 **excess** 초과한; 초과[량] **contaminate** 오염시키다; 악영향을 주다 **residue** 잔류[잔여](물) **regulation** 규제, 규정 **irrigation** 관개, 물을 끌어들임 **indicative of** ~을 나타내는[시사하는] **evident** 분명한, 명백한 **environmentally-friendly** 친환경적인(= **eco-friendly**) **achievable** 달성할 수 있는; 성취할 수 있는 **proposition** 처리할 일; 제의; 명제

43~45 장문 43 ③ 44 ④ 45 ⑤

소재 두 부모님 간의 신기한 인연

해설 43. (A)는 결혼식 전날 필자가 자신의 부모님과 Steve의 부모님이 잘 어울릴 수 있을지 걱정하는 내용이다. 이어서 결혼식 예행연습 날 부모님들이 만나고, 결혼식 후 Steve의 부모님 댁으로 가는 동안 불안해하는 필자의 심경이 나오는 (C)가 나오고, Steve의 부모님 댁에 도착해서 그의 부모님과 필자의 아버지가 20년 전 인연이 있었음이 밝혀지는 (D)가 이어진 후, 필자의 어머니가 20년 전의 만남에 대해 추가적인 이야기를 하는 (B)로 마무리하는 순서가 적절하다. 따라서 정답은 ③ '(C)-(D)-(B)'이다.
44. (d)는 Steve를 가리키고, 나머지는 모두 필자의 아버지를 가리킨다.
45. (D)에서 20년 전 필자의 아버지만 Steve의 부모님을 만난 것을 알 수 있으므로 ⑤는 글의 내용과 일치하지 않는다.

해석 (A) 내가 결혼하기 전날, 한 가지 걱정거리가 나를 괴롭혔다. ① Steve와 나는 자란 환경이 달랐다. 나는 애리조나 주(州) 스카츠데일 출신의 도시 여자였다. 그는 오클라호마 주에서 태어나 캔자스 주에서 자랐다. 그의 아버지는 목사였고, (a) 나의 아버지(= 필자의 아버지)는 트럭 운전사였다. 그래도 대학 신입생 시절 생물학 수업 시간에 나를 괴롭히던 그 소년은 곧 내 마음을 얻었다. 졸업반이 되자 그가 청혼을 했고, ② 우리는 졸업식 이틀 후 대학 교회에서 결혼하기로 했다. 우리 부모님과 Steve의 부모님이 축하해 주러 차를 몰고 오실 것이었다. 서로 너무 멀리 떨어져 살다 보니, 양가 부모님들은 만난 적이 없었다. 게다가 우리 부모님은 그렇게 외향적이지는 않으셨다. 부모님들이 잘 어울리실 수 있을까?
(C) 결혼식 예행연습을 한 후 저녁 식사 자리에서, 나는 Steve의 부모님이 내 아버지를 호기심을 갖고 쳐다보시는 것을 보았다. "Lana, 신경 쓰지 마. 두 분이 그저 (c) 그(= 필자의 아버지)가 낯익어서 그러시는 거야."라고 Steve가 말했다. 나는 그것이 좋은 의미이기를 바랐다. 결혼식과 피로연은 멋지게 진행되었고, 그 후 우리는 가족 식사를 하러 Steve의 부모님 댁으로 향했다. 나는 그곳에 도착할 때까지 걱정이 되었다. "나는 우리 없이 부모님들께서 잘 지내실 거라고 확신해."라고 Steve가 내게 말했다. ④ (d) 그(= Steve)는 나를 안심시키려고 노력했지만, 내 마음의 조바심은 멈추질 않았다.
(D) 우리가 마침내 (그의 부모님 댁에) 차를 댔을 때, 아버지들끼리 마당에서 즐겁게 거니시는 모습을 보자 안심이 되었다. "우리가 서로 어떻게 알고 있는지 알아냈단다."라고 Steve의 아버지께서 말씀하셨다. 20년 전에 아버지는 장거리 운전을 하다가 눈보라로 인해 어쩔 수 없이 오클라호마 주로 우회하게 되었다. "그날은 일요일 아침이어서 나는 트럭을 길가에 세우고는 예배드리러 교회에 들렀지."라고 아버지가 말씀하셨다. ⑤ "끝나고 나서 목사님과 사모님께서 같이 식사하자고 (e) 나(= 필자의 아버지)를 집으로 초대하시더구나." "그게 우리 부부였단다!"라고 Steve의 아버지께서 말씀하셨다.
(B) 나중에, 나는 어머니께 수년 전 아버지와 Steve의 아버지와의 만남에 내가 얼마나 놀랐는지를 말했다. "그뿐만이 아니란다."라고 어머니가 말씀하셨다. "네 아버지가 운전 중에 많은 사람을 만났었다만, 엄마는 (b) 그(= 필자의 아버지)가 Steve 부모님에 대해 말했던 것을 명확하게 기억한단다. ③ 아버지는 그 두 분에게 무척 감동을 받으셨지. 또래 자녀들을 둔 것도 재미있다고 생각하셨고…. 그리고 아버지께서 한 말씀을 더 하셨지." "어떤 말씀이요?"라고 내가 물었다. "우리 애들 중 한 명이 그분들 같은 가족에게 시집간다면 뿌듯하겠다고 하셨단다."

어휘 (A) **minister** 목사; 장관 **bother** 괴롭히다; 귀찮게 하다 **graduation** 졸업(식) **outgoing** 외향적인, 사교적인 **get along** 사이좋게 지내다; 살아가다; (일이) 되어가다 (B) **impressed** 감동[감명]받은, 인상 깊게 생각하는 (C) **rehearsal dinner** 결혼식 전날의 만찬 **reception** 피로연(결혼이나 출생 따위의 기쁜 일을 널리 알리기 위하여 베푸는 연회); 접수처 **head to** ~로 향하다[가다] **butterflies in the stomach** 안절부절 못함, 초조함 (D) **pull up** (차를) 대다[멈추다] **figure out** 알아내다, 이해하다; 계산하다 **force** (어쩔 수 없이) ~하게 하다 **detour** 우회하다; 우회로 **pull over** (길 한쪽으로) 차를 대다 **service** 예배; 근무; 봉사

실전 모의고사 08

본문 p.111

18 ④	19 ⑤	20 ④	21 ②	22 ②	23 ①	24 ①	25 ⑤	26 ⑤	27 ⑤
28 ④	29 ③	30 ⑤	31 ②	32 ③	33 ①	34 ②	35 ③	36 ③	37 ②
38 ③	39 ④	40 ③	41 ④	42 ③	43 ④	44 ④	45 ②		

18 글의 목적 ④

소재 리더십 프로그램 성공에 대한 감사 편지

해설 리더십 프로그램이 Hunters and the Campaign이라는 단체와 학생들에게 긍정적인 영향을 주며 성공했음을 알리면서 그 프로그램을 위해 대학에 방문했던 외부 인사에게 보내는 감사 편지이므로 정답은 ④이다. 마지막 문장(~, I want to express to you our tremendous appreciation.)에 감사 표현이 잘 드러나 있다.

해석 Richardson 씨께,
주제문 저는 귀하께서 제2회 Presidential Public Leadership Program을 위해 저희 대학을 방문하신 동안 귀하를 직접 만날 기회를 가져 기뻤습니다. Roosevelt(루스벨트) 생가 복원 위원회의 의장으로서 저는 이 프로그램의 성공에 대해, 또한 이 프로그램이 Roosevelt 생가 복원과 관련된 또 다른 단체인 Hunters and the Campaign에 가져온 인식에 대해 큰 기쁨을 표하고 싶습니다. 이 프로그램은 학생들이 경력과 삶에 관한 선택을 할 때 되돌아보게 될 경험이었다고 저는 확신합니다. 주제문 저는 저희 대학의 모든 직원과 학생을 대표하여 귀하께 크나큰 감사를 표하고 싶습니다.
Billy Wright 드림

구문 [5행~10행] As chair of the Committee ~, / I wish to express our great pleasure / **at** *the success* (of the program) and *the recognition* [(that) it has brought to Hunters and the Campaign, *another organization* (involved in the restoration of Roosevelt House)].
전치사 at의 목적어 자리에 두 개의 명사구가 병렬구조를 이루고 있다. it has brought ~ Roosevelt House는 선행사 the recognition을 한정하는 목적격 관계대명사절로, 여기서 it은 앞의 the program을 받는다. another organization 이하는 Hunters and the Campaign을 보충 설명하는 동격어구이다.

어휘 **in person** 직접, 자기 스스로 **chair** 의장, 위원장 **committee** 위원회 **restoration** 복원; 회복 **recognition** 인식, 알아봄; 인정 **involved in** ~에 관련된 **reflect upon** 되돌아보다; 곰곰이 생각하다 **on behalf of** ~을 대표[대신]하여 **tremendous** 굉장한, 거대한 **appreciation** 감사; 감상; 평가

19 심경 변화 ⑤

소재 부상으로 인한 우울함과 아버지의 위로

해설 Chad는 당분간 축구를 할 수 없게 되어 꿈을 이룰 수 없게 된 우울한 상황이었지만, 지금은 강해 보이는 아버지도 과거에 비슷한 경험을 했었다는 이야기를 듣고는 자신도 괜찮아질 거라고 위로를 받게 되었다. 따라서 Chad의 심경 변화로 가장 적절한 것은 ⑤ '우울한 → 위안을 받은'이다.

해석 Chad는 침실 벽에 공을 느릿느릿하게 튀기며 침대 가장자리에 앉았다. 대학에 가서 축구를 하겠다는 그의 꿈은 더는 가능한 일이 아니었다. 의사들은 그에게 최소 6개월 동안 다시 축구를 할 수 없을 것이라고 말했다. 주제문 그는 한숨을 쉬고는 창문 너머로 끝도 없는 회색 하늘을 내다봤다. 아버지가 Chad의 방으로 들어오셨을 때, '왜 나야?'라고 그는 생각했다. Chad의 아버지는 항상 그에게 무관심해 보여서, 그는 다음에 무슨 일이 일어날지 예상하지 못했다. 아버지는 그의 옆에 앉아 팔로 그를 감싸고는, 오래 전 자신의 스포츠 경력이 끝난 것에 대해 말씀하셨다. 주제문 이것은 그가 전에는 전혀 본 적이 없는 아버지의 모습이었고, 그는 이 이야기로 신뢰를 받아 내면에서 따뜻함을 느꼈다. 만약 자신의 아버지가 비슷한 상황을 겪고 오늘날 그가 아는 강한 남자가 되었다면, 아마 Chad도 괜찮을 것이다.

① 편안한 → 혼란스러워하는
② 우울한 → 낭만적인
③ 불안해하는 → 들뜬
④ 즐거워하는 → 슬픈

구문 [11행~13행] This was *a side of his father* [(which[that]) he'd never seen before], // and he felt a warmth inside him / from being trusted with this story.
[ ] 부분은 목적격 관계대명사가 생략된 관계대명사절로 a side of his father를 수식한다.

[13행~16행] If his own father suffered through a similar situation and became *the strong man* [(who(m)) he knew today], // perhaps Chad **would** be okay, too.
동사 suffered와 became이 접속사 and로 연결되어 병렬구조를 이루고, 여기서 suffered와 became은 가정법 과거가 아닌 직설법 과거로서 과거의 일을 사실 그대로 표현한 것이다. [ ] 부분은 목적격 관계대명사 who(m)가 생략된 관계사절로 the strong man을 수식한다. would 역시 가정법 시제가 아니라 '~일 것이다'란 의미인 will의 과거형이다.

어휘 **edge** 가장자리, 모서리; 끝; (칼의) 날 **lazily** 느릿느릿하게; 나태하게 **bounce** 튀기다 **possibility** 가능성 **sigh** 한숨을 쉬다; 한숨 **indifferent** 무관심한, 냉담한 **warmth** (마음 · 태도 등이) 따뜻함; 온기 **suffer** (부상 · 패배 등을) 겪다[당하다]; 시달리다; 고통받다

20 필자 주장 ④

소재 감정 표출 방법

해설 화가 쌓이도록 내버려뒀을 때 나타나는 문제점을 지적한 다음, 감정을 그때그때 올바른 대상에게 이야기하라는 내용이므로 필자의 주장으로 적절한 것은 ④이다.

해석 많은 사람이 다른 사람에게 무언가를 하지 말라고 요청할 때 불편함을 느끼기 때문에, 무언가가 자신들을 화나게 하면 화가 마음속에 쌓이도록 내버려 둔다. 그러고 나서 그들이 말을 하게 되면, 쓸데없이 화가 난 것처럼 들리고, 종종 그들은 자신의 화를 부적당한 사람에게 돌린다. 주제문 분명하고 침착하게 즉시 그리고 올바른 대상에게 감정을 이야기하는 것이 훨씬 낫다. 예를 들어, 당신이 비흡연자고 당신 옆의 누군가가 담배에 불을 붙인다면, 정중하게 당신 근처에서 담배를 피우지 말라고 요청하라. 거기에 앉아서 괴로워하며 화내지 말고, 당신이 얼마나 흡연자를 싫어하는지 친구에게 불평하지 마라. 그 흡연자는 당신이 불편해한다는 걸 전혀 몰랐을 수도 있다. 다른 사람의 무지와 배려 없는 것 때문에 괴로워하지 말고, 그 문제를 해결할 수 없는 사람들에게 불평하지도 마라.

구문 [1행~2행] Many people are uncomfortable / **asking** others **not to do** something, ~.
asking 이하는 '때'를 나타내는 분사구문으로, when they(=many people) ask ~로 바꿔 쓸 수 있다. 「ask A not to-v」 구문은 'A에게 v하지 말 것을 요청하다'의 의미로, to부정사를 부정할 때는 부정어를 to 앞에 쓴다.

[9행~10행] Don't sit there **suffering and getting angry**, ~.

suffering and getting angry는 동시동작을 나타내는 분사구문으로 '~하면서'로 해석한다.

[13행~14행] Don't **let** other people's ignorance and inconsiderateness (V: let, O: other people's ignorance and inconsiderateness) **cause** you **to suffer**, ~. (C: cause you to suffer)

사역동사 let은 목적격보어로 원형부정사를 취하므로 동사원형 cause가 왔다. 목적격보어는 「cause A to-v (A가 v하게 하다)」의 구조로 쓰였다.

어휘 **direct** (시선·주의·노력 등을) 돌리다, 향하게 하다; 직접적인 **be unaware of** ~을 알지 못하다; ~을 눈치 채지 못하다 **discomfort** 불편, 불쾌 **ignorance** 무지(無知); (사물·사실을) 알지 못함 **inconsiderateness** 배려하지 않음, 경솔함

21 밑줄 함의 ②

소재 글쓰기의 규칙

해설 본문의 교사는 학생들의 과제를 흥미로운 부분까지만 읽고 평가함으로써 학생들이 처음부터 끝까지 독자의 흥미를 사로잡는 글을 쓰도록 유도했으므로, 그가 가르쳐준 '한 가지 엄중한 규칙'은 ② '독자의 주의 집중을 처음부터 끝까지 유지해라.'이다.

해석 옛날에 학생의 과제물이 자신의 흥미를 사로잡는 한에서만 그것을 읽을 거라고 선언한 교사가 있었다. 보고서가 지루해지자마자 그녀는 읽는 것을 멈추고 자신이 읽은 부분에만 점수를 매기곤 했다. 그것이 숙제의 처음 절반, 혹은 첫 4분의 1만 읽는다는 것을 의미한다면, 학생에게는 그저 너무 안 된 일이었다. 그녀는 말하곤 했다. "주의 집중 기간은 짧습니다! 지루한 TV 프로그램을 보거나 지루한 음악을 듣는 사람은 없습니다. 그들은 재미있는 것으로 바꿀 겁니다. 주제문 지루한 글을 읽는 사람은 없습니다! 여러분의 독자를 여러분의 처음 몇 문장으로 끌어당길 수 없다면 그들은 사라져 버릴 겁니다!" 이 교사의 학생들은 지루한 주제를 피했고 구식 문체에 느리게 흘러가는 줄거리로 글을 쓰지 않았다. 그들은 훌륭한 작가가 되었다. 이유는 명확하다. 그들은 교사로부터 한 가지 엄중한 규칙을 배울 수 있었던 것이다.

① 글쓰기를 더 잘하고 싶으면 계속 연습하라.
③ 말하고자 하는 바를 분명하고 간결한 방식으로 말하라.
④ 당신의 글에 정직한 피드백을 제공할 사람을 찾아라.
⑤ 당신이 그것을 쓰면 독자가 그것을 흥미롭게 읽을 거라고 믿어라.

구문 [3행~5행] **As soon as** a report became dull, // she would stop reading and grade *only the part* [(that) she had read ●].

접속사 as soon as는 '~하자마자'의 뜻이다. [ ]는 앞에 목적격 관계대명사가 생략되었으며 only the part를 수식한다.

어휘 **declare** 선언하다 **paper** 과제(= report) **dull** 지루한 **grade** 점수[등급]를 매기다; 등급; 학년 **attention** 주의 집중 **span** 기간 **hook** 끌어당기다 **old-fashioned** 구식의 **style** 문체 **plot** 줄거리, 구성 **hard and fast** 엄중한 [선택지 어휘] **concise** 간결한; 명료한

22 글의 요지 ②

소재 비관주의가 더 유용한 경우

해설 낙관주의가 비관주의보다 더 낫다는 의견이 있지만, 위험한 상황에서는 오히려 비관주의가 낙관주의보다 유용한 감정 상태여서, 미래의 예측할 수 없는 부정적인 변화에 더 잘 대비할 수 있게 해준다는 내용의 글이다. 비관주의의 유용한 측면을 강조한 내용이므로 글의 요지로 가장 적절한 것은 ②이다.

해석 배가 바다로 1마일 나간 곳에서 뒤집힐 때, 해안까지 헤엄칠 수 있는 자신의 능력에 대한 낙관주의는 치명적이다. 외국을 침략할지 결정할 때, 따뜻한 환영을 받는 것에 관한 낙관주의는 역사의 전 과정을 나쁜 쪽으로 변화시키는 재앙을 초래할 수 있다. 낙관주의를 비관주의보다 우수한 것으로 보는 경향은 뿌리 깊은 환상이다. 주제문 낙관주의는 호의적인 상황에서 유용하지만, 비관주의는 위험한 상황에서 유용하다. 운 좋은 사람들에게 지금의 삶은 옛날보다 대단히 더 안전하고 더 안심할 수 있으므로 비관주의가 덜 필요하다. 하지만 비관주의를 막는 것의 의도치 않은 결과가 생길 수 있다. 세상은 예측하기 힘든 많은 방식으로 더 좋아질 것이고, 예측하기 힘든 다른 방식으로 더 나빠질 것이다. 주제문 따라서 비관주의는 문제가 아니라 유용한 감정 상태이다.

구문 [13행~14행] The world will be better in *many ways* [and] worse in *others* [that are hard to predict].

in others는 in other ways를 축약한 표현이다. [ ] 부분은 many ways와 others를 동시에 수식한다.

어휘 **overturn** 뒤집히다 **optimism** 낙관주의(↔ **pessimism** 비관주의) **shore** 해안, 물가 **deadly** 치명적인 **invade** 침략하다 **catastrophe** 재앙, 참사 **for the worse** 나쁜 쪽으로 **superior to** ~보다 우수한 **favorable** 호의적인 **vastly** 대단히, 엄청나게 **secure** 안심하는, 안전한; 확실한 **unintended** 의도하지 않은 **consequence** 결과 **block** 막다

23 글의 주제 ①

소재 문화가 스트레스의 원인에 미치는 영향

해설 각 문화마다 사람들이 겪는 주요 스트레스의 형태가 크게 다르고(cultures vary greatly in the predominant forms of stress their people experience), 스트레스의 경험과 평가에 있어 문화가 그 맥락을 결정한다(culture sets the context in which people experience and appraise stress)는 내용이므로, 주제로는 ① '문화가 스트레스의 원인에 미치는 영향'이 가장 적절하다.

해석 (사랑하는 사람의 죽음과 같은) 어떤 종류의 사건들이 아마도 사실상 모든 인간 사회에서 스트레스를 주는 것으로 여겨지기는 하지만, 주제문 문화는 사람들이 겪는 지배적인 스트레스의 형태에 있어 굉장히 달라진다. 분명히, 몬트리올이나 필라델피아와 같은 현대의 서구 도시들에서 마주치는 일상의 어려움들은 아프리카나 남미의 토착 사회에서 겪는 일상의 어려움들과는 상당히 다르다. 주제문 사실상, 문화는 사람들이 스트레스를 경험하고 평가하는 맥락을 설정한다. 어떤 경우에서는, 특정한 문화 집단이 그 집단에게 특유한, 널리 퍼져 있는 스트레스에 노출될 수도 있다. 예를 들어, 1999년 코소보에서의 알바니아인들에 대한 인종 청소와 2004년 인도네시아와 동남아시아 지역들에서의 쓰나미로 인한 엄청나고 광범위한 파괴는 이러한 사회들에서 뚜렷이 구별되는 색다른 형태의 스트레스였다.

② 스트레스가 없는 사회에 대한 비현실적인 갈망들
③ 스트레스를 주는 사건들의 보편적인 특성들
④ 각 사회 특유의 스트레스에 대한 해결책들
⑤ 문화적 맥락과 상관없는 스트레스에 대한 반응들

구문 [5행~9행] Obviously, *the challenges of daily living* (encountered in modern, western cities like Montreal or Philadelphia) (S) / are (V) quite different from *the day-to-day difficulties* (experienced in *indigenous societies* (in Africa or South America)).

첫 번째, 두 번째 ( ) 부분은 분사구로 각각 앞의 the challenges of daily living과 the day-to-day difficulties를 수식한다. 세 번째 ( ) 부분은 전명구로서 앞의 indigenous societies를 수식한다.

[12행~17행] For example, the ethnic cleansing ~ [and] *the devastating and widespread destruction* (from *the tsunami* (in Indonesia ~ in 2004)) / **were** *extraordinary forms of stress* (distinctive to these societies).

문장의 주어는 the ethnic ~ in 2004이며 동사는 were이다.

어휘 **virtually** 사실상, 거의 **vary** 서로 다르다 **predominant** 지배적인, 우세한; 두드러진 **encounter** 마주치다; 만남 **context** 맥락, 전후 사정 **appraise** 평가하다; 살피다 **expose** 노출시키다; 폭로하다 **pervasive** 널리 퍼져 있는, 만연하는 **ethnic cleansing** 인종 청소(어떤 지역·국가에서 특정 인종을 몰아내는 정책) **devastating** 엄청난, 대단히 파괴적인 **destruction** 파괴, 파멸; 말살 **extraordinary** 색다른; 엄청난; 비범한 **distinctive** 뚜렷이 구별되는; 특유의 [선택지 어휘] **irrespective of** ~와 상관없는

24 글의 제목 ①

소재 인간의 유전자에 내재된 공격성

해설 인간의 공격적 성향이 생존 가능성을 향상시켜 주면서 결국 인간의 유전자 속에 남아 전해지게 되었을 것이고, 이러한 공격성이 영역권과 결부되면서 전쟁이 불가피할 것이라는 내용의 글이다. 즉, 전쟁이 인간의 유전자 속에 내재된 공격성에 기인한다는 것을 설명하는 글이므로 제목으로 가장 적절한 것은 ① '전쟁은 우리의 유전자 속에 있는가?'이다.

해석 몇몇 과학자들에 따르면, 인간은 전쟁의 존재에 대해 영장류 조상들에게 최소한 어느 정도는 감사해도 된다. 인류 진화의 초기 단계 동안, 공격적인 행동이 생존 가능성을 향상시키고, 증가하는 수의 개인의 유전자 속에 암호화되었을지도 모른다. 생태학자들과 사회 생물학자들은 공격적 성향이 한 세대에서 다음 세대로 유전적으로 전해졌을지도 모른다고 믿는다. 이러한 견해의 가장 유명한 지지자들 중 한 사람이 생태학자 Konrad Lorenz이다. 다른 생태학자들처럼 Lorenz는 그의 연구를 인간 이외 동물들의 행동으로 향해 왔다. 주제문 이 연구에서 그는 공격성이 하등동물들에게서 그렇듯이 인간에게도 본능이라고 결론지었다. Lorenz는 공격성을 영역권과 결부시킨다. 동물들이 자신의 둥지, 굴, 그리고 영역을 방어하는 것과 마찬가지로, 인간은 자신의 국가를 방어하기 위해 전쟁을 한다. 이러한 이론으로부터 전쟁이 타고난 욕구에서 생기기 때문에 그것(=전쟁)은 아마 불가피할 것이라는 결론이 나온다.

② 평화의 황금시대
③ 전쟁이 없는 세상을 상상해 보라
④ 공격성의 변화
⑤ 공격적 행동에 대처하기

구문 [17행~19행] It follows from this theory that because war stems from a natural urge, it(=war) is likely inevitable.
(It: 가주어 / that ~: 진주어)

「It follows that ~」은 '~라는 결과[결론]가 나오다'의 뜻이다. it은 가주어이고 that절이 진주어이다. this theory는 앞 문장의 내용(인간은 동물처럼 자신의 영역을 지키기 위해 싸운다)을 가리킨다.

어휘 **primate** (동물) 영장류 **ancestor** 조상 **existence** 존재, 실재 **evolution** 진화 **aggressive** 공격적인 *cf.* **aggression** 공격(성) **odds** (어떤 일이 있을) 가능성 **encode** 암호로 바꾸다; 부호화하다 **gene** 유전자 **sociobiologist** 사회 생물학자 **transmit** 전송하다 **genetically** 유전적으로 **advocate** 지지자, 옹호자; 지지[옹호]하다 **other than** ~ 외에 **instinct** 본능; 직감 **territoriality** 영역권, 세력권 **burrow** 굴; 굴을 파다 **range** 영역, 분포 범위; 다양성 **stem from** ~에서 생겨나다[기인하다] **urge** 욕구, 충동; 강력히 권고하다; 재촉하다 **inevitable** 불가피한, 필연적인 [선택지 어휘] **golden age** 황금기, 전성기 **transformation** 변화, 변환, 변형

25 도표 이해 ⑤

소재 실업률 변화 추이

해설 전체 실업률과 청년 실업률의 차이는 2017년에 가장 작았고 2014년에 가장 컸으므로 ⑤는 greatest와 smallest가 서로 바뀌었다.

해석 〈실업률 (2013~2017)〉

주제문 위 도표는 지난 5년간 전체 실업률과 15~29세의 청년 실업률을 비교한 것이다. 전체 기간 동안, 청년 실업률은 전체 실업률보다 훨씬 높았다. ① 전체 실업률은 3.1퍼센트에서 3.7퍼센트의 범위인 반면, 청년 실업률은 7.3퍼센트에서 8.3퍼센트에 이르렀다. ② 전체 실업률은 2014년과 2015년에 최고치에 도달했다가 2017년에 3.1퍼센트로 떨어졌다. ③ 한편, 청년 실업률은 2014년에 최고치를 기록한 다음 2017년에 최저로 떨어졌다. ④ 전체 실업률은 2014년과 2015년 사이에 아무 변화가 없었던 반면, 청년 실업률은 0.3퍼센트 포인트 감소했다. ⑤ 또한, 두 실업률 사이의 차이는 2017년에 가장 컸고, 2014년에 가장 작았다.

구문 [10행~12행] Meanwhile, the youth unemployment rate hit a record high in 2014 / **before dropping** to its lowest point in 2017.

before dropping ~은 분사구문으로, 분사구문의 접속사는 주로 생략되지만, 의미를 명확하게 나타내기 위해 접속사를 생략하지 않고 그대로 쓰기도 한다. before it dropped ~로 바꿔 쓸 수 있다.

어휘 **unemployment** 실업, 실직 상태 **compare A with B** A를 B와 비교하다 **range from A to B** (범위가) A에서 B에 이르다 **reach[hit] a record high** 최고치에 이르다 **meanwhile** 한편; 그 동안에

26 내용 불일치 ⑤

소재 James Hubert Blake의 음악 인생

해설 Sophie Tucker가 'It's All Your Fault'란 노래를 James Hubert Blake와 함께 부른 것이 아니라 자신의 쇼에서 그 노래를 사용하면서 Blake가 작곡가로서 유명해진 것이므로 ⑤는 틀린 내용이다.

해석 James Hubert Blake는 1883년 볼티모어에서 ① 예전에 노예였던 부모의 여덟 번째 아이로 태어났으며, 유아기를 넘겨 살아남은 유일한 아이였다. Blake는 다섯 살 때 음악 수업을 받기 시작했는데, ② 신앙심이 깊었던 그의 어머니는 그가 결코 '신을 섬기지 않는 음악'을 하지는 않을 것이라고 주장했지만, 그는 래그타임을 발견하자마자 그녀의 원칙을 무시했다. ③ 15세 때, 그는 어머니 몰래 돈을 벌기 위해 피아노를 연주하기 시작했다. 그는 겨우 12세 때 ④ 그의 유명한 노래 'Charleston Rag'의 선율을 처음으로 작곡했지만, 16년이 흐를 때까지 그 곡을 종이에 적지 않았다고 알려져 있다. 32세에 그는 Noble Sissle이라는 가수를 만나 함께 'It's All Your Fault'를 작곡했다. ⑤ 유명한 가수이자 코미디언인 Sophie Tucker가 자신의 쇼에 이 노래를 삽입하자, Blake와 Sissle은 순식간에 일류 작곡가로 변신하게 되었다.

구문 [5행~6행] ~, but he ignored her rule // **the minute** (that) he discovered ragtime.

the minute (that)은 '~하자마자'의 뜻으로 부사절을 이끄는 접속사로 쓰였다.

어휘 **ex-** (접두사) 이전의(=former) **slave** 노예 **infancy** 유아기; (발달의) 초기 **religious** 신앙심이 깊은; 종교적인 **insist** 주장하다; 고집하다 **ungodly** 신을 경외하지 않는 **without A's knowledge** A 몰래, A에게 알리지 않고 **compose** 작곡하다; 구성하다 **put down** (종이에) 적다 **incorporate** (일부로) 포함하다; 통합시키다; 설립하다 **transform A into B** A를 B로 바꾸다[변형시키다]

27 안내문 불일치 ⑤

소재 농장 체험학습 안내

해설 안내 정보(Helpful Info)의 마지막 내용에서 안내문을 가져가면 The Adams Market의 물건 중 한 개를 25퍼센트 할인 받을 수 있다고 했으므로 ⑤가 안내문의 내용과 일치하지 않는다.

해석

Adams 농장

학부모님들께,

귀하의 자녀가 곧 저희 농장에 체험학습차 방문하게 되어 정말 기쁩니다! Adams 농장은 40에이커 규모로서 농산물로 놀이를 즐길 수 있는 농장입니다.

부모님들의 일정이 허락한다면 자녀분과 함께 참석하실 것을 권해드리고 싶습니다. ① 이 체험학습은 10시에 시작하여 1시 15분경에 끝납니다. ② 입장료는 1인당 6달러입니다. 도착하신 뒤에 곧장 The Adams Market에 들러서 ③ 입장료를 내시고 (입장에) 필요한 손목 밴드를 받아 가시기 바랍니다.

안내 정보:

④ 모든 행사는 야외에서 열리므로 날씨에 대비하여 옷을 입고 오시기 바랍니다. 카메라 가져오는 걸 잊지 마세요!

쿠폰: ⑤ The Adams Market에 이 안내 편지를 가지고 오셔서 한 가지 물건의 가격을 25퍼센트 할인받으세요.

농장에서 학부모님들을 만나 뵙길 바랍니다!

어휘 **field trip** 체험학습 **agri-entertainment** 농산물로 오락을 즐기는 **approximately** 대략 **admission** 입장(료) **wristband** 손목 밴드

28 안내문 일치 ④

소재 반려동물용 식수 펌프

해설 영하의 온도에 노출될 수 있는 장소에 설치하지 말고 직사광선을 피하라고 했으므로 ④가 안내문의 내용과 일치한다.

해석

> **신선한 분수 펌프**
>
> 사람들과 마찬가지로 반려동물들도 건강을 위해 물을 필요로 합니다. ① Fresh Fountain Pump는 신선하고 깨끗한 식수의 지속적인 공급에 대한 여러분의 반려동물의 필요에 부응합니다.
>
> 주의:
>
> 이것은 애완동물용 식수 분수 펌프입니다.
> - ② 펌프를 수영장이나 사람들이 수중에 있는 상황에서 사용하지 마십시오.
> - ③ 이 펌프는 섭씨 35도까지의 수온에서 사용하기에 적합합니다.
> - 이 펌프를 인화성이 있는 액체와 함께 사용하지 마십시오.
> - ④ 영하의 기온에 노출될 수 있는 장소에 이 기구를 설치하거나 보관하지 마십시오. 펌프를 직사광선으로부터 보호하십시오.
> - 펌프가 마르지 않도록 하십시오. ⑤ 펌프는 물에 완전히 담겨져 있어야 합니다.

어휘 **immerse** (액체 속에) 담그다; 몰두하다 **suitable for** ~에 적합한[알맞은] **inflammable** 가연성의, 타기 쉬운 **liquid** 액체 **appliance** 기구, 장비 **shelter** (위험 등으로부터) 보호하다; 피하다 **run dry** (물이) 말라버리다; 고갈되다 **completely** 완전히

29 밑줄 어법 ③

소재 단일 관점의 문제점

해설 ③ 문장의 주어이자 telling의 의미상 주어인 not one subject는 this(ACE 붕대가 다 떨어졌다는 말)를 직접 하는 사람이 아니고 듣는 사람이므로, telling을 수동의 의미가 되도록 being told로 바꿔 써야 한다.

오답 분석 ① pass by는 문맥상 '지나가는'의 의미로 앞의 명사 people을 꾸미는 현재분사가 되어야 한다. 「tell+O+to-v (O에게 v하라고 말하다)」의 문맥은 어색하다. ② 「ask+O+to-v」는 'O에게 v해달라고 부탁하다'의 뜻이다. ④ 「had+S´+p.p., S+might have p.p.」는 원래 형태가 「If+S´+had+p.p., S+might have p.p.」인 가정법 과거완료 표현이며, If가 생략되고 had와 주어가 도치된 형태이다. '~했다면 …했을지도 모른다'의 의미이다. ⑤ that a sprained ~ an ACE bandage는 앞의 the single thought에 대한 동격절이다.

해석 주제문 내가 대학원에서 수행한 실험은 단일 관점의 문제점을 탐색한 것이었다. 그것은 도움에 대한 각기 다른 요청의 효과성을 검토하는 시험적 연구였다. 동료 연구자가 붐비는 보도에 서서 지나가는 사람들에게 자신이 무릎을 삐었고 도움이 필요하다고 말했다. 누군가가 멈추면, 그녀는 그 사람에게 근처 약국에서 ACE 붕대를 사다 달라고 부탁했다. 도움을 주는 사람이 약사에게 요청하는 동안 나는 가게 안에 서서 귀를 기울였는데, 약사는 ACE 붕대가 다 떨어졌다고 말해주겠다는 동의를 사전에 했었다. 이 말을 들은 후에, 우리가 연구한 25명 중에 단 한 사람의 피실험자도 약사에게 다른 것을 추천해줄 수 있는지 물어볼 생각을 못했다. 사람들은 약국을 나섰고 '환자'에게 빈손으로 돌아가서 그 소식을 전했다. 우리는 그녀가 덜 구체적인 도움을 요청했더라면 그것(= 붕대)을 받을 수 있었을 거라고 추측했다. 그러나 삔 무릎에는 ACE 붕대가 필요하다는 단일한 사고로만 행동했기 때문에 누구도 다른 종류의 도움을 찾으려 노력하지 않았다.

구문 [8행~11행] I stood inside the store [and] listened / while the helpful person gave the request to *the pharmacist*, // **who** had agreed ~ bandages.
동사 stood와 listened가 병렬구조를 이룬다. who 이하는 the pharmacist에 대한 추가적인 설명을 제시한다.

어휘 **graduate school** 대학원 **perspective** 관점; 원근법 **pilot** (대규모로 시행하기 전에 소규모로) 시험[실험]하는 **fellow** 동료 **investigator** 연구자; 수사관 **sprain** 삐다 **bandage** 붕대 **pharmacist** 약사 **be out of** ~이 다 떨어지다 **victim** (범죄·질병·사고 등의) 피해자, 환자, 희생자 **speculate** 추측하다 **act on** ~에 따라 행동하다

30 밑줄 어휘 ⑤

소재 끊임없이 변화를 추구하는 인간의 인식

해설 인간은 변화와 움직임을 탐색하도록 진화했으며, 아무 변화가 없는 정체 상태는 우리의 인식이 제대로 기능하지 못하도록 지장을 초래한다. 따라서 우리는 수용과 정체를 장려하는 것이 아니라 막기 위해 노력할 것이므로 ⑤의 encourage를 discourage로 바꿔 써야 한다.

해석 주제문 인간의 인식은 ① 기능하기 위해 변화와 움직임에 의존한다. 진화는 우리를 이런 식으로 구축해왔다. 눈을 깜박이지 않고 몇 초 동안 텅 빈 벽 응시하기를 시도해보면, 아무것도 보이지 않을 때까지 이미지가 희어지는 것을 알게 될 것이다. 눈의 시각적 작동은 움직임과 변화에 반응한다. 우리의 다른 인식 체계 부위 역시 마찬가지이다. 그것(= 다른 인식 체계)에 연속적으로 동일한 투입을 부여하면 그것은 산출로 가질 만한 가치가 있는 것을 많이 생산하기를 ② 중지한다. 물속의 상어처럼, 우리는 계속해서 움직일 필요가 있으며, 그렇지 않으면 인지적으로 죽는다. 과학 역시 우리의 ③ 부단한 본성에 대한 가장 위대한 광고를 나타낸다. 어떤 이론이 확립된 통설이 되자마자, 창의적인 사람들은 우리가 완전히 다른 출발의 가정에서 시작해야 하고 자료의 ④ 참신한 해석을 추구해야 한다는 가능성을 탐색하기 시작하기 때문이다. 수용과 정체를 ⑤ 장려하기(→ 막기) 위한 이러한 부단한 움직임이 없다면, 우리는 기초 과학이 제공할 수 있는 진보나 흥분을 갖지 못할 것이다.

구문 [7행~9행] **Feed** them the same inputs successively // **and** they cease to produce *very much* (worth having as output).
명령문 다음의 and는 '그러면'의 뜻이다. 참고로 명령문 다음의 or는 '그렇지 않으면'의 뜻이다. ( ) 부분은 형용사구로 very much를 수식하며, 「worth v-ing」는 'v할 가치가 있는'의 뜻이다.

[12행~16행] **For** as soon as a theory becomes the established orthodoxy, / creative minds begin to explore the possibility that we must begin ~ data.
접속사 For는 '~이므로'의 뜻이며, 원래는 「S+V, for S´+V´」의 형태로 문장 중간에만 쓰는데 이 문장에서는 주절이 생략된 것으로 볼 수 있다. 접속사 For 다음에 이어지는 〈S´+V´〉는 creative minds begin이다. as soon as는 '~하자마자'라는 의미의 접속사이다. that절은 the possibility에 대한 동격절이다.

어휘 **cognition** 인식, 인지 *cf.* **cognitive** 인식의 **evolution** 진화 **stare at** ~을 응시하다 **blink** 눈을 깜박이다 **bleach** 희어지다, 표백되다; 바래다 **successively** 연속적으로 **cease** 중지하다 **restless** 부단히 활동하는, 끊임없는 **assumption** 가정, 가설 **novel** 참신한, 새로운 **interpretation** 해석 **stasis** 정체, 정지 **fundamental** 기초의, 근본적인

31 빈칸 추론 ②

소재 미디어에 의해 간과되는 축산업의 불합리성

해설 축산업의 불합리성과 폭력성은 예컨대 휘발유 가격이나 할리우드 스타들의 뉴스에 비해 터무니없을 정도로 미디어 보도에서 외면당하며 대중 담론에서 부재하여 육류 섭취를 정당화하는 데 기여한다는 내용의 글이다. 이러한 외면 혹은 부재와 가장 가까운 전략은 ② '생략'임을 추론할 수 있다.

해석 주제문 미디어가 육류 섭취에 대한 정당성을 강화하는 한 가지 방법은 생략을 통해서이다. 당신은 농장 동물들에 대한 폭력적인 처우와 도축 산업의 부패한 관행에 대한 미디어 폭로 기사를 얼마나 자주 보았는가? 이것을 변동하는 휘발유 가격이나 할리우드의 패션 실수에 제공되는 보도의 양과 비교해 보라. 우리들 대부분은 수십억의 동물들, 수백만의 사람들과 생태계 전체가 그토록 정당화되지 않는 폭력으로 수익을 얻는 산업에 의해 조직적으로 착취당한다는 사실보다 1갤런의 휘발유에 5센트를 더 지불해야 한다는 사실에 대해 더 분노한다. 그리고 우리들 대부분은 우리가 먹는 동물들에 대해서 알고 있는 것

보다 스타들이 오스카상 시상식에 입고 가는 것에 대해서 더 많이 안다. 고기를 얻기 위해 매년 죽임을 당하는 백억 마리의 동물들과 현대의 동물 농업의 관행이 불러온 파괴적인 결과는 대중 담론에서 눈에 띄게 부재하는 상태로 남아 있다.
① 단순화 ③ 과도한 강조 ④ 투명성 ⑤ 일반화

구문 [5행~7행] **Compare** this **with** the amount of *coverage* (afforded to fluctuating gas prices or Hollywood fashion blunders).
「compare A with B」는 'A와 B를 비교하다'의 뜻이다. ( )는 수동의 의미로 coverage를 수식한다.

[7행~11행] Most of us are **more** outraged over having to pay five cents more for a gallon of gas **than** over the fact that billions of animals, ~ are systematically exploited by *an industry* [that profits from such unjustified violence].
over ~ a gallon of gas와 over the fact ~ such unjustified violence가 비교 대상이다. that ~ violence는 the fact에 대한 동격절이다. [ ] 부분은 an industry를 수식하는 주격 관계사절이다.

어휘 **reinforce** 강화하다 **justification** 정당화 **treatment** 처우, 대우 **corrupt** 부패한 **practice** 관행, 관례; 실천 **slaughter** 도축 **coverage** 보도[방송] **afford** 제공하다; ~할 여유가 되다 **fluctuate** 변동하다 **blunder** 실수 **outrage** 격분하게 만들다 **entire** 전체의 **systematically** 조직적으로 **exploit** 착취하다 **destructive** 파괴적인 **consequence** 결과 **contemporary** 현대의 **agricultural** 농업의 **conspicuously** 눈에 띄게, 두드러지게 **absent** 부재하는 **discourse** 담론

32 빈칸 추론 ③

소재 안절부절못하는 행동이 주는 인상

해설 안절부절못하는 행동(fidgeting)은 상대방에게 신뢰감을 주지 못한다는 것이 글의 주된 내용이다. fidget의 의미를 모른다고 하더라도, Nixon이 대통령 후보 토론회에서 이마를 닦는 등의 불안해하는 행동(nervous movements)을 한 것이 선거 패배의 원인이었다는 예시에서 빈칸에 들어갈 말이 ③ '쓸데없는 동작을 하지 않도록'임을 추론할 수 있다.

해석 보통 사람이 거짓말을 할 때 감정적으로 각성되어서 안절부절못하기 시작한다. 그러나 우리는 거짓말을 할 때뿐만 아니라 불편함을 느낄 때도 안절부절못한다. 하지만 주제문 안절부절못하는 모습은 보는 사람에게 무언가 옳지 않거나 당신이 무언가에 대해 거짓말을 하고 있다는 느낌을 주게 된다. 1960년 9월 25일 방송된 Richard Milhous Nixon과 John Fitzgerald Kennedy의 대통령 후보 텔레비전 토론회를 생각해 보라. 정치 전문가들은 카메라에 비친 이마 닦는 모습 등 Nixon의 불안해하는 움직임이 그를 선거에서 패배하게 했다고 추측한다. 주제문 만일 당신이 이야기하고 있는 것이 정말 중요하고 사람들이 당신을 믿고 신뢰할 만하다고 여기길 원한다면, 쓸데없는 동작을 하지 않도록 노력하라.
① 듣는 이의 기분을 간파하도록
② 진실한 감정을 드러내도록
④ 당신이 잘 알고 있는 것에 대해 얘기하도록
⑤ 청중과 눈을 맞추도록

구문 [4행~6행] Fidgeting(S), however, will make(V) an observer(O) sense(C) **that** something isn't right [or] **that** you are lying about something.
동사 make가 사역동사로 쓰여 목적격보어로 원형부정사(sense)가 쓰였다. 목적격보어 내에서 sense의 목적어 역할을 하는 두 개의 명사절이 등위접속사 or로 연결된 구조이다.

어휘 **arouse** 각성시키다; 깨우다 **fidget** 안절부절못하다, 조바심 내며 부스럭거리다 **observer** 관찰자 **broadcast** 방송[방영]하다 **speculate** 추측하다; 사색하다, 깊이 생각하다 **mop** (땀 등을) 닦아 내다; 대걸레로 닦다 **count** 중요하다; (수를) 세다 **reliable** 믿을 수 있는 **trustworthy** 신뢰할 수 있는 [선택지 어휘] **detect** 간파하다, 탐지하다 **reveal** 드러내다, 누설하다

33 빈칸 추론 ①

소재 악몽의 테마가 갖는 보편성

해설 서로 다른 문화에서도 사람들은 공포, 수치심, 상실감, 죽음과 같이 악몽이 나타내는 동일한 무의식적인 상징들을 지닌다(people all ~ and so on)고 했으므로 악몽의 테마가 비슷하다는 것을 알 수 있다. 따라서 빈칸에 가장 적절한 것은 ① '놀랍게도 보편적인 것 같다'이다.

해석 주제문 악몽의 테마는 놀랍게도 보편적인 것 같다. 서로 다른 문화에 걸쳐 이루어져 온 몇몇 연구에서는 가장 보편적인 (꿈의) 시나리오가 꿈꾸는 사람이 쫓기거나, 공격당하거나, 혹은 죽음을 눈앞에 두는 것과 관련 있다. 다른 여러 시나리오들은 학교에서 발표 중 마비되거나 심지어 사람들 앞에서 발가벗겨지는 것 같이 수치스러운 상황에 놓이는 생각, 혹은 중요한 약속이나 시험에 늦는 것 같이 있어야 할 곳에 있지 않은 자신을 발견하는 생각과 관련이 있을지 모른다. 여러 문화에 걸쳐 그 줄거리가 상당한 유사성을 보이지만, 우리의 악몽 속에 나타나는 사람들은 그럼에도 불구하고 마치 우리만큼 다양하다. 경찰관, 학교 선생님, 친구, 가족, 그리고 전혀 모르는 무서운 정체불명의 권력자가 우리 지역, 이웃, 집에 불쑥 나타났다 사라질 수 있다. 주제문 악몽 속의 인물, 배경, 줄거리 전개는 각기 매우 다를 수 있지만, 그러나 결국 전 세계 사람들은 공포, 수치심, 상실감, 죽음이라는 운명 등에 대한 무의식적 상징들을 똑같이 지니고 있는 것 같다.
② 매우 무서운 주제를 다룬다
③ 힘 있는 사람들이 우리를 어떻게 겁주는지를 보여준다
④ 각 사람이 지닌 특정한 욕망을 설명해준다
⑤ 상당히 단순하면서도 복잡한 측면을 나타낸다

구문 [5행~10행] Other different scenarios(S) may involve(V) *the thought*(O) (**of** being in a shameful situation—being paralyzed during a school presentation or even being naked in public—[or] finding oneself not in the right place—being late for an important meeting or an exam).
( ) 부분 전체는 목적어 the thought를 수식하는 전명구이다. of의 목적어인 두 개의 동명사구(being ~, finding ~)가 or로 연결되어 있다. 대시(—) 이하는 각각 앞의 동명사구를 보충 설명해준다.

[11행~12행] ~, *the people* [that appear in our nightmares] are nevertheless **as** varied **as** we are (varied).
원급 비교 「A as ~ as B」는 'A가 B만큼 ~하다'란 의미이다.

어휘 **theme** 테마, 주제 **nightmare** 악몽 **scenario** 시나리오, 각본 **imminent** 눈앞에 둔, 임박한 **shameful** 수치스러운, 부끄러운 *cf.* **shame** 부끄러움, 수치심 **paralyze** 마비시키다 **naked** 벌거벗은 **storyline** 줄거리, 구성(= **plot**) **immense** 엄청난, 어마어마한 **similarity** 유사성 **varied** 다양한 *cf.* **vary** 서로 다르다 **faceless** 정체불명의, 얼굴 없는 **authority** 권력, 권위 **figure** 인물; 모양; 수치 **pop** 불쑥 나타나다 **setting** 배경; 환경 **twist** 전개; 전환; 비틀기 **infinitely** 대단히; 무한히 **unconscious** 무의식적인 **metaphor for** ~에 대한 상징 *cf.* **metaphor** 은유 **mortality** 죽을 운명; 사망률 [선택지 어휘] **universal** 보편적인 **subject matter** 주제 **simplicity** 단순함(↔ **complexity** 복잡함)

34 빈칸 추론 ②

소재 소리를 전기 에너지로 변환하는 기술

해설 음파를 전기로 전환해주는 기술을 이용해 대화 또는 혼잡한 도로에서 발생하는 소리를 에너지원으로 이용할 수 있다(Not only ~ noisiest roads.)고 했으므로 수다스러운 사람들이 ② '전 세계의 차세대 재생 에너지의 원천이 될 수도 있다'는 내용이 들어가는 것이 문맥상 적절하다.

해석 주제문 미래에는 수다스러운 사람들이 전 세계의 차세대 재생 에너지의 원천이 될 수도 있다. 한국의 과학자들은 칼라민 로션의 주성분을 음파를 전기로 전환해주는 미세한 물질로 바꾸었다. 연구진들은 스피커가 전파를 소리로 바꾸어주듯이, 소리를 전력 자원으로 바꾸는 그 반대의 과정도 가능하다고 설명했다. 그 연구는 소형 음향 패널의 제조 산업으로 이어질 수 있을 것이다. 전화 통화에서 (발생한) 에너지를 끌어 모은 후, 이 패널들은 그 사람이 통화하고 있던 휴대전화를 포함해 모든 전자기기를 충전하는 데 사용될 수 있

다. 이 기술은 자가 충전하는 휴대전화 개발에 사용될 수 있을 뿐만 아니라, 나라에서 가장 붐비고 소음이 심한 도로 위에 소리를 모으고 에너지를 발생시키는 거대한 패널을 설치함으로써 국가 전기 공급망에도 증가한 에너지를 제공해 줄 수 있을 것이다.
① 에너지 보존에 훨씬 더 많이 신경 쓸 것이다
③ 국가의 최대 전기 사용자가 될 것이다
④ 연구진들이 통신 기술을 개발하는 데 도움을 줄 수 있을 것이다
⑤ 가장 최근에 출시된 전자기기를 갖고 싶어 할 것이다

구문 [9행~12행] After **they** collect energy from a phone call, // these panels could **be used to charge** any electrical device, / including *the cell phone* [(that[which]) the person had been talking on ●].
부사절의 they는 주절의 주어 these panels를 지칭한다. 「be used to-v」는 'v하는 데 사용되다'는 뜻이다. including의 목적어 the cell phone은 목적격 관계대명사절의 수식을 받고 있다. the cell phone은 관계대명사절 내에서 전치사 on의 목적어에 해당한다.

[12행~15행] **Not only** could(조동사) this technology(S) be used(V) to invent a self-charging cell phone, / **but** it(= this technology) could **also** provide ~ / through the placement ~.
「not only A but also B (A뿐 아니라 B도)」의 구조로, 부정어인 Not only가 문두에 위치하면서 「조동사+주어+동사」의 어순으로 도치되었다.

어휘 **chatty** 수다스러운 **ingredient** 성분, 재료 **convert A into B** A를 B로 전환[개조]시키다 **sound wave** 음파 *cf.* **electric signal** 전파 **transform A into B** A를 B로 변형시키다 **electrical** 전기의, 전기와 관련된 **lead to A** A로 이어지다[초래하다]; A를 이끌다 **manufacturing** 제조업 **panel** 패널, 판 **charge** 충전하다, 채우다 *cf.* **self-charging** 자가 충전식의 *cf.* **rechargeable** 재충전할 수 있는 **device** 장치, 기구 **boost** 증가, 증대 **grid** (전기·가스) 공급망 **placement** 설치, 배치 **generate** 발생시키다, 만들어내다 [선택지 어휘] **conservation** 보존, 보호 **renewable** 재생 가능한 **aid A in v-ing** A가 v하도록 돕다 **release** (상품을) 출시[발표]하다; 방출하다 **electronic** 전자의

35 무관한 문장 ③

소재 페이스북의 보안 기능 추가

해설 소셜 네트워크 사이트인 페이스북이 보안 수준을 강화하는 새로운 기능을 추가했다는 내용의 글이다. 반면에 ③은 온라인 뱅킹의 장점에 관한 내용이므로 글의 흐름과 무관하다.

해석 주제문 페이스북은 전 세계 수백만 명의 사용자들을 위해 웹사이트에 사생활과 보안 수준을 향상시키는 새로운 보안 기능을 추가했다. 그 변화는 세계에서 가장 큰 소셜 네트워크 사이트에서 사생활 보호가 미흡한 것에 대한 많은 불만과 부정적 여론 이후에 생겨났다. 이렇게 새로운 기능이 추가됨에 따라 사용자들은 이제 온라인 뱅킹 웹사이트와 비슷한 수준의 보안 옵션을 갖게 되었다. 게다가 온라인 뱅킹은 당신의 돈을 관리하는 쉽고 안전한 방법이며 당신의 모든 계좌로의 빠르고 쉬운 접근을 제공한다. 이 기능을 사용하여, 사용자는 자신이 개인적으로 권한을 부여한 특정 컴퓨터와 휴대전화에서만 자신의 계정에 접근 가능하도록 할 수 있다. 만약 승인되지 않은 장치를 통해 접근이 시도되면, 사용자는 이메일이나 SMS로 통지받아 그것이 성공하기 전에 그 시도를 차단할 수 있다.

구문 [6행~9행] With the addition of this new feature, / users now have *the option of security* [that's of a similar level to **that** of online banking websites].
[ ] 부분은 the option of security를 수식하는 주격 관계사절이며, 관계사절 내의 that은 the option of security를 지칭한다.

어휘 **feature** 특징; 얼굴 생김새 **mass** 대량의; 대중의; 큰 덩어리 **public opinion** 여론 **account** (예금) 계좌; (인터넷) 계정 **accessible** 접근 가능한 **personally** 개인적으로 **authorize** 권한을 부여하다 *cf.* **unauthorized** 승인[공인]되지 않은 **attempt** 시도(하다) **notify** 알리다, 통지하다

36 글의 순서 ③

소재 낯선 음악을 이해하려는 노력

해설 개인의 취향과 사회적 배경에 따라 음악의 선호도가 달라질 수 있다는 주어진 글의 내용에 대해 (B)의 for instance에서 예를 들어 부연설명하고 있다. (C)는 이러한 사실에 대한 반론으로(However, ~) 익숙하지 않은 음악도 이해하려고 노력하면 즐길 수 있다고 한 뒤, 마지막 (A)에서 그러한 노력이 가지는 의미를 정리하고 있다. 따라서 정답은 ③ '(B)-(C)-(A)'이다.

해석 활기가 넘치고 활동적인 음악 문화는 삶을 풍요롭게 해주고, 주변 사람 모두에게 삶을 더 짜릿하고 흥미롭게, 그리고 의미 있게 만들어준다. 아름다움은 그것을 보는 사람의 눈에만 있는 것이 아니라 귀에도 있으며, 주제문 노래나 한 편의 기악곡을 즐기는 것은 어느 정도 듣는 사람의 개인적 취향과 사회적 배경에 달렸다.
(B) 예를 들어, 평범한 서양인에게 동아시아의 전통 음악은 그 표현 방식이 매우 낯설어서 아마도 이상하게 들릴 것이고 심지어 듣기가 불편할 정도로 어려울 수 있다.
(C) 그러나 음악적 관습에 대한 자신의 선입견을 내려놓고 익숙하지 않은 음악적 맥락을 이해하려고 노력할 수 있는 사람들은 그러한 음악이 더 다가가기 쉽고 즐겁다고 생각하게 될 것이다.
(A) '다른 것'에 대해 귀와 마음의 눈을 엶으로써 사람들은 새로운 다른 문화와 더 잘 관계 맺고 상호작용할 수 있다.

구문 [16행~20행] However, *people*(S) [who can set aside ~ the unfamiliar music] will find(V) **it**(O) more accessible and enjoyable(C).
find가 목적격보어를 취하는 SVOC의 구조로 쓰이면 'O가 C라는 것을 알다'라고 해석한다. it은 바로 앞 문장에 등장한 the traditional music of East Asia를 가리킨다.

어휘 **vibrant** 활기 넘치는; (색·빛이) 선명한 **enrich** 풍요롭게 하다; 부유하게 만들다 **beholder** 보는 사람; 구경꾼 **to a certain extent** 어느 정도까지는, 다소 **engage with** (이해심을 갖고) ~와 관계를 맺다 **mode** 방식, 유형 **set aside** 제쳐놓다; 무시하다; (나중을 위해) 떼어놓다 **preconception** 선입견 **convention** 관습, 관례 **accessible** 접근하기 쉬운; 이해하기 쉬운

37 글의 순서 ②

소재 화학물질에 따라 달라지는 불꽃 색

해설 주어진 글은 소금이나 소다를 불에 대면 어떤 일이 생길지에 대한 물음이다. 이에 대한 대답으로 소금을 불에 대면 노란색 불꽃이 된다는 내용의 (B)가 이어지는 것이 자연스럽고, (A)의 the light from this flame은 실험에서 생긴 노란 불꽃을 의미하므로 (B) 다음에 오는 것이 적절하다. (C)는 주석과 초석의 불꽃 색깔에 대해 설명한 후 내용을 요약하고(To sum up, ~) 있으므로 ② '(B)-(A)-(C)'의 순서가 적절하다.

해석 만일 당신이 부엌을 어둡게 하고, 소량의 소금이나 소다를 드라이버나 양철 조각 끝에 놓고, 그 소금이나 소다를 가스 불에 대면 무슨 일이 발생할까?
(B) 가장 작은 소금 알갱이라도 무색의 거의 보이지 않는 불꽃이 진한 노란색 빛을 띠게 만들 것이다. 노란색은 화학 원소인 나트륨의 증기 때문인데, 그것(= 나트륨)은 일반 소금의 성분들 중 하나이다.
(A) 만일 당신이 이 불꽃의 빛을 프리즘에 통과시키면, 이 빛이 스펙트럼 상에서 한 가지 색깔만을 갖고 있다는 것을 발견하게 될 텐데, 스펙트럼의 노란색 부분에 있는 좁은 부분 외에는 아무것도 없을 것이다. 나트륨을 함유하는 그 어떤 화학물질이든지 이와 동일한 색깔의 빛을 낼 것이다.
(C) 마찬가지로, 가스 불속에 넣은 소량의 주석이나 초석 유액은 불꽃이 독특한 라일락 색을 띠게 한다. 주제문 요약하자면, 화학 첨가물에 따라 불꽃은 다른 색으로 보인다. 만약 당신이 어떤 화학물질이 무슨 색을 내는지 안다면 당신이 원하는 언제든 다양한 색으로 불이 타게 할 수 있을 것이다.

어휘 **tin** 양철 **flame** 불꽃, 화염 **spectrum** (빛의) 스펙트럼, 빛띠; 범위, 영역 **sodium** 나트륨 **give off** (냄새·빛 등을) 내다[방출하다] **speck** 알갱이, 입자; 점, 작은 얼룩 **invisible** 보이지 않는 **take on** (색·성질 등을) 띠다 **glow** 불빛; 빛나다 **vapor** 증기 **chemical** 화학적인; 화학물질 **element** (화학) 원소; 요소 **component** (구성) 성분, 요소 **introduce into** ~ 속에 넣다 **peculiar** 독특한 **additive** 첨가물, 첨가제

38 문장 넣기 ③

소재 연구 프로젝트의 윤리성 심사

해설 주어진 문장의 this protection이 ②의 뒤에 나오는 a way that does not violate the rights of people who participate를 가리키고 있고, ③ 이후에 나오는 this panel은 주어진 문장의 a local panel을 가리키므로 주어진 문장은 ③에 들어가는 것이 가장 적절하다.

해석 좋은 연구 설계를 선택하는 것은 단지 어떤 특정 방법을 선택하는 것 이상을 요구한다. 주제문 연구원들은 자신들이 사용하려고 하는 방법이 윤리적인지 알아내야 한다. 즉, 연구를 설계할 때, 연구자들은 참가하는 사람들의 권리를 침해하지 않는 방식으로 그렇게 해야(= 설계해야) 한다. 모든 연구 프로젝트가 이러한 보호 조치를 가지고 있는지 확실히 하기 위해, 연구자들은 모든 자료 수집 전에 전문가와 지역 사회 대표자들로 구성된 지역 심사원단의 공식 검토를 위해 제안된 연구를 제출해야 한다. 이 심사원단의 승인이 있어야만 과학자들은 자신들의 연구를 시작할 수 있다. 만약 검토 심사원단이 제안된 연구의 어떤 측면을 승인하지 않는다면, 그 연구원은 심사원단의 승인을 얻기 위해 그 측면들을 수정하여 다시 제출해야 한다. 마찬가지로, 연구의 한 구성 요소가 바뀔 때마다 검토 심사원단은 반드시 통지를 받고 승인을 해야 한다.

구문 [12행~13행] Only with the approval of this panel (부사구) can (조동사) scientists (S) begin (V) their study.

only가 이끄는 부사구가 문두에 위치하면서 도치가 일어나 「부사구+조동사+S+V」의 어순이 되었다.

어휘 **ensure** 확실히 하다 **investigator** 연구자, 조사자 **proposed** 제안된 **formal review** 공식 검토 **panel** 심사원단; 판 **representative** 대표자; 대표적인 **prior to** ~에 앞서 **ethical** 윤리적인 **violate** 위반하다; 침해하다 **approval** 승인, 인정; 찬성 *cf.* **approve** 승인하다; 찬성하다 **aspect** 측면, 양상 **revise** 수정하다, 교정하다 **component** 구성 요소 **alter** 바꾸다, 변경하다

39 문장 넣기 ④

해설 유인원의 통찰력을 통한 학습

해석 ④를 전후로 논리적인 비약이 있다. ④의 앞에서 오랑우탄은 여러 가지 시도를 해보지만 보상을 획득하는 데 계속해서 실패하다가 ④ 다음 문장에서 오랑우탄은 바로 문제를 해결한다. 따라서 '오랑우탄에게 갑자기 통찰력이 떠올랐다'는 주어진 문장은 ④에 위치해야 한다.

해석 주제문 유인원에게 통찰 학습의 사례가 있다는 몇몇 보고가 있다. Lethmate Gebrauch는 다음의 연속적인 사건들을 기술하며 어린 오랑우탄의 통찰력을 시사한다. 오랑우탄은, (플라스틱 관 안에 있는) 달콤한 음식에 닿아서 그것을 밖으로 밀쳐낼 수 있도록 투명한 플라스틱 관 안으로 넣을 수 있는 긴 막대를 받았다. 오랑우탄은 단 음식이 무엇인지 알고 있었지만, 그것을 얻기 위해 막대를 도구로 사용하는 방법은 알지 못했다. 그는 관을 물어뜯고 그 도구를 집어넣으려고 애썼지만 성공하진 못했다. 그러고 나서 그는 물러나 앉았는데, 그 도구를 가지고 틀에 박힌 반복 행동을 수행하기 시작하면서, 겉보기에 좌절한 것처럼 보였다. 그때 그는 관을 다시 흘긋 보았고, 명백히 이번에는 그에게 통찰력이 떠오른 것 같았다. 그는 일어나서 막대를 가지고 관으로 걸어갔고, 관에 그것을 집어넣어 단 음식을 획득했다. 물론 그가 단 음식을 먹음으로써 보상을 받았지만, 이것은 단지 연속적인 사건들의 끝에 있던 것일 뿐이었고, 문제는 불현듯 떠오른 통찰력으로 해결된 것처럼 보였다.

어휘 **glance** 흘긋 보다 **apparently** 명백히; 겉보기에는, 외관상으로 **insight** 통찰력 **sequence** 연속(적인 사건) **rod** 막대 **transparent** 투명한 **bite (bit-bitten)** 물어뜯다, 물다 **stereotyped** 틀에 박힌, 진부한 **repetitive** 반복적인 **reward** 보상하다 **flash** (감정·생각 등이) 갑자기 떠오름

40 요약문 완성 ③

소재 주고받는 이익의 형태로 보는 친밀함의 정도

해설 요약문을 보면, 이익을 주고받는 상황에서 그 이익이 '어떠할' 때, 인식되는 '무엇'이 더 컸는지 찾아야 함을 알 수 있다. 두 가지 형태의 이익을 되돌려 주는 방식을 보고 피실험자들이 두 사람 사이의 우정의 질을 평가하는(evaluate the quality of the friendship between the two) 실험이므로 (A)에는 'closeness(친밀함)'가 적절하다. 또한 다른 형태로 이익을 되돌려 줄 때 친밀함이 더 높다고 인식하였으므로, (B)에는 'unrelated(관련이 없는)'나 'dissimilar(비슷하지 않은)'가 적절하다. 따라서 정답은 ③이다.

해석 한 실험에서, 피실험자들은 두 사람 사이의 일련의 상호 작용에 대한 짧은 이야기를 읽도록 요청을 받았다. 이 이야기에서 한 사람은 다른 사람에게 직장까지 태워달라는 것과 같은 어떤 부탁을 했다. 그 이야기의 절반에서는 호의를 받은 사람이 그다음에 상대방에게 똑같은 이익(예를 들어, 만약 직장까지 차를 얻어 타고 갔으면, 그들도 상대방을 직장까지 태워다 주는 것)을 제공하였고, 그 이야기 중 절반에서는 호의를 받은 사람이 그다음에 상대방에게 다른 종류의 이익(예를 들어, 만약 직장까지 차를 얻어 타고 갔으면, 상대방에게 점심을 사주는 것)을 제공하였다. 피실험자들은 이 이야기들을 읽은 후에 두 사람 사이의 우정의 질을 평가해 달라고 요청을 받았다. 주제문 피실험자들은 똑같은 이익을 교환한 사람들은 다른 형태의 이익을 교환한 사람들보다 덜 친밀하다고 말했다. 왜 이런 평가를 내렸는지에 대한 질문을 받았을 때, 피실험자들은 똑같은 이익을 교환하는 것을 분명히 친밀한 우정과는 관련이 없는, 빚을 갚는 형식으로 해석했다고 말했다.

⬇

이익을 주고받는 상황에서 그 이익이 (B) 비슷하지 않은 것일 때, 인식되는 (A) 친밀함이 더 컸다.

구문 [17행~21행] **Asked** why they made these assessments, / subjects said // that they interpreted the exchange of the same benefits / as a form of repayment, something [that they evidently did not associate ● with close friendship].

Asked ~ assessments는 분사구문으로 When subjects were asked ~ assessments와 같은 의미이다. a form of repayment와 something ~ friendship이 동격 관계이며, 관계사절 that ~ friendship은 앞의 something을 수식한다. something은 관계사절 내에서 「associate A with B (A를 B와 관련시키다)」 구문의 A에 해당한다.

어휘 **account** 이야기, 설명 **a series of** 일련의 **favor** 부탁; 호의, 친절 **recipient** 받는 사람, 수령인 **subsequently** 그다음에, 나중에 **assessment** 평가 **interpret** 해석[이해]하다 **repayment** (빚을) 갚음, 상환 **evidently** 분명히, 눈에 띄게 [선택지 어휘] **availability** 이용 가능성 **tangible** 유형의; 만질 수 있는 **substantial** 상당한; 크고 단단한 **impact** 충격, 영향; 충격[영향]을 주다 **immediate** 즉각적인; 직접적인

41~42 장문 41 ④ 42 ③

소재 부정적 뉴스 청취로 인한 생각의 오류

해설 41. 언론의 자유가 더욱 커지고 첨단 기술이 발달한 덕에 많은 소식을 접하지만, 주로 나쁜 소식, 재난, 위기 뉴스를 듣게 되어 세상이 좋아지고 있는데도 세상이 나빠진다는 착각에 빠진다는 내용의 글이다. 그러므로 ④ '나쁜 뉴스의 끊임없는 흐름은 그 자체로 오류다'가 글의 제목으로 가장 적절하다.

① 저널리즘의 윤리와 표준
② 언론의 자유가 어떻게 작동하는가
③ 거대한 과학기술이 오보를 억제한다
⑤ 선택적 보도: 실제 거짓을 말하며 간파하는 것

42. 예시로 든 미국에서의 범죄는 1990년 약 1,450만 건에서 2016년에는 950만 건으로 떨어졌다. 그러므로 (c)의 '상승하는(growing)'은 '하락하는(downward)'으로 바꾸어 써야 적절하다.

해석 우리는 전쟁, 기근, 자연재해, 질병, 대량 해고, 테러 행위 등 전 세계에서 끊임없이 쏟아지는 부정적 뉴스에 시달린다. 점진적 개선에 대한 이야기는 그것들이 극적인 규모로 일어나고 수백만 명에게 강한 영향을 줄 때조차도 신문 1면에 (a) 거의 실리지 않는다. 그리고 언론 자유의 증가와 발전하는 기술 덕분에 우리는 과거 어느 때 보다 더 많이, 더 많은 재난에 대해 듣는다. 이렇게 더 좋아진 보도는 그 자체가 인류 발전의 표시이지만 그것은 정반대의 느낌을 만들어낸다. 동시에 활동가와 로비스트는 전반적 추세가 명백하게 발전하고 있다 하더라도 어떤 추세의 어느 일시적인 하락을 세상의 끝인 것처럼 보이도록 교묘히 어떻게든 만들어내서 세상을 소란케 하는 과장으로 우리를 (b) 겁준다. 예를 들어 미국에서는 1990년대 이후로 강력 범죄율이 (c) 늘어나는(→ 줄어드는) 추세다. 1990년에는 1,450만 건을 약간 밑도는 범죄가 보도되었다. 2016년에는 그 수치는 950만 건 한참 아래였다. 거의 매년 일어나는 끔찍하거나 놀라운 일이 벌어질 때마다 위기라는 보도가 나왔다. 대다수의 사람들은 거의 대부분의 때에 강력 범죄가 점점 더 악화되고 있다고 믿는다. 그리고 이것이 우리에게 만들어내는 파멸에 이르고 있다는 느낌은 우리가 과거를 기억하지 (d) 못함으로 인해 더욱 심해진다. 주제문 그러나 뉴스 안건은 사실 요점을 놓치고 있다. 상황은 호전되고 있다. 우리는 1년 전, 또는 10년 전, 또는 50년 전에 훨씬 더 많은 끔찍한 사건이 있었다는 것을 기억하지 못한다. (e) 악화에 대한 이런 착각은 어떤 사람들에게는 큰 스트레스를 주고 어떤 사람들은 희망을 잃게 만든다. 타당한 근거도 없이.

구문 [11행~15행] At the same time, activists and lobbyists skillfully manage to ^{V}**make** ^{O}*every dip in a trend* ^{C}**appear** to be the end of the world, // even if the general trend is clearly improving, / scaring us with alarmist exaggerations.
동사 manage의 목적어 역할을 하는 밑줄 친 부분에서 사역동사 make의 목적어로 every dip in a trend가 나왔고 목적격보어로 원형부정사 appear가 쓰였다. even if ~ improving은 양보를 나타내는 삽입절이고, scaring 이하는 분사구문이다.

어휘 **subject A to B** B로 하여금 A에 시달리게[당하게] 만들다 **famine** 기근, 기아 **mass** 대량의, 많은; 덩어리 **layoff** 정리[일시] 해고 **scale** 규모, 범위 **impact** 강한 영향[충격]을 주다 **progress** 진보, 발달 **activist** (정치 · 사회 운동) 활동가, 운동가 **lobbyist** 로비스트, 의안 통과 운동가, 원외 활동가 **dip** (일시적인) 하락[감소] **alarmist** 세상을 소란케 하는 (사람), 불필요한 우려를 자아내는 **exaggeration** 과장 **violent crime rate** 강력 범죄율 **figure** 수치, 숫자 **horrific** 끔찍한, 무서운 **majority** 대다수 **doom-laden** 파멸에 이르는, 파멸을 예고하는 **intensify** 심해지다, 강화하다 **inability** ~할 수 없음, 무능(력) **agenda** 안건, 의제 **illusion** 착각, 오해; 환상 **deterioration** 악화, 퇴보 **good reason** 타당한 이유 [선택지 어휘] **ethics** 윤리(학) **curb** 억제[제한]하다 **flawed** 결함[흠]이 있는

43~45 장문

43 ④ 44 ④ 45 ②

소재 겉모습만 보고 판단하지 마라

해설 43. (A)에서 젊은이가 현자에게 그의 허름한 옷차림의 연유를 물은 이후에 현자가 반지를 금 한 덩이에 팔아오는 과제를 수행해오면 답을 해주겠다고 말하는 (D)가 오고, 젊은이가 반지를 그 값에 팔지 못하고 돌아오자 금을 파는 상인에게 가보게 하는 (B)가 이어져야 한다. 마지막 (C)에서 금을 파는 상인이 막대한 금을 지불하고 그 반지를 사겠다고 했는데, 그 이유가 바로 젊은이가 던진 질문에 대한 대답이 되므로 ④ '(D)-(B)-(C)'의 순서가 알맞다.

44. (d)는 '금을 파는 상인'을 나타내지만, 나머지는 모두 '젊은이'를 가리킨다.

45. (B)에서 상인들이 젊은이에게 반지 값으로 은 한 덩이 이상은 주지 못하겠다고 해서 결국 반지를 다시 가지고 돌아왔으므로 ②가 글의 내용과 일치하지 않는다.

해석 (A) 옛날 이집트에 Zunnun이라는 이름의 유명한 현자(賢者)가 살았다. 어느 날 젊은이가 그의 집에 와서 말하길, "스승님, ① 저는 스승님이 어째서 그렇게 간소하고 초라하게 옷을 입고 계신지 이해하지 못하겠습니다. 스승님이 사실 수 있는 가장 좋은 옷을 입는 것이 더 좋지 않을까요?"
(D) Zunnun은 (e) 그(= 젊은이)에게 그저 미소를 짓고는 그의 손가락에서 반지를 빼서 이렇게 말했다. "내가 네 질문에 대답해주겠다. 하지만 먼저 너는 이 반지를 시장에 가져가서 금 한 덩이를 받고 팔아야 한다." 색이 흐릿한 반지를 그 현자의 손에서 가져가면서 젊은이는 속으로 생각했다. ⑤ '금 한 덩이라고? 이런 보잘것없는 반지를 그렇게 비싼 값에 파는 건 불가능해! 하지만 난 내 질문에 대한 답을 듣고 싶으니 해봐야지.'
(B) 그 젊은이는 재빨리 시장에 갔다. (a) 그(= 젊은이)는 그 반지를 직물 상인, 채소 장수, 정육점 주인, 생선 장수에게 내놓았다. ② 아무도 금 한 덩이를 기꺼이 지불하려고 하지 않았다. 그래서 (b) 그(= 젊은이)는 Zunnun에게 돌아와 보고했다. "스승님, 아무도 은 한 덩이 이상은 주지 않겠답니다." Zunnun은 웃으며 말했다. "이제 이 길 끝에 있는 금을 파는 상인의 가게에 가서 그 반지를 주인에게 보여 주거라. 네가 원하는 가격을 말하지 말고 그저 그가 네게 반지에 얼마를 지불할 것인지를 물어 보거라."
(C) 그 젊은이는 (c) 그(= 젊은이)가 가라고 얘기 들은 가게를 찾았다. 그는 돌아와서 "스승님, ③ 그 금을 파는 상인이 제게 금 천 덩이를 반지 값으로 주겠답니다! (d) 그(= 금을 파는 상인)는 그 반지를 다른 상인들보다 2천 배나 높은 값으로 평가했습니다!"라고 말했다. Zunnun은 다시 웃으며 부드럽게 말했다. "여보게, 그것이 네 질문에 대한 대답이다. 주제문 겉만 보고 가치를 빨리 결정하지 말거라. 시장에 있는 상인들은 그렇게 해서 놋쇠를 보았지만, ④ 금을 파는 상인은 면밀히 살펴서 다이아몬드와 금을 보았단다."

구문 [(C) 1행~2행] The young man found *the shop* [**to which** he was told to go].
관계대명사절은 he was told to go to the shop에서 the shop을 목적격 관계대명사 which로 바꾸고, 전치사 to와 관계대명사 which를 동시에 절 앞으로 보낸 형태이다.

어휘 **(A) humbly** 초라하게; 겸손하게 **afford** (금전적 · 시간적) 여유가 되다 **(B) textile** 직물 **butcher** 정육점 주인 **trader** 상인, 무역업자 **(C) value** (가치를) 평가하다; 가치 **swift** 재빠른, 신속한 **appearance** 겉모습, 외모; 출현, 나타남 **brass** 놋쇠, 황동 **(D) dull** (색 등이) 분명치 않은, 희미한; 머리가 둔한 **worthless** 쓸모없는, 가치 없는

실전 모의고사 09

본문 p.125

18 ②	19 ⑤	20 ①	21 ①	22 ⑤	23 ②	24 ②	25 ⑤	26 ③	27 ⑤
28 ③	29 ④	30 ①	31 ③	32 ④	33 ①	34 ⑤	35 ③	36 ②	37 ①
38 ④	39 ⑤	40 ②	41 ③	42 ④	43 ③	44 ②	45 ④		

18 글의 목적 ②

소재 고등학교 연극 공연 안내

해설 고등학교 연극부의 학기말 공연을 소개하며 연극 관람을 독려하는 글이다. 글 중반의 I wholeheartedly recommend it ~ loves the theater와 마지막의 See you at the theater!에 잘 드러나 있듯이 학교 연극 공연 관람을 권하는 내용이므로 정답은 ②이다.

해석 독자 여러분,
Crestford 고등학교 연극부가 학년의 마지막 연극을 무대에 올릴 그 때가 다시 돌아왔습니다. 지난 공연들은 우리의 가장 훌륭한 연극부 학생들의 재능과 함께 우리의 소중한 연극 강사인 David Banff의 재능을 돋보이게 했습니다. 올해의 〈오즈의 마법사〉 공연도 예외가 아니어서, 약간의 흥미진진한 변화와 함께 원작의 정신을 담아내는 데 성공했습니다. 주제문 이 연극에 대해서는 그저 대단한 것이라고 밖에는 할 말이 없고, 저는 연극을 사랑하는 누구에게나 진심으로 이것을 권합니다. 또한 올해 Banff 선생님이 은퇴를 예정하고 있기에 활동하는 그의 작품을 볼 마지막 기회입니다. 입장권 가격은 학생 할인도 없어서 좀 비쌀 수 있지만 수익은 모두 연극부를 지원하는 것에 쓰입니다. 그러니 제 생각으로는 가치 있는 대의입니다. 주제문 극장에서 만납시다!
기고자, Maria Vasquez

구문 [7행~10행] This year's performance of *The Wizard of Oz* is no exception, / **managing** to capture the spirit of the original / with a few exciting changes.
managing 이하는 분사구문으로 앞에 나온 내용을 부연 설명한다. and it(= this year's performance) manages to capture ~로 바꾸어 쓸 수 있다.

어휘 **put on** 무대에 올리다, 공연하다 **highlight** 돋보이게 하다, 강조하다 **beloved** 소중한, 사랑하는 **instructor** 강사, 지도자 **exception** 예외 **capture** 담아내다; 포착하다; 붙잡다 **nothing but** 오직, 그저 ~일 뿐 **wholeheartedly** 진심으로, 전적으로 **mark** 예정하다; 표시하다 **retirement** 은퇴 **go toward** ~에 쓰이다; ~에 도움이 되다 **cause** 대의명분, 큰 목적; 원인 **contributor** 기고자; 공헌자

19 심경 변화 ⑤

소재 이상한 토끼와의 마주침

해설 She는 강둑에 앉아 할 일이 없어 언니가 읽는 책을 엿보았지만 그것도 재미없어서 지루해하다가(bored), 이상한 토끼를 보고 호기심이 생겨서(curious) 쫓아가는 상황이므로 정답은 ⑤ '지루한 → 호기심 있는'이다. 참고로 이 글은 〈이상한 나라의 앨리스〉의 도입부이다.

해석 주제문 그녀는 강둑 위에서 언니 옆에 앉아 아무 할 일 없이 있는 것이 매우 지루해지기 시작했다. 한두 번 언니가 읽고 있는 책을 엿보았지만, 그 책에는 그림도 대화문도 없었다. "그림도 대화문도 없는 책이 무슨 소용이람?" 갑자기 분홍색 눈을 한 하얀 토끼가 그녀 옆을 가까이 달려 지나갔다. 그런 모습에서 아주 많이 놀라운 점은 전혀 없었다. 주제문 하지만 그 토끼가 정말로 자기 조끼 주머니에서 시계를 꺼내어 쳐다본 다음 서둘러 갔을 때, 그녀는 자리에서 갑자기 일어섰다. 왜냐하면 조끼 주머니나 그 안에서 꺼내볼 시계를 가진 토끼는 한 번도 본 적이 없다는 생각이 문득 그녀의 머릿속에 떠올랐기 때문이다. 그래서 그녀는 그 토끼를 쫓아 들판을 가로질러 달려갔다.

① 슬픈 → 기쁜
② 동정하는 → 겁먹은
③ 외로운 → 질투 난
④ 짜증 난 → 당황한

구문 [10행~12행] ~, **for** it flashed across her mind / that she had never before seen *a rabbit* (with either a waistcoat-pocket or a watch to take out of it).
(it: 가주어, that she had ~: 진주어)
여기서 for는 앞서 말한 내용의 '이유'가 되는 절을 이끄는 등위접속사로 쓰였다. it은 가주어이고 that절이 진주어이다. with 이하의 전명구는 a rabbit을 수식하며 「either A or B (A이거나 B)」 구문이 쓰였다.

어휘 **bank** 둑, 제방; 은행 **peep into** 엿보다, 몰래 훔쳐보다 **remarkable** 놀랄 만한, 주목할 만한 **waistcoat** (남자용) 조끼 **start to one's feet** 갑자기 일어서다 **flash across one's mind** 문득 머리에 떠오르다, 갑자기 생각나다 *cf.* **flash** (생각이) 불현듯 들다; 휙 지나가다; 번쩍이다; 비추다

20 필자 주장 ①

소재 불안을 극복하는 방법

해설 역사상 가장 위대한 선수조차 불안을 겪는데 이를 극복하는 방법은 경기를 시작하는 것, 즉 일단 행동을 실행하는 것이라는 내용의 글이다. 따라서 필자의 주장으로 가장 적절한 것은 ①이다.

해석 나는 여러 해 전에 한 스포츠 기자가 Bill Russell과 했던 인터뷰를 아주 흥미롭게 보았다. Bill Russell은 NBA 역사상 가장 위대한 선수 중 하나이자 보스턴 셀틱스에 많은 우승을 안겨주는 데 도움을 준 사람이다. 이 인터뷰에서 스포츠 기자는 명예의 전당에 오른 사람(= Russell)에게 경기 전에 긴장한 적이 있는지 물었다. Russell은 말했다. "전 매 경기 전에 토해요." 그것은 심한 불안이다. Bill Russell은 자신의 불안을 어떻게 극복했을까? 그는 경기를 시작했다. 일단 경기가 시작되면 불안은 사라졌다. 행동이 핵심이었다. 이러한 전략은 우리에게도 효과가 있을 것이다. 주제문 때때로 불안을 극복하는 유일한 방법은 무언가를 하느라 분주해지는 것이다. 그 지점에서 두 가지 일 중 하나가 발생할 것이다. 불안에 사실 아무런 근거가 없었다면, 그것(= 불안)은 활동의 질풍 속에서 사라질 것이다. 불안의 원인이 정당했다면, 우리는 적어도 그것에 관해 무언가를 하고 있으므로 여전히 어떤 안도감을 얻을 것이다.

구문 [2행~5행] Bill Russell is one of the greatest players / in the history of the National Basketball Association, *a man* [who **helped bring** multiple championships to the Boston Celtics].
밑줄 친 두 어구는 서로 동격 관계이다. [ ]는 a man을 수식하는 주격 관계대명사절이다. help는 목적어로 to부정사나 원형부정사를 쓸 수 있는데, 여기서는 원형부정사(bring)가 쓰였다.

[5행~7행] In this interview, the sports reporter asked (V) the Hall of Famer (IO) **if** he ever got nervous before a game (DO).
ask의 직접목적어로 접속사 if가 이끄는 명사절이 쓰였다. 여기서 if는 '~인지 (아닌지)'의 뜻이다.

어휘 **intrigue** 강한 흥미[호기심]를 불러일으키다 **multiple** 많은, 다수의 **Hall of Famer** 명예의 전당에 오른 사람 **vomit** 구토하다 **anxiety** 불안 **overcome** 극복하다 **strategy** 전략 **basis** 근거 **dissolve** 사라지다; 녹다 **flurry** 질풍 **legitimate** 정당한, 적법한 **relief** 안도

21 밑줄 함의 ①

소재 자신의 강점이나 약점에 집착하지 않는 태도

해설 세계 인구의 다수가 자신의 강점에 집중하는 것이 성공에 유리하다고 생각하지 않으며, 모든 문화권에서 노년층은 자신의 약점에 개의치 않고 자기 자신을 있는 그대로 받아들인다는 내용의 글이다. 노년층이 '끈질기게 남아있는 균열에 도배하는 것의 무용함'을 깨달았다는 말은 ① '그들은 자신의 약점을 고치려고 노력할 필요가 없다'는 것을 깨달았다는 의미로 이해할 수 있다.

해석 강점에 가장 많이 집중하는 문화는 미국이며, 인구의 41퍼센트가 자신의 강점을 아는 것이 그들을 가장 많이 향상시키는 데 도움이 될 거라고 말한다. 강점에 가장 적게 집중하는 문화는 일본과 중국이다. 오직 24퍼센트만이 성공의 핵심이 그들의 강점에 있다고 믿는다. 그러나 그 범위에도 불구하고, 다음의 일반적인 결론이 진실이다. 주제문 세계 인구의 다수는 향상의 비결이 자신의 강점에 대한 깊은 이해에 있다고 생각하지 않는다는 점이다. 흥미롭게도, 모든 문화에서 자신의 약점에 가장 덜 집착하는 집단은 가장 나이든 집단, 즉 55세 이상의 사람들이었다. 약간 더 나이 많고 약간 더 현명한 이 집단은 아마 자아수용 정책을 습득했을 것이다. 그들은 끈질기게 남아있는 균열에 도배를 하는 것의 무용함을 깨달았다.
② 그들은 자신의 약점을 극복하기 위해 계속해서 노력할 필요가 있다
③ 그들은 자기 자신의 강점에 집중하고 그것을 극대화해야 한다
④ 그들은 성취에 대한 접근법을 바꿀 기회를 가진다
⑤ 그들은 어려운 시기에 현실적인 기대를 설정해야 한다

구문 [1행~4행] The most strengths-focused culture is the United States, / **with** *41 percent of the population* **saying** that knowing their strengths will **help** *them* **improve** the most.
「with+O+분사」는 'O가 ~한 채로'의 뜻으로, 여기서는 현재분사 saying이 쓰여 목적어와 목적격보어가 능동 관계임을 나타낸다. saying의 목적어로 쓰인 that절에서 help의 목적격보어로 원형부정사(improve)가 쓰였다.

어휘 **strength** 강점(↔ **weakness** 약점) **lie in** ~에 있다 **range** 범위 **general** 일반적인 **conclusion** 결론 **hold true** 진실이다 **fixate (on)** (~에) 병적으로 집착하게 하다 **acquire** 습득하다 **measure** 조치, 정책 **self-acceptance** 자아수용 **futility** 무용(無用), 소용없음 **paper** 도배하다 **persistent** 끈질긴, 지속하는 **crack** 갈라진 틈 [선택지 어휘] **correct** 고치다, 수정하다 **maximize** 극대화[최대화]하다 **vary** 변화를 주다; 달라지다 **approach** 접근(법) **challenging** 어려운, 힘든; 도전적인

22 글의 요지 ⑤

소재 공정 거래 상품 구입을 통한 윤리적 소비 실천

해설 '공정 거래' 표시가 붙어 있는 상품을 구입함으로써 다국적 기업이 아니라 일반 농민의 경제에 보탬이 될 수 있다는 내용이다. 즉, 윤리적 소비가 부의 재분배에 기여할 수 있다는 요지를 전달하므로 정답은 ⑤이다.

해석 주제문 당신의 소비 습관이 당신을 아주 많은 사람들의 삶에 직접적으로 연결시킨다. '공정 거래'나 '윤리적 소비'라는 용어를 들어본 적이 있는가? 당신의 커피가 어디에서 왔는지 생각해본 적이 있는가? 세계 커피의 대부분은 농장 노동자들에게 적은 임금을 지급함으로써 자신의 상품 가격을 낮출 수 있는 다국적 기업에 의해 생산된다. 이러한 회사들과 경쟁하기 위해서 (다국적 기업이 아닌) 전통적인 방식의 농민들은 불공정한 가격에 그들의 농산품을 팔도록 강요받고, 따라서 그들은 가난의 굴레에 갇히게 된다. 하지만 '공정 거래'라는 라벨이 붙은 커피는 공정한 가격을 지급받은 농민들에 의해서 생산된 것이다. 공정 거래 커피를 사서 마시는 것은 윤리적 소비와 관련된 하나의 본보기일 뿐이다. 주제문 그것(= 윤리적 소비)은 돈을 받을 만한 가치가 있는 더 많은 사람들에게 돈을 준다. 자, 상품을 사기 전에 라벨을 읽어 보고 당신이 윤리적인 구매를 하고 있는지 살펴보라.

어휘 **consumption** 소비 **fair trade** 공정 거래 *cf.* **fair** 공정한(↔ **unfair** 불공정한) **ethical** 윤리적인, 도덕적인 **multinational corporation** 다국적 기업 **wage** 임금, 보수 **trap** 가두다; 덫[함정]에 빠뜨리다; 덫 **poverty** 가난, 빈곤 **label** 라벨[상표]을 붙이다; 라벨, 상표 **deserve** ~을 받을 만하다

23 글의 주제 ②

소재 자녀가 최종 기한을 지키게 하는 것의 의미

해설 자녀가 최종 기한을 지키지 않았을 때 또 기회를 주면, 아이들은 정해진 무언가를 지키지 않아도 이익을 얻을 수 있다고 여기게 되어 시간 관리를 배우는 데 좋지 않다는 내용의 글이므로, 이 글의 주제로는 ② '자녀에게 최종 기한을 지키게 하는 것의 중요성'이 가장 적절하다.

해석 주제문 자녀에게 방을 청소할 30분의 시간이 주어지면, 부모는 30분 후에 확인할 의무가 있다. 그 일(= 청소)이 행해지지 않아서 부모가 자녀에게 돌아가서 그것을 끝내도록 지시한다면, 그것이 자녀에게 최종 기한의 의미(혹은 그 일에 있어서 30분의 의미)에 관해 무엇을 가르쳐 주겠는가? 자녀는 진정한 최종 기한, 즉 최후통첩이 없었다는 것을 곧 깨닫는다. 최종 기한이 지난 후에 자녀에게 "거기로 돌아가서 그것을 해라!"라고 지시하는 것은 자녀에게 시간 관리에 대해 가르쳐 주지 못한다. 그것은 자녀에게 논쟁을 벌일 추가적인 기회가 있다는 것을 가르쳐 준다. 누구도 그런 종류의 실행을 필요로 하지 않는다. 너무 많은 제2의 기회는 아이들이 말을 듣지 않아도 되고, 검사에 불합격해도 되고, 사람들을 화나게 해도 되고, '자기가' 하고 싶을 때 일할 수 있으며, 그래도 이익을 얻을 수 있다는 것을 아이들에게 가르쳐 준다.
① 아이들이 집안일을 하도록 동기 부여하는 방법
③ 자녀의 잘못된 행동에 대한 보상의 결과
④ 시간 관리 기술을 아이들에게 가르치는 것의 이점
⑤ 자녀와 부모 간의 흔한 오해

구문 [8행~10행] V'Ordering O'a child C'to "Get back in there and do it!" (S) / after the deadline has expired fails (V) to teach a child about time management. (O)
주어는 Ordering으로 시작하는 동명사구이고 동사는 fails이다. order는 목적격보어로 to부정사를 취한다.
[12행~15행] Too many second chances (S) teach (V) kids (IO) // (that) they can (DO) **disobey**, **fail** inspection, **irritate** people, and **do** tasks when they feel like doing them, and still **reap** the benefits.
that절 내의 동사 disobey, fail, irritate, do, reap은 조동사 can 뒤에 오는 동사원형이 and에 의해 병렬연결된 구조이다.

어휘 **be obligated to-v** v할 의무가 있다 **expire** (기한이) 만료되다, 만기가 되다 **management** 관리; 경영 **disobey** (사람 · 명령 등을) 따르지 않다, 거역하다 **inspection** 검사, 점검 **irritate** 짜증나게 하다, 거슬리게 하다 **reap** (결실을) 얻다; (농작물을) 수확하다 [선택지 어휘] **chore** (가정의) 잡일; 하기 싫은 일 **enforce** (법을) 집행[시행]하다; 강요하다 **consequence** 결과, 영향(력); (영향 등의) 중요성

24 글의 제목 ②

소재 인간의 털이 빠진 이유

해설 감정에 따라 변하는 피부색을 통해 상대방의 감정을 읽을 수 있듯이, 털이 더 적은 것이 감정 신호를 보내는 데 더 유리하기 때문에 인간의 털이 빠졌을 것이라는 주장을 소개하는 글이다. 따라서 제목으로 가장 적절한 것은 ② '인류는 어떻게 털이 빠지게 되었는가'이다.

해석 우리의 얼굴은 화가 났을 때 주홍색으로, 당황했을 때는 붉은색으로 바뀌어서 우리의 강한 감정을 드러낸다. 이제, 캘리포니아 공과대학의 신경생리학자 Mark Changizi

는 우리의 색 구별 능력이 이러한 감정 신호를 더 잘 해석하기 위해 발달했을 수도 있다고 주장한다. 그는 또한 이 특성이 왜 우리가 '벌거벗은 원숭이'가 되었는지 설명해 줄 수 있다고 주장한다. Changizi는 맨얼굴과 맨엉덩이의 영장류(개코원숭이, 고릴라, 그리고 인간을 포함하는 집단)는 붉어진 피부에 매우 민감한 시력을 가지고 있는 반면, 완전히 털로 덮여 있는 영장류는 그렇지 않다는 것을 발견했다. 이 시각적 민감도는 매우 유리한 사교적인 기술인, 친구나 적의 감정을 읽을 수 있는 능력을 향상시키지만 피부가 완전히 털로 덮여 있으면 소용이 없다. 주제문 따라서 털이 더 적은 것이 신체가 감정 신호를 보내는 데 더 유리하기 때문에 오랜 세월에 걸쳐 우리는 털이 빠졌을 수 있다.

① 영장류의 감정을 읽는 방법
③ 정교한 인간의 시력에서 오는 혜택
④ 인간의 시력은 원숭이의 시력과 어떻게 다른가
⑤ 어떻게 인간과 다른 영장류가 진화했는가

구문 [7행~10행] Changizi found // **that** barefaced and bare-bottomed primates (S′) *a group* [that includes baboons, gorillas, and humans] have (V′) *vision* (O′) [that's highly sensitive to increased redness in the skin], ~.

found의 목적어인 that절의 주어는 barefaced ~ primates, 동사는 have이다. a group ~ humans는 주어를 부연 설명하는 동격어구이다. 목적어인 vision을 주격 관계대명사 that이 이끄는 절이 수식하고 있다.

어휘 **reveal** 드러내다 **scarlet** 주홍색 **rage** 분노, 격분; 몹시 화내다 **embarrassment** 당혹감 **neurobiologist** 신경생리학자 **evolve** 발달하다, 진화하다 **interpret** 해석[이해]하다 **trait** 특성, 특징 **ape** 유인원 **barefaced** 맨얼굴의; 뻔뻔스러운 **primate** 영장류 **sensitive** 민감한 *cf.* **sensitivity** 민감도; 감수성 **foe** 적(군) **advantageous** 유리한, 이로운 [선택지 어휘] **sophisticated** 정교한, 매우 복잡한

25 도표 이해 ⑤

소재 캐나다와 멕시코 간의 무역량

해설 도표에 제시된 첫 해인 2015년의 수출액은 450만 캐나다 달러, 마지막 해인 2019년의 수출액은 610만 캐나다 달러이므로 총 증가액은 160만 캐나다 달러이다. 따라서 200만 캐나다 달러 이상 증가했다는 ⑤는 잘못된 설명이다.

해석 〈캐나다의 멕시코와의 무역〉

주제문 이 도표는 2015년에서 2019년까지 5년간 캐나다와 멕시코 간의 연간 무역 가치를 100만 캐나다 달러 단위로 보여준다. ① 이 5년 중 2018년에는 멕시코로의 수출액이 최대가 되어, 690만 캐나다 달러의 기록을 세웠다. ② 2017년에는 수입액이 수출액을 조금 웃돌았다. ③ 그 후, 캐나다의 총 수입액은 매년 줄어들었다. ④ 2019년에 수입 가치는 수출 가치보다 훨씬 적었지만, 그보다 4년 전에는 수출액과 수입액 간의 차이가 겨우 70만 캐나다 달러에 불과했다. ⑤ 이 5년간의 기간 중 처음과 비교하여 2019년의 캐나다의 수출액은 가치가 200만 캐나다 달러 이상 증가했다.

어휘 **value** 가치; 값 **set a record** 기록을 세우다 **volume** 양, 부피; 음량; 책 **slightly** 조금, 약간 **outdo (outdid-outdone)** 앞지르다, 능가하다

26 내용 불일치 ③

소재 천연 피부 질환 치료제 '용의 피'

해설 '용의 피'를 섭취하는 것이 아니라 피부 질환 부위에 직접 발라서 치료하므로 ③이 틀린 내용이다.

해석 ① '용의 피'는 수세기 동안 남아메리카의 원주민 부족들이 사용해온 천연 수액이다. 그 수액은 아마존의 우림 지대에 서식하는 나무인 Croton lechleri(크로톤 레치레리)에서 나오는데, 나무가 잘리거나 상처를 입었을 때 수액이 나오는 것이 마치 나무가 피를 흘리고 있는 것처럼 보여서 ② 주민들이 *Sangre de Drago*(스페인 어로 '용의 피')라고 이름을 붙였다. ③ 용의 피는 벌레에 물리거나 쏘인 곳, 베인 상처, 화상, 발진 등의 피부 질환 외부에 바른다. 수액은 일종의 액체 붕대로 사용되어, 매일 수차례 상처 부위에 직접 문질러 바르고 말린다. 이 수액은 상처 부위를 덮어서 감염으로부터 지켜주고, ④ 출혈과 통증을 줄이며, 치유 과정을 촉진시키는 막을 만든다. ⑤ 수액 속에 함유된 특별한 알칼리성 화학물질이 이 나무의 치유 능력의 원천이라고 여겨지고 있다.

구문 [11행~13행] It creates *a layer* [**that** seals affected areas **to protect** against infections, **(to) reduce** bleeding and pain, and **(to) speed up** the healing process].

'결과'를 나타내는 부사적 용법의 to부정사구 3개가 and로 병렬연결된 구조이다. '~해서 (그 결과) v하다'로 해석하는 것이 자연스럽다.

어휘 **tribe** 부족, 종족 **rainforest** 열대 우림 **local** 주민, 현지인; 지역의 **apply** (크림 등을) 바르다; 적용하다; 지원하다 **externally** 외부적으로, 외부에서 **rash** 발진 **liquid** 액체의 **rub** 문지르다 **affect** (신체 부위에) 질병이 발생하다; 영향을 미치다 **layer** 막, 층, 겹 **seal** 덮다; 밀봉하다 **infection** 감염, 전염 **alkali** 알칼리(성) **chemical** 화학물질; 화학의

27 안내문 불일치 ⑤

소재 식중독 처치

해설 일반적인 설사 증상은 3일간 지속되면 병원에 가야 하지만, 심한 탈수 증세가 동반되는 경우에는 즉시 병원에 가야 한다고 했으므로 ⑤가 안내문과 일치하지 않는다.

해석

식중독 처치

1. 메스꺼움과 구토 조절
- ① 구토가 멈출 때까지 단단한 음식을 피하세요. 그리고 크래커, 바나나, 밥, 빵 같은 가볍고 자극 없는 음식을 드세요.
- ② 탄산수를 한 모금 마시면 구토를 방지하는 데 도움이 될 수도 있습니다.
- 튀기거나 기름지거나 맵거나 단 음식을 드시면 안 됩니다.
- ③ 의사에 묻지 않고 메스꺼움이나 설사를 방지하는 약을 복용해서는 안 됩니다. 그 약들은 몇몇 종류의 설사를 더욱 악화시킬 수도 있습니다.

2. 병원에 가야 할 때

다음과 같이 설사가 나면 즉시 병원에 가야 합니다.
- 설사가 3일 이상 지속될 때
- ④ 해산물이나 버섯 종류를 먹은 후에 설사가 날 때
- ⑤ 심한 탈수 증세가 함께 보이는 설사가 날 때

어휘 **food poisoning** 식중독 **treatment** 처치, 치료; 대우, 취급 **nausea** 메스꺼움 **vomit** 토하다 **solid** 단단한; 고체의 **bland** (맛이) 자극적이지 않은; 특징 없는 **sip** 한 모금 마시다, 홀짝이다 **soda** 탄산수 **diarrhea** 설사 **medication** 약물 **severe** 심각한 **dehydration** 탈수(증)

28 안내문 일치 ③

소재 제습기 보상 판매 행사

해설 ENERGY STAR의 검증된 제습기로 교체하면 전기료를 일 년에 60달러까지 절약할 수 있다고 했으므로 ③이 안내문의 내용과 일치한다.

해석

보상 판매 행사

날짜: 6월 20일~22일 (금요일~일요일)
장소: ① 온타리오 주(州) 전역의 Brant Power 상점
방법: ② 여러분의 오래되고 성능이 떨어진 제습기를 가지고 오셔서 교체품 ENERGY STAR 상표의 검증된 제습기를 구입하는 데 쓸 50달러짜리 쿠폰으로 교환하세요.

이 행사는 여러분이 새로 나온 에너지 효율이 높은 전기 기구를 구입하는 데 50달러를 절약할 수 있는 기회일 뿐만 아니라, 보상 판매 행사를 통해 여러분이 오래된 기기

를 ENERGY STAR의 검증된 기기로 교체하면 이제부터는 ③ 전기료를 일 년에 60달러까지 절약하는 즐거움을 추가로 얻을 수 있습니다.

필요 요건:
오래된 제습기는 10년 이상 된 것이어야 하며 ④ 사용할 수 있는 상태의 것이어야 합니다. ⑤ 여러분이 쓰던 제습기는 책임지고 폐기될 것입니다.

어휘 **trade-in** 보상 판매(쓰던 물건을 새 물건 값의 일부로 보상받아 구입하는 것) **inefficient** 성능이 떨어지는; 비효율적인 **dehumidifier** 제습기 **replacement** 교체, 대체 *cf.* **replace** 교체하다 **qualified** 검증된; 자격이 있는 **appliance** (전기) 기구 **additional** 추가적인 **ongoing** 계속 진행 중인 **discard** 폐기하다, 버리다 **responsibly** 책임지고, 확실히

29 밑줄 어법 ④

소재 새로운 정신적 분야의 탐색

해설 ④ 사역동사 let 다음에 the flow of water, in the form of rivers가 목적어이며, 목적격보어 자리에는 원형부정사를 써야 하므로 indicating을 indicate로 바꿔 써야 한다.

오답 분석 ① what ~ each mountain은 tell의 직접목적어이다. 명사절이므로 접속사 혹은 명사절을 이끄는 관계대명사 what을 사용해야 하는데, what 이하가 주어가 없는 불완전한 구문이므로 관계대명사 what을 사용한다. ② where ~는 '~한 곳'의 의미를 가지는 관계부사절이다. 앞에 the place 등의 선행사가 생략되었다. ③ that helped them explore는 useful strategies를 수식하는 관계대명사절이다. they could use 역시 앞에 목적격 관계대명사 which[that]가 생략되어 useful strategies를 수식한다. ⑤ to guide 이하는 strategies를 수식하는 형용사적 용법으로 쓰였다. you can draw upon 역시 앞에 목적격 관계대명사 which[that]가 생략되어 strategies를 수식한다.

해석 수 세기 전에 탐험가들이 새로운 변경 지대를 여행했을 때, 그들에게는 따라갈 자취나 각 산의 다른 쪽에 무엇이 있는지를 말해주는 지도가 없었다. 대신에 그들은 자기 자신의 길을 만들고 자기 자신의 지도를 그려야 했다. 주제문 마찬가지로 당신이 새로운 정신적 분야를 탐사할 때, 따를 수 있는 어떠한 단계별 지시나 규칙 없이 당신 자신의 길을 개척해야 한다. 결국 당신은 아마 누구도 이제껏 가보지 않은 곳을 가는 것이므로, 누가 당신에게 그곳에 도달할 수 있는 지시를 어떻게 제공할 수 있겠는가? 그러나 지리 탐험가들은 자신들이 사용할 수 있는 탐험에 도움이 되는 유용한 전략을 학습했다. 그들은 주변의 지형을 보기 위해 높은 산에 올라갔고, 강의 형태로 나타나는 물의 흐름으로 불필요한 등반을 포함하지 않는 경로가 나타나 보이게 했다. 이와 유사하게, 창의적인 문제 해결 과정 속에서 당신을 이끌어줄 의지할 수 있는 전략들이 있다.

어휘 **frontier** 변경 (지대), 새로운 분야 **trail** 자취; 자국 **instruction** 지시 **geographic** 지리학의, 지리적인 **indicate** 나타내다 **analogously** 유사하게 **draw upon** ~에 의지하다

30 네모 어휘 ①

소재 후각의 중요성

해설 (A) 냄새 수용기관은 후천적으로 얻어지는 것이 아니라 본래 비강 뒤쪽에 '위치하고' 있는 것이므로 situated가 적절하다. obtain은 '얻다, 획득하다'의 의미이다.
(B) 맛을 느끼는 데 있어서 코가 혀보다 더 중요하다는 내용에 이어 인간의 후각이 미각보다 더 '민감하다'는 것을 강조하는 문장이므로 sensitive가 알맞다. sensible은 '합리적인, 분별 있는'의 의미이다.
(C) 마지막 문장의 This data는 뇌 속에 '기록된' 정보를 의미하므로 recorded가 적절하다. erase는 '지우다, 없애다'란 뜻이다.

해석 주제문 우리가 맛볼 수 있는 가능한 모든 것들을 먹고, 마시고, 맛보는 것에 관해서, 우리의 코는 혀의 미뢰보다 훨씬 더 중요하다. 만약 우리에게 비강의 뒤쪽에 (A) 위치한 냄새 수용기관이 없다면, 우리는 아마도 김치와 사과의 차이점조차 구별할 수 없을 것이다. 인간의 후각은 미각보다 훨씬 더 (B) 민감하고, 수천 가지의 서로 다른 냄새를 식별할 수 있다. 우리가 태어난 그 순간부터, 우리가 냄새 맡는 모든 것들을 그 냄새를 맡는 경험에 동반되는 느낌과 또 다른 감각과 함께 우리의 뇌 속에 (C) 기록된다. 이 정보는 우리의 생존을 위해 중요하며, 심지어 우리의 기분과 기억을 형성하기도 한다.

구문 [9행~13행] From *the moment* [(that) we are born], / *everything* [that we smell] is recorded in our brains / along with *the feelings and other sensations* [that accompany those smelling experiences].
세 개의 [ ]는 모두 앞의 명사(구)를 수식하는 관계사절이다. the moment (that)은 여기서 전치사 from의 목적어로 쓰였지만, '~하자마자, ~하는 순간에'라는 뜻의 접속사로도 쓰인다.
e.g. **The moment** they met, they recognized each other right away.
(만나자마자 그들은 서로를 곧바로 알아보았다.)

어휘 **when it comes to A** A에 관한 한 **savor** 맛보다; 맛 **flavor** 맛, 풍미; 맛을 내다 **taste buds** (혀의) 미뢰[맛봉오리] **aroma** (기분 좋은) 냄새, 향기 **receptor** (인체의) 수용기[감각기] **sensation** 감각, 느낌 **accompany** 동반하다

31 빈칸 추론 ③

소재 행복을 결정하는 요소

해설 일란성 쌍둥이와 이란성 쌍둥이를 대상으로 행복 수준에 대해 연구한 결과, 일란성 쌍둥이가 환경에 관계없이 비슷한 행복 수준을 보였으며, 사람들은 저마다 행복의 '설정 값'을 타고나므로 다사다난한 일상에서 행복의 수준이 오르내려도 행복 수치는 결국 이 타고난 설정 값으로 회귀한다는 내용의 글이다. 따라서 행복의 거의 절반을 설명하는 것은 ③ '유전적(genetic)' 요소임을 알 수 있다.

해석 David Lykken과 Auke Tellegen은 1,300쌍의 일란성 쌍둥이와 이란성 쌍둥이가 보고한 행복 수준을 검사했다. 일란성 쌍둥이들은 비슷한 행복 수준을 보고한 반면 이란성 쌍둥이들은 보고한 행복감에 있어서 더 큰 차이를 보였다. 이러한 결과는 쌍둥이들이 함께 양육된 가정에서뿐만 아니라 따로 떨어져 양육된 쌍둥이들에서도 발견되었다. 주제문 그들은 행복의 거의 절반은 유전적 요소로 설명될 수 있다는 결론을 내렸다. 나머지 절반은 인생의 매일의 상승과 하강으로 결정된다. 다시 말해서 모든 사람들은 가정의 온도 조절 장치가 집 안에서 특정 온도를 유지하도록 설정되어 있는 것과 동일한 방식으로 행복에 대하여 특정 '설정 값'을 가지고 태어난다. 비극과 즐거움이 당신의 행복 수준에 영향을 미칠지도 모른다. 그러나 문이나 창문을 열어서 찬 공기를 들인 후에 집의 온도가 온도 조절 장치의 설정 값으로 돌아올 것처럼 결국 당신은 당신의 설정 값으로 회귀할 것이다.
① 문화의 ② 시간의 ④ 우연한 ⑤ 지리적인

구문 [6행~7행] These results were found not only in families of *twins* (raised together) but (also) in *twins* (reared apart).
「not only A but (also) B (A뿐만 아니라 B도)」 구문이 쓰였으며 raised together와 reared apart는 각각 앞의 명사 twins를 수식한다.

어휘 **identical twins** 일란성 쌍둥이 **fracternal twins** 이란성 쌍둥이 **exhibit** 보이다; 전시하다 **variation** 차이, 변화 **well-being** 행복, 안녕 **rear** 양육하다, 기르다 **account for** 설명하다 **ups and downs** 오르내림 **set point** 설정 값 **thermostat** 온도 조절 장치 **let in** ~을 들어오게 하다

32 빈칸 추론 ④

소재 인간의 모순성

해설 인간은 자신을 다른 동물들보다 뛰어나다고 생각하지만 그들의 희생자가 되기도 하고, 이성과 지성을 가졌지만 어리석은 행동을 하며, 세상에 위대한 예술품과 동시에 흉측한 산물을 남기기도 하는 등 ④ '역설의 화신'과 같은 면모를 보인다고 할 수 있다.

해석 어떤 먼 행성에서 온 한 방문자가 인간의 역사에 대해 어떻게 생각할지를 상상해 보자. 멀리서 인간사 박물관을 내려다보자. 주제문 그 방문자는 거의 확실히 인간이 역설의 화신이라는 결론을 내릴 것이다. 그들(= 인간)은 확실히 그저 동물에 불과하지만, 자신이 특별하다고 생각하는 것 같다. 그들은 자신을 불멸이라고 생각하지만, 죽는다. 그들은 자

신을 만물의 영장이라고 생각하지만, 매우 많은 다른 종의 먹이가 된다. 그들은 뛰어난 정신을 갖고 있지만, 이것은 단지 그들을 어리석음과 불합리로 이끌 뿐이다. 인간들은 협동적인 동물이지만, 또한 몹시 이기적이다. 그들은 위대한 예술을 창작할 수 있지만, 세상에 흉측한 난잡함을 남긴다. 그들은 관용과 이해를 옹호하지만, 자신의 신념을 위하여 서로를 고문한다. 먼 곳의 관찰자가 혼란스러운 것도 당연하다.

① 신비한 순환
② 고통의 총합
③ 일단의 오류
⑤ 역사의 모든 복합물

구문 [7행] They **think of** themselves(A) **as** immortal(B), yet they die.

「think of A as B」는 'A를 B로 생각하다'의 뜻이다. A의 themselves와 같은 재귀대명사는 목적어가 주어와 지칭하는 바가 동일할 때 사용한다. B에는 형용사를 쓰는 것이 가능하다.

어휘 **from afar** 멀리서 **immortal** 불멸의(↔ **mortal** 죽음을 면할 수 없는) **lord of creation** 만물의 영장 **folly** 어리석음 **unreason** 불합리, 부조리 **intensely** 몹시, 강렬하게 **mess** 난잡, 엉망진창 **advocate** 옹호하다 **tolerance** 관용; 인내(력) **torture** 고문하다, 괴롭히다 **might well** ~하는 것도 당연한 일이다 [선택지 어휘] **fallacy** 오류 **embody** 구현하다, 구체화하다 **composite** 복합물, 합성물

33 빈칸 추론 ①

소재 노인의 청력 상실 원인

해설 청력 저하는 노화의 결과일 뿐만 아니라 두뇌 능력의 저하 때문에도 생길 수 있다는 연구 결과에 관한 글이다. 빈칸에는 청력 저하에는 노화 이외의 다른 원인도 있을 수 있다는 내용이 와야 하므로 ① '청력이 유일한 문제가 아닐 수도 있다'가 가장 적절하다.

해석 식당이나 파티장과 같은 곳에서 주변 소음에 둘러싸여 있을 때 노인들은 누군가가 말하는 것을 이해하는 데 종종 어려움을 겪고, 그래서 많은 사람들은 노인들의 청력이 나이가 듦에 따라 저하된다고 생각한다. 주제문 하지만 한 연구조사에 따르면 청력이 유일한 문제가 아닐 수도 있다. 연구진들은 자기공명영상법(MRI)을 사용하여 36명의 노인과 젊은 성인을 대상으로 뇌 정밀검사를 실시하면서 특정 단어를 구별하는 능력을 테스트했는데, 그 단어들 중 일부는 알아듣기 어렵도록 걸러졌다. 연구진들은 일반적으로 노인이 청취가 어려운 환경에서 단어를 구별하는 데 있어 젊은 성인에 비해 현저히 뒤떨어진다는 것을 발견했다. 그 연구 결과는 노화로 인해 야기되는 청력 상실의 한 종류인 노인성 난청이, 귀가 듣는 것을 처리하지 못하는 뇌의 불능 또한 포함한다는 것을 우리가 더 잘 이해하도록 도와줄 것이다.

② 노인의 청력은 특정 소리를 듣는 데만 문제가 있다
③ 젊은이들의 청력 또한 자연히 저하될 수 있다
④ 이러한 종류의 청력 상실을 치료하는 많은 방법이 있다
⑤ 주변 소음 정도가 가장 큰 문제이다

구문 [7행~10행] ~, the researchers performed *brain scans* (on 36 older and younger adults) // as they tested *their ability* (**to identify** *certain words*), // **some of which** had been filtered / **to make** them difficult to understand.

계속적 용법으로 쓰인 which는 certain words를 가리키며, some of which ~는 and some of them ~의 의미와 같다. to identify certain words는 their ability를 수식하는 형용사적 용법이고, to make ~ understand는 '목적'을 나타내는 부사적 용법의 to부정사구이다.

[13행~17행] The findings(S) could **help**(V) us(O) better **understand**(C) *presbycusis*, a type of *hearing loss* (brought on by aging) [**that** also involves *the brain's inability* (to process what the ears hear)].

help는 SVOC 구조일 때 목적격보어로 원형부정사 또는 to부정사를 취할 수 있다. presbycusis와 a type ~ by aging은 동격을 이루며, that이 이끄는 관계사절이 presbycusis를 수식하고 있다.

어휘 **have trouble v-ing** v하는 데 어려움을 겪다 **senior citizen** 노인, 고령자 **deteriorate** 저하되다, 악화하다 **magnetic resonance imaging (MRI)** 자기공명영상법 **scan** 정밀검사; 훑어보기 **filter** 거르다, 여과하다 **in general** 일반적으로 **significantly** 상당히, 크게 **challenging** 어려운, 도전적인 **condition** (복수형) 환경, 상황 **finding** (보통 복수형) 연구[조사] 결과 **presbycusis** 노인성 난청 **loss** 상실, 손실 **bring on** ~을 야기[초래]하다 **inability** 무능, 불능(↔ **ability** 능력)

34 빈칸 추론 ⑤

소재 대화를 지속하는 방법

해설 대화를 지속하려면 상대방의 질문에 대해 단답형으로 답하지 말고 상대방이 의견을 말할 수 있도록 한두 문장을 덧붙이라고 했으므로(All it takes ~ comment on.) 빈칸에는 ⑤ '질문에 절대 겨우 한 문장으로 대답하지 마라'가 들어가는 것이 적절하다.

해석 당신은 한 회의에 참석해 있고, 모든 사람들이 "고향이 어디세요?"라고 묻고 있다. 당신이 "아, 저는 아이오와 주(州)의 머스커틴 출신입니다"라고 답하거나, 또는 그 밖에 사람들이 들어 본 적도 없는 곳을 답한다면 멍한 시선 외에 무엇을 기대할 수 있겠는가? 당신이 세계인(世界人)이고 마이애미나 로스앤젤레스에 사는 세련된 대도시 거주자라 할지라도 당신의 고향 출신인 사람을 제외하고는 모두 당황한 표정이 역력함을 느끼게 될 것이다. 다른 이들은 '다음에 무슨 말을 해야 하나?'라고 생각하면서 빠르게 머리를 짜내고 있을 것이다. 내가 사람들에게 '저는 뉴욕 출신입니다'라고 말할 때, 그들이 뭐라고 말할 것인가? 주제문 "고향이 어디세요?"라는 질문에 절대 겨우 한 문장으로 대답하지 마라. 물어본 사람이 연료 탱크를 채울 수 있게 그에게 얼마간의 연료를 주어 그 사람, 즉 너무나도 확실히 무언가를 갈망하고 있는 대화 상대가 당신이 말한 것이나 질문한 것에 대해 의견을 말하거나 대답하여 그 대화가 계속 이어질 수 있게 하는 것은 대화상 예의의 문제이다. 필요한 것이라고는 출신 도시에 대해 한두 문장을 덧붙여 당신의 대화 상대가 의견을 말할 수 있게 하는 것이다.

① 질문을 절대 하지 않음으로써 더 나은 대화 상대가 되어라
② 질문을 받을 때 무례하게 답하지 마라
③ 질문과 같은 적당히 소소한 이야깃거리를 만들어내는 법을 배워라
④ 질문을 하기 전에 질문 받는 사람의 고향에 대해 추측하라

구문 [12행~16행] It's(가주어) *a matter* (of conversational politeness) to give(진주어) IO the asker DO some fuel for his tank // **so that** he(S'), so obviously a hungry communicator, can **keep**(V') the conversation(O') **going**(C') / by commenting about [or] (by) replying to *something* [(that) you have said or asked].

「so that ~」은 '~하도록'의 뜻으로 '목적'을 나타낸다. 「keep+O+C」는 'O가 계속해서 C하게 하다'란 뜻으로, 목적어와 목적격보어의 관계가 능동일 때 목적격보어로 현재분사(v-ing)를 쓴다. 「by+v-ing」는 'v함으로써'란 의미이며 전치사 about과 to는 모두 something을 목적어로 한다.

[16~18행] *All*(S) [(that) it takes] is(V) *an extra sentence or two* (about your city)(C) [**that** your conversational partner can comment on ●].

all이 '모든 것'을 의미할 때는 주로 단수 취급한다. 목적격 관계대명사 that의 선행사는 an extra sentence or two about your city이며, ●는 관계대명사절에서 비어 있는 목적어 자리를 가리킨다.

어휘 **convention** 회의; 관습 **blank** 멍한, 무표정한 **stare** 시선; 바라보다 **cosmopolitan** 세계인(여러 나라와 문화에 대해 잘 아는 사람) **urbane** 세련된, 도시풍의 **dweller** 거주자 **panic (panicked-panicked)** 공황상태에 빠지다[빠지게 하다] **but** ~을 제외하고(= **except**) **rack one's brain** 머리를 쥐어짜다 *cf.* **rack** 괴롭히다 **fuel** 연료; (에너지원이 되는) 동력 **comment about[on]** ~에 대해 견해를 밝히다 [선택지 어휘] **impolitely** 무례하게, 버릇없이 **take a guess** 추측하다 **response to A** A에 대한 대답[반응]

35 무관한 문장 ③

소재 19세기 약장수 공연과 현대의 약 사기 판매

해설 19세기 약장수 공연과 현대의 약 사기 판매 행위를 연결 지어 설명하는 내용인데, ③은 제약 회사에서 발간하는 소식지에 넣은 광고와 문구가 현대 광고의 시작이 되었다는 내용이므로 글의 흐름에서 벗어난다.

해석 순회하는 약장수 공연은 19세기 미국 오락에 있어 일반적인 볼거리였다. 그 쇼의 코미디와 음악 공연은 노동자들의 일상생활에 즐거운 기분 전환을 제공했다. 일단 관중이 모여들면, 언제나 '의사' 누구누구라고 주장하는 출중하게 생긴 신사가 만병통치약을 판매하기 위한 공연을 펼쳤다. 비록 의사들이 벌이는 맛보기 공연이 그들의 제품에 대한 선전 문구를 터무니없이 과장했지만, 장사는 대개 잘되었다. 제약 회사들이 수많은 광고와 혼합된 재미있는 인용어구를 넣은 소식지를 발간하면서 이 기간 동안 현대적인 개념의 광고가 생겨났다. 주제문 오늘날, 이러한 공연은 과거의 일이 되었지만, 약과 관련된 사기와 속임수는 (과거의 일이) 아니다. 19세기 상대측(=약장수들)처럼, 현대의 사기꾼들은 자신을 건강 전문가로 위장하고 고통, 노화, 죽음에 대한 일반적인 공포를 이용하여 '기적'의 치료제를 판다.

구문 [4행~7행] Once a crowd **had assembled**, // *a distinguished-looking gentleman*, / **who** always claimed to be "Doctor" somebody, / **began** a performance ~.
Once는 접속사로 쓰여 '일단 ~하면'이란 뜻을 나타낸다. 공연을 시작한 것(began)보다 관중이 모여든 것이 시간상 먼저이므로 과거완료 시제(had assembled)가 쓰였다. who가 이끄는 관계대명사절이 삽입되어 주어인 a distinguished-looking gentleman을 보충 설명하고 있다.

[13행~14행] Today, these shows are things of the past, // but medical fraud and trickery are not (things of the past).
not 다음에 반복되는 어구 things of the past가 생략되었다.

어휘 **feature** 볼거리; 특징, 특색 **routine** 루틴(공연의 일부로 정해져 있는 동작·농담 등); 판에 박힌 일 **diversion** 기분 전환, 오락 **assemble** 모이다; 불러 모으다 **distinguished-looking** (외모가) 출중한 **aim at** ~을 목표로 하다 **cure-all** 만병통치약 **outrageously** 터무니없이 **exaggerate** 과장하다 **quotation** 인용구 **fraud** 사기 **trickery** 속임수 **counterpart** 대응 관계에 있는 사람[것], 상대방 **disguise oneself as** 자신을 ~로 변장하다 **take advantage of** ~을 이용하다

36 글의 순서 ②

소재 성취동기 조절

해설 주어진 글은 식욕과 성취동기는 본능적인 것이어서 그 존재는 우리가 어떻게 할 수 없다는 도입 설명이고, (B)에서는 But 이후에 우리가 그것들을 통제할 수 있다고 하면서 먼저 '식욕'의 통제에 대해 설명하고 있다. (A)에서는 같은 방식으로(In the same way) '동기'도 통제할 수 있다고 한 뒤, 먼저 동기를 무디게 하는 측면을 설명하고 있다. (C)는 (A)의 마지막 내용에 대한 대조(on the other hand)의 내용으로, 동기를 자극하는 측면에 대해 설명하고 있다. 따라서 글의 순서는 ② '(B)-(A)-(C)'가 자연스럽다.

해석 식욕은 인간에게 본능적이다. 성취동기 또한 마찬가지이다. 우리는 그것들(=식욕과 성취동기)을 만들고자 노력할 필요가 없는데, 그것들이 이미 존재하고 있기 때문이다. 우리는 식욕과 동기를 가지고 태어나고 그것들은 본능적이기 때문에 (식욕과 동기는) 그것들의 존재에 대한 우리의 지식을 앞선다.

(B) 그러나 이는 우리가 그것들을 통제할 수 없다는 것을 의미하지는 않는다. 우리는 식욕을 조절하는 방법을 이미 알고 있다. 우리는 식욕을 줄이기 위해 식사 전에 물을 많이 마시거나 식욕을 높이기 위해 짭짤한 감자칩을 한 움큼 먹을 수 있다.

(A) 같은 방식으로 우리는 성공하려는 동기를 무디게 하거나 예리하게 할 수 있다. 만약 당신이 끊임없이 걱정하며 쉬운 인생을 기다린다면, 당신은 성공에 대한 동기를 줄이게 될 것이다.

(C) 반면에, 만약 당신이 좋아하고 당신에게 자극을 주는 활동을 하며 당신의 시간을 채운다면 당신의 동기는 늘어날 것이다. 주제문 목표를 향해 동기를 키워가라. 그러면 당신의 커져가는 동기는 성공을 추구하는 것을 더 쉽게 해줄 것이다.

구문 [1행~2행] Appetite is instinctive in humans. **So** is *motivation* (for achievement).
(is: V, motivation (for achievement): S)
「so+(조)동사+주어」는 '(주어)도 역시[또한] 그러하다'의 의미를 갖는 도치구문으로, so는 앞 문장의 내용(instinctive in humans)을 받는다.

어휘 **appetite** 식욕; 욕구 **instinctive** 본능적인; 직관적인 **exist** 존재하다 *cf.* **existence** 존재 **predate** ~보다 앞서 오다[존재하다] **dull** 무디게 하다, 둔하게 하다(↔ **sharpen** 예리하게 하다) **regulate** 조절하다, 규제하다 **a handful of** 한 움큼의 **crisp** ((보통 복수형)) 얇게 썬 감자칩 **care about** ~을 좋아하다, ~에 마음을 쓰다 **stimulate** 자극하다 **cultivate** 기르다, 함양하다; 경작하다 **pursuit** 추구; 추적

37 글의 순서 ①

소재 과학기술의 발전으로 인한 'literacy'의 의미 변화

해설 'literacy'의 전통적인 개념과 오늘날의 개념을 대비하여 설명하는 글이다. 주어진 글에서 단순히 글을 읽고 쓰는 능력을 의미하는 전통적인 'literacy'에 대해 소개하고, 마지막 But 이하의 문장과 함께 (A)에서 다양한 미디어에서 정보를 만들어내는 오늘날의 'literacy' 개념을 소개하고 있다. (C)에서는 다양한 미디어의 예를 나열하면서 미디어 관련 능력이 필수적임을 언급하고, (B)에서는 이러한 능력을 갖추지 못했을 경우에 대한 설명과 함께, 오늘날 필요한 'literacy'의 능력에 대해서 종합적으로 설명하며 마무리하고 있다. 따라서 글의 순서는 ① '(A)-(C)-(B)'가 적절하다.

해석 인쇄된 문자가 미디어를 지배하던 때, 'literacy'의 뜻은 단순히 읽고 쓰는 능력, 또는 그 사회의 생각을 이해하고 의사소통하기 위해 언어를 사용하는 능력일 뿐이었다. 주제문 하지만 최신 과학기술이 읽고 쓸 줄 안다는 것의 의미를 바꾸었다.

(A) 오늘날 'literacy'는 단순히 읽고 쓸 줄 아는 것 이상이다. 그것은 다양한 미디어에서 정보를 사용하고 만들어 내는 능력을 갖추는 것이다. 디지털 시대는 우리가 이해해야 하는 정보의 양, 범위, 속도를 바꾸고 있다.

(C) 그리고 오늘날 대부분의 사람들은 텔레비전, 인터넷, 다른 과학기술들에서 정보의 대부분을 얻는다. 그러므로 이런 미디어 관련 능력을 갖추는 것은 필수적이다.

(B) 이런 능력을 갖추지 못한 사람들은 뒤처질 것이다. 오늘날 읽고 쓸 줄 알기 위해서는 인쇄물과 인쇄물이 아닌 것을 포함한 모든 형태의 미디어를 통해, 그리고 그 미디어를 가지고 정보를 해독하고 이해하며 창조할 수 있어야 한다.

구문 [2행~4행] ~, the definition of literacy was simply *the ability* (to read and write), or *the ability* (to use language / to understand and communicate ideas in a society).
(the definition of literacy: S, was: V, simply ~: C)
SVC의 구조로, 보어가 or로 병렬연결된 두 개의 명사구로 이루어져 있다. the ability는 to부정사구의 수식을 받으며, to understand and communicate ~는 '목적'을 나타내는 부사적 용법이다.

어휘 **dominate** 지배하다; 우세하다 **definition** 정의 **literacy** 읽고 쓸 줄 아는 것 *cf.* **literate** 읽고 쓸 줄 아는 **emerging** 최신의, 최근 생겨난 **transform** 바꾸다 **range** 범위 **be[get] left behind** 뒤처지다 **decode** (암호 등을) 해독하다

38 문장 넣기 ④

소재 아나사지인들이 보금자리를 떠난 이유

해설 아나사지인들이 자신들이 건설한 도시를 떠나 종적을 감춘 이유에 관한 여러 가지 설을 나열하고 있는 글이다. 주어진 문장은 첫 번째 설에 관한 내용이므로 여러 가지 설이 있다는 설명 바로 다음인 ④에 오는 것이 적절하다. 뒤에 또 다른 가설이 제시되면서 글이 자연스럽게 연결되는 것을 확인할 수 있다.

해석 아나사지인들은 약 1,500년 전 메사 베르데 지역에 번성한 문화를 이룩했던 지적인 종족이었다. 그러나 1,200년대 후반에 아나사지인들은 등에 짊어질 수 있는 것만을 가지고 갑자기 보금자리를 떠나 수수께끼처럼 이전해버렸다. 주제문 아나사지인들이 그 지역

을 떠나야 하는 타당한 이유가 분명히 있었겠지만, 아무도 정말 그들이 떠난 이유를 알지 못한다. 많은 설이 있다. 한 가지 이유는 가뭄으로 인해 그들이 다른 지역으로 이동할 수밖에 없었다는 것인데, 이것이 유일한 이유이었을 리는 없다. 그들은 또한 이웃 부족과의 싸움에서 졌을지도 모르고, 또는 그곳에 끔찍한 질병이 발병했을 수도 있다. 아마도, 아나사지인들로 하여금 그들이 협곡 절벽에 지은 정교한 석조 도시를 떠나게 한 것은 바로 여러 가지 복합적 요인이었을 것이다.

구문 [14행~16행] Most likely, **it was** *a combination of factors* **that caused** the Anasazi **to leave** *the elaborate stone cities* [that they built in the canyon walls].
V′ O′ C′

「it is[was] ~ that ...」 강조구문으로 주어 a combination of factors를 강조하고 있다. 동사는 caused로 SVOC 구조를 이끌며 목적격보어로 to부정사가 쓰였다.

어휘 **drought** 가뭄 **force A to-v** A가 v하도록 하다 **sophisticated** 지적인; 세련된, 교양 있는; 정교한 **flourish** 번성[번영]하다 **mysteriously** 수수께끼처럼, 신비하게 **tribe** 부족, 종족 **outbreak** (질병 · 전쟁 등의) 발생, 발발 **combination** 조합, 결합 **elaborate** 정교한, 정성 들여 만든 **canyon** 협곡, 계곡

39 문장 넣기 ⑤

소재 바람직한 코치의 태도

해설 주어진 문장은 역접의 접속사 However로 시작하여 번복이 불가피하다면 운동선수들에게 그 이유를 설명해주는 것이 좋다는 내용이므로, 돌변을 피해야 한다는 내용과 체조 코치가 방침을 바꿀 때 선수들에게 충분히 설명해주는 예시 사이인 ⑤에 들어가는 것이 가장 적절하다.

해석 돌변은 예를 들어 어떤 코치가 하나의 활동에서 두 번째 활동으로 옮겨 갔다가 마치 마음이 변했다는 듯이 다시 첫 번째 활동으로 전환할 때 일어난다. 예를 들어, 체조 코치가 자기 선수들에게 화요일은 평균대와 철봉을 연습하는 날이 될 거라고 말하지만, 그의 운동선수들이 평균대와 철봉을 연습할 준비를 하고 화요일에 도착하자, 그는 그들에게 마루운동과 도마 연습을 할 거라고 말한다. 그러다가 연습 도중에 그는 그들에게 평균대와 철봉이 있는 곳으로 가라고 지시한다. 이 변동은 연습 활동의 흐름을 엉망으로 만들뿐만 아니라 또한 코치가 무엇을 해야 할지 확신하지 못하고 있다는 생각을 운동선수들에게 전달한다. 주제문 돌변을 피하는 것이 중요하다. 하지만 그러한 번복을 하는 것이 꼭 필요하게 되는 경우에는, 왜 그 전환이 일어나는지를 자신의 운동선수들에게 설명해 주는 것이 현명하다. 예를 들어, 체조 코치가 잠시 회의를 위해 선수들을 모아 놓고 "오늘 평균대와 철봉 연습을 할 거라고 어제 내가 여러분에게 말했다는 것을 알고 있지만, 내일 우리가 (마루운동용) 스프링 플로어를 사용할 수 없을 것이기 때문에 오늘 마루운동의 정해진 과정을 연습하겠다."라고 말할 수 있다.

구문 [1행~3행] However, if it becomes necessary to make such a reversal, // it is **advisable** that the coach **explain** to his athletes / why the switch is occurring.
(it: 가주어, to make such a reversal: 진주어 / it: 가주어, that ~ occurring: 진주어)

조건절과 주절에 모두 「가주어-진주어」 구문이 쓰였으며, 진주어 자리에는 각각 to부정사구와 that절이 쓰였다. 주관적 판단이나 감정을 나타내는 말(advisable) 뒤에 오는 that절에는 「(should) 동사원형」이 오며, 여기서는 should가 생략되어 동사원형 explain이 쓰였다. why ~ occurring은 explain의 목적어 역할을 하는 의문사절이다.

어휘 **reversal** 뒤바꿈; 전환, 반전 **advisable** 현명한; 권할 만한 **athlete** 운동선수 **transition** 이동, 변화 **gymnastics** 체조 **beam** 평균대 **midway** 도중에 **instruct** 지시하다; 가르치다 **ruin** 엉망으로 만들다 **convey** 전달하다 **gather** 모으다 **routine** 정해진 과정[순서]; 틀에 박힌 일

40 요약문 완성 ②

소재 경험과 판단의 정확성 실험

해설 요약문을 보면, 경험이 많은 영역에서는 '무엇'이 분석을 이길 수 있지만, 익숙하지 않은 영역에서는 '어떠한' 판단이 신중한 점검에 의해서만 내려질 수 있는지 찾아야 한다. 경험과 판단의 정확성에 관한 실험에서, 디자이너 핸드백을 많이 소유해 본 사람들은 핸드백의 진품 여부를 판단하는 데 있어서 직감에 의존해야 하는 상황에서 더 정확한 판단을 했고, 반대로 그렇지 않은 사람들은 더 자세히 살펴보는 과정이 필요했다. 즉, (A)에는 'intuition(직관)', (B)에는 'sound(올바른, 타당한)'가 가장 적절하다.

해석 경험과 판단의 정확성을 실험하고자 설계되었던 한 실험에서, Erik Dane은 사람들에게 열 개의 디자이너 핸드백을 보고 그것들이 진짜인지 가짜인지를 판단하도록 했다. 참가자 절반에게는 추측하는 데 겨우 5초의 시간만 주어졌는데, 그것이 그들로 하여금 자신들의 직감에 의존하도록 만들었다. 나머지 절반에게는 30초가 주어졌는데, 그것이 그들로 하여금 특징들을 조사하고 분석하도록 했다. Dane의 팀은 또한 그들(=실험 참가자들)의 핸드백과 관련된 경험을 측정했다. 일부는 많은 경험을 가졌고, Coach나 Louis Vuitton에서 만든 핸드백을 세 개 이상 가지고 있던 반면, 다른 사람들은 디자이너 가방을 만져본 적이 없었다. 주제문 경험이 풍부한 핸드백 소지자들은 그들에게 30초의 시간이 있었을 때보다 겨우 5초만 있을 때 22퍼센트 더 정확했다. 하지만 핸드백에 대해 전혀 아는 것이 없던 사람들에게는 자신들의 무의식적인 판단이 도움이 되지 않았다. 그들은 한 걸음 물러나서 그 핸드백들을 평가해야 할 필요가 있었다.

⬇

우리가 경험이 많은 영역에서는 (A) 직관이 분석을 이길 수 있지만, 익숙하지 않은 영역에서는 (B) 올바른 판단은 세심한 검토에 의해서만 이루어질 수 있다.

구문 [8행~12행] Dane's team also measured their handbag experience — some had a lot, / **owning** more than *three handbags* (made by Coach or Louis Vuitton), // whereas others had never touched a designer bag.

콤마(,) 이하의 owning ~ Louis Vuitton은 앞의 some had a lot을 보충 설명해준다. ( ) 부분은 과거분사구로 앞의 three handbags를 수식한다.

어휘 **judgmental** 판단(상)의; 재판(상)의 *cf.* **judge** 판단하다; 재판하다 *cf.* **judgement** 판단(력); 재판, 심판 **accuracy** 정확(성) *cf.* **accurate** 정확한; 정밀한 **fake** 가짜의, 거짓된 **instinct** 직감; 본능 **inspect** 조사하다 **analyze** 분석하다 *cf.* **analysis** 분석 **feature** 특징; 특징으로 삼다 **measure** 측정하다; 조치 **own** 소유하다; 자기 자신의 **automatic** 무의식적인, 반사적인; 자동의 **verdict** 판단; 평결 **assess** 평가하다; 재다, 가늠하다 [선택지 어휘] **flexible** 융통성 있는; 유연한 **hasty** 성급한, 서두르는 **arbitrary** 자의적인; 멋대로의

41~42 장문 41 ③ 42 ④

소재 완전히 보편적이지는 않은 꽃의 선호와 그 이유

해설 41. 세계 대부분의 문화권에서 꽃에 대한 애호가 있지만 아프리카에서는 꽃에 대한 애호가 부재하는 것처럼 보이는데, 이것에 대한 이유를 분석한 글이므로 제목으로 가장 적절한 것은 ③ '꽃에 대한 선호는 보편적인가?'이다.

① 인간들은 왜 꽃을 사랑하는가?
② 꽃의 다양성은 어떻게 생겨났나?
④ 미에 대한 취향의 다양성과 보편성
⑤ 세계 문화에서 꽃의 상징적인 의미

42. (d)가 있는 문장에서 세계에서 재배되는 꽃 중 오직 극소수만이 아프리카에서 나왔다고 했기 때문에 아프리카 꽃의 종의 범위는 '아시아나 북미의 제한된 정도'가 아니라 '광범위한 정도'에 미치지 못한다고 서술해야 문장 내의 모순이 없다. 따라서 restricted를 extensive 등으로 바꿔 써야 한다.

해석 우리는 그저 꽃을 사랑하여 그것을 아름답다고 인식하고, 이것이 꽃을 소중하게 만든다. 주제문 그러나 대부분의 세계 문화권(동양과 서양, 과거와 현재)에서의 꽃의 역할을 연구한 잉글랜드의 인류학자 Jack Goody에 따르면, 꽃에 대한 사랑은 거의 보편적이지만 완전히 (a) 보편적인 것은 아니라고 한다. '완전히는 아님'은 아프리카를 지칭하는데, 그곳에서 꽃은 종교 의식이나 일상적인 사회적 예식에서 거의 아무런 역할도 맡지 않는다. 아프리카인들은 재배되는 꽃을 좀처럼 기르지 않으며, 아프리카의 예술이나 종교에서 꽃의 형상은 좀처럼 등장하지 않는다. Goody는 아프리카에서의 꽃의 문화의 (b) 부재에 대해 두 가지 가능한 설명을 제시한다. 한 가지 설명은 사람들이 먹을 것을 충분히

얻기 전까지는 꽃에 주의를 기울일 여유가 없다는 것이다. 꽃이 잘 발달한 문화는 아프리카 대부분이 역사적으로 부양할 수 없었던 (c) 사치이다. 다른 설명은 아프리카의 생태이다. 세계에서 재배되는 꽃 중 상대적으로 극소수가 아프리카에서 나왔고, 이 대륙의 꽃 종의 범위는 예컨대 아시아 혹은 심지어 북미의 (d) 제한된(→ 광범위한) 정도에 도저히 미치지 못한다. 그러나 한 가지 질문이 우리 모두의 마음속에 남아있다. 이것은 꽃의 아름다움이 제 눈의 안경이라는 뜻인가? 만약 그렇다면, 왜 그토록 많은 다른 민족들이 그렇게 많은 다른 시대와 장소에서 그 생각을 해냈을까? Goody가 지적하는 대로, 아프리카인들은 다른 사람들이 꽃의 문화를 도입한 곳이면 어디에서든 그것을 재빨리 채택했다. 아마 꽃에 대한 사랑은 모든 사람들이 (e) 공유하는 애호겠지만, 환경이 무르익고서야, 주변에 많은 꽃이 있고 멈춰서 그것의 향을 맡을 충분한 여가가 생기고서야 비로소 스스로 피어날 수 있는 것(애호)일 것이다.

구문 [28행~32행] Maybe the love of flowers is *a predilection* [(which[that] all people share], but it's *one* [that can**not** itself flower **until** conditions are ripe—**until** there are lots of flowers around and enough leisure to stop and smell them].
첫 번째 [ ]는 앞에 목적격 관계대명사 which[that]가 생략되어 a predilection을 수식한다. 두 번째 [ ]는 one을 수식하며, it's one에서 it은 the love of flowers를, one은 a predilection을 각각 지칭한다. 「not A until B」는 'B하고서야 비로소 A하다'의 뜻이다.

어휘 **anthropologist** 인류학자 **not quite** 완전히 ~하지는 않은 **universal** 보편적인 **refer to** 지칭하다, 언급하다 **observance** 의식; 준수 **ritual** 예식, 의식 **domesticate** 재배하다; 길들이다 **imagery** 형상, 심상 **ecology** 생태 **nowhere near** 도저히 미치지 못하는 **restrict** 제한하다 **Beauty is in the eye of the beholder.** 제 눈에 안경 (아름다움은 보는 사람의 눈 속에 있는 것이다.)
[선택지 어휘] **diversity** 다양성 **universality** 보편성

43~45 장문

43 ③ 44 ② 45 ④

소재 옷 쇼핑 성향이 다른 두 딸

해설 43. (A)는 필자 부부가 옷 구입에 관해 큰딸아이와 의견이 달라 늘 다퉜다는 내용이다. 따라서 그 뒤에는 부부가 큰딸에게 옷 구입을 위한 용돈을 한꺼번에 주는 방법을 써서 성공했다는 (C)가 이어지는 것이 적절하다. 다음으로 작은딸에게도 같은 방법을 썼지만 두 딸의 성향이 달랐다는 내용의 (D)가 나오고, 작은딸의 다른 성향을 구체적으로 설명하는 (B)가 마지막에 오는 것이 자연스럽다. 따라서 정답은 ③ '(C)-(D)-(B)'이다.

44. (b)는 작은딸을 가리키고, 나머지는 모두 큰딸을 가리킨다.

45. (C)에서 필자 부부는 큰딸에게 용돈을 한 번에 주고 그것을 어떻게 쓸지 스스로 결정하도록 했으므로 ④가 글의 내용과 일치하지 않는다.

해석 (A) 내게는 두 딸이 있다. 큰딸이 사춘기에 들어섰을 때, ① 나와 내 아내는 통제권을 잡으려는 부모 대 사춘기 자녀 간의 흔한 싸움을 경험했다. 종종, 우리 딸과의 싸움은 옷을 구입하는 것에 관한 것이었다. ② 그 아이는 유행에 민감하며 고급 취향을 가지고 있어서, (a) 그녀(=큰딸)가 '필요로 하는 것'에 관한 생각이 우리의 생각과는 달랐다.
(C) 그러자 우리는 한 가지 아이디어를 냈다. 우리는 딸과 옷을 구입할 수 있는 용돈을 협상해서 합리적인 가격의 옷 여러 벌에 대한 돈을 할당해 주었다. 우리는 딸에게 일정 금액의 돈을 한 번에 주었으며, 그러면 ④ (c) 그녀(=큰딸)는 그것을 어떻게 쓸지를 결정할 수 있었다. 그것은 신통하게 효과가 있었다. 옷에 대한 말싸움은 그쳤고, 우리는 딸의 사춘기의 나머지 기간을 더 중요한 것들에 관해 (d) 그녀(=큰딸)와 싸우며 보낼 수 있었다.
(D) 나와 내 아내는 우리의 성공에 아주 만족스러워서 작은딸에게도 똑같이 하기로 결심했다. 하지만 두 딸은 매우 다르다. ⑤ 큰딸은 만족할 줄 아는 사람(satisfier)인 반면, 작은딸은 적어도 옷에 관해서는 최대한의 것을 추구하는 사람(maximizer)이다. 이것이 의미하는 바는 큰딸은 옷을 사라고 준 용돈을 받아서 (e) 자신(=큰딸)이 좋아하는 것을 샀고, 자신이 지나쳤던 대안들(=다른 옷들)에 대해 결코 마음을 쓰지 않았다는 것이다.
(B) 이것은 작은딸에게는 그리 쉽지 않은 일이었다. ③ 매번 쇼핑을 할 때마다 이 옷 혹은 저 옷을 사는 것이 정말로 가장 최선의 일인지에 대한 고민이 생겼다. 자신이 구입한 것을 두 달 후, 유행이 바뀌었을 때 후회하지 않을까? 이러한 일은 작은 딸에게는 너무 벅찬 일이었던 것이다. (b) 그녀(=작은딸)에게 이 모든 자유를 주는 것은 진정한 호의가 아니었다. '옷을 사는 자유'는 그녀에게 많은 걱정을 주고 기쁨은 거의 주지 못했다.

구문 [(D) 1행~2행] My wife and I were **so** pleased with our success **that** we decided to do the same with ~.
「so ~ that ...」 구문으로 '매우 ~해서 …하다'란 뜻이다.
[(D) 5행~8행] What this meant (S) was (V) that (C) $^{S'}$the older one $^{V'1}$took her clothing allowance, $^{V'2}$bought *things* [(that[which]) she liked], and never $^{V'3}$worried about *alternatives* [that she was passing up].
what이 이끄는 명사절이 주어이고, that절이 보어인 SVC의 구조이다. that절 내에는 3개의 동사가 and로 연결되어 있다.

어휘 **(A) adolescence** 사춘기, 청소년기 *cf.* **adolescent** 사춘기의; 청소년(의) **struggle** 싸움; (오랜 기간의) 노력 **battle** 싸움, 전투 **style-conscious** 유행에 민감한 *cf.* **conscious** 의식하는 **(B) accompany** 수반하다, 동시에 일어나다; 동행하다 **distress** 고민, 걱정 **genuine** 진정한; 진짜의 **favor** 호의, 친절; 호의를 보이다; 찬성하다 **liberation** 자유 **(C) negotiate** 협상하다 **allowance** 용돈 **allocate** 할당하다, 배분하다 **reasonably** 합당하게, 적당하게 **work like a charm** 신통하게 잘 듣다 **argument** 말싸움, 논쟁 **(D) with regard to A** A에 관한 **alternative** 대안, 선택 가능한 것 **pass up** (기회 · 제안 등을) 지나치다

실전 모의고사 10

본문 p.139

18 ⑤	19 ①	20 ②	21 ②	22 ③	23 ③	24 ③	25 ④	26 ④	27 ④
28 ③	29 ③	30 ④	31 ③	32 ⑤	33 ②	34 ①	35 ④	36 ③	37 ④
38 ③	39 ③	40 ②	41 ⑤	42 ②	43 ①	44 ⑤	45 ③		

18 글의 목적 ⑤

소재 물품 수령에 관한 안내

해설 두 번째 문장에서 이 편지가 지불 확인과 배송 준비를 알리는 것을 목적으로 한다고 하였다. 이어지는 내용이 배송된 물품에 파손의 흔적이 있을 경우의 대처법, 물품 수령 시 요구되는 행동, 배송 사고 발생 시 회사의 방침 등을 설명하고 있는데, 이를 종합하면 물품 수령 시의 주의사항을 안내하는 것이 주목적이라고 할 수 있다. 따라서 정답은 ⑤이다.

해석 소중한 고객님께,
주문해주셔서 감사드립니다. 주제문 이 편지는 지불이 되었음을 확인해 드리고 배송 준비에 대해 알려 드리기 위한 것입니다. 저희는 귀하의 물품을 완벽한 상태로 배송하기 위해 각별히 주의하고 있습니다. 그러므로 포장에 충격이나 누손의 흔적이 있을 경우 배송 수령을 거부하시기를 제안드립니다. 배송을 수령하시는 즉시, 인수증에 서명하시기 전에 포장을 열어 물품을 검사해 주시기 바랍니다. 이것이 가능하지 않을 경우, 물품 상태에 관한 귀하의 우려를 양식에 표시해 주시기 바랍니다. 저희 회사는 모든 운송 위험에 대해 책임이 있으며, 불만 내용을 설명한 편지와 함께 상품이 반환되면 고객님의 지불 금액을 환불해 드릴 것입니다.
감사합니다.
고객 서비스 부서

구문 [5행~8행] Therefore, **should** the packaging show signs of impact or leakage, // we **suggest** // (that) you (should) **refuse** to accept the delivery.
「should+주어+동사」는 희박한 가능성(혹시라도 ~한다면)을 나타내는 가정법이며, if를 생략하고 조동사인 should를 문장 앞으로 도치시킨 형태이다. suggest가 '제안하다'의 의미일 때 당위성을 나타내는 that절의 동사는 「(should) 동사원형」이 된다.

어휘 **confirm** 확인하다 **delivery** 배달 **arrangement** 준비; 배열 **utmost** 최대의, 최고의 **merchandise** 상품, 제품 **impact** 충격; 영향 **leakage** 누손, 누출 **receipt** 인수, 수령; 영수증 **be invited to-v** v하도록 (정중히) 요청되다 **indicate** 표시하다, 나타내다 **concern** 우려, 걱정; 관심사 **state** 상태; 지위; 국가 **refund** 환불하다 **as long as** ~하는 한 **explanatory** 설명적인; 해석하는 **complaint** 불만, 불평

19 심경 변화 ①

소재 새로 온 직원에게 느낀 질투심

해설 Sarah는 동료들을 돕는 것에서 기쁨을 얻고 우쭐한(flattered) 느낌도 있었으므로 자부심(proud)을 느꼈을 것이다. 그러나 같은 부서에 새로운 직원이 오고 동료들이 모두 그녀에게 도움을 요청하는 것을 보고 부당하다고 여기며 질투(jealous)를 느꼈으므로 정답은 ①이다.

해석 Sarah는 몇 년 동안 한 무역회사의 기술 부서에서 일해 왔고, 그녀는 동료들이 그녀에게 컴퓨터 관련 질문을 하는 것에 익숙했다. 그녀는 항상 도움이 되기 위해 최선을 다했으며 심지어 방해받는 것을 즐기기까지 했다. 주제문 그녀는 그들로부터 그렇게 많은 친절한 칭찬을 듣고 우쭐한 느낌이었다. 그리고 나서 Kelly가 그녀의 부서로 합류했다. Sarah는 Kelly와 함께 일하는 게 즐거웠고 그녀가 그들의 회사 직원들에게 훌륭한 증원 직원이라고 생각했다. 오래지 않아 Sarah는 사람들이 컴퓨터 문제로 Kelly에게 모이기 시작했다는 것을 알아차렸다. 처음에 Sarah는 방해받는 일에서 벗어나게 되어 안심했다. 하지만 그때 그런 생각이 그녀에게 들었다. 더 이상 아무도 그녀를 필요로 하지 않는다고. Sarah는 자신이 그저 또 다른 회사 직원이라는 느낌이 들었다. 많은 생각이 그녀의 머릿속을 질주했다. "왜 그녀가 갑자기 전문가인 거지? 그녀는 그저 신참자일 뿐인데. 내가 그들의 질문에 더 잘 답할 수 있어! 주제문 Kelly가 나보다 더 많은 관심을 받는 건 공정하지 않아."
② 불안한 → 고마운 ③ 무관심한 → 기쁜
④ 기쁜 → 수치스러운 ⑤ 기대하는 → 실망한

구문 [5행~6행] She **felt** *herself* **flattered** to hear so many nice compliments from them.
지각동사 feel이 「feel+O+C(p.p.) (O가 ~된 것을 느끼다)」 형태로 사용되었다. herself와 같은 재귀대명사는 주어와 지칭하는 바가 같은 목적어에 쓰는 표현이다.

[15행~16행] It's not fair that Kelly gets more attention than I **do**.
It은 가주어이고 that 이하가 진주어이다. do는 대동사로 get attention을 지칭한다.

어휘 **department** 부서 **be used to v-ing** v하는 것에 익숙하다 **colleague** 동료 **interruption** 방해, 중단 **flatter (oneself)** 우쭐해지다 **compliment** 칭찬 **company** 함께 있음 **addition** 추가된 사람[물건] **before long** 오래지 않아 **flock** 모이다 **be rid of** ~에서 벗어나다 **hit** (생각이) 떠오르다 **race** 질주하다 **expert** 전문가 **newcomer** 신참자 **fair** 공정한

20 필자 주장 ②

소재 라이브 공연 활성화의 필요성

해설 인기 있는 밴드 외에는 음원으로 수익을 창출하는 것이 어려우므로 음악인들이 수익을 낼 수 있도록 라이브 공연 문화를 활성화해야 한다는 내용의 글이다. 따라서 필자의 주장으로 가장 적절한 것은 ②이다.

해석 최근 한 유명 밴드가 팬들이 그 밴드의 최신 앨범을 다운로드하는 데 원하는 만큼 돈을 낼 수 있다고 발표했다. 다른 음악가들은 벌써 이들의 전례를 따라가고 있는데, 이것은 이를 바라보는 몇몇 사람들로 하여금 그것이 음악 산업에서의 새로운 수익 모델의 시초라고 주장하게 했다. 이것은 탄탄한 밴드들에게는 좋은 일일지도 모르는데, 왜냐하면 이들은 기꺼이 돈을 낼 수백만 명의 팬들을 확보하고 있기 때문이다. 그러나 그 밖에 모든 사람들은 음악을 듣는 데 돈을 지불할 사람들을 확보하는 것이 점점 더 어려워지고 있다. 음악인들이 돈을 벌 확실하고 유일한 방법은 라이브 공연을 통해서이다. 주제문 우리는 라이브 음악 현장을 다시 활성화하고 그것을 일상적인 문화 중 하나로 만드는 데 모든 노력을 쏟아야 한다. 관심을 높이는 한 가지 방법은 우리가 가서 음악가들이 연주하는 것을 볼 수 있는 공연 장소와 축제의 수와 질을 높이는 것이다.

구문 [1행~3행] A famous band recently announced // that fans can pay **whatever** they want / **to download** the band's latest album.
복합관계사 whatever가 pay의 목적어가 되는 명사절을 이끄는 구조이다. whatever는 '~하는 것은 무엇이라도'란 뜻으로 anything that으로 바꿔 쓸 수 있다. 뒤에 나오는 to부정사구는 '~하기 위해서'란 뜻의 부사적 용법으로 쓰였다.

[8행~9행] However, everyone else is finding it(가목적어) **harder and harder** to get listeners to pay for music.(진목적어)
「find it ~ to-v」의 구조로 진목적어인 to부정사구를 가목적어 it이 대신하고 있다. 「비교급 and 비교급」은 '점점 더 ~한'이란 뜻이다.

[12행~15행] One way (to enhance awareness) / is by increasing *the number and quality* (of *venues and festivals* [**where** we can go and see artists play]).
S V C

One way to enhance awareness가 주어이며, by 이하 전명구가 be동사의 보어 역할을 하고 있다. where가 이끄는 관계부사절이 선행사인 venues and festivals를 수식하고 있다.

어휘 **announce** 발표하다 **latest** 최신의 **lead** 전례; 모범; 선도, 솔선 **prompt A to-v** A가 v하도록 자극하다 **observer** 지켜보는 사람, 관찰자 **claim** 주장하다; 요구[청구]하다 **dawn** 시초, 시작; 새벽 **business model** 수익 모델 **well-established** 기초가 탄탄한, 안정된 **willing to-v** 기꺼이 v하는 **performance** 공연 **make an effort to-v** v하려고 노력하다 **re-energize** 다시 활성화하다 **scene** 현장; 장면 **enhance** 높이다, 강화하다 **awareness** (중요성에 대한) 관심, 의식 **venue** (회담 등의) 장소

21 글의 요지 ②

소재 시의 음악성을 해치는 번역

해설 시는 '말로 만들어진 음악'인데 다른 나라 언어로 번역할 경우 설령 의미는 보존된다고 해도 소리와 운율의 음악적 요소는 번역 과정에서 상실되므로 시를 다른 언어로 번역한다는 것은 거의 불가능하다는 내용의 글이다. 따라서 글의 요지로 가장 적절한 것은 ②이다.

해석 시는 의미와 소리 전체의 말의 예술이다. 규칙적인 간격으로 나오는 음절 패턴은 시의 형태와 운율을 규정하지만, 시에서 음악성을 만들어내는 핵심 요소는 바로 소리이다. 사실, 자유시로 구성될 때조차도 시는 말로 만들어진 음악이다. 특이한 조합이 언어의 선율적인 면을 끌어낸다. 의미와 소리 간의 관계를 엮어내는 절묘한 기술이 시적 기교의 정수이다. 주제문 그래서 시를 원문 외의 언어로 번역하는 것은 거의 불가능하다. 많은 경우 의미가 보존된다는 게 사실이라 해도, 소리와 원래의 운율은 돌이킬 수 없게 상실된다. 시의 운율적이고 음악적인 측면을 완전히 이해하기 위해, 운문은 원어로, 크게 소리 내어, 번역 없이 향유되어야 한다.

구문 [4행~5행] ~ but **it is** *sound* **that** is *the key factor* (for developing musicality in a poem).

「it is ~ that ...」 강조구문은 it is와 that 사이의 표현을 강조하며 '…한 것은 바로 ~이다'의 뜻이다. 여기서는 주어인 sound를 강조하였다.

[11행~13행] **If** it is true that often the sense is preserved, // sound and original rhythm are irretrievably lost.
가주어 진주어

여기서 If는 '~일지라도'의 뜻으로 쓰였다.

어휘 **poetry** (집합적) 시(詩) *cf.* **poem** (한 편의) 시 *cf.* **poetic** 시의 **entirety** 전체, 온전함 **syllable** 음절 **regular** 규칙적인; 정기적인 **interval** 간격 **rhythm** 운율; 리듬 **factor** 요소, 요인 **musicality** 음악성 **be composed of** ~로 구성되다 **free verse** 자유시 *cf.* **verse** 운문 **unusual** 특이한, 흔치 않은 **combination** 조합 **bring out** 끌어내다 **melodic** 선율의 **aspect** 측면 **subtle** 절묘한; 미묘한 **weave** 짜다, 엮다 **essence** 본질, 정수 **craft** 기교; 공예; 기술 **translate A into B** A를 B로 번역하다 *cf.* **translation** 번역 **other than** ~ 외에 **original** 원문, 원작; 본래의; 독창적인 **sense** 의미; 감각 **preserve** 보존하다 **irretrievably** 돌이킬 수 없게 **grasp** 이해하다, 파악하다

22 글의 주제 ③

소재 천재들이 창조성을 발휘하는 방식

해설 천재들이 자신들의 창조성을 어떻게 드러내게 되는지 설명하는 글이다. 그들은 영감을 받으면 장시간 집중하는 사이사이에 반드시 정체기를 가지며, 이 정체기는 생각을 발효시키는 단계로 창조적 과정에 꼭 필요하다고 설명하고 있다. 따라서 정답은 ③ '천재들이 창조성을 드러내는 방법'이다.

해석 주제문 천재의 한 가지 특징은 고도의 집중력이며, 그것은 종종 순환하는 방식으로 표현된다. 다시 말해, 천재의 성격은 때로 양극단을 통합시키는 것처럼 보인다. 즉, 영감을 받으면 천재는 해결책이 자신의 머릿속에서 아직 생생한 동안에 그것을 실현하기 위해 하루에 스무 시간을 일할지도 모른다. 이러한 강도 높은 활동 기간들은 명백한 정체기인 것처럼 보이지만 실제로는 발효의 시간들(= 아이디어가 숙성되는 시간들) 사이사이에 흩어져 있는 경향이 있는데, 이것은 창조적인 과정에 필요한 부분이다. 천재들은 아이디어들을 구체화할 여지를 만들 필요성을 이해하는데, 그 이유는 창조성이 외적 상황이 아닌 적절한 내적 상황에서 생기기 때문이다. 그러한 단계는 완전히 (주의가) 산만한 상태에 의해 자주 이루어지는데, 우리는 모두 고속도로에서 교통 체증 속에 앉아 있는 동안 복잡한 문제들에 대한 해답을 찾아낸 사람들에 관한 이야기들을 알고 있다.

① 창의적인 아이디어에 지속적으로 집중하는 것의 이점
② 환경이 개인의 독창성에 미치는 영향
④ 천재들에게 짜임새 있는 휴식 기간의 중요성
⑤ 천재들이 집중력을 높이는 가장 좋은 방법

구문 [6행~9행] ~ these periods of intense activity tend to be scattered with intervals of *apparent stasis* [**that** are actually times of *fermentation*], // **which** is a necessary part of the creative process.

주격 관계대명사 that이 이끄는 절은 선행사 apparent stasis를 수식하며, 관계대명사 which는 계속적 용법으로 쓰여 선행사 fermentation을 부연 설명한다.

[9행~12행] Geniuses understand *the need* (to make *space for ideas* **to crystallize**), // **for** creativity occurs under appropriate inner, not outer, circumstances.
S V O

for ideas는 to crystallize의 의미상 주어이다. creativity 앞에 쓰인 for는 '이유'를 나타내는 등위접속사로, 앞서 말한 내용에 대해 부가적인 이유를 설명한다. '그 이유는 ~이기 때문에'로 해석한다.

어휘 **intensity** 집중, 전념; 강도 *cf.* **intense** 강렬한, 극심한 **in a ~ fashion** ~하는 방식으로 **cyclic** 순환하는, 주기적인 **incorporate** 통합시키다 **polar** (자석의) 양극의; 북극[남극]의 **extreme** 극단(적인 상태); 극도의 **scatter** 흐트러뜨리다 **interval** (두 사건 사이의) 간격; (연극 등의) 중간 휴식 시간 **apparent** 명백한, 분명한 **fermentation** 발효 (작용) **crystallize** (사상 · 계획 따위를) 구체화하다; 결정체를 이루다 **circumstance** (주로 복수형) 상황, 환경 **distraction** 주의산만; 기분 전환, 오락 (활동) **freeway** 고속도로 [선택지 어휘] **consistent** 지속적인, 끊임없는 **ingenuity** 독창성; 기발한 재주 **concentration** 집중

23 글의 제목 ③

소재 초기 이슬람 건축 양식의 특징

해설 초기 이슬람의 건축 양식이 복잡한 문양의 장식을 통해 신성함을 추구했다는 내용의 글이다. 따라서 글의 제목으로 가장 적절한 것은 ③ '신성함: 초기 이슬람 예술의 디자인의 동인(動因)'이 가장 적절하다.

오답 분석 ⑤ 정교한 문양을 통해 종교적 신성함을 추구했다는 것이 글의 요지이므로, 이슬람 장식이 정교하다는 일부 내용만 다룬 표현은 글의 제목으로 적절하지 않다.

해석 초기 이슬람 건축가들과 예술가들은 그들 종교의 주장에 대한 물질적인 뒷받침과 증거를 제공하는 웅장한 물리적 배경을 만들어내기 위해 노력했다. 주제문 신(神)이 모든 앎의 원천이라고 주장하는 이슬람교는 신성한 요소로서의 수학적 법칙을 특히 강조했다. 우아하고 복잡한 기하학적 구성은 신의 무한한 지혜를 암시하는 것으로 생각되었고, 이슬람교의 장인들은 사원과 집의 벽을 이런 무늬의 반복되는 연속으로 뒤덮었다. 깔개나 유리잔의 정말 기분 좋게 복잡한 이런 장식이 홀의 내부를 완전히 뒤덮으면 그것은 거의 환각 경험을 만들어낸다. 재미없고 실용적인 일상의 물건들만 보는 데 익숙한 눈이라도, 그런 홀 안에서라면 일상과 전혀 관련이 없는 세계를 상상할 수 있었을 것이다. 그러한 정교하면서도 놀랍도록 복잡한 장식은 속세의 제약이 없는 정신, 인간의 결점으로 변질되지 않은 더 고귀한 존재, 그래서 완전히 복종할 가치가 있는 신의 작품처럼 보였다.

① 이슬람 예술에서의 세속성과 신성
② 모스크 건축물이 주는 심리적 효과
④ 이슬람 역사에서의 순수 수학과 기하학
⑤ 이슬람 실내 디자인의 정교한 장식

구문 [12행~15행] *Eyes* (accustomed to looking at **nothing but** the dull and practical objects of daily life) could, inside such a hall, imagine a world ~.

Eyes는 분사구 accustomed ~ life의 수식을 받으며, nothing but은 '오직, 단지'의 뜻이다.

[16행~20행] Such delicate yet extraordinarily complex decoration seemed like *the product* (**of** *a mind* (without earthly limitations)), (**of** *a higher being* (uncorrupted by human failings)), and therefore (**of** *a God* [(who is) worth surrendering to completely]).

the product를 뒤에서 수식하는 of가 이끄는 전명구 세 개가 and therefore로 연결되어 병렬구조를 이룬다.

어휘 **Islamic** 이슬람교의 **architect** 건축가 *cf.* **architecture** 건축(물); 건축 양식 **strive to-v** v하려고 노력하다 **backdrop** (주위) 배경; (사건 등의) 배경 **divine** 신성한; 신(神)의 *cf.* **divinity** 신; 신성; 신학 **elegant** 우아한 **geometry** 기하학적 배열; 기하학 **imply** 암시하다 **infinite** 무한한 **Muslim** 이슬람교도; 이슬람교의(=**Islamic**) **artisan** 장인, 기능공 **mosque** 이슬람교 사원, 모스크 **sequence** (일련의) 계속, 연속 **ornamentation** 장식(물)(=**decoration**) **intricate** 복잡한; 난해한 **accustomed to A** A에 익숙한 **dull** 재미없는, 지루한; 무딘 **association** 관련, 연합 **delicate** 섬세한; 민감한 **extraordinarily** 놀랍도록; 엄청나게 **earthly** 속세의; 지구의 **uncorrupted** 타락하지 않은 **failing** 결점; 실패 **surrender** 굴복[항복]하다; 넘겨주다 [선택지 어휘] **domestic** 집안의; 가정의; 국내의

24 도표 이해 ③

소재 국가별 밤늦은 취침 비율

해설 오전 1시 이후에 잠자리에 드는 사람들의 비율은 대만이 가장 높고 그다음이 홍콩이므로 ③이 잘못된 설명이다.

해석 〈자정 이후 취침하는 올빼미족 상위 5개국〉

주제문 이 도표는 대체로 밤늦게 자는 사람 수의 측면에서 상위 다섯 개 국가를 보여준다. ① 포르투갈이 오전 12시에서 1시 사이에 자는 사람들의 가장 높은 비율을 나타냈고, 근소한 차로 스페인, 그리고 한국이 그 뒤를 이었다. ② 오전 12시에서 1시까지의 취침 시간 범주에서 한국과 그다음 국가인 홍콩 사이에는 무려 8퍼센트 포인트 차이가 났다. ③ 오전 1시 이후에 자는 사람들의 경우, 홍콩이 가장 높은 비율을 나타냈고, 대만이 두 번째로 높았다. ④ 전반적으로 포르투갈 사람들 중 75퍼센트가 자정을 넘겨 취침한다고 말했고, 대만 사람들과 한국 사람들이 그 뒤를 이었다. ⑤ 오전 12시에서 1시 사이의 취침 시간대에서 사람 수가 가장 많은 나라와 가장 적은 나라의 차이가 12퍼센트 포인트였던 반면, 자정 이후의 범주에서는 그 차이가 단지 6퍼센트 포인트였다.

구문 [5행~7행] There was quite a difference, of 8%p, / between Korea and the next country in the 12-1 a.m. bedtime category, Hong Kong.

a difference와 8%p는 동격이며, between이 이끄는 전명구에서 the next country와 Hong Kong도 동격 관계이다.

어휘 **night owl** 올빼미족, 밤늦게까지 활동하는 사람(↔ **early bird** 일찍 일어나는 사람) **in terms of** ~의 측면[관점]에서 **as for[to]** ~에 관해서는, ~은 어떤가 하면

25 내용 불일치 ④

소재 기념비 디자이너 Maya Ying Lin

해설 Maya Ying Lin이 디자인한 기념비는 처음에는 전통적인 디자인과 달라 비난받았지만, 곧 가장 사랑받는 명소 중 하나가 되었다고 했으므로 ④가 글의 내용과 일치하지 않는다.

해석 누가 스물한 살의 나이에 전국 건축 대회에서 우승하는 것을 꿈꾸겠는가? 1980년에 중국계 미국인인 Maya Ying Lin은 Washington, D.C.의 ① 베트남전 참전용사 기념비를 디자인하도록 1,400명의 예술가 중에서 선발되었다. ② 대회에 나갔을 때 그녀는 Yale 대학의 건축과 학생이었다. 그녀는 ③ 베트남전에서 죽은 58,000명의 군인들의 이름이 새겨져 있는 500피트의 검은 화강암으로 된 V자형 벽을 디자인했다. 처음에는 그것이 전통적인 기념비와 너무 달랐기 때문에 몇몇 사람들은 그 디자인을 맹비난했다. ④ 그러나 놀랄 만큼 단순하지만 강력한 그 기념물은 곧 가장 사랑받는 명소 중 하나가 되었다. 결과적으로 Maya Lin은 존경받는 건축가가 되었고, ⑤ 다른 많은 중요한 기념비들을 디자인하도록 선택되었다.

구문 [7행~9행] She designed *a 500-foot black granite V-shaped wall* [on which are carved the names of *the 58,000 soldiers* (killed in the Vietnam War)].

[ ]는 a 500-foot black granite V-shaped wall을 수식한다. on which 다음에는 are carved가 동사이고 the names of ~ War가 주어인 도치구문이 나온다. ( ) 부분은 수동의 의미로 the 58,000 soldiers를 수식한다.

어휘 **architectural** 건축의 **competition** 대회 **veteran** 참전 용사; 베테랑[전문가] **memorial** 기념비 **granite** 화강암 **carve** 새기다 **attack** 맹비난하다; 공격하다 **astonishingly** 놀랄 만큼 **beloved** 가장 사랑하는, 인기 많은 **attraction** 명소

26 안내문 불일치 ④

소재 수확물 상자 판매

해설 Harvest Box는 9월과 10월에는 두 번 구매할 수 있고 학년 중 나머지 달에는 한 번씩 이용이 가능하다고 했으므로 ④가 안내문의 내용과 일치하지 않는다.

해석

수확물 상자

신선한 농산물
여러분의 교실 바로 밖에 농산물 시장을 두는 것과 같습니다. ① Harvest Box는 알맞은 가격으로 고품질 농산물 구입을 원하는 학생들을 위한 프로그램이며 동시에 지역 농장을 지원합니다.

선택 사항
- ② Value Box: 12파운드의 제철 과일과 채소가 ③ 8달러 50센트입니다.
- Local Box: 25파운드의 제철 과일과 채소가 ③ 16달러 50센트입니다.

④ Harvest Box는 9월과 10월에는 두 번씩 이용할 수 있고, 학년의 나머지 달에는 한 달에 한 번씩 이용할 수 있습니다. ⑤ 상자의 개수가 한정되어 있어서 선착순으로 판매하므로 주문을 서두르세요.

모든 구매 목록과 수취 일정은 교내에 게시된 행사 일정을 확인하세요.

어휘 **locate** (특정 위치에) 두다; 정확한 위치를 찾아내다 **produce** 농산물; 생산하다 **affordable** (가격이) 알맞은, 감당할 수 있는 **remainder** 나머지 **first come, first served** 선착순

27 안내문 일치 ④

소재 벼룩시장 참가 안내

해설 공지사항에서 판매대는 선착순으로 이용 가능하며 예약할 수 없다고 했으므로 ④가 안내문의 내용과 일치한다.

해석

HBS 벼룩시장

HBS 벼룩시장은 일 년 내내(① 우천에 상관없이) 매달 셋째 주 토요일 오전 6시부터 오후 2시까지 열립니다. ② 판매자들은 오후 3시까지는 주차장에서 나가주셔야 하고, 그렇지 않으면 추가 비용이 판매자들에게 부과됩니다.

시간
개장: 오전 6시 (정문)
폐장: 오후 3시 (모든 출입구)

요금
• 나란히 배치된 판매대 두 칸은 15달러입니다.
• ③ 일렬로 배치된 판매대 세 칸은 25달러입니다.

공지
④ 판매대는 선착순으로 이용 가능하며 예약은 할 수 없습니다. ⑤ 여러분이 지불한 구획보다 판매대 크기가 초과되었을 때에는 추가로 15달러가 부과될 것입니다. 더 많은 정보를 원하시면 (400) 620-3400로 저희에게 연락하시기 바랍니다.

어휘 **flea market** 벼룩시장 **year round** 연중 계속되는 **stall** 가판대 **side by side** 나란히 **in a row** 일렬로 **reserve** 예약하다 **exceed** 초과하다

28 네모 어법 ③

소재 포디즘(Fordism)

해설 (A) enable은 목적격보어로 to부정사를 취하므로 to purchase가 적절하다. 「enable A to-v」는 'A가 v할 수 있게 하다'란 의미이다.
(B) 콤마 앞에 「주어(Ford)+동사(pioneered)+목적어(the development ~ methods)」 형태의 완전한 절이 오므로 (B) 이하는 부사구 역할을 하는 분사구문이 되어야 한다. 주어인 Ford가 조립 라인을 도입한 것이므로 the assembly line을 목적어로 취할 수 있는 현재분사 introducing이 알맞다.
(C) 뒤에 「주어(Fordism)+동사(would reverse)+목적어(the downturn)」 형태의 완전한 절이 오므로 자신이 이끄는 명사절 안에서 주어, 목적어, 보어 역할을 하는 what은 올 수 없다. 문맥상 '희망=포디즘이 경기 침체를 뒤집을 것'이란 뜻이므로, the hope와 동격인 명사절을 이끄는 접속사 that이 알맞다.

해석 주제문 미국에서 '포디즘'은 노동자들이 자동차와 같이 자신들의 노동으로 생산한 제품을 구매할 수 있게 해주는 높은 임금을 통해 폭넓은 번영과 높은 기업 이익이 달성될 수 있다고 생각하는 경제 원리이다. 포디즘은 1910년경에 자동차 산업에서 Henry Ford가 거둔 성공의 결과로 만들어진 단어이다. Ford는 대량 생산 방법을 발전시키는 데 선도적인 역할을 했으며, 1913년에 이르러 조립 라인을 도입했다. 그는 상대적으로 저렴한 Model T 자동차를 1,000만 대나 팔아 엄청난 돈을 벌었고, 그의 직원들은 세계에서 가장 많은 임금을 받는 공장 노동자들이 되었다. 좀 더 넓은 관점에서 포디즘은 능률증진운동의 일부였으며, 그것은 미국의 진보 시대를 특징지었다. 대공황이 시작됐을 때 미국의 정책은 포디즘이 경기 침체를 뒤집을 것이라는 희망을 품고 높은 임금을 유지하는 것이었다.

구문 [1행~5행] In the USA, "Fordism" is *an economic theory* [**which** V'considers // O'**that** widespread prosperity and high profits for corporations / can be achieved through *high wages* [**that** enable workers to purchase the products of their labor, such as automobiles]].
which 이하는 an economic theory를 한정하는 주격 관계대명사절이다. that절이 considers의 목적어 역할을 하고 있다. 이 목적어절 안에서 주격 관계대명사 that이 이끄는 절이 high wages를 수식하고 있다.

어휘 **prosperity** 번영 **coin** (신조어 등을) 만들어내다; 동전 **pioneer** 선도하다; 개척하다 **mass production** 대량 생산 **assembly line** (대량 생산의) 조립 라인 **relatively** 상대적으로, 비교적 **vast** (수·양 등이) 막대한; 거대한 **fortune** 부; 재산; 운 **perspective** 관점, 견해 **progressive** 진보적인; 진보주의의 **era** 시대, 시기 **the Great Depression** (1929년 미국에서 시작된) 세계 대공황 **reverse** (방향·순서 등을) 뒤집다, 반대로 하다 **downturn** (경기의) 침체, 하강

29 밑줄 어휘 ③

소재 돈에 관한 역설

해설 기부를 하면 무의식적으로 지출을 줄여 결국 돈을 절약하게 되지만, 그렇지 않으면 무분별하게 돈을 쓰게 돼 결국 부(富)를 잃게 된다는 내용의 글이다. 기부를 했는데도 돈을 절약하게 되는 이유는 무의식적으로 재정적 '자유'를 누리는 것이 아니라, 그와 반대로 소비를 '억제'하기 때문이라는 의미가 되어야 하므로 ③의 freedom은 restraint 등이 되어야 한다.

해석 주제문 돈에 관한 위대한 심리적 ① 역설은 어려움에 처한 사람들에게 돈을 주면 비록 자신의 소비습관에 주의해야 하더라도 부유함을 느낀다는 것이다. 그에 따른 모순이 생기는데, 돈을 주는 바로 그 행위 자체가 소비의 ② 축소를 가져오고, 그에 따라 돈의 절약을 이끌 수 있기 때문이다. 이는 기부를 한 후, 무의식적인 생각이 재정적인 ③ 자유(→ 억제)를 행사하도록 할 것이기 때문이다. 한편, 어떤 사람들은 전혀 기부하지 않고 우아한 옷가지, 거창한 휴가 등, 자기 자신에게만 돈을 쓰면 더 부유함을 느낄 거라 생각한다. 무의식적인 생각이 그들에게 그러한 ④ 자기중심적 사고에 대해 괴로움을 주더라도, 그들은 자신의 방식을 바꿀 수 없고 곧 들어오는 수입과 관련한 재앙이 닥친다. 그들은 ⑤ 무분별한 재정적 선택으로 부(富)를 잃는다.

구문 [1행~4행] The great psychological *paradox* (concerning money)(S) is(V) **that** if you give money to *people* (in need), // you feel rich // even if you have to watch your spending habits.(C)
보어가 that절인 SVC 구조의 문장이다. that절은 「if절+주절+even if절」로 이루어졌다.

어휘 **psychological** 심리의, 정신의 **paradox** 역설 **concerning** ~에 관한 **in need** 어려움에 처한 **subsequent** 그다음의, 차후의 **contradiction** 모순; 반박, 반대 **give away** ~을 줘버리다 **lead to A** (결과로) A를 이끌다 **hence** 따라서, 그러므로 **unconscious** 무의식적인 **push A to-v** A가 v하도록 밀어붙이다, 요구하다 **exercise** 행사하다, 실행하다 **financial** 재정의 **donation** 기부 *cf.* **donate** 기부하다 **elegant** 우아한, 품격 있는 **egotism** 자기중심(주의); 이기주의 **reckless** 무모한, 신중치 못한

30 지칭 대상 ④

소재 도서 자동판매기를 고안한 Richard Carlile

해설 ④는 기계를 이용해 책을 사려는 구매자(The purchaser)를 가리키고, 나머지는 모두 Richard Carlile을 가리킨다.

해석 주제문 1822년에 Richard Carlile이라는 영국의 서적 판매업자이자 자유사상가는 (자동판매기가) 검열관과 경찰을 막아 줄 것으로 ① 그(=Carlile)는 기대하며 자동판매기를 고안했다. 그 당시에 Carlile과 소수의 다른 서적판매업자들과 출판업자들은 영국 언론의 자유를 확립하기 위해 애쓰고 있었다. Carlile과 그의 직원 중 몇 사람은 Thomas Paine의 〈이성의 시대〉와 같은 품목을 판매했다는 이유로 투옥된 적이 있었다. 그런 (부당한) 체포가 또 일어나는 것을 막기 위해 ② 그(=Carlile)는 기계로 책을 판매하기로 결심했는데, 그렇게 함으로써 서적 판매인은 법적으로 신원이 확인될 수 없다고 믿었다. Carlile은 ③ 그(=Carlile)의 기기(=자동판매기)를 묘사하면서 "가게 안에는 판매 중인 모든 출판물이 쓰여 있는 다이얼이 있습니다. 구매자가 들어와서 다이얼의 지침(指針)을 자신이 원하는 출판물 쪽으로 돌리면 돈을 넣자마자 그 출판물이 ④ 그(=the purchaser)의 앞으로 떨어집니다."라고 썼다. 하지만 법정은 여전히 그에게 책임을 물었으며, ⑤ 그(=Carlile)의 직원 중 한 명에게 그 기기를 통해 불쾌감을 주는 문헌을 팔았다고 유죄를 선고했다.

구문 [1행~4행] In 1822, *an English bookseller and freethinker* (named Richard Carlile)(S) designed(V) *a vending machine*(O) [(which) **he hoped** would provide protection from censors and the police].
a vending machine을 수식하는 관계사절에서 주격 관계대명사가 생략된 형태로, 주격 관계대명사는 바로 뒤에 「S+V」 형태의 삽입절(he hoped)이 나올 때 흔히 생략된다.

e.g. The boy [(who) **I thought** was very healthy] suddenly fell ill.
(내가 생각하기에 매우 건강했던 소년이 갑자기 병이 났다.)

[12행~13행] In the shop(부사구) is(V) *a dial*(S) [**on which** V′is written S′every publication for sale].

두 문장 A dial is in the shop.과 Every publication for sale is written on the dial.을 관계대명사를 이용하여 연결한 것으로, 부사구인 In the shop이 문두로 나가면서 주어와 동사가 도치되었고, 관계대명사절 내에서도 긴 주어가 문장의 균형상 뒤로 가고 동사가 그 앞에 위치하였다.

어휘 **freethinker** (특히 종교적 가르침에서) 자유사상가 **vending machine** 자동판매기 **censor** 검열관; 검열하다 **a handful of** 소수의; 한 줌의 **publisher** 출판업자 *cf.* **publication** 출판(물) **struggle** 애쓰다, 투쟁하다 **legally** 법률상, 합법적으로(↔ **illegally** 불법적으로) **identify** (신원 등을) 확인하다; 동일시하다 **device** 장치, 기구 **hand** 지침(指針): 지시 장치에 붙어 있는 바늘); 도움 **deposit** (돈을) 넣다, 예금하다; 퇴적시키다; 보증금; 예금; 침전물 **court** 법정 **hold A responsible (for B)** (B에 대하여) A에게 책임을 묻다 **convict A of B** B에 대하여 A에게 유죄를 선고하다 **offensive** 불쾌한, 모욕적인; 공격의 **literature** 문헌; 문학

31 빈칸 추론 ③

소재 지능과 연관이 있는 유아기 행동

해설 유아기 때의 행동으로 어린 시절의 지능 지수뿐만 아니라 청소년기의 학업 성취도를 예측할 수 있으며, 유아는 자신의 행동을 통해 세상에 대한 것들을 배우고 다른 사람들의 행동과 의도를 이해한다는 내용이다. 이러한 내용은 행동과 지능이 ③ '분리할 수 없는' 것임을 보여준다.

해석 주제문 유명한 한 연구에서 아이들이 생후 5개월 때 할 수 있었던 행동들은 네 살 때와 열 살 때의 지능 지수뿐 아니라 열네 살 때의 학업 성취도까지 예측한다고 밝혀졌다. 이런 행동들에는 유아들이 한 번에 몇 초 동안 자신들의 머리와 어깨를 들 수 있는 때인 '(아이를) 엎어 놓는 시기', 그들이 스스로 앉을 수 있게 되는 때, 그리고 그들이 얼마나 자주 손을 뻗어 물체를 붙잡으려고 시도했는지가 포함됐다. 연구자들은 행동에서 사고로의 연결이 부모의 지능이나 교육 수준이 아니라 유아의 신체적 능력에 의해 설명된다는 것을 보여줄 수 있었다. 아이들이 스스로 똑바로 앉을 수 있을 때 그들의 손을 자유롭게 뻗어서 물체를 잡을 수 있고, 이것은 그들이 그렇지 않으면 배우지 못할 세상에 대한 것들을 배울 수 있게 해 준다. 유아들은 자신들의 행동이 자신들의 환경을 변화시킬 수 있다는 것을 배웠고, 이것은 다른 사람들의 행동과 의도에 대한 그들의 이해를 형성하는 것을 도왔다. 주제문 요컨대, 행동과 지능은 분리할 수 없다.

① 물려받는 ② 예측할 수 없는 ④ 발달 중인 ⑤ 관계없는

구문 [9행~12행] The researchers were able to show // that *the link* (from action to thought) was explained / not by the parents' intelligence or education level(A) but by the infants' physical capabilities(B).

that ~ capabilities는 show의 목적어가 되는 명사절이다. by the parents' ~ level과 by the infants' ~ capabilities는 「not A but B」 구문으로 연결되어 병렬구조를 이룬다.

[13행~15행] ~, their hands are free to reach out and grab objects, // **which** allows them to learn *things about the world* [that they wouldn't (learn) otherwise].

which 이하는 주절 전체를 선행사로 하며 and it allows ~ wouldn't otherwise로 풀어 쓸 수 있다. wouldn't 다음에는 learn이 생략되었다.

어휘 **academic** 학업의 **achievement** 성취 **tummy time** (아기의 상체 힘을 길러 주기 위해) 엎어 놓는 시기 *cf.* **tummy** 배, 복부 **infant** 유아 **attempt** 시도하다 **object** 물건; 대상; 목표 **intelligence** 지능 **physical** 신체의; 물리적인 **capability** 능력, 역량 **otherwise** 그렇지 않으면; 그 외에는 **shape** 형성하다; 형태, 모양 **intention** 의도

32 빈칸 추론 ⑤

소재 침팬지의 과장된 도움 요청 신호

해설 영장류는 공격자에게서 자신을 구해줄 수 있는 서열 높은 침팬지나 인간이 주위에 있을 때 비명을 과장한다(magnify their cries)고 했으므로, 빈칸에는 ⑤ '두려움의 신호(= 비명)를 과장한다'가 들어가는 것이 가장 적절하다.

해석 주제문 스코틀랜드의 St. Andrews 대학교 연구원들은 침팬지들이 위협을 당하거나 공격받고 있을 때 서열이 더 높은 다른 침팬지들에게 도움을 얻기 위해 두려움의 신호를 과장한다는 것을 발견했다. 침팬지들이 타격과 같은 심한 공격을 당하고 있을 때 고음의 긴 비명을 지른다는 것은 이미 알려져 있었다. 하지만 이 연구가 알아낸 것은 그 공격자에게 도전할 수 있는 더 높은 서열의 침팬지나 인간이 그 지역에 있을 때 영장류는 자신의 비명을 과장한다는 것이다. 이 연구의 리더인 Katie Slocombe 박사는 "더 높은 지위의 동물들이 주위에 없을 때 비명 소리는 보통 수준이지만, 그런 동물들이 있을 때 공격받고 있는 침팬지는 실제 공격의 정도보다 훨씬 더 끔찍하게 들리도록 비명을 지릅니다."라고 말했다.

① 심하게 부상을 입은 척한다
② 훨씬 더 공격적으로 싸운다
③ 가능한 한 조용히 있는다
④ 비명 같은 신호를 보낸다

구문 [8행~11행] But what the study found(S) was(V) // that the primates magnify their cries // when there is *a higher-ranking chimp or human* in the area [who could challenge the aggressor].(C)

what ~ found가 문장의 주어이고 that절이 보어인 SVC의 구조이다. 주격 관계대명사절 who ~ aggressor는 a higher-ranking chimp or human을 수식한다.

어휘 **rank** 계급, 지위 **high-pitched** 고음의 **prolonged** 오래 끄는, 장기의 **subject A to B** A에게 B를 당하게 하다 **aggression** 공격 *cf.* **aggressor** 공격자, 침략자 **primate** 영장류 **magnify** 과장하다; 확대하다 **higher-status** 더 높은 지위의 *cf.* **status** 지위; 신분, 자격; 상황 [선택지 어휘] **transmit** 보내다; 전하다 **exaggerate** 과장하다

33 빈칸 추론 ②

소재 사물 실재의 조건

해설 우주에 책 외에는 아무것도 없을 때까지 책이 계속 팽창하면 결국 그 책이 사라질 것이라 했다. 이는 '한 가지 사물 외에 아무것도 존재하지 않는 상황이 되면 그 사물조차 사라질 것이다'란 뜻으로 하나의 사물이 존재하려면 그 사물 외에 다른 것이 존재해야 한다는 내용이 빈칸에 들어가야 적절하므로 정답은 ② '다른 것들도 존재해야 한다'이다.

해석 누군가가 당신에게 "사물이 존재하는 걸까?"라고 묻는다면 당신은 다음과 같은 말을 할지 모른다. "무슨 소리야? 당연히 사물은 존재하지! 네 주위를 둘러봐. 실재하고 물리적으로 만질 수 있는 것들이 어디에나 있어. 모든 것들이 너와 나랑은 관계없이 (독립적으로) 존재하고 있어!" 그러나 만약 이 질문이 "어떤 하나의 사물, 즉 의자나 다른 물체가 존재하도록 하는 것이 무엇일까?"라면 어떻게 될까? 그 답을 찾을 수 있는 한 가지 방법은 특정한 사물, 예를 들어 책이 온 우주에 책 외에는 아무것도 없을 때까지 계속해서 팽창한다고 상상해 보는 것이다. 그것에 어떤 일이 일어날까? 그 책은 아마 사라질 것인데 온 우주에 그 책이 아닌 것은 아무것도 없기 때문이다. 이것은 실재에 대한 매우 기본적인 개념이다. 주제문 즉, 어떤 하나의 사물이 존재하기 위해서는 다른 것들도 존재해야 한다.

① 그 똑같은 것이 존재해서는 안 된다
③ 우리는 그것에 적절한 이름을 지어줘야 한다
④ 그것은 독특한 특징이 있어야 한다
⑤ 그것이 다른 것들과 상관없이 존재해야 한다

구문 [7행~10행] *One way* (to find the answer) is to imagine a specific thing — say, a book — expanding and expanding // until there is **nothing** in the universe **except** the book.

nothing except는 only의 의미로 밑줄 친 문장은 There is only the book in the universe.와 같다.

어휘 **physical** 물리적인; 육체의 **tangible** 만질 수 있는; 유형(有形)의 **independently of** ~와 관계없이 **specific** 특정한; 뚜렷한 **expand** 팽창하다 **concept** 개념, 발상 [선택지 어휘] **distinctive** 독특한; 뚜렷이 구별되는

34 빈칸 추론 ①

소재 서머타임제가 건강에 미치는 영향

해설 빈칸 이후에 실제 시간이 조정되더라도 체내 생체 시계는 이에 적응하지 못한다(It seems ~ not adjust.)고 한 후, 이에 대한 연구 결과의 예를 나열하며 논지를 뒷받침하고 있다. 마지막 문장에서 신체 시간과 실제 시간이 다를 때 인체에 미칠 수 있는 부정적 영향을 언급하고 있으므로 빈칸에 가장 적절한 것은 ① '의도하지 않은 건강상의 결과를 일으킬 수 있다'이다.

해석 전 세계적으로 일광 절약 시간제(=서머타임제)는 에너지를 절약하는 한 가지 방법으로 오랫동안 장려되어 왔다. 주제문 그 제도가 실제로 에너지를 절약하는지 아닌지는 여전히 논란의 여지가 있지만, 여러 연구에서 1시간의 조정이 의도하지 않은 건강상의 결과를 일으킬 수 있다는 것이 정말 확실해 보인다. 시계가 1시간 빨라지거나 늦어져도 체내 생체 시계, 즉 그 주변 환경과 조화를 이루기 위해 일광을 이용하는 신체의 24시간 주기 리듬은 적응하지 않는 듯 보인다. 예를 들면 55,000명의 사람이 참가한 한 연구에서 과학자들은, 피실험자들이 휴무일에 일광 절약시가 아니라 표준시에 자는 경향이 있다는 것을 발견했다. 그리고 그들이 잠에서 깨어나는 시간은 동트는 시간이 계절에 의해 서서히 바뀜에 따라 달라졌다. 다른 연구들에서 과학자들은, 봄철에 사람들이 가장 활발히 움직이는 지수가 실제 시계보다는 체내 시계와 더 일치한다는 것을 발견했다. 연구들은 체내 시간과 시계가 나타내는 시간 사이의 이러한 괴리가 제대로 쉬지 못함, 수면 장애, 부족한 수면 시간을 초래할 수 있음을 시사한다.

② 우리의 체내 생체 시계가 재조정되는 것과 관련이 있다
③ 확실히 하루를 더 건강하게 시작하는 방법이다
④ 수면 장애가 있는 사람들에게 유익한 효과가 있다
⑤ 여름보다는 봄에 더 쉽게 이루어질 수 있다

구문 [2행~5행] **Whether** it **does** (S) is (V) still a matter of debate (C), // but it (가주어) **does** seem clear from studies // that a one-hour time adjustment ~ health consequences (진주어).

Whether가 이끄는 명사절이 문장의 주어로 쓰였다. Whether절에 쓰인 does는 saves energy를 받는 대동사이고, it 뒤에 쓰인 does는 동사 seem을 강조한다.

[15행~18행] Studies **suggest** // **that** *this disconnect* (between body time and clock time) (S') **can result in** (V') restlessness, sleep disruption, and shorter sleep duration (O').

여기서 suggest는 '제안하다'가 아니라 '암시하다, 시사하다'의 의미로 쓰였다. 이때 that절의 동사는 시제, 인칭, 수에 맞춘다.

cf. The doctor **suggested** that surgery **(should) be** postponed until he is getting better.
(의사는 그가 더 좋아질 때까지 수술을 미뤄야 한다고 제안했다.)

어휘 **daylight saving time** 일광 절약 시간제, 서머타임제《여름철에 표준시보다 1시간 시계를 앞당겨 놓는 제도》 **a matter of debate** 논란의 여지가 있는 문제 **adjustment** 조정, 수정; 적응 *cf.* **adjust** 적응하다; 조정하다 **internal** 내부의 **in tune with** ~와 조화[일치]를 이루어; 리듬을 맞추어 **subject** 피실험자; 주제 **peak** 최고조(의) **disconnect** 괴리, 단절; 연결을 끊다 **result in** (어떤 결과를) 가져오다 **restlessness** 제대로 쉬지[잠들지] 못함; 안절부절못함 **disruption** 방해, 중단 [선택지 어휘] **unintended** 의도하지 않은 **disorder** 장애, 이상

35 무관한 문장 ④

소재 문제를 조기에 인식하는 것의 중요성

해설 개구리를 찬물에 넣고 물을 서서히 덥히면 개구리가 온도 변화를 못 느끼고 죽는 것처럼, 우리 삶의 문제도 천천히 몰래 다가와서 우리가 그것을 인식하기도 전에 그 문제에 매몰되어 버릴 수 있으므로, 문제점을 인식하고 작은 문제라도 바로 처리하는 것이 바람직하다는 내용의 글이다. 따라서 동기나 인내 부족에 관한 내용인 ④는 글의 흐름과 무관하다.

해석 개구리가 뜨거운 물속에 빠지면, 개구리는 갑작스런 열 변화에 매우 빨리 반응해서 해를 입지 않은 채로 뛰어나올 것이다. 하지만 개구리가 차가운 물에 넣어진 후에 그 물을 매우 천천히 덥힌다면, 개구리는 익어서 죽을 때까지 거기에 계속 머물러 있을 것이다. 문제점들을 고려할 때 그 개구리를 염두에 두는 것이 유용하다. 우리 삶에서 가장 어렵고 중요한 문제 중 다수가 서서히 몰래 우리에게 다가온다. 심지어 그 문제점들이 거기에 존재한다는 것조차 인식하기 전에, 우리는 그 문제들에 깊이 빠진다. 동기나 인내의 부족은 특히 다루기 어려운 문제인데 그 이유는 그러한 것이 다른 문제들을 해결할 수 있는 당신의 능력 또한 제한하기 때문이다. 주제문 문제점들을 인지하는 것은 그에 대한 해결책을 찾는 데 필수적이며, 소소한 문제점들이 발생할 때 처리하는 것이 그 문제점들이 너무 커서 고칠 수 없는 문제로 커질 때까지 무시하는 것보다 낫다.

구문 [13행~15행] ~ **dealing** with small problems **as** they arise is better than **ignoring** them **until** they build up into *problems* (too big to fix).

두 개의 동명사구 dealing with ~ they arise와 ignoring them ~ to fix가 비교되고 있으며, 각각의 동명사구에 as와 until이 이끄는 부사절이 포함된 형태이다. too big to fix는 「too+형용사+to-v (너무 ~해서 v할 수 없는)」 구문으로 problems를 후치 수식한다.

어휘 **sudden** 갑작스러운 **bear A in mind** A를 명심하다 **sneak up on** ~에게 몰래 다가오다[다가가다] **gradually** 서서히 **be immersed in** (곤경·비탄 등에) 빠지다, ~에서 헤어나지 못하다 **deal with** 다루다, 처리하다 **arise** 발생하다, 생기다 **build up into** ~으로 커지다[키우다]

36 글의 순서 ③

소재 한국의 두뇌 유출 현상

해설 한국의 두뇌 유출 현상의 변화를 설명한 글이다. 먼저 주어진 글과 (B)의 앞부분에서는 30년 동안 경제적 요인 때문에 지적 자본이 높은 보수를 주는 나라로 흘러 들어갔다는 내용을 설명한 후에 (B)의 However 이하에서 다른 요인들을 언급하고 있다. 그중 하나인 한국의 유교에 관해 설명하는 (A), (C)의 순서를 결정하는 단서는 (A)의 처음에 나온 It이다. It은 (C)에서 처음 언급된 Confucianism을 가리킨다. 문맥상으로도 유교에 대한 일반적인 설명이 있은 후, 그것이 일자리를 결정하는 데 미친 영향을 언급하는 것이 자연스러우므로 ③ '(B)-(C)-(A)'의 순서가 적절하다.

해석 '두뇌 유출' 현상과 미국에서 박사 학위를 받은 한국 과학자와 기술자의 관계에 대한 30년간의 연구는 이러한 전문가들의 귀국 여부 결정에 있어서 경제적인 요인이 주요했다는 것을 보여준다.

(B) 두뇌 유출 현상에서 지적 자본은 가장 높은 보수를 제공해주는 나라로 흘러간다. 주제문 그러나 이 연구는 대안들 사이의 경제적 차이가 좁아지면, 다른 요인이 한국의 과학자와 기술자의 결정에서 더 중요하게 된다는 것을 발견했다.

(C) 특히, 이 연구는 유교적 가치가 중대한 영향을 주었다는 것을 시사한다. 유교는 한국 사회의 기반이 되는 고대 사상 체계이다.

(A) 이는 국가에 대한 충성과 의무를 강조하는데, 이것이 미국보다는 고국에서 일자리를 선택한 한국의 과학자와 기술자의 결정에 주요했다는 것이 발견되었다. 확실히 문화적 분석이 한국의 두뇌 유출 현상을 이해하는 데 필수적이다.

구문 [1행~4행] *A study* (S) (of three decades of the phenomenon of "brain drain" and *its relationship* (to *Korean scientists and engineers (KSEs)* [who earned a PhD in the US]), / shows (V) (that) economic factors ~ (O).

주어는 A study, 동사는 shows로 주어 뒤에 오는 수식어구가 길어진 형태이다. who가 이끄는 관계대명사절이 Korean scientists and engineers (KSEs)를 수식하고 있다.

어휘 phenomenon (복수형 phenomena) 현상 drain 유출, 배출 PhD (= Doctor of Philosophy) 박사 학위 central 중요한; 중심의 loyalty 충성 opt for ~을 선택하다 analysis 분석 intellectual 지적인, 지능의; 지식인 capital 자본; 수도 alternative 대안; 양자택일 Confucian 유교의, 공자의 *cf.* Confucianism 유교 underpin 지탱하다, 버팀목이 되다

37 글의 순서 ④

소재 성격이 행복에 미치는 영향

해설 인생에서 일어나는 사건과 개인의 성격이 행복에 영향을 주는 정도를 알아보는 연구가 있었다는 주어진 글 다음에 영향을 주는 정도를 구체적으로 설명하는 (C)가 이어지고, 같은 종류의 일이 같은 사람에게 반복적으로 일어난다는 (C)의 마지막 문장의 내용에 대해 운이 좋은 사람과 그렇지 못한 사람의 경우를 들어 설명하고 있는 (A)가 이어져야 한다. 다음으로 (A)의 마지막 문장에 언급된 연구자들의 틀린 가정(성격과 인생에서 일어나는 사건이 행복에 별개로 영향을 미칠 것이다)을 대신하여(Instead) 실제로 얻어진 연구 결과(성격 자체가 사람들에게 일어난 것에 가장 강력한 영향을 미친다)가 언급되는 (B)가 이어져야 하므로, 정답은 ④ '(C)-(A)-(B)'이다.

해석 한 연구에서, 연구자들은 어떻게 인생의 사건들과 성격이 사람들의 행복에 영향을 주는지 알아보기 위해 수년 동안 빅토리아 주(州) 주민들을 인터뷰했다. 그들은 사람의 성격과 그들에게 일어난 일을 비교하여, 그것들이 안녕과 행복에 영향을 주는 정도를 알고 싶어 했다.

(C) 이를테면, 성격이 행복에서 40퍼센트를 차지할 수도 있고, 반면에 인생의 사건들이 60퍼센트를 차지할 수도 있었다. 그렇지 않으면 아마도 성격이 더 중요하다고 밝혀질 수도 있었다. 연구가 진행되자, 같은 종류의 일이 반복해서 같은 사람에게 계속 발생한다는 것이 명백해졌다.

(A) 운이 좋은 사람은 계속해서 운이 좋았다. 마찬가지로, 관계 불화와 실직과 같은 나쁜 경험을 많이 겪은 사람은 나쁜 일에 연달아 직면하는 것처럼 보였다. 성격과 인생의 사건들이 행복에 별개로 영향을 미칠 것이라는 그 연구자들의 가정은 틀렸다.

(B) 주제문 대신, 성격 그 자체가 사람들에게 발생한 일에 가장 강력한 영향을 미쳤다. 낙관주의자들은 긍정적인 경험을 더 많이 한 반면, 비관주의자들은 부정적인 경험을 더 많이 했다.

구문 [4행~6행] They wanted to know *the extent* [**to which** a person's personality versus *the things* [**that** happened to them] / affected well-being and happiness].

to which에서 to는 to the extent(~의 정도까지)라는 표현에서 나온 전치사이며, which는 the extent를 받는다. that은 the things를 수식하는 절을 이끈다.

어휘 resident 주민, 거주자 personality 성격, 인격 extent 정도 versus ~와 비교[대비]하여; (경기 등에서) -대(對) likewise 마찬가지로 breakup 불화, 파탄 assumption 가정, 추정 separate 별개의, 분리된; 분리하다 optimist 낙관주의자(↔ pessimist 비관주의자) account for (비율 · 부분을) 차지하다; 설명하다 whereas 반면에 alternatively 그렇지 않으면, 그 대신에

38 문장 넣기 ③

소재 미국으로 이민 온 아시아인들

해설 글의 첫 문장에서 이 글이 아시아인의 미국 이민에 관한 내용임을 알 수 있다. 주어진 문장은 더 많은 비숙련 노동자가 중국으로부터 들어왔다는 내용으로, 이 앞에 이미 숙련공들의 이주가 한 번 더 있었음을 짐작할 수 있다. 따라서 주어진 문장은 The earliest immigrants에 대한 설명과 These later arrivals에 관한 언급 사이인 ③에 오는 것이 적절하다.

해석 주제문 아마 대략 1만 2천 년 전에 시베리아에서 이주한 북아메리카 원주민을 포함하지 않으면, 미국으로 간 최초의 대규모 아시아인 이민은 19세기 중반에 있었다. 이때는 캘리포니아의 골드러시 기간이었고, 많은 중국인들은 '금광'의 꿈에 매료되었다. 가장 초기 이민자는 대개는 부유하고 기술이 있는 중국인들로, 이들은 배를 이용한 항해를 할 여유가 있었다. 주제문 그러나 머지않아 더 많은 비숙련공들이 중국으로부터 들어오기 시작했다. 이 후기의 이민자들은 초기의 이민자들과 다르게, 장시간의 힘들고 더럽고 위험한 일을 매우 적은 보수를 받고도 기꺼이 받아들였다. 그들은 '값싼 노동력'으로 여겨졌기 때문에 이렇게 근면한 중국인은 많은 미국인의 분노를 샀다. 미국인들은 당연히 그들에게 속해야 하는 일자리와 재산을 그 새로운 이민자들이 가져가고 있다고 느꼈다.

어휘 unskilled 숙련되지 않은, 미숙한(↔ skilled 숙련된) large-scale 대규모의 immigration (입국) 이민, 이주 *cf.* immigrant 이민자 gold rush 골드러시(새로운 금광이 발견되어 많은 사람들이 몰려드는 현상) lure 유혹하다 afford (경제적 · 시간적으로) ~할 여유가 있다 passage 항해, 여행; 통과; (글의) 단락 settler 이민자; 개척자 willingly 기꺼이, 자진해서 in return for ~의 보수로; ~의 답례로 resent 분개하다 rightfully 당연하게 belong to A A에 속하다

39 문장 넣기 ③

소재 '생산적 실패' 그룹과 '직접 지도' 그룹의 학습 효율성 차이

해설 주어진 문장이 In contrast(대조적으로)로 시작하면서 생산적 실패 그룹의 이야기를 전개하므로 주어진 문장 앞에는 직접 지도 그룹에 관한 내용이 있어야 한다. 직접 지도 그룹의 이야기는 ③ 앞에서 마무리되므로 주어진 문장은 ③에 위치해야 한다.

해석 주제문 최근 연구는 어려움과 실수를 도입하는 것이 교실에서 매우 효과적일 수 있다는 것을 보여준다. 예를 들어, 교육학자인 Kapur와 Bielaczyc가 수행한 연구에서 학생들은 '생산적 실패' 그룹이나 '직접 지도' 그룹에 배정되었다. 직접 지도 그룹의 학생들은 복잡한 수학 문제에 관한 전형적인 수업을 끝마쳤다. 그 과정에서 교사는 학생들이 성공적으로 문제를 풀도록 도움을 주었다. 대조적으로, 생산적 실패 그룹의 학생들은 복잡한 문제를 받고 나서 그룹으로 동료 급우들과 함께 그 문제를 풀기 위해 노력했다. 문제는 매우 어려웠고 생산적 실패 그룹은 그 문제를 풀 수 없었다. 마지막 수업 시간에, 교사는 생산적 실패 그룹이 실패한 시도를 분석하는 것을 도와주었고 올바른 풀이 방법을 제공해 주었다. 최종 시험에서, 생산적 실패 그룹은 더 간단한 문제뿐 아니라 복잡한 문제 모두에서 직접 지도 그룹보다 더 좋은 성적을 거두었다.

어휘 productive 생산적인 fellow 동료, 동년배; (남자를 가리켜) 녀석, 친구 attempt 시도하다, 애써 해보다; 시도 educationalist 교육학자 assign 배정하다 complete 끝마치다; 작성하다; 완전한 typical 전형적인 analyze 분석하다 score 점수를 받다 straightforward 간단한, 쉬운; 솔직한

40 요약문 완성 ②

소재 추론보다 추측에 근거한 인간의 행동 결정 방식

해설 먼저 요약문을 보면, 이 글이 인간에 대한 어떤 통념을 서술한 것임을 추론할 수 있다. 글의 첫 문장이 통념에 해당하는데, a reasoning animal은 rational decision makers로 바꿔 표현할 수 있다. rational은 '이성적인, 합리적인'이란 뜻으로, 감정(emotion)이 아닌 추론(reasoning)에 입각하여 결정이나 사고를 하는 것이다. 한편, 글 중간의 But 이하부터 제시된 최근의 연구 조사 결과는 이러한 통념을 바로잡는 '사실'에 해당한다. 즉, 인간은 추론이 아닌 shots in the dark(억측), suggestion(암시), guess(추측)에 의거하여 결정을 내린다고 하였는데, 이는 assumption(가정)과 일맥상통한다.

해석 예전에 인간은 추론하는 동물로 여겨졌다. 인간은 어떤 의견을 형성하거나 행동 방식을 결정하기 전에 그 문제에 찬성하고 반대하는 이유 중 적어도 일부를 저울질하고 어느 정도 단순한 추론 과정을 실행한다고 생각되었다. 그러나 최근의 연구 조사는 이 생각이 사실이 아님을 보여주었다. 주제문 우리의 의견과 행동 대부분은 오히려 막연한 추측에 가깝다. 실제로, 몇몇 권위자들은 순수한 추론 행위라는 것은 보통의 사람들에게 있어서는 매우 드물다고 단언한다. 중대한 결정과 지대한 영향을 끼치는 행동은 주로 암시의 힘에 의해 이루어지고 결정된다. '주로'라는 단어에 주목해라. 왜냐하면 간단한 사고, 그리고 심사숙고한 추론조차도 종종 추측에 의해 결론 내려지며, 생각하는 사람(= 인간)은 터무니없게도 자신의 결정이 처음부터 끝까지 온전한 추론에 근거한다고 생각하기 때문이다.

⬇

인간은 (A) 이성적인 결정을 내리는 존재라는 생각이 일반적으로 받아들여졌지만, 실제로는 (B) 가정이 그러한 문제에 더 중요한 역할을 한다.

구문 [2행~6행] It was supposed that before forming an opinion or deciding on a course of conduct // he **weighed** at least some of the reasons for and against the matter, and **performed** a more or less simple process of reasoning.
(가주어 / 진주어)
It은 가주어이고 that 이하가 진주어인 구문이다. that절은 부사절(before ~ conduct)과 주절(he weighed ~ reasoning)로 구성되며, 주절의 동사 weighed와 performed는 and로 병렬연결되어 있다.

[13행~17행] Notice that word "primarily," // **for** simple thought, and even mature reasoning, often concludes with a guess, and ~ based on solid deduction.
여기서 for는 '이유'를 나타내는 접속사이므로 '~ 때문에'로 해석한다.

어휘 **reason** 추론[추리]하다; 이성; 이유 **conduct** 행동; 수행 **shot in the dark** 막연한 추측, 억측 **authority** 권위자; 권한; (주로 복수형) 당국 **momentous** 중대한 **far-reaching** 지대한 영향을 가져올 **primarily** 주로; 우선 **suggestion** 암시, 시사; 제안 **mature** 심사숙고한; 성숙한; 잘 익은 **absurdly** 터무니없이; 어리석게 **solid** 완전한; 고체의 **deduction** 추론; 공제(액) [선택지 어휘] **flexibility** 유연성; 융통성; 탄력성 **convention** 관습, 풍습 **integrated** 통합된 **insight** 통찰력; 이해, 간파

41~42 장문

41 ⑤ 42 ②

소재 영국의 '미키마우스' 학위 제도의 장단점

해설 41. 이 글은 영국의 직업 교육 학위인 '미키마우스' 학위에 관한 것으로, 그것에 대한 찬반 의견을 차례대로 보여주고 있으므로 ⑤ '미키 마우스 학위: 유용한 혁신인가, 형편없는 아이디어인가?'가 글의 제목으로 가장 적절하다.
① 미키마우스 학위의 사실과 허구
② 미키마우스 학위는 어떻게 어디에서 취득하는가
③ 왜 미키마우스 학위가 열등하다고 여겨지는가?
④ 직업을 얻는 것이 대학 공부의 목적인가?

42. 빈칸 뒤에 대학이 학생 증가로 시설비와 연구비를 더 벌 수 있다는 내용이 나온다. 이는 ② '재정적' 이익에 해당한다.
① 심리적 ③ 문화적 ④ 학문적 ⑤ 이론적

해석 학생들은 보통 물리학, 경제학, 또는 역사학에서 학위를 얻으려고 대학에 간다. 그러나 영국에서는 승마 연구나 방향 요법 같은 덜 전통적인 과목에서 대학 학위를 얻는 것이 이제 가능하다. 이러한 학위는 비공식적으로 '미키마우스' 학위라고 알려져 있다. 만화 캐릭터의 이름에서 따온 '미키마우스'라고 불리는 것은 아마추어 같은 것으로 여겨진다. 주제문 그러나 새롭게 만들어진 대학에서 흔히 제공하는 이러한 학위들이 정말로 기성 대학이 주는 전통 학위보다 열등한가?
이러한 학위에 찬성하는 사람들은 공부하는 것이 학문에 대한 사랑과 교육에 대한 존경을 촉진하기 때문에 사회는 모든 분야에서 많은 대학 졸업자들을 갖는 것으로부터 이익을 얻는다고 말한다. 그들은 또한 이러한 새로운 과정이 진지한 연구를 필요로 한다고 주장한다. 예를 들어, 서핑 연구는 기상학, 생물학, 경영학을 포함한다. 사회적인 이익뿐만 아니라, 재정적 이익도 있다. 더 많은 대학생들은 대학이 시설을 개선하고 연구를 늘리기 위한 더 많은 돈을 의미한다. 더군다나 특수 훈련은 많은 고용주들에게 관심을 끌 수가 있다.
그러나 어떤 사람들은 제빵 기술 같은 분야에서의 훈련이 직장과 기술학교에서 습득되어야 하고, 대학은 사람들이 직업을 찾는 것을 도와주기보다는 지식을 촉진하기 위해 존재한다고 주장한다. 그들은 정치가들이 대학 졸업생의 수를 늘리기를 원하는데, 이러한 '미키마우스' 학사 과정을 개설하는 것이 고등교육 수준을 유지하지 않고도 이것(= 정치가들이 원하는 것)을 이루어낸다고 말한다. 그들은 또한 만약 이러한 학위가 폐지되면, 더 많은 장학금이 '진정한' 대학 과목을 공부하는 사람들에게 돌아갈 것이라고 주장한다.

구문 [6행~8행] **Taken** from the name of the cartoon character, / *anything* (termed "Mickey Mouse") is considered amateurish.
Taken ~ character는 분사구문으로 주어 anything termed "Mickey Mouse"를 부연 설명하고 있다. ( ) 부분은 과거분사구로 anything을 후치 수식한다.

어휘 **degree** 학위; 정도 **physics** 물리학 **informally** 비공식적으로; 격식 없이 **term** 칭하다, 이름 짓다 **amateurish** 아마추어 같은, 서투른 **inferior** 열등한 **conventional** 전통적인, 관습적인 **established** 기성의, 확립된 **in favor of** ~에 찬성[지지]하여 **meteorology** 기상학 **facility** (주로 복수형으로) 시설 **attractive** 관심을 끄는 **acquire** 습득하다, 얻다 **further** 촉진하다, 진전시키다 **abolish** 폐지하다 **scholarship** 장학금 (제도) [선택지 어휘] **innovation** 혁신

43~45 장문

43 ① 44 ⑤ 45 ③

소재 서점 직원과 공통점 찾기

해설 43. Jessica가 서점에서 잡지를 읽고 있는 내용 다음에 서점 직원이 눈치를 주며 빤히 쳐다보는 (B)가 이어지는 것이 자연스럽다. Jessica가 책을 골라 계산대에서 줄을 선 내용 다음에는 직원을 마주하고 말을 건네는 (D)가 와야 적절하다. Jessica가 직원의 이름표를 보고 말을 걸었으므로 그다음에는 직원이 그에 대한 답을 하고 둘이 서로 이야기를 나누는 (C)가 와야 한다.
44. (e)는 서점 직원을 가리키는 반면 나머지는 모두 Jessica를 가리킨다.
45. (C)에서 아버지에게서 낚시를 배운 사람은 서점 직원이 아니라 Jessica임을 알 수 있으므로 ③이 글의 내용과 일치하지 않는다.

해석 (A) Jessica는 한 신문사의 기자로 일하고 있었다. 어느 겨울, Jessica는 공항에 있었는데 눈에 발이 묶여 서점에서 잡지를 읽고 있었다. 그녀는 결국 (잡지) 하나를 살 작정이었지만 ① 구입할 생각이 없는 잡지를 읽고 있었다. 그것은 시시한 이야깃거리를 다루는 잡지였다. 그녀는 "서서 먹는 칼로리를 계산에 넣지 않는 것처럼 읽지만 사지 않는 시시한 이야기도 계산에 넣지 않는 거야."라고 혼잣말을 했다.
(B) 계산대 뒤의 여자는 "그거 살 건가요?"라는 듯 Jessica를 엄청나게 빤히 쳐다보고 있었다. Jessica는 책 선반 뒤에 숨었다. (a) 그녀(= Jessica)는 그 기사를 다 읽고 나서 시시한 잡지를 내려놓고 사려고 했던 잡지를 골랐다. (b) 그녀(= Jessica)는 줄을 서서 기다리면서 ② 그 직원이 손님들에게 전혀 미소 짓지 않고 정중한 대화를 묵살하는 것을 알아차렸다. 그녀는 자기 일을 지겨워하는 것 같았다.
(D) 마침내 (d) 그녀(= Jessica) 차례가 되었을 때 Jessica는 아주 무뚝뚝한 얼굴과 마주했다. 직원은 긴 금발에 고양이 눈 모양의 안경을 쓰고 있었다. 직원이 책을 포장하고 있는 동안 Jessica는 ⑤ "난 정말로 당신의 금발을 가졌으면 좋겠네요."라고 말했다. 점원은 반쯤 놀라면서 얼굴이 미소로 환히 빛나면서 올려다보았다. "글쎄요, 제 머리카락이 예전처럼 좋지는 않아요."라고 (e) 그녀(= 서점 직원)는 겸손하게 말했다. 그때 Jessica는 "Eddie Joe"라는 그녀의 이름표를 흘끗 보았다. Jessica는 미소 지으며 물었다. "아버지 이름을 따라 지었나요?"
(C) 약간 머뭇거린 후, 그녀는 미소 지으며 말했다. "예, 그분들은 아들을 원했거든요." Jessica는 말했다. "제 부모님도 그러셨어요. ③ 저는 여섯 살 때쯤 낚시하는 법을 배웠답니다." 그녀(= 서점 직원)는 (c) 그녀(= Jessica)도 아버지 이름을 따라 이름이 지어졌냐고 물었다. Jessica는 아니라고 말했지만 그녀는 실망하지 않았다. 그녀는 Jessica의 이야기에 연결시켰다. "저는 물건들을 만드는 법을 배웠어요. ④ 우리 아버지는 목수였거든요. 저는 톱질하고 측량하고 못을 칠 수 있답니다." Jessica와 Eddie는 그때 둘 다 미소를 짓고 있었다. 그들은 이야기를 주고받았고 그것이 그들 둘 다의 기분을 좋게 만들었다.

구문 [(D) 4행~5행] ~, Jessica said, "I really wish I **had** your blond hair."
밑줄 친 부분은 가정법 과거 시제로 I wish 다음에 과거동사 had가 나온 것은 현재 사실과는 다른 것을 가정하는 것이다.

[(D) 5행~6행] The clerk looked up, **half-startled**, *her face* **beaming** with a smile.
half-startled와 her face beaming ~은 모두 동시동작을 나타내는 분사구문이다. her face는 분사 beaming의 의미상 주어이다.

어휘 (A) **snowbound** 눈 때문에 발이 묶인, 눈에 갇힌 **count** 계산에 넣다; 중요하다 (B) **stare** 빤히 쳐다보기, 응시 **rack** 선반 (C) **name after** ~의 이름을 따서 명명하다 **match** 연결시키다, 맞추다 **measure** 측량하다 **pound** 마구 치다, 세게 두드리다 **trade** 주고받다, 교환하다 (D) **grumpy** 무뚝뚝한, 기분이 언짢은 **startled** 놀란 **beam** 환하게 미소 짓다, 기쁨으로 빛나다 **modestly** 겸손하게, 얌전하게 **catch sight of** 흘끗[언뜻] 보다

실전 모의고사 11

본문 p.153

18 ⑤	19 ④	20 ②	21 ②	22 ②	23 ⑤	24 ③	25 ③	26 ②	27 ⑤
28 ③	29 ③	30 ①	31 ④	32 ③	33 ①	34 ②	35 ②	36 ④	37 ③
38 ③	39 ⑤	40 ④	41 ④	42 ④	43 ⑤	44 ②	45 ②		

18 글의 목적 ⑤

소재 제설 작업에 대한 주민 협조 요청

해설 도로를 깨끗하고 안전하게 유지하려면 부동산 소유자들이 눈을 도로 쪽으로 밀어내지 말고 사유지 위로 치워야 한다는 내용이므로 글의 목적으로 적절한 것은 ⑤이다.

해석 링컨셔 주민 여러분께
우리 도시의 도로 근로자들은 도로가 깨끗하고 안전하게 유지되도록 책임집니다. 주제문 그러나 눈을 도로에서 자신들의 사유지 위로 날려 보내거나, 삽으로 퍼내거나, 치워줄 수 있는 부동산 소유자분들의 도움도 필요합니다. 저희는 또한 부동산 소유자분들께서 도시 조례 7조 1항을 명심해 주시기를 요청합니다. 이 조례는 거주자들이 자신의 사유지에 있는 눈을 도로 위로 치우는 것을 금지합니다. 길 위에 쌓인 눈은 재빨리 얼음 더미로 굳는데, 이것은 제설 차량의 운전사들이 쉽게 감지할 수 없습니다. 트럭의 제설기가 얼음을 치게 되면 제설기가 트럭에서 뜯겨 나갈 수 있고, 그러면 트럭이 제어할 수 없는 상태로 회전할 수도 있습니다. 단단히 굳은 얼음은 도로를 이용하는 모든 이에게 똑같이 위험하므로 여러분의 도로를 깨끗이 유지해서 저희에게 도움을 주시기 바랍니다.
관리부 부장 Jim Mckay 드림

구문 [9행~11행] *Snow* (deposited on the roads) / quickly compacts into *mounds of ice*, // **which** cannot easily be detected by our snowplow drivers.
(Snow: S, compacts: V)
which 이하는 mounds of ice를 보충 설명하는 계속적 용법의 관계대명사절이다.

어휘 **resident** 주민; 거주하는 **property** 부동산, 소유지; 재산 **blow** 날려 보내다; (입으로) 불다 **shovel** 삽으로 뜨다 **plow** (도로 등을) 제설하다; 제설기 *cf.* **snowplow** 제설기, 제설차 **bear in mind** 명심하다, 유념하다 **prohibit A from v-ing** A가 v하는 것을 금지하다 **deposit** 퇴적시키다; 놓다; 맡기다 **compact** (단단히) 다지다; 조밀한; 소형의 **mound** 더미; 흙무더기 **detect** 발견하다, 탐지하다 **rip off** 뜯어내다, 벗겨내다 **hazardous** 위험한

19 심경 변화 ④

소재 비버 댐에서 새끼 곰과 마주친 일화

해설 Matt는 덤불에서 정체를 알 수 없는 소리를 듣고 '두려워(frightened)' 팔의 털이 곤두서고 숨을 거의 쉴 수 없을 정도였으나, 소리를 낸 것이 작은 새끼 곰이었음을 알게 된 후 '긴장이 풀려(relaxed)' 웃을 만한 상황으로 바뀌었다.

해석 소년들은 비버 댐에 다시 가기로 결정했다. Matt는 Attean의 뒤쪽에서 걷고 있었는데, 그때 Attean이 갑자기 멈춰 섰다. Matt는 아무것도 이상한 점을 볼 수 없어 말을 하려고 입을 열었는데, Attean이 재빨리 손을 들어 올려 Matt를 조용히 시켰다. 그때 앞에 있는 덤불에서 소리가 들렸다. 그것은 뱀이나 덫에 걸린 동물의 그것(=소리) 같지는 않았다. 이것은 천천히 무겁게 움직이는 무언가의 움직임이었다. 주제문 그는 팔의 털이 곤두서는 것을 느낄 수 있었다. 그는 자신의 근육을 단단하게 하고, 거의 숨을 쉬지 않으면서 Attean의 옆에 섰다. 낮은 덤불이 옆으로 휘어졌다. 나뭇잎 사이로 갈색 머리가 쑥 나왔다. 강아지의 그것(=머리)보다 컸고, 두터운 털로 덮여 있었다. 그것은 작은 새끼 곰이었다. Matt는 작은 눈이 호기심에 그들을 들여다보고, 갈색 코는 인간 소년의 낯선 냄새로 찡그려지는 것을 볼 수 있었다. 주제문 그 작은 동물은 너무나 웃기게 생겨서 Matt는 거의 크게 웃을 뻔했다.

① 걱정하는 → 짜증 난
② 안도한 → 긴장한
③ 부러워하는 → 기쁜
⑤ 기대하는 → 실망한

구문 [12행] (The head was) Bigger than **that** of a dog, / and (it was) covered in thick fur.
(that = the head)
주어와 be동사가 의미상 추론 가능하므로 생략되었고, that은 반복을 피하기 위하여 사용된 대명사이다.

[13행~15행] Matt could **see** *the little eyes* **peering** at them curiously, *the brown nose* **wrinkling** at the strange smell of human boy.
(see: V, the little eyes: O1, peering ~: C1, the brown nose: O2, wrinkling ~: C2)
「지각동사 see+O+C」 구조이며, 동작을 강조하기 위해 목적격보어 자리에 현재분사가 쓰였다.

어휘 **halt** 멈추다 **unusual** 이상한(↔ **usual** 평소의, 일반적인) **underbrush** 덤불 **stir** (약간) 움직이다; 휘젓다 **scarcely** 거의 ~ 않는 **thrust (through)** 밀치고 나아가다 **cub** (육식 포유동물의) 새끼 **peer** 자세히 들여다보다, 응시하다; 동료 **wrinkle** 찡그리다, (얼굴에) 주름을 잡다; 주름

20 필자 주장 ②

소재 민주주의와 경제 성장의 관계

해설 민주주의는 경제 성장에 유리한 체제일 수 있지만 민주주의 국가라고 해서 모두 경제 성장을 이루는 것은 아니며, 전제 국가나 1당 관료제 국가가 경제 성장을 이루는 경우에서 볼 수 있듯이 민주주의가 경제 성장을 보장하는 것은 아니라는 내용이므로, 필자의 주장으로 가장 적절한 것은 ②이다.

해석 민주주의는 개인들이 안전한 환경에서 자신의 경제적 목표를 추구할 수 있고 실제로 그렇게 하도록 장려받는 것을 보장하는 패키지의 일부이다. 그러므로 그것은 경제적인 성공, 그리고 그에 따른 군사적 성공을 가져오는 경향이 있다. 주제문 그러나 민주주의가 자동으로 경제 성장을 가져오지 않는다는 점은 확실하다. 1930년대 미국의 경기 침체를 포함하여 경제적 하강이 있었던 민주 사회의 역사상 시기를 집어내는 것이 가능하다. 둘째로, 놀라운 경제 성장을 보이는 오늘날의 중국에서처럼 대부분의 민주 국가보다 일시적으로 더 성공한 전제 국가의 형태가 있다. 싱가포르, 혹은 몇몇 사람들이 주장하기로 일본과 같은 1당 관료제 국가가 있는데, 이 국가들은 (민주주의라는) 단어의 보통의 의미에서의 민주주의 없이 놀라운 성장을 거두어 왔다. 주제문 그러므로 민주주의가 (경제) 성장의 보증도 아니고 유일한 길도 아니다.

구문 [6행~9행] **It** is possible **to point** to *periods* (in the history of democratic societies, / including the recession in the United States in the 1930s), // **where** there has been economic decline.
It은 가주어이고 to point ~ economic decline 전체가 진주어이다. where 이하의 관계사절은 periods를 부연 설명한다.

[15행~17행] So democracy is **neither** a guarantee of growth **nor** is it the only path.
「neither A nor B」는 'A도 아니고 B도 아니다'의 뜻이다. nor는 부정어이므로 뒤에 「동사(is)+주어(it)」 어순으로 도치되었다.

어휘 **pursue** 추구하다 **generate** 일으키다; 발생시키다 **hence** 따라서 **recession** 불경기, 불황 **autocracy** 전제 국가[정치] **temporarily** 일시적으로 **bureaucratic** 관료 정치의; 관료의 **extraordinary** 놀라운, 비범한 **guarantee** 보증(서) **path** 길, 경로

21 밑줄 함의 ②

소재 질병에 대한 표준 지침의 허점

해설 질병에 대한 표준 지침이 일정 조건에 있는 대부분의 사람들에게 효과가 있을지라도 모든 개개인에게 완벽하게 적용될 수는 없다는 내용의 글이다. 'None of us is us.'에서 첫 번째 us는 '일반적인 보통 사람들'을, 두 번째 us는 실험이 가정한 '통제된 상황의 표준 집단'을 나타낸다. 따라서 '우리들 중 누구도 우리가 아니다.'라는 말은 ② '질병에 대한 지침이 모두에게 효과가 있는 것은 아니다.'라는 의미를 포함한다.

해석 〈뉴욕 타임스〉지에 실린 Barry Meier의 최근 기사는 같은 병을 앓고 있는 다른 환자들을 치료하는 지침을 정하는 것의 문제점을 논했다. 예를 들어, 당뇨병에 대한 하나의 일련의 지침을 만드는 것이 돈은 절약해줄지 몰라도, 어떤 사람들은 다른 사람들에게는 도움이 되는 치료로 인하여 심각한 건강상의 결과를 겪게 될 것이다. 지침을 바꾸거나 일부 사람들이 주장하는 대로 더 엄격한 연구를 요구하는 것으로는 이 문제가 사라지지 않을 것이다. 지침이 근거를 두고 있는 연구가 아무리 정확해도, 일부 사람들은 고통을 겪게 될 것이다. 의학적 연구에는 복용량, 투여 횟수, 연구 대상 집단, 환경, 질병의 고통에 대한 정의 등 숨겨진 결정들이 있으며, 여기에 대하여 이러한 것들 중 어느 하나라도 약간만 바꾸면 연구 결과가 바뀔 수 있다. 연구는 오직 확률만을 산출할 뿐이지 절대적인 사실을 산출하지는 않는다. 주제문 자료가 단지 표준적(즉, 같은 환경에 있는 대부분의 사람들에게 사실일 수 있다는 것)이라는 점을 고려하면, 확실히 어떤 사람들에게는 그것이 사실이 아닌 것으로 입증될 것이다. 우리들 중 누구도 우리가 아니다.

① 우리는 건강에 대한 부정적인 사고방식을 없애야 한다.
③ 우리의 건강을 평가하기 위해 사용되는 지침은 일시적이다.
④ 건강을 다루기 위해 새로운 지침을 채택할 필요가 있다.
⑤ 환자들은 유용한 의학적 혁신을 더 빠르게 접할 기회를 가져야 한다.

구문 [9행~11행] **No matter how** accurate *the research* is [that the guidelines are based on], // some people will suffer.
「no matter how+형용사/부사+S+V」는 '~가 아무리 …하더라도'의 뜻이다. [ ]는 the research를 수식하는 관계사절이다.

어휘 **diabetes** 당뇨병 **rigorous** 엄격한, 철저한 **dosage** 복용량 **administer** (약을) 투여하다; 관리하다 **population** 집단, 개체군; 인구 **severity** 고통, 쓰라림; 격렬함 **yield** 산출하다; 양도하다 **probability** 확률 **absolute** 절대적인 **given that** ~을 고려하면 **normative** 표준적인

22 글의 요지 ②

소재 모서리 없는 공간의 편안함

해설 날카로운 모서리를 없앤 공간이 얼마나 자유로울지 상상해 보라고 한 후, 곡선 형태의 공간이 더 자연에 가깝고 편안함을 준다고 이야기하고 있으므로 글의 요지로 적절한 것은 ②이다.

해석 주택에서도 아파트에서도 마찬가지로, 우리는 상자로 시작하고 그 속에 모든 것을 맞추어 넣는다. 상자 안에 또 상자 (이런 식으로). 그것이 어떻게 여러분이 생활하는 거리, 동네, 기찻길, 기타 등등의 밖으로까지도 적용되는지 생각해 보라. 날카로운 모서리를 없애 버리고 모든 것을 더 매끄럽게 만들면 얼마나 자유로울지 상상해 보라. 다음에 여러분이 비행기를 탔을 때, 창밖으로 그 그리드(=격자 모양으로 나 있는 거리나 구역)를 내려다보며, 그것이 우리가 살아가는 데 정말 이상적인 방식인지 생각해 보라. 모든 선이 곡선이라면 어떨까? 이음매가 없는 것이 가능한데 교차점을 만들 이유가 무엇인가? 모서리는 마찰의 접점이며, 먼지가 모이는 곳이다. 이제 각지지 않은 객실이 있는 비행기 내부를 생각해 보라. 그것이 불러일으키는 편안한 누에고치 같은 느낌에 대해 생각해 보라. 주제문 모서리와 직각이 없는 것이 더 편한 공간을 만드는 데 도움이 된다. 자연에는 직각이 없다. 빈 백 의자와 태내(胎內) 같은 공간에서 편안함을 찾을 수 있음을 우리는 안다. 왜 그에 맞서려 하나?

구문 [4행~6행] Imagine // how liberating it would feel **to eliminate** the sharp edges and (to) **make** everything more seamless.
(it: 가주어, to eliminate: 진주어)
가주어 it이 진주어 to eliminate ~ more seamless를 대신한다. to eliminate ~와 (to) make ~는 and로 병렬 연결되었다.

어휘 **liberating** 해방감을 느끼게 하는 **eliminate** 제거하다 **edge** 모서리, 끝 **seamless** (끊김 없이) 아주 매끄러운; 이음매 없는 **grid** 그리드, 격자 (무늬) **intersection** 교차점; 교차로 **friction** 마찰; 갈등 **angleless** 각이 없는 **cocoon-like** 누에고치 같은 **evoke** (감정·기억을) 불러일으키다, 환기시키다 **absence** 없음; 부재, 결석 **right angle** 직각 **make for** ~에 도움이 되다[기여하다] **casual** 편한; 평상시의; 우연한 **womb-like** 태내(胎內) 같은

23 글의 주제 ⑤

소재 공적인 감정 표현과 사적인 감정 표현의 차이

해설 공적인 감정 표현과 사적인 감정 표현이 다를 수 있다는 내용으로, 'This split between our public and private emotional lives'가 글의 주제를 명시적으로 보여준다. 따라서 정답은 ⑤ '공적인 그리고 사적인 감정생활 사이의 차이'이다.

해석 어떤 의미에서 감정 표현은 극장과 같다. 주제문 우리 모두에게는 감정을 느끼는 숨겨진 장소인 무대 뒤편과, 우리가 드러내기로 선택한 감정들을 보여 주는 사회적 영역인 무대 앞 공간이 있다. 우리의 공적인 그리고 사적인 감정생활 사이의 이러한 분리는 매장에서 일하는 직원이 손님들을 대할 때 행동이 어떻게 변하는지와 비슷하다. 감정 표현은 고객들과 상호 작용할 때 더 흔히 주의 깊게 관리되며, 무대 뒤편에서는 덜 관리되는데, 이 차이는 (고객의 입장에서) 당혹스러울 수 있다. 큰 주일학교의 교장은 그 설교가 영감을 주고 진지하게 생각하게 하는 목사에 대해 나에게 불평했다. "그는 표현력이 완전히 부족하고 또한 매우 이해하기 어려워요. 저는 그가 제게 말하는 것의 많은 부분을 어떻게 받아들여야 할지 모르겠어요. 그와 함께 일하는 것이 너무 힘들어요." 적절하게 감정을 표현하는 데 서투른 것은 중대한 장애가 될 수도 있을 것이다.

① 무대에서 감정을 조절하는 다양한 방법들
② 우리가 감정을 드러내는 것이 어렵다고 느끼는 이유
③ 사람들 앞에서 사적인 감정을 숨길 필요성
④ 감정을 적절하게 표현하는 것의 건강상의 이점

구문 [1행~4행] We all have a backstage, *the hidden zone* [where we feel our emotions], and a stage front, *the social arena* [where we present *the emotions* [(that[which]) we choose to reveal]].
where가 이끄는 두 개의 관계부사절이 각각 앞의 the hidden zone과 the social arena를 수식한다. a backstage와 the hidden zone, a stage front와 the social arena은 서로 동격이다.

어휘 **backstage** 무대 뒤; 사생활 **arena** 활약 무대; 경기장, 공연장 **split** 쪼개짐; 나누다 **interact** 상호 작용하다 **unfortunate** 당혹스러운; 유감스러운; 불운한 **minister** 성직자; 장관 **sermon** 설교 **inspiring** 영감을 주는; 고무하는, 자극하는 **thought-provoking** 진지하게 생각하게 하는 **unexpressive** 표현력이 부족한 **appropriately** 적절하게; 어울리게 **handicap** 장애; 불리한 조건 [선택지 어휘] **conceal** 숨기다

24 글의 제목 ③

소재 가설 검증을 위한 반복 실험

해설 일회적 실험 결과는 단지 우연의 산물일 수도 있으므로, 과학자는 실험을 여러 번 되풀이해야 하고 다른 과학자들의 검증도 받아야 한다는 내용이므로 제목으로 가장 적절한 것은 ③ '과학: 가설 검증을 위한 실험의 반복'이다.

해석 실험은 때때로 전적으로 우연히 발생하여 되풀이될 수 없는 결과를 내놓는다. 그러므로 가설을 받아들이기 전에 연구자들은 결과가 타당하다는 것을 확신하기 위하여 그 실험을 여러 번 되풀이한다. 가설이 타당하여 인정되기 위해서는 별도로 연구하는 또

다른 과학자가 같은 실험을 되풀이하여 본질적으로 똑같은 결과를 낼 수 있어야 한다. 다른 변수들이 간과되지 않았다는 점을 확실히 하기 위하여 대안 실험 역시 행해져야 한다. 여러 다른 접근법들이 가설이 틀렸음을 입증하는 데 실패할 경우에만 그것은 정확하다고 생각될 것이다. 그때조차도, 그 가설의 인정은 새로운 정보가 밝혀지면 변경의 대상이 된다. 주제문 따라서 과학자의 목표는 무언가를 입증하는 것이 아니라, 조사되고 있는 현상의 더욱 정확한 설명을 성취하기 위해 그것을 여러 번 실험하는 것이다.

① 실험을 설계하기 위한 과학적 방법의 사용
② 관찰: 가설 형성의 전제 조건
④ 결정적인 하나의 실험이 가설을 이론으로 만든다
⑤ 과학은 과정이 아니라 결론에 관한 것이다

구문 [5행~8행] *Another scientist* (working separately) must be able to repeat the same experiments and (to) get essentially the same results / *for a hypothesis* to be valid and accepted.
to repeat ~ experiments와 (to) get ~ results 부분은 and로 연결된 병렬구조이며, for a hypothesis는 to be valid and accepted의 의미상 주어이다.

[10행~12행] Only if many different approaches fail to disprove a hypothesis (부사절) will (조동사) it (S) be considered (V) accurate; ~.
Only if ~ 절이 문두로 나오면서 「조동사+주어+동사원형」 어순의 도치가 일어났다.

어휘 **purely** 전적으로, 순전히 **by chance** 우연히 **duplicate** 두 번 되풀이하다; 복사하다 **hypothesis** 가설 **guarantee** (어떤 일이 있을 것임을) 확신하다; 보장하다 **valid** 타당한, 유효한 **essentially** 본질적으로 **alternative** 대안(의) **conduct** 실행하다; 지휘하다; 안내하다 **ensure** 반드시 ~하게 하다 **variable** 변수 **disprove** 틀렸음을 입증하다 **be subject to** ~의 대상이다; ~의 지배를 받다 **come to light** 밝혀지다, 알려지다 **phenomenon** 현상 **investigate** 조사하다 [선택지 어휘] **prerequisite** 전제 조건 **formation** 형성(과정) **decisive** 결정적인; 결단력 있는

25 도표 이해 ③

소재 미국의 학교 폭력 발생률

해설 2009년 이후에 2010년, 2011년, 2013년의 범죄율은 같지만 2012년의 범죄율은 약간 낮다. 따라서 4년 연속 같은 수치를 유지했다는 ③은 틀린 설명이다.

해석 〈미국 학교에서의 폭력 범죄 비율〉
주제문 이 그래프는 미국 학교에서 (발생한) 학생 천 명당 폭력 범죄 비율을 보여준다. 이 자료는 2007년부터 2017년까지 (범위를) 아우르며 12세에서 18세 사이의 학생들을 포함한다. ① 2007년부터 2009년까지 폭력 범죄 비율은 천 명당 학생 피해자 10명에서 13명으로 꾸준히 상승했다. ② 하지만 일반적으로 믿는 것과 달리, 학교에서의 폭력 범죄는 2009년 이후로 두 번의 작은 상승에도 불구하고 전반적으로 급격히 하락했다. ③ 낮아진 범죄율은 2009년 이후에 4년 연속 같은 수준을 유지했다. ④ 그 비율은 계속해서 떨어져 2015년 가장 낮은 수치에 도달했지만, 2016년에는 다시 조금 상승했다. ⑤ 2017년의 폭력 범죄 비율은 2009년 비율의 반에도 미치지 못했다.

어휘 **crime** 범죄 **steadily** 꾸준히 **victim** 피해자, 희생자 **dramatically** 급격하게, 극적으로 **despite** ~에도 불구하고 **consecutive** 연속적인 **go on to-v** 계속해서 V하다

26 내용 불일치 ②

소재 사향소

해설 사향소는 비바람을 막아주는 외피가 있어 추위를 신경 쓰지 않으며, 추위를 피하기 위해서가 아니라 먹이를 찾기 위해 무리 지어 다닌다고 했으므로 ②가 글의 내용과 일치하지 않는다.

해석 ① 사향소는 수컷이 내뿜는 사향(麝香) 같은 향에서 그 이름을 얻었는데, 그 향은 수소의 눈 아래에 있는 샘에서 만들어진다. 수컷과 암컷 둘 다 2피트까지 이를 수 있는 뿔을 가지고 있다. 사향소는 북극의 기후를 신경 쓰지 않는데, 왜냐하면 그들의 외피는 '모든 비바람을 막아주는' 보증을 갖춰 나오기 때문이다. ② 사향소는 충분한 먹이를 찾기 위해 20에서 30마리의 무리를 이루어 다닌다. 공격을 받으면, 다 자란 소들은 새끼들을 안에 안전하게 두며 원을 형성할 것이다. ③ 다 자란 소들은 바깥을 향하고 그들의 날카로운 뿔을 적에게 대항하는 무기로 사용할 것이다. ④ 사향소는 내부 열 생산을 증대시키기 위해 대량의 먹이를 먹으며 풀, 이끼와 버드나무를 먹고 산다. 수소들은 한 소가 멀리 가버릴 때까지 그들의 머리를 함께 격렬하게 들이받음으로써 번식 권리를 얻으려 경쟁할 것이다. ⑤ 수소가 일반적으로 암소보다 수명이 짧은 것은 놀랍지 않다!

구문 [1행~3행] The musk ox gets its name from *the musk-like perfume* [(which[that]) the male gives off], // **which** is produced by glands beneath the bull's eyes.
[ ]는 앞에 목적격 관계대명사 which[that]가 생략되었으며 the musk-like perfume을 수식한다. which는 the musk-like perfume을 지칭하며 which 이하는 the musk-like perfume에 대한 추가적인 설명을 제시한다.

[8행~9행] When (they are) attacked, the adults will form a circle **with** *the young* **safe** inside.
When과 attacked 사이에 they(= the adults) are가 생략되어 있다. 「with+O+형용사」는 'O가 ~한 채로'의 뜻이다.

어휘 **ox** 소, 황소(복수형 **oxen**) **give off** 내뿜다 **gland** (분비)선(腺), 샘 **horn** 뿔 **mind** 신경 쓰다; 싫어하다, 꺼리다 **Arctic** 북극의 **outfit** 차림; 의복; 장비 **weatherproof** 비바람을 막아주는 **warranty** 보증(서) **herd** (짐승의) 무리, 떼 **adequate** 충분한; 적절한 **internal** 내부의(↔ **external** 외부의) **feed on** ~을 먹고 살다 **lichen** 이끼 **willow** 버드나무 **breeding** 번식 **life span** 수명

27 안내문 불일치 ⑤

소재 강연 및 책 사인회 행사

해설 〈Love〉는 책 사인회 행사에서 판매될 것이라고 했으므로 ⑤가 안내문의 내용과 일치하지 않는다.

해석

현대 사진 예술 센터

아티스트의 강연 및 책 사인회
작가: Joyce Evans
① 시간: 11월 18일 화요일 오후 6시~7시 30분
장소: MPAC(현대 사진 예술 센터)의 White Space
입장료: 무료

후원자 파티
시간: 11월 18일 화요일 오후 8시~9시 30분
입장료: 1인당 75달러, 또는 ② 2인 125달러

③ Joyce Evans는 그녀의 최신작 〈Love〉를 선보일 뿐만 아니라 순수 예술가이자 사진 편집 작가로서의 자신의 경력과 작품에 대해 이야기할 것입니다. ④ 〈Love〉는 9년간에 걸쳐 그녀의 아이들과 함께 찍은 어머니 시절/어린 시절 프로젝트의 몹시 친밀한 사진들을 보여줍니다. 강연 후에 책 사인회가 이어지며 그 행사에서 ⑤ 〈Love〉가 판매될 것입니다. 자리를 예약하려면 신청서 양식을 작성해주세요.

구문 [12행~14행] Joyce Evans will discuss her career and work as a fine artist ~ (A) **as well as** introduce her most recent book, *Love*. (B)
「A as well as B」는 'B뿐만 아니라 A도'의 의미로 「not only B but (also) A」와 같다.

어휘 **book signing** 책 사인회 **patron** 후원자 **editorial** 편집(상)의; 사설[논설](의) **intensely** 몹시, 강렬하게 **intimate** 친밀한 **complete** 작성하다; 완료하다; 완전한

28 안내문 일치 ③

소재 음악 축제 안내

해설 캠핑 입장권 하나당 캠핑장 출입 손목 밴드를 4개 제공한다고 했으므로 ③이 안내문의 내용과 일치한다.

해석

Valley 음악 축제

① Valley 음악 축제가 밴쿠버에서 북쪽으로 약 45분 정도이고 휘슬러에서 남쪽으로 30분 거리에 위치한 Centennial Field에서 열립니다.

(음악) 축제 입장권
② 페스티벌 입장권은 환불되지 않으며, 세금과 요금이 포함된 정가는 여러분이 구입하시기 전에 공개될 것입니다.

캠핑
캠핑장 이용이 가능하며, ③ 캠핑 입장권 한 장에 10'×12' 크기의 땅과 캠핑장 출입 손목 밴드 4개를 드립니다.

④ 매표소 시간
8월 8일 금요일 오후 2시~오후 10시
8월 9일 토요일 정오~오후 10시
8월 10일 일요일 정오~오후 10시

개장 시간
금요일 오후 5시 — ⑤ 매일 개장 후 두세 시간 후에 음악회가 시작됩니다. 정확한 시간은 음악 축제가 열리기 전 주중에 게시될 것입니다.

어휘 **valley** 계곡 **take place** 개최하다 **approximately** 대략 **non-refundable** 환불되지 않는 **plot** 조그마한 땅; 음모, 계획; 줄거리 **wristband** 손목 밴드 **box office** 매표소 **exact** 정확한 **post** 게시[공고]하다 **prior to** ~ 이전에

29 밑줄 어법 ③

소재 피드백이 기분에 미치는 영향

해설 ③ whether ~ partners가 문장의 주어이므로 이에 대한 문장의 동사가 필요하다. 또한 문맥상 과거시제로 쓰여야 하므로 making을 made로 바꾸어 써야 한다.

오답 분석 ① performance의 주체는 an expert가 아니고 participants이기 때문에 복수형 소유격 their가 적절하다. ② 문제(question)가 '연구하는' 것이 아닌 '연구되는' 것이므로 수동의 의미를 나타내는 과거분사 investigated가 적절히 쓰였다. ④ 선행사 the only thing을 수식하는 주격 관계대명사 that이 적절히 쓰였다. ⑤ 비교급 형용사 worse를 강조하는 부사로 쓰여 적절하다.

해석 한 연구에서, 참가자들은 동영상 강의를 만들어 달라는 요청을 받았다. 한 '전문가'가 참가자들의 (강의) 수행에 대해 상세한 피드백을 주었다. 참가자들은 같은 과제를 수행하는 파트너 한 명과 함께 (강의를) 실시했다. 연구되고 있던 문제는, 피드백이 참가자들의 기분에 어떻게 영향을 미치는가 하는 것이었다. 주제문 행복을 느끼는 사람들은 그들의 파트너에게 주어지는 피드백을 그들이 들었는지 아닌지가 영향을 미치지 않았다. 대조적으로, 불행을 느끼는 사람들은 매우 많은 영향을 받았다. 한 참가자가 긍정적인 피드백을 받았는데, 그녀의 파트너가 더 좋은 피드백을 받았다면, 그 참가자의 기분은 더 나빠졌다. 이와 같이 불행을 느끼는 사람들에게 중요한 유일한 것은 마치 그들이 그들의 파트너와 비교해서 어떻게 했나인 것처럼 보였다. 당신은 상당히 훌륭한 교사이지만 다른 교사들이 더 훌륭하다는 말을 듣는 것보다, 당신은 상당히 능력 없는 교사이지만 다른 교사들이 훨씬 더 능력 없다는 말을 듣는 것이 더 낫다.

구문 [14행~17행] (It is) **Better** to be told // that you're a pretty bad teacher but that others are even worse **than** to be told // that you're a pretty good teacher but that others are better.

가주어 It과 be동사 is가 생략된 비교급 구문으로 to be told that ~ even worse와 to be told that ~ are better를 비교한다. be told의 목적어로 각각 두 개의 that절이 but에 의해 병렬구조로 연결되어 있다.

어휘 **expert** 전문가 **detailed** 상세한 **alongside** ~와 함께; ~ 옆에 **investigate** 연구[조사]하다 **make no difference** 영향을 미치지 않다, 차이가 없다 **affect** 영향을 미치다 **in comparison to** ~와 비교해서

30 네모 어휘 ①

소재 나쁜 습관을 없애려는 접근법의 문제점

해설 (A) 나쁜 습관을 없애고자 하는 우리의 접근법의 문제점을 다루고 있으므로 접근법에 '결함이 있다(faulty)'는 것이 문맥상 적절하다. desirable은 '바람직한'이란 뜻이다.
(B) 뒷문장에서 나쁜 습관을 없애는 것이 삶에 '상실감'을 만들어낸다고 했는데, 이는 '박탈감(deprivation)'과 의미가 통한다. satisfaction은 '만족감'이란 뜻이다.
(C) 한때 즐거움을 제공했던 나쁜 습관을 삶에서 제거하는 것은 상실감을 만들어내고, 그 상실감을 채우기 위해 곧 옛날 행동으로 돌아가게 되므로 이러한 종류의 변화는 '지속 가능하지(sustainable)' 않다. temporary는 '일시적인'이란 뜻이다.

해석 우리에게 몇 가지 나쁜 습관이 있다는 것을 우리는 안다. 그것들이 없으면 우리가 더 나을 것이라는 것도 우리는 안다. 우리는 변하려고 여러 번 모두 노력해 왔고 성공의 정도는 다양했다. 하지만 그 변화는 충분히 깊거나 지속된 적이 한 번도 없었다. 주제문 문제는 이 문제에 달려드는 우리의 접근법에 (A) 결함이 있다는 것이다. 우리는 나쁜 습관을 들이고 그것을 하는 것을 멈추려고 그저 열심히 노력하는 경향이 있다. 우리는 무언가를 하지 않으려고 우리의 모든 의지를 모은다. 이것이 우리 마음속에 (B) 박탈감을 만들어낸다. 우리는 그것(=잘못된 행동)을 즐겼기 때문에 잘못된 행동이 무엇이든 했다. 그러니까 우리는 실제로 즐거움을 제공했던 어떤 것을 제거하고 있고, 우리 삶에서 상실감을 만들어내고 있는 것이다. 당연히 이런 종류의 변화는 (C) 지속 가능하지 않다. 조만간에 우리는 그 상실감을 다시 채워야 할 것이고 필연적으로 그 옛날 행동으로 돌아갈 것인데, 그것이 우리가 그 상실감을 채울 수 있는 유일한 방법이기 때문이다.

구문 [10행~11행] We did **whatever** the wrong behavior was // because we enjoyed **it**.
whatever ~ was는 did의 목적어이며 whatever는 '~한 것이면 무엇이든지'의 뜻이다. it은 whatever ~ behavior was를 지칭한다.

어휘 **be better off** 더 잘되다 **degree** 정도; 등급; (온도 따위의) 도(度) **lasting** 오래 가는, 영속하는 **approach** 접근법; 접근하다 **attack** 덤벼들다; 공격하다 **will** 의지 **sooner or later** 조만간, 머잖아 **inevitably** 필연적으로

31 빈칸 추론 ④

소재 감정 발생의 필요조건인 '동일시'

해설 신문에서 먼 나라의 비극적인 소식을 읽으면 슬픔을 느끼더라도 그 슬픔이 오래 지속되지는 않는데, 이는 동정심이 없어서가 아니라 비극적인 소식에 감정적으로 연결되는 개인적인 ④ '동일시(identification)' 과정이 일어나지 않았기 때문이라고 추론할 수 있다.

해석 주제문 부정적인 감정을 위한 핵심적 필요조건은 동일시이다. 이것은 당신이 일을 개인적으로 받아들인다는 것을 의미한다. 당신은 발생한 일을 당신에 대한 개인적인 공격으로 해석한다. 당신 자신을 부정적인 상황과 개인적으로 연관 지을 수 없다면, 당신은 그것에 대해 긍정적이든 부정적이든 어떠한 감정도 생성하는 데 어려움을 겪을 것이다. 신문에서 천 명의 사람들(남성, 여성, 그리고 어린이)이 중국 북부에서 홍수에 휩쓸려 익사했다는 것을 신문에서 읽는다면, 당신은 어떤 슬픔을 느끼고 나서 십중팔구 거의 혹은 아무런 감정 없이 페이지를 휙 넘겨 다음 주제로 넘어갈 것이다. 당신이 (사고의) 영향을 받은 사람들 중 누구도 알지 못하거나 심지어 세계의 그 지역에 관해 많이 알지 못하므로, 당신은 그 비극과 동일시하지 않는다. 그 결과 당신은 그것에 대해 어떠한 부정적인 감정도 경험하지 않는다. 이것은 당신이 다른 누군가의 경험이나 아픔에 연민을 느끼지 못한다는 의미가 아니라, 당신이 감정적으로 관여하게 되지 않았음을 의미한다.
① 부인 ② 기만 ③ 성찰 ⑤ 합리화

구문 [7행~12행] **If** you **read** in the paper that a thousand people ~ drowned by a flood in northern China, you **would feel** some sorrow ~ no emotion.
「If+S'+과거동사 ~, S+would+동사원형 ...」의 가정법 과거 구문으로 '~한다면 …할 것이다'로 해석한다.

어휘 **requirement** 필요조건, 요건 **interpret** 해석하다 **associate A with B** A를 B와 연관 짓다 **generate** 생성하다, 발생시키다 **drown** 익사하다 **sorrow** 슬픔 **flip** (책장을) 휙 넘기다 **equate with** ~와 동일시하다 **compassion** 연민, 동정심 **involved** 관여하는, 관련된

32 빈칸 추론 ③

소재 유년기 기억상실의 이유

해설 빈칸 문장에서 언어활동 이전의 기억은 '어떠하지' 않을 경우에 소실되는지 파악해야 한다. 유년기 기억상실(childhood amnesia)은 아이들이 어떤 사건을 말로 표현할 수 있는 능력의 유무에 달려 있다는 내용이므로, 언어활동 이전의 기억은 ③ '언어로 옮겨지지' 않을 때 소실된다는 것을 추론할 수 있다.

해석 우리 대부분은 삶의 첫 3~4년에 대한 아무런 기억이 없다. '유년기 기억상실'이라 알려진 그 현상은 한 세기가 넘도록 심리학자들을 당황하게 해왔고 우리는 여전히 그것을 충분히 이해하지 못한다. 그러나 한 가지 답을 시사해주는 연구가 시작되고 있다. 즉, 자서전적인 기억은 아마도 우리가 서로에게 들려주는 이야기들로 시작될지도 모른다는 것이다. 한 아이가 어떤 사건이 일어난 시점에서 그 사건에 대해 말로 표현할 수 있는 능력이 그들이 몇 달 혹은 몇 년 뒤에도 그것을 얼마나 잘 기억하는지를 예측해 준다는 것은 어느 정도 사실이다. 한 연구 집단은 흔한 유년기 부상으로 사고가 나서 응급실에 실려 온 유아들을 면담하는 것으로 이 연구를 수행했다. 사건 당시 그것에 관해 말할 수 있었던 26개월이 넘은 유아들은 그것을 5년 후에도 기억해냈지만, 반면 사건에 관해 말을 못했던 26개월 미만의 유아들은 거의 또는 전혀 기억해내지 못했다. 주제문 이것은 아이가 말을 하기 이전의 기억이 언어로 옮겨지지 않을 경우 소실된다는 것을 시사해 준다.
① 또래들과 공유되지
② 트라우마와 관련되지
④ 정기적으로 기록되지
⑤ 장기 기억으로 부호화되지

구문 [7행~10행] It(가주어) is true to some extent that(진주어) ^{S}*a child's ability* (to verbalize about an event at *the time* [**that** it happened]) ^{V}predicts ^{O}how well they remember it months or years later.
It은 가주어이고 that ~ years later가 진주어이다. 진주어절 내에서 주어는 to부정사구의 수식을 받아 길어졌고, 동사는 predicts, 목적어는 간접의문문인 how well ~ later이다. [ ] 부분은 선행사 the time을 수식해주는 관계사절로, 관계부사 when을 대신해 that이 쓰였다.

어휘 **phenomenon** (복수형 **phenomena**) 현상 **puzzle** 당황하게[어리둥절하게] 하다 **suggest** 시사하다; 제시[제안]하다 **autobiographical** 자서전적인 **to some extent** 어느 정도까지는 **verbalize** 말로 표현하다 **conduct** 수행(하다); 행동(하다); 지휘하다; (열 · 전기 · 소리 등을) 전도하다 **toddler** 유아, 아장아장 걷는 아기 **emergency department** 응급실 **recall** 기억해내다; 회수하다 **whereas** 반면에 **preverbal** 아이가 말을 하기 이전의 [선택지 어휘] **peer** 또래 (집단); 동료 **associated with** ~와 관련된 **trauma** 트라우마, 정신적 외상; 충격적인 경험 **encode** 부호화하다, 암호로 바꾸다

33 빈칸 추론 ①

소재 소비자의 충동소비에 의존하는 판매 전략

해설 To this end부터 충동구매를 유도하는 전략들을 제시하고 있으므로 판매자들의 전략이 의존하는 것은 ① '충동소비에 대한 우리의 나약함'이라 할 수 있다.

해석 주제문 소매상점, 광고업, 마케팅 전략들은 충동소비에 대한 우리의 나약함에 상당히 의존한다. 그것(=충동소비에 대한 우리의 나약함)이 바로, 두어 가지 전략을 예로 들자면, 팝업 광고와 정보성 광고가 우리에게 매우 효과적으로 영향을 미치는 이유 중 하나이다. 판매자들은 우리를 전적으로 완벽히 지배하고, 그들은 구매자의 심리와 의지력이 발휘될 가망성이 전혀 없다는 것을 알고 있다. 이를 실현하기 위해 계산대 쪽에 마음을 끄는 간식거리가 손쉽게 닿을 수 있는 위치에 놓이며, 웹사이트에서는 당신이 상품 하나를 장바구니에 담자마자 할인가의 다른 상품들을 곧바로 추천해주고, 마네킹들은 같이 연출하면 매우 잘 어울려서 당신이 통째로 구매할 수밖에 없는 옷과 장신구로 꾸며진다. 소매상인들은 당신이 계산대 앞에서 지갑을 손에 들고 있는 경우, 이미 구매하고 있는 물품을 보완해주는 물품 구매에 대해 두 번 생각해보지 않을 것을 알고 있다. 따라서 바로 그 시점에 당신은 점원에게서 '특별 할인'을 받거나 이런 저런 물품도 원하는지 질문을 받게 되는 것이다.
② 쇼핑을 편하게 하려는 우리의 욕구
③ 더 저렴한 가격대의 상점들을 비교하려는 우리의 욕구
④ 소비자의 요구를 이해하기 위한 연구조사
⑤ 적절한 매체에 적절한 광고를 배치하는 타이밍

구문 [7행~13행] ~, tempting snacks are placed ~ at checkout counters; websites instantly suggest ~ **as soon as** you place ~; mannequins are styled in *clothes and accessories* [**that** look **so** good together (**that**) you **simply have to buy** the whole look].
3개의 절이 세미콜론으로 대등하게 연결된 하나의 문장이다. 두 번째 절은 「S+V ~ as soon as ...」의 구조로 '…하자마자 ~하다'의 의미이다. 세 번째 절에서는 that 이하가 clothes and accessories를 수식하며, that절은 「so ~ (that) ...」 구조로 '매우 ~해서 …하다'의 의미이고, 「simply have to-v」는 'v할 수밖에 없다'로 해석한다.

[17행~18행] ~, so **it is** *here* **that** you are given "special offers" by sales clerks and (you are) asked ^{O}**if** you also want this or that.
「it is ~ that ...」 강조구문이 쓰여 부사 here를 강조하고 있다. 여기서 if는 '~인지 아닌지'란 뜻으로 명사절을 이끈다.

어휘 **retail** 소매상(의) *cf.* **retailer** 소매업자 **pop-up ad** (인터넷) 팝업 광고 *cf.* **pop-up** 팝업의, 갑자기 튀어나오는 **infomercial** 인포머셜(**information+commercial**), 정보성 광고(상품에 대한 상세한 정보를 제공하는 광고) **to name but a few** 몇 가지 예를 들어 **work on** ~에 영향을 미치다 **merchandiser** 판매자 **have power over** ~을 지배하다 **willpower** 의지력 **stand no chance (of)** (~할) 가능성이 전혀 없다(=**not stand a chance**) **to this end** 이를 실현하기 위해, 이러한 목적으로 **tempting** 마음을 끄는 **mannequin** 마네킹 **complementary** 상호 보완적인 [선택지 어휘] **on impulse** 충동적으로 *cf.* **impulse** 충동 **appetite** 욕구; 식욕

34 빈칸 추론 ②

소재 감정 교환을 통해 닮아가는 부부

해설 빈칸 문장으로 보아, 매일 감정을 교환하는 것이 '어떠한' 정도로 상대방을 내면화하는지 찾아야 한다. 결혼 생활을 오래하면 서로의 외모가 닮게 되어 남들이 부부임을 쉽게 알아본다는 실험 결과를 통해서, 부부가 매일 감정을 교환하는 것이 ② '누구라도 그들이 얼마나 많이 서로에게 속해 있는지를 알 수 있을' 정도로 서로를 내면화한다는 것을 알 수 있다.

해석 주제문 얼굴 표정과 신체 언어를 통한 기분 전달은 대단히 강력해서 매일 그렇게 하는 사람들은 말 그대로 닮아가기 시작한다. 이것은 오랜 부부들의 인물 사진을 가지고 실험되었다. 한 세트의 사진은 그들의 결혼식 날 찍힌 것이고, 다른 한 세트의 사진은 25년 후에 찍힌 것이었다. 이들 남자와 여자의 각각의 사진을 받은 뒤, 피실험자들은 유사성에 따라 그들을 짝지어 보라고 요청받았다. 노년기에 찍은 사진 세트에서는, 그들은 누가 누구와 결혼했는지 결정하는 데 아무런 문제가 없었다. 하지만 더 젊은 나이에 찍힌 사진에서는, 피실험자들은 그 일에 실패했다. 따라서 부부는 서로 닮아 있는데, 이것은 그들이 자신과 닮은 상대방을 선택하기 때문이 아니라 세월이 흐르면서 그들의 이목구비가 점점 비슷해지기 때문이다. 유사성은 연구에서 가장 큰 행복을 보고한 부부에게서 가장 강했다. 주제문 매일 감정을 교환하는 것은 누구라도 그들이 얼마나 많이 서로에게 속해 있는지를 알 수 있을 정도로 한 사람을 상대방에게 '내면화하도록' 하는 것으로 보이며, 그 반대도 마찬가지이다.

① 신체적인 외모는 그들에게 관심사가 아닐
③ 건강의 부정적인 결과가 개선될 것이라고 예상이 될
④ 그것이 그들로 하여금 상대방이 무슨 생각을 하는지 알게 할
⑤ 그들이 항상 서로의 감정이 다치지 않게 할

구문 [6행~8행] **Presented** with separate portraits of these men and women, / human subjects were asked ~.
Presented ~ women은 수동 분사구문으로 After they were presented ~ women으로 바꿔 쓸 수 있다.

[16행~18행] *Daily sharing* (of emotions) apparently leads one partner to "internalize" the other, ~ / to the point that anyone can see how much they belong together.
the point와 that ~ together는 동격을 나타낸다.

어휘 **transfer** 전달; 이동 **via** ~을 통해[경유하여] **on a daily basis** 매일 **literally** 말 그대로 **portrait** 인물 사진; 초상(화) **separate** 각각의; 분리된 **subject** 피실험자; 주제; 과목 **similarity** 유사(성), 닮은 점 **resemble** 닮다 **feature** 이목구비; 특징 **apparently** 보아[듣자] 하니; 분명히 **internalize** 내면화하다 **vice versa** 그 반대도 마찬가지이다 [선택지 어휘] **appearance** 외모, (겉)모습; 출현, 등장 **outcome** 결과

35 무관한 문장 ②

소재 지구의 자전 속도 계산

해설 지구를 돌면서 햇빛을 놓치지 않고 따라가려면 얼마나 빨리 이동해야 하는지를 계산함으로써 지구의 자전 속도가 얼마나 빠른지를 이해하기 쉽게 설명한 글이다. ②는 태양의 크기를 지구와 비교한 내용이므로 글의 흐름과 무관하다.

해석 주제문 **지구를 돌면서 햇빛을 놓치지 않고 따라가려면 얼마나 빨리 이동해야 할까?** 논쟁의 편의를 위해서 적도에서 이 과제를 수행한다고 가정하고, 다음 계산 방법을 사용한다. 지구의 지름은 12,756킬로미터이고 둘레는 40,074킬로미터이다. 지구의 전체 원둘레가 태양 아래를 하루 안에 통과한다. 만약 태양이 속이 비어 있는 구(球)라면, 약 백만 개의 지구가 그 안에 들어갈 것이다. 하루는 거의 정확히 24시간으로 이루어진다. 그래서 적도에서 지구 표면 위를 이동해야 하는 속도는 하루 (24)시간으로 (지구의) 둘레를 나눈 것이 된다. 그것은 시속 1,670킬로미터가 되는데, 음속의 약 1.33배 혹은 '포뮬러 원' 경주 자동차의 최고 속도보다 5배 이상 빠른 속도이다.

구문 [9행~12행] ~, *the speed* [(that) you would have to travel / over the surface of Earth at the Equator] is *the circumference* (divided by the number of hours in the day).
the speed와 you 사이에 관계부사 that이 생략되었다.

어휘 **travel** 이동하다; 여행하다 **globe** 지구 **assume** 가정하다 **for A's sake** A를 위하여 **equator** 적도 **calculation** 계산 **diameter** 지름, 직경 **sphere** 구(球); 구면 **consist of** ~로 이루어지다 **surface** 표면 **come to** (총계가) ~이 되다

36 글의 순서 ④

소재 개인의 이익에 유리한 협력

해설 이기적으로 보이는 유전자들도 신체 기관의 형성을 위해서는 서로 협력하는 것과 같이, 조직에서도 개인의 이익을 위해 협력하는 것이 더 생산적이라는 내용이다. (C)는 예시를 통해(for instance) 주어진 글의 내용을 부연 설명한다. (A)와 (B)는 사회 조직 내에서의 협동에 관한 내용으로 (A)의 첫 문장은 (C)에 연결되고 (B)의 연결사 But과 그 뒤에 이어지는 내용은 (A)의 마지막 문장에 연결된다. 따라서 자연스러운 글의 순서는 ④ '(C)-(A)-(B)'이다.

해석 Richard Dawkins는 유전자의 본래 관심은 자기 복제를 하는 데 있기 때문에 이기적이지만, 자기 자신을 보존하기 위해 이타적으로 행동할 수 있다고 주장했다.
(C) 예를 들어, 수천 개의 유전자는 (신체의) 기관을 만들기 위해 함께 움직이는데, 인간의 심장을 만드는 데 1,195개의 유전자가, 그리고 인간의 뇌를 만들어내는 데에는 3,195개의 유전자가 함께한다. 이 개별 유전자들은 유전자 풀의 가혹한 환경 속에서 혼자 지내는 것은 도움이 되지 않는다는 사실을 이해했음에 틀림없다.
(A) 이것은 조직에서도 마찬가지다. 일반적으로, 같은 회사의 같은 직급으로 근무하는 직원들은 모두 같은 일자리, 프로젝트 업무에서의 같은 권한, 그리고 같은 특별 수당을 바랄 것이다.
(B) 그러나 그들은 매일 함께 팀을 이루어 일하는데, 그것이 그들을 더 행복하고 더 생산적이게 하며 승진하거나 연말 보너스를 받을 가능성을 높여주기 때문이다. 주제문 우리는 모두 이기적이지만 가장 똑똑한 사람들은 협력이 자기 이익에 좋다는 사실을 알고 있다.

구문 [17행~20행] These individual genes **must have figured out** // that it doesn't pay to be alone / in the harsh environment of the gene pool.
「must have p.p.」는 '~했음에 틀림없다'는 의미로 과거의 일에 대한 단정적 추측을 나타낸다. 이어지는 that절의 it은 가주어, to be 이하는 진주어이다.

어휘 **gene** (생물) 유전자 *cf.* **gene pool** 유전자 풀(어떤 생물 종의 모든 개체가 가지고 있는 유전자 전체) **replicate oneself** 자기 복제를 하다 **altruistically** 이타적으로 **preservation** 보존, 보호 **productive** 생산적인; 이익을 내는 **It pays to-v** v하는 것이 도움이 되다[좋은 결과를 내다] **harsh** 가혹한; 거친

37 글의 순서 ③

소재 '가족 조각' 미술 치료법

해설 가족 조각 미술에 대해 설명한 주어진 글 다음에는 환자가 첫 번째 단계로 진흙 덩어리를 받아서 가족들의 인물상을 만들어보는 (B)가 나온다. 환자가 만든 인물상이 치료를 위한 정보를 줄 수 있다는 (B)의 마지막 문장에 대한 예시(For example)로 아버지의 인물상을 크게 만드는 것이 아버지를 두려워하는 것을 나타낼 수 있다는 (C)가 나온다. (C)의 후반부에는 환자가 만들어놓은 가족 인물상들을 배치하는 활동이 제시되며 (A)에서는 이 활동이 가족 간의 문제를 나타내줄 수 있다는 내용이 나온다. (A)의 This는 (C)의 후반부에 나온 '가족 인물상들을 배치하기'를 가리킨다.

해석 다른 미술 치료 기법만큼 인기 있진 않지만, 가족 조각은 미술 치료에 대한 더욱 촉각적인 접근법이란 점에서 독특하다. 주제문 **이 기법은 심리치료사 Virginia Satir에 의해 처음 개발되었으며 환자가 자신의 가족에게 갖고 있는, 다른 상황에서라면 기꺼이 표현하지 못하거나 아예 표현할 수 없는 내면의 감정을 드러내주려 한다.**
(B) 환자는 몇 개의 진흙 덩어리를 제공받고 나서 진흙을 각 가족 구성원 개인에 대한 묘사로 주조해 보라는 지시를 받는다. 환자가 각 인물상을 만드는 방식은 치료사에게 필수적인 정보를 제공할 수 있다.
(C) 예를 들어, 자신의 아버지를 두려워하는 환자는 그 인물상을 다른 인물상과 비교했을 때 크고 위협적인 것으로 조각할 수도 있다. 몇몇 치료사들은 그 과정을 한 단계 더 진척시켜서 환자에게 조각상들을 서로와 관련하여 놓아보라고 요청할 수 있다.
(A) 이것은 특정 개인들 간의 문제를 확인해줄 수 있다. 예를 들어 환자가 어머니의 조각품을 나머지 가족으로부터 멀리 떨어진 곳에 둔다면, 그것은 어머니가 소원하다는 것을 나타낼 수도 있다.

구문 [3행~7행] This method **was** first **developed** by psychotherapist Virginia Satir and **seeks** to unlock *the inner feelings* [(which[that]) a patient has toward his/her family] [that the patient is otherwise unwilling or unable to express].
동사 was developed와 seeks가 병렬구조를 이룬다. 두 개의 [ ]는 모두 the inner feelings를 수식하는 관계사절이다.

[15행~16행] *The way* [the patient creates each figure] can **provide** the therapist **with** vital information.
[ ]는 관계부사절로 The way를 수식한다. 선행사가 the way이므로 관계부사 how를 쓰지 않는 것에 유의한다. 「provide A with B (A에게 B를 제공하다)」는 「provide B for A」로 바꾸어 쓸 수 있다.

어휘 **sculpt** 조각하다; 형상을 만들다 *cf.* **sculpture** 조각품 **tactile** 촉각의 **psychotherapist** 심리치료사 **unlock** 열다; 드러내다 **indicate** 나타내다 **lump** 덩어리 **mold** (틀에 넣어) 만들다, 주조하다 **representation** 묘사, 표현 **figure** 인물상 **menacing** 위협적인 **in comparison to** ~와 비교할 때 **situate** 위치시키다, 두다

38 문장 넣기 ③

소재 기후 변화의 주범인 목축

해설 주어진 문장에서 yet 앞의 절은 숲 개간을 통한 땅의 개발을, yet 뒤의 절은 이산화탄소를 없애는 데 필수적인 숲의 역할을 언급하고 있다. 따라서 목축을 위해 개발된 땅의 비율을 언급하는 문장과 목축으로 인한 이산화탄소 배출량을 언급하는 문장 사이인 ③에 들어가는 것이 가장 적절하다.

해석 주제문 고기와 유제품에 대해 점점 더 늘어가는 우리의 욕구는 특히 기후 변화라는 영역에서 환경적 재앙을 불러올 것이다. 목축은 현재 지구상의 전체 지표면의 30퍼센트를 전부 차지하며, 그중 대부분은 풀을 뜯어 먹는 양과 소를 위한 영구 목초지이다. 이는 세계의 기름진 농경지 중 33퍼센트를 포함하는데, 이는 가축에게 먹일 곡물을 재배하는 데 사용된다. 이 땅의 많은 부분은 넓은 영역의 숲을 개간하는 것으로 이용 가능하게 되었지만, 숲은 대기에서 이산화탄소를 제거하는 데 정말로 필수불가결한 것이다. 목축으로 인한 이산화탄소 배출은 인간과 관련된 세계 총 이산화탄소 배출량의 9퍼센트를 나타낸다. 하지만 아산화질소와 메탄가스는 대기 온난화에 있어 이산화탄소보다 훨씬 더 강력하다. 그리고 세계 아산화질소 배출량의 65퍼센트와 메탄가스 배출량의 37퍼센트는 가축에서 나온다.

구문 [9행~11행] This includes *33 percent of the world's fertile agricultural land*, // **which** is used to grow *grain* (to feed the livestock).
which 이하는 33 percent ~ land를 보충 설명하는 계속적 용법의 관계사절이다. to feed 이하는 grain을 수식한다.

어휘 **clear** 개간[개척]하다 **vast** 광대한, 거대한 **vital** 대단히 중요한; 생명에 꼭 필요한 **atmosphere** 대기; 분위기 **appetite** 욕구; 입맛, 식욕 **dairy product** 유제품 **be a recipe for** ~을 초래하기 십상이다 **livestock** 가축 **take up** (시간·장소 등을) 차지하다 **permanent** 영구적인 **pasture** 목초지, 목장 **graze** 풀을 먹다 **fertile** 비옥한; 다산(多産)의 **agricultural** 농경의, 농업의 **grain** 곡물, 곡식 **emission** 배출; 발산

39 문장 넣기 ⑤

소재 아동 도서 속 성역할의 변화

해설 주어진 문장에 however가 쓰였으므로 바로 앞에 이와 대조적인 내용이 나와야 한다. 주어진 문장은 소년이 비전통적 행위를 하는 경우는 여전히 드물다는 부정적 내용이므로, 이 문장 앞에는 아동 도서에서의 긍정적인 성역할 변화가 언급되어야 한다. 아동 도서의 남녀 주인공 성별 비율이 비슷해졌다는 내용이 ⑤의 앞 문장까지 나오고, ⑤ 뒤의 문장에서 this, too, will change의 this는 주어진 문장의 that boys ~ doing housework를 가리키므로, 주어진 문장은 ⑤에 들어가는 것이 적절하다.

해석 성(性) 연구 학자들은 1970년대에 아동용 그림책을 조사하여 여자 아이들이 주인공이 되는 일이 드물다는 것을 발견했다. 조금이라도 그림이 실리면 여자 아이들은 수동적이고 인형처럼 표현되는 경향이 있는데 반해, 남자 아이들은 활동적이고 모험적이었다. 그들(=남자 아이들)은 독립심과 자신감을 필요로 하는 일들을 하는 것으로 보인 것에 반해, 여자 아이들은 조력자로 등장했다. 여권주장자들은 그 불균형을 바로잡기 위해 이런 고정관념에 이의를 제기하고 강한 여자 아이 등장인물이 나오는 아동용 책을 출판하기 시작했다. 그 결과, 오늘날 아동용 책은 대략적으로 같은 수의 남자 아이와 여자 아이를 주인공으로 한다. 하지만 연구원들은 남자 아이들이 더 어린 아이들을 돌보거나 집안일을 하는 것 같은 비전통적인 행위를 하는 것은 아직 거의 보이지 않는다고 항의한다. 주제문 성역할은 계속해서 진화하므로, 이것 역시 바뀔 거라 추정하는 것이 온당하다.

어휘 **gender** 성(性), 성별 **leading** 주연의, 주역의; 뛰어난 **character** 등장인물, 배역; 성격 **at all** (조건) 적어도, 조금이나마 **passive** 수동적인, 소극적인 **feminist** 여권주장자, 남녀동권론자 **protest** 항의하다, 이의를 제기하다 **stereotype** 고정관념; 전형 **imbalance** 불균형, 불안정 **evolve** 진화[발달]하다

40 요약문 완성 ④

소재 사회 집단을 통한 비교와 정체감 형성

해설 다른 사람들은 우리의 수행이 어느 정도인지에 대한 평가의 준거가 되기도 하고, 우리의 자아 개념과 자아 존중감에도 연결되어 있다고 하였으므로, 다른 사람들의 집단은 우리의 수행을 평가하기 위한 사회적 '비교(comparisons)'로서뿐만 아니라 우리의 '정체성(identity)'을 구성하기도 한다는 내용으로 요약할 수 있다.

해석 사회 집단에 속해서 다른 사람들과 교제하는 것은 우리가 의미 있는 삶을 만들어내는 것을 돕는 것보다 훨씬 더 많은 일을 한다. 주제문 다른 사람들의 눈을 통해 우리 자신에 대해 숙고하는 것은 또한 중요한 정체성 기능을 수행한다. 우리가 자기 평가에 참여할 수 있는 것은 오직 사회적 비교를 통해서 뿐이다. 시험 후 당신의 점수가 게시된 때에 대해 생각해보라. 당신은 단순히 당신이 얼마나 해냈는지를 확인했는가, 아니면 당신의 점수를 다른 사람들의 점수와 비교해봤는가? 왜 그랬는가(=왜 비교해봤는가)? 물론 그것은 점수가 다른 사람들과 관련해서만 좋은 것으로 혹은 나쁜 것으로 여겨지기 때문이다. 그러나 다른 사람들은 비교 지점 이상의 역할을 수행할 것이다. 다른 사람들은 또한 자아의 일부가 되도록 내면화될 것이다. 우리가 친분을 맺고 동료애와 사회적 유대를 위해 참여하고자 다른 사람들의 집단을 찾아 나설 때, 이러한 타인의 집단들은 우리 자신의 일부로 여겨지게 된다. 우리는 자아 감각에 사회적 구성 요소를 발달시킨다. 주제문 즉, 우리의 자아 개념과 자아 존중감은 우리가 속한 사회적 집단과 연결되어 있다.

⬇

다른 사람들의 집단은 우리의 수행을 평가하기 위한 사회적 (A) 비교로서뿐만 아니라 우리의 (B) 정체성의 사회적 구성요소로서의 역할도 한다.

구문 [5행~6행] **It is** *only through social comparisons* **that** we may engage in self-evaluation.
「It is ~ that ...」은 '…한 것은 바로 ~이다'라는 뜻의 강조구문이며, 이 문장에서는 only through social comparisons가 강조되고 있다.

어휘 **associate with** ~와 교제하다; ~와 연관 짓다 **reflect on** ~에 대해 숙고하다 **self-evaluation** 자기 평가 **post** 게시하다 **internalize** 내면화하다 **bonding** 유대 **component** 구성 요소 **self-esteem** 자아 존중감 [선택지 어휘] **approval** 승인 **hierarchy** 계급, 계층 **authorities** 관계자; (정부)당국 **existence** 존재; 생존

41~42 장문 41 ④ 42 ④

소재 시를 읽을 때 뇌에서 일어나는 일

해설 41. 태아 때에도 시를 읽는 소리를 들으면 심박동수가 빨라지는 것으로 보아 인간의 두뇌에는 시에 반응하는 내재된 무언가가 있는 것 같다. 시를 읽는 것은 뇌 속에서 자아 성찰이 일어나는 것과 비슷한 작용을 일으킨다. 또한 어떤 연구에 의하면 시에 대한 지식이 없는 사람도 시의 규칙을 따른 문장을 읽으면 두뇌에서 기쁨의 감정을 표현한다. 이러한 내용을 종합하면 글의 제목으로 가장 적절한 것은 ④ '시를 읽을 때 당신 뇌에 발생하는 일'이다.

① 시가 당신의 삶을 바꿀 수 있을까?
② 시, 음악과 그것들 간의 관련성
③ 시는 오늘날 우리 세상에 왜 중요한가?
⑤ 시를 읽는 것은 우리의 기억과 언어에 영향을 미친다

42. 실험에 의하면 피실험자들은 시의 규칙을 잘 준수한 문장을 읽을 때 뇌에서 기쁨의 반응을 나타냈으므로, 인간은 무작위성이 아니라 질서와 규칙을 사랑함을 알 수 있다. 따라서 (d)의 randomness를 order 혹은 patterns로 바꿔 써야 한다.

해석 주제문 두뇌가 시에 어떻게 반응하는지와 두뇌가 왜 그런 식으로 반응하는지는 별개의 문제이다. 과학자들은 꽤 오랫동안 답을 찾으려고 시도해왔다. 어머니가 시를 암송하는 것을 들을 때 열 달을 다 채운 태아의 심박동수가 증가한다는 발견과 같은 새로운 사실은 아마 시적 소리에 반응하는, 인간의 두뇌 속에 (a) 내재된 무언가가 있을지도 모른다는 점을 암시한다. 과학자들은 또한 두뇌가 과거를 되돌아보며 자기 성찰을 할 때와 비슷한 방식으로 시에 반응한다는 것을 밝힌다. 이것은 시를 읽는 것이 또한 (b) 자기 성찰을 위한 공간을 제공해준다는 것을 의미한다. 그리고 2017년 연구에서는 우리가 시에 대해 배운 적이 없어도 그것에 (c) 긍정적으로 반응하는 것 같다고 나온다. 하나의 행 내에서 운문 형식과 압운에 대한 대단히 엄격한 규칙을 가지고 있는 'cynghanedd'라 불리는 전통적 형식의 웨일스어 시가 있다. 연구자들은 웨일스어를 사용하지만 'cynghanedd'에 대한 지식은 전혀 없는 자원자들을 모집하여 그들에게 문장들을 제시했는데, 그중 일부는 'cynghanedd'의 규칙을 따랐고 다른 문장들은 어떤 방식에서 그것을 위반했다. 문장들이 규칙에 완벽히 들어맞았을 때 자원자들의 두뇌는 기쁨을 나타냈고, 그것들이 어쩐지 틀에서 벗어났을 때 두뇌는 시어를 덜 좋아했다. 이것이 정확히 입증하는 바는 분명하다. (d) 무작위성(→ 질서)에 대한 인간의 사랑은 우리 자신이 시의 특성을 이해함에 있어 어떠한 배경지식도 갖고 있지 않더라도 언어에 대한 우리의 반응의 형태로 언뜻 내비칠 수 있다. 이것이 또한 아마도 우리가 가사와 랩에 그토록 (e) 강하게 반응하는 이유일 것이다.

구문 [4행~8행] *Revelations* (like the discovery that full-term fetuses increase their heart rates // when they **hear** *their mothers* **reciting** poetry) suggest that perhaps there's something inherent in *the human brain* [that responds to poetic sounds].
(Revelations = S, suggest = V)
주어는 Revelations, 동사는 suggest이고, ( )는 전명구로 주어를 수식한다. 전명구 내에 밑줄 친 the discovery와 that절은 서로 동격 관계이다. 동격절 속의 when절에서 지각동사 「hear+O+C(v-ing) (O가 C하고 있는 것을 듣다)」 구문이 쓰였다.

[19행~21행] ~ and **presented** them **with** *sentences*, some of which obeyed the rules of *cynghanedd* and others of which violated **them** in some way.
「present A with B」는 'A에게 B를 제시하다'의 뜻이다. some of which와 others of which에서 which는 모두 앞에 나온 sentences를 가리키며, them은 the rules of *cynghanedd*를 가리킨다.

어휘 **A is one thing B is another** A와 B는 별개이다 **revelation** 폭로(된 사실), 뜻밖의 새 사실 **full-term** 열 달을 다 채우는 **heart rate** 심박동수 **recite** 암송하다 **inherent** 내재하는 **introspect** 자기 성찰하다 **self-reflection** 자기 성찰 **verse** 운문, 시 **rhyming** 압운 맞추기 **mold** 주형, 틀 **be keen on** ~을 아주 좋아하다 **show through** (언뜻) 드러나 보이다, 비치다 **specific** 특성 **lyric** 가사; 서정시

43~45 장문

43 ⑤ 44 ② 45 ②

소재 아버지가 아끼는 차를 긁은 아들

해설 43. (A)는 Bob의 아버지가 차를 얼마나 아껴왔는지에 관한 내용이다. 시간의 흐름상 그 뒤에는 갓 운전면허를 딴 Bob이 자동차를 운전해서 주유소로 가는 (D), 주유소에서 나오는 길에 차를 긁은 사건이 일어난 (C), 그리고 Bob이 집으로 돌아와 차가 망가진 것을 아버지에게 알리는 (B)의 순서로 연결되는 것이 가장 자연스러우므로 정답은 ⑤ '(D)-(C)-(B)'이다.

44. (b)는 the damage, 즉 '캐딜락의 파손 부분'을 가리키고, 나머지는 모두 아버지가 소유한 1958년형 캐딜락을 가리킨다.

45. (B)에서 Bob은 아버지와 함께 자동차의 파손 부분을 살펴보았는데 그 정도가 상당했다고 했으므로 ②가 글의 내용과 일치하지 않는다.

해석 (A) ① Bob의 아버지는 자동차 판매원으로, 그가 소유한 1958년형 캐딜락은 그의 자랑이자 기쁨이었다. 그것은 오히려 배처럼 생긴 종류의 차였고, 거대했으며, 위로 높이 곡선으로 뻗은 후미 장식 판이 붙어 있었다. (a) 그것(=아버지 소유의 1958년형 캐딜락)은 아이처럼 돌봐졌고, 밤새 밖에 세워져 있는 일이 없었으며, 매주 토요일마다 성실하게 세차되고 왁스칠되었다. 그것은 한 남자의 소중한 자동차의 빛나는 표본이었다.

(D) Bob은 16세가 되어 ④ 운전면허증을 이제 막 땄고, (e) 그 캐딜락(=아버지 소유의 1958년형 캐딜락)을 운전해보고 싶은 욕망이 실로 충만했다. 그래서 그의 친절한 아버지는 그에게 3달러를 주며 기름을 넣어 오라고 보냈다. 자부심과 젊은이다운 열정으로 가득 찬 ⑤ Bob은 주유소로 차를 몰고 가서 주유원이 차에 기름을 넣고 창문을 닦아주는 동안 얼굴에 아주 큰 미소를 지으며 차 안에 앉아 있었다.

(C) 그러고 나서 생각할 수도 없는 일이 일어났다. Bob이 주유소를 떠날 때 커브를 급하게 돌면서 ③ 콘크리트 기둥에 (d) 차(=아버지 소유의 1958년형 캐딜락)의 옆면을 긁은 것이다. 그는 속이 울렁거렸다. 잠시 그는 도망갈 생각을 했다. 화내고 실망할 아버지를 대할 생각을 하니 끔찍했다. 그는 천천히 집 쪽으로 차를 돌렸다.

(B) 차를 조심스럽게 주차한 후, 그는 머리를 숙인 채 들어가 그의 아버지에게 말했다. ② 그들은 함께 나와 파손 부분을 점검했는데, (b) 그것(=파손 부분)은 상당했다. 그들은 영원처럼 느껴지는 시간 동안 거기에 서 있었고, 그의 아버지는 말이 없었다. 결국 Bob은 떨리는 목소리로 "아빠, 제가 어떻게 하길 바라세요?"라고 말했다. 그의 아버지가 주머니에서 천천히 2달러를 꺼냈다. 그는 Bob에게 그 2달러를 주면서 그의 눈을 똑바로 바라보고, "아들아, 난 네가 다시 가서 (c) 그것(=아버지 소유의 1958년형 캐딜락)에 기름을 좀 더 채우고 오는 게 좋을 것 같구나."라고 말했다.

구문 [(A) 4행~6행] It was cared for like a baby, / never left outside overnight, / and faithfully washed and waxed every Saturday.
cared for, left, washed, washed and waxed는 모두 It was에 연결된다.

[(B) 8행~9행] **Handing** it to Bob and **looking** him straight in the eye, / he said, ~.
(him = Bob, he = Bob's father)
Handing ~ Bob과 looking ~ eye는 연속동작을 나타내는 분사구문으로, 의미상 주어는 주절의 주어와 같은 he(= Bob's father)이다.

어휘 (A) **tail fin** 자동차의 후미 장식 판; 꼬리지느러미 **overnight** 밤새도록, 하룻밤 동안 **faithfully** 성실히, 충실하게 **wheel** ((복수형)) 자동차; 바퀴 (B) **bowed** 머리를 숙인, 굽은 **considerable** 상당한, 적지 않은 **eternity** 영원, 영구 **trembling** 떨리는, 전율하는 **look A in the eye** A를 똑바로 보다 (C) **unthinkable** 생각할 수도 없는, 상상할 수 없는 **pull out of** ~을 떠나다 **cut the corner** (자동차가 커브에서 측면을 따라 돌지 않고) 보도로 가로질러 가다 **scrape** 긁다 **pillar** 기둥 (D) **burst with** ~으로 충만하다 **get behind the wheel** 운전하다 **enthusiasm** 열정, 열의 **attendant** 종업원, 점원

실전 모의고사 12

본문 p.167

18 ④	19 ②	20 ④	21 ①	22 ⑤	23 ⑤	24 ④	25 ③	26 ④	27 ④
28 ④	29 ⑤	30 ④	31 ⑤	32 ③	33 ①	34 ④	35 ③	36 ①	37 ④
38 ③	39 ④	40 ④	41 ③	42 ④	43 ④	44 ③	45 ③		

18 글의 목적 ④

소재 기부 가능 지역을 확대하는 방안 제안

해설 봄철 대청소를 하면서 나온 불필요한 물건들을 더 많이 기부받아 홍수 피해자들을 돕자는 내용의 글이다. 이를 위해 기부 물품을 수집하는 트럭이 시 경계 밖의 더 먼 시골 지역까지 가는 것을 제안하고 있으므로 글의 목적으로 적절한 것은 ④이다.

해석 관계자분께,
우선, 봄철 대청소 기부 운동(Spring Clean Donation Drive)을 위해 일하시는 모든 분의 노력에 대하여 경의를 표할 뿐입니다. 샌디 시 지역사회의 아주 많은 가구들에 영향을 준 참혹한 홍수 이후, (저는) 돕기 위해 무언가 해야만 할 것 같았습니다. 홍수 피해자들을 돕기 위해 불필요한 가정용품을 수거해 그것들을 다시 팔아서 수천 달러가 모금되었습니다. 주제문 저의 유일한 바람은 수거 트럭이 더 먼 시골 지역으로 보내지는 것입니다. 귀 자선단체에 물품을 기부하고 싶어 하는 많은 사람들이 샌디 시 경계 밖에서 살고 있습니다. 기부를 늘리는 방법으로 이것을 고려해 주시고 계속 좋은 일 해주시기 바랍니다!
Heather Nandall 드림

구문 [11행~13행] There are *many of us* (living outside the Sandy City limit) [who would love to donate items to your charity].
living ~ limit와 who가 이끄는 관계절이 동시에 many of us를 수식하고 있다.

어휘 **to begin** 우선; 처음에는 **nothing but** 오직, 그저 **donation** 기부 *cf.* **donate** 기부[기증]하다 **drive** (조직적인) 운동 **tragic** 참혹한, 비극적인 **flooding** 홍수, 범람 **household items** 가정용품, 살림살이 **raise** (자금 등을) 모으다; 들어 올리다; 기르다 **victim** 피해자, 희생자 **rural** 시골의, 지방의 **limit** 경계, 한계; 제한하다 **charity** 자선[구호] 단체; 자선

19 심경 변화 ②

소재 연극 악평을 접한 후의 심경

해설 Edward는 자신의 연극이 성공적이라 생각하고 좋은 평들을 기대하며 컴퓨터를 켰으나, 좋지 않은 평들을 확인하자 당혹감에 얼굴이 붉어지며 연락을 피할 방법을 생각하는 상황으로 바뀌었다. 따라서 정답은 ② '희망찬 → 당혹스러운'이다.

해석 Edward는 더는 침대에 누워있을 수 없었다. 주제문 자신의 연극에 관한 평이 분명 지금쯤 온라인상에 있을 것이었고, 그는 그 평들을 몹시 읽고 싶어 했다. 어쨌든 그 연극은 성공적이었던 것 같았다. 더 이상 기다릴 수 없어서 그는 침대에서 뛰쳐나와 노트북 컴퓨터를 켰고, 좋은 소식을 읽기 위해 앉았다. 주제문 그러나 첫 번째 평은 그가 기대했던 것이 아니었다. 그 글쓴이의 부정적인 어조로 인해 약간 실망한 채 Edward는 또 다른 평을 빠르게 찾았다. 이것은 훨씬 안 좋았다! '독창성이 없는', '졸음이 오게 하는', 그리고 '지루한'이라는 단어를 보자 Edward의 얼굴은 살짝 붉어지기 시작했다. 그는 그 평에 댓글을 달고 싶었지만, 그렇게 하는 것이 훨씬 안 좋은 것처럼 보일 것이라는 걸 깨달았다. 그래서 그는 자신의 노트북 컴퓨터를 닫고 블라인드를 치고는 침대 안으로 다시 기어가서 전화 오는 것을 어떻게 피할지 생각해 내려고 애썼다.
① 불만족스러운 → 안도한
③ 들뜬 → 부러워하는
④ 우울한 → 고마워하는
⑤ 좌절한 → 기쁜

구문 [4행~6행] **No longer** (**being**) **able to wait**, // he jumped out of bed, switched on his laptop, and sat down to read the good news.
No longer able to wait는 이유를 나타내는 분사구문으로 being이 생략되었으며, Because he was no longer able to wait와 같은 의미이다. 밑줄 친 세 개의 동사(구)가 접속사 and로 연결되어 병렬구조를 이루고 있다.

[7행~8행] (**Being**) **Slightly let down** by the author's negative tone, / Edward quickly searched for another review.
Slightly ~ tone은 이유를 나타내는 수동 분사구문으로 Because he was slightly let down ~ tone과 같은 의미이다.

어휘 **review** (책 · 연극 등의) 평론, 논평(=comment) **be eager to-v** 몹시 v하고 싶어 하다 **jump out of** ~에서 뛰쳐나오다 **let A down** A를 실망시키다, A의 기대를 저버리다 **tone** 어조; 음색; 기풍, 풍조 **shade** 색조; 음영; 그늘 **uninspired** 독창성이 없는; 활기 없는, 지루한 **lazy** 졸음이 오게 하는; 게으른 **realize** 깨닫다, 인식[자각]하다 **crawl** 기어가다

20 필자 주장 ④

소재 초심자의 마음

해설 불교 선종에는 선입견과 과거 경험에 얽매이지 않고 처음의 마음으로 사물을 인식하는 '초심자의 마음'이라는 개념이 있는데, 이는 독단적인 사고에 대한 해법이 될 수 있으며, 전문적 지식을 갖춘 사람들은 자신의 지식을 버릴 필요는 없지만 이러한 '초심자의 마음'을 가지고 새로운 경험에 마음을 여는 자세가 필요하다고 하였다. 따라서 필자의 주장으로 가장 적절한 것은 ④이다.

해석 심리학자들이 얼어붙은 사고를 연구할 때, 그들은 그것을 '독단적 인식'이라고 부른다. 심리학자의 정의에서 그것은 '개인의 사전 의견 혹은 기대를 강화하는 방식으로 정보를 처리하는 경향'이다. 선종은 독단적 인식과 완전히 반대되는 사고 양식에 대한 개념을 갖고 있다. 그것은 '초심자의 마음'이라 불린다. 그것은 선입견을 갖지 않고, 당신의 과거 경험에 근거를 두어 자동적으로 가정하지 않고 심지어 마치 일상적인 상황을 처음 마주치는 것처럼 그것을 인식하는 접근법을 지칭한다. 그것은 당신이 당신의 전문 지식을 버리는 것을 의미하는 것이 아니라, 당신이 그것(=전문 지식)에도 불구하고 새로운 경험에 마음을 연 상태로 있는 것을 의미한다. 우리들 대부분은 초심자의 마음과 독단적 인식이라는 극단 사이의 어딘가에 해당하는 인식적 양식을 가지고 있다. 주제문 어떠한 분야에서도 이상적인 전문가는 대단히 폭넓고 깊이 있는 지식을 갖추고 있으면서도 초심자의 마음을 많이 유지하는 사람이다.

구문 [7행~11행] It refers to *an approach* [in which you have (V'1) a lack of preconceptions / and perceive (V'2) even routine situations // **as if** you are encountering them for the first time, / without automatically making *assumptions* (based on your past experience)].
[ ]는 an approach를 수식하는 관계사절이다. 관계사절 내에서 동사 have와 perceive가 병렬구조를 이룬다. as if는 '마치 ~인 것처럼'의 뜻이다.

[11행~13행] That does**n't** mean // (that) you discard your expertise (A), / **but** that you remain open to new experience despite it (B).

「not A but B (A가 아니라 B)」 구문이 쓰였다. A, B에 해당하는 자리에 공통적으로 mean의 목적어인 that절이 왔는데, 첫 번째 that절에서는 접속사 that이 생략되어 있다.

어휘 **dogmatic** 독단적인 **cognition** 인식, 인지 *cf.* **cognitive** 인식의, 인지의 **process** 처리하다 **reinforce** 강화하다 **prior** 이전의 **Zen Buddhism** 선종 **opposed to** ~에 반대하는 **refer to** 가리키다, 언급하다 **preconception** 선입견 **encounter** (우연히) 마주치다 **assumption** 가정, 추측 **discard** 버리다 **expertise** 전문적 지식[기술] **extreme** 극단; 극단적인 **ideal** 이상적인; 이상 **breadth** 폭, 너비 **depth** 깊이 **to a large extent** 대단히, 매우

21 글의 요지 ①

소재 유아 쇠약증

해설 아기들이 신체 접촉의 부족으로 인해 유아 쇠약증으로 고통받거나 사망했고, 신체 접촉을 많이 한 병원의 유아 사망률이 낮아졌다. 이는 신체 접촉이 아이의 건강에 중요하다는 의미이므로 요지로는 ①이 가장 적절하다.

해석 20세기 초 영국에서는 많은 아기가 당시 '유아 쇠약증(marasmus)'이라고 불리는 병으로 사망했는데, 이것은 그리스어로 '쇠약해짐'을 뜻한다. 아주 빈곤한 지역에 있는 일부 보육원에서는 유아 사망률이 100퍼센트에 달했고, 심지어 가장 부유한 집과 시설에서조차도 아기들은 유아 쇠약증을 앓았다. 주제문 마침내, 아기들이 사실은 신체 접촉의 결핍으로 병에 걸린다는 것이 밝혀졌다. 그들(=아기들)을 안거나 쓰다듬어 주지 않았기 때문에 그 결과 그들은 쇠약해져서 사망했다. 이것을 알아낸 후, 한 병원의 간호사들은 반드시 하루 종일 아기들을 안고 돌아다니거나, 아니면 아기들과 신체 접촉을 했다. 곧 이 병원의 유아 사망률이 65퍼센트에서 10퍼센트 이하로 떨어졌고, 이것은 간호사들이 했던 것이 아기들에게 매우 중요한 것임을 확인시켜 주었다.

구문 [1행~3행] ~, many infants died from *a condition* [**that** was then called *marasmus*], // **which** means "wasting away" in Greek.
that이 이끄는 관계사절이 a condition을 수식하고, 계속적 용법으로 쓰인 which가 이끄는 절이 앞의 marasmus를 부연 설명한다.

어휘 **infant** 갓난아기, 유아 **condition** 질환, 문제; 상태 **waste away** 쇠약해지다, 수척해지다 **orphanage** 보육원 **district** 지역; 행정구 **mortality** 사망률; 죽을 운명 **institution** (보호) 시설; 기관, 협회 **suffer from** ~을 앓다; ~으로 고통받다 **lack** 결핍, 부족 **stroke** 쓰다듬다, 어루만지다 **ensure** 반드시 ~하게 하다, 보장하다 **interact with** ~와 상호작용하다, 서로 영향을 끼치다 **vital** (생명 유지에) 필수적인, 매우 중요한

22 글의 주제 ⑤

소재 민주주의 국가들이 권력 남용을 막는 이유와 방법

해설 글의 전반부에는 권력에 대한 대중들의 감정이 부정적이라는 것, 즉 어떤 이유로 민주주의 정치 시스템이 권력을 견제하는지가 주로 서술되고 있고, 후반부에는 권력 집중을 막는 제도적 장치로 미국 헌법의 예가 소개되고 있다. 따라서 주제로 가장 적절한 것은 ⑤ '민주주의 국가들이 권력 남용을 막는 이유와 방법'이다.

해석 많은 사람들이, 권력이 그것을 가장 적극적으로 추구하는 사람들에게는 주어지지 말아야 한다고 느낀다. 권력과 권력을 추구하는 사람들에 대한 이러한 일반적인 반감 때문에 Rosabeth Moss Kanter는 "권력을 가진 사람은 그것을 부인하고, 권력을 원하는 사람은 그것을 갈망하는 것처럼 보이고 싶어 하지 않으며, 권력의 음모에 관여하는 사람은 비밀리에 가담한다."라고 쓰고 있다. 주제문 권력과 권력을 가진 사람들에 대한 우리의 감정을 고려하면, 민주주의 정치 시스템이 권력에 대한 견제 방안을 가지고 있는 것은 놀랍지 않다. 이 시스템들은 또한 권력이 절대적이 되거나 극소수 사람들의 손에 집중되는 것을 방지하는 방식으로 권력을 분배하는 방안들을 구체적으로 명시하고 있다. 미국의 건국자들은 이 문제를 두고 의견 충돌을 일으켰다. 그들의 헌법상의 해결책은? 정부의 한 기관에 권력이 집중되는 것을 막으면서 다수의 권력으로부터 소수의 이익을 보장하는 메커니즘을 확립하는 것이었다. 미국 헌법의 권리장전은 (정부가) 아무리 강력하더라도 정부가 축소할 수 없는 개인의 권리를 구체적으로 명시함으로써 권력을 견제한다.

① 평화적이고 민주적인 권력 이양의 필요성
② 권력 투쟁을 해결하려는 정치적 노력의 역사
③ 사회에서 사람들의 권력 갈망의 결과
④ 정치적 권력을 민주주의 국가에서 행사하는 것의 중요성

구문 [14행~17행] Establish *mechanisms* [**that** prevent the concentration ~ government and **that** protect the interests of minorities against ~ the majority].
주격 관계대명사 that이 이끄는 두 개의 절이 and로 연결되어 선행사 mechanisms를 수식한다.

어휘 **withhold** 주지 않다, 보류하다; 억제하다 **antipathy** 반감, 혐오감 **given** ~을 고려하면 **democratic** 민주주의의 **check** 견제; 확인; 억제 **specify** 구체적으로 명시하다 **distribute** 분배하다 **clash over** ~에 대해 (의견이) 충돌하다[대립하다] **constitutional** 헌법의, 입헌의; 체질의 *cf.* **constitution** 헌법; 구성; 체질 **mechanism** 메커니즘(특정한 기능을 수행하는) 구조, 기계 장치 **branch** 지국, 분점 **minority** 소수(↔ **majority** 다수) **Bill of Rights** 권리장전 [선택지 어휘] **shift** 이동; 교대; 변화; 방향을 바꾸다 **consequence** 결과

23 글의 제목 ⑤

소재 인간 복제의 한계

해설 첫 번째 문장에서 복제를 통해 같은 사람을 여럿 만들 수 있을 것이라는 생각이 틀렸음을 지적한 뒤 유전자를 완벽하게 복제하더라도 개인의 미래 또한 같을 수는 없다는 것을 쌍둥이를 예로 들며 설명하고 있다. 따라서 이 글의 제목으로 가장 적절한 것은 ⑤ '인간 복제에 대한 오해'이다.

해석 치료용의 생물 복제를 통해 우리가 예컨대 여러 명의 David Beckham으로 이뤄진 축구팀이나 여러 명의 Martin Luther King이 참가하는 평화 운동, 혹은 여러 명의 J. K. Rowling이 일하는 출판사를 만들어낼 수 있다고 생각하는 것은 간단히 말해서 완전히 잘못된 생각이다. 문제는, 우리가 한 개인의 유전자 구성을 완전히 복제할 수 있다 하더라도 그 개인의 미래는 여전히 예견할 수 없다는 데 있다. 같은 가정과 학교에서 쌍둥이로 자라났지만 재능이나 호불호는 여전히 매우 다른 수천 명의 일란성 쌍둥이들을 보기만 해도, 똑같은 유전자가 똑같은 인생을 만들지 않음을 알 수 있다. 주제문 점점 더 정교해진 연구는 우리가 유전자 작용에 대해 더 잘 알게 될수록 맞춤형 인간을 생산하기가 불가능하다는 것이 더 명확해짐을 보여주고 있다.

① 어떻게 인간이 복제되는가
② 인간 복제의 이점
③ 일란성 쌍둥이와 인간 복제
④ 인간 복제를 금지해야 하는 이유들

구문 [7행~12행] We only **need** look at *the many thousands of identical twins* [who, **although** *(they are)* **raised** *in the same home and schools as their twin*, are still very different / in talents and likes and dislikes], and we can see that identical genes do not make identical lives.
크게는 두 개의 절, We only need ~ dislikes와 we can see ~ lives가 등위접속사 and로 연결된 구조이다. 여기서 need는 뒤에 동사원형 look이 나오므로 조동사로 쓰였다. the many thousands of identical twins를 수식하는 주격 관계대명사절 안에 양보의 분사구문 although raised ~ their twin이 삽입된 형태로 이 분사구문의 주어는 관계대명사절의 주어(who = the many ~ identical twins)와 동일하기 때문에 생략되었으며, 의미를 확실히 하기 위해 접속사 although를 분사 앞에 남겨두었다.

[12행~15행] Increasingly sophisticated research is showing // that **the better** we understand gene function, / **the more obvious** the impossibility of producing a made-to-order human being.
「the+비교급 ~, the+비교급 ...」 구문은 '~하면 할수록 더 …하다'라는 뜻이다.

어휘 **therapeutic** 치료용의 **cloning** 생물 복제 *cf.* **clone** 복제하다 **publishing house** 출판사 **genetic** (생물) 유전의 *cf.* **gene** 유전자, 유전인자

makeup 구성, 구조 **identical twins** 일란성 쌍둥이 *cf.* **identical** 똑같은, 동일한 **talent** 재능, 소질 **likes and dislikes** 호불호, 좋아하는 것과 싫어하는 것 **increasingly** 점점 더, 더욱 더 **sophisticated** 정교한; 교양 있는, 세련된 **function** 작용, 기능 **obvious** 분명한 **made-to-order** 맞춤의, 주문한 [선택지 어휘] **misconception** 오해

24 도표 이해 ④

소재 온라인 쇼핑의 예상 소비와 실제 소비 비교

해설 두 그래프에서 차이가 가장 적은 것은 100달러 이상 소비를 한 경우이므로 ④가 잘못된 설명이다.

해석 〈온라인 구매에서의 소비〉

주제문 위의 도표는 쇼핑객 표본에 의해 보고된 대로 온라인 구매에서의 예상 소비와 실제 소비를 비교하고 있다. ① 전반적인 추세는 사람들이 예상했던 것보다 더 많이 소비했다는 것이다. ② 도표에 따르면, 온라인에서 100달러 이상을 소비한 사람들의 비율이 가장 높았던 반면, 10~49달러를 소비한 사람들의 비율이 가장 낮았다. ③ 10달러 미만을 소비한 사람들은 이 도표에서 두 번째로 높은 비율을 차지했다. ④ 예상 소비와 실제 소비의 차이가 가장 적은 경우는 50~99달러 범주였다. ⑤ 이와 반대로, 예상 소비와 실제 소비의 차이는 10달러 미만을 소비할 때 가장 컸다.

어휘 **compare** 비교하다 **trend** 추세, 경향 **account for** (~의 비율을) 차지하다; 설명하다 **on the contrary** 반대로

25 내용 불일치 ③

소재 미국 육군 사관학교(United States Military Academy)

해설 George Washington이 독립전쟁 기간에 사관학교 설립의 필요성을 절감한 것이 이 학교의 설립 계기가 됐다고 했으므로, 독립전쟁은 이 학교 설립 이전에 발생한 것임을 알 수 있다. 이 학교 졸업생들이 활약한 것은 독립전쟁이 아니라 남북전쟁이므로 ③이 글의 내용과 일치하지 않는다.

해석 United States Military Academy는 ① West Point로도 알려졌는데, 뉴욕시에서 북쪽으로 대략 50마일 떨어져 있는 아름다운 허드슨 계곡에 자리 잡고 있다. 1802년 Thomas Jefferson에 의해 설립된 이 학교는 ② 미국에서 가장 오래된 사관학교이다. ③ 미국 독립전쟁 기간에 George Washington은 군사 장교들을 훈련할 학교가 긴급히 필요하다는 것을 깨달았고, 이것이 이 학교의 설립으로 이어졌다. ④ 미국 남북전쟁에서 남부 연합 측을 지휘한 Jefferson Finis Davis와 북부 연합 측을 지휘한 장군인 Ulysses S. Grant는 둘 다 West Point의 졸업생이었다. 이 학교에 입학하려면 지원자들은 17세에서 23세의 나이로, ⑤ 대학 진학 적성 검사(SAT)에서 높은 점수를 받아야 하며, 훌륭한 도덕적 성품을 지녀야 한다.

구문 [6행~8행] ~, George Washington realized // (that) *an academy* (to train army officers) was urgently needed, // **which** led to the establishment of the academy.
계속적 용법의 관계대명사 which는 앞 절 전체 내용을 받는다.

어휘 **approximately** 대략 **scenic** 경치가 좋은, 아름다운 **establish** 설립하다, 세우다 *cf.* **establishment** 설립 **urgently** 긴급히, 다급하게 **general** 장군; 일반적인 **graduate** 졸업생; 졸업하다 **candidate** 지원자; 후보자 **scholastic** 학교의, 학교 교육의 **aptitude** 적성 **moral** 도덕적인, 품행이 단정한; 도덕(상)의

26 안내문 불일치 ④

소재 피트니스 회원 특전

해설 종합 건강 평가는 무료로 받을 수 있다고 했으므로 ④가 안내문의 내용과 일치하지 않는다.

해석

Max 피트니스 센터

4월은 휴식의 달입니다!
Max 피트니스 센터의 4월의 체력 도전반에 가입하시고 ① 4월 14일까지 무료 등록을 누리세요! ② 오리엔테이션은 모든 신입 회원들에게 권장되는 무료 서비스입니다. 오리엔테이션은 30분 정도만 소요되며 피트니스 센터의 규칙, 규정, 프로그램, 판촉 상품을 살펴보게 될 것입니다.

회원권 특전
- 이곳의 ③ 피트니스 전문가들과 함께 여러분의 운동 목표를 논의하여 그 목표가 유연성, 유산소 운동 능력, 체력, 체중 감량 중에서 어느 것인지 결정합니다.
- ④ 무료 피트니스 평가는 종합적인 건강을 평가하기 위해 고안되었으며, 이 평가에는 체성분 검사와 유연성 측정이 포함됩니다.
- ⑤ 60분간의 일대일 개인 트레이닝은 여러분의 목표를 다루는 데 도움을 줄 것입니다.

어휘 **relaxation** 휴식 **enrollment** 등록 **recommend** 권장하다, 추천하다 **regulation** 규정 **promotion** 판촉 상품 **workout** 운동 **flexibility** 유연성 **aerobic** 유산소 운동의 **complimentary** 무료의; 칭찬하는 **assessment** 평가 *cf.* **assess** 평가하다 **overall** 종합적인, 전반적인 **body composition** 체성분 **measurement** 측정 **address** (문제 · 상황 등을) 다루다; 연설하다; 말을 걸다

27 안내문 일치 ④

소재 약 사용법 안내

해설 눈에 들어가지 않게 주의하고, 들어갔을 경우 물로 씻어내야 한다고 했으므로 ④가 안내문의 내용과 일치한다.

해석

Biofin 사용법

이 약을 바르기 전에 손을 씻으세요. ① 감염된 피부를 순하거나 비눗기 없는 세안제로 부드럽게 닦은 다음 가볍게 두드려 말리세요. ② 이 약을 보통은 하루에 한 번씩 또는 의사의 지시대로 얇게 바르세요.

주의사항
- 입술 안쪽 부위나 코/입의 안쪽에 바르지 마세요.
- 베였거나 찰과상을 입은 곳, 또는 ③ 햇볕에 탄 피부에는 바르지 마세요.
- ④ 이 약이 눈에 들어가지 않도록 하세요. 이 약이 눈에 들어가면 많은 양의 물로 씻어 내세요.
- ⑤ 이 약을 다른 사람과 같이 사용하지 마세요.

상태가 좋아지지 않거나 악화되면 의사에게 문의하세요.

어휘 **apply** (크림 등을) 바르다; 적용하다; 지원하다 **medication** 약, 치료 **affected** (병에) 걸린; 영향을 받은 **pat dry** 가볍게 두드려 말리다 **layer** 막, 층, 겹 **scraped** 찰과상을 입은; 긁힌 **sunburned** 햇볕에 심하게 탄 **flush** 물로 씻어 내리다; 얼굴이 붉어지다 **condition** 상태; 질환

28 밑줄 어법 ④

소재 상대방의 말을 경청하는 것의 중요성

해설 ④ which 이하가 완전한 절이므로 관계대명사는 적절치 않다. so preoccupied에 대응하여 접속사 that을 쓰면 「so ~ that ... (너무 ~해서 …하다)」 구문이 되어 적절하다.

오답 분석 ① is는 주어 One에 대응되는 단수 동사이다. ② to be (sure)는 '~하기 위하여'라는 의미를 가지는 to부정사구로서 문맥상 적절하다. ③ that은 명사절을 이끄

는 접속사이며, that절은 shows에 대한 목적어 역할을 한다. ⑤ 전치사 by의 목적어로 동명사 asking과 listening이 and로 연결되어 병렬구조를 이룬다.

해석 주제문 당신이 느낄 수 있는 어떠한 수줍음 및 사회적 불안을 극복하는 가장 빠른 방법 중의 하나는 상대방에게 질문한 후 그들의 진짜 감정과 관심을 이해하려고 노력하는 것이다. 그들이 말하는 동안 그들의 답변을 잘 경청하라. 후속 질문을 하고 이해를 했는지 체크하라. 당신이 이해했는지를 확실히 하기 위해 그들이 했던 말을 당신 자신의 언어로 다시 반복하여 말해보라. 코치 Lou Holtz가 말하는 것처럼 '모든 사람들의 첫 번째 질문은 이것이다. 당신은 저에게 관심이 있으십니까?' 경청은 당신이 정말로 관심이 있음을 보여준다. 대부분의 사람들은 자기 자신과 자신의 삶의 세부사항에 너무나 정신이 팔려 있어서 다른 사람들에게 거의 주의를 기울이지 않는다. 당신이 반대로 행동하여 그들의 관심을 이해하려고 노력함으로써, 그들에게 질문하고 그들이 말할 때 그들의 말을 잘 들어줌으로써 그들과 공감할 때, 그들은 당신을 좋아하고 당신과 협력하기를 원할 것이다.

구문 [1행~4행] One of *the fastest ways* for you (to overcome *any shyness and social anxieties* [(which[that]) you may feel]) is **to** ask questions of the other person and then try to understand their true feelings and concerns.
주어는 One이고 동사는 is이다. ( )는 the fastest ways를 수식하는 형용사구이고, for you는 ( )의 의미상 주어이다. [ ]는 앞에 목적격 관계대명사 which[that]가 생략되어 any shyness and social anxieties를 수식한다. to 다음의 동사원형 ask와 try가 and로 연결되어 병렬구조를 이룬다.

어휘 **shyness** 수줍음 **follow-up** 후속의 **preoccupied** 정신이 팔린 **empathize** 공감하다

29 밑줄 어휘 ⑤

소재 실패의 인내를 통한 성공

해설 이 글은 복잡한 사물이나 시스템을 향상시키는 방법이 일부러 고장을 내는 것이라고 하면서 실패에 대해 인내심을 가지라고 이야기하고 있다. 이러한 맥락에서 마지막 문장의 부정적인 결과, 즉 고장이나 실패는 '피할' 것이 아니라 성공을 얻기 위해 '받아들여야' 하는 것이므로 ⑤의 preventing을 embracing 등으로 고쳐야 한다.

해석 주제문 사물, 특히 복잡한 사물을 보다 좋게 만들기 위해 그것을 고장 내야 한다는 관련된 생각이 실패를 받아들인다는 생각 속에 포함되어 있다. 보통 복잡한 시스템을 향상시키는 유일한 방법은 그것을 강제로 다양한 방식으로 실패하게 함으로써 그 시스템의 ① 한계를 시험하는 것이다. 소프트웨어는, 우리가 만드는 가장 복잡한 물건 중에 하나인데, 일반적으로 그것을 ② 고장 내는 방법을 체계적으로 찾아내도록 기술자를 고용함으로써 품질을 검사받는다. 마찬가지로, 고장 난 복잡한 장치를 수리하는 한 가지 방법은 실제 기능 장애가 있는 곳의 ③ 정확한 위치를 찾아내기 위해 그 장치의 다양한 기능에 의도적으로 부정적인 결과(일시적인 고장)를 억지로 생기게 하는 것이다. 과학자가 외부인을 흔히 당황하게 하는 실패에 ④ 인내심을 갖고 있는 것과 마찬가지로, 훌륭한 기술자는 때로는 기술자가 아닌 사람을 놀라게 하는, 물건을 고장 내는 일들을 존중한다. 주제문 그러나 부정적인 결과를 ⑤ 방지하는(→ 받아들이는) 습관은 성공을 얻는 가장 근본적인 비결 중 하나이다.

구문 [1행~3행] Wrapped up in the idea of embracing failure is the related notion of breaking things to make them better — particularly complex things.
(V: is, S: the related notion ~ complex things; the related notion = breaking things ~)
「S+be+p.p.」의 수동태 문장에서 p.p.를 강조하기 위해 「p.p.+be+S」의 어순으로 도치되었다. the related notion과 breaking things ~ complex things는 동격 관계이다.

[8행~10행] Similarly, *one way* (to troubleshoot *a complicated device* [that's broken]) is to deliberately force negative results ~.
to troubleshoot ~ broken은 to부정사의 형용사적 용법으로 one way를 수식하며, 그 안의 관계대명사절 that's broken은 a complicated device을 수식한다.

어휘 **embrace** 받아들이다; (껴)안다 **notion** 생각, 관념 **force A to-v** A를 v하게 강제[강요]하다 **systematically** 체계적으로 **crash** (컴퓨터를) 고장 내다; 충돌(하다); 추락(하다) **complicated** 복잡한(= complex) **deliberately** 의도적으로, 고의로 **temporary** 일시적인; 임시의 **locate** ~의 정확한 위치를 찾아내다; (특정 위치에) 두다 **trick** 비결, 요령; 속임수

30 지칭 대상 ④

소재 햇빛을 받으면 기분이 좋은 이유

해설 ④는 멜라토닌(melatonin)을 가리키고 나머지는 모두 햇빛(sunlight)을 가리킨다.

해석 주제문 사람들은 왜 일반적으로 햇빛을 받을 때 더 기분이 좋을까? 아마도 가장 분명한 답은 모두가 ① 그것(= 햇빛)이 없으면 죽으리라는 것을 알고 있다는 것이다. 가장 기본적인 심리적 차원에서, ② 그것(= 햇빛)은 사람들이 더 안전하고, 더 자신감 있고, 더 활기차게 느끼게 한다. 좀 더 과학적인 차원에서의 또 다른 답은 신경과학자들이 우리의 뇌에 관해 밝혀내고 있는 놀라운 발견들에 있다. ③ 그것(= 햇빛)이 없으면, 우리의 뇌는 멜라토닌을 생산하기 시작하는데, 이 호르몬은 체온을 낮추고 뇌의 활동을 줄이도록 돕는다. 이것은 우리가 잠들게 도와준다. 하지만 너무 많은 ④ 그것(= 멜라토닌)은 우울증의 한 원인이 되는 것으로 여겨지기 때문에 햇빛이 그것의 생산을 억제한다는 것은 다행한 일이다. 게다가, ⑤ 그것(= 햇빛)은 뇌에서 세로토닌과 노르아드레날린의 수치를 높이는 것으로 보이는데, 이것들은 우리의 기분을 정말 좋게 해주는 호르몬들이다. 이것이 바로 길고 어두운 겨울이 그렇게 지겨울 수 있는 이유이다.

어휘 **in general** 일반적으로(= generally) **obvious** 분명한, 명백한 **psychological** 심리적인, 정신적인 **lie in** ~에 있다 **neuroscientist** 신경과학자 **reveal** 밝히다, 드러내다 **in the absence of A** A가 없으면 **depression** 우울(증) **it's a good thing[job] that** ~해서 다행이다[잘됐다] **shut off** 멈추다 **appear** ~인 것처럼 보이다; 나타나다 **drag** 지겨운 것; 끌다

31 빈칸 추론 ⑤

소재 몽구스의 동정심

해설 이 글은 〈예시+주제〉의 구조로, 제시된 예를 통해서 주제문의 빈칸에 들어갈 몽구스 사회가 가진 '특성'을 추론해야 한다. 몽구스 사회에서 아픈 몽구스가 생기면 나머지 몽구스들이 그의 먹이나 잠자리에 편의를 봐주고 호의를 베푼다는 예들은 몽구스 사회가 가진 ⑤ '동정심'을 보여준다고 할 수 있다.

해석 자신의 책 〈Mongoose Watch〉를 쓰려고 동물 행동을 연구하는 동안, 영국의 동물 행동학자 Anne Rasa는 난쟁이 몽구스 한 마리가 만성 신장 질환으로 병들었을 때, 동료들에게서 다르게 대우 받는 것을 발견하고는 깜짝 놀랐다. 다른 몽구스들은, 몽구스 사회 서열 속에서의 그(= 병에 걸린 몽구스)의 지위를 감안했을 때, 보통 때 먹었을 것보다 병에 걸린 동물(= 몽구스)이 훨씬 더 일찍 먹을 수 있도록 허용했다. Rasa에게 정말 놀라웠던 것은, 지배하는 위치에 있는 수컷이 먹고 있던 음식의 똑같은 부분을 한입 먹는 것까지도 그 아픈 몽구스에게 허용되었다는 것인데, 그것은 보통 때는 결코 일어나지 않을 일이었다. 병에 걸린 그 몽구스가 기어오르는 능력을 잃었을 때, 몽구스 집단 전체는 상자와 같은 높은 물체 위에서 자는 것에 대한 확실한 선호를 포기했다. 대신, 그들은 모두 아픈 그 친구와 함께 바닥에서 잠을 자는 것을 택했다. 주제문 이러한 예들은 몽구스 '사회'가 동정심을 갖고 있음을 보여준다.
① 창의성 ② 자제심 ③ 흥미 ④ 존경심

구문 [5행~7행] The other mongooses permitted the ill animal to eat much earlier / than he normally would have (eaten), / **considering** his rank ~.
normally would have 다음에는 eaten이 생략되어 있다. considering 이하는 능동 의미의 분사구문이다.

어휘 **dwarf** 난쟁이 **chronic** 만성적인 **kidney** 신장 **peer** 동료, 또래; 응시하다 **rank** 지위 **to A's astonishment** A에게 놀랍게도 **bite** 한입; 물기 **dominant** 지배적인, 우세한 **entire** 전체의 **decided** 명확하고 확실한, 결정적인 **preference** 선호 **elevate** 올리다 **opt** 선택하다

32 빈칸 추론 ③

소재 훌륭한 기념물의 조건

해설 빈칸 다음에 이어지는 예시에서 전쟁 병동의 구체적인 묘사 대신 간호사의 눈에 담긴 동정심만으로도 병사의 연약함을 전달하기에 충분하다고 했으므로 훌륭한 기념물은 ③ '모든 것을 상세하게 묘사할' 필요가 없다고 할 수 있다.

해석 훌륭한 기념물은, (그것이) 기념하고 있는 사건 동안의 경험(된 것)을 관람자들이 실제로 느끼도록 가장 잘 돕는 방식으로 만들어져야 한다. 주제문 그러나 훌륭한 기념물을 만든다고 해서 반드시 모든 것을 상세하게 묘사할 필요는 없다. 이러한 기념물의 좋은 예로 '병사와 간호사'가 있다. 이 기념물은 전쟁 병동을 보여주고 있지만, 수술대나 기타 의료 시설을 담고 있지는 않다. 이것은 병사의 연약함을 뛰어나게 전달하고 있는데, 병사를 돕기 위해 해줄 수 있는 것이 거의 없을 때 관람자들은 병사의 고통을 더 잘 느끼게 되기 때문이다. 그리고 간호사가 보이는 약간의 동정의 눈빛만으로도 기념물을 효과적인 것으로 만들기에 충분하다. 이 기념물은 관람자들이 결코 똑같은 상황에 놓이고 싶지 않게 한다.

① 그 시대정신을 반영할
② 작가의 의도를 표현할
④ 그 목적에 대한 대중 인식을 필요로 할
⑤ 관람자들에게 호의적인 평을 받을

어휘 **memorial** 기념물, 기념관 *cf.* **memorialize** 기념하다 **observer** 관람자, 관찰자 **not necessarily** 반드시 ~은 아닌 **battlefield** 전장, 싸움터 **ward** 병동, 병실 **surgical** 수술의, 외과용의 **facility** (복수형) 시설, 설비 **convey** 전달하다 **vulnerability** 연약함, 상처받기 쉬움 **hint of** 약간의 **sympathy** 동정(심); 공감 [선택지 어휘] **era** 시대 **intention** 의도 **depict** 묘사하다, 그리다 **favorable** 호의적인; 찬성인

33 빈칸 추론 ①

소재 효과적인 읽기 전략

해설 글을 읽을 때에는 전체의 내용과 흐름을 먼저 훑어보는 것이 정보를 정확히 파악하는 데 효과적이라는 요지의 글이다. 예로 든 조각 맞추기 퍼즐의 경우에도 전체 그림을 보고 났을 때 하나의 조각이 의미하는 것이 더 잘 이해된다는 내용이 되어야 하므로 빈칸에는 ① '이미 전체 그림을 보았을'이 들어가야 한다.

해석 주제문 좀 더 효과적인 읽기를 위한 첫 번째 단계는 실제로 읽기 전에, 쓰인 정보를 전체적으로 빨리 훑어보는 것이다. 이는 여러분의 두뇌가 그 정보를 받아들이고 그 특정한 주제에 대해 생각하도록 준비시킨다. 이는 산에 오르기를 시작하기 전에 가능한 최선의 길을 선택할 수 있도록 한 걸음 물러나서 산을 바라보는 것과 유사하다. 또한, 여행을 시작하거나 고속도로에 이르기 전에 지도를 보는 것과도 같다. 전반적인 목적과 글의 흐름을 이해하는 것은 각각의 부분에 이르렀을 때 당신이 그것을 한데 종합하고 정확하게 이해하는 것을 돕는다. 당연히, 조각 맞추기 퍼즐의 한 조각은 이미 전체 그림을 보았을 때 이해가 더 잘되고 더 쉽게 자리를 맞출 수 있다.

② 마침내 퍼즐의 테두리를 완성할
③ 색깔에 따라 각각의 조각을 분류할
④ 그것이 매우 독특한 모양을 가지고 있음을 볼
⑤ 좀 더 자신감을 갖고 각각의 어려움에 맞설

어휘 **effective** 효과적인 **entirety** 전체; 완전한 상태 **particular** 특정한 **material** 자료; 소재; 물질 **piece together** 종합하다; ~을 잇다 [선택지 어휘] **border** 테두리, 가장자리; 경계 **sort** 분류하다 **distinctive** 독특한, 뚜렷이 구별되는

34 빈칸 추론 ④

소재 디지털화된 현대 예술 기록의 문제점

해설 빈칸 문장으로 보아 '무엇'에 관한 중요한 의문을 제기할 수 있는지를 찾아야 한다. 현대 예술가들이 자신들의 견해를 전자적 형태로 제시해 왔는데, 이 자료들은 삭제가 될(be deleted) 가능성이 있고, 내구성(endurance)이 확실하지 않으므로 ④ '미래에 현대 예술 기록들의 이용 가능성'에 의문이 든다는 내용이 되는 것이 가장 적절하다.

해석 현대의 예술가들은 강의, 인터뷰, 에세이, 그리고 다양한 새로운 형식으로 자신들의 견해를 제시해 왔다. 이메일, 문자와 음성 메시지, 그리고 다른 가상의 공개 토론장이 편지와 일지를 거의 대체해 버렸다. 많은 예술가들이 블로그, 채팅, 그리고 요즘에는 몇몇 소셜미디어 계정을 가진 세련된 웹사이트를 가지고 있다. 이런 새로운 가능성들은 전문가들만이 아니라 청중들도 정보를 제공받고 예술가들과의 의미 있는 대화에 참여할 수 있게 해준다. 주제문 그러나 이런 흥미로운 전자 플랫폼에는 잠재적인 문제가 있다. 유형의 문서와는 달리, 이메일과 다른 전자적 문자, 시각, 그리고 청각 자료는 삭제될 수도 있고, (실제로) 자주 삭제된다. 심지어 그것들이 저장되어 있을 때도, 시간이 경과한 이후의 디지털 매체의 내구성은 여전히 알려져 있지 않다. 이것은 미래에 현대 예술 기록들의 이용 가능성에 관한 중요한 의문을 제기한다.

① 예술의 진정한 정의에 대해 합의하는 것의 어려움
② 언제 현대 예술이 전통 예술로 바뀌는지
③ 예술이 의미를 제공할 의무가 있어야 하는지
⑤ 왜 예술과 실물은 의식적으로 함께 연결되어 있는지

구문 [7행~9행] These new possibilities (S) **allow** (V) the audience (O), / (not just specialists), / **to be informed** (C1) / and **to engage** (C2) in meaningful dialogues with artists.

명사구 not just specialists가 문장 중간에 삽입된 형태이다. 「allow+O+to-v (O가 v하는 것을 허용하다)」 구조로 목적격보어인 to be informed와 to engage in ~ artists가 and로 연결되어 병렬구조를 이룬다.

어휘 **contemporary** 현대[당대]의; 동시대의 (사람) **novel** 새로운; (장편) 소설 **format** 형식; 형태 **virtual** (컴퓨터) 가상의; 사실상의 **public forum** 공개 토론장 **all but** 거의 **sophisticated** 세련된; 정교한 **account** 계정; 계좌 **specialist** 전문가, 전공자 **engage in** ~에 참여하다 **platform** 플랫폼(사용 기반이 되는 컴퓨터 시스템이나 소프트웨어) **tangible** 유형(有形)의, 만질 수 있는 **endurance** 내구성; 지구력 **raise** (문제를) 제기하다; 들어 올리다 [선택지 어휘] **conventional** 전통적인; 관습적인 **be obligated to-v** v할 의무가 있다 **availability** 이용 가능성; 유효성 **consciously** 의식적으로, 자각하여

35 무관한 문장 ③

소재 격한 감정 상태에서 높아지는 기억력

해설 격한 감정 상태에서 겪은 사건의 사소한 것까지 생생하게 기억할 수 있는 이유는 그때 뇌가 화학적 변화를 겪기 때문임을 설명하는 내용의 글이다. 반면에 ③은 긴장 완화 기법에 관한 내용이므로 글의 흐름과 무관하다.

해석 주제문 격한 감정 상태에서 경험한 사건들은 기억하기 더 쉽다. 화재를 겪은 소녀는 작은 것, 이를테면 자신이 그때 입고 있었던 드레스의 무늬를 생생하게 기억할지 모른다. 기억이 강화된 것은 사건 그 자체에 대한 감정 때문이 아니라 충격적인 사건이 일어날 때 뇌가 화학적 변화를 겪는다는 사실 때문이다. 긴장 완화 기법은 뇌가 격한 감정을 완화하고, 두려움을 유발하는 자극을 (사건) 현장의 사소한 일처럼 다루도록 도와준다. 사람이 매우 감정이 격한 상태일 때, 뇌는 특별한 호르몬을 방출하는데, 이것은 신경을 유난히 (모든 일에) 수용적으로 만들어서 가장 사소한 사항까지도 기록될 수 있게 한다. 감정적으로 격한 경험의 기억에 사소한 일들이 양적으로 유난히 많은 것은 이러한 경험들이 상기될 때마다 시간이 천천히 지나간다고 느끼는 것을 설명해 줄지도 모른다.

구문 [5행~8행] Heightened memory is not caused by the emotion of the event itself but (caused) by the fact that the brain goes through chemical changes when the shocking event occurs.

「not A but B」 구문이 사용되었으며 'A가 아니라 B'로 해석한다. the fact와 that절은 동격 관계이다.

어휘 **vivid** 생생한, 선명한 **heightened** 강화된, 고조된 **chemical** 화학적인; 화학물질 **neutralize** 완화[중화]하다; 무효로 하다 **stimulus** (복수형 **stimuli**) 자극(제) **nerve** 신경 **exceptionally** 유난히, 더욱, 특별히 **receptive** 수용적인, 선뜻 받아들이는 **insignificant** 사소한, 중요하지 않은 **intense** 격렬한, 강렬한 **account for** 설명하다; (비율을) 차지하다 **recall** 상기하다, 기억해 내다; 회수[리콜]하다

36 글의 순서 ①

소재 아이의 발달에 있어 부모의 역할

해설 주어진 글 뒤에는 앞서 언급된 과정에서(in the progress) 부모들이 자녀 교육에 과도한 열성을 보이게 될 수 있음을 언급한 (A)가 이어지는 것이 적절하다. 다음으로는 (A)에 대해 예를 들어(for example) 설명하는 (C)가 오고, 부모가 적극적으로 나서는 (C)와는 대조적으로(On the other hand) 부모가 아이의 학습을 돕지 않는 경우에 빚어질 수 있는 결과를 언급하는 (B)가 마지막에 오는 것이 자연스럽다. 따라서 정답은 ① '(A)-(C)-(B)'이다.

해석 갓 부모가 된 모든 이들은 자신의 아기가 개개의 새 기술을 숙련해나가는 표시들을 기쁘고 자랑스럽게 지켜본다. (아기가 한) 첫 번째 말, 첫 걸음마, 읽기나 쓰기 능력을 보여주는 첫 징조 같은 것들 말이다.

(A) 그 진행 과정에서 느끼는 기쁨 때문에 부모들은 아기에게 너무 일찍 너무 많은 것을 배우게 하려고 서두르고 싶어질지도 모른다. 주제문 하지만 발달을 서두르는 것은 아이들을 과도하게 조바심 내게 하고 성과 중심적으로 만들 수 있다.

(C) 예를 들어, 부모가 너무 일찍 아기에게 글씨를 쓰거나 그림을 그리게 적극적으로 장려하면, 아기는 부모를 기쁘게 하기 위해 너무 열심히 노력하다가 연필을 제대로 잡는 것조차 못하는 시기에 실패감에 시달릴 수 있다.

(B) 주제문 반면, 아이들이 부모로부터의 칭찬과 더불어 나이에 적합하고 (부모의) 지도를 받는 많은 활동들을 못하게 되면, 그들의 타고난 호기심과 용기를 잃게 될지도 모른다.

어휘 **mastery** 숙련, 숙달 **be tempted to-v** v하고 싶어지다 **rush** 서두르다 **overly** 지나치게 **anxious** 조바심내는 **performance** 성과, 성적 **oriented** ~ 지향적인, ~ 우선의 **deny** (남이 원하는 것을) 허락하지 않다; 거절하다; 부인하다 **age-appropriate** 나이에 적합한 **combine A with B** A와 B를 결합시키다; A와 B를 겸비하다

37 글의 순서 ④

소재 추위를 막아주는 눈

해설 주어진 문장은 식물 위에 덮인 눈이 혹독한 추위로부터 식물을 보호한다는 내용이다. 눈 덮인 회양목의 예를 제시하는 (C)가 그 뒤에 오고, 식물뿐만 아니라 눈이 땅속에 사는 생물을 보호하기도 한다는 내용의 (A)가 그다음에 오는 것이 자연스럽다. (A)가 땅속에 사는 생명체를 죽일 수 있을 만큼 겨울 기온이 낮게 떨어진다는 내용으로 끝나므로, 눈이 이러한 것을 예방한다는 내용의 (B)가 그 뒤에 와야 한다. 따라서 정답은 ④ '(C)-(A)-(B)'이다.

해석 주제문 연약한 부분이 극심한 추위로 인해 죽게 될 식물들은 공기가 채워진 덮인 눈 덕분에 혹독한 날씨로부터 차단되면 종종 살아남게 된다.

(C) 예를 들어, 눈이 내려 회양목을 덮는다면 정원사는 그것을 털어내고 싶을 수도 있다. 그러나 회양목 위에 덮인 눈을 그대로 두는 게 더 현명하다. 그렇지 않으면, 공기와 바람의 극심한 기온이 쉽사리 그것(= 회양목)을 죽일 수 있다.

(A) 주제문 게다가, 덮인 눈은 무수히 많은 수의 곤충, 벌레, 달팽이 그리고 땅속의 다른 많은 작은 생물체를 보호한다. 겨울의 대기 온도는 지표 바로 아래 살고 있는 수많은 유기체를 죽일 수 있을 만큼 쉽사리 낮게 떨어질 수 있다.

(B) 그러나 눈이 이것을 막아준다. 지표와 쌓인 눈의 바닥 사이에 보존된 공기층은 단열재로 작용하여 그 아래 생물체가 얼어 죽는 것을 막을 만큼 충분한 온기를 유지한다.

구문 [1행~3행] *Plants* [**whose** tender parts would be killed by extreme cold] often survive // **if** they are insulated from a severe climate / by an air-filled snow blanket.
(Plants: S, survive: V)

「주절+조건 부사절」의 구조이다. 주어(Plants)가 관계대명사절의 수식을 받아 길어졌다.

[9행~13행] *The layer of air* [**that** is preserved between the surface of the soil and the base of the snowfall] acts as an insulator, / **preserving** *enough warmth* (**to stop** the creatures beneath **from freezing**).

문장 전체의 주어는 The layer of air, 동사는 acts이다. 주어는 that이 이끄는 관계대명사절의 수식을 받고 있다. 「between A and B」는 'A와 B 사이에'의 뜻이다. preserving 이하는 '동시동작'을 나타내는 분사구문이다. ( )는 enough warmth를 수식하는 형용사적 용법의 to부정사구이며, 「enough+명사+to-v」는 'v하기에 충분한 (명사)'로 해석하는 것이 자연스럽다. 「stop A from v-ing」는 'A가 v하는 것을 막다'란 뜻이다.

어휘 **tender** 부드러운, 연한 **insulate** 고립시키다, 격리하다; 단열[절연, 방음]하다 *cf.* **insulator** 단열재 **severe** 심한, 맹렬한 **blanket** 전면을 덮는 것; 담요 **untold** 셀 수 없는, 막대한; 밝혀지지 않은 **creature** 생물 **plunge** 추락하다; 뛰어들다; 내던지다 **organism** 유기체, 생물 **surface** 표면 **layer** 층, 겹 **preserve** 보존하다, 간직하다 **beneath** ~의 바로 밑에 **be tempted to-v** v하고 싶어지다

38 문장 넣기 ③

소재 에버글레이즈 습지의 물 부족 현상

해설 주어진 문장은 사람들과 자연이 에버글레이즈에서 물을 빼내는 데 합심하고 있다는 내용이며 ③ 이후에 이에 대한 구체적인 예가 제시되고 있으므로, 주어진 문장은 ③에 들어가는 것이 가장 적절하다.

해석 에버글레이즈 지역은 플로리다 주(州) 남부에서만 발견되는 거대한 참억새 늪지대를 특징으로 하는 아열대 습지이다. 물은 이 독특한 환경에 필수적이다. 이 지역은 오키초비 호수가 수천 년 넘게 범람하면서 형성되었다. 이런 연례적인 범람은 늘 이 습지에 다양한 식물과 동물을 부양하는 데 필요한 신선한 물을 공급했다. 주제문 불행히도 사람들과 자연이 에버글레이에서 소중한 물을 빼내는 데 합심하고 있다. 예를 들어, 마이애미 강, 리틀 강, 뉴 강이 모두 그 지역에서 많은 물을 제거한다. 하지만 더 안 좋은 것은 지난 세기에 지어진 댐과 운하들로, 그것들이 매년 일어나는 범람을 막기 때문이다. 이러한 범람이 없으면 에버글레이즈는 생존할 수 없다. 개간과 복구 사업들이 이 독특한 생태계를 살리려는 희망으로 시작되었다.

구문 [3행~5행] The Everglades region is *a subtropical wetland* (**featuring** *vast sawgrass marshlands* (**found** only in southern Florida)).

featuring 이하는 a subtropical wetland를 수식하며, 이 분사구 안의 또 다른 분사구 found ~ Florida는 vast sawgrass marshlands를 수식한다. wetland와 feature는 능동 관계이므로 현재분사를, marshlands와 find는 수동 관계이므로 과거분사를 썼다.

[12행~13행] But worse are *the dams and canals* [**that** were built last century], / **as** they prevent annual flooding.
(worse: C, are: V, the dams and canals: S)

보어를 문두에 두어 강조하고, 수식어구 때문에 길어진 주어를 동사 뒤로 보낸 도치구문이다. [ ] 부분은 the dams and canals를 수식하는 주격 관계대명사절이다. 여기서 접속사 as는 '이유'를 나타낸다.

어휘 **unite** 연합하다 **subtropical** 아열대의 **wetland** 습지대 **feature** ~을 특색으로 삼다 **vast** 거대한, 광대한 **marshland** 늪지대, 습지대 *cf.* **marsh** 늪, 습지 **vital** 필수적인; 생명의 **canal** 운하, 수로 **restoration** 복구, 복원, 회복 **ecosystem** 생태계

39 문장 넣기 ④

소재 굴곡을 따라 달리는 트랙 경기가 폐지된 이유

해설 주어진 문장 앞에는 선수가 실내경기를 포기할 정도로 심각한 제약이 나와야 하는데 ④의 앞부분에 굴곡이 심하고 레인 폭이 좁은 200미터 실내 트랙에 대한 진술이 나와 있고 ④의 뒷부분에는 '이는 안쪽 레인이 불리하기 때문이다'라는 진술이 나오므로 주어진 문장은 ④에 위치해야 한다. 주어진 문장에서 such a severe restriction은 ④의 앞부분에 있는 '굴곡이 심하고 레인 폭이 좁은 트랙'을 지칭한다.

해석 여러분은 굴곡을 따라 전속력으로 달려야 하는 200미터 경기와 같은 트랙 경기에서 안쪽 레인을 갖는 것이 가장 좋은지 바깥쪽 레인을 갖는 것이 가장 좋은지 궁금하게 여긴 적이 있는가? 육상 선수들은 강한 선호를 가지고 있다. 키가 큰 주자들은 안쪽 레인

의 더 심한 굴곡을 지나가는 것이 완만한 바깥쪽 레인의 굴곡에 비해 더 어렵다고 느낀다. 단거리 주자가, 트랙 둘레가 불과 200미터밖에 되지 않아서 굴곡이 훨씬 더 심하고 레인 폭이 1.22미터에서 1미터로 줄어드는 실내에서 경주할 때, 그 상황은 훨씬 더 심각하다. 이것은 매우 심한 제약이어서 (경기 기록상으로 가장 느린 예선 통과자가 되어) 최종 결승에서 안쪽 레인을 배정받은 선수가 실내 선수권 대회의 최종 결승에 참가하지 않는 것이 흔한 일이 되었다. 주제문 이것은 안쪽 레인에서는 이길 가능성이 너무나 낮아지고 상당한 부상 위험이 있기 때문이었다. 그 결과 이 경기는 실내 선수권 대회의 경기 목록에서 대부분 사라졌다.

구문 [1행~4행] This was **such** *a severe restriction* **that** it became common for *the athlete* [who drew the inside lane for the final] (by being the slowest qualifier on times) not to take part in the final in indoor championships.
「such ~ that ...」은 '너무 ~해서 …하다'의 뜻이며, 「such a(n)+형용사+명사」의 어순을 따른다. that절에서 it은 가주어, not to take ~ championships 부분이 진주어이며 for the athlete은 to부정사의 의미상 주어이다. [ ] 부분은 the athlete을 수식한다.

[8행~10행] Tall runners find it *harder* to get round the tighter curve of the inside lane / than **that** of the gentle outer lanes.
it은 가목적어이고 to get round ~ outer lane이 진목적어이며 harder는 목적격 보어이다. than 다음의 that은 the curve를 지칭한다.

어휘 **severe** 심한 **restriction** 제약 **athlete** 운동선수, 육상 경기 선수 **lane** (경주 등의) 레인; 차선 **take part in** ~에 참가하다 **final** 결승전 **championship** 선수권 대회 **sprint** 전력질주하다 *cf.* **sprinter** 단거리 주자 **bend** 굽이, 굽은 곳 **preference** 선호 **gentle** 완만한, 심하지 않은 **width** 폭, 너비 **considerable** 상당한

40 요약문 완성 ④

소재 먹이와 장소를 연관 짓는 쥐의 학습 능력

해설 처음에 먹이 없이 실행했던 방의 선호도 검사에서 쥐가 선호하지 않았던 방은, 그곳에서 자신들이 좋아하는 먹이를 얻게 되자 선호하는 방으로 바뀌었다. 이는 쥐들이 먹이와 장소를 '연관 짓고(associate)' 맛있는 먹이에 대한 노출이 발생한 방을 '선호하는(prefer)' 쪽으로 바뀌었음을 의미한다.

해석 주제문 한 연구에서 쥐가 먹이와 장소에 어떻게 반응하는지를 조사했다. 처음에 연구자들은 쥐들 간의 방에 대한 선호를 검사했다. 쥐들은 그들의 장소를 자유롭게 선택했고, 어느 방에도 먹이는 없었다. 그러고 나서 쥐들은 실험 당시에는 배고프지 않은 상태였는데, 두 그룹으로 나뉘었다. 첫 번째 집단은 자신에게 호감이 덜 가는 방에서 단맛이 많이 첨가된 시리얼을 받았다. 두 번째 집단은 자신이 선호하는 방에서 보통의 먹이를 받았다. 다음에 두 번째 집단은 덜 선호하는 방에서 고열량, 고지방 간식을 받은 반면, 첫 번째 집단은 자기가 선호하는 장소에서 보통의 먹이를 받았다. 그러고 나서 처음의 방 선호 실험이 반복되었다. 다시 쥐들은 자신의 장소를 자유롭게 선택했고, 다시 각 방에는 먹이가 없었다. 연구 결과는 분명했다. 이전의 선택과는 관계없이, 두 집단의 쥐들은 단맛이 첨가된 시리얼이나 고지방 간식을 먹었던 방을 선택하는 법을 학습했다.

⬇

당분이나 지방이 많은 먹이에 노출된 것은 실험의 쥐들이 먹이를 장소와 (A) 연관 짓고 노출이 발생한 장소를 (B) 선호하도록 길들였다.

구문 [8행~10행] The second group was fed standard food in *the chamber* [(which[that]) it preferred].
[ ]는 앞에 목적격 관계대명사 which[that]가 생략된 관계사절로 the chamber를 수식한다.

[17행~20행] Regardless of their previous choices, / both groups of rats had learned to choose *the chamber* [where they had eaten **either** sweetened cereals **or** high-fat snacks].
[ ]는 the chamber를 수식하는 관계부사절이다. 「either A or B」는 'A나 B 둘 중 하나'의 뜻이다.

어휘 **location** 장소, 위치 **preference** 선호(도) *cf.* **prefer** 선호하다, 좋아하다 **chamber** 방 **locale** 장소, 현장 **less-favored** 호감이 덜 가는 **snack** 간식 **initial** 처음의; 머리글자의 **finding** 연구 결과 **regardless of** ~와 관계없이 **exposure** 노출 **condition** 길들이다, 훈련시키다; 조절[조정]하다 [선택지 어휘] **confuse** 혼란시키다, 어리둥절하게 만들다

41~42 장문 41 ③ 42 ④

소재 음식에 대한 거부감이 다이어트에 미치는 영향

해설 41. 마지막 문장 The secret is to not let food become a bugaboo, a dark monster that runs our life.에 글의 요지가 나타나 있다. 즉, 음식을 두려워하지 말고 자연스럽게 대하라는 내용이므로 ③ '다이어트의 비결: 음식이 당신의 친구가 되게 하라!'가 제목으로 가장 적절하다.
① 매일 더 적게 먹고 더 많이 움직여라
② 포만감이 들기 전에 멈추는 것을 기억하라
④ 끈기: 성공적인 다이어트의 핵심
⑤ 감각으로 말고 지성으로 먹어라(= 먹고 싶다고 먹지 말고 생각하고 먹어라)

42. 지방은 다른 영양 공급원이 없을 때 신체가 생존을 위해 활용하는 것인데, 사람들이 다이어트 실패에 대한 불안을 느낄 때 지방을 만들어내는 화학반응이 자극되어 살찌게 된다는 내용이다. 지방은 '생존'을 위해 활용하는 것이므로 지방이 만들어지는 과정은 ④ '자기 보호적' 과정이라고 표현할 수 있을 것이다.
① 노화를 방지하는 ② 스트레스에 의한 ③ 다이어트 중심의 ⑤ 체중을 줄이는

해석 다이어트에 관해 "음식만 봐도 살이 쪄요."라는 유명한 우스갯말이 있다. 매우 존경받는 한 체중 조절 분야 강사는 사실 이 말에도 다소 사실성이 있다고 말했다. 그녀는 두려움의 감정이 자기 보호적 과정을 활성화하는 신체의 화학반응을 이끌어낸다고 설명했다. 이런 반응의 부산물 중 하나가 음식 저장고인 지방을 만들어내는 것이다. 지방은 다른 영양 공급원이 없을 때 당신의 신체가 생존을 위해 활용하는 것이다. 체중이 늘어나는 것을 걱정하는 사람들은 자신들의 다이어트를 중단하는 것에 죄의식을 느끼고 (다이어트에) 실패하는 것을 두려워하기 때문에 군침이 도는 음식에 둘러싸였을 때 종종 불안해한다. 이러한 불안은 지방을 만들어내는 신체의 작용을 자극한다. 그것이 어떤 사람들은 결코 체중을 감량할 수 없는 것처럼 보이는 이유이다. 주제문 즉, 체중 감량에 대해 걱정하는 것이 바로 체중이 (줄지 않고) 그대로이게 하는 원인인 것이다!
자연스러운 상태에서는 우리는 음식을 위협으로 보지 않지만 만약 우리가 효과가 없었던 많은 다이어트를 해왔다면 우리는 이것(= 음식)을 유혹, 시험과 실패의 상징으로 볼 것이다. 가끔씩 기름진 별미를 포함해서 수많은 즐길 만한 음식을 먹는데도 완전한 건강 상태에 있고 멋져 보이는 많은 사람들이 있다. 주제문 비결은 음식이 두려운 것, 즉 우리 인생을 통제하는 어둠의 괴물이 되게 하지 않는 것이다.

구문 [9행~13행] *People* [who are worried about gaining weight] often become anxious // **when** (they are) **surrounded** by mouthwatering food, // **as** they feel guilt about breaking their diet and fear failing.
(People = S, become = V, feel = V'1, fear = V'2)
when과 surrounded 사이에는 「주어+be동사」가 생략되었으며, 이는 분사구문에 접속사가 생략되지 않은 형태로 볼 수도 있다. 여기서 as는 '이유'를 나타낸다.

어휘 **activate** 활성화시키다; 작동시키다 **byproduct** 부산물 **reserve** 비축, 축적; 남겨두다; 보유하다 **nutrition** 영양 **mouthwatering** 군침이 도는 **guilt** 죄책감 **stimulate** 자극하다 **precisely** 바로, 정확히 **trigger** (반응·사건을 유발한) 계기, 도화선; 유발하다; (총의) 방아쇠 **occasional** 가끔의 **delicacy** 별미, 진미; 연약함; 섬세함 **bugaboo** 두려운 것, 걱정거리

43~45 장문 43 ④ 44 ③ 45 ③

소재 Joe와 이웃을 화해시켜준 목수

해설 43. Joe가 하나 있는 이웃과 송아지 때문에 말다툼하다가 말을 안 하게 되는 (A) 다음에는 몇 년 동안 계속 말을 안 했다는 (D)가 오는 것이 자연스럽다. Joe에게 목수가

찾아오자 울타리를 세워줄 것을 요청하는 내용 다음에는 목수가 승낙하는 (B)가 와야 하고, 울타리 대신 다리를 만든 목수를 야단치러 가는 내용 다음에는 목수의 의도로 이웃과 화해하게 되는 (C)가 오는 것이 적절하다.

44. (c)는 Joe를 가리키는 반면 나머지는 모두 목수를 가리킨다.

45. (C)에서 Joe에게 다가와 사과한 사람은 이웃이다. 이 때 목수는 Joe에게 윙크하며 미소 짓고 있었으므로 ③은 글의 내용과 일치하지 않는다.

해석 (A) 노인 Joe는 여러 해 동안 그의 맞은편에 살고 있는 한 이웃이 있는 농부였다. Joe와 그의 이웃은 서로밖에 없었다. 어느 날 오후 그들이 창문 밖에서 송아지를 발견했을 때까지는 종종 그들이 나눈 말들은 하루 종일 그들이 한 유일한 말이었다. 이웃이 "이봐, 밖에 있는 내 송아지를 보게."라고 말했다. Joe가 대답했다. "어떤 바보라도 무늬를 보고 그 송아지가 내 것이라는 걸 알 수 있을 거네." ① 그들은 말다툼을 시작했고 무자비한 말들은 침묵으로 끝나기에 이르렀다.

(D) ④ 몇 달이 몇 년이 되었지만 (그들 사이에) 말은 결코 나오지 않았다. 어느 날 떠돌이 목수가 Joe의 문을 두드렸다. 그는 일이 필요했기에 Joe는 그를 자기 집에 들어오라고 청했다. Joe는 "저기 개울이 보이시오? 넌더리나는 내 바보 이웃이 저걸 만들었소. 그놈은 단지 나를 화나게 하려고 쟁기를 들고 도랑을 파서 물을 채웠소."라고 말했다. (e) 그(= 목수)는 고개를 끄덕였다. Joe는 말했다. "⑤ 난 당신이 울타리를 세우기를 바라오. 정말로 높은 울타리를 말이요. 그러면 내가 이 바보를 다시는 볼 필요가 없지."

(B) 목수가 대답했다. "제가 당신을 행복하게 만들어줄 일을 할 수 있을 것 같군요." (a) 그(= 목수)와 Joe는 다음 날 ② Joe가 시내에서 하루를 보내는 동안 목수가 목재를 가져다가 울타리를 세우기로 합의했다. 다음 날 Joe가 집으로 돌아왔을 때 그는 목수가 해놓은 일을 보았다. 울타리 대신 (b) 그(= 목수)는 개울을 가로지르는 다리를 만들었다. 몹시 화가 난 Joe는 목수에게 따끔하게 한마디 하기 위해 내려가기 시작했다.

(C) 그러나 그가 목수를 만나기도 전에 이웃이 다리를 건너와 그를 힘껏 껴안았다. "Joe, 자네는 나보다 더 큰 사람일세. 난 다리를 만들 용기를 전혀 갖지 못했을 거야. 날 용서해 줄 수 있나?" ③ Joe는 그를 다시 껴안고 "용서할 게 없네."라고 속삭이고 (c) 그(= Joe)에게 윙크하고 미소 짓는 목수를 힐끗 쳐다보았다. Joe는 목수에게 가지 말라고 했지만 (d) 그(= 목수)는 해야 할 다른 일이 있다고 말했다.

구문 [(A) 3행~4행] Often *the words* [they spoke] **would** be *the only words* [they said] all day, ~.
[ ] 부분은 각각 앞에 나온 the words를 수식하는 관계대명사절이다. 조동사 would는 과거의 습관이나 동작을 나타낸다.

어휘 (A) **spy** 찾아내다, 발견하다 **calf** 송아지 **marking** 반점, 무늬 **cruel** 무자비한, 지독한 (B) **carpenter** 목수 **creek** 개울, 시내 **furious** 몹시 화가 난, 격노한 **give a person a piece of one's mind** 남에게 거침없이 의견[잔소리]을 말하다 (B) **whisper** 작은 소리로 이야기하다, 속삭이다 **glance** 흘끗 보다 **stay around** (어떤 장소에서) 떠나지[가지] 않다 (D) **damned** 넌더리나는, 지긋지긋한 **plow** 쟁기 **ditch** 도랑, 개천 **flood** 물을 대다

12

고난도 모의고사 13

본문 p.181

18 ⑤	19 ①	20 ①	21 ④	22 ②	23 ②	24 ④	25 ⑤	26 ③	27 ④
28 ⑤	29 ④	30 ⑤	31 ②	32 ⑤	33 ②	34 ②	35 ③	36 ④	37 ②
38 ④	39 ⑤	40 ②	41 ⑤	42 ③	43 ⑤	44 ④	45 ④		

18 글의 목적 ⑤

소재 미술대회 출품작의 기준 미달 통보

해설 환경 보존 미술 대회인 만큼 작품 재료 중 최소한 90퍼센트는 재활용품을 사용해야 하는데 출품한 작품이 그 요건을 충족하지 못해 반환될 것임을 알리는 내용이므로 글의 목적으로는 ⑤가 가장 적절하다.

해석 Samantha Park 님께,
생태 축제의 환경 보존 미술 대회에 출품해주신 것에 감사드립니다. 매년 우리는 아마추어 화가와 전문 화가로부터 똑같이 수백 개의 출품작을 받습니다만, 귀하의 작품이 명백하게 보여주는 재능과 관심사를 거의 보여주지 못합니다. 불행히도 환경 파괴 없는 지속 가능성과 환경 의식의 증진을 위해서 우리는 대회 지침 시행에 있어 엄격함을 유지해야 합니다. 이러한 것들 중 하나는 출품작이 금속이든 플라스틱이든 유리든 아니면 다른 종류의 재료든 간에, 반드시 최소한 90퍼센트의 재활용된 내용물을 사용해야 한다는 것을 명시하고 있습니다. 주제문 심사숙고 끝에 우리 심사위원들은 귀하의 출품작이 이런 자격 요건을 충족하지 않는다고 결정 내렸습니다. 귀하의 작품은 우편으로 다음 주 중 반환될 것입니다. 참여해주신 것에 감사드리며 화가로서 귀하의 활동에 행운을 빕니다.
축제 조직위원 Kate Ling 드림

구문 [10행~13행] One of these states // that entries must use at least 90% recycled content, // **whether** that *be* metals, plastic, glass, **or** another type of material.
that entries ~ material 전체는 동사 states의 목적어절이고, 「whether A or B」는 'A이든지 B이든지'의 뜻으로 양보의 부사절을 이끈다. 이러한 의미의 whether절에서 be동사는 원형이 흔히 쓰이는데, is를 써도 의미 차이는 거의 없다.

어휘 **submission** 제출; 제안; 항복 **sustainable** (환경 파괴 없이) 지속 가능한 *cf.* **sustainability** 지속 가능성 **amateur** 아마추어, 애호가 **alike** 똑같이, 둘 다 **in the interest of** ~을 위해서 **awareness** 의식, 관심 **enforcement** 시행, 실시 **guideline** 지침 **state** 명시하다; 진술하다 **entry** 출품작; 참가자 **content** 내용물; 함유량 **consideration** 숙고; 고려 **rule** 결정을 내리다, 규정하다; 지배하다 **qualification** 자격 **requirement** 요건, 필요조건

19 심경 변화 ①

소재 이상한 소리에 놀란 Jennifer

해설 Jennifer는 집안에서 들려오는 수상한 소리에 무서웠지만(frightened), 소리의 정체가 아버지였다는 것을 알고 안도했으므로(relieved) 심경 변화로 가장 적절한 것은 ① '무서운 → 안도한'이다.

해석 Jennifer는 글쓰기를 멈추고 집안 깊숙한 곳 어디선가 들려오는 둔탁하고 긁는 듯한 소리를 들었다. "여보세요." 그녀는 외쳤다. "거기 누구 있어요?" 아무도 그녀에게 대답하지 않았다. 천천히, 조용히, 그녀는 일어나서 계단을 내려가기 시작했다. 검은 (빛의) 웅덩이가 그녀 앞에서 소용돌이쳤다. 쿵! 지하실 문이 쾅 닫혔고 밀려드는 시원한 바람이 그녀를 휩쓸고 지나갔다. 주제문 그녀는 손이 떨리는 것을 느꼈다. Jennifer는 마지막 몇 개의 계단을 살금살금 내려갔고, 아버지의 침실로 쏜살같이 달려들었다. 그녀는 그의 무거운 손전등을 움켜잡고 전원을 켜서 부엌문을 향해 조금씩 나아갔다. "아! 너 때문에 놀랐잖아." 그녀의 아빠가 조명을 켜려고 뒷걸음치며 말했다. "저 때문에 놀라셨다고요?!" Jennifer가 손이 떨리는 채로 말했다. "미안하다 얘야. 내 열쇠가 오늘 밤에 잘 안 되더라고. 그리고 집 앞이 어두워서 네가 집에 없는 줄 알았어. 지하실 창을 억지로 열고 안으로 기어들어왔지." "다음에는 그냥 초인종을 누르세요." 주제문 Jennifer가 안도의 한숨을 쉬며 말했다.
② 화난 → 창피한
③ 불안한 → 기쁜
④ 분노한 → 만족한
⑤ 걱정하는 → 확신하는

구문 [12행~13행] "I scared you?!" said Jennifer, her hands **shaking**.
her hands shaking은 분사구문이며 여기에서 her hands는 shaking의 의미상 주어이다. 주절의 주어(Jennifer)와 부사절의 주어(her hands)가 다른 경우 분사구문에서 주어를 생략하지 않고 그냥 둔다.

어휘 **dull** 둔탁한 **scrape** 긁다 **pool** 웅덩이 **swirl** 소용돌이치다 **slam** 쾅 닫히다 **rush** 돌진, 쇄도 **sweep (swept-swept)** 휩쓸다 **tiptoe** 발끝으로 살금살금 걷다 **dart** 쏜살같이 달리다 **grab** 붙잡다 **inch** 조금씩 움직이다 **crawl** 기다 **a sigh of relief** 안도의 한숨

20 필자 주장 ①

소재 제품 홍보의 역동성

해설 시간이 흘러도 홍보 메시지의 효과가 있으려면 시대의 상황에 맞게 계속해서 바뀌어야 한다는 내용의 글이다. 따라서 필자의 주장으로 가장 적절한 것은 ①이다.

해석 혁신에 대해 결과 중심의 접근법을 취하는 회사들은 일단 결과가 충족되면 그것(=결과)은 더 이상 향상의 가능성이 없다는 것을 인정한다. 어떤 상품의 한 가지 장점을 계속해서 광고하는 메시지들은 고객들에게 영향력을 잃을 것이다. 주제문 이것은 기업의 메시지 전달이 계속 효과적이기 위해서는 시간이 흐름에 따라 (그에) 적응해야 한다는 것을 의미한다. '오염보다 더 강하다'는 것은 그런 특징이 특이한 장점을 나타낼 때는 세탁 세제를 위해서 좋은 메시지일 수도 있으나, 일단 모든 구할 수 있는 상품들이 '오염보다 더 강하다'면, 그 메시지는 의미가 없게 된다. 그것은 그 상품이 가지고 있을 수 있는 다른 어떤 이점들을 다른 결과들과 연결하지 못하고, 따라서 그 상품의 진정한 가치를 더 이상 전하지 못한다. 주제문 가치는 변하기 때문에 혁신은 역동적이어야 하고, 메시지 전달도 그러해야 한다. 더는 관련이 없는 메시지를 고수하고 있는 것은 판매와 성장을 더디게 할 뿐이다.

구문 [11행~14행] It fails to connect *any other advantages* [(which [that]) the product may have with other outcomes] and, therefore, no longer communicates the true value of the product.
문장의 동사 fails와 communicates는 and로 연결되어 병렬구조를 이루고 있다.

어휘 **outcome-driven** 결과 중심의, 성과 주도의 **approach** 접근(하다) **innovation** 혁신, 쇄신 **detergent** 세제 **feature** 특징 **represent** 나타내다, 의미하다; 대표하다 **dynamic** 역동적인 **relevant** 관련 있는, 적절한; 유의미한

21 밑줄 함의 ④

소재 다이어트 할 때의 영양상의 딜레마

해설 다이어트를 할 때는 단 음식을 먹지 않으려는 자제심을 가져야 하지만, 자제심을 갖기 위해서는 포도당이 필요하므로 단 음식을 먹어야 한다는 '영양상의 딜레마'를 설명하

는 글이다. 즉, 이 딜레마는 ④ '먹지 않기 위해 단 음식을 갈망해야 하는 것'이다.

해석 동기 부여가 잘 된 다이어트 수행자는 종종 영양상의 딜레마에 갇혀 있다. 최근의 실험실 연구에서 자제심 과제를 수행한 대학생들은 자신이 단 음식에 대한 더 큰 욕망을 가지게 되었음을 깨달았다. 다음 과제 동안 간식을 먹는 것을 허락받았을 때, 전에 자제심을 발휘했던 사람들이 달콤한 간식을 더 많이 먹었지만, 다른 (짭짤한) 간식은 더 먹지 않았다. 당신이 다이어트를 해본 적이 있고, 자신이 초콜릿이나 아이스크림에 대한 저 밀고 들어오는 갈망에서 벗어날 수 없음을 깨달은 적이 있으면, 이것은 억압된 욕망이 당신에게 돌아와서 계속 붙어 따라다니는 것 이상의 문제이다. 자제심이 혈류의 포도당을 고갈시키기 때문에 달콤한 음식은 특히 저항하기 어렵게 된다. 주제문 먹지 않기 위해서는 의지력이 필요하지만, 의지력을 갖기 위해서는 먹을 필요가 있다. 타당한 생리적 근거가 있다. 몸은 그것이 자제심을 발휘함으로써 혈류의 포도당을 고갈시켰음을 '알고' 있으며, 그것은 또한 단맛이 나는 음식이 일반적으로 에너지가 풍부한 포도당을 주입받는 가장 빠른 방법이라는 것도 알고 있는 것 같다.

① 체중 감소 없이 다이어트하기
② 다이어트를 그만두기 위해 자제심 사용하기
③ 먹으면서 다이어트를 하려는 유혹에 저항하기
⑤ 적절한 영양을 섭취하면서 다이어트 지속하기

구문 [5행~7행] **When** (they are) **allowed** to snack during the next task, // *those* [who had previously exerted self-control] ate more sweet snacks, / but not other (salty) snacks.

When과 allowed 사이에 they are가 생략되어 있다. [ ] 부분은 주어 those를 수식하는 관계사절이며 동사는 ate이다. but not other (salty) snacks는 but didn't eat more other (salty) snacks를 줄여 쓴 표현이다.

[7행~11행] If you've ever been on a diet and found yourself unable to escape *those intrusive cravings* (for chocolate or ice cream), // this is more than a matter **of** *repressed desires* **coming** back to haunt you.

과거분사 been과 found가 have에 이어져 병렬구조를 이룬다. coming ~ you는 전치사 of의 목적어로 쓰인 동명사구이며, repressed desires는 동명사 coming의 의미상 주어이다.

어휘 **motivated** 동기 부여가 된 **be trapped in** ~에 갇히다 **catch-22** 딜레마, 진퇴양난 **self-control** 자제심 **snack** 간식(을 먹다) **previously** 이전에 **exert** 발휘하다, 행사하다 **intrusive** 밀고 들어오는, 침입하는 **craving** 갈망, 열망 *cf.* **crave** 갈망[열망]하다 **repress** 억누르다 **haunt** (생각 등이) 늘 붙어 따라다니다; (유령이) 출몰하다 **deplete** 고갈시키다 **glucose** 포도당 **bloodstream** 혈류 **willpower** 의지력, 자제심 **sound** 타당한, 믿을 만한 **physiological** 생리(학)적인 **infusion** 주입, 투입 [선택지 어휘] **temptation** 유혹 **intake** 섭취; 흡입 **nutrition** 영양; 영양 공급

22 글의 요지 ②

소재 문명 간 교류

해설 우리는 우리 주변의 사물을 우리 사회가 발견했다고 생각하기 쉽지만, 사실 거의 모든 물건은 다른 문명의 것을 모방하고, 교역하고, 차용한 결과물이라는 내용이므로 ②가 글의 요지로 가장 적절하다.

해석 우리는 우리 주변의 사물은 우리의 사회가 발견했다는, 혹은 적어도 기본적으로 (우리 사회에 맞게) 조정했다는 생각에 쉽사리 빠져든다. 그러나 잠시만 생각해 보면 당신은 거의 모든 것들이 다른 문명에서 발명되었다는 것을 발견할 것이다. 잉글랜드는 특히 이것의 명확한 예인데, 왜냐하면 대륙 근처의 작은 섬의 일부이며 무역을 하는 제국이어서, 그 나라(=잉글랜드)는 자기 문화의 거의 전부를 해외에서 끌어왔기 때문이다. 적어도 18세기까지는 음악, 미술, 건축, 과학, 지식에서 대개 차용의 결과가 아니었던 것이 거의 없다. 우리가 세계의 다른 어떤 지역을 가도 마찬가지일 텐데, 어딜 가도 특징적으로 '지역적인' 것들 중 많은 것이 타 지역으로부터 수입된 것이다. 주제문 하나의 문명은 외제 수입품들로 이루어진 한 바구니이다. 우리는 빌리고, 모방하고, 교역하고, 훔친 다음 편리하게 잊어버린다.

구문 [1행~3행] We easily slip into the idea that the things around us were **discovered**, or at least basically **adapted**, by our own society.

that절은 the idea를 부연 설명하는 동격절이다. that절에서 과거분사 discovered와 adapted가 병렬구조를 이룬다.

[9행~12행] There is scarcely *anything*, (in music, painting, architecture, science and knowledge, / up to the eighteenth century at least), [**that** was not largely the result of borrowings].

[ ]는 anything을 수식하는 주격 관계대명사절이다. in ~ at least의 전명구를 괄호로 묶으면 문장 구조를 파악하기 쉽다.

[12행~15행] The same **would be** true // **if** we **went** to *any other part of the world*, // **where** many of the characteristically 'local' things were imported from elsewhere.

「S+would+동사원형, if+S'+동사의 과거형」의 가정법 과거 구문으로 '~한다면 …할 것이다'로 해석한다. where 이하는 any other part of the world를 보충 설명한다.

어휘 **slip into** ~에 빠지다 **adapt** 적응시키다, 적합하게 하다 **civilization** 문명 **obvious** 명확한 **continent** 대륙 **imperial** 제국의 **suck in** ~을 끌어들이다 **scarcely** 거의 ~않다 **architecture** 건축(술) **borrowing** 차용 **characteristically** 특징적으로 **import** 수입하다; 수입품 **imitate** 모방하다

23 글의 주제 ②

소재 교육 지출의 경제 효과

해설 교육 분야에 대한 지출이 경제적 이득을 가져다주지 못한다고 생각하는 사람들이 있지만, 교육은 각종 직업 교육 실시와 사회 전반에 걸친 지식 확산, 그리고 새로운 지식과 기술을 갖춘 노동 인구 세대 공급 등의 역할을 수행하며 경제 성장을 견인하고 있다는 내용의 글이다. 따라서 글의 주제로 가장 적절한 것은 ② '교육 지출이 경제 성장에 미치는 영향'이다.

해석 주제문 어떤 사람들은 교육에의 지출이 생산성이나 성장에 직접적인 증가를 전혀 만들어내지 못한다고 주장하지만, 이것은 사회에서 발생하는 교육 지출에 대한 많은 즉각적인 수익을 무시하는 것이다. 특히 고등 교육에서뿐만 아니라 농업 기관, 직업 교육, 그리고 낮은 수준의 교육과의 다른 연결을 통하여, (교육) 지출은 그 세대에서의 상대적으로 빠른 수익과 사회 전반에 걸친 지식의 확산에 잠재적으로 기여한다. 교육 지출은 또한 일반적으로 보통교육 기간으로 포착되지 않는 성취 요소인 평생 학습을 목표로 삼음으로써 국가의 경제적 성과를 꽤 빠르게 향상시킬 수 있다. 뿐만 아니라 많은 교육 투자는 은퇴하거나 사망한 직원들을 새로운 직원들로 교체한다. 새로운 직원들이 인구 집단에 수년간의 경험을 더해 주지 못할 수도 있지만, 그들은 그야말로 더 최근의 지식과 기술을 구현하며, 이는 더 높은 GDP로 바뀔 수 있다.

① 엘리트 교육에서 대중 교육으로의 변천
③ 현대 사회에서 전통적 교육의 한계
④ 교육을 통해 실업률을 줄이는 방법들
⑤ 은퇴자들을 위해 평생 교육을 장려하는 것의 필요성

어휘 **expenditure** 지출 **productivity** 생산성 **immediate** 즉각적인 **institute** 기관, 협회 **vocational** 직업의 **contribute** 기여하다; 원인이 되다 **relatively** 상대적으로 **diffusion** 확산, 발산 **fairly** 꽤, 상당히 **target** 목표로 삼다 **lifelong learning** 평생 학습 **attainment** 성취, 달성 **replace A with B** A를 B로 교체하다 **embody** 구현하다 **translate into** ~로 바뀌다 [선택지 어휘] **transition** 변천, 이행 **retiree** 퇴직자

24 글의 제목 ④

소재 망각

해설 망각은 두뇌의 쇠퇴 현상이 아니며 오히려 새로운 정보를 계속 받아들이기 위한 두뇌의 전략이라는 내용의 글이므로, 제목으로 가장 적절한 것은 ④ '망각: 두뇌의 적절한 기능'이다.

해석 전통적으로 망각은 두뇌에 기록되고 저장된 정보가 시간의 흐름에 따라 수동적으로 쇠퇴하는 것으로 간주되어왔다. 그러나 어떤 기억은 햇빛에 노출된 종이 위의 잉크처럼 그저 서서히 흐릿해져가는 것일지 몰라도, 최근의 연구에 의하면 망각은 보통 정교한 세포와 분자의 메커니즘에 의해 조정되는 삭제를 수반하는, 더욱 의도적인 것이라 한다. 그리고 건망증이 반드시 결함 있는 기억의 징후인 것은 아니다. 사실 똑똑한 기억 체계는 망각을 필요로 한다는 것이 컴퓨터 모형과 동물 실험에서도 계속 드러났다. 실패를 의미하기는커녕, 망각은 투입되는 정보를 처리하는 데 있어 두뇌의 최전선 전략일지도 모른다. 주제문 두뇌의 기억 체계의 생물학적 목표는 정보를 보존하는 것이 아니라 오히려 두뇌가 타당한 결정을 내리도록 돕는 것이기 때문에 망각은 필수적이다.

① 망각은 정신을 더 편안하게 한다
② 건망증은 무엇의 징후일 수 있을까?
③ 기억하는 것은 모든 지혜의 어머니이다
⑤ 망각 이면의 과학과 그것(= 망각)을 극복하는 방법

구문 [1행~3행] Traditionally, forgetting has **been regarded as** a passive decay over time of *the information* (recorded and stored in the brain).
「be regarded as A」는 'A로 간주되다'의 뜻이다. ( )는 수동의 의미로 the information을 수식한다.

어휘 **passive** 수동적인 **decay** 쇠퇴, 부패 **fade away** 서서히 사라지다[약해지다] **expose** 노출시키다 **intentional** 의도적인 **erasure** 삭제, 말소 **arrange** 조정하다; 배열하다 **elaborate** 정교한; 공들인 **cellular** 세포의 **molecular** 분자의 **mechanism** 메커니즘, 방법 **forgetfulness** 건망증 **faulty** 결함 있는; 불완전한 **over and over** 계속해서 **computational** 컴퓨터를 사용한; 계산에 관한 **signify** 의미하다 **frontline** 최전선 **preserve** 보존하다 **sound** 타당한, 믿을 만한

25 도표 이해 ⑤

소재 영국, 미국, 호주의 물 사용량

해설 영국의 가정 내 물 소비량은 16퍼센트, 미국은 12퍼센트로, 영국이 4퍼센트 포인트 적게 사용한 것이 아니라 더 많이 사용하였으므로 ⑤가 틀린 설명이다.

해석 〈2020년 영국, 미국, 호주의 물 소비량〉

주제문 이 파이 도표는 2020년 영국, 미국, 호주의 물 사용량을 비교한다. ① 미국과 영국 두 나라에서는 전체 물의 약 50퍼센트가 산업 분야에서 소비되었고, 이것은 이 나라들에서 다른 분야들과는 상당한 차이가 나는 가장 많은 물 소비 주체였다. ② 반면에, 호주에서는 농업이 가장 많은 물 소비 주체였고, 그것은 전체 사용량의 50퍼센트 이상을 차지했다. ③ 농업은 미국에서 전체의 약 5분의 2를 차지하면서 두 번째로 많은 소비 분야였던 반면, 영국에서는 같은 분야(= 농업)가 3분의 1만 차지했다. ④ 호주에서는 3분의 1이 산업(분야)에서 소비되었다. ⑤ 가정은 세 나라에서 모두 가장 적은 양의 물을 소비했는데, 영국의 16퍼센트는 미국보다 4퍼센트 포인트 적고, 호주보다 7퍼센트 포인트 많은 양이다.

구문 [9행~11행] Agriculture was the second biggest consumer in the USA, / **taking** about *two fifths* of the total, // while in Britain the same sector took just about *a third*.
taking ~ total은 부대상황을 나타내는 분사구문으로 and it took ~으로 바꿔 쓸 수 있다. 분수를 표시할 때 분자는 기수, 분모는 서수로 쓰고 분자가 2 이상일 때는 분모에 -s를 붙인다.

어휘 **usage** 사용량; 사용(법) **industrial** 산업의 *cf.* **industry** 산업 **sector** 분야, 부문 **substantial** 상당한, 많은 **margin** 차이; 이익; (책의) 여백 **agriculture** 농업 **household** 가구(家口); 가족

26 내용 불일치 ③

소재 베이스 비올 연주자 Marin Marais의 경력

해설 Marin Marais는 Lully의 합주단에서 '비올 연주자'로 일했다고 했으므로 ③이 일치하지 않는다.

해석 ① Marin Marais(마랭 마레)는 17세기 전환기(= 17세기에서 18세기로 넘어가는 시기) 프랑스 최고의 베이스 비올 연주자였다. Marais는 자신의 전 생애를 파리에서 보냈다. 그가 당대 최고로 유명한 비올 연주자이자 교사였던 ② Sainte-Colombe(쌩뜨 꼴롱브)의 지도 아래 공부했던 것 외에 그의 어린 시절에 대해 알려진 바는 거의 없다. 1679년에 그는 '왕을 위한 정규 비올 연주자'가 되었는데, 1725년에 은퇴할 때까지 그 직책을 보유했다. Marais는 또한 Lully(륄리)의 지도 아래 작곡을 공부했고, 그 후에 ③ 그의 합주단에서 비올 연주자로 그의 경력 내내 그와 함께 일했다. Lully는 Marais가 그의 네 편의 오페라인 〈Alcide〉 (1693년), 〈Ariane et Bacchus〉 (1696년), 〈Alcione〉 (1706년), 그리고 〈Sémélé〉 (1709년)를 작곡하는 것을 독려했을 것이다. ④ 네 작품 모두 Lully의 양식에서 매우 많이 볼 수 있는 다소 전형적인 5막 비극이며 상당한 성공을 거두어서, 〈Alcione〉는 1771년까지도 상연되었다. 그러나 Marais가 오늘날 기억되는 것은 ⑤ 베이스 비올을 위한 가장 위대하고 가장 중요한 작곡가로서이다.

구문 [12행~15행] All four are rather typical five-act tragedies very much in Lully's style, / and were considerably successful, / *Alcione* **being staged** as late as 1771.
동사는 are와 were가 병렬구조를 이루고 있으며, being staged 이하는 분사구문이고 *Alcione*는 분사의 의미상 주어이다.

[15행~17행] **It is** *as the greatest and most important composer for the bass viol*, however, **that** Marais is remembered today.
「It is ~ that ... (…한 것은 바로 ~이다)」 강조구문으로, as the greatest ~ the bass viol이 강조되고 있다.

어휘 **bass** 베이스 (음), 최저음 **other than** ~외에 **prominent** 유명한; 중요한; 두드러진 **retirement** 은퇴 **composition** 작곡 *cf.* **compose** 작곡[작문]하다; 구성하다 *cf.* **composer** 작곡가 **subsequently** 그 뒤에 **ensemble** (소규모) 합주단, 앙상블 **act** (연극 등의) 막 **considerably** 상당히; 많이 **stage** 무대에 올리다; 무대

27 안내문 불일치 ④

소재 공항 분실물 보관소 이용 안내

해설 전화로 사전 예약하면 근무 시간 이후에도 물건을 찾을 수 있다고 했으므로 ④가 안내문의 내용과 일치하지 않는다.

해석

분실물 보관소

Tucson 국제공항 분실물 보관소는 주 터미널의 수하물 찾는 층에 있습니다.

- ① 공항터미널, 주차장 건물, 공항 주차장에서 발견된 물건들은 30일 동안 안전하게 보관된 후에 처분됩니다.
- ② 비행기 기내에서 잃어버리거나 놓고 내린 물건은 해당 항공사에 연락하시기 바랍니다.

발견된 물건들을 어떻게 요청해서 되돌려 받나요?

여러분은 다음과 같이 (잃어버린) 물건의 반환을 정할 수 있습니다.

- 현장 수령: 여러분이 적합하게 물건을 확인할 수 있다면, ③ 평일 오전 9시부터 오후 4시까지의 정상 근무시간에 물건을 가져가셔도 됩니다. 여러분은 근무시간에 (520) 573-8156으로 전화해서 ④ 근무시간 후 물건을 찾아가는 것을 사전 조정해 놓을 수도 있습니다.
- 미국 우편: ⑤ 여러분이 배송료를 지불할 경우, 보관소에서 미국 우편으로 (부피가) 작은 물건들을 돌려드릴 수 있습니다.

어휘 **lost and found** 분실물 보관소 **baggage claim** (공항의) 수하물 찾는 곳 **level** (건물의) 층; 수준 **securely** 안전하게; 확실히 **disposition** 처분, 정리; 성향 **claim** (자기 권리나 재산이라고 여겨) 요청[요구]하다; (~이 사실이라고) 주장하다 **arrange** 정하다; 미리 준비하다, 정리하다; 배열하다 **on-site** 현장의, 현지의 **business hours** 근무시간, 영업시간

28 안내문 일치 ⑤

소재 자원봉사자 모집 안내

해설 개인 교사 신청서가 처리되면 필수 오리엔테이션과 교육을 받아야 한다고 했으므로 ⑤가 안내문의 내용과 일치한다.

해석

> **자원봉사자 모집**
> 여러분이 이곳 CHS(보육원)에서 저희의 파트너가 되어 저희가 돌보는 어린이들을 도울 수 있는 다양한 방법들이 있습니다.
>
> **CHS에서 자원봉사 하는 법:**
> ① 단체:
> • 조경 업무, 벽화 그리기 등 — 본 보육시설을 안전하고 아름답게 꾸며주세요.
>
> ② 개인:
> • 요리: 식사 준비와 정리 돕기
> • ③ 벼룩시장: 가격표 달기, 물건 분류하기, 행사에서 물건 판매하기
> • ④ 특별 행사: 특정한 필요가 생기면 연락드릴 수 있도록 등록해 주세요.
>
> **개인교사 업무:**
> 신청서를 작성하여 저희에게 메일로 보내주세요. ⑤ 신청서가 처리되면 여러분은 필수 오리엔테이션과 훈련을 받게 됩니다.
>
> CHS의 생활을 변화시키려는 저희를 돕는 데 관심을 가져주신 여러분께 감사드립니다!

어휘 **landscape** (나무 · 꽃 등을 심어) 조경을 하다; 풍경 **facility** ((보통 복수형)) 시설; 설비; 재능 **tag** 가격표를 달다 **sort** 분류하다 **tutor** 가정교사로 가르치다; 가정교사 **application** 지원(서); 적용 **required** 필수인, 필요한

29 밑줄 어법 ④

소재 공감과 동정의 차이점

해설 ④ what절에서 it은 가주어이고 to be ~ shoes가 진주어이다. what ~ like는 '~는 어떠한가'의 뜻이다. likely를 쓰면 it's 이하가 완전한 문장이 되므로 앞에 what을 쓸 수 없다. what 다음에는 주어나 목적어가 없는 불완전한 구문이 나온다.

오답 분석 ① 「with+O+v-ing」는 'O가 v한 채로'의 뜻이다. ② similar는 appear와 대응되는 형용사인데(appear는 보어를 가지는 동사이며, 보어 자리에는 부사가 아닌 형용사를 사용한다), 「형용사+as+S′+be[appear]」는 '비록 ~이지만'의 뜻이다. ③ where 이하는 관계부사절로 뒤에 완전한 절이 이어지며, empathy에 대한 설명을 제시한다. ⑤ a person이 듣는 상황이 아니라 '자신의 말이 들려지는[전달되는] 것'을 느낀다고 해야 문맥에 맞으므로 feel 다음의 보어로 과거분사를 사용했다.

해석 주제문 공감과 동정의 개념 간에는 다소 큰 차이가 있으며, 후자가 사람들이 사용하는 다소 잘 알려진 단어이다. 그것들은 비슷해 보일지 모르지만, 매우 구별되는 의미와 용법을 가지고 있다. 소셜 미디어 전문가인 Chloe Chong에 따르면, 동정심은 다른 사람이 고통받고 있다는 인식에서 나타나며, 이는 상대방의 고통이나 괴로움이 지각되는 공감과 대조를 이룬다. 동정은 청하지 않은 충고를 하거나 무슨 일을 해야 할지를 듣는 것을 요구한다. 공감은 적극적인 경청을 요구한다. 이 경우에 공감은 다른 사람의 입장에 서본다는 것이 어떠할지를 느끼는 능력을 의미한다. 동정의 가장 좋은 표현은 '가엾기도 해라.'이다. 그것은 그 사람의 역경에 대한 연민을 자아낸다. 공감의 가장 좋은 표현은 '어떤 느낌인지 이해가 가. 정말 힘들 것 같다.'이다. 이것은 어떤 사람으로 하여금 자신의 말이 전달되었다는 느낌을 갖게 도와준다.

구문 [6행~7행] ~, the feeling of sympathy emerges from the recognition that another person is suffering, ~
(the recognition = that ~)

that절은 the recognition에 대한 동격절이다.

어휘 **empathy** 공감, 감정이입 **sympathy** 동정, 연민 **the latter** 후자 **distinct** 구별되는, 별개의 **usage** 용법 **recognition** 인식, 인지 **be in someone else's shoes** 다른 사람의 입장이 되어보다 **plight** 역경

30 밑줄 어휘 ⑤

소재 자극적인 뉴스에 대한 인간의 심리적 반응

해설 침략자가 마을에 불을 지른 상황에서 도태되었을 유전자는 '동요[불안]'를 장려하는 유전자가 아니라 (동요를 장려하는 유전자는 이러한 위급 상황에서 순기능을 한다) '침착함'을 장려하는 유전자였을 것이므로 ⑤의 agitation을 calmness로 바꿔 써야 한다.

해석 특정 종류의 뉴스는 상당히 과대 보도되며, 다른 뉴스는 상당히 과소 보도된다. 이러한 ① 불균형은 합리적인 공공 정책의 왜곡과 같은 주요 문제로 이어진다. 그러나 그것은 ② 낙관할 만한 이유이다. 상황이 실제보다 더 나쁘다고 믿도록 세뇌되고 있음을 일단 깨달으면, 당신은 약간의 용기를 내어 햇빛 속으로 나아갈 수 있다. 기만은 어떻게 발생하는가? 문제는 인간의 깊숙한 ③ 심리적 반응에서 시작된다. 우리는 추상적인 사실보다 ④ 극적인 이야기에 더 강하게 반응하도록 체계가 잡혀 있다. 인간은 이것이 그렇게 된, 그럴 만한 역사적, 진화적 이유를 쉽게 상상할 수 있다. 침략자가 당신 마을의 오두막에 방금 불을 질렀다는 소식은 즉각적인 반응을 요구한다. 그러한 상황에서 ⑤ 동요(→ 차분함)를 자극하는 유전자는 오래 전에 다 타버렸을 것이다(= 이미 사라졌을 것이다). 우리 마을이 지금은 세계이지만, 우리는 여전히 본능적으로 동일한 방식으로 반응한다.

구문 [11행~13행] One can readily imagine *possible historical and evolutionary reasons* [why this might be **so**].

[ ]는 관계부사절로 앞의 possible ~ reasons를 수식한다. so는 앞 문장의 내용(인간이 추상적인 사실보다 극적인 이야기에 더 강하게 반응하게 되어 있다)을 지칭한다.

[13행~15행] The news that an invader has just set fire to a hut in your village demands immediate response.
(S: The news, V: demands, The news = that ~)

that절은 The news에 대한 동격절이며, 주어 The news에 대응되는 동사는 demands이다.

어휘 **distortion** 왜곡; 뒤틀림 **rational** 합리적인, 이성적인 **optimistic** 낙관적인 **deception** 기만, 속임 **take place** 발생하다, 일어나다 **be wired to-v** v하도록 (설계)되어 있다, v하는 경향이 있다 **abstract** 추상적인 **readily** 쉽게 **evolutionary** 진화의 **invader** 침략자 **set fire to** ~에 불을 지르다 **hut** 오두막 **agitation** 동요, 불안 **instinctively** 본능적으로

31 빈칸 추론 ②

소재 예술계에 관한 '근거 없는 믿음'과 '사실'

해설 빈칸 문장의 '사실(the facts)'이란 많은 예술가들이 정규 학교 교육, 즉 예술계의 관행 속에서 훈련을 받는다는 것이고, '근거 없는 믿음(myths)'이란 예술가들이 학교의 가르침에 영향받지 않는 개인주의자라는 것이다. 이러한 '근거 없는 믿음'이 '사실'보다 더 강하게 대중들의 의식을 지배하기 때문에 학교 교육이 미술계에 미치는 영향력을 인식하지 못하는 것이라고 했으므로, '사실'과 '근거 없는 믿음'이 충돌할 때 '사실'은 ② '무시된다'는 것을 추론할 수 있다.

해석 오늘날 우리 대부분은 예술적 창의성이 과도하게 계획되었거나 조직된 것이 아니고 자발적이라고 믿는다. 우리는 우리의 예술가들이 예술학교에서 가르치는 일반적인 관념이나 고루한 미술관 큐레이터에 의해 영향받지 않고 고립되어 일하는 강한 개인주의자라고 생각하기를 좋아한다. 그러나 우리가 갖고 있는 이 시대의 창의성에 대한 근거 없는 믿음에 대해 많은 것이 그러하듯이, 이러한 생각은 19세기에 이르러서야 나타났다. 20세기 후반에는, 예술가는 전통을 거부하는 사람이라는 생각이 훨씬 더 강하게 대중들의 의식을 지배했다. 동시에 역설적이게도, 예술가들은 예술계의 관행 속에서 훈련을 받으려고 점점 더 많은 수가 예술학교에 입학하고 있었다. 오늘날 미국에서는 역사의 어느 다른 때보다도 더 많은 비율의 예술가들이 예술 석사 학위를 가지고 있다. 그러나 미술계에서 정규 학교 교육의 증가하는 영향력을 인식하는 사람은 우리 중에 거의 없다. 주제문 일반적으로 사실과 우리가 가진 창의성에 대한 근거 없는 믿음이 충돌할 때 사실이 무시된다.
① 드러난다 ③ 변형된다 ④ 보존된다 ⑤ 인정된다

구문 [8행~10행] ~, the idea **that** the artist is *a person* [who rejects convention] took an even stronger hold on the popular consciousness.
(S: the idea, V: took, the idea = that ~)

that은 동격절을 이끄는 접속사이며, that ~ convention은 앞에 나온 the idea의 내용을 담고 있다.

어휘 **spontaneous** 자발적인, 자연히 일어나는 **individualist** 개인주의자 **isolation** 고립 **prevailing** 일반적인, 널리 퍼진; 우세한 **contemporary** 현대의; 동시대의 **myth** 근거 없는 믿음, 사회적 통념 **emerge** 나타나다, 등장하다 **convention** 전통, 관습 **take a hold on** ~을 지배하다 **ironically** 역설적이게도 **proportion** 비율, 부분; 균형 **formal** 정규적인; 공식적인; 형식적인 **fine art** 미술 **clash with** ~와 충돌하다

32 빈칸 추론 ⑤

소재 문화권에 따라 다른 소비자 선택의 의미

해설 서양에서는 선택이 자기표현의 일환이며 소비를 통해 자신만의 개성과 특별함을 나타내 보이려는 다양화 편향을 드러내지만, 집단을 강조하는 문화권에서는 소비가 대인 관계적 과제여서 개인 표현에 별 관심을 두지 않는다고 하였다. 이렇듯 문화권에 따라 소비자 선택의 의미가 달라지므로 소비자 선택을 이해할 때는 소비자가 자신을 ⑤ '별개의 개인 혹은 타인과 연결된' 것으로 생각하는지가 중요하다는 것을 알 수 있다.

해석 주제문 우리가 우리 자신을 별개의 개인 혹은 타인과 연결된 것으로 생각하는지는 소비자 선택을 이해함에 있어서 중요하다. 서양 문화에서 소비자 선택은 자기표현의 행위로 여겨진다. 고유성은 바람직하며 소비는 외부 세계에 당신 자신을 표현하는 한 방법이며, 그래서 우리는 '특별함'의 느낌을 얻기 위한 시도로 우리의 구매를 다양화한다. 행동경제학에서 이것은 다양화 편향이라 한다. 이 선택이 자기표현의 한 행위일 때 그것은 개인에게 대단히 중요해지고, 선택이 결여되거나 선택하지 못한 것이 미치는 심리적 영향은 더 커지게 되어, 다양성 추구와 같은 전략으로 이어지게 된다. 그러나 개인보다 집단을 강조하는 문화에서는 소비자 선택이 종종 대인관계적 과제인데, 이것은 자기 자신을 가장 우호적인 관점에서 보여주는 결정을 하는 것의 성공 혹은 실패가 그렇게 큰 관심사는 아님을 뜻한다. 이어서 최근 연구는 다양화 편향이 이러한 문화적 맥락에서는 더 약하다는 것을 보여주었다.

① 완전히 이성적인 존재 혹은 그렇지 못한 존재인
② 유행에 민감한 혹은 민감하지 않은
③ 마케팅의 영향을 알고 있는
④ 상류층의 일원 혹은 하류층의 일원인

어휘 **uniqueness** 고유성, 유일함 **diversification** 다양화 **bias** 편향, 편견 **interpersonal** 대인관계에 관한 **portray** 보여주다, 나타내다; 묘사하다 **favorable** 호의적인 **concern** 관심(사); 걱정 **subsequently** 이어서; 차후에 [선택지 어휘] **rational** 이성적인, 합리적인 **fashion-conscious** 유행에 민감한

33 빈칸 추론 ②

소재 음악 검열의 오랜 역사

해설 빈칸 문장의 '어떤' 충동이 음악만큼 오래된 것인지를 글에서 추론해야 한다. 고대 그리스 철학자인 Plato의 언급은 빈칸 문장을 상술하는 구체적인 예시에 해당한다. 또한 17세기 영국, 19세기 이탈리아의 사례를 종합하면, 빈칸에 가장 적절한 것은 ② '음악의 영향력을 두려워하여 음악을 검열하려는'이다.

해석 주제문 음악의 영향력을 두려워하여 음악을 검열하려는 충동은 음악 그 자체만큼이나 오래된 것이다. 음악의 유형에서 발견된 잠재적인 도덕적 손상에 대한 Plato(플라톤)의 우려는 기록상 가장 오래된 사례들 중 하나를 나타낸다. Plato는 "감시자들은 기존의 질서에 반하는 음악의 새로운 흐름을 끊임없이 감시해야 하고, 그들의 권력을 최대로 활용하여 그것을 경계해야 한다."라고 말한 것으로 기록되어 있다. 17세기 영국에서 허가받지 않은 발라드는 벌금이나 징역에 이를 수 있었던 한편, 19세기 이탈리아에서 모든 오페라의 대본은 검열 과정의 대상이었다. 주제문 인류의 역사 내내, 음악은 두려움의 원천이었고 억압의 대상이었다. 모든 대륙에서 모든 세기에 걸쳐 특정한 소리나 연주자들을 침묵하게 하려고 자신들의 권력을 이용하는, 교회로서든 국가로서든 권력 안에 있는 사람들을 봐왔다.

① 음악을 다른 사람을 조종하기 위해 사용하려는
③ 지금까지 들어본 적 없는 멜로디로 사람들을 놀라게 하려는
④ 비범한 음악적 재능이 있는 사람들을 통제하려는
⑤ 우울할 때 음악으로 우리 자신을 위로하려는

구문 [2행~4행] Plato's concern with *the potential moral damage* (**to be found** in types of music) marks one of the earliest recorded examples.
( ) 부분은 the potential moral damage를 꾸며주는 to부정사구로, 잠재적인 도덕적 손상이 '발견되는' 것이므로 수동의 관계를 표현하는 수동부정사 to be found가 쓰였다.

어휘 **urge** 충동, 욕구; 촉구하다 **moral** 도덕적인, 도덕상의 **overseer** 감독자 **watchful** 경계하는, 주의 깊은 **innovation** 혁신, 획기적인 것 **counter to** ~에 반대인 **established** 기존의, 확립된; 인정받는 **to the best of** ~하는 한, ~이 미치는 한 **unlicensed** 무허가의(↔ **licensed** 허가받은) **imprisonment** 구금, 투옥 **be subject to** ~의 대상이다; ~의 지배를 받다 **repression** 억압, 탄압; (감정 등의) 억누름 [선택지 어휘] **manipulate** (교묘하게) 조종하다; (사물을 능숙하게) 다루다 **censor** 검열하다 **unheard-of** 지금까지 들어본 적 없는, 전례가 없는 **soothe** 위로하다, 달래다; (감정 · 통증 등을) 진정시키다

34 빈칸 추론 ②

소재 인간 인식의 간접성

해설 우리는 세상을 직접적으로 감지하는 것이 아니라 감각기관을 통해 들어온 데이터를 두뇌에서 가공한 후 두뇌가 형성하여 제시해준 세상의 모형을 인식하는 것이므로, '의자를 본다'는 말은 자신이 직접 의자를 본다는 말이 아니라 ② '우리의 두뇌가 의자의 정신적인 모형을 창조했고' 우리는 그 모형을 인지할 뿐이라는 의미이다.

해석 철학자들은 '현실'의 본질, 그리고 우리가 경험하는 세계가 진짜인지 환상인지에 대해 수 세기 동안 논해왔다. 주제문 그러나 현대 신경 과학은 우리의 모든 인식은 환상으로 여겨져야 한다는 점을 우리에게 가르쳐준다. 그것은 우리가 우리 감각의 미가공 데이터를 처리하고 해석하여 오직 간접적으로만 세상을 인식하기 때문이다. 우리의 무의식적 처리는 세상의 모형을 형성한다. 예를 들어 당신은 주변을 둘러볼 때, 삼차원 공간을 들여다보고 있다는 느낌을 가질 것이다. 그러나 당신은 그러한 삼차원을 직접적으로 감지하는 것이 아니다. 대신에 당신의 두뇌가 망막으로부터 들어온 다수의 편평한 이차원 데이터를 읽고 삼차원의 감각을 형성한다. 당신의 무의식적 정신은 이미지를 가공하는 일을 너무 잘해서 당신이 당신 눈의 이미지를 거꾸로 전환시키는 안경을 쓴다면, 잠시 후에 당신은 사물을 바른 면이 위에 있는 모습으로 다시 보게 될 것이다. 그리고 나서 안경을 벗으면 당신은 세상을 다시 거꾸로 보겠지만, 잠시뿐이다. 그러므로 '의자가 보여'라고 말할 때, 우리가 진정으로 의미하는 바는 우리의 두뇌가 의자의 정신적인 모형을 창조했다는 것이다.

① 우리 앞에 의자라는 물리적 물체가 있다
③ 우리가 볼 수 있는 것은 의자에서 반사된 빛뿐이다
④ 우리는 우리가 서 있는 곳에서 눈에 보이는 것을 볼 수 있을 뿐이다
⑤ 의자는 객관적인 지칭이며, '나'는 관찰자이다

구문 [13행~17행] Your unconscious mind is **so** good at processing images **that** if you **were fitted** with *glasses* [that turn the images in your eyes upside down], // after a short while you **would see** things right side up again.
「so ~ that ...」은 '너무 ~해서 …하다'의 뜻이다. 「be good at v-ing」는 'v를 잘하다, 능숙하다'의 뜻이다. that절에서는 「If+S'+동사의 과거형, S+would+동사원형(~한다면 …할 것이다)」의 가정법 과거 표현이 사용되었다. [ ]는 glasses를 수식하는 관계사절이다.

어휘 **illusion** 환상 **neuroscience** 신경 과학 **perception** 인식, 인지 *cf.* **perceive** 인식[인지]하다 **process** 처리하다, 가공하다 **interpret** 해석하다 **raw data** 미가공 데이터 **three-dimensional** 삼차원의, 입체적인 **an array of** 다수의 **retina** 망막 **sensation** 감각 **be fitted (with)** (~로) 장착되다 **upside down** 거꾸로 [선택지 어휘] **physical** 물리적인 **mental** 정신의 **visible** (눈에) 보이는 **reference** 지칭; 언급; 참고

35 무관한 문장 ③

소재 언어의 표층 구조와 심층 구조

해설 언어의 표층 구조와 심층 구조를 설명하는 글로, ①, ②에 그 개념을 설명하는 예시 문장이 나오고 ④의 The sentence는 ②에 나온 "Jane hit the man with a bat"을 가리킨다. 그런데 ③은 글을 쓸 때 애매함을 피하기 위해 단순하게 쓰는 것이 좋다는 내용이므로 글의 흐름을 단절시킨다.

해석 주제문 언어학은 문장의 표층 구조(문장을 말하거나 쓰는 방식)와 문장의 심층 구조(문장을 이해하는 방식)에 차이를 두어 구별한다. 예를 들어, 'Jane이 화요일에 의사에게 말했다.'라는 문장의 표층 구조는 하나의 분명한 의미, 즉 심층 구조가 있다. 그러나 'Jane hit the man with a bat'이라는 문장은 'Jane이 방망이를 들고 있는 남자를 때렸다'나 'Jane이 방망이를 사용하여 남자를 때렸다'를 의미할 수 있다. 훌륭한 작가는, 같은 생각이 단순한 방식이나 복잡한 방식으로 표현될 수 있다면, 애매모호함을 피하기 위해 단순한 방식이 더 낫다는 것을 알고 있다. 그 문장은 두 개의 심층 구조가 있지만, 당신은 무의식적으로 그 문장이 어느 한 쪽만 의미하는 것으로 이해했을 것이다. 당신은 그 특정한 의미를 무의식적으로 처리했기 때문에, 우리가 나머지 다른 의미를 당신에게 제시할 때까지 아마도 당신은 그 다른 의미를 생각조차 못했을 것이다.

어휘 **linguistics** 언어학 **make[draw] a distinction between A and B** A와 B를 구별하다 **surface structure** (문법) 표층 구조 **deep structure** (문법) 심층 구조 **ambiguity** 애매모호함

36 글의 순서 ④

소재 동물의 크기, 체온, 수명 사이의 관계

해설 작은 동물은 표면적 대 부피의 비율이 높아서 체온 손실이 크다는 주어진 글 뒤에는 생쥐와 벌새처럼 몸집이 작은 동물을 예시로 드는 (C)가 와야 한다. 작은 동물들은 체온을 유지하기 위해 더 많은 칼로리를 연소함에 따라 물질대사가 빨라지게 되는데, 빠른 물질대사 속도는 수명의 단축을 의미한다는 내용의 (A)가 나온 뒤, 그와 반대 경우인 몸집이 큰 동물에 대해 설명하는 (B)가 마지막에 와야 한다. 따라서 ④ '(C)-(A)-(B)'의 순서가 알맞다.

해석 주제문 동물은 표면을 통해 체온을 잃기 때문에, 표면적 대 부피의 비율이 더 높으면 더 큰 체온 손실을 초래할 수 있다. 이것이 더 작은 몸집을 가진 동물들이 더 많은 체온을 잃는 이유이다.

(C) 그 결과, 생쥐나 벌새는 일정한 체온을 유지하기 위해 많은 칼로리를 연소시켜야 한다. 이는 온혈동물들이 몸집이 커짐에 따라 물질대사 속도가 줄어드는 주된 이유이다. 작은 포유동물들은 상대적으로 더 많은 체온을 생산하도록 진화하였다.

(A) 그것들의 더 빠른 물질대사 속도는 그것들이 그만큼 오래 살지 못한다는 것을 의미한다. 작은 동물들은 큰 동물들보다 수명이 더 짧은 경향이 있고, 온혈동물은 냉혈동물보다 수명이 더 짧은 경향이 있다.

(B) 반대로, 큰 동물들은 노력을 덜 들이고도 따뜻한 몸을 유지할 수 있는데, 이로 인해 그들은 더 오래 살 수 있게 된다. 더 느리게 뛰는 심장을 가진 큰 동물들은 심장마비가 훨씬 더 후에 일어날 것이다.

구문 [6행~8행] Small animals tend to have shorter lives ~, and warm-blooded animals (tend to have) shorter lives ~.
warm-blooded animals 다음에 반복되는 동사구 tend to have가 생략되어 있다.

[15행~17행] This is *the main reason* [**that**, among warm-blooded animals, metabolic rate declines with increasing body size].
[ ] 부분은 the main reason을 수식하며, that은 이유를 나타내는 관계부사 why로 바꾸어 쓸 수 있다.

어휘 **surface** 표면 **ratio** 비율 **rate** 속도; 비율 **warm-blooded** 온혈의 **cold-blooded** 냉혈의 **conversely** 반대로; 역으로 **hummingbird** 벌새 **constant** 일정한, 꾸준한 **mammal** 포유동물 **evolve** 진화하다 **relatively** 상대적으로

37 글의 순서 ②

소재 강우(强雨)의 과학적 원리

해설 증발로 인해 수증기가 상승한다는 주어진 글 다음에는 이 수증기가 낮은 온도층에 도달했을 때 응결이 발생한다는 내용의 (B)가 나온다. 응결이 일어나면 수증기가 무거워져서 땅으로 떨어진다는 (B) 다음에는 however로 이어지면서 강우가 전부 다 땅에 도달하는 것은 아니라는 내용의 (A)가 나온다. 공기 중에서 증발하는 물방울, 땅에 떨어지는 강우를 제외하고 바다에 떨어지는 강우를 논한 (C)가 마지막으로 나온다. 따라서 정답은 ② '(B)-(A)-(C)'이다.

해석 호수와 강에서 빗물 배수관과 새 물통에 이르기까지, 물이 있는 곳이면 어디에서나 증발은 발생한다. 주제문 이 모든 따뜻한 수증기는 상승하기 시작하여, 수십억 개의 다른 물 분자와 합류하여 아찔하게 상승해 대류권으로 진입한다.

(B) 마침내 수증기는 더 낮은 온도층에 도달하여 작은 먼지, 꽃가루나 오염 입자 둘레에서 응결한다. 주제문 응결 과정이 지속됨에 따라 작은 물방울들은 바람이 지탱하기에는 지나치게 커져서 지표면을 향한 급락을 시작한다.

(A) 그러나 모든 강우가 땅에 도달하는 것은 아니다. 그중 일부는 아래로 내려오는 길에 대기 중으로 다시 직접 증발한다. 남아있는 것이 비, 눈, 우박 혹은 진눈깨비의 형태로 마침내 땅에 도달하며, 그 과정에서 때로는 소풍을 망치거나 학교를 닫게 한다.

(C) 강우가 바다에 떨어지면 당장 순환이 다시 시작될 준비가 된 것이며, 그것이 바로 대다수의 빗방울과 눈송이에 일어나는 일이다. 결국 바다는 지표면의 70퍼센트가 넘는 영역을 뒤덮고 있어서 (강우가 떨어질) 커다란 과녁이 된다.

구문 [8행~11행] What's left(S) finally reaches(V) the ground / in the form of rain, snow, hail, or sleet, / sometimes **ruining** picnics [or] **closing** schools in the process.
what이 이끄는 명사절이 주어이며, 동사는 reaches이다. sometimes 이하는 분사구문이며 ruining과 closing이 or로 연결되어 병렬구조를 이룬다.

[14행~17행] **As** the condensation process continues, // the droplets become **too** big *for the wind* **to support**, // and they begin a plunge / toward the surface.
접속사 As는 '~함에 따라'의 뜻으로 쓰였다. 「too ... for A+to-v」는 'A가 v하기에는 지나치게 …한'의 뜻이다. for the wind는 to support의 의미상 주어이다.

어휘 **evaporation** 증발 **storm drain** 빗물 배수관 **birdbath** 새 물통 **vapor** 증기 **molecule** 분자 **dizzying** 아찔한, 어지러운 **ascent** 상승 **precipitation** 강수[강우](량) **hail** 우박 **sleet** 진눈깨비 **condense** 응결[응축]하다 *cf.* **condensation** 응결, 응축 **particle** 입자 **pollen** 꽃가루 **droplet** 작은 방울 **plunge** 급락 **snowflake** 눈송이

38 문장 넣기 ④

소재 '달콤함'을 이용한 식물의 번식

해설 ④의 앞 문장에서는 식물과 동물이 공생 관계를 맺어왔다고 했는데 ④의 다음 문장에서는 식물이 씨앗이 완전히 익을 때까지는 동물에게 달콤한 과육을 제공하지 않는 행동을 보여주고 있으므로 두 문장이 논리적으로 연결되지 않는다. '식물이 포식자에게 착취당하지 않기 위해 조치를 취한다'는 주어진 문장이 ④에 위치하면, 이러한 식물의 행동에 대한 이유가 제시되어 글의 흐름이 자연스럽게 연결된다.

해석 주제문 달콤함은 진화에서 힘이 된다는 점이 입증되었다. 씨앗을 당분과 영양분이 많은 과육 속에 덮어둠으로써, 사과와 같은 열매를 맺는 식물들은 단것을 좋아하는 포유류의 성향을 이용하는 기발한 방법을 생각해냈다. 과당과 교환하여, 동물들은 씨앗에 운송을 제공하여 식물이 자신의 범위를 확장하게 해준다. 이러한 웅장한 공진화 거래의 당사자들로서, 단맛에 대한 가장 강한 기호를 가진 동물들과 가장 크고 가장 달콤한 과일을 제공하는 식물들은 함께 번성하고 증식했으며, 오늘날 우리가 보는 종, 그리고 현재의 우리라는 종으로 진화했다. 식물은 예방책으로서 자신을 먹는 자들의 탐욕으로부터 씨앗을 보호하기 위해 확실한 조치를 취했다. 그것들(= 식물)은 씨앗이 완전히 익기 전까지 달콤함과 색깔을 발달시키는 일을 연기했다. 그 전에(= 씨앗이 완전히 익기 전에) 과일은 주의를 끌지 않는 녹색이며 입에 안 맞는 경향이 있다. 사과와 같은 일부 경우에, 식물은 달콤한 과육만 섭취되는 것을 확실히 하기 위해 씨앗에 독을 발달시켰다.

구문 [9행~13행] As parties to this grand co-evolutionary bargain, / *animals* (with the strongest inclination for sweetness) [and] *plants* (offering the biggest, sweetest fruits) prospered together [and] multiplied, / **evolving** into *the species* [(which[that]) we see ●, and are ●, today].

(S: animals ~ fruits / V1: prospered / V2: multiplied)

전명구와 현재분사구가 각각 수식하는 animals와 plants가 and로 연결되어 문장의 주어로 쓰였다. 동사는 prospered와 multiplied이다. evolving 이하는 분사구문이며, the species는 관계사절 내에서 see의 목적어이자 are의 보어에 해당한다. (= we see the species, and we are the species, today)

어휘 **precaution** 예방책 **take a step** 조치를 취하다 **greed** 탐욕, 식탐 **evolution** 진화, 발달 *cf.* **evolve** 진화하다, 발달하다 **nutritious** 영양분이 많은 **flesh** 과육; 살 **hit on** ~을 (우연히) 생각해내다 **ingenious** 기발한, 독창적인 **exploit** 이용하다; 착취하다 **mammalian** 포유류의 **sweet tooth** 단것을 좋아함 **in exchange for** ~와 교환하여, ~ 대신에 **transportation** 운송, 수송 **expand** 확장[확대]하다 **co-evolutionary** 공진화의 **bargain** 거래 **inclination** 기호, 좋아함; 성향; 기울기 **prosper** 번성하다 **multiply** 증식[번식]하다 **hold off (on)** (~을) 미루다, 연기하다 **mature** (과일 등이) 익다, 숙성하다 **inconspicuously** 주의를 끌지 않게, 눈에 띄지 않게 **unpalatable** 입[구미]에 안 맞는

39 문장 넣기 ⑤

소재 Jenner의 천연두 백신

해설 주어진 문장은 Jenner의 백신 기법을 다른 과학자들은 사용할 수 없었다는 내용으로 Jenner의 기법의 단점을 기술하고 있으므로, Jenner의 발견의 성공적인 측면만을 기술하다가 However로 내용이 전환된 이후인 ⑤에 들어가는 것이 알맞다.

해석 주제문 1796년 Edward Jenner(에드워드 제너)의 천연두 백신 접종법의 발견은 천연두 예방에 매우 중요했다. 이 일이 있기 전에 일부 사람들은 그 병(= 천연두)을 피하기 위해 자신의 몸을 약한 케이스의 천연두에 노출시키는 접종법을 시도했지만, 더 약한 형태의 천연두와 천연두에 대한 저항력을 연결시켜본 사람은 아무도 없었다. Jenner의 발견은 영국 정부에 의해 채택되어 모든 사람들에게 백신 접종을 무료로 제공했고 마침내 그것(= 백신 접종)을 의무화해서 그 결과 많은 생명을 구했다. Jenner의 연구는 또한 백신 접종이 성공할 수 있음을 보여주었는데, 이는 다른 과학자들을 고무시켰다. 주제문 그러나 그것(= 백신 접종)은 천연두 외의 질병을 예방하는 데 있어서는 특별히 중요하지 않았다. 천연두 백신은 특수한 경우였고 후대의 백신은 다른 방식으로 효과를 냈는데, 이는 다른 과학자들이 Jenner와 동일한 방법을 사용할 수 없음을 의미했다. 이것은 Jenner가 백신이 작용하는 방식을 이해하지 못했고, 따라서 그 이론이 다른 질병에 적용될 수 없었기 때문이다.

구문 [1행~4행] The smallpox vaccine was a special case / and later vaccines worked in a different way, // **which** meant other scientists could not use **the same** method **as** Jenner.

which는 앞 문장 전체(The smallpox ~ a different way)를 가리킨다. 「the same A as B」는 'B와 같은 A'의 뜻이다.

[7행~11행] Before this, / some people **had tried** the method of inoculation—exposing themselves to mild cases of smallpox / to avoid the disease, // but nobody **had made** *the link* ([between] milder forms of pox [and] a resistance to smallpox).

Before this(Jenner의 종두법 이전 시대)는 과거보다 더 이전의 일이므로 had tried, had made와 같이 과거완료 시제가 쓰였다. ( )는 the link를 수식하는 전명구로 「between A and B (A와 B 사이의)」 구조가 쓰였다.

어휘 **vaccination** 백신[예방] 접종 **prevention** 예방 **expose** 노출시키다 **resistance** 저항력 **compulsory** 의무적인, 강제적인 **inspire** 고무[격려]하다; 영감을 주다 **other than** ~ 외에 **be applied to** ~에 적용되다

40 요약문 완성 ②

소재 노래에 대한 정보 유무에 따른 인지 차이

해설 노래의 제목을 알고 두드리는 사람은 그 두드림을 듣고서 답하는 사람들이 노래를 이해하는 것이 아니라 단지 분절된 두드림 소리로 인식하고 있다는 것을 생각할 수 없었다는 내용의 글이다. 즉, 두드리는 사람은 듣는 사람이 그 노래에 대한 지식이 '없다는' 것을 '상상할' 수 없었다는 것이 실험의 내용이므로 정답은 ②이다.

해석 1990년에 Stanford 대학의 Elizabeth Newton은 자신의 대학 동기들에게 연구에 참가해달라고 요청했다. 각각의 학생들은 두 가지 역할인 '두드리는 사람' 혹은 '듣는 사람' 중 하나를 배정받았다. 두드리는 사람들은 '생일 축하합니다'와 '징글벨'과 같은 25개의 인기 있는 곡 목록을 받았다. 그들은 손가락으로 테이블에 선율을 두드려야 했고, 듣는 사람들은 노래를 맞춰야 했다. 그들은 그러고 나서 듣는 사람들 중 몇 프로가 그들이 두드린 노래를 맞출 수 있을지 추측해보라는 요청을 받았다. 두드리는 사람들은 평균적으로 듣는 사람들 중 50퍼센트가 듣고 있던 노래를 맞출 거라고 추정했다. 실제로 그들이 두드리는 것을 들은 참가자들은 노래 중 겨우 2.5퍼센트만을 맞출 수 있었다. 왜 그럴까? 주제문 두드릴 때 그들은 머릿속에서 노래를 듣고 있었다. 그러나 듣는 사람들이 듣고 있던 것이라곤 다수의 분절된 두드림뿐이었다는 것을 그들은 알지 못했다.

⬇

실험에 따르면, 두드리는 사람들이 일단 노래에 대한 지식을 얻으면, 듣는 사람들에게 그 지식이 (B) 없을 거라고 (A) 상상할 수 없었다.

구문 [8행~10행] They were then asked to guess / what percentage of listeners would be able to guess *the song* [(which[that]) they had tapped ●].

밑줄 친 부분은 간접의문문 명사절로 guess에 대한 목적어 역할을 한다. [ ] 부분은 the song을 수식하는 목적격 관계대명사 which[that]가 생략된 관계사절이다.

어휘 **invite** 요청하다; 초대하다 **peer** 동년배, 동료 **assign** 배정[할당]하다 **tapper** 두드리는 사람 *cf.* **tap** 톡톡 두드리다; 두드리기 *cf.* **tap out** (리듬에 맞춰) ~을 두드리다 **tune** 곡, 곡조; 선율 **a bunch of** 다수의 **disconnect** 연결을 끊다 [선택지 어휘] **utilize** 이용하다 **expand** 확장하다

41~42 장문 41 ⑤ 42 ③

소재 과학에서 작용하는 '선물하기'의 원리

해설 41. 과학계의 연구는 불확실하고 보상도 보잘것없지만, 선대들이 이루어낸 결과물을 바탕으로 업적을 이루고, 다시 자신의 연구 결과를 과학계에 기여하는 상호 보답적인 '선물하기'의 원리가 작용하고 있다는 내용의 글이므로 제목으로 가장 적절한 것은 ⑤ '과학적 지식 추구에 있는 선물하기의 원리'이다.

① 선물하기의 윤리학: 보상 없이 줘라
② 우리의 과학 지식 추구는 결코 끝나지 않을 것이다
③ 선물하기에서 지름길을 택하는 것의 결과
④ 과학의 혜택은 현대 세계에서 왜 중요한가

42. 과학적 발견은 선배 과학자들의 연구결과를 토대로 발전하고 새로운 과학적 발견이 후대를 위한 새로운 토대가 된다고 했으므로 '우연적'인 것이 아니라 오랫동안 '누적된' 성질을 갖는다고 할 수 있다. 따라서 (c)의 accidental을 cumulative(누적적인) 등으로 바꿔 써야 한다.

해석 넓은 의미로 보면, 선물은 단지 선물인 것이 아니라 다른 사람에게 즐거움을 주거나 인상을 남기기 위해 행해지는 많은 것들이 될 수 있다. 선물이 무엇이든, 그것에는 여러 요소가 있다. 음식에서 시(詩), 승리한 전투에서 수학의 새로운 이론에 이르기까지 어느 것이든 (a) 외적인 '물질적' 요소가 있다. 그런 다음 그 이면에는 선물의 '정신'이 있는데, 이는 그것이 나타내는 상징적 관계이다. 주고받는 방식과 답례품에서 표현되는 감사는 모두 (b) 사회적 관계를 표현한다. 그것들은 개인이 존중을 보이고, 자신의 개성을 표현하고, 존경을 얻게 해준다.
주제문 과학 지식의 추구는 선물 행위의 거대한 연결망으로 볼 수 있다. 연결망에서 다른 사람들에게 제시되는 것은 단지 물질적인 것 이상이다. 과학자는 자신의 동료에게 제시하

는 새로운 사실이나 이론을 발견할 수 있다. 과학자의 정신 중 일부가 그 이론에 투자된다. 게다가 선물은 새로운 지식이 이전의 연구결과들을 토대로 발전하여 보답의 의무를 수립하는 경향이 있다. 따라서 각각의 과학적 발견은 (c) 우연적(→ 누적적)인데, 단지 그것이 다양한 새로운 이해를 열어주기 때문만이 아니라, 다른 사람들에게 무언가를 되돌려줄 의무를 부과하기 때문이다.
선물은 너무 (d) 계산적이어서는 안 된다. 과학자들이 무엇이 빠르게 '성과를 낼지'를 끊임없이 생각하고 있다면, 실질적인 위험과 장기간의 노력을 요하는 종류의 기본 과학에 착수하는 일은 결코 없을 것이다. 대부분의 의미 있는 과학은 꽤나 정신 나간 짓이며, 오랫동안 예감을 따르고, 매우 작은 보상을 얻기 위해 분투하고, 지름길과 단기적 이득을 포기한다. 과학자는 누구를 위해 그토록 (e) 무익한 일을 하는가? 다른 사람들(소수 집단의 친구들과 동료들, 교사들과 학생들, 자신의 이름에 영광을 베풀어줄 사회)을 위해서, 후세를 위해서지만, 항상 상대방에 대한 선물로 (그러는 것이다).

구문 [1행~3행] In the wider sense, a gift is **not just** a present **but** can be *many things* (done to please or impress another).
「not just A but B」는 '단지 A가 아니라 B'의 뜻이다. ( )는 수동의 의미로 many things를 수식하는 분사구이다.

[19행~21행] Furthermore, the gift tends to set up the obligation to reciprocate, **with** *new knowledge* **building** on earlier findings.
「with+O+v-ing」는 'O가 v하면서[한 채로]'라는 뜻의 분사구문이다.

어휘 **counter-** 반대의, 역의 **esteem** 존경 **set up** 수립하다 **obligation** 의무 **reciprocate** 보답하다, 답례하다 **accidental** 우연한 **pay off** 성공하다, 성과를 내다 **undertake (undertook-undertaken)** 착수하다 **fairly** 꽤 **shortcut** 지름길 **unprofitable** 무익한 **pupil** 학생 **honor** ~에게 영광을 베풀다 **posterity** 후세, 후대 [선택지 어휘] **ethics** 윤리학 **quest** 탐색(하다)

43~45 장문

43 ⑤ 44 ④ 45 ④

소재 도축장에서 도망친 소

해설 43. 암소 Emily가 도축장에서 도망친 내용인 (A) 다음에는 Emily가 숲 속에 몸을 숨기는 (D)가 와야 하고, 신문에 Emily의 이야기가 실린 내용 다음에는 Meg이 기사를 읽고 도축장 주인에게서 Emily를 사기로 하는 (C)가 오는 것이 적절하다. 마지막으로는 Meg이 Emily를 은신처로 데려오고 방문객들이 그녀를 보러오는 (B)가 오는 것이 자연스럽다.

44. (d)는 Meg을 가리키는 반면 나머지는 모두 Emily를 가리킨다. 도축장 주인이 Emily를 파는 상대가 Meg임에 유의한다.

45. (C)에서 소 주인은 처음에 Meg에게 500달러짜리 소를 350달러에 팔겠다고 제안했지만 결국 1달러에 팔았다. 따라서 ④는 본문의 내용과 일치하지 않는다.

해석 (A) 1995년 11월, 암소 Emily는 뉴잉글랜드 도축장의 줄에 서서 도축장으로 향하는 문을 통과할 차례를 기다리고 있었다. ① 도축 시설의 일꾼들이 휴식을 하러 갔을 때 Emily는 5피트 울타리를 용케 뛰어넘어 필사적으로 도망쳤다. 그녀는 숲속을 지나 도망쳤는데 놀란 ② 도축장 일꾼 무리가 그녀를 쫓아갔지만 소용이 없었다. "이 소는 내가 본 소 중에서 가장 빠른 소 중 하나예요."라고 한 직원이 기자에게 말했다.
(D) 혹독하게 추운 40일 동안 Emily는 작은 시골 마을인 매사추세츠 주(州) 홉킨턴의 숲이 우거진 지역에서 추적자들로부터 몸을 숨었다. 그리고 Emily가 도망친 도축장의 소유주가 그녀를 생포하기로 결심했지만 지역 사람들은 그녀의 자유를 향한 탈출에서 (e) 그녀(= Emily)를 돕기로 결심했다. 사람들은 뒷마당에 그녀를 숨겨주고 먹을 것을 주었다. 짧은 기간 동안 Emily는 인기를 얻었고 ⑤ 그녀의 이야기는 지역 신문에 대서특필되었다.
(C) Meg Randa가 지역 신문에서 그 이야기를 읽었을 때, 그녀는 Emily를 어떻게 하면 잡히는 것에서 구해낼 수 있을까에 대해 곰곰이 생각해보았다. Meg은 도축장 주인에게 전화를 걸기로 결심했고 그녀가 상황을 해결하기를 원하며 (c) 그녀(= Emily)에게 살 장소를 마련해주고 싶다고 말했다. ④ 주인인 Frank Arena는 처음에는 그녀에게 소를 350달러에 팔겠다고 내놓았다. 그러나 그의 손녀 Angela의 강력한 권유로 그는 그 500달러짜리 암소를 (d) 그녀(= Meg)에게 단돈 1달러에 파는 데 동의했다.
(B) Meg은 크리스마스이브에 그녀를 Peace 성당의 은신처에서 살게 데려왔다. 곧 암소 Emily의 소식이 전국과 전 세계에 퍼졌다. (a) 그녀(= Emily)는 전국적인 유명인사이며 국민 영웅이 되었고, 그녀의 용기에 감탄한 세계 도처로부터의 방문객들이 그녀를 보러 왔다. (b) 그녀(= Emily)는 많은 사람들에게 채식주의로 가는 길에 나서도록 영감을 주었고 곧 동물 권리와 ③ 채식주의의 대표자가 되었다.

구문 [(C) 3행~6행] Meg decided to place a call to *the owner* (of the slaughterhouse) and said // (that) she wanted to resolve the situation and to provide a place for her to live.
she wanted ~ live는 동사 said의 목적어절이고, 동사 wanted 뒤에는 목적어 역할을 하는 밑줄 친 두 개의 to부정사구가 병렬구조를 이루고 있다.

어휘 **(A) slaughterhouse** 도축장 *cf.* **slaughter** 도축, 도살 **kill floor** 도축장 **manage to-v** (용케) v해내다, v하는 데 성공하다 **run for one's life** 죽어라하고 도망치다 **flee (fled-fled)** 달아나다, 도망하다 **to no avail** 아무 효과가 없어, 헛되이 **(B) sanctuary** 은신처, 성소 **abbey** 성당, 대수도원 **folk** 국민, 민족 **bravery** 용기 **embark on** ~에 착수하다, 나서다 **vegetarianism** 채식주의 **representative** 대표자 **(C) resolve** 해결하다 **urge** 강력히 권고하다, 설득하다 **(D) frigid** 추운, 혹한의 **pursuer** 추적자 **wooded** 숲이 많은, 나무가 우거진 **flight** 탈출, 도피; 비행 **popularity** 인기

고난도 모의고사 14

본문 p.195

18 ⑤	19 ①	20 ⑤	21 ③	22 ⑤	23 ②	24 ③	25 ②	26 ④	27 ④
28 ④	29 ⑤	30 ③	31 ①	32 ④	33 ⑤	34 ②	35 ④	36 ②	37 ④
38 ④	39 ⑤	40 ①	41 ④	42 ④	43 ④	44 ④	45 ④		

18 글의 목적 ⑤

소재 자원봉사자들에 대한 안전 관리 촉구

해설 오솔길과 강 청소 활동에 참여한 자원봉사자가 위원회 측에 보낸 편지로, 참가하는 어린 자원봉사자들이 맨손으로 위험한 쓰레기를 치운 것을 보고 내년 행사에서는 안전에 유의해 줄 것을 당부하고 있다. 따라서 글의 목적으로 가장 적절한 것은 ⑤이다.

해석 관계자분께,
저는 먼저 오솔길과 강 청소 위원회의 노력을 칭찬하는 것으로 시작하겠습니다. 연례 대청소 행사를 개최함으로써 귀하의 단체는 우리 시의 하천 제방에서 수많은 쓰레기와 폐기물을 제거했습니다. 오랜 거주자로서 저는 귀하가 만들어 낸 변화가 엄청나다고 확신을 갖고 말할 수 있습니다. 주제문 그렇긴 해도 저는 자원봉사자들, 특히 어린 자원봉사자들의 안전에 대해 약간의 염려가 있습니다. 처음 하는 자원봉사자로서 저는 잠재적으로 위험한 활동이 여럿 있는 것을 보고 무척 놀랐습니다. 나이 든 회원들이 무거운 물품들을 불안정한 지면 위의 가파른 경사면으로 들어 올리는 동안 열 살이나 열한 살 정도의 어린 자원봉사자들은 맨손으로 깨진 유리와 다른 위험한 것들을 치우고 있었습니다. 누군가가 심하게 다치는 것이 그저 시간문제인 것으로 보입니다. 주제문 내년 대청소를 준비하실 때에는 이를 고려해주시기 바랍니다.
Brian Spencer 드림

구문 [6행~8행] As a long-time resident, / I can confidently say // that *the difference* [(which[that]) you have made] is huge.

that ~ is huge는 say의 목적어가 되는 명사절이고, [ ] 부분은 목적격 관계사 which[that]이 생략된 관계사절로 that절의 주어인 the difference를 수식한다.

어휘 **pathway** 오솔길 **cleanup** 대청소 **committee** 위원회 **loads of** 수많은 **bank** 제방, 둑 **resident** 거주자, 주민 **confidently** 확신을 갖고 **that being said** 그렇긴 해도 **concern** 염려, 걱정 **potentially** 잠재적으로 **bare hands** 맨손 **slope** 경사면 **it's only a matter of time** (~은) 그저 시간문제일 뿐이다(언젠가 분명히 일어날 일임을 뜻함) **take A into consideration** A를 고려[참작]하다

19 분위기 추론 ①

소재 절벽에서 떨어지는 차

해설 절벽 아래로 떨어지는 차 안에 운전자가 안전벨트도 매지 않은 채 구르고 있는 상황이므로 분위기로 가장 적절한 것은 ① '긴박한'이다.

해석 차를 돌리는 것은 항상 까다롭다. 나는 캘리포니아의 산라파엘 외곽의 언덕 위 외진 곳에 사는데, 그곳은 거대한 나무들로 가득 찬 숲으로 둘러싸여 있다. 저단 기어로 산을 올라가야 집으로 가는 도로에 이르는데, 그 길은 차 한 대가 간신히 지나갈 수 있는 폭이고, 가파른 낭떠러지 앞에서 끝난다. 나는 몸을 돌려 차를 천천히 후진했다. 바로 그때 햇빛이 반짝하면서 눈이 안 보였다. 나는 손을 들어 눈을 가렸다. SUV의 왼쪽 뒷부분이 떨어지면서 나는 덜컹거림을 느꼈다. 차가 부드러운 흙에 미끄러져 굴렀다. 나는 아직 안전벨트를 매지 않고 있었던 상태였는데 차를 다 돌리기까지 (안전벨트 착용을) 기다리고 있는 중이었다. 주제문 차가 산비탈을 굴러 내려갈 때 나는 차 안에서 구르고 있었다.

② 평화로운 ③ 음산한 ④ 흥미진진한 ⑤ 단조로운

구문 [3행~6행] You have to drive up the mountain in low gear / to get to *our driveway*, // **which** is barely wide enough for one car and ends at a steep drop-off.

주격 관계대명사 which는 our driveway를 선행사로 취하며, 관계사절의 동사 is와 ends가 접속사 and로 병렬 연결되어 있다.

어휘 **remote** 외딴 **surround** 둘러싸다 **driveway** (집 앞) 차도 **barely** 간신히; 겨우 **drop-off** 낭떠러지 **back up** 차를 후진시키다 **blind** 앞이 안 보이게 만들다; 눈이 먼; 맹목적인 **tumble** 뒹굴다; 굴러 떨어지다

20 필자 주장 ⑤

소재 성문 헌법의 자유 보장

해설 성문 헌법은 다양한 해석이 가능하고, 프랑스, 이탈리아, 독일이 200년간 성문 헌법이 있었음에도 압제에서 완벽히 벗어날 수 없었듯이 성문 헌법 자체만으로 자유를 보장할 수 없다는 내용의 글이다. 따라서 필자의 주장으로 가장 적절한 것은 ⑤이다.

해석 사람들은 우리가 성문 헌법을 통해 우리의 통치자들과 다수의 횡포에 대항해 더 잘 보호받을 거라고 말해왔다. 확실히 미국 헌법은 고귀한 문서이며, 개인의 자유와 양심의 자유를 보장한다. 그러나 그것(= 성문 헌법)은 그것이 보존한 원칙이 매우 모호하고 일반적인 자명한 이치로 영국의 불문 정치 체제에서 옮겨온 명확한 생각의 성명서였기 때문에 효력이 있었다. 그것은 다른 사람들에 의해 완전히 다른 방식으로 해석될 수 있으며 해석되어왔다. 침묵과 생략으로 그것은 자유를 증가시키기보다는 오히려 파괴할 수 있다. 주제문 성문 헌법은 그 자체로 전혀 자유의 보증이 아니다. 프랑스인들, 이탈리아인들, 그리고 독일인들은 지난 200년에 걸쳐 많은 성문 헌법이 있었지만, 이것이 압제로부터 그들을 보호해주지는 않았다.

구문 [6행~9행] But it has worked // because *the principles* [(which[that]) it preserved •] were very vague and general truisms, a statement of *the obvious ideas* (transferred from the unwritten British political system).

[ ] 부분은 앞에 목적격 관계대명사 which[that]가 생략되어 the principles를 수식한다. ( ) 부분은 수동의 의미로 the obvious ideas를 수식한다. very ~ truism과 a statement ~ system은 동격 관계이다.

어휘 **ruler** 통치자 **tyranny** 횡포, 압제; 폭정 **constitution** 헌법 *cf.* **written constitution** 성문 헌법 **noble** 고귀한 **guarantee** 보장(하다) **liberty** 자유 **conscience** 양심 **principle** 원칙, 원리 **vague** 모호한 **truism** 자명한 이치; 진부한 문구 **statement** 성명서; 진술 **interpret** 해석하다 **omission** 생략; 소홀, 태만 **in themselves** 그 자체로, 본질적으로

21 밑줄 함의 ③

소재 자아인식의 우월성 편향

해설 사람들은 자신이 다른 사람들보다 더 우수하다고 생각하고 자신의 상황을 다른 사람에 비해 낙관적으로 바라보는데, 이것이 우리의 자아가 '블랙홀'과 같다는 것을 보여

준다고 하였다. 즉, 모든 것을 빨아들이는 블랙홀처럼 우리 자신에 대한 우월성 편향도 그러하다는 의미이므로, 밑줄 친 부분은 ③ '우리의 자아인식이 우리의 우월성 편향에 의해 왜곡된다'는 의미로 이해할 수 있다.

해석 다른 사람들과 잘 지낼 수 있는 자신의 능력을 판단해보라는 요청을 받았을 때, 고등학교 졸업반 학생들 중 60퍼센트는 자신이 상위 10퍼센트에 속한다고 평가했고, 25퍼센트는 자신이 상위 1퍼센트에 속한다고 생각했다. 그리고 자신의 리더십 기량에 관한 질문을 받았을 때, 오직 2퍼센트만이 자신을 평균 아래라고 평가했다. 교사들이라고 더 현실적인 것도 아니었다. 대학 교수 중 94퍼센트는 자신이 평균 이상의 일을 한다고 말했다. 한 연구에서 직장의 직원들은 스스로에게 자신의 기량에 대해 너무 많이 공을 돌려서, 유의미한 피드백을 제공하는 것을 어렵게 했다. CEO들 또한 특히 새로운 시장이나 새로운 프로젝트에 진입할 때 (예를 들어 자기 회사의 주가에 도움이 된다기보다는 해가 되는 인수를 제안하는 것) 자신의 판단에 확신을 보였다. 마찬가지로, 사람들은 자기 자신의 건강 위험에 대해 다른 사람들의 그것과 비교하여 비현실적일 정도로 낙관적이다. 주제문 이러한 예들은 우리의 자아가 블랙홀과 같다는 것을 보여준다.

① 우리는 성공에 집중하고 실패를 무시하는 경향이 있다
② 우리의 기억은 우리의 기대에 의해 조작될 수 있다
④ 우리는 유효성이 더 큰 사건의 가능성을 과대평가한다
⑤ 우리의 의식은 우리의 믿음을 반박하는 새로운 증거를 거부한다

구문 [8행~10행] In one study, employees in the workplace gave themselves too much credit for their skill, / **making** it difficult to give meaningful feedback.
making 이하는 분사구문이다. it은 가목적어이고 to give ~ feedback이 진목적어이며, 「make+it+형용사+to-v」는 'v하는 것을 ~하게 하다'의 뜻이다.

[13행~14행] ~ for example, proposing *takeovers* [that hurt, **rather than** helped, the price of their company's stock].
[ ] 부분은 takeovers를 수식하는 관계사절이다. 「A rather than B」은 'B라기보다는 오히려 A'의 뜻으로 A를 강조하는 표현이다. 밑줄 부분은 hurt와 helped의 공통 목적어이다.

어휘 **get along with** ~와 잘 지내다 **rate** 평가하다(=assess) **credit** 공로; 인정; 칭찬 **confidence** 자신감 **step into** ~을 시작하다, 발을 들여놓다 **novel** 새로운; 소설 **takeover** 기업 인수 **stock** 주식; 재고 **optimistic** 낙관적인, 낙천적인 [선택지 어휘] **manipulate** 조작하다; 조종하다, 다루다 **self-perception** 자아인식 **distort** 왜곡하다; 뒤틀다 **superiority bias** 우월성 편향 *cf.* **bias** 편향, 선입견 **overestimate** 과대평가하다 **likelihood** 가능성 **availability** 유효성, 유용성 **consciousness** 의식 **contradict** 반박하다; 모순되다

22 글의 요지 ⑤

소재 사회적 관계를 촉진하는 온라인 소통

해설 온라인 소통이 통념과 달리 기존에 확립되어 있는 오프라인상의 관계를 더 친밀하게 강화시켜준다는 긍정적 측면에 관한 내용이다. 따라서 글의 요지로 가장 적절한 것은 ⑤이다.

해석 연구자들은 (서로) 직접 만나는 사교적인 아이들과 온라인상에서 낯선 이들과 잡담하는 고립된 외톨이로 어린이들이 구분될 수 없다는 것을 알게 되었다. 후자인 소수 어린이들은 정말로 존재하며, 그들의 인터넷 사용이 그들의 문제를 악화시키는 한 주목을 받을 만하다. 그러나 십 대들이 외로운 호기심이라는 이유로 낯선 이들과 교류한다는 초기의 가정은 도전받고 있다. 주제문 다시 말해서, 인터넷은 기존의 사회적 관계를 약화시킨다기보다는 촉진하는 것 같다. 오늘날의 풍요로운 매체 환경에서, 오프라인에서뿐만 아니라 온라인에서도 소통하지 않는 사교적인 십 대는 희귀한 사람이며, 온라인에서 그들은 기존에 확립되어 있는, 흔히 지역 친구들과 주로 소통하는데, 가장 강력한 유대는 기존의 지역적 배경에 집중되어 있기 때문이다. '부자가 더 부유해진다'는 가설은 특히 컴퓨터의 인스턴트 메시지에 작용하는데, 일대일 온라인 의사소통으로 제공되는 자기 노출이 친밀함을 북돋아 관계를 강화시키기 때문이다.

구문 [10행~14행] ~, *the sociable teenager* [who does not communicate online **as well as** offline] is a rarity, // and online, they communicate mainly with already established, ~, / *the strongest ties* **being centered** on pre-existing local contexts.
[ ] 부분은 the sociable teenager를 수식하며 「A as well as B (B뿐만 아니라 A도)」 구문이 쓰였다. the strongest ties being centered 이하는 분사구문이며 the strongest ties는 분사의 의미상 주어이다.

[16행~18행] ~ **as** *the self-disclosure* (provided by one-to-one online communication) encourages intimacy and thus strengthens relationships.
여기서 접속사 as는 '이유'를 나타낸다. as절에서 주어는 the self-disclosure이고 ( ) 부분은 수동의 의미로 the self-disclosure를 수식한다. 동사는 encourages와 strengthens가 and로 연결되어 병렬구조를 이루고 있다.

어휘 **sociable** 사교적인 **face to face** 마주 대하여, 직면하여 **loner** 혼자 있기를 더 좋아하는 사람 **the latter** 후자(↔ **the former** 전자) **minority** 소수; 미성년자 **deserve** ~을 받을 만하다 **insofar as** ~하는 한에 있어서는 **assumption** 가정, 추측 **foster** 촉진시키다; 조성하다 **undermine** 약화시키다 **rarity** 희귀(한 사람) **establish** 확립하다; 수립하다 **hypothesis** 가설 **self-disclosure** 자기 노출[폭로] **intimacy** 친밀함

23 글의 주제 ②

소재 외래종 유입으로 인한 부정적 영향

해설 생태계에 수많은 도입종(=외래종)의 침입이 있어 왔는데 그것의 영향은 예측할 수 없고 때로 파괴적이라는 내용이므로 주제로 가장 적절한 것은 ② '외래종의 예기치 않은 부정적 영향'이다.

해석 농업의 초창기부터 인간은 씨앗, 식물, 그리고 동물을 지구상의 한 지역으로부터 다른 지역으로 옮겨왔다. 감자가 안데스 산맥으로부터 유럽으로 도입되었을 때처럼, 새로운 종의 새로운 지역으로의 도입은 매우 빈번하게 의도적이었다. 히아신스가 빅토리아 호수에 침범해 햇빛이 드는 광범위한 지역을 빼앗음으로써 그 호수를 거의 막아 버렸을 때처럼, 때때로 종의 도입은 의도적이지 않다. 주제문 인간은 부작용과 의도하지 않은 결과들에 대한 이해가 거의 없이 지구의 생태계를 오랫동안 재배치해오고 있다. 어떤 도입종(=외래종)은 대단히 파괴적인 잡초 역할을 하여 적절한 방어 능력이 부족한 생태계를 점령한다. 해충과 병원균은 한 장소에서 다른 장소로 쉽게 옮겨간다. 대개 그러한 도입종의 결과는 복잡하고, 보통 예측할 수 없으며, 그리고 때로는 자생종(=토종)과 지역 생태계의 기능에 파괴적인 영향을 미친다.

① 침입종이 빨리 번지는 이유
③ 외래종을 새로운 지역에 도입하는 방법들
④ 자생종 보호의 필요성
⑤ 외래 침입종의 의도적 도입

구문 [14행~18행] In general, *the consequences* (of such introduced species) are complex, typically unpredictable, and occasionally devastating to native species and to the functioning of the local ecosystems.
보어인 형용사 complex, unpredictable, devastating이 병렬구조를 이루고 있다. to native species와 to the functioning of the local ecosystems 또한 병렬구조로 devastating에 연결된다.

어휘 **agriculture** 농업 **intentional** 의도적인, 고의로 한(↔ **unintentional** 고의가 아닌, 무심코 한) **invade** 침입하다 *cf.* **invasive** 침입하는; 급속히 퍼지는 **choke** 막다, 메우다; 숨이 막히다 **deprive A of B** A에게서 B를 빼앗다[박탈하다] **rearrange** 재배열하다, 재정리하다 **ecology** 생태(계)(=**ecosystem**); 생태학 **consequence** 결과; 영향 **devastating** 대단히 파괴적인, 황폐시키는 **take over** 양도받다; 접수하다; 장악하다 **pest** 해충, 유해 동물 [선택지 어휘] **exotic** 외래의(=**alien**)

24 글의 제목 ③

소재 테크놀로지로 구분되는 과거와 현재

해설 전통 사회에서는 과거를 중시했으나 현대 사회에서는 테크놀로지의 발달로 인하여 사람들의 관심의 초점이 미래로 옮겨갔으며, 사람들은 테크놀로지가 부재했던 과거를 낯설게 느낀다는 내용의 글이다. 따라서 글의 제목으로 가장 적절한 것은 ③ '테크놀로지는 우리를 과거로부터 단절시킨다'이다.

해석 대부분의 전통 사회에서 사람들은 과거로 시선을 돌리는 경향이 있었다. 그들은 그들의 조상을 존경했고, 전통을 유지하려고 노력했으며, 기억되는 세계에서 살았다. 대조적으로, 우리에게는 점점 더 과거가 낯선 이들이 살았던 외국이 된다. 대부분의 사람들은, 특히 미국이나 중국 같은 빠르게 변화하는 사회에서는 과거보다 미래에 대해 훨씬 더 많이 생각하는 경향이 있다. 테크놀로지가 역할을 한다. 인쇄술, 나침반, 화약이라는 위대한 발명은 17세기 철학자들이 더 이상 고대인들과 같지 않다고 느꼈다는 것을 의미했다. 이제 우리는 보통 전기, 자동차, 사진술과 현대 의학이 있기 이전에 살았던 사람들은 틀림없이 (우리와) 매우 달랐을 거라고 느낀다. 주제문 테크놀로지의 변화는 너무 빨라서 인터넷, 휴대폰, 유전공학과 최신 세대의 무기 이전의 세계는 우리에게 가르쳐주는 것이 거의 없는 다른 세계인 것처럼 보인다.

① 과거가 미래를 결정하는가?
② 과거는 현재와 미래이다
④ 테크놀로지 변화는 왜 일어났나
⑤ 테크놀로지 변화: 편익 향상

구문 [11행~13행] Now we often feel // that *those* [who lived before electricity, cars, photography and modern medicine] **must have been** very different.

[ ] 부분은 those를 수식한다. 「must have p.p.」는 '~했음에 틀림없다'의 뜻으로 과거에 대한 단정적 추측을 나타낸다.

[14행~17행] Technological change is **so** rapid // **that** *a world* (before the Internet, ~ and the latest generation of weapons) seems a different one, / with little to teach us.
(S′: a world / V′: seems / C′: a different one)

「so ~ that ...」은 '너무 ~해서 …하다'의 뜻이다. that절에서 주어는 a world이고 동사는 seems이다.

어휘 **tend to-v** v하는 경향이 있다 **look to** ~로 시선을 돌리다; 기대하다 **admire** 존경하다; 감탄하다 **ancestor** 조상, 선조 **retain** 유지[보유]하다 **play a part** 역할을 하다 **compass** 나침반 **gunpowder** 화약 **the Ancients** 고대인 (특히 고대 그리스인 · 로마인) **genetic engineering** 유전공학 **generation** 세대; (전기 등의) 발생, 생성 [선택지 어휘] **enhance** 향상시키다 **benefit** 이익, 혜택

25 도표 이해 ②

소재 전 세계 지역/국가별 가구당 피부양자 수 변화

해설 인도와 북아프리카/중동은 피부양자 수가 2040년에 감소하는 것이 맞지만, 북미는 피부양자가 더 많아지는 지역에 속하므로 ②는 도표와 일치하지 않는다. North America를 South America로 바꿔 써야 한다.

해석 〈2020년과 2040년의 각 가정 내 근로자 한 사람당 피부양자 평균 수〉
주제문 위 그래프는 2020년, 그리고 2040년에 그럴 것으로 예측되는, 지역별 가정 내 직업이 있는 각 사람에 의해 부양되는 사람 수를 보여준다. ① 가정에서 고용된 한 사람당 피부양자의 총 평균은 2020년에 1.23명이었으며, 2040년에는 1.37명으로 증가할 것으로 예상된다. ② 전반적으로, 인도, 북아프리카/중동, 북미 세 지역을 제외한 많은 지역들은 2020년보다 2040년에 근로자 한 사람당 피부양자가 더 많아질 것으로 예상된다. ③ 중국은 비록 2020년과 2040년 사이의 증가 폭이 전 지역 중 가장 크긴 해도, 2020년과 2040년 둘 다 가장 낮은 피부양자 수치를 보여주고 있다. ④ 반면에, 북아프리카/중동 근로자들은 2020년에 2.04명의 피부양자로 가장 큰 부양 부담을 졌다. ⑤ 비록 그들의 부담이 2040년에는 1.83명의 피부양자로 줄어들 것으로 예상되나, 북아프리카/중동은 여전히 근로자 한 사람당 피부양자 평균 수가 전 지역에서 가장 큰 곳으로 남게 될 것이다.

구문 [1행~3행] The graph above shows the number of *people* (supported by each employed person in the household / for each region in 2020 / and **as** (it is) predicted for 2040).

supported 이하의 과거분사구가 앞의 people을 수식한다. as predicted에서 as는 '~하는 대로'의 의미로 쓰인 접속사이며 as와 predicted 사이에 'it(=the number) is'가 생략되어 있다.

어휘 **support** 부양(하다); 지지(하다) **household** 가정, 가구 **dependent** 피부양자, 부양가족; 의존하는 **margin** 차이; 여백, 가장자리 **burden** 부담, 짐

26 내용 불일치 ④

소재 북부 흉내지빠귀

해설 북부 흉내지빠귀는 낮 시간 내내 지저귀지만, 밤 시간에는 종종 지저귄다고 했으므로 밤에 항상 지저귀는 것은 아니다. 따라서 ④가 글의 내용과 일치하지 않는다.

해석 만약 당신이 집 밖에서 끝없는 일련의 ① 10종 혹은 15종의 다른 새의 지저귐을 들어왔다면, 당신의 마당에 북부 흉내지빠귀가 있을지도 모른다. 북부 흉내지빠귀는 ② 북아메리카에서 흔히 발견되는 유일한 흉내지빠귀이다. 흉내지빠귀들은 ③ 다람쥐와 개구리가 내는 소리 같은 동물의 소리를 흉내 낼 수 있다. 새들은 가혹한 날씨 (기간) 동안에 남쪽으로 이동할 수도 있다. 그들은 ④ 낮 시간 내내 그리고 종종 밤까지 지저귀는데, 밤 시간의 지저귐은 보름달이 뜬 동안 더 많이 발생한다. 대부분의 지저귐은 짝짓기 철 동안 암컷에게 인상을 주기 위해 자신의 방대한 레퍼토리를 사용하는 수컷에 의해 행해진다. 암컷 북부 흉내지빠귀는 비록 보통 수컷보다 더 조용하게는 하지만, 역시 지저귄다. ⑤ 암컷은 여름에는 좀처럼 지저귀지 않고 수컷이 영역에서 멀리 나가있을 때만 보통 지저귄다.

구문 [5행~7행] The mockingbirds can imitate animal sounds, such as **those** (made by squirrels and frogs).

those는 animal sounds를 지칭한다. ( ) 부분은 수동의 의미로 those를 수식한다.

[8행~10행] They sing all through the day and often into the night, **with** *nighttime singing* **occurring** more during a full moon.

「with+O+v-ing」는 'O가 v한 채로, v하면서'의 뜻이다.

어휘 **a string of** 일련의 **mockingbird** 흉내지빠귀 **imitate** 흉내 내다 **harsh** 가혹한 **repertoire** 레퍼토리, 노래 목록 **mating season** 짝짓기 철 **rarely** 좀처럼 ~않는 **territory** 영역; 영토

27 안내문 불일치 ④

소재 고등학생 대학 체험일 안내

해설 어떤 전공 수업이든 들을 수 있다고 했으므로 ④가 안내문의 내용과 일치하지 않는다.

해석

대학 체험일

이 날은 어떤 날인가?
① 대학 체험일은 고등학교 학생들에게 Nebraska 대학 링컨 캠퍼스를 하루 동안 방문할 수 있는 기회를 제공합니다. ② 이는 모든 규모의 단체 방문을 수용할 수 있도록 고안되었습니다.

다뤄지는 시간별 주제
학과 공부:
학업 시간은 직접 해보는 수업 경험입니다. ③ 교실에서 UNL 교수단과 학생들과 함께 시간을 보내게 될 것입니다. ④ 그들은 관심 있는 어느 전공과도 연관된 강의를 들을 수 있습니다.

학생 생활:
학생들은 다음에 대해 알 수 있습니다.
- 학생 자치회
- 동아리/단체
- ⑤ 기숙사: 일반실을 돌아봅니다.
- 식당: 요리와 식당 분위기를 경험해 봅니다.

어휘 **access** 입장, 접근; 접근하다 **accommodate** 수용하다; (숙박을) 제공하다 **session** (단체 활동) 시간 **cover** 다루다; (범위에) 걸치다, 포함하다 **academic** 학문의 *cf.* **academics** 학과 공부 **hands-on** 직접 해 보는 **faculty** 교수단 **student government** 학생 자치회 **residence hall** 기숙사, 생활관 **cuisine** 요리(법) **atmosphere** 분위기; 대기

28 안내문 일치 ④

소재 지역 사회 공방과 암벽 클라이밍 체육관의 제휴 안내

해설 Artisans Asylum 회원은 12월 31일까지 BKB에 등록하면 연간 회원권을 10퍼센트 할인받는다고 했으므로 ④가 안내문과 일치한다.

해석

암벽 클라이밍 체육관 제휴

Artisans Asylum은 매사추세츠 주(州) 서머빌에 위치한 ① 비영리 지역 사회 공방입니다. 저희와 새롭게 이웃이 된 ② Brooklyn Boulders(BKB)와의 제휴를 발표하게 되어 정말 기쁩니다!

단순한 암벽 클라이밍 체육관을 넘어, Brooklyn Boulders는 새로운 유형의 지역 사회 공간을 제공해 드립니다. BKB의 성대한 개업과 저희와의 제휴를 축하하여 BKB는 Artisans Asylum 단체에게 다음의 한시적 제안을 제공하고 있습니다.

- ③ 이번 주 7월 29일부터 8월 4일까지 Artisans Asylum의 모든 현 회원들과 자원봉사자들을 대상으로 하는 무료 클라이밍
- ④ 12월 31일까지 등록하는 현 회원들께 1년 회원권 10% 할인
- ⑤ 12월 31일까지 등록하는 헌신적인 Artisans Asylum의 자원봉사자께 1년 회원권 15% 할인

금주 후반에 있을 성대한 개업식에 참석해 주세요!

어휘 **gym** 체육관(=**gymnasium**) **partnership** 제휴 **artisan** 장인, 기능 보유자 **asylum** 보호 시설, 피난처 **non-profit** 비영리의 **craft studio** 공방 **boulder** (크고 둥근) 바위, 옥석 **in honor of** ~을 축하하여 **extend** 베풀다; 연장하다 **limited-time-only** 한시적 **annual** 일 년의 **sign up** (강좌에) 등록하다 **dedicated** 헌신적인

29 밑줄 어법 ⑤

소재 실수에서 배우지 못한 피자 가게 부자(父子)

해설 ⑤ 주절의 동사의 형태가 would have improved인 것을 통해 가정법이 쓰인 문장임을 알 수 있고, ⑤는 앞 문장의 never learned ~와 반대되는 상황을 가정한 것이므로, 과거 사실에 대해 가정하는 가정법 과거완료(had p.p.)를 써서 If they had learned ~가 되어야 한다. learned 이하를 생략하면 had만 남게 되므로 did를 had로 고쳐야 한다.

오답 분석 ① 선행사 the first pizza place를 대신하는 주격 관계대명사 that을 쓴 것은 어법상 옳다. ② 동사 were의 보어가 필요하므로 형용사 rude를 쓴 것은 어법상 옳다. ③ '~하는 곳에서'라는 의미로 부사절을 이끌고 있으므로 어법상 적절하다. ④ 앞에 나온 동사 learned를 받는 대동사로 did를 쓴 것은 어법상 옳다. 「nor+V+S」는 '~도 또한 아니다'의 뜻이다.

해석 내가 아는 나보다 나이 많은 한 남자가 자신이 사는 작은 도시로 이전한 첫 번째 피자 가게 이야기를 내게 해 주었다. 그 피자는 형편없었고 주인은 무례했지만, 그는 마을에서 유일하게 이용 가능한 것(=마을에서 유일한 피자 가게)을 갖고 있었다. 그래서 그는 엄청난 돈을 벌고 일찍 은퇴했다. 그는 그 피자 가게를 두 아들에게 물려주었는데, 그 두 아들은 똑같이 형편없는 피자를 만들었고 꼭 아버지와 똑같이 무례했다. 그러나 이제 시간이 흘러, 다른 경쟁자들이 그 지역 시장에 들어왔고, 더 이상 이곳은 마을에서 유일한 피자 가게가 아니었다. 그 가게는 곧바로 문을 닫게 되었다. 원래의 주인은 전에 한 번도 행해진 적이 없는 곳에서 어떤 일을 한 최초의 사람이었기 때문에 운이 좋았다. 하지만 자신의 실수가 무엇인지 결코 알지 못했으며, 두 아들도 또한 그랬다(=실수를 알지 못했다). 만약 그들이 그것을 알았더라면, 그들은 고객 서비스뿐만 아니라 제품의 품질도 개선했을 것이다. 나는 도대체 무엇이 잘못되었는지 궁금해하면서 그저 침울하게 서성이고 있는 그 두 아들의 현재의 모습을 상상할 수 있다.

어휘 **lousy** 형편없는; 나쁜 **rude** 무례한, 예의 없는 **the only game in town**: 유일하게 이용 가능한 것 **retire** 은퇴하다; 물러가다 **competitor** 경쟁자 **local** 지역의 **in no time** 곧바로, 즉시 **original** 원래의; 독창적인 **quality** 품질; 자질; 특성, 특징 **mope around**: 침울하게 서성거리다 **on earth** (의문문을 강조하여) 도대체 **go wrong** (일이) 잘못되다

30 밑줄 어휘 ③

소재 인간의 에너지와 빛 에너지의 유사점

해설 천재는 한 번에 한 가지 대상에 자신의 에너지를 집중시키는 것과는 달리 일반적인 사람들은 다양한 일들을 한다고 했으므로 그들의 에너지를 '분산시킨다'고 할 수 있다. 따라서 ③ gathers는 disperses 등으로 바꿔야 한다.

해석 주제문 인간의 에너지는 빛 에너지와 ① 유사하다. 그것(=인간의 에너지)이 발산되면 평범한 백열전구에서처럼 그것은 평범한 방식으로 일을 해낸다. 하지만 레이저 광선에서처럼 그 똑같은 에너지를 단 하나의 목표에 초점을 맞출 때에는 어떤 종류의 장애물도 ② 관통할 수 있는 힘을 갖게 된다. 마찬가지로, 일반적인 사람들은 다양한 일들로 자신의 에너지를 ③ 모은다(→ 분산시킨다). 대조적으로, '천재'인 사람은 자신의 에너지를 한 번에 한 가지 추구 대상을 향하는 데 이용하며, 다른 사람들보다 훨씬 더 많은 것들을 ④ 성취한다. 이러한 에너지 ⑤ 집중의 원리는 큰 무리의 사람들, 즉 조직의 노력을 생각할 때에도 적용된다. 그러한 조직의 성공은 조직의 사람들이 기꺼이 투입하는 에너지의 양과 단 하나의 갈망하는 목적을 향해 그러한 에너지를 이용하고 향하게 하는 능력과 직접적으로 관련되어 있다.

구문 [13행~17행] The success of that organization / is directly related to *the amount of energy* [(which[that]) its people are willing to invest], and to *its ability* (to harness and direct those energies toward a single, burning purpose).
related에 연결되는 전명구 to the amount of energy ~ to invest와 to its ability ~ burning purpose가 병렬구조를 이룬다. 선행사 the amount of energy를 수식하는 관계사절에서 목적격 관계대명사 which[that]가 생략되었다.

어휘 **resemble** 유사하다, 닮다 **release** 발산하다; 풀어주다; 방출하다 **penetrate** 관통하다; 뚫고 들어가다 **obstacle** 장애(물), 방해(물) **pursuit** (시간과 에너지를 들여 하는) 일, 활동; 추구 **direct** ~로 향하다; 직접적인 **concentration** 집중 **burning** 갈망하는; 불타는

31 빈칸 추론 ①

소재 초연하기

해설 성공과 쾌락에 집착하고 실패와 고통을 두려워하며 살지 말고 이것들로부터 거리를 두면, 삶에서 진정으로 중요한 것에 집중할 수 있고 인생의 아름다운 순간을 순수하게 즐길 수 있다는 삶의 전략을 가장 잘 나타낸 표현은 ① 'detachment(거리 두기, 초연)'이다.

해석 우리 모두는 삶이 쾌락과 고통, 위안과 역경의 혼합임을 안다. 아마 당신은 쾌락이 당신을 결코 떠나지 않기를 바라며 쾌락에 매달리는 경향이 있을 것이고, 고통이 결코 끝나지 않으리라 두려워하며 고통에 압도될 것이다. 주제문 그러나 초연을 연습하기 시작하면, 현명한 속담에서 말하듯이 이 또한 지나가리라는 것을 알고서, 심지어 어떤 유머 감각마저 갖고 어려운 순간을 견뎌낼 수 있을 것이다. 이 모두는 당신이 의지하는 모든 것이 어떤 특정 순간에라도 바스러질 수 있음을 두려워하며 끊임없는 불안 속에서 살 필요가 있다는 것을 의미하지 않는다. 오히려 그 반대다. 주제문 성공과 실패로부터, 쾌락과 고통으로부터 거리를 두는 것은 당신을 언제나 존재하고 안정적이고 안전한 유일한 것인, 당신의 순수한 의식과 순수한 사랑의 중심과 다시 연결되게 해줄 것이다. 마찬가지로 당신은 인생의 아름다운 순간이 끝나리라는 두려움으로 더럽혀지지 않은 상태로 그것을 즐길 것이다. 그것은 의심할 여지없이 끝날 것이므로.
② 선견지명 ③ 융통성 ④ 관찰 ⑤ 낙천성

구문 [8행~11행] All this doesn't mean // that you need to live in constant insecurity, / **fearing** that *everything* [(that) you rely upon] could crumble at any given moment.
fearing 이하는 분사구문이다. [ ]는 앞에 목적격 관계대명사 that이 생략되어 everything을 수식한다.

[15행~18행] In the same way, you will enjoy the beautiful moments of life / without being tainted / by the fear that they will end — as **they** undoubtedly **will**.
that ~ end는 the fear에 대한 동격절이다. as절에서 they는 the beautiful moments of life를 지칭하며 will은 will end를 의미한다.

어휘 **comfort** 위안, 위로 **hardship** 역경, 어려움 **cling to** ~에 매달리다 **overwhelmed** 압도된 **endure** 견디다, 참다 **as a saying goes** 속담에서 말하듯이 **insecurity** 불안 **crumble** 바스러지다; 무너지다 **invariably** 언제나, 변함없이 **stable** 안정적인 **taint** 더럽히다, 오염시키다 **undoubtedly** 의심할 여지없이

32 빈칸 추론 ④

소재 자기 분야에 대해 폭넓은 관점을 얻는 것의 중요성

해설 인도의 한 수학자가 고립된 상태로 연구 활동을 한 결과, 수학의 지식 기반을 새로이 넓히지 못하고 이미 알려진 지식을 재발견했을 뿐이라는 내용의 글로, 빈칸 문장은 처음에 ④ '자기 분야에 대한 폭넓은 관점을 얻었더라면' 헛된 수고를 하지 않아도 되었을 것이라는 내용이 되는 것이 가장 적절하다.

해석 주제문 사람들이 자신들에게는 독창적이지만 전에 이미 생각된 적이 있는 아이디어를 떠올릴 때, 우리는 (어떤 분야에 대한) 지식의 결여가 창의적인 성과에 미치는 영향을 매일 본다. 이러한 현상의 눈에 띄게 비참한 사례는 지금까지 가장 뛰어난 수학적 사상가들 중 한 명으로 여겨지는 인도의 수학자 Srinivasa Ramanujan의 경우이다. 외부 세계와의 접촉이 없었기 때문에, 그는 모르고 서양 수학에서는 이미 알려져 있는 것 중 많은 것을 단독으로 '재발견하는' 데 인생의 많은 시간을 보냈다. 만약 처음에 자기 분야에 대한 폭넓은 관점을 얻었더라면, 그는 이러한 대단하지만 헛된 일을 피할 수 있었을 것이고, 대신에 자신의 상당한 재능을 수학의 지식 기반을 다시 만들어 내는 것이 아니라 발전시키는 데로 향하게 했을 것이다.
① 자신의 직업에서 성공했다면
② 자신의 창의성 부족을 극복했다면
③ 자신의 능력에 대한 확신을 쌓았다면
⑤ 자신의 마음을 진정시키고 창의성을 증대시켰다면

구문 [1행~4행] We see *the effects* (of lack of knowledge) on creative performance every day, // when people come up with *ideas* [that are original for them] but [that nevertheless have been thought of before].
두 개의 [ ]는 주격 관계대명사절로 ideas를 수식하며, but으로 연결되어 병렬구조를 이룬다.

[11행~15행] **Had** he first **gained** a broad perspective of his field, // he **could have avoided** this amazing yet useless career and instead **turned** his considerable talents to **advancing**, not **reworking**, the mathematical knowledge base.
Had he first gained는 If he had first gained로 바꿔 쓸 수 있다. 「If+S'+had p.p. ~, S+could+have p.p. ...」는 가정법 과거완료로 과거 사실에 대한 반대 상황을 가정하며, '~했다면 …할 수 있었을 것이다'의 뜻이다. could have 다음의 과거분사 avoided와 turned가 and로 연결된 병렬구조이다. the mathematical knowledge base는 advancing과 reworking의 공통 목적어이다.

어휘 **come up with** ~을 생각해내다 **original** 독창적인; 본래의 **strikingly** 눈에 띄게, 두드러지게 **pitiful** 측은한 **phenomenon** (복수형 **phenomena**) 현상 **brilliant** 뛰어난, 훌륭한; 빛나는, 반짝이는 **unknowingly** 모르고, 알아채지 못하고 **considerable** 상당한 **advance** 발전시키다 [선택지 어휘] **get ahead** 성공하다, 출세하다; 앞서다 **perspective** 관점; 원근법

33 빈칸 추론 ⑤

소재 코끼리의 자기 인식 능력

해설 동물이 거울 속 자신의 이미지를 보고 자신을 만지는 것은 자기 자신을 인식할 수 있다는 것인데, 코끼리가 거울을 본 후에 자신의 머리에 있는 페인트 자국을 만졌다는 것은 코끼리도 이러한 능력을 가지고 있다는 것을 의미한다. 따라서 빈칸에 가장 적절한 것은 ⑤ '자기 인식 능력을 가지고 있다'이다.

해석 주제문 코끼리는 자기 인식 능력을 가지고 있다는 것이 밝혀졌다. "코끼리의 사회적 복잡성, 잘 알려져 있는 이타적인 행동, 그리고 말할 것도 없는 큰 뇌는 코끼리를 거울 앞에서 검사를 받을 타당한 후보 동물이 되도록 만들었다."라고 애틀랜타에 있는 Emory 대학의 심리학자 Joshua Plotnik가 말했다. 과거에는 (인간을 포함한) 소수의 유인원과 큰돌고래만이 이런 능력을 지니고 있다고 여겨졌다. 이 분야에서 유인원과 돌고래에게 행해졌던 이전의 실험처럼 실험 대상 동물이 보통 볼 수 없는 곳에 페인트 자국을 남긴 다음, 거울 속의 이미지에 대한 그 동물의 반응을 관찰함으로써 그 능력이 판단되었는데, 자신을 만지는 것은 그 동물이 거울 속의 이미지를 자기 자신으로 동일시하는 것을 나타내고, 반면에 거울을 만지는 것은 실험 대상 동물이 다른 동물을 살펴보고 있다는 것을 암시하는 사회적 행동을 보여준다. 실험된 코끼리는 거울을 본 후에 자기 머리에 있는 페인트 자국을 만졌다.
① 복잡한 사회 체계를 가지고 있다
② 긍정적인 자아 이미지를 발달시킨다
③ 다른 동물들과 의사소통을 한다
④ 남의 시선을 의식하는 방식으로 행동한다

구문 [9행~13행] As with *previous research* (carried out ~ on apes and dolphins), / it was measured / **by** putting a paint mark on *a place* [(that[which]) the subject would normally be unable to see ●], and then observing his reaction to a mirror-image ~.
( ) 부분은 과거분사가 이끄는 형용사구로 앞의 previous research를 수식한다. 전치사 by의 목적어로 동명사 putting과 observing이 콤마(,)와 접속사 and로 연결되어 병렬구조를 이룬다. [ ] 부분은 a place를 대신하는 목적격 관계대명사가 생략되었으며, a place는 관계대명사 절에서 see의 목적어에 해당한다.

어휘 **complexity** 복잡성 **altruistic** 이타적인, 이타주의의 **logical** 타당한; 논리적인 **species** (생물) 종(種) **ape** 유인원 **faculty** 능력; 학부; 교수진 **previous** 이전의 **measure** 판단하다; 측정하다; 척도; 조치 **subject** 실험 대상자; 주제; 과목 **indicate** 나타내다; 가리키다 **identify** 동일시하다; 밝히다 **whereas** 반면에 **investigate** 조사[연구]하다; 수사하다 [선택지 어휘] **operate** 행동하다; 작동하다; 수술하다 **self-conscious** 남의 시선을 의식하는; 자의식이 강한 **capacity** 능력; 용량 **self-awareness** 자기 인식

34 빈칸 추론 ②

소재 업무에 따른 뇌의 분화

해설 공간 능력을 특히 필요로 하는 런던 택시 기사의 후위 해마를 조사해보니 경력이 오래된 택시 기사일수록 후위 해마의 크기가 더 컸다는 내용의 글이다. 결국 우리의 뇌는 일정한 것이 아니라 필요에 따라 적응하는 것이므로 빈칸에는 ② '우리가 부과하는 요구에 반응하여 적응한다'가 들어가는 것이 가장 적절하다.

해석 런던의 택시 운전사들은 세계에서 가장 복잡한 도시들 중 하나를 훌륭하게 운전한다. 영국의 신경과학자인 Eleanor Maguire와 그녀의 동료들은 그 택시 기사들의 뇌를 MRI 정밀검사를 했고 그것들을 다른 사람들의 뇌 검사와 비교했다. 택시 기사가 아닌 다른 사람들과 대조적으로, 숙련된 택시 기사들은 상당히 큰 후위 해마를 갖고 있었는데, 그것은 공간 표상을 기억해 내는 것을 전문적으로 하는 뇌의 부분이다. 더욱이 택시 기사의 해마의 크기는 각 운전자의 경험과 직접적으로 상관관계가 있었다. 즉, 운전 경력이 길수록 후위 해마의 크기는 더 컸다. 그것은 공간 업무가 택시 기사들의 뇌를 활발하게 바꾸고 있다는 것을 강력하게 시사했다. 이것은 바이올린 연주자들, 점자를 읽는 사람들, 명상 수련하는 사람들에 대한 연구와 완벽하게 일치했다. 주제문 우리의 뇌는 우리가 부과하는 요구에 반응하여 적응한다.
① 정보를 연결하여 패턴을 식별한다

③ 새로운 길보다 익숙한 길을 따라가는 것을 선호한다
④ 우리가 경험하는 불편함에 대한 보상 신호를 만든다
⑤ 예기치 못한 사건을 신속하게 통제할 수 있는 능력을 가지고 있다

구문 [12행~13행] That strongly **suggested** // that spatial tasks **were** actively changing taxi drivers' brains.
동사 suggest는 목적절에 직설법 동사(were)가 오면 '제안하다'의 뜻이 아니고 '시사하다'의 뜻을 나타낸다.

어휘 **famously** 훌륭하게; 유명하게 **navigate** 운전하다; 항해하다 **neurologist** 신경과학자 **colleague** 동료 **conduct** 수행하다 **posterior** 뒤의 (↔ **anterior** 앞의) **specialize in** ~을 전문으로 하다 **spatial** 공간의 **representation** 표현, 묘사 **correlate** 상관관계를 보여주다 **consistent** 일치된, 조화된 **Braille** 점자 **meditation** 명상 **practitioner** 실천하는 사람 [선택지 어휘] **adapt** 적응하다 **in response to** ~에 응하여 **reward** 보상

35 무관한 문장 ④

소재 북극의 척박한 생활환경

해설 북극 지역의 척박한 자연환경과 자원 부족에 대해 설명하는 글이다. 자원의 부족에 대한 내용이 이어지는 가운데 먹이 그물의 변화로 인한 영향을 언급한 ④는 글의 흐름에 어울리지 않는 문장이다.

해석 세계에서 가장 척박한 환경인 북극권 위쪽 지역에 사는 사람들은 문화와 언어가 다양하고, 필요에 의해 매우 강인하고 기략이 풍부할 수밖에 없다. 주제문 결핍은 북극 생태계를 가장 잘 묘사하는 단어인데, 그곳에서는 활력을 불어넣는 태양 에너지만이 부족한 자원인 것은 아니다. 심지어 하루에 20시간 동안 (햇빛이 비쳐서) 밝은 여름철 동안에도 태양 광선은 얼어붙은 심토(心土)를 녹일 정도로 강하지 않다. 그러나 극심한 추위보다도, 자원의 부족이 북극 사람들이 살아가는 삶의 방식을 잘 보여준다. 먹이 그물의 변화는 북극지방의 삶을 위협하는 것뿐만 아니라 지구의 기후에도 나쁜 영향을 줄 수 있다. 이곳에서는 식물이 거의 자랄 수 없고, 나무도, 목재도, 상점도, 자동차도, 발전된 세상에서 우리가 매일 당연히 여기는 것이 아무것도 없다.

구문 [4행~7행] Scarcity is *the word* [**that** best describes *the Arctic ecosystem*], // **where** life-giving solar energy is not *the only resource* [**that** is in short supply].
where가 이끄는 관계부사절이 선행사인 the Arctic ecosystem을 보충 설명하고 있으며 that이 이끄는 주격 관계대명사절은 각각의 선행사를 수식한다.

어휘 **inhabit** 살다, 서식하다 **harsh** 황량한, 거친 **the Arctic Circle** 북극권 **necessity** 필요(성) **resourceful** 기략이 풍부한, 수완이 비상한, 능숙한 **scarcity** 결핍, 부족(=**lack**) **ecosystem** 생태계 **life-giving** 활기를 띠게 하는, 생기를 주는 **in short supply** (공급이) 부족한 **ray** 광선 **thaw** 녹이다 **subsurface** 지표 밑의 **severe** 심한, 맹렬한 **define** 명백히 보여주다; 정의를 내리다 **food web** 먹이 그물 **take A for granted** A를 당연시하다

36 글의 순서 ②

소재 상관관계와 인과관계의 차이

해설 주어진 글에서는 상관관계를 논했으므로, 그다음에는 우선 상관관계를 논한 (A)나 (B)가 나와야 한다. 그런데 (A)에는 however라는 반박의 표현이 있으므로 주어진 글 다음에 (A)가 바로 올 수 없다. 따라서 (B)가 이어진다. 두 현상 간에 양/음의 관계가 있는 것이 상관관계라고 한 (B) 다음에는 however로 이어지며 '이것이 반드시 인과관계라는 뜻은 아니다'라는 (A)가 이어진다. (A)의 This는 '두 현상 간에 양/음의 관계가 존재하는 것'을 나타낸다. (C)는 인과관계에 대한 내용이므로 (A)까지 상관관계를 논한 후에 마지막에 나오게 된다.

해석 주제문 이제까지 저술된 모든 통계학 서적은 '상관관계는 인과관계가 아니다'라는 구절을 포함하고 있다. 그것은 사실 단순한 개념이다. 두 개의 정보 간의 상관관계는 그것들이 관련되어 있다는 것을 의미한다.
(B) 두 현상의 측정에서 상관관계가 양의 관계라면, 한 현상의 양이 오를 때 다른 현상의 양도 그렇게 된다(= 오른다). 상관관계가 음의 관계이면, 그것들의 양은 반대 방향으로 움직인다.
(A) 그러나 이것은 하나가 나머지 하나를 일으키고 있다는 뜻은 아니다. 빈번하게 소변을 봐야 한다는 것은 당뇨병과 상관관계가 있지만, 하루에 여러 번 화장실을 이용해야 한다는 것이 당뇨병을 유발하는 것은 아니다(또한 당신이 이미 당뇨병에 걸렸다는 뜻도 아니다).
(C) 인과관계는 상관관계보다 한 단계 더 나아간다. 그것은 한 변수(운동)의 값의 어떠한 변화도 다른 변수(소모된 열량)의 값의 변화를 일으킬 것임을 일컫는데, 이는 한 변수가 다른 변수를 발생하게 한다는 것을 의미한다.

구문 [7행~9행] ~, but **needing** to use the bathroom many times a day (S) does not cause (V) diabetes (**nor** does **it** mean // you already have **it**).
동명사구 주어가 쓰여 단수형 does를 썼다. nor와 같은 부정어 다음에는 「부정어+조동사+주어+동사원형」 순으로 도치가 일어난다. does 다음에 나온 it은 needing to use the bathroom many times a day를 지칭하며, have 다음에 나온 it은 diabetes를 지칭한다.

[10행~12행] If the correlation in the measurement of two phenomena is positive, // when the measure of **one** goes up, // **so** too *does* **the other**.
two phenomena 가운데 하나는 one, 나머지 하나는 the other로 지칭하였다. 「so+동사+주어」는 '…도 또한 그렇다'의 뜻이다. does는 goes up에 대응된다.

어휘 **statistics** 통계(학); 통계 자료 **phrase** 구(절) **correlation** 상관관계 *cf.* **correlate** 상관관계를 보여주다 **causation** 인과관계 **urinate** 소변을 보다 **diabetes** 당뇨병 **measure** 분량, 양; 정도 **variable** 변수; 변하기 쉬운

37 글의 순서 ④

소재 음악 저작권 보장 기간

해설 주어진 글의 마지막에 있는 a time limit(시간상의 제한)에 대해 (C)에서 녹음은 50년의 기간, 작곡은 저작자 사후 70년의 기간이 지나면 만료된다는 구체적인 설명을 하고 있으므로 (C)가 가장 먼저 나와야 한다. (A)의 첫 번째 문장의 This is ~ a considerable period of time이 (C)의 '50년'과 '70년'을 가리키므로 (C) 다음에는 (A)가 와야 한다. 또한, (A)에 나와 있는 Paul McCartney의 자작곡이 보호받는 기간(사후 70년)과는 대조적으로 앨범에 대해서는 재산권의 보호 기간이 상대적으로 짧은 것과 그 이유를 (B)에서 설명하고 있으므로 (B)가 마지막에 와야 한다. 따라서 글의 순서는 ④ '(C)-(A)-(B)'가 적절하다.

해석 주제문 음악의 권리 소유자에게 부여된 '당연한' 독점권은 그것의 시행에 있어 제한이 있다. 이것은 입법 기관에 음악 사용자들(방송업자들과 다른 사람들)의 경제적 이해관계가 행사하는 압력이 반영된 것이다. 예를 들어, 이 재산권은 시간상 제한이 있다.
(C) 50년이 지나면 음악 녹음의 저작권은 끝이 나게 되며, 누구라도 그것의 복제품을 대중들에게 유포할 수 있다. 음악의 작곡과 관련된 경우에는 저작자가 죽고 난 뒤 70년이 지나면 저작권이 종료된다.
(A) 물론, 이것은 상당한 기간이다. 만약 Paul McCartney(폴 매카트니)가 2030년까지 산다면, 그의 자작곡들뿐만 아니라 고인이 된 John Lennon(존 레논)과 함께 작곡한 곡들도 최소한 21세기 말까지 저작권이 남아 있게 된다.
(B) 대조적으로, 1962년에 발표된 Beatles(비틀즈)의 초창기 앨범은 2012년에 공공의 영역에 들어갔다. 이러한 재산권에 대한 두 기간의 차이는 원저자의 남아 있는 기운(= 작곡가의 저작권)이 음반의 '산업적인' 의미(= 앨범의 저작권)보다 더 많이 보상 받는 것을 보장한다는 생각을 드러낸다.

구문 [14행~18행] *The disparity* (between these two periods of property rights) (S) / discloses (V) the idea (O) that (=) the residual aura of authorship (S′) guarantees (V′) / that this will be more highly rewarded / than the "industrial" connotation of recording (O′).

the idea와 that the residual ~ recording은 동격 관계이다. that this ~ recording은 동사 guarantees의 목적어이다.

어휘 **natural** 당연한; 타고난; 자연의 **monopoly** 독점(권), 전매 **operation** 시행, 실시; 운용 **reflection** 반영; 반사 **exert** 행사하다, 가하다 **legislature** 입법 기관, 입법부 **property right** 재산권 **composition** 작곡(법); 작품; 구성(요소들) *cf.* **compose** 작곡하다 **late** 고인이 된 **copyright** 저작권 **disclose** 드러내다; 밝히다, 폭로하다 **residual** 남은, 잔여(의) **aura** 기운, 분위기 **authorship** (원)저자; 저작, 저술 **connotation** 함축(된 의미) **issue** 유포하다; 발표하다; 발행하다 **where A is concerned** A가 관련된 경우에 **expire** 종료[만료]되다, 만기가 되다

38 문장 넣기 ④

소재 '중력 렌즈'를 통한 우주 탐사

해설 ④를 전후로 논리 구조를 살펴보면, ④의 앞 문장에서는 '우주 배경 복사가 예전에는 에너지가 높고 뜨겁고 밝았다'고 했지만, ④의 다음 문장에서는 '그것이 희미하여 연구하기 어렵다'고 하여 두 문장 간에 논리적인 괴리가 있다. 이 두 문장 사이에 But으로 시작하는 주어진 문장이 위치하면, '처음에는 에너지가 높았던 빛이 우주가 팽창함에 따라 파장이 길어졌고, 그 결과 그 빛이 이제는 희미해져서 연구하기 어렵게 되었다'는 논리 구조로 자연스럽게 연결된다. ④ 다음 문장의 It은 주어진 문장의 microwave radiation을 지칭한다.

해석 주제문 중력 렌즈는 먼 우주를 탐색하기 위한 도구이다. 그것은 전자기 스펙트럼 전 범위의 빛에 작용하여, 우주 마이크로파 배경이라 불리는, 빅뱅에서 나온 빛의 최후의 희미한 떨림을 연구하는 데 사용될 수 있다. 이것은 우주의 탄생으로부터 대략 37만 년 후에 우주 전역으로의 여정을 시작한 빛의 분산된 배경이다. 그것은 예전에는 매우 에너지가 높고 뜨거웠으며, 아마 별의 표면만큼 밝았을 것이다. 그러나 우주의 팽창은 그 빛의 파장을 늘렸고, 우리는 오늘날 그것을 마이크로파 복사로 본다. 그것은 희미하여 연구하기 어렵다. 중력 렌즈는 빅뱅의 마지막 반향을 담고 있는 이러한 잔여 복사의 변화와 변동을 관찰할 수 있는 방법을 제공한다.

구문 [13행~16행] Gravitational lensing offers *a way* (**to observe** changes and fluctuations in *this remnant radiation* [that contains the last echoes of the Big Bang]).
( )는 a way를 수식하는 형용사적 용법의 to부정사구이며, 그 안의 [ ]는 this remnant radiation을 수식하는 관계사절이다.

어휘 **expansion** 확장, 확대 **stretch** 늘이다, 펴다 **wavelength** 파장, 주파수 **microwave radiation** 마이크로파 복사 *cf.* **radiation** (빛 · 열 등의) 복사; 복사 에너지 **gravitational lens[lensing]** 중력 렌즈 **electromagnetic** 전자기의 **faint** 희미한, 약한 **tremor** (약간의) 떨림 **cosmic** 우주의 **disperse** 흩뜨리다; 확산[분산]시키다 **fluctuation** 변동, 오르내림 **remnant** 나머지의 **echo** 반향, 메아리

39 문장 넣기 ⑤

소재 알타미라 동굴 벽화

해설 주어진 문장은 그림의 연대를 추측하는 것인데 also라는 표현이 있으므로 주어진 문장 앞에는 그림의 연대와 관련된 내용이 선행되어야 한다. 또한 ⑤를 전후로 논리 구조를 살펴보면, '동굴 벽화가 약 35,000년 전의 것이다'와 '이것은 수백 세대가 수천 년에 걸쳐 그림에 수정과 첨가를 가했음을 의미한다'라고 했는데 두 문장은 논리적으로 연결되지 않는다. '벽화가 단일 시기에 그려진 것이 아니라 20,000년에 걸쳐서 그려진 것일 수 있다'는 주어진 문장이 ⑤에 위치하면, '동굴 벽화들은 35,000년 전 것인 진품이다 — 또한 이 벽화들은 20,000년에 걸쳐 완성된 것 같다 — 이것은 수백 세대가 그림의 완성에 기여했다는 의미이다'라는 자연스러운 흐름이 완성된다.

해석 동굴 벽화에 대한 최초의 주요 발견은 고고학자 Marcelino de Sautuola가 스페인의 알타미라 동굴을 우연히 발견했을 때인 1876년에 나왔다. 소재는 대개 사슴, 말과 들소 떼를 포함한 거대 동물로 구성되었고, 그것들은 숯과 황토로 만들어진 물감을 사용하여 창작되었다. 그 그림들은 아주 세세하고 정교해서 Sautuola의 동시대인들은 그에게 위조를 했다고 비난했다. 그들은 고대인들이 그렇게 비범한 예술 작품을 만들 능력이 있었다는 것을 믿지 않으려고 했다. 나중에 드러난 것처럼, 그 그림들은 완전히 진품이었으며 우리는 이제 그것들이 3만 5천 년이나 이전에 그려졌다는 것을 알고 있다. 또한 방사성 탄소에 의하면 그 그림들은 단일 시기가 아닌 2만 년의 세월에 걸쳐 완성되었을지도 모른다. 주제문 그 연대 결정이 정확하다면, 이것은 초기 인류의 수백 세대가 수천 년에 걸쳐 그림을 수정하고 그들 자신이 그린 형상들을 더했음을 의미할 것이다.

구문 [16행~19행] ~ this would mean // that hundreds of generations (S′) of early humans retouched (V′1) the drawings and added (V′2) their own figures / over the course of millennia.
that절에서 주어는 hundreds ~ humans이며 동사 retouched와 added가 and로 연결되어 병렬구조를 이룬다.

어휘 **as opposed to** ~와 반대로 **session** (특정) 시간, 기간 **archaeologist** 고고학자 **stumble upon** ~을 우연히 발견하다 **subject matter** 주제, 소재 **consist of** ~으로 구성되다 **herd** 떼 **bison** 들소 **charcoal** 숯; 짙은 회색 **elaborate** 정교한 **contemporary** 동시대인 **accuse A of B** B의 이유로 A를 비난하다 **forgery** 위조 **authentic** 진짜의, 진품인 **dating** 연대 결정 **retouch** 수정하다 **millennia (millennium**의 복수형**)** 천 년

40 요약문 완성 ①

소재 의미 전달이 아닌 창조력 표현으로서의 예술 활동

해설 먼저 요약문을 보면, 예술가의 창조는 때때로 의미를 '무엇(A)'하기보다는 예술가 자신의 '무엇(B)'을 발휘하는 것을 의도한다는 내용이다. 글의 첫 문장에서, 예술 작품은 때때로 관람객에게 경험을 전달하기보다 창의적으로 표현하고자 하는 예술가의 의도로 만들어진다고 했다. 이어 나오는 예시에서 사람들은 자신의 행동에 대해 다른 사람이 어떻게 반응할지에 대한 생각을 하지 않은 채로 자신의 생각이나 감정을 표현한다는 내용이 이를 뒷받침한다. 따라서 (A)에는 '전달하다(convey)'가, (B)에는 '창조력(creativity)'이 들어가는 것이 적절하다.

해석 주제문 예술 작품은 종종 관람객들에게 특정한 경험을 일으키도록 만들어지기도 하지만, 때로 예술가들의 이러한 의도는 예술적 상상력을 창의적으로 표현하려는 의도보다는 부차적인 것이다. 잠시 행동에 대해 일반적으로 생각해보라. 예를 들어, 좋아하는 스포츠 팀을 보고 있는 사람들을 떠올려보라. 실제 경기장에서 보는 것이든 술집에서 보는 것이든, 경기의 중요한 시점에서 사람들은 기대감의 몸짓을 하거나 충고의 갈채를 보내는 경향이 있다. 상황에 따라 이러한 행동은 팀에게는 긴박감을, 혹은 술집의 다른 이들에게는 반감을 전달하기 위해 수행되는 것일지도 모른다. 하지만 사람들은 보통 다른 사람들이 뭐라고 생각할지, 혹은 그들이 어떻게 반응할지에 대해 생각하지 않고 이런 식으로 자신을 표현한다. 우리가 감정, 생각, 태도를 표현하기 위해서 하는 행동에 다른 사람들이 어떻게 반응할지에 대한 생각을 할 필요는 없다. 적어도 일부 (예술) 작품들은 단지 이런 종류의 행동의 전형으로 이해되어야 한다.

⬇

> 때때로 예술가의 창조는 어떤 의미를 (A) 전달하거나 관람객의 반응을 이끌어내는 것이 아니라, 자신의 (B) 창조력 발휘가 의도된 것이다.

구문 [7행~9행] **Whether** it is at an actual match **or** in a bar, // at crucial periods in a game, / people tend to gesture in anticipation, or (to) cheer in exhortation.
whether는 or와 함께 '~이든 …이든 간에'라는 의미를 나타내는 양보의 접속사로 쓰였다. tend의 목적어인 to gesture ~ anticipation과 (to) cheer ~ exhortation은 or로 대등하게 연결되었다.

[15행~18행] *Actions* (S′) [(that) we perform] [through **which** we intend to express our feelings, thoughts, and attitudes] need not have thought (V) (**for** (O) how others may respond).

주어인 Actions는 두 개의 관계사절이 수식하고 있다. how가 이끄는 의문사절은 전치사 for의 목적어로 쓰였다.

어휘 **secondary** 부차적인, 이차적인; 제2의 **crucial** 중요한, 결정적인 **anticipation** 기대; 예상 **urgency** 긴급, 위기 **disgust** 반감, 혐오; 메스꺼움 **embodiment** (특질을 보여주는) 전형; 구체화 **exercise** (역량을) 발휘(하다), (권력 · 권리 등을) 행사(하다); 연습(하다) [선택지 어휘] **conceal** 감추다, 숨기다 **distort** (사실 · 생각을) 왜곡하다; (형체를) 비틀다

41~42 장문 41 ④ 42 ④

소재 경쟁자 수와 동기부여의 상관관계

해설 41. 경쟁자가 다수 존재하는 상황에서는 동기부여가 약해져서 수행 성과가 낮아진다는 내용의 글이므로 제목으로 가장 적절한 것은 ④ '경쟁이 오르면 동기부여는 내려간다'이다.
① 경쟁: 최고의 동기 요인
② 경쟁은 보상으로 동기를 부여하는 것이다
③ 경쟁은 일부에게는 동기부여가 되지만 모두에게 그런 것은 아니다
⑤ 기분이 좋을수록 사고방식은 더욱 경쟁적이게 된다

42. 경쟁자의 총 수가 많으면 개인 경장자의 동기부여는 증가하는 것이 아니라 감소하므로, (d)의 increased를 diminished 등으로 바꿔 써야 한다.

해석 일반적인 통념에 의하면 우리의 가장 강력한 경쟁 동기 요인들 중 하나는 사회적 (a) 비교라고 한다. 우리는 자기 자신을 다른 사람들과 비교하자마자 그들과 경쟁하기 시작한다. 그러나 <심리과학>지에 출간된 새로운 연구에 의하면 우리가 경쟁하는 사람들의 (b) 수는 경쟁하고자 하는 우리의 동기에 직접적인 영향을 미친다고 나온다. 여기에 한 예가 있다. Jessica는 열 명의 다른 학생들과 함께 교실에 앉아 있다. 그녀는 주변을 둘러보고, 경쟁적인 조망을 평가하고, 이 작은 집단에 대하여 자신이 잘할 가능성이 괜찮다고 결정한다. 강사는 입자물리학 시험지를 배부하고, Jessica는 이 학급에서 최고 성적에 들겠다는 동기부여가 된 상태로 힘차게 착수한다. Jason은 시험을 치기 위해 다른 교실에 도착하는데, 그것은 Jessica의 교실보다 훨씬 더 크다. 사실 그것은 열 배 더 크며, Jason은 백 명의 학생들이 있는 한 무리에서 좌석을 찾아야 한다. 강사는 시험지를 배부하고 Jason은 경쟁적 우위를 느끼지 못한 채로 시작한다.
주제문 Jessica의 결심과 비교하여 Jason이 느끼는 동기부여의 (c) 결여는 심리학자들이 N효과라고 지칭하는 것이다. 이 효과는 전체 경쟁자들의 증가가 개인 경쟁자들에게 (d) 증가된(→ 감소된) 동기부여를 야기할 때 발생한다. 연구자들은 다섯 개로 구성된 일련의 연구를 통해 이 효과를 평가했다. 첫 번째 연구에서는 다년간에 걸쳐서 특정한 장소에서 몇 명의 사람들이 시험을 쳤는지를 고려하여 SAT와 CRT(인지 반영 테스트) 점수를 검토했다. 다른 변수들에 대한 통제를 했을 때조차도 연구자들은 시험 응시자의 수와 점수 간의 의미 있는 역의 상관관계를 발견했다. 더 많은 사람들이 시험에 응시할수록 점수는 (e) 더 낮아졌다.

구문 [12행~14행] The instructor passes out the particle physics exam, / and Jessica is off and running, / **motivated** to score among the best in this class.
motivated 이하는 수동의 의미를 가지는 분사구문이며, motivated to-v는 'v하려는 동기를 부여받은'의 뜻이다.

[30행~33행] ~, researchers found a significant inverse correlation between the number of test takers and scores: **the more** people taking the test, **the worse** the scores.
「a correlation between A and B」는 'A와 B 사이의 상관관계'의 뜻이다. 「the 비교급 ~, the 비교급 ...」은 '~하면 할수록 더 …하다'의 뜻이다.

어휘 **conventional wisdom** 일반 통념, 속된 지혜 **have it that** ~라고 주장하다 **mighty** 강력한 **motivator** 동기 요인 **illustration** 실례, 예 **odds** 가능성 **pass out** 분배하다, 나눠주다 **particle physics** 입자물리학 **off and running** 힘차게 일에 착수하는 **competitive edge** 경쟁적 우위 *cf.* **edge** 우위; 모서리 **resolve** 결심 **in light of** ~을 고려하여 **venue** 장소 **variable** 변수 **inverse correlation** 역상관관계 *cf.* **inverse** 역(逆)의, 정반대의 [선택지 어휘] **mindset** 사고방식[태도]

43~45 장문 43 ④ 44 ④ 45 ④

소재 승리를 누린 현명한 방법

해설 43. Singer에게 한 달간 야간 근무가 주어진 (A) 다음에는 그녀가 낮에 활동하는 사람이라서 야근에서 벗어나려고 방법을 모색하는 (D)가 오는 것이 자연스럽다. Singer가 Wells에게 퀴즈를 제안하는 내용 다음에는 Singer가 퀴즈에서 이기는 (B)가 오고 마지막에 승리 후 Singer의 처신에 대한 내용인 (C)가 이어지는 것이 적절하다.

44. (d)는 편집장 Wells를 가리키는 반면 나머지는 모두 Singer를 가리킨다.

45. (C)에서 Singer가 내기에서 상사를 이긴 후의 곤란한 상황을 타개하기 위해 Wells가 일부러 져주었다고 말했을 뿐, 실제로 Wells가 일부러 진 것은 아니다.

해석 (A) 주제문 이기는 것은 멋진 일이다. 그것은 직업에 도움이 될 수 있고 종종 성공으로 이어진다. 그렇더라도 결국 중요한 것은 우리가 행운을 어떻게 다루느냐는 것이다. 그것은 기자 Ellen Singer가 야간 근무로 일하는 것을 피하려는 행동에서 배운 것이다. 그녀의 신문 편집장인 ① Linda Wells는 그녀에게 (a) 그녀(= Singer)로서는 악몽 같은 과제를 주었는데, 즉 한 달간 야간 근무로 일하는 것이었다.
(D) ⑤ 천성적으로 '낮에 활동하기를 좋아하는 사람'인 그녀는 먼저 합리적으로 그 임무에서 자신이 배제되도록 그녀를 설득하려고 했다. 그것은 효과가 없었다. 그러고 나서 필사적으로 그녀는 연예에 대한 자기의 지식을 유리하게 이용하려고 했다. Singer는 Wells가 퀴즈에서 자기를 이길 수 있다면 (e) 그녀(= Singer)가 야간 근무를 1개월이 아니라 6개월을 할 것이라고 편집장에게 내기를 걸었다. 반면에 Singer가 이기면 그녀는 1년간 야간 근무를 면제받게 되는 것이다.
(B) 게다가 (b) 그녀(= Singer)는 자기가 원하는 어떤 것에 대해서든 한 달 동안 글을 쓰도록 할당받을 것이다. 퀴즈 주제는 텔레비전 연속극인 'Bewitched'가 되었고 ② Singer는 쉽게 이겼다. 이제 더 큰 도전이 왔다. 그녀는 상사를 이겼다는 곤란한 상황을 처리해야 했다. 우선 Singer는 자신의 자유로운 한 달을 이용해 (c) 그녀(= Singer)와 신문이 ③ 찬사를 받은 훌륭한 기사를 썼다.
(C) 자신의 승리를 축하하는 대신 그녀는 듣는 모든 사람들에게 ④ 그녀의 편집장이 그녀를 격려하기 위해 일부러 그녀를 이기게 해주었다고 말했다. 편집장은 긍정적인 결과에 대해 어느 정도 인정을 받게 되어 당연히 기뻐했다. 또한 (d) 그녀(= Wells)는 Singer가 그녀의 '승리' 뒤에 행동했던 정중한 태도를 잊지 않았다. Singer는 현명하게 이긴 것이 주는 단기적인 포상을 포기했다. 그녀는 자신의 '승리'를 자신과 다른 사람들을 위한 '승리'를 만들어내는 장기적인 직업상의 관계에 투자했다.

어휘 (A) **fortune** 운, 운명 **in the long run** 결국에는 **move** 행동, 조치 **night shift** 야간 근무 (B) **allot** 할당하다, 주다 **turn out** (일 · 진행 · 결과가 특정 방식으로) 되다[되어 가다] **tricky** 곤란한, 까다로운 **at liberty** 풀려난, 자유로운 (C) **on purpose** 일부러, 고의로 **inspire** 격려하다, 고무하다 **understandably** 당연히 **credit** 신망, 인정 **gracious** 공손한, 정중한 **pass up** 거절하다, 포기하다 (D) **day person** 낮에 활동하기를 좋아하는 사람 **argue A out of B** A를 설득하여 B를 그만두게 하다 **desperate** 필사적인, 절박한 **turn A to one's advantage** A를 유리하게 이용하다 **bet** 내기하다 **exempt** 면제하다, 없애주다

14

고난도 모의고사 15

본문 p.209

18 ② 19 ⑤ 20 ⑤ 21 ③ 22 ③ 23 ③ 24 ② 25 ③ 26 ⑤ 27 ④
28 ⑤ 29 ② 30 ⑤ 31 ③ 32 ① 33 ④ 34 ⑤ 35 ② 36 ④ 37 ⑤
38 ③ 39 ② 40 ① 41 ② 42 ② 43 ③ 44 ⑤ 45 ②

18 글의 목적 ②

소재 쓰레기 처리 관련 법 시행에 따른 의무 훈련 공지

해설 쓰레기 처리와 관련된 새로운 법의 시행과 함께 회사의 쓰레기 처리에 관한 의무 훈련이 실시된다는 것을 공지하는 내용이므로 정답은 ②이다. there will be a mandatory training session this Thursday에 글의 목적이 잘 드러나 있다.

해석 직원 여러분께 알려 드립니다.
여러분이 이미 알고 있다시피 뉴포트 시는 쓰레기 처리와 관련된 새로운 법을 시행합니다. 이 법안들의 다수는 기업체의 재활용을 특히 목표로 삼고 있습니다. 수년에 걸쳐, 우리는 여기 Dunbar 전자에서 환경적으로 책임을 다하기 위해 최선을 다해왔지만 우리가 완벽한 것은 전혀 아닙니다. 주제문 새로운 법률적 요구를 지키기 위해서 우리는 다수의 우리 습관들을 새롭게 할 필요가 있을 것입니다. 첫 단계는 모두가 재활용과 쓰레기 감소에 대해 한층 더 잘 이해하는 것입니다. 주제문 이것을 이루기 위해서 이번 목요일에 의무 훈련 시간이 있을 것입니다. 불편하게 해드려 죄송하지만 모두가 이 문제의 중요성을 깨달을 수 있으리라 확신합니다. 자세한 사항을 알려면 구내식당의 공지 게시판을 확인하시고, 제시간에 도착하시기 바랍니다. 감사합니다.
총괄 관리자 Andy Spade 드림

어휘 **put in place** 시행하다 **disposal** 처리, 처분 **aim** 목표로 삼다; 겨냥하다 **far from** 전혀 ~이 아닌 **meet** 충족시키다; 만나다 **legal** 적법한, 합법의 **requirement** 요구; 필요조건 **update** 새롭게 하다, 갱신하다 **practice** 습관; 관행; 실행 **reduction** 감소 **accomplish** 이루다, 성취하다 **mandatory** 의무적인, 필수의 **session** (특정한 활동을 위한) 시간, 기간 **inconvenience** 불편 **announcement** 공고, 알림 **lunchroom** 구내식당

19 심경 변화 ⑤

소재 로스쿨에서 받은 합격 소식

해설 필자는 장학금을 주는 로스쿨에 합격하기를 바라는데, 한 입학사정관이 전화를 걸어 좋은 소식이 있다며 나중에 괜찮을 때 전화해 달라고 말했다. 이때 필자는 매우 '고대하는(anticipating)' 심정이었을 것이다. 그러나 다시 전화를 걸었을 때 입학사정관은 장학금에 대한 언급은 없이 합격 소식만 전해주어서 필자는 '실망(disappointed)'하였으므로 심경 변화로 가장 적절한 것은 ⑤이다.

해석 나는 재정적 도움을 주는 몇몇 로스쿨에 지원했고, 그 과정은 거절로 넘쳐났다. 어느 날 두 친구와 차로 쇼핑몰에서 돌아오던 중, 주제문 나는 캘리포니아 대학교 Berkeley의 입학사정관에게서 걸려온 전화를 받았다. 그녀는 얘기하기에 괜찮은지 물었고 나는 그녀에게 운전 중이라 안 된다고 말했다. 그녀는 말했다. "좋아요, 하지만 가능한 한 빨리 저에게 전화해 주세요. 좋은 소식이 있어요." 나는 전화를 끊고 친구들에게 통화에 관해 말했다. 그들 중 한 명이 말했다. "아마 그녀가 너에게 장학금을 제안하려고 전화했나 봐." 나는 말했다. "네 말이 맞으면 좋겠다." 그리고 나는 잠시 Berkeley에서의 학교생활을 상상해 봤다. 기숙사로 돌아오자마자 나는 그녀에게 전화했고 그녀는 말했다. "축하합니다! Berkeley에 합격했어요." 주제문 나는 그녀에게 전화해준 데 대해 예의를 갖춰 감사를 표했고 전화를 끊고 나서 내 상황에 대해 한탄하는 일로 돌아갔다. 나는 혼자 생각했다. "그래서 어쩌라고? 어쨌든 내가 갈 수 있을 것 같진 않아. 난 로스쿨을 다닐 여유가 없어. 내가 바라는 건 장학금이야."

① 긴장한 → 화난 ② 불안한 → 안도한
③ 의심하는 → 확신하는 ④ 우울한 → 만족한

어휘 **apply to** ~에 지원하다 **award** 주다, 수여하다 **financial** 재정의 **aid** 도움 **flood** 쇄도하다 **admissions officer** 입학사정관 **get off** 그만하다 **scholarship** 장학금 **for a while** 잠시 동안 **as soon as** ~하자마자 **dorm** 기숙사 (=**dormitory**) **lament** 한탄하다

20 필자 주장 ⑤

소재 사생활 보호의 필요성

해설 인간이 사회화되기 위해서는 혼자 있는 시간이 필요하며, 사생활의 상실이 생기면 인간이 사회화될 수 있는 자원을 보충할 수 없게 되고 심리적 문제도 생긴다는 내용이므로, 필자의 주장으로 적절한 것은 ⑤이다.

해석 인간은 모든 동물들 중에서 사회적으로 가장 발달했다. 다른 인간과의 상호 작용은 인간에게 있어 하나의 환경적 필수 사항이다. 어떠한 인간도 완전히 혼자 섬으로 살아남을 수 없다. 어떠한 인간도 섬이 되기를 원하지 않는다. 하지만 모든 인간은 자신만의 방, 말하자면 자신이 물러나서 외부 세계의 소문과 비상 신호에 방해받지 않고 홀로 있을 수 있는 보호 구역을 가짐으로써 사회화되기 위한 자신의 자원을 보충하기를 원하고 필요로 한다. 주제문 나는 서양인들이, 특히 미국에서, 겪고 있는 사생활 상실의 증가는 무엇보다도 개인이 인간으로서 자신이 해야 하는 올바르고 건강한 것들이 무엇인지를 발견할 수 있는 기회를 늘리기보다 감소시키는 역할을 하고 있다고 말하려고 한다. 그리고 이러한 사실로부터 어떤 심각한 심리적 결과들이 생겨난다는 것도 (말하려고 한다).

구문 [10행~16행] I am going to suggest // that *the increasing loss of privacy* [from which Western man is suffering, ~,] (S') / serves, ~, (V') / to reduce ~ the chances of the individual being able to discover / what *those things* are [that are right ~ to do].

첫 번째 [ ] 부분은 「전치사+관계대명사」가 이끄는 관계사절로서 the increasing loss of privacy를 수식한다. the chances와 the individual ~ to do가 of로 연결되어 동격 관계를 이룬다. 두 번째 [ ]는 those things를 수식하는 관계사절로, what이 이끄는 절의 주어가 길어져서 균형을 맞추기 위해 동사 뒤로 보냈다.

[16행~17행] And (I am going to suggest) that from this fact (장소의 부사구) spring (V') certain serious psychological consequences (S').

장소의 부사구가 문장 앞에 나와 주어와 동사가 도치되었고, I am going to suggest가 앞 문장과 중복되어 생략되었다.

어휘 **interaction** 상호 작용 **necessity** 필수(품); 필요(성) **entirely** 완전히 **resource** 자원; 재료 **as it were** 말하자면, 다시 말해 **retire** 물러나다; 은퇴[퇴직]하다 **undisturbed** 방해받지 않는 **serve** ~의 역할을 하다; 도움이 되다; (서비스를) 제공하다; 근무[복무]하다 **spring from** ~로부터 생겨나다 **psychological** 심리적인 **consequence** 결과; 영향(력)

21 밑줄 함의 ③

소재 민주주의에 대한 오해

해설 뉴기니 사람들이 활주로만 지으면 '화물'이 나타날 거라고 믿었던 것과 마찬가지로, 우리는 민주주의만 도입하면 온갖 혜택이 자동적으로 뒤따를 거라고 혼동하는 '정치적인 화물'의 열성적 지지자가 되었다. 즉, '정치적 화물의 열성적 지지자'라는 것은 ③ '민주주의가 번영을 가져온다고 믿는 사람들'을 의미하는 것이다.

해석 뉴기니의 지역에 사는 사람들은 백인들이 도착했을 때, 그들이 자주 비행장을 건설했다는 것을 알아차렸다. 그리고 나서 비행기가 도착해서 대량의 가치 있는 물건들 혹은 '화물'을 쏟아내곤 했다. 분명 비행장이 핵심인 것 같았다. 그것(= 비행장)이 비행기들을 끌어들였다. 그래서 사람들은 희망에 차서 비행장을 건설한 후 화물이 도착하기를 기다렸다. 그들은 실망했다. '민주주의'에 대해 우리도 마찬가지가 되었다. 우리는 민주주의가 많은 경우 소비자 성공과 어떤 형태의 자유와 연관되는 것을 관찰해왔다. 민주주의는 물건을 가져다준다고 우리는 느낀다. 우리가 나서서 전 세계에 '민주주의를 건설'하면, 민주주의에 연결된 혜택이 자동으로 따라올 거라는 결론을 내린다. 우리가 투표함을 꺼내 놓으면, 나머지도 곧 일어나리라. 그러나 우리는 정치적인 화물의 열성적 지지자가 되었다. 우리는 마찬가지로 실망할 것이다. 주제문 우리는 '민주주의'가 많은 다른 것들의 결과임을 잊었다. 그것(= 민주주의)은 우리가 높이 평가하는 것들의 원인인 것만큼이나 결과이기도 하다.

① 민주주의를 자본주의와 혼동하는 사람들
② 민주주의가 평등을 보장한다고 주장하는 사람들
④ 민주주의를 자유와 마찬가지인 것으로 간주하는 사람들
⑤ 민주주의가 최고의 정부 형태라고 생각하는 사람들

구문 [5행~7행] So people hopefully built airfields and then waited *for the cargo* **to arrive**.
(V1: built, V2: waited)
동사 built와 waited가 병렬구조를 이룬다. for the cargo는 to arrive의 의미상 주어이다.

[17행~19행] It is **as much** the consequence **as** the cause of *things* [(which[that]) we appreciate].
「as 원급 as ~ (~만큼 …하다)」의 원급 비교구문이 쓰였다. [ ] 부분은 목적격 관계대명사가 생략되었으며 앞의 명사 things를 수식한다.

어휘 **airfield** 비행장 **desirable** 가치 있는; 바람직한 **cargo** 화물 **observe** 관찰하다; 준수하다 **be associated with** ~와 연관되다 **set out** 착수하다, 출발하다 **voting box** 투표함 **enthusiast** 열성적 지지자 **appreciate** 진가를 인정하다 [선택지 어휘] **confuse A with B** A와 B를 혼동하다 **capitalism** 자본주의 **equality** 평등 *cf.* **equal** 동등하다; 동등한 **prosperity** 번영, 번성 **regard A as B** A를 B로 간주하다[여기다]

22 글의 요지 ③

소재 색상 관련 단어 유무와 색상 인지 사이의 관계

해설 어떤 언어는 색상에 대한 세분화된 어휘가 없지만 그렇다고 해서 그 언어 사용자들이 색조의 미묘한 차이를 인식하지 못하는 것은 아니라는 내용의 글이므로, 요지로 가장 적절한 것은 ③이다.

해석 각각의 언어는 색상 명명(命名)에 관해 자기만의 특성을 가지고 있다. 전 세계 문화 집단은 색깔에 대해 다르게 말한다. 어떤 집단에는 심지어 색깔에 대한 단어가 없다. 네팔에서 나와 함께 일하는 사람들 간에는 'pingya'라는 한 단어만 있는데, 이는 파란색과 녹색 둘 다 의미한다. 주제문 그들이 (색상) 차이를 말할 수 없으면 (색상) 차이를 볼 수는 있을까? 답에 대한 실마리는 러시아어에 대략 연한 파랑과 진한 파랑을 의미하는 '파랑'에 해당하는 두 단어가 있다는 사실로 제시된다. 우리(= 영국인)를 연구하는 러시아인 인류학자는 우리가 두 개의 파란색을 (단어로) 구별할 수 없으므로, 옥스퍼드 대학과 캠브리지 대학의 보트 레이스 팀이 서로를 분간할 수 없을 거라는 논리적이지만 잘못된 결론에 도달할지도 모른다. 내가 나의 네팔 친구들에게 질문했을 때, 그들은 당연히 녹색 풀과 파란 하늘 간의 차이를 볼 수 있다고 말했다.

구문 [7행~9행] A clue to the answer is given / by the fact that in Russian there are *two words for 'blue'* [**which** roughly mean light and dark blue].
the fact와 that절은 서로 동격 관계이다. which는 two words for 'blue'를 받는 주격 관계대명사이다.

[9행~13행] *A Russian anthropologist* (studying us) might come to the logical, but incorrect, conclusion that because we cannot differentiate the two blues, // the Oxford and Cambridge boat race teams could not tell each other apart.
that절은 the logical, but incorrect, conclusion에 대한 동격절이다. that절이 because절과 주절로 이루어진 구조이다.

어휘 **peculiarity** 특성; 특이함 **clue** 실마리, 단서 **roughly** 대략; 거칠게 **anthropologist** 인류학자 **come to a conclusion** 결론에 도달하다 **logical** 논리적인 **differentiate** 구별하다 **tell ~ apart** 분간하다, 구별하다

23 글의 주제 ③

소재 색채가 풍부한 식단의 필요성

해설 많은 사람들이 고기와 곡물 위주의 '갈색' 식단을 먹고 있는데, 색채가 풍부한 과일과 채소를 풍부하게 구성한 알록달록한 식단이 건강에 많은 이로움을 준다는 내용의 글이므로 주제로 가장 적절한 것은 ③ '색채가 더욱 풍부한 음식을 먹는 것의 건강상의 이점들'이다.

해석 많은 사람들의 접시는 고기와 정제 곡물로 베이지색과 갈색인 경향이 있다. 이러한 음식이 풍부한 식단은 고지방과 고콜레스테롤을 제공하지만 영양상의 우수함은 거의 없다. 국립 암 연구소는 '스펙트럼을 맛보세요'라는 캠페인을 시작했다. 그들은 사람들이 원색 그룹(빨강, 노랑, 주황, 녹색, 파랑, 자주, 그리고 흰색)으로 구성된 과일과 채소를 먹도록 장려하고 있다. 왜 그런가? 색채가 아주 풍부한 과일이 많이 담겨있는 식단은 당신에게 심장마비와 당뇨병을 예방하는 데 도움이 되기 위해 필요한 이로운 합성물을 준다. 또한 색채가 풍부한 채소는 당신의 혈압을 조절하고, 일부 암을 예방하고, 시력 상실이 오지 않도록 보호해준다. 더 많은 색이 보일수록 더 좋다. 국립 암 연구소 프로그램의 관리자인 Loreli Disogra는 말한다. 주제문 "접시에 색채가 보일 때 당신은 당신이 자기 자신을 위해 좋은 일을 하고 있다는 것을 아는 겁니다. 당신의 저녁 접시를 화가의 캔버스로 생각하세요."

① 정크 푸드가 건강에 미치는 해로운 영향들
② 색채가 풍부한 음식을 고르고 먹어보는 것에 대한 조언들
④ 색채가 풍부한 음식이 우리의 감각에 구미가 당기는 이유들
⑤ 당신의 몸에 맞는 건강한 식품을 고르는 방법들

구문 [8행~11행] *A diet* (rich in the most colorful fruits) gives you *the beneficial compounds* [that you need to help prevent a heart attack and diabetes].
( )는 주어 A diet를 꾸미는 형용사구이며 동사는 gives이다. [ ]는 관계사절로 the beneficial compounds를 수식한다.

어휘 **refined** 정제된; 세련된 **launch** 시작[착수]하다 **savor** 맛보다, 음미하다 **primary color** 원색 **compound** 합성물, 혼합물 **diabetes** 당뇨병 **think of A as B** A를 B로 생각하다 [선택지 어휘] **appeal** 관심[흥미]을 끌다

24 글의 제목 ②

소재 문명 이전과 이후의 인간의 폭력성

해설 문명 이전의 사회가 평화로웠을 거라는 통념과는 달리 사실 원시시대는 대단히 폭력적인 사회였으며, 현재 전쟁과 폭력으로 인한 사망률은 과거에 비해 현저히 낮아졌다는 내용의 글이므로 제목으로 가장 적절한 것은 ② '인간은 그 어느 때보다 (현재) 덜 폭력적이다'이다.

해석 겨우 수십 년 전만 해도 많은 학자들은 평화로운 야만인이라는 신화를 믿었는데, 이는 전쟁을 국가 이전의 사회에서는 존재하지 않았던, 근대 문명의 부산물로 묘사한다. 인류학자인 Steven LeBlanc은 이러한 신화가 틀렸음을 입증하며, 대다수의 원시적

인, 국가 이전의 사회는 적어도 간헐적인 전쟁에 참여했음을 지적한다. 일부 사회에서의 폭력으로 인한 사망률은 50퍼센트 정도에 달했다. 주제문 사실 문명은 전쟁의 문제를 일으키기는커녕 명백히 우리가 그 문제를 해결하는 데 도움을 주고 있다. 피투성이의 20세기에 1억 명의 남성, 여성, 어린이들이 전쟁과 관련된 원인으로 죽었다. 우리의 폭력 비율이 평균적인 원시 사회만큼 높았다면 총합은 20억 명이었을 것이다. 게다가 둘 이상의 국가의 군대 간의 재래식 전쟁과 심지어 내전조차도 최근 수십 년 동안 덜 흔한 것이 되었다. 우리는 지금 주로 게릴라전, 폭동, 테러, 혹은 정치학자 John Mueller가 '전쟁의 잔재'라고 부르는 것들을 대하고 있다.

① 전쟁은 범죄에 어떻게 영향을 미치는가?
③ 인간이 전쟁을 하는 것이 당연한가?
④ 현대 시대: 갈등과 폭력의 새로운 시대
⑤ 인간 사회는 왜 과거보다 더 폭력적인가

구문 [1행~4행] Just a few decades ago, many scholars believed in *the myth of the peaceful savage*, // **which** depicts war as *a by-product of modern civilization* [**that** did not exist in pre-state societies].

which는 계속적 용법의 관계대명사로 the myth of the peaceful savage를 부연 설명하는 관계사절을 이끌고, that은 a by-product of modern civilization을 수식하는 관계사절을 이끈다.

[12행~14행] The total **would have been** 2 billion // **if** our rates of violence **had been** / as high as in the average primitive society.

「If+S′+had p.p., S+조동사 과거형+have p.p. (…했다면 ~했을 것이다)」의 가정법 과거완료 구문이 쓰였다.

어휘 **savage** 야만인 **depict A as B** A를 B로 묘사하다 **by-product** 부산물 **civilization** 문명 **pre-state** 국가 이전의 **disprove** 틀렸음을 입증하다 **vast** 광대한 **primitive** 원시적인 **engage in** ~에 참여하다 **occasional** 가끔의 **warfare** 전쟁 **mortality rate** 사망률 **far from** 결코 ~이 아닌, ~이기는커녕 **apparently** 명백히 **blood-soaked** 피투성이의 **violence** 폭력 *cf.* **violent** 폭력적인 **conventional** 재래식의, 전통적인; 관습적인 **civil war** 내전 **primarily** 주로; 근본적으로; 최초로 [선택지 어휘] **era** 시대, 시기 **conflict** 갈등; 충돌

25 도표 이해 ③

소재 미국 내 부의 분배

해설 설문조사 참가자들은 상위 두 번째 그룹인 20퍼센트가 소유한 부의 비율이 20퍼센트를 조금 넘을 것으로 추정했지만, 실제 그들이 소유한 부의 비율은 10퍼센트이다. 즉, 설문조사 참가자들은 실제 비율보다 더 많게 추정한(overestimated) 것이므로 ③에서 더 적게 추정했다는(underestimated) 것은 잘못된 설명이다.

해석 〈미국 내 부의 실제적, 추정적, 이상적 분배〉

주제문 위 그래프는 미국 내 부의 실제적 분배뿐만 아니라 추정적, 이상적 분배에 대해서도 미국인들에게 물은 설문조사의 결과를 보여준다. ① 실제 수치는 가장 부유한 미국인들이 전체 부의 85퍼센트를 소유하고 있고 하위 40퍼센트의 미국인들이 전체 부의 1퍼센트 미만을 공유하고 있어 인상적인 모습을 보여준다. ② 그러나 자신들의 추정치에 관한 질문을 받았을 때, 미국인들은 가장 부유한 사람들이 전체 부의 반을 조금 넘게 소유하는 반면에 중간 20퍼센트는 10퍼센트를 약간 넘게 소유한다고 추정했다. ③ 사실, 설문 조사 참가자들은 두 번째로 높은 20퍼센트가 소유한 부의 비율을 거의 12퍼센트 포인트만큼 더 적게 추정했다. ④ 더욱이, 설문조사에 참여한 사람들은 두 번째로 가난한 미국인들이 부의 10퍼센트 미만을 소유하지만, 최하위 20퍼센트는 부의 약 3~4퍼센트를 소유할 것이라고 추정했다. ⑤ 그럼에도 불구하고, 설문조사 응답자들은 자신들의 이상은 훨씬 더 평등한 나라라고 말했고, (이상적인) 그 나라에서는 최하위가 10퍼센트를 약간 넘는 부에, 그리고 최상위는 이러한 부의 양(=10퍼센트)의 약 세 배 정도(=30퍼센트)에 접근했다.

구문 [4행~7행] The actual numbers paint a striking picture, / **with** *the wealthiest Americans* **holding** 85% of all wealth and *the bottom 40% of Americans* **sharing** less than 1% of all wealth.

「with+명사+v-ing」는 부대상황을 나타내는 분사구문으로, 「명사+v-ing」 두 개가 and로 연결되어 병렬구조를 이루고 있다.

[16행~19행] Still, the survey respondents said // (that) their ideal was *a much more even country*, // **where** the bottom had access to a little over 10% of wealth and the top (had access to) around three times this amount.

said의 목적어절에서 접속사 that이 생략되었다. 관계부사 where가 이끄는 절이 a much more even country를 보충 설명해준다.

어휘 **survey** (설문)조사 **estimation** 추정(치); 판단 **distribution** 분배; 분포 **ideal** 이상적인; 이상 **A as well as B** B뿐만 아니라 A도 **striking** 인상적인; 주의를 끄는 **hold** 소유하다; 잡고 있다 **underestimate** (비용 · 규모 등을) 너무 적게 추정하다; 과소평가하다 **furthermore** 더욱이, 게다가 **respondent** (조사에서) 응답자 **even** 평등한, 균등한; 평평한 **have access to A** A에 접근[출입]할 수 있다

26 내용 불일치 ⑤

소재 Horace Greeley의 정치 인생

해설 Horace Greeley가 대통령 선거에 출마한 것은 맞지만, 근소한 차이가 아니라 큰 차이로 패배했으므로 ⑤가 글의 내용과 일치하지 않는다.

해석 1811년 2월 3일에 태어난 Horace Greeley는 뉴햄프셔의 애머스트에 있는 가난한 집안 출신의 미국 정치인이었다. 20세의 나이에 그는 ① 뉴욕으로 이주했고, 그곳에서 그는 정치 관련 기사를 작성하고 수정하면서 생계를 꾸려나갔다. 1841년, 그는 ② 당대 훌륭한 신문사들 중 하나인 'Tribune'을 창립했다. 그는 정치에도 관심이 있었는데 1848년에 ③ 뉴욕 주(州) 대표로서 미국 의회 의원에 마침내 선출되었다. 1854년, 그는 공화당 설립을 도왔는데, 이는 꽤 진보적이라고 여겨졌다. 그는 ④ 미국 남북전쟁 동안 Abraham Lincoln의 강력한 지지자였으며, 후에 Andrew Jackson에 반대하는 운동을 했다. 1872년, ⑤ Greeley는 스스로 대통령 선거에 출마했지만, 결국 큰 차이로 패배했다. 그의 아내는 선거 불과 5일 전에 사망했으며, Greeley는 (아내가 사망한 지) 3주 후 세상을 떠났다.

구문 [9행~10행] In 1854, / he helped to found *the Republican Party*, // **which** was considered quite progressive.
V′ C′

the Republican party를 선행사로 하는 which가 이끄는 관계대명사절은 원래 SVOC 구조(people considered the Republican Party quite progressive)이던 것을 수동태로 표현한 것이다.

어휘 **politician** 정치인 *cf.* **politics** 정치(학) *cf.* **political** 정치와 관련된, 정치적인 **make one's living** 생계를 꾸리다 **edit** 편집[교정]하다 **found** 창립[설립]하다; ~에 기초하다 **eventually** 마침내, 결국 **Congress** (미국) 의회 **representative** 대표(자); 대표하는 **Republican Party** (미국) 공화당 **progressive** 진보적인; 점진적인 **campaign against** ~에 반대하는 운동을 하다 **run for** ~에 출마하다 **defeat** 패배시키다, 이기다; 패배 **margin** (득표수 등의) 차이; (책 페이지의) 여백; 이윤

27 안내문 불일치 ④

소재 잡지 구독 신청 안내

해설 인쇄본을 구독하면 기본적으로 e-book 구독 시 얻을 수 있는 모든 혜택을 얻게 된다고 하였다. 이는 인쇄본 구독 시 e-book을 무료로 함께 받아보게 된다는 의미이므로 ④가 안내문의 내용과 일치하지 않는다.

해석

HG 잡지를 구독하세요!

① e-book 구독(1년/12권) 15달러
포함 사항:
- 디지털 포맷의 최신호가 있는 월간 이메일
- 각각 18개의 이야기와 ② 주목을 받았던 6편의 인터뷰를 담은 연 2회 발행하는 두 권의 모음집

③ 인쇄본 구독(1년/12권) 30달러 (미국 내 주소에 한함)
포함 사항:
• 페이퍼백 잡지
④ 이것은 e-book 구독 시의 모든 사항에 '추가한' 것입니다!

구독 갱신
여러분이 이미 구독자이며 구독을 갱신하고 싶으시면 여기를 클릭하셔서 구매하시기 바랍니다. ⑤ 이전에 구독 시 사용했던 이메일 주소와 다른 이메일을 사용하고 계시면 이전 이메일 주소도 포함해 주셔야 합니다.

어휘 **subscribe** (신문 · 잡지 등을) 구독하다; (자선 단체에 정기적으로) 기부하다 *cf.* **subscription** 구독(료); 기부(금) *cf.* **subscriber** 구독자; 기부자, 후원자 **issue** 발행물 **biannual** 연 2회의 **paperback** 페이퍼백(종이 한 장으로 표지를 한 저렴한 보급판 책) **edition** 판, 책 **renewal** 갱신 *cf.* **renew** 갱신하다; 재개하다

28 안내문 일치 ⑤

소재 인턴 모집 안내

해설 자격 요건에서 개발도상국(developing country)에서의 경험이 필요하다고 했으므로 ⑤가 안내문의 내용과 일치한다.

해석

프로젝트-E를 위한 인턴 과정

① 프로젝트-E는 에티오피아의 고아들에게 시장 지향적인 직업 교육을 제공합니다.

I. 제공
• 젊고 동기부여가 된 팀에서의 고무적인 업무 분위기
• ② 이동과 숙박을 위한 재정 지원

II. 업무
• 에티오피아 업체 및 국제 기업, 정부 및 NGO 단체들과의 네트워킹
• ③ 새로운 학생 선발, 사업 제휴 협상, 워크숍 준비

III. 자격 요건
• ④ 학생들은 대학교 2년을 수료했어야 합니다.
• 뛰어난 영어 회화 및 작문 능력, 훌륭한 IT 지식
• ⑤ 개발도상국에서의 경험
• 높은 수준의 의사소통 능력과 팀 업무 능력

IV. 지원
jasper@email.com로 이력서와 자기소개서를 첨부한 이메일을 보내주세요.

어휘 **internship** 인턴 과정 **market-oriented** 시장 지향적인 **vocational** 직업상의 **orphan** 고아; 고아로 만들다 **inspiring** 고무하는 **atmosphere** 분위기; 대기 **financial** 재정의, 재정적인 **accommodation** 숙박 시설, 숙소 **NGO** 비정부 기구(**non-governmental organization**) **negotiate** 협상하다 **application** 지원, 신청; 적용, 응용 **résumé** 이력서 **cover letter** 자기소개서

29 밑줄 어법 ②

소재 공인되지 않은 전기의 문제점

해설 ② their 전후로 모두 절이 나오므로, their와 같은 단순 대명사가 아니라 절을 연결할 수 있는 관계대명사가 필요하다. 선행사 people과 뒤에 나오는 명사 jealousy가 소유 관계이므로 their를 소유격 관계대명사 whose로 바꿔 써야 한다.

오답 분석 ① where ~ everyone was fighting은 관계부사절로서 앞의 an ~ party를 수식한다. where 이하는 완전한 절이므로 관계부사가 알맞게 사용되었다. ③ 클로즈업은 '사물의 실제 모습보다' 커 보이게 만든다는 의미인데, 현재의 실제 모습(they really are big)을 나타낼 때 쓰는 것은 be동사의 현재형이므로 are를 쓴 것은 적절하다. ④ when 다음에 it(= a camera) is가 생략된 것으로 볼 수 있는데, 카메라는 '조작되는' 것이므로 수동의 의미를 나타내는 과거분사가 알맞다. ⑤ what we carry in our own hearts는 sees의 목적어 역할을 하는 명사절로서 sees와 what절 사이에 부사구 in others가 위치한 형태이다. what 이하가 목적어가 없는 불완전한 절이고 타동사인 sees 이후에는 목적어로 쓰일 수 있는 명사절이 나와야 하므로, 관계대명사 what을 쓴 것은 알맞다.

해석 당신이 한 파티에 가서 말다툼하고 있는 사람들 무리에 카메라의 초점을 맞춘 채 한쪽 구석에 앉아있다고 가정해보자. 그 파티는 어떻게 표현될 것인가? 그것은 즐거운 시간을 보낸 사람이 아무도 없고 모두가 싸우고 있는 불쾌하고 좌절감을 안기는 파티로 묘사될 것이다. 이것이 '공인되지 않은' 전기에 대해 곤란한 점이 그토록 많은 이유이다. 그것은 다른 사람의 인생에 대한 오직 한 사람의 인식일 뿐이다. 그리고 많은 경우 이러한 견해는 자신의 질시로 인해 일을 왜곡하는 데 강한 흥미를 갖게 된 사람들이 제공하는 것이다. 주제문 **문제는 전기의 견해가 오직 저자의 '카메라 앵글'로만 제한되어 있다는 것이며, 우리 모두는 카메라가 현실을 왜곡한다는 것을, 클로즈업은 사물을 실제보다 더 커 보이게 만들 수 있다는 것을 알고 있다.** 그리고 전문적으로 조작될 때, 카메라는 현실의 중요한 부분을 최소화하거나 흐릿하게 할 수 있다. Ralph Waldo Emerson이 말한 대로, 우리들 각자는 우리 마음속에 담아두고 있는 바를 다른 사람들 속에서 본다.

어휘 **represent** 표현하다, 나타내다; 대표하다 **unauthorized** 공인되지 않은 **biography** 전기 **vested interest in** ~하는 것에 대한 강한 흥미 **distort** 왜곡하다 **manipulate** 조작하다 **expertly** 전문적으로 **blur** 흐릿하게 만들다

30 밑줄 어휘 ⑤

소재 어린이의 낙관적 태도가 미래에 미치는 영향

해설 우리는 조금씩, 세대에 걸쳐 세상을 바꾸며 우리가 만든 혁신은 자손들에게 전해지고, 그들은 그것을 바탕으로 새로운 아이디어를 낸다. 즉, 인간의 삶을 더 나은 방향으로 바꿔놓는 변화의 성질은 '점진적인' 것이므로, 인간의 삶을 결코 더 나은 방향으로 바꿔주지 못하는 변화는 '급진적인' 변화임을 추론할 수 있다. 따라서 ⑤의 gradual을 radical로 바꿔 써야 한다.

해석 주제문 **인간에게 어린이란 단지 종의 생물학적 연속보다 더 깊게 흐르는 방식으로 낙관주의와 연결된다.** 낙관주의는 본질적으로 미래에 대한 ① 이성적인 평가의 문제가 아니다. 그것은 판단이라기보다는 태도이다. 그리고 그것은 가장 특징적으로 인간적인 태도이며, 우리의 DNA에 구축되어 있는 것이다. 인간 진화의 가장 위대한 이점은 미래에 존재할 수 있는 가능한 우주들을 상상하고 그것들을 실제로 만드는 방법을 알아내는 우리의 ② 타고난 능력이다. 그것은 현재의 세계에 대한 더 나은 ③ 대안을 찾아내는 능력이며, 우리는 심지어 가장 어린 아이들이 하는 공상적인 가상 놀이에서도 그것을 볼 수 있다. 전례 없고 예측 불가능한 방식으로 물리적, 사회적 세계를 변화시키는 이러한 능력은 우리의 특징적으로 ④ 연장되어 있는 인간 유년기, 즉 장기간의 보호받는 미성숙 상태와 몹시 밀접한 관계가 있다. 우리는 조금씩, 세대에 걸쳐 세상을 바꾼다. ⑤ 점진적인(→ 급진적인) 변화가 인간의 삶을 더 나은 쪽으로 바꿔놓는 적은 결코 없었다. 우리는 우리 자신의 혁신과 그것(= 혁신)이 창조하는 새로운 세상을 우리 아이들에게 전해준다. 그리고 그들은 새로운 아이디어를 상상한다.

구문 [7행~10행] The greatest human evolutionary advantage is *our innate ability* (to imagine *possible universes* [that could exist in the future]) and (to figure out how to make **them** real).
our innate ability를 to부정사가 이끄는 두 ( ) 부분이 수식한다. [ ]는 possible universes를 수식하는 관계사절이다. 두 번째 ( )에서 them은 possible universes를 지칭한다.

[19행~21행] We pass on our own innovations and *the new worlds* [(which[that]) **they** create] to our children ~.
밑줄 친 부분은 pass on의 두 목적어이다. [ ]은 앞에 목적격 관계대명사 which[that]가 생략되어 the new worlds를 수식하며, they는 our own innovations를 지칭한다.

어휘 **optimism** 낙관주의 **continuation** 연속, 계속 **assessment** 평가 **characteristically** 특징적으로 **innate** 타고난, 선천적인 **pretend play** 가상 놀이 **unprecedented** 전례 없는 **be bound up with** ~와 밀접한 관계가 있다 **immaturity** 미성숙, 미숙[상태] **transform** 변형시키다, 완전히 바꿔놓다 **for the better** 더 나은 쪽으로 **pass on** 전달하다

31 빈칸 추론 ③

소재 사과의 '민주적' 특징

해설 좋은 사과는 혈통이나 교배의 도움 없이 자력으로, 같은 땅에서 동등한 기회를 가지고 능력에 따라 위대한 결과물을 만들어낼 수 있다는 내용의 글로 이러한 특징을 종합하면 사과를 ③ '민주적인(democratic)' 과일이라 칭할 수 있을 것이다.

해석 주제문 명성 있는 성직자인 Henry Ward Beecher는 사과가 진정 민주적인 과일이라고 말했다. 거의 어디에서나 기꺼이 자라며, 방치당하든 학대당하든 버려지든, 그것은 스스로를 돌볼 수 있고, 우수함의 결실을 맺을 수 있다. 19세기 묘목 과수원에서 나타난 Horatio Alger 사과 또한 어떤 의미에선 '자수성가'했는데, (이는) 다른 많은 식물들에 관해서는 논할 수 없는 것이다. 예를 들어 위대한 장미는 주의 깊은 품종 개량, 즉 귀족 부모(교배자의 말을 빌리자면 '엘리트 계통')의 계획적인 이종 교배의 결과물이다. 위대한 사과는 그렇지 않으며, 혈통이나 품종 개량과 관계없이 '수많은 독창적이지 않은 사람들'과 구별된다. 미국의 과수원, 혹은 적어도 Johnny Appleseed 과수원은 꽃 피우고 열매 맺는 능력사회이며, 이곳에서는 출신 혹은 유산과 관계없이 모든 사과 씨앗은 동일한 토양에 뿌리를 내리고, 어떠한 묘목도 위대함에 있어서 동등한 기회를 가진다.

① 독립적인 ② 관대한 ④ 수익성이 있는 ⑤ 다목적의

구문 [3행~5행] (Being) Happy to grow just about anywhere, / whether (it is) neglected, abused or abandoned, / it is able to take care of itself, and to be fruitful of excellence.

Happy to grow just about anywhere는 앞에 Being이 생략된 분사구문이다. whether 다음에는 it is가 생략되어 있다. 두 밑줄 친 부분은 공통으로 is able 다음에 연결된다.

어휘 **renowned** 명성 있는, 유명한 **clergyman** 성직자 **neglect** 방치하다 **abuse** 학대하다 **abandon** 버리다, 포기하다 **fruitful of** ~이 풍부한, ~을 잉태한[밴] **seedling** 묘목 **orchard** 과수원 **self-made** 자수성가한 **breeding** 품종 개량, 육종(育種) **deliberate** 계획적인, 고의의 **crossing** 이종 교배 **aristocratic** 귀족인 **distinguish A from B** A를 B와 구별하다 **host of** 많은 **unoriginal** 독창적이지 않은 **without reference to** ~에 관계없이(=**regardless of**) **ancestry** 혈통, 가계 **heritage** 유산

32 빈칸 추론 ①

소재 생존 전략으로서의 상호 교환

해설 빈칸 문장으로 보아, 위기관리의 일종이면서 생존 전략인 것이 무엇인지를 찾아야 한다. 이어지는 수렵 채집인들의 예시에서 사냥 성공으로 얻은 동물을 함께 나누는 것이 추후 다른 이의 (사냥의) 성공에서 자신의 이익을 보장한다고 했으므로, 빈칸에는 ① '협조적인 상호 교환'이 들어가는 것이 가장 적절하다.

해석 주제문 인간의 역사가 보여주듯이 협조적인 상호 교환은 위기관리의 일종으로, 매우 유용한 생존 전략이다. 그것은 아주 오래된 기술이다. 그것 없이는, 인류, 그리고 수많은 동물의 종은 오래전에 멸종되었을 것이다. 우리는 (먹이의) 이용 가능 여부에서 먹이 공급이 변화되기 쉬운 모든 종들에게서 그것(=협조적인 상호 교환)을 보게 된다. 당신이 (원시시대의) 수렵 채집인이라고 상상해보자. 어느 날 당신은 운이 좋아 사슴 한 마리를 잡는다. 당신은 그것을 하루 만에 전부 먹을 수는 없을 것이고 냉장고는 여전히 수세기 떨어져 있다. 당신은 사슴을 집단과 나누기로 결정하는데, 그것은 당신의 운이 굉장하지 않을 때 다른 이의 (사냥의) 성공에서 이익을 보게 될 것을 보장해준다. 당신 친구들의 배는 당신의 냉장고 역할을 한다. 그것은 경제적 성장 및 부의 창출을 위한 필수적인 요소이다. 그것 없이 세계 경제는 없을 것이고 경제도 전혀 없을 것이다.

② 문화적 적응
③ 경쟁적인 대립 관계
④ 기발한 발명
⑤ 경계 태세에 있는 것

구문 [3행~5행] **Without it**, humanity—and countless species of animals—**would be** long extinct.

주절의 동사 형태가 would be인 것으로 보아 현재 사실의 반대를 표현하는 가정법 과거 문장이다. Without은 'If it were not for ~ (~이 없다면)'로 바꿔 쓸 수 있다.

어휘 **demonstrate** 보여주다, 입증하다 **strategy** 전략, 계획 **humanity** 인류; 인간성 **extinct** 멸종된 **be subject to A** A되기 쉽다; A의 대상이다 **availability** 이용할 수 있음 **hunter-gatherer** 수렵 채집인 **ensure** 보장하다 **belly** 배, 복부; 위 **serve** 역할을 하다; 도움이 되다 **ingredient** 재료, 성분; 구성 요소 [선택지 어휘] **cooperative** 협동의, 협조적인 **interchange** (생각·정보의) 교환 **adaptability** 적응성, 순응성; 융통성 **rivalry** 경쟁 (의식)

33 빈칸 추론 ④

소재 아동기의 인지적 공감 능력 발달

해설 24개월 이전의 어린 아이들은 인지적 공감 능력이 없어서 자기 자신의 관점으로 생각하지만, 24개월 이후부터는 인지적 공감 능력이 발달하여 다른 사람의 관점에서 생각할 수 있다는 내용이다. 즉, 2~3세의 아이들은 ④ '자기 자신의 관점 외의 관점을 상상하는' 능력을 가지고 있음을 알 수 있다.

해석 주제문 아동 발달 연구에서 현재 합의된 사항은 2~3세만큼 어린 아이들이 자기 자신의 관점 외의 관점을 상상하는 초보적 능력을 가지고 있다는 것이다. 나는 그것을 내 쌍둥이 아이들에게서 보았다. 그들이 18개월 정도 되었을 때, 내 아들이 울고 있으면 (쌍둥이) 누이가 그에게 자신의 장난감 강아지를 주어서 그를 달래려고 애쓰곤 했다. 그러나 그들이 24개월에 이르게 되자, 그가 울면 그녀는 더 이상 그에게 자신의 작은 강아지를 주지 않았고, 그에게 그가 가장 좋아하는 장난감 고양이를 건네주면 그가 훨씬 더 기뻐할 거라는 것을 깨달았다. 이것이 인지적 공감 혹은 관점 취하기에 관한 모든 것이다. 그것은 상상력의 도약을 이루고 다른 사람들은 우리 자신의 것과는 다른 취향, 경험, 세계관을 가지고 있다는 것을 인식하는 것을 포함한다. 주제문 인지적 공감이 딱 자아와 타자 간의 구별이 나타나기 시작하는 때인 유년기 초반에 자연스럽게 발달한다는 바로 그 사실은 인간이 공감 능력이 내재된, 선천적으로 사회적인 생물임을 우리에게 말해준다.

① 혼자서 외부 자극을 탐색하는
② 그들이 말하지 않은 의도를 이해시키는
③ 다른 사람들의 감정과 표정을 흉내 내는
⑤ 그들의 흥미를 불러일으키는 활동에 몰입하는

구문 [14행~18행] The very fact (S) that cognitive empathy develops ~ childhood — just *at the time* [when the distinction between self and other begins to emerge] — tells (V) us (IO) that human beings are inherently *social creatures* [that are wired for empathy]. (DO)

that ~ emerge는 동격절로 앞에 나온 The very fact의 구체적 내용을 담고 있다.

어휘 **consensus** 합의, 의견 일치 **elementary** 초보의, 초급의 **comfort** 위로하다 **cognitive** 인지의 **empathy** 공감 **perspective** 관점 **leap** 도약 **worldview** 세계관 **distinction** 구별; 차이 **emerge** 나타나다; 드러나다 **inherently** 선천적으로, 타고난 **wired** 내재된; 배선이 된; 유선의 [선택지 어휘] **external** 외부의(↔ **internal** 내부의) **intention** 의도 **mimic** 흉내 내다, 따라 하다 **immerse** 몰두하다; 담그다

34 빈칸 추론 ⑤

소재 친환경 소비자의 유형 비교

해설 친환경 소비자는 '진보적 소비자 운동가' 유형과 '반 소비자 운동가' 유형으로 구분할 수 있는데, 전자는 친환경적인 제품을 소비하고 그렇지 않은 제품은 불매함으로써 기업의 제조 및 유통 관행을 바꾸는 '질적' 접근법을 택하지만, 후자는 이와 대조적으로 '양적' 접근법을 택한다고 하였다. 즉, '반 소비자 운동가'의 주요 목표는 ⑤ '분별 있게 소비하는 것이 아니라 덜 소비하는 것을 의미한다'고 할 수 있다.

해석 녹색(= 친환경) 소비자 행동은 환경주의자들과 사회과학자들 간의 논쟁의 프리즘으로서의 기능을 하게 되었다. 간단한 만큼이나 단순한 한 논쟁은 '진보적 소비자 운동가'와 '반 소비자 운동가'를 맞붙게 한다. 주제문 전자(= 진보적 소비자 운동가)에게는 환경 위기의 뿌리가 대중 소비의 속성에 있다. 그들은 변화를 이끌어내는 소비자의 능력을 강조

한다. 환경 위기에 대한 인식이 확산됨에 따라, 그리고 개인 소비자들이 친환경 제품과 서비스를 선택하며 반응함에 따라, 대중 시장의 구매력은 기업들이 친환경 성향 소비자에 의해 시장에서 회피될까 봐 두려워서 그들의 제품과 제조 및 유통 과정을 '친환경적으로 하도록' 강요하게 될 것이다. 주제문 대조적으로, 금욕적 경향의 '극렬 친환경론자'(= 반소비자 운동가)에게, 위기는 소비의 질보다는 양에서 비롯된 것이다. 그들에게 있어서 주요 목표는 분별 있게 소비하는 것이 아니라 덜 소비하는 것을 의미한다.

① 소비자들이 가능한 한 많이 구매하게 하는 것이다
② 사회과학자의 기법을 적용하는 것이 될지도 모른다
③ 친환경적인 제품에 관하여 지식을 공유하는 것이다
④ 친환경적이면서 그들의 자아상도 고양시켜주는 것이 될 것이다

구문 [16행~17행] ~ the crisis **results** less **from** the quality (A) than **from** the quantity (B) of consumption.

result from은 '~에서 비롯되다'의 뜻으로 from 다음에 '원인'이 제시된다. 「less A than B」는 'A라기보다는 B'의 뜻이다.

어휘 **function as** ~로서의 기능을 하다 **prism** 프리즘 **dispute** 논쟁(하다) **straightforward** 간단한 **set A against B** A를 B와 맞붙게 하다[겨루게 하다] **liberal** 진보적인; 자유주의의; 인색하지 않은 **counter-** 반(反)-, 역(逆)- **the former** 전자(↔ **the latter** 후자) **mass** 대중; 덩어리; 대량의 **opt for** ~을 선택하다 **distribution** 유통 **for fear of** ~할까 봐 (두려워서) **leaning** 성향, 경향 *cf.* **lean** 기대다 **inclined** 경향이 있는 **primary** 주요한; 기본적인; (순서·단계상) 최초의, 초기의 [선택지 어휘] **self-image** 자아상 **disceringly** 분별 있게; 통찰력 있게

35 무관한 문장 ②

소재 객관성의 부정적 측면과 뉴스의 역할

해설 객관적인 사실은 항상 특정 관점만을 옹호하며 이의를 제기할 수 없기 때문에 청중의 활동과 참여를 막는다는 부정적 측면이 있으므로, TV 뉴스 역시 객관성을 앞세워 특정 관점만을 옹호하지 말고 다양한 사회적 입장과 그 속에 담긴 다양한 관점을 제시해야 한다고 주장하는 글이다. 객관성의 부정적 측면에 대한 설명에서 TV 뉴스가 객관적이기보다는 다양한 관점을 제시해야 한다는 내용으로 이어져야 하는데, 객관성이 존재할 수 없는 경우에 대한 설명인 ②는 글의 자연스런 흐름을 단절시킨다.

해석 객관성은 변장을 한 권위이다. '객관적인' 사실은 항상 특정한 관점을 옹호하며, 그러한 (사실의) '객관성'은 권력 과시의 일부로서만 존재할 수 있다. 더욱 중요한 것은, 객관적인 사실에는 이의를 제기할 수 없다는 것이다. 즉, 객관성은 청중의 활동과 참여를 막는다. 오랜 기간 확고했던 사실들을 두고 몇몇 사람들이 논쟁하기를 고집한다면 객관성은 존재할 수 없다. 주제문 그러므로 TV 뉴스는 '객관적'이기보다는, 연속극의 시각처럼 가능한 한 불분명한 위계를 가진 다양한 관점들을 제시해야 한다. 그것(=TV 뉴스)이 다루는 사건이 더 복잡할수록, 그 사건을 이해하는 다양한 사회적 입장 사이의 상반된 주장들이 더 많이 개방적이고 있는 그대로 남겨져야 한다. 뉴스 진행자와 기자는 일어난 일에 대한 최종적인 진실을 말하는 데 관심을 덜 가져야 하고, 그 대신 그 일을 이해하는 다양한 방식과 그런 다양한 방식 속에 새겨진 다양한 관점을 제시해야 한다.

구문 [8행~11행] **Rather than** being "objective," (B) therefore, / TV news should present *multiple perspectives* [**that**, like those(=perspectives) of a soap opera, have **as** unclear a hierarchy **as possible**] (A).

「A rather than B (B보다는 오히려 A)」 구문에서 A와 B는 문법적으로 성격이 대등해야 하므로, B에 should present와 병렬을 이루는 be가 쓰여야 하는데, rather than이 이끄는 구가 주절의 앞이나 뒤에 이어질 때는 원형부정사나 v-ing 형태로 자주 쓴다. that은 주격 관계대명사로 multiple perspectives를 수식하는 관계사절을 이끈다. 「as ~ as possible (가능한 한 ~한)」 구문에 명사가 쓰이면 「as+형용사(unclear)+a(n)+명사(hierarchy)」의 어순이 된다.

[11행~14행] **The more complex** *the events* [(that) it describes ●]. / **the more** *the contradictions* (among *the different social positions* [**from which** to make sense of them]) should be left open and raw.

「the+비교급 ~, the+비교급 ...」 구문은 '~할수록 더욱 더 …하다'란 뜻을 나타낸다. the events 뒤에는 목적격 관계대명사가 생략되었으며 ●는 원래 목적어가 위치했던 자리이다. from which to make sense of them은 「전치사+관계대명사절」이 「전치사+관계대명사+to-v ~」로 축약된 것이다.

어휘 **objectivity** 객관성 *cf.* **objective** 객관적인 **in disguise** 변장[가장]하고 *cf.* **disguise** 변장하다; 숨기다; 변장 **point of view** 관점, 견해 **insist** 주장하다, 우기다 **perspective** 관점; 원근법 **soap opera** 연속극, 드라마 **hierarchy** 위계질서; 계급, 계층 **contradiction** 반박; 모순 **make sense of** ~을 이해하다 **raw** 가공되지 않은; 날것의 **anchor** (뉴스) 앵커; 닻(을 내리다); 고정시키다 **inscribe** (이름 등을) 새기다

36 글의 순서 ④

소재 노화로 인한 질병을 정상적인 것으로 생각하는 것의 문제

해설 '정상적인(normal)'이란 어휘의 의미를 폭넓고 다양하게 사용하는 것의 문제점을 제시하며, 특히 노화의 과정에서 얻어지는 질병을 정상적인 것으로 간주하는 관행을 지적하는 내용의 글이다. 주어진 문장에 이어 예시가 시작되는 (C)가 가장 먼저 오고, 지시대명사 This로 시작하는 (A)가 (C)에 제시된 상황을 받고 있으므로 그 뒤에 이어져야 한다. 그리고 역접의 연결사 However로 시작하는 (B)가 이어져 (A)에 제시된 일반적인 통념을 반박하며 마무리하는 것이 가장 자연스럽다. 따라서 정답은 ④ '(C)-(A)-(B)'이다.

해석 우리는 '정상적인'이라는 단어를 '평범한, 예상되는, 평균적인, 중간의, 흔한, 일반적인, 최적의' 등 많은 다른 방식으로 생각한다. '정상적으로 작동하는'은 보통 '문제가 없는'을 뜻한다. 주제문 연령과 관련된 변화의 경우에서와 같이, 우리가 '정상적인'을 흔하거나 예상되는 것과 연관시킬 때 문제는 시작된다.

(C) 예를 들어, 연령 증가와 관련된 많은 부정적인 변화들이 매우 흔하기 때문에 '정상적인' 것으로 간주된다. 노년기의 만성 질환도 마찬가지이다. 대부분의 고령자들은 복합적인 진단을 받고 여러 가지 처방에 의지해 산다.

(A) 단지 매우 흔하다는 이유로 흔히 이것은 정상적인 것으로 간주된다. 의사들은 "그것은 단지 노화의 일부이자, 우리가 그만큼 오래 사는 것에 대해 지불하는 대가입니다."라고 진단을 설명함으로써 그 잘못된 생각을 흔히 영속시킨다. 우리는 나이 든 사람들이 이러한 질병을 앓게 될 것으로 예상한다.

(B) 그러나 정의에 의하면 질병이란 '올바른' 기능을 하는 것으로부터의 단절을 나타낸다는 의미에서 정상적이지 않다. '정상적인'이란 말은 그것이 사용되는 방식에서 사실은 '노화'라는 말보다 더 나쁠 수도 있다.

구문 [8행~10행] Doctors often perpetuate the misconception / by explaining diagnoses as: // "It's just part of aging, *the price* [(which [that]) we pay for living so long]."

콤마는 동격을 나타내며, the price를 수식하는 [ ]에는 목적격 관계대명사 which 또는 that이 생략되었다.

[16행~18행] Many of *the negative changes* (S) (associated with increasing age), / for example, / are considered (V) "normal" (C) // because they are so common.

( ) 부분이 the negative changes를 수식하며 동사는 are considered이다. 주절은 원래 SVOC 구조(We consider many of the negative changes associated with increasing age "normal.")이었던 것을 수동태로 바꾸어 동사 뒤에 목적격보어가 남은 형태가 되었다.

어휘 **normal** 정상적인, 보통의(↔ **abnormal** 비정상적인) **mean** 중간의, 평균의; 인색한, 못된; 의미하다 **optimal** 최적의, 최상의 **operate** 작동[가동]하다; 운용하다 **associate** 연관시키다, 연상하다 **misconception** 잘못된 생각; 통념 **diagnosis** (복수형 **diagnoses**) 진단 **folk** 사람들; 민요; 민속[민간]의 **by definition** 정의에 의하면; 당연히 **disconnect** 단절, 분리(하다) **chronic** 만성적인(↔ **acute** 급성의) **prescription** 처방(전)

37 글의 순서 ⑤

소재 지구의 자전축 이동

해설 주어진 글은 지구의 북쪽 축이 100년에 0.5도 정도로 매우 천천히 이동한다는 내용이며, (C) 또한 '하늘 상에 거대하고 좁은 원을 그리는 행성 축'에 대한 내용이므로 주어진 글과 내용상 이어진다. (C)의 This motion은 이러한 행성 축의 작은 움직임을 지칭한다. (B)는 지구의 북쪽 축이 아닌 지구의 경사각에 대해 추가적으로(Further complicating the picture ~) 제시하고 있으므로 (C) 다음에 나온다. (A)의 '각도가 작을 때'와 '각도가 클 때'는 (B)에 나온 경사각의 변화 폭인 '21.5도 ~ 24.5도'의 범위 내를 지칭하는 것이므로 (A)는 (B) 다음에 나온다. 따라서 글의 순서는 ⑤ '(C)-(B)-(A)'가 적절하다.

해석 금세기에 지구의 북쪽 축은 북극성(폴라리스)을 향해 있다. 그러나 이것이 항상 이렇지는 않을 텐데, 멈추어 넘어지기 직전의 팽이처럼 지구의 축이 한 세기에 약 0.5도 정도로 매우 천천히 이동하기 때문이다.

(C) 이러한 운동은 세차운동이라고 불리는데, 이것은 행성 축이 (원을 그리는 것을) 다 완수하는 데 거의 26,000년이 걸리는 하늘 상의 거대하고 좁은 원을 그리게 만든다. 그래서 대략 11,000년 후에 지구는 태양에 7월에는 더 가까워지고 12월에는 더 멀어질 것이다. 이는 오늘날의 상황과는 반대이다. 26,000년 후에는 상황이 현재 방식으로 되돌아올 것이다.

(B) 그림을 더 복잡하게 만드는 것은 지구의 23.5도 기울기 역시 시간이 지나며 바뀌고, 21.5도에서 24.5도까지 변하는 완전한 한 주기를 거치는 데 대략 41,000년이 걸린다는 사실이다.

(A) 각도가 더 작을 때는 중위도에서 계절적 차이가 덜할 것이다. 더 큰 각도에서는 차이가 증폭될 것이다. 이러한 경사각의 변화가 우리 행성을 휩쓰는 주기적인 빙하기를 일으키는 주요 요인 중 하나라고 생각된다.

구문 [8행~11행] **It**'s thought **that** *this change* (in tilt angle) is *one of the main factors* [that causes *the periodic ice ages* [that sweep across our planet]].

It은 가주어이고 that this change ~ planet 전체가 진주어이다. one of the main factors를 수식하는 관계사절 안에 the periodic ice ages 수식하는 관계사절이 포함된 구조이다.

[12행~15행] Further complicating the picture (C) is (V) the fact (S) that Earth's 23.5-degree tilt changes over time too, / **taking** about 41,000 years **to run through** *a full cycle* [that varies / from about 21.5 to 24.5 degrees].

동사는 is이고 주어는 the fact 이하인 도치구문이다. that ~ degrees는 the fact를 설명하는 동격절이다. taking 이하는 분사구문이며, 「take+시간+to-v」는 'v하는 데 (시간)이 걸리다'의 뜻이다.

어휘 **axis** 축 **Polaris** 북극성(= the North Star) **top** 팽이 **fall over** 넘어지다 **angle** 각도 **seasonal** 계절의, 계절에 의한 **variation** 차이, 변화 **latitude** 위도 **amplify** 증폭시키다 **tilt angle** 경사각 *cf.* **tilt** 기울기; 기울다 **periodic** 주기적인 **ice age** 빙하기 **complicate** 복잡하게 만들다; 복잡한

38 문장 넣기 ③

소재 인쇄술과 예술이 의학 발전에 미친 영향

해설 ③ 이전은 인쇄술의 발달이 유럽 전역의 의료 전문가들 간의 소통을 향상시키고 지식을 공유하는 데 도움이 되었다는 내용이고, ③ 이후는 Vesalius의 책에 실제로 사실적인 삽화가 많이 담겨 해부학의 이해를 향상시키는 데 도움이 되었다는 내용이다. 즉, ③ 이후부터는 그림의 역할을 강조하고 있으므로 '예술이 사실적인 상을 구상하는 데 도움이 되어 예술도 의학에 기여했다'는 내용의 주어진 문장은 ③에 들어가는 것이 가장 적절하다.

해석 주제문 인쇄술은 르네상스 동안 의사들과 의학 교수들이 그들의 발견과 연구를 서로 더 효율적으로 공유하는 데 도움이 되었다. 인쇄술은 의학 연구의 사본을 대량 생산하는 것을 더 쉽고 더 저렴하게 만들었고, 따라서 유럽 전역의 의사들 간의 의사소통을 개선했다. 예를 들어, 인쇄술의 발달은 Vesalius(베살리우스)의 책 모음인 〈인간 신체의 구조〉가 의료 전문인들 사이에서 널리 판매되는 것을 가능하게 해주었다. 주제문 예술이 인간 신체의 더 사실적이고 실물과 똑같은 상을 만드는 데 도움이 되었으므로 예술 또한 영향을 미쳤다. Vesalius의 책에는 그가 인간 신체에 수행했던 해부로부터 화가들이 그린 200점이 넘는 삽화가 들어 있었다. 이 책들은 과거의 것과 달랐는데, 과거에는 화가들이 좀 더 이차원적인 양식으로 그렸고 실물로는 좀처럼 그리지 않았다. 이것은 의사들이 이용할 수 있는 인간 신체의 훨씬 더 정확한 묘사가 나타났음을 의미했으며, 그들은 해부학에 대한 이해를 향상시키기 위해 이것을 사용했다.

구문 [6행~8행] Printing **made it** *easier and cheaper* **to mass-produce** copies of medical research, / therefore **improving** *communication* (among doctors from across Europe).

it은 가목적어이고 to mass-produce ~ research가 진목적어이다. 「make+it+형용사+to-v」는 '~하는 것을 v하게 만들다'의 뜻이다. therefore improving 이하는 분사구문이다.

[12행~14행] Vesalius's books **had** *over 200 illustrations* [which **were drawn** by artists from *dissections* [(which[that]) he **had carried out** on the human body]].

첫 번째 [ ]는 over 200 illustrations를 수식하는 관계사절이다. 관계사절 내의 두 번째 [ ]는 앞에 목적격 관계대명사 whicih[that]가 생략되어 있으며 dissections를 수식한다. 해부를 수행한 것이 그림을 그려서(were drawn) 책에 들어간(had) 것보다 이전의 일이므로 had carried out과 같이 과거완료 시제를 썼다.

어휘 **have an impact** 영향을 미치다 **lifelike** 실물과 똑같은 **mass-produce** 대량 생산하다 **illustration** 삽화, 도해 **carry out** 수행하다 **two-dimensional** 이차원의, 평면적인 **style** 양식 **accurate** 정확한 **portrayal** 묘사 **anatomy** 해부학

39 문장 넣기 ②

소재 고대시대 동물 도축의 정당화

해설 주어진 문장은 신들에게 동물을 바친 것이 도축이 인간의 욕망이 아닌 신들의 바람인 것으로 돌려 도축을 정당화하기 위함이었다는 내용이다. 이에 대한 예시가 ② 뒤에 For example, in ancient Greece, ~에서 이어지므로 주어진 문장은 ②에 들어가는 것이 가장 적절하다.

해석 현대에만 사람들이 동물을 죽이는 것에 대해 점차 불편하게 느끼게 되었다는 생각은 (현대의 사람들을) 우쭐하게 하는 생각이다. 주제문 생명을 빼앗는 것은 중대하며, 사람들은 수천 년간 그것을 정당화하려고 시도해왔다. 종교와 의식은 우리가 도덕적 비용을 평가하도록 돕는 데에 결정적인 역할을 해왔다. 북미 원주민들과 그 밖의 다른 수렵 채집인들은 생명을 포기해 줘서 먹는 이들이 살도록 해준 것에 대해 그들의 먹잇감에 감사해하곤 했다. 많은 문화는 희생된 동물들을 신들에게 바쳐 왔는데, 아마도 도축을 요구한 것이 자신들의 욕망이 아니라 바로 신들의 바람이었다는 것을 스스로 확신하게 하는 방법으로서였다. 예를 들어, 고대 그리스에서, 도축을 책임진 사제들은 제물로 바쳐진 동물의 이마에 성수(聖水)를 뿌리곤 했다. 그 짐승은 곧바로 머리를 흔들곤 했고, 이것은 승인의 표시인 것으로 받아들여졌다. 도축이 반드시 존중받지 못하는 것은 아니다. 이러한 모든 사람들에게 의식은 그들이 먹은 것을 받아들이도록 허용했다.

구문 [5행~7행] The idea (S) that only in modern times have people become uneasy about killing animals is (V) a flattering one.

주어는 The idea이고 동사는 is이며, 사이의 that절은 The idea와 동격을 이룬다. that절 안에서 only in modern times가 앞으로 나오면서 도치가 일어나, 「조동사(have)+주어(people)+동사(become)」의 어순이 되었다.

어휘 **sacrificial** 희생의; 제물로 바쳐진 **convince** 확신시키다, 납득시키다 **slaughter** (가축의) 도살; 학살, 살육 **uneasy** 불안한, 우려되는; 불편한 **flattering** 아첨하는, 추켜올리는; 위안의 **momentous** 중대한, 중요한 **ritual** 의식, 의례 **crucial** 결정적인, 중대한 **moral** 도덕의 **priest** 사제, 성직자 **sprinkle** 뿌리다, 끼얹다 **holy water** 성수(聖水) **brow** 이마 **promptly** 지체 없이, 즉시 **assent** 찬성, 승인; 찬성하다

40 요약문 완성 ①

소재 스스로 유발한 의존성의 발달 실험

해설 피실험자들은 쉬운 산수 문제를 처음에는 잘 풀 수 있었지만 하급자의 직함을 달아보고 활동한 후에는 잘 못 풀게 되었으므로, '동일한(equal)' 능력을 갖고서도 어떤 '꼬리표(labels)'를 달아봤는지가 수행에 영향을 미친 셈이다.

해석 주제문 심리학자 Ellen Langer는 스스로 유발한 의존성이 어떻게 발달하는지를 알아보기 위해 몇 가지 실험을 고안했다. 그녀는 여행하는 사람들은 다소 독립적이고 자신감이 있을 것 같다는 가정 하에 공항에서 실험을 수행했다. 이러한 실험 중 하나의 첫 번째 단계에서, 피실험자들은 쉽게 풀 수 있는 산수 문제들을 받았다. 2단계에서 그녀는 피실험자들을 자신의 능력에 의문을 제기하도록 유도할 것 같은 입장에 두었다. Ellen Langer는 어떤 사람들에게는 '조수' 직함을, 다른 사람들에게는 '상관' 직함을 주고, 그들이 모두 자기 역할에 적절한 방식으로 임무를 수행하게 했다. 3단계에서 모든 피실험자들은 자기가 1단계에서 성공적으로 완수했던 것과 동일한 종류의 쉬운 산수 문제로 돌아왔다. '조수'가 되었던 사람들은 이제 원래 풀었던 것의 겨우 절반 정도만 문제를 잘 풀었다.

⬇

실험들이 시사하는 바는, 피실험자들이 (A) 동일한 능력을 갖고 참가하기 시작했어도, 그들이 취했던 (B) 꼬리표가 그들의 수행에 영향을 미쳤다는 것이다.

구문 [4행~6행] ~, on the assumption that *people* [who travel] **are likely to** be somewhat independent and self-assured.
that ~ self-assured는 the assumption에 대한 동격절이다. 「be likely to-v」는 'v할 것 같다, v하기 쉽다'의 뜻이다.

[11행~13행] Ellen Langer gave some the title of "assistant" and (gave) others (the title of) "boss," / and **had** them all **perform** tasks / in *a manner* (appropriate to their roles).
others "boss,"는 gave others the title of "boss,"를 간단히 나타낸 표현이다. had them all perform은 사역동사 「have+O+원형부정사 (O가 v하게 하다)」 구문이다. ( ) 부분은 a manner를 수식한다.

어휘 **self-induced** 스스로 유발한, 자기 유도의 *cf.* **induce** 유발[유도]하다 **somewhat** 다소 **self-assured** 자신감 있는; 자기 만족의 **phase** 단계, 국면 **arithmetic** 산수의 **competence** 능력 **title** 직함, 칭호 **assume** 취하다[띠다]; 맡다; 가정하다; ~인 척하다

41~42 장문 41 ② 42 ②

소재 환경에 따른 행동 변화

해설 41. 피실험자들은 지저분한 환경에 비해 깨끗한 환경에서 쓰레기를 버리는 확률이 훨씬 적었는데, 여기에서 무질서한 환경이 책임감을 약화시킨다는 결론이 도출되었다. 이를 반영하면 제목으로 가장 적절한 것은 ② '무질서의 징후가 사회 규범을 약화시킨다'이다.
① 범죄 행위: 정황과 결과
③ 분별력 있는 삶이 정돈된 환경을 만든다
④ 우리 공동체의 범죄를 어떻게 줄일 수 있을까?
⑤ 사회 규범을 위반할 때 무슨 일이 생기는가?

42. 깨끗한 환경에서 피실험자들이 쓰레기를 버리는 확률은 확연히 낮아졌으므로 정돈된 환경은 책임감을 감소시키는 것이 아니라 발전시키는 것을 알 수 있다. 따라서 (b)의 reduces를 fosters 등으로 바꿔 써야 한다.

해석 한 연구에서 사회심리학자들은 대형 병원 주차장에 있는 139대의 차에 전단지를 놔두었다. 그들은 그 차의 운전자들이 전단지를 쓰레기통에 넣을지, 아니면 대신에 그것들을 주차장에 놔둬서 버릴지에 대해 호기심을 가졌다. 몇몇 차 운전자들이 주차장 엘리베이터에서 나타나기 전에, 연구자들은 버려진 전단지, 사탕 포장지와 커피 컵을 주차장 전역에 흩뿌려놓았다. 다른 때에 그들(= 연구자들)은 주차장 바닥에서 모든 담배꽁초와 쓰레기를 마지막 하나까지 치워서, 쓰레기를 버리는 것이 (a) 부적절하다는 생각을 전달했다. 주차장이 이미 쓰레기로 뒤덮여 있었을 때는 모든 운전자들 중 거의 절반이 쓰레기를 버렸지만 (쓰레기의 토대 위에 쓰레기를 하나 더 올려두는 것이 뭐 대수겠는가?), 주차장에 티끌 하나 없었을 때는 오직 열 명 중 한 명의 운전자들만이 쓰레기를 버렸다. 주제문 이 연구는 정돈된 환경이 책임감을 (b) 감소시킨다(→ 발전시킨다)는 것을 보여주었다. 연구자들은 환경적 신호가 사람들의 행동을 (c) 형성하는지를 알아보기 위해 또 다른 전환을 첨가했다. 그들은 조수에게 일부 운전자들이 엘리베이터를 나서는 바로 그때 땅에 원치 않는 전단지를 눈에 띄게 떨어뜨리라고 요청했다. 이 (d) 고의적인 행동은 운전자들의 주의를 주차장의 기존 상태로 끌어들여, 그것이 이미 쓰레기로 가득 차있음을 강조하거나, 그 조수가 자기의 버려진 전단지를 무심하게 버리기 전에는 그것이 얼마나 깔끔했는지를 강조했다. 조수가 운전자들의 주의를 주차장의 상태로 끌었을 때, 겨우 6퍼센트만 깨끗한 주차장에 쓰레기를 버린 반면 이미 어수선한 주차장에서는 극적으로 더 높은 비율인 54퍼센트가 쓰레기를 버렸다. 주제문 운전자들은 그 장소(= 주차장)의 일반적 표준을 이해하여 가장 적절한 것으로 보이는 행동을 (e) 채택했다.

구문 [9행~12행] At other times, they removed every last cigarette butt and piece of trash ~, **conveying** the idea that littering was inappropriate.
conveying 이하는 부대상황을 나타내는 분사구문이고, 밑줄 친 두 부분은 동격 관계이다.

[23행~28행] This intentional act drew the drivers' attention / to the existing state of the parking lot, **either** emphasizing // that it was already full of litter, **or** highlighting **how neat it was** // before the assistant indifferently cast aside his discarded flyer.
「either A or B」는 'A나 B 둘 중 하나'의 뜻이고, A와 B 자리 모두 분사구문이 위치해 있다. highlighting의 목적어로 의문사 how가 이끄는 간접의문문 「how+형용사+주어+동사」가 쓰였다.

어휘 **flyer** 전단지 **litter** (쓰레기를) 버리다(= **discard, cast aside**) **scatter** 흩뿌리다 **cigarette butt** 담배꽁초 **atop** 꼭대기에 **spotless** 티끌 하나 없는 **orderly** 정돈된; 질서 있는 **twist** 전환 **cue** 신호 **conspicuously** 눈에 띄게 **highlight** 강조하다 **neat** 깔끔한 **cluttered** 어수선한 **given** ~이 주어지면, ~이라고 가정하면 **prevailing** 일반적인, 보통의; 우세한 **norm** 규범 [선택지 어휘] **disorder** 무질서 **undermine** 약화시키다 **sensible** 분별력 있는

43~45 장문 43 ③ 44 ⑤ 45 ②

소재 뇌 부상으로 성격이 변한 Willie

해설 43. (A)는 사람들과 잘 어울리던 성격의 Willie가 두 번의 자동차 사고를 당해 머리를 조금 다쳤지만, 의사는 걱정할 것 없다고 말했다는 내용이다. 그러나 사고 이후 Willie는 성격이 변하여 주변 사람들과 점점 멀어졌고, 스스로 조치가 필요하다고 느껴 전문의의 연락처를 알아냈다는 내용의 (C)가 이어지고, 검사 결과 그의 성격이 변하게 된 이유가 뇌의 이상 때문이었음이 밝혀졌다는 내용의 (D)가 이어져야 적절하다. 마지막으로 증상을 완화해 주는 약물 치료를 한 결과, 상태가 호전되어 다시 예전의 모습을 되찾았다는 내용의 (B)가 오는 것이 자연스럽다. 따라서 정답은 ③ '(C)-(D)-(B)'이다.

44. (e)는 Willie가 치료를 위해 찾은 전문의를 가리키며, 나머지는 모두 Willie를 지칭한다.

45. (B)에서 상태가 호전된 이후에도 약물 치료를 계속 받아 왔다고 했으므로 ②가 일치하지 않는다.

해석 (A) Willie는 모든 사람과 잘 어울리는 그런 종류의 사람이었다. 그는 전도유망한 미래가 있는 뛰어난 학생이었다. 그의 자동차가 사고로 가드레일을 들이받으면서 계기판에 머리를 부딪치기 전까지는 말이다. 비록 멍한 느낌이 들긴 했지만, Willie는 괜찮은 것처럼 보였다. 하지만 3개월 후, ① 운전 중에 개를 치지 않으려고 급격하게 방향을 바꾸다가 또 다른 사고를 당했고, 그는 이번에는 응급실로 보내져야 했다. Willie를 검사한 후에 의사는 그에게 걱정할 것 없다고 말했다. (a) 그(=Willie)는 단지 가벼운 머리 부상만 입었을 뿐이라는 것이었다.
(C) 하지만 이어지는 몇 달간, Willie는 그것이 자신의 삶에 문제를 일으키고 있음을 알게 되었다. 그의 모든 태도와 행동이 변하기 시작했다. ③ (c) 그(=Willie)는 이제 툭하면 화를 냈고, 늘 화가 나 있었다. 그의 성급함과 끊임없이 터져 나오는 화는 친구들과 가족을 멀어지게 만들기 시작했다. 그는 자신을 통제할 수 없다는 것과 너무 늦기 전에 그것을

멈춰야 한다는 것을 깨달았다. ④ 그는 친구에게 전화했고, 그 친구가 (d) 그(=Willie)에게 전문의의 전화번호를 알려주었으며, 당장의 위기는 모면하게 됐다.

(D) Willie는 의사에게 두 번의 사고와 감정 기복의 심각함을 설명했다. ⑤ (e) 그(=전문의)는 즉시 뇌 검사를 지시했고, 그 검사로 (뇌의) 이상이 밝혀졌다. (뇌의) 두 부위가 지나치게 활성화되어 있었다. 한 부위는 뇌의 왼쪽에 있었는데, 그곳의 기능 장애는 흔히 편집증이나 폭력성과 관련이 있다. 두 번째 부위는 뇌 앞부분의 위쪽 중앙 구역이었고, 그 부위는 사람이 한 곳에서 다른 곳으로 자유롭게 주의를 전환할 수 있게 해준다. 그 뇌 검사는 편집증, 불같은 성질, 그리고 부정적인 생각과 같은 변화들을 분명하게 설명해주었다.

(B) 다음 단계는 분명했다. Willie는 그의 증상들을 완화하는 약을 처방받았는데, 뇌의 이상에 대한 전용 치료제와 부정적인 생각에서 빠져나오게 도와주는 항우울제였다. 몇 주간의 치료 후, 그 결과는 극적이었다. Willie는 유머 감각을 되찾기 시작했고, 친구들이나 가족과도 다시 연락을 시작했다. ② (b) 그(=Willie)는 그 이후로 외상으로 유발된 뇌의 문제를 억제하기 위해 약물 치료를 계속 받아왔고, 지금은 당신이 앞으로 만날 수도 있는 가장 친절한 사람들 중 한 사람이 되었다.

어휘 **(A) promising** 전도유망한, 촉망되는 **collide** 충돌하다 **dashboard** (자동차의) 계기판 **guard rail** (도로의) 가드레일 **dazed** (정신이) 멍한 **sharply** 급격하게; 날카롭게 **(B) prescribe** (의사가) 처방하다 **medication** 약물 (치료) *cf.* **be on medication** 약물 치료를 받고 있다 **abnormality** 이상, 기형 **get unstuck from A** A에서 빠져나오다[벗어나다] *cf.* **unstuck** 붙어 있지 않은 **regain** 되찾다, 회복하다; 되돌아가다 **trauma** 외상, 부상; (정신적) 트라우마 **induce** 유발하다; 유도[설득]하다 **(C) demeanor** 태도; 처신, 품행 **have a short fuse** 걸핏하면 화를 내다, 성미가 급하다 **irritability** 성급함, 화를 잘 냄 *cf.* **irritable** 짜증을 (잘) 내는; 화가 난 **flare** (순간적으로 확 타오르는) 불길; (잠깐 동안) 확 타오르다; 버럭 화를 내다 **temper** (화내는) 성질 **alienate** (사람을) 소원하게 하다 **avert** (사고 · 위험을) 피하다; (눈 · 생각 등을) 돌리다 **(D) severity** 심각(성), 가혹함 **mood swing** (조울증 등에서 볼 수 있는) 기분의 두드러진 변화 **dysfunction** 기능 장애; 역기능 **be associated with** ~와 관련되다 **fiery** (성질이) 불같은; 불타는